INTRODUCTION TO HUMAN SERVICE NETWORKS

History, Organization and Professions

Robert P. Scheurell
School of Social Welfare
University of Wisconsin-Milwaukee

UNIVERSITY
PRESS OF
AMERICA

Lanham • New York • London

Copyright © 1987 by

University Press of America,® Inc.

4720 Boston Way
Lanham, MD 20706

3 Henrietta Street
London WC2E 8LU England

Printed in the United States of America

British Cataloging in Publication Information Available

Library of Congress Cataloging-in-Publication Data

Scheurell, Robert P.
  Introduction to human service networks.

  Includes bibliographies and index.
  1. Social service—United States.   2. Social networks—
United States.   3. Public welfare—United States.   I. Title.
II. Title: Human service networks.
HV31.S33   1987   361'.973   87-10525
ISBN 0-8191-6420-8 (alk. paper)

All University Press of America books are produced on acid-free
paper which exceeds the minimum standards set by the National
Historical Publication and Records Commission.

DEDICATION

To my wife Sally and children
Lynn and Laura

ACKNOWLEDGEMENTS

A number of faculty colleagues at the University of
Wisconsin-Whitewater, University of Wisconsin-Oshkosh, the
Wisconsin Conservatory of Music, Psychiatric Services, Columbia
Hospital and the University of Wisconsin-Milwaukee have
volunteered their time and effort to review specific chapters
and provide comments for revision, expansion, and deletion of
material in various sections. Those individuals who have
volunteered their time and effort include the following:
Charles Zastrow (Social Welfare), University of
Wisconsin-Whitewater; Donald Martin (Sociology), University of
Wisconsin-Oshkosh; Virginia Langrehr (Consumer Affairs),
University of Utah; Ronald Lewis (Social Work), University of
Arizona; Peter Baime (Music), Wisconsin Conservatory of Music
and Milton Silva, Director of Psychiatric Services at Columbia
Hospital, and Professor of Psychiatry, Medical College of
Wisconsin, Milwaukee, Wisconsin (mental health).

The following individuals are all affiliated with the
University of Wisconsin-Milwaukee: Robert Magill (Social Work);
Walter Trattner (History); Leo Muskatevc (Music); Rolf Hickman
(Art); Robert Holzhauer (Social Work); Ann Meyer (Rehabilitation
Counseling); Thomas Lynch (Military Science); Clarke Hagensack
(Political Science); Richard Cummings (Education); Paul Tutwiler
(Information and Library Science); Ellen Hochstedler (Criminal
Justice); John Conley (Criminal Justice); Christine Dunning
(Criminal Justice); William Feyerherm (Criminal Justice); Ernest
Spaights (Social Work); Philip Lerman (Employment); Elvira de
Silva (Social Work); Karen Robison (Nursing); Alan Meyer
(Business); Adrian Chan (Education); Roger McNeely (Social
Work); Victor Green (History); Dennis Staral (Graduate
School-APA certification) and William Winter, University of
Wisconsin-Extension and Vice President of Wisconsin Volunteers
in Criminal Justice.

In addition to faculty colleagues, the author wishes to
acknowledge the typists who in addition to typing skills had
made various changes in editing the book, such as Mary Ann
Riggs, Dorothy Brostowiz, Jan Downey, Lorraine Haeffel and Sonya
Baime. Other individuals who supplied information for the book
include Gordon Farr Milwaukee Psychiatric Hospital, Bruce Badin
Veteran's Administration, Suzanne Harman Columbia Hospital, John
St. John Sacred Heart Rehabilitation Hospital and Jane Thompson
Neighborhood House.

Robert P. Scheurell, 1987
University of Wisconsin-Milwaukee

INTRODUCTION TO HUMAN SERVICE NETWORKS:

HISTORY, ORGANIZATION AND PROFESSIONS

Page

TABLE OF CONTENTS

LIST of FIGURES and CHARTS

xi

PREFACE

Most textbooks on human services and social work focus on either broad terminology, concepts, processes of working with people or specific fields of practice, such as health, poverty, corrections etc. There is no existing book which attempts to interrelate the broad field of human services and the specific profession of social work. A basic organizing thesis of this book is that social services are provided within a context of societies social networks (social institutions) and to obtain an overview of the delivery of social services and the professions involved, one needs to look at each social network (social institution). Each social network (social institution) has a specific function and an occupation or profession which is dominant. As the United States moves further into a service economy (some authors refer to it as a service-information economy), it is anticipated the delivery of social services will be expanding into some social networks which have not been heavily involved in the delivery of social services, such as aesthetic, information and referral and military. On the other hand, some of the other social networks which have been traditionally identified with the delivery of social services will be decreasing the social service component, such as corrections, income maintenance, and others will continue to provide social services and either maintain their emphasis on social service delivery or expand services, such as the religious, physical health and rehabilitation networks.

The system for the delivery of social services in the United States today is undergoing slow but fundamental changes, partly as a consequence of the emerging service/information economy and partly as a consequence of the more fiscally conservative trend of the 1980s which encourages the religious, economic, and mutual support networks to provide more social services. This book is not a traditional textbook since it provides a voluminous amount of concrete information for the reader and is designed as a reference text for libraries, school guidance counselors at the secondary level, postsecondary guidance counselors and students. This book can also be of use to those who are teaching the introductory courses in social work, social welfare, human services and to sociologists who are interested in the sociology of occupations and professions.

INTRODUCTION

ORGANIZATION of the TEXT

The major thesis of the author is that the broad area known as human services and the specific profession of social work are highly interdependent and related to society's institutions and other human service professions. That is, to understand social work as a profession one needs to see where this profession interacts with other professions in the delivery of social services within the same social network (social institution). Consequently, the focus of this text is on the description of social networks (social institutions) and where the human service occupations and professions fit into each social network and where social work as a profession fits into each social network. The text is organized into five separate but related parts.

1.   OVERVIEW of SOCIAL ORGANIZATION and HUMAN SERVICES-- Chapter 1 discusses the concepts of a service economy, social organization, human services, and social welfare. Chapter 2 discusses the concepts of human services and helping professions, with a conceptual distinction made between the "professional helper" and the "helping professions." Chapter 3 discusses social work as an example of one of the helping professions. The model used to discuss social work can be used to analyze any of the other professions identified within the text.

2.   NON-HUMAN SERVICE NETWORKS--Included in this section are those social networks which have as their primary function a non-human service. Chapter 4 discusses the aesthetic network, Chapter 5, economic, Chapter 6, military and Chapter 7 the political network.

The format for each chapter in sections 2, 3 and 4 is to discuss for each social network it's size, historical development, organizational context, services provided, occupations and professions, dominate occupations and professions, the role of social work, the role of the personal social services, services for special populations and a brief discussion of some issues. This format provides a frame of reference so the reader knows exactly what to expect within each chapter.

3.   GENERAL HUMAN SERVICE NETWORKS--Included in this
section are those social networks which have as their primary
function a general human service in society. Chapter 8
discusses the education network, Chapter 9, environment
protection, Chapter 10, information and referral, Chapter 11,
judicial, Chapter 12, protective service, Chapter 13, legal,
Chapter 14, leisure and recreation, and Chapter 15, religious
network.

4.   SPECIFIC HUMAN SERVICE NETWORKS (SOCIAL WELFARE)--
Included in this section are those social networks which have as
their primary function a specific social problem or human
service, which is called social welfare. Chapter 16 discusses
the corrections network, Chapter 17, employment and manpower,
Chapter 18, housing, Chapter 19, income maintenance, Chapter 20,
mental health, Chapter 21, mutual support, Chapter 22, personal
social services, Chapter 23, physical health, and Chapter 24,
rehabilitation (disability) network.

5.   SPECIAL POPULATIONS and MAJOR THEMES and ISSUES--
Chapter 25 discusses special populations (Asians, Blacks,
European Ethnic, Native Americans, Same Sex Preference, Spanish
Speaking and Women) and Chapter 26 is a discussion of the major
themes of the text and issues which will be with us the for next
10-20 years.

SECTION 1

OVERVIEW of SOCIAL ORGANIZATION and HUMAN SERVICES

The United States has been described by some economists as a service society and by some social critics as a service/information economy. As society and the economic network changes, the traditional terminology to describe social welfare and human services may be inadequate. The author proposes a different perspective in looking at old problems.

This section focuses on a conceptual overview strongly influenced by sociological literature. In chapter 1, the focus is a description of a service economy and from that concept looking at society and how it is organized in terms of social institutions (social network). Each social network (Social Institution) is viewed as having a primary function which may or may not be human services. This chapter conceptually distinguishes between social networks which do not have a human service as their primary function and those social networks which do have a human service as a primary function (General Human Services). A conceptual distinction is made between the general human service network and specific human service network (social welfare). Chapter 2 discusses the concept of profession and develops a conceptual distinction between a professional helper and a helping profession. A model is then presented of the commonalities and differences between specific human service professions. This model can be used to analyze any profession. Chapter 3 analyzes social work as one of the helping professions. The model used to analyze social work can be used to analyze any profession.

CHAPTER 1

SERVICE ECONOMY and SOCIAL ORGANIZATION*

"This country (United States) is pioneering in a
stage of economic development. We are now in a
"service economy," that is, we are the first
nation in the history of the world in which more
than half of the employed population is not
involved in the production of food, clothing,
housing, automobiles, and other tangible
products." (Fuchs, 1965:1)

INTRODUCTION

The above statement by Victor Fuchs in 1965 was prophetic
since it forecast a new age of economic development with a
redefinition of what is of economic significance. Traditionally, the average individual perceives economics as a discussion of goods production in private industry, growth rates,
employment rates and financial cycles, i.e., inflation versus
deflation, boom versus recession, etc. Most individuals do not
perceive two economically significant items: the growing predominance of the service industries (public and private), and
the relationship of the economic network to the utilization of
finite natural resources (ecology). A service economy shifts
the focus of concern from goods producing industries and a heavy
use of finite natural resources to service producing industries
and heavy use of human resources. Within the context of service
industries, some economists, such as Arthur Pearl (1973) are
viewing the human services as a solid base for an economic
network which is more ecologically sound.

Human services are part of a broader economic and sociological system, consequently, one should have a notion of how
society is organized and the interdependence between all of the
elements in society. This chapter provides a brief overview of
a service economy, social organization, and where the human
services fit into society and its organization. A classification of societal networks (social institutions) is developed,
with a definition of human services and social welfare.

A SERVICE ECONOMY

When one refers to the economy, one usually has in mind a
system of economics where one discusses corporations, the
production of goods, and their allocation and distribution to a

3

population. In a service economy, the focus of economics becomes broader, focusing on the quality of life, and the majority of workers are employed in service industries. If the economy becomes more service-oriented, then service industries, including the human services and helping professions, become a significant part of the economy and not an ancillary or peripheral aspect. It is this trend toward a service economy which is discussed by Arthur Pearl (1973), Solomon Barkin (1966), and Alan Gartner (1974).

The United States, as indicated earlier, has moved into a new stage of economic development called the "service economy." The phenomenon of a service economy is not restricted to the United States. The United States was the first country in the world to enter this stage of economic development.[1]

Figures for employment in the United States are shown in Figure 1-1 for 1982 and projections for 1995. Employment is classified by the form of industrial production, goods or services. Goods producing industries include manufacturing, contract/construction, mining, and agriculture. Service producing industries include transportation and public utilities, trade, financial, insurance, real estate, services and miscellaneous, and government, including military (also called public administration). These figures indicate that the bulk of employment in the United States is in the service industries. In 1982, 72.4 percent of the work force was employed in service industries, and 27.6 percent of the work force was employed in goods producing industries. The anticipated number of people employed is expected to increase to 127.5 million in 1995 with 92.7 million or 72.7 percent in service producing industries and 34.8 million or 27.3 percent in goods producing industries.

DEVELOPMENT of SERVICE INDUSTRIES

The trend of having more people employed in service-producing industries rather than goods-producing industries has been slow yet constant since 1900. Figure 1-2 shows the number and percentage of the work force employed in service-producing industries from 1900-1995. Using the 1900 figures as a base, there has been a steady growth of service producing industries of 38.7 percent of the work force to 1980, and a projected growth of 40.7 percent of the work force to 1995. There was a corresponding decline in agriculture using the 1900 figures as a base of 32.2 percent of the work force to 1980 and a projected decline of 33.0 percent of the work force to 1995, and a decline of 7.5 percent in goods producing industries to 1980 and a projected decline of 8.7 percent of the work force to 1995.

Figure 1-1

Number and Percent of the Work Force by Major Industry
in 1982 and Projected for 1995*

| Industry | Number and Percent of Work Force | | | |
| | 1982 | | 1995 | |
	Number Employed in Thousands	Per-cent	Number Employed in Thousands	Per-cent
Goods Producing				
Manufacturing	19,234	18.8	23,491	18.4
Contract/Construction	5,491	5.4	7,925	6.2
Mining	742	.7	864	.7
Agriculture/Forestry/ Fisheries	2,815	2.7	2,550	2.0
TOTAL	28,282	27.6	34,830	27.3
Service Producing Industries				
Transporation & public utilities	5,543	5.4	7,637	5.2
Trade	22,536	22.0	28,545	22.4
Financial, insurance & real estate	5,899	5.8	6,685	6.0
Service & miscellaneous	24,252	23.7	32,636	25.6
Public Administration (Government, including military)	15,803	15.5	17,230	13.5
TOTAL	74,033	72.4	92,733	72.7
GRAND TOTAL	102,315	100.0	127,563	100.0

Source: Adapted from United States, Department of Commerce, Bureau of the Census, Statistical Abstract of the United States: 1986 (106th Ed.), Washington, DC: U.S. Government Printing Office, 1985, p. 405.

Figure 1-2

Percent of the Work Force in Various Industries for the United Sta~

1900-1995*

Time Period	Industrial Classification		
	Goods Producing Industries		Service Producing Industries
	Agricultural	Other Goods Producing	
1900	35	34	32
1910	28	38	34
1920	24	41	35
1930	22	36	42
1940	19	35	46
1950	12	39	48
1960	8	38	54
1970	4.3	30.1	65.6
1980	2.8	26.5	70.7
1990	2.2	25.4	72.4
1995	2.0	25.3	72.7

Sources: Adapted from Victor Fuchs. The Service Economy, op cit, p. 30; and United States Department of Labor, Occupational Outlook 1986-87 Edition, Washington, D.C.: U.S. Government Printing Office, 1986, pp. 13-22 and United States Department of Commerce, Bureau of the Census, Statistical Abstract of the United States: 1986 (106th Ed.), Washington, DC: U.S. Government Printing Office, 1985, p. 405.

The previous figures showing the growth of the service industries do not specify services (including social work). There has been a steady growth in the number of individuals employed in professional services in the United States. In 1900 there were an estimated 4.88 professional employees per 1,000 population, and in 1950, 6.61 professional employees per 1,000 population.[2] The professional services included in the above figures include lawyers, physicians, dentists, college teachers, clergymen and military officers. It is difficult to historically trace the precise number of social workers in the United States. One method to determine the growth of a field is through the number of individuals holding membership in a professional association. For social work, there were 1,800 members in the American Association of Social Workers in 1921 which became the Natonal Association of Social Workers in 1955. In 1984 there were over 90,000 members in the National Association of Social Workers. The development of service industries as the major means of employment is consistent with trends occurring in other industrialized nations, such as Canada, England, France, Germany, etc.

WHY a SERVICE ECONOMY

The economy of a society is related to its natural and human resources, degree of technology, density of population, values, beliefs and, of course, politics. Historically, one can view Western industrial societies moving into and out of different economic and technological systems with periods of rapid, and slow adjustment and change. A generalized view of Western technological and economic development is shown in Figure 1-3. In different historical periods one can identify a specific technological and economic system. The assumption made by economic writers who write about the service economy is that the United States has entered a new and different stage of technological and economic development. Some authors, such as Kleinberg (1973) and Galbraith (1978) have referred to this new economic system as a "social industrial technology and Naisbitt (1984) a "service information" economy."

The reasons for the change from an industrial goods-producing economy to a service-producing economy are complex, with no one cause. Technological development is a major factor in this change, since industrial goods can be produced with a smaller percentage of the labor force (labor intensive). That is, fewer people need to be engaged in the production of survival items, such as clothes, food, shelter, etc. Along with the smaller number of people needed to produce goods, there has been a corresponding increase in money available to the consumer, an increase in non-working hours, and an increase in consumer demand for services. As industrial workers are able to

Figure 1-3

Idealized Historical Model of Economic and Technological Development

	Aspect of Technological and Economic Development		
Time Period	Technological Base	Economic System	Predominant Energy Resource
Tomorrow	Smaller corporate organization and labor-extensive (lower production per working unit)	Human economics	Human/natural resources
Today	Corporate industry and labor intensive (high production per working unit)	Welfare society economics	Natural/human resources
1900	Industrial	Capitalism	Natural resources
1800	Agriculture	Developing capitalism	Developing natural resources
1600	Small industry (an agriculture base)	Mercantilism	Human resources
1200	Agricultural	Feudalism	Human/resources

supply their basic needs of clothing, housing and shelter with less of their income, they are looking for other consumer items of a materialistic or a quality of life nature. Materialistic goods, such as television, cars, refrigerators, etc., need repair or servicing. Non-materialistic goods, refers to those which address one's quality of life. When one looks at the quality of life, it is more difficult to measure what one is obtaining, and more hours of work are needed to accomplish a task (labor extensive). Many hours of counseling for a marital problem, for example, may be necessary to produce some results.

There is a growing awareness our industrial technology is incompatible with nature (high natural resource consumption). In an age where ecology and the ecological balance is taking on more importance, it seems logical to seek an economic system which is compatible with nature (less natural resource consumption) and is ecologically sound. A service-oriented economic system takes on this characteristic since the primary resource used in the economic system is human resources. The current, more conservative economic and political trend in the United States in the 1980s is a movement which will delay the development of the service economy, but will not negate the trend toward a service economy. The impact of the 1980s is to shift the major focus of service industries from professional services and social service programs in the public area to other areas of service industries, such as military (public administration), finances, utilities, and the private sector of the economy, such as private practice, religious, and private agencies.

In effect, Reaganomics is not altering the move toward a service economy, but is shifting the focus of what part of the service industries will have predominance, and how social services are funded and organized.

SERVICES and MISCELLANEOUS CLASSIFICATION of SERVICE INDUSTRIES

When one looks for services to people and the professions providing these services, where would one look for them in the service industry classification? In general, one will find services for people under the classification services and miscellaneous and government including military (now called public administration).

A commonly accepted classification of industries in the service category of service industries is as follows: business and repair, entertainment and recreation, personal service and professional and related services.

BUSINESS and REPAIR - refers to industries, such as advertising, commercial research, computer and data processing, automotive repair, electrical repair, protective services, etc.

ENTERTAINMENT and RECREATION - refers to industries, such as commercial sports, playgrounds, theater and motion pictures, concerts, opera, etc.

PERSONAL SERVICES - refers to industries, such as hotels, motels, beauty and barber shops, dressmaking, funeral service etc.

PROFESSIONAL and RELATED - refers to industries, such as engineering, accounting, health, education, legal service, social service, etc.[3]

Figure 1-4 shows a more detailed classification of these industries.

The professional and related services can be viewed as those which focus on problem solving, which can be classified as indirect, or direct professional services.

Indirect professional services are impersonal in the sense that the professions in this industrial classification have as their primary objective the solving of mathematical, structural, transportation, planning and design problems. The indirect professional services have a variety of related occupations and professions which can be called professional problem solvers. These are occupations and professions which have something other than personal problems of people as their immediate concern. Some examples of problem solver occupations and professions include engineer, architect, accountant and bookkeeper.

Direct professional services are personal in the sense that the professions in this industrial classification have as their primary objective the solving of technical and personal concerns as they relate directly to people and their personal problems. The direct personal services have a variety of related occupations and professions which can be called professional helpers. These are occupations and professions which have problems of people as their immediate concern. This group of occupations and professions may or may not use interaction or a relationship with people as one of the means of working on a problem. Some examples of professional helper occupations and professions include education, social work, law, psychiatry, psychology, medicine, nursing, medical record administration, clinical laboratory technician and library and information science. (See Chapter 2 for a detailed discussion on occupations and professions.)

Figure I-4

Generalized Categories of Industries in the Service and Miscellaneous
Classification of Service Industries*

Business and and Repair	Entertainment and Recreation	Personal Service	Professional and Related
vertising rvices to .ellings mmercial esearch Devel- opment and esting Labs siness Management nd Consulting mputer and Data rocessing tective and Pro- ective Services siness Service ot Classified tomotive Service nd Repair ectrical Repair sc. Repair: lacksmith ocksmith, etc.	Theater and Motion Picture Bowling Alleys, Billard and Pool Halls Miscellaneous: Commercial Sports Concessions Amusement Parks Concerts Bathing Beach Playgrounds Recreation Dance Halls and Studios Etc.	Private Household Hotel and Motel Lodging Laundry, Cleaning Beauty Shops Barber Shops Funeral Service and Crematoriums Shoe Repair Dressmaking Miscellaneous: Baby Sitting Brothel Escort Service Genealogical Research, etc.	Indirect Engineering, Archi- tecture, Surveying Accounting, Auditing, Bookkeeping Direct Health Practitioners Hospitals Nursing and Personal Care Legal Services Elementary and Second- ary Education College and University Business Trade and Vocational Schools Libraries Job Training and Voca- tional Rehabilitation Child Day Care Residential Care Social Services Religious Organizations Miscellaneous: Consulting Lecturer Psychological Testing etc.

ot an exhaustive list. This list is a sampling of the types of industries under each
rvice category. There is some overlapping between various categories such as
ofessional and business. For example, a lawyer providing a legal service who has a
ivate office is under professional, yet the same person may have a part-time office in
e business sector. Similarly an individual in the detective and protective service
ea of business and repair may also be employed in the social service area of
ofessional and related industries. United States Department of Commerce, Bureau of
e Census, Occupational Outlook 1986-87 Edition, Washington, D.C.: U.S. Government
inting Office, 1986, pp. 13-22 and United States Department of Commerce, Bureau of the
nsus, 1980 Census of Population. Classified Index of Industries and Occupations Final
ition, Washington, D.C.: U.S. Government Printing Office, 1982.

11

The professional services sector of the service industries is where one predominantly finds the professional helpers. As our economy moves more into the service area, professional helpers can be found in all of the institutions of our society. To grasp the importance of social services existing in all of society's institutions, one needs to have a concept of what is meant by a social institution.

SOCIAL ORGANIZATION

All societies throughout history have developed some form of social structure or organization, some less specialized or less complex (the Wasusu tribe of Brazil) and others more specialized or complex (United States of America). The organization of a society is a reflection of the following factors: natural resources available, geography, population density, climate, level of technology, and the values or cultural attributes of a population. Social organization can be defined as "the process of merging social actors into ordered relationships which become infused with cultural ideas."[4] As individuals interact with each other over time, a predictable or stable form of behavior develops in a dyadic (two person) social system. If this relationship expands to a larger number of people, a group is formed which will have a mutuality of interest and expectations regarding appropriate or non-appropriate behavior. The group is developing a value system regarding behavioral expectations and a culture of its own. When expectations of behavior develop, one can begin to identify different groups because boundaries are formed between groups based upon behavioral expectations, similarity of interest or similarity of socioeconomic position in society.

LEVEL of SOCIAL ORGANIZATION

From different groups one can expand the perception of society's organization to larger and more abstract parts, such as organizations, associations, networks of association, etc. Figure 1-5 ideally represents a society's organization beginning with the individual and their relationship to other parts of a society.

Society in this diagram represents a clam shell with layer after layer of higher-order abstractions of society, yet the individual is a central component with the concept of values and culture interwoven into all levels of organization. The two side arrows ideally represent the degree of personal involvement of the individual in society and the varying level of abstraction of society beginning with the individual. This diagram is a graphic description of the levels of social organization as discussed in Olsen's "The Process of Social Organization"

12

(1968). The typology of social organization from a low order to a high order of abstraction used by Olsen is summarized as follows:

Population	–	Unorganized individuals from which social organization develops.
Aggregate	–	A collectivity of people, spontaneous in origin and temporary in nature.
Social Class	–	A loosely ordered collectivity based upon socio-economic status.
Group	–	Members who know and identify with each other.
Family	–	A group characterized by kinship.
Community	–	A series of groups localized by a territorial or identification basis.
Association	–	An organization more or less purposefully created for the attainment of relatively specific and limited goals.
Network	–	A functionally specialized organization that links together numerous associations, groups and other types of organizations. [Author's note: this is commonly referred to as a social institution.]
Society	–	A broad type of organization which dominates all others.
Confederation	–	A loosely organized combination of societies.
Web of Organization	–	The overlapping of organizations.[5]

ASSOCIATIONS and NETWORKS

The major concepts in social organization useful for understanding where professional services are utilized in society are that of association and network. The concept of association refers to organizations which have developed to obtain specific,

13

FIGURE 1-5

GENERAL MODEL OF SOCIETAL ORGANIZATION*

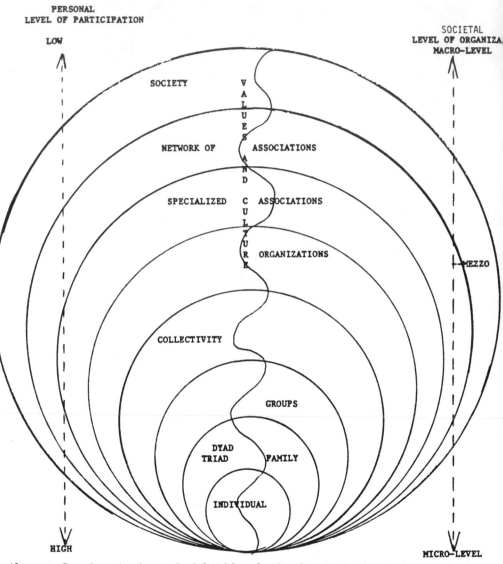

*Source: From <u>Introduction to Social Welfare Institutions</u> by Charles Zastrow, Revised Ed.,
p. 73, Homewood, Illinois: Copyright (c) The Dorsey Press, 1978, 1982.

14

and at times limited, goals. The major forms of associations can be classified according to who is the primary benefactor of the association. A typology of associations used by Olsen (1968) and others, is as follows:

Business Association   —   primary benefactor is the person or the corporation to make money. An examples is a business corporation.

Mutual Aid Association   —   primary benefactor is the member of an association. Examples are a labor union or employee association.

Service Association   —   primary benefactor is the client. The general breakdown of service associations is: tertiary (focus on domestic and quasi-domestic tasks), quarternary (focus is facilitating the division of labor), and quinary (focus is to change or improve ones life style). Examples are a social service department, alcohol or drug treatment agency.

Commonweal Association   —   primary benefactor is the community or society. Examples are a law enforcement agency or the Social Security Program.[6]

The primary associations of concern in looking at the professional helper occupations and professions and services are service and commonweal types of associations, which have as their primary benefactor or focus of concern services to individuals and groups (service associations) or to the total community (commonweal associations). These two types of associations incorporate most activities and programs which have been commonly referred to as social service, human service, and social welfare.

The next level of social organization of importance in looking at a system of delivering professional services is the formation of a cluster of associations with similar interests, goals, and functions into a specific network (social institution). A network exists when different associations interlock. Figure 1-6 shows an ideal model of a network. (One could use

15

more than 6 points of intersection to show the interlocking between each one.)

A network would contain certain types of associations which are dominant, such as business or service, however, other types of associations would belong to the same network such as mutual and commonweal. For example, the economic network consists of business, mutual aid, service and commonweal associations, but the dominant types are business and mutual aid associations. The income maintenance network consists of all four types of associations but the dominant ones are those which use public expenditures, such as service and commonweal. Figure 1-7 shows a specific example of the interrelatedness of the various types of associations into what is commonly called the economic and income maintenance (welfare) network. The concept of network is used instead of the term "institution" in order to highlight the complexity and variability of what one commonly calls a social institution.

MAJOR NETWORKS

Society has a large number of identifiable networks of associations which have a specific function. Figure 8 graphically portrays the major networks of association (social institution) in a society.

One can see from Figure 1-8 that all of these networks affect the individual, the family and the community, as well as overlap with each other. It is a graphic representation of a dynamic and flexible system of networks or institutions.

FUNCTION of SOCIETAL NETWORKS - Each of the networks identified in Figure 1-8 has a specific function or purpose in society, such as allocation of power (politics), defense (military), financial assistance (income maintenance) and prevention and curing of physical illness (medical health) etc. Regardless of the primary purpose of a network of association, a network has a non-social service and a social service function.[7] For example, the military network is designed for defense, however, in accomplishing this purpose a series of social services have been developed for military personnel to use. The physical health network is designed to prevent and cure diseases, a social service, yet many medical personnel, such as lab technicians and researchers, do not work directly with people. The educational network transmits knowledge and culture, yet has a social service function of guidance and counseling and a non-social service function of research.

16

FIGURE 1-6

MODEL OF THE CONCEPT NETWORK

NETWORKS 1-6 AND THEIR
INTERCONNECTEDNESS

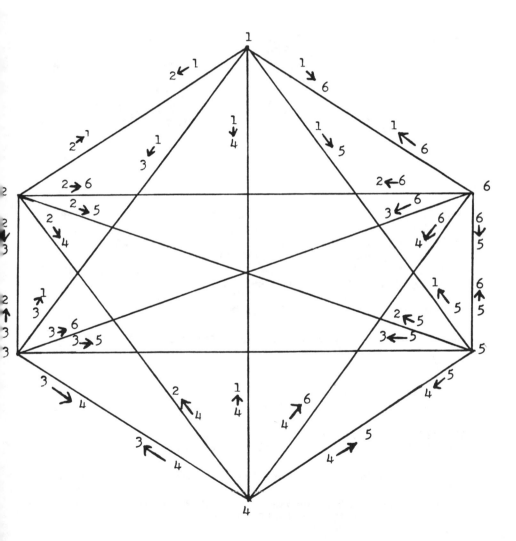

Figure 1-7

Relationship of Types of Association to
a Network of Associations*

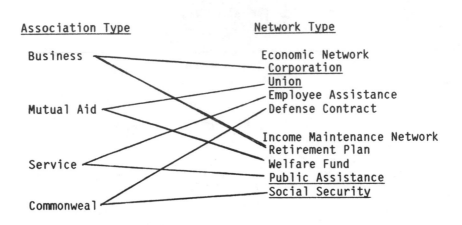

Association Type   Network Type

Business   Economic Network
                                    Corporation
                                    Union
                                    Employee Assistance
Mutual Aid   Defense Contract

                                    Income Maintenance Network
                                    Retirement Plan
Service   Welfare Fund
                                    Public Assistance
                                    Social Security
Commonweal

*Due to the complexity of showing schematically all of the net-
works of associations, only two are shown here to graphically
portray the ideal interrelatedness between association types and
the overall network of associations known as social institutions. This model can be used to look at any other network such
as education, legal, corrections, mental health etc.

The underlined examples are the dominant ones in the network.

    Figure 1-9 identifies the major social networks, their
primary function, and a dominant occupational group or groups.[8]

In looking at the networks in Figures 1-8, 1-9 and 1-10, one
should be aware of five significant concepts:

    1. Each societal network has a primary function.

    2. Each societal network has both a non-social service and
        a social service component.

FIGURE 1-8

MAJOR SOCIETAL NETWORKS OF ASSOCIATIONS

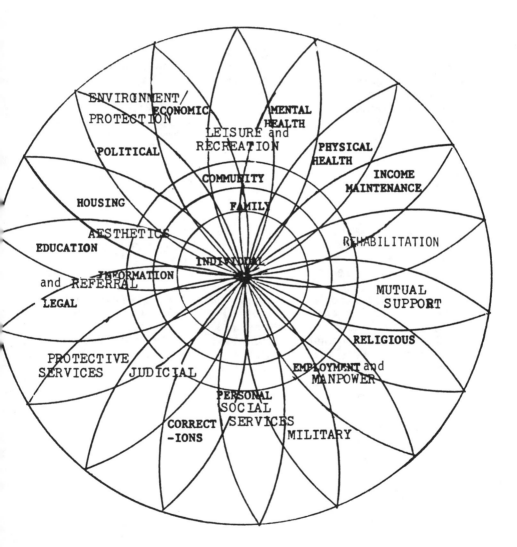

3. Each societal network is interrelated with other networks.

4. Each societal network has a dominant occupation and profession.

5. Social science and other professions are involved in all of the social networks, and specific occupations and professions are involved in more than one social network.

One of the social networks which needs more elaboration is that of the personal social service network.

PERSONAL SOCIAL SERVICE NETWORK - One of the social networks identified in Figure 1-8 is the personal social service network. Figure 1-10 is an elaboration of that social network. The personal social service network has as its primary function the amelioration or resolution of individual and group problems. In a sense, this network is a residual network in that problems which are not the primary concern of other networks are the focus of this network.[9] The personal social service network also has responsibility for programs with special populations which includes Asians, Blacks, European Ethnics, Native Americans, Same Sex Preference, Spanish Speaking and Women.

Although the personal social service network is an autonomous network, this network and its services overlap with all other networks as shown in Figure 1-11, using child welfare and alcohol and drug rehabilitation programs as examples.

The personal social services consist of a large collection of social services which can be classified in four ways: protective, utilitarian, developmental and socialization, and rehabilitative and therapeutic services. Figure 1-12 shows this classification of the personal social service network with a number of examples of each one.

Figure I-9

Social Networks, Their Function, and Dominant
Occupation and Profession

Network	Function	Dominant Occupation and Profession	Service Orientation
Aesthetic	self-expression/ creativity	cluster of fine arts professions	secondary
Corrections	punishment/ rehabilitation of offenders	cluster of social science disciplines and professions	primary
Economic	allocation, distribution and production of goods and services	business (personnel) manager)	secondary
Education	transmission of knowledge, culture and values	education/teacher and guidance counselor	primary
Employment and Manpower	access to, finding and maintaining employment	cluster of social science/manpower disciplines, vocational counselor	primary
Environment Protection	consumerism conservation, family planning	home economics/urban life specialists, natural scientists	secondary
Housing	develop and improve housing	cluster of social science disciplines	primary
Income Maintenance	financial assistance	social work and related social sciences	primary
Information and Referral	access, collecting and maintaining material	library and information science	primary
Judicial	determination of guilt and innocence	lawyers/judges	primary
Legal	providing order in one's relation with others and society	lawyers	primary

21

Figure I-9 continued

Network	Function	Dominant Occupation and Profession	Service Orientation
Leisure and Recreation	physical and emotional outlet for people	education/recreation/ leisure specialist	primary
Mental Health	prevention and treatment of mental disturbances	cluster of professions (psychology, nursing, psychiatry, social work)	primary
Military	defense	officer	secondary
Mutual Support	supporting individuals having a problem	no specific group, many volunteers	primary
Personal Social Service	resolution of personal problems	cluster of professions (psychology, psychiatry, social work, human service)	primary
Physical Health	prevention and treatment of physical illness	medicine, nursing, allied health professions	primary
Political	distribution and allocation of power	politician	secondary
Protective service	protection of society and prevention of crime	law enforcement/ private security	primary
Rehabilitation	retraining of individuals because of physical, emotional disability	rehabilitation counselor	primary
Religious	Humankind's relationship to a supreme being and a code of behavior	theologian/clergy/ pastoral counselor	primary

FIGURE 1-10

MODEL OF THE PERSONAL SOCIAL SERVICES
(not covered in Figure 1-8)

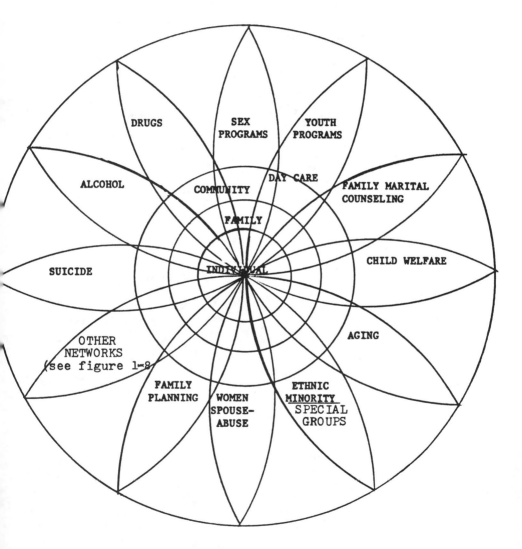

Figure I-II

Idealized Relationship of Selected Personal Social Services
to other Societal NetworkS

EXEMPLARY PROGRAMS IN THE
PERSONAL SOCIAL SERVICE NETWORK

SOCIETAL NETWORK

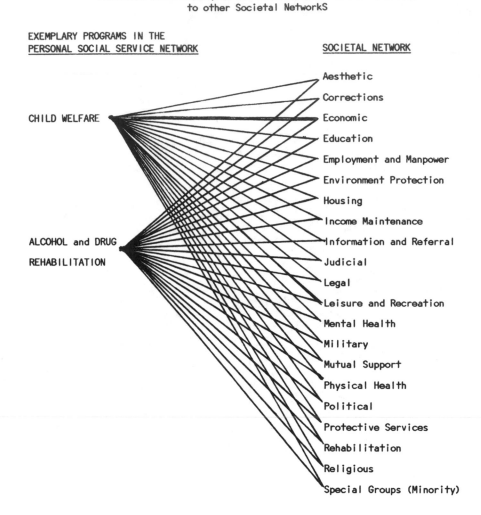

24

Figure I-12

Some Examples of Programs in the Personal Social Service Network*

Protective Services
    Child Care
    Child Welfare and Protection (abuse, adoption, foster care, neglect)
    Assessment for Courts, Schools, Camps
    Family Violence (spouse abuse)
    Sexual Violence (rape)
    Probation and Parole Services
    Consumer Protection for the Aged, and other groups

Utilitarian Services
    Advocacy and Legal Services
    Community Coordination, Planning and Organizing
    Day Care Facilities
    Financial Assistance (Social Security, Supplemental Security Income,
     Public Assistance)
    Food Stamps, Surplus Commodities
    Homemakers
    Information and Referral
    Personnel Work
    Institutional Services (medical, mental, corrections, mentally retarded,
     etc.)

Developmental and Socialization Services
    Volunteer and self help program development
    Child Development
    Community Centers for Youth, Families and the Aged
    Family and Marital Counseling
    Family Planning
    Divorce and Bereavement Counseling
    Immigrant Services
    Services to Minorities and Women
    Program Evaluation and Research

Rehabilitative and Therapeutic Services
    Sexual Counseling and Therapy
    Alcohol, Drugs, Sexual Assault Counseling
    Mutual Support Groups
    Rehabilitation (physical, vocational)
    Employment Counseling, Evaluation and Placement

*Source: This list of services are examples drawn from a variety of resources including the following: Alfred Kahn. Social Policy and Social Services, New York, NY: Random House, Inc., 1973, pp. 13, 28-30; Ralph Dolgoff and Donald Feldstein. Understanding Social Welfare. New York, NY: Harper Row Publishers, 1980, pp. 216-222; David Macarov. The Design of Social Welfare, New York, NY: Holt, Rinehart and Winston, Inc., 1978, pp. 7-15.

SOCIAL NETWORKS and HUMAN SERVICE NETWORKS

At this point no prior attempt has been made to define human services. It has been suggested that in a service economy some form of social service is found in all societal networks. Since social services are found in all social networks, there are difficulties in clearly distinguishing between terms like social service, human service and social welfare.

The definitional and conceptual problems confronting someone attempting to define these terms with clarity are tremendous. Some authors simply state "services to humans or whenever one person is employed to be of service to another." Erickson (1976) and others equate the term "human service" and "social welfare."[10] Further definitional problems in distinguishing these terms are a consequence of the perspective or beginning point one assumes in attempting to define social services, human services, and social welfare. For example, one can focus on the form of social services provided, the setting in which social services are provided, the population and clientele to be served, the social problem to be resolved or the professions involved.

This section attempts to define these terms from the social service and the network (social institution) perspective. The term social service means a communal response (public or private) of programs and activities to meet individual and group needs. These programs and activities can be organized within a highly structured network like education or physical health, or a more loosely structured network like personal social services, or a secondary aspect of a network like the economic and military. That is, social services as a system of programs and activities are found in all social networks. The term human services as programs and activities means the same as social service.[11]

Although programs and activities known as social services and human services are found in all social networks, not all social networks have as their primary function the delivery of social services or human services. Using the perspective of societal networks, the term human service network can be defined as those networks which have as their primary function the delivery of social services.

Of those social networks described in Figures 1-8, 1-9 and 1-10, the following can be identified as <u>not having</u> social services as their primary function and are not part of the human service network, but they do contain a social service element:

- Aesthetic

- Economic

- Environment protection

- Military

- Political

Those social networks <u>having</u> as their primary function the delivery of social services and are part of the human service networks are as follows:

- Corrections

- Education

- Employment and manpower

- Housing

- Income maintenance

- Information and referral

- Judicial

- Legal

- Leisure and recreation

- Mental health

- Mutual support

- Personal social service

- Physical health

- Protective service

- Rehabilitation

- Religious

Those networks identified as human service networks share
ideally the following common attributes which distinguish these
networks from other societal networks, and distinguish the human
service industries from other service industries. These common
ideal philosophical characteristics include the following:

1. Consumer or service orientation (consumer is direct
    benefactor),

2. Reliance on interpersonal contact in providing services,

3. End product is usually intangible (affective/cognitive
    quality),

4. Consumers have a right to the service (quality of
    service should be unrelated to one's ability to pay),

5. Consumers should have a right to participate in deci-
    sions which affect them,

6. Public has a legitimate concern for the quality of
    services,

7. Central concern is serving people.[12]

HUMAN SERVICE NETWORKS and the DELIVERY of SOCIAL SERVICES

The previous listing of societal networks forms an overall
boundary for looking at human service organizations. The human
service network as a broad area of concern consists of a large
variety of organizations: some of which are specialized and
others non-specialized, some work directly on personal problems
and others indirectly on personal problems, some are large-scale
bureaucracies, others are small organizations, some are
legalistic and legal-code oriented and others are process and
relationship-oriented, some require a high level of educational
achievement, i.e., professionalism, and others do not.

There is a tendency to equate the terms "human service" and
"social welfare." In looking at the types of social services
provided and the types of societal networks used in providing
social services, it is clear there is a major difference between
the generalized concept of human services and the more specific
concept of social welfare. For example, the legal network and
education network are quite different than the income maintenance and personal social service networks.

HUMAN SERVICE and SOCIAL WELFARE NETWORKS

The human service network consists of a variety of disparate or different forms of networks, but they have a common element of the primacy of a consumer and problem orientation versus a societal orientation. The social networks identified as human service can be further classified into whether the focus of the network is on the general population or general social problem or on a specific population or specific social problem. Using this classification, the human service networks can be classified as follows:

General Human Service Networks	Specific Human Service Networks (Social Welfare)
- Education	- Corrections
- Information and Referral	- Employment and Manpower
- Judicial	- Housing
- Legal	- Income Maintenance
- Leisure and Recreation	- Mental Health
- Protective service	- Mutual Support
- Religious	- Personal Social Service
	- Physical Health
	- Rehabilitation

The term social welfare means those social networks which are classified as human service networks which have as their primary population for the delivery of social services, a specific population group or a specific social problem.[13] The use of this definition clearly makes a distinction between various networks and implicitly highlights the varied occupations and professions found delivering some form of social service in one of the networks (see Figure 1-9).

IMPLICATIONS of a SERVICE ECONOMY

The current industrial system is based on: a division between public and private enterprise, a large multi-corporation model, uses skilled and unskilled employees, and full-time workers. Some potential consequences of a service oriented economic network are as follows:

29

1. Growing significance of the public sector and the government to provide employment. The United States since 1945 has pursued as a goal full employment. The private economic network has never generated sufficient employment to achieve the goal of full employment since 1920. In the 1980's, there has been a trend to reduce the role of the federal government in generating employment. The result of this trend has been to increase the role of local and state government and local private agencies in the implementation of social service programs.

2. Advanced education or training required. Many of the human service positions, even at low levels, require some form of training. In effect, regulation of the human services would be based upon training and competence and not on competition and profit.

3. Labor extensive. More workers will be needed for service industries. In human service industries there is a lower level of productivity per worker than in manufacturing industries, therefore, more workers per unit of production will be necessary.

4. Female employment. Since the service industries do not rely on physical labor, there will be an expanded market for female employment.

5. Part-time employment. Along with the female orientation of the service industries, there should be an expectation of more part-time employment since the needs of people are not on an eight-to-five hour basis.

6. Older population. Since part-time employment is acceptable in the service industries, it is anticipated there will be a more open market for employment of an older population, for example, part time employment for retired individuals.

7. A consumer orientation. Since the primary benefactor in service industries is the consumer, there will be more questions regarding the role and participation of the consumer in the development, implementation and accountability of services.

8. Intangible products. Since the service industries rely on the affective domain in working with people, it is extremely difficult to ascertain the direct benefit to the recipient. This means that service industries will have to rely more upon personal relationships than in the past.

9. Small business organization. Manufacturing of tangible products, such as cars, refrigerators, etc., in the business corporation has led to the large, impersonal multi-corporation. The level of employment for a particular corporation varies anywhere from 5,000 employees plus. In the provision of social services, the service industries will rely more on a personal relationship between the consumer and the service provider, consequently there should be a different form of business organization. Organizationally, bureaucracy and small numbers of employees will dominate. Many human services are currently implemented through a bureaucracy. Although the bureaucracy in human services seems large, they are small in comparison to large multi-level corporations. Fuchs (1965) makes this point by indicating that in 50 percent of the service sector, half of the employees are in firms with fewer than 20 workers. Although hospitals are large, more than half of the hospitals have less than 500 employees. Government, which is commonly called a huge bureaucracy, in reality is a series of smaller bureaucracies and the majority of governmental units have less than 500 employees. In addition, many of the service industries, including human services, are run by small non-profit businesses.

10. Since the level of business organization is smaller, there should be more personalization of the work world. The organization of business must be on a smaller level and the span between the service provider and the recipient reduced.

11. Role confusion and diffusion. As a consequence of moving into a service oriented economic network, there is a high degree of role confusion and diffusion between occupations and professions in the service industries, human service networks and within the human service professions themselves. For example, some quasidomestic services, such as bartenders, beauticians and prostitutes are receiving education in the recognition of mental illness and techniques of crisis intervention. The question is, does this type of education make them a full participant within the human services at a paraprofessional level. The problem of suicide is treated by a variety of professions, such as social work, psychiatry, psychology, nursing, etc. Do the approaches taken by each of these professions vary or are they the same?[14]

Most of the professions are expanding their traditional roles, with a consequence of identity crisis and boundary problems. For example, when one talks about psychiatric work, some of the techniques utilized by a psychologist, psychiatrist, psychiatric nurse, psychiatric social worker, school guidance counselor, human service worker and pastoral counselor are very similar. What is glossed over is the fact that these professions come from very specific occupational, professional and educational backgrounds, and their value orientation and knowledge base are somewhat different.

Other implications of a service economy are discussed in social science literature, such as the cyclical nature of employment, role of the huge multi-level corporations is declining, and the difficulty in assessing production outcomes. It is difficult to predict the actual consequences for industrial reorganization based upon a service oriented economic network, yet it is clear that the type of industrial management we are accustomed to will be changing. It was indicated earlier that although the United States is now developing a service economy, other nations, such as Canada, Sweden, Switzerland and Denmark have reached a similar point in their economic systems.

SUMMARY

The development of a service economy is a relatively recent phenomenon, since 1965 in the United States. This chapter provided a brief overview of societal organization to show the relatedness of various networks of association (social institutions) and how each has a social service function. A typology of service industries was presented to show the location of human services within the overall structure of society. The concepts social service, human service and social welfare were defined. A number of implications of a service society were discussed, including the concept that a human service oriented economic network is ecologically sound in an age where natural resources are beginning to dwindle. Because of the complexity of the concepts used in this chapter, a summary chart (Figure 1-13) is included as a guide.

Figure 1-13

Summary of Chapter 1

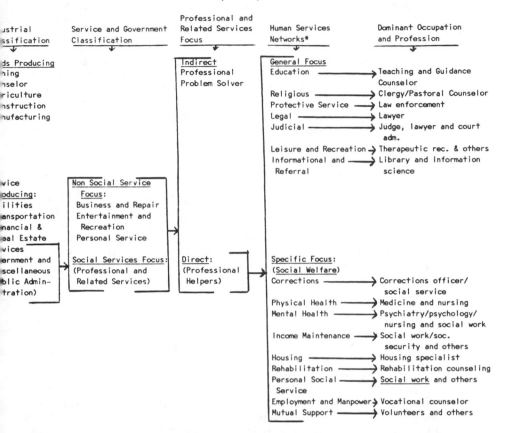

Industrial Classification	Service and Government Classification	Professional and Related Services Focus	Human Services Networks*	Dominant Occupation and Profession
Goods Producing: Mining, Counselor, Agriculture, Construction, Manufacturing		Indirect Professional Problem Solver	General Focus: Education → Teaching and Guidance Counselor; Religious → Clergy/Pastoral Counselor; Protective Service → Law enforcement; Legal → Lawyer; Judicial → Judge, lawyer and court adm.; Leisure and Recreation → Therapeutic rec. & others; Informational and Referral → Library and Information science	
Service Producing: Utilities, Transportation, Financial & Real Estate, Services, Government and Miscellaneous (Public Administration)	Non Social Service Focus: Business and Repair, Entertainment and Recreation, Personal Service / Social Services Focus: (Professional and Related Services)	Direct: (Professional Helpers)	Specific Focus: (Social Welfare): Corrections → Corrections officer/social service; Physical Health → Medicine and nursing; Mental Health → Psychiatry/psychology/nursing and social work; Income Maintenance → Social work/soc. security and others; Housing → Housing specialist; Rehabilitation → Rehabilitation counseling; Personal Social Service → Social work and others; Employment and Manpower → Vocational counselor; Mutual Support → Volunteers and others	

*The following networks were not included as a human service network: military – military officer; economy – personnel manager; aesthetic – art, dance, music therapy; political – politician; environment protection – nature of professions, including home economics and consumer affairs. Although each of these networks has a social service element, the primary concentration of the network is not the delivery of social services.

FOOTNOTES

*This chapter was reviewed for comments by Donald Martin, Professor of Sociology, University of Wisconsin-Oshkosh, Oshkosh, Wisconsin.

1. For a fuller discussion of the trends toward a service economy in the industrialized world, see Solomon Barkin, Manpower Problems in the Service Sector. Paris, France: Organization for Economic Cooperation and Development, 1966; and George Stigler, Trends in Employment in the Service Industries. Princeton, NJ: Princeton University Press, 1956.

2. George Stigler, op cit., p. 108.

3. This classification of service industries is adapted from the United States Department of Commerce, Bureau of the Census, Occupational Outlook 1986-87 Edition, Washington, D.C.: U.S. Government Printing Office, 1986, pp. 13-22 and United States Department of Commerce, Bureau of the Census. 1980 Census of Population: Classified Index of Industries and Occupations: Final Report, Washington, D.C.: U.S. Government Printing Office, 1982.

4. The author draws heavily upon the work of Marvin Olsen, The Process of Social Organization. New York, NY: Holt, Rinehart and Winston, Inc., 1968, for the discussion on social organization. This frame of reference is used since it utilizes the concept of network, highlights the inter-relatedness of the varied aspects of society and the limita-tions of social organization based upon natural resources, such as population, geography, etc. This approach allows one to realize the important of eco-systems and ecological perspectives in understanding human society.

5. Marvin Olsen, op cit., pp. 86-102.

6. Marvin Olsen, op cit., p. 95. The material on the organiza-tion of society is adapted in part from Charles Zastrow. Introduction to Social Welfare Institutions. Homewood, IL: Dorsey Press, 1982, pp. 71-74 and is reproduced in part with the permission of Dorsey Press.

7. The term "service function" is used broadly to make a distinction between whether a primary function of a network is working with people to resolve personal problems or to cope with broader societal issues. The term "service function" means the delivery of social services. For example, the primary purpose of education is to transmit

knowledge and cultural values, however, secondarily, educators become involved in personal problems of the students and broader societal issues.

8. The family as a network is not specifically described, since all other networks affect the family and vice versa.

9. The term "personal social service" and its application to a specific network of associations is rather recent in the United States, beginning in the late 1960s. For a general review of the personal service concept see: Robert Morris. <u>Social Policy of the American Welfare State</u>. New York, NY: Harper and Row Publishers, 1979; and Ralph Dolgoff and Donald Feldstein. <u>Understanding Social Welfare</u> 2nd Ed. New York, NY: Longman Inc., 1984.

10. Examples of the various ways in which the terms "social services" and "social welfare" have been defined are as follows: <u>social service perspective</u> in Alfred Kahn. <u>Social Policy and Social Services</u>. New York, NY: Random House, Inc., 1973; <u>setting perspective</u> in Arthur Fink. <u>The Field of Social Work</u>. New York, NY: Holt, Rinehart and Winston, Inc., 1978; <u>population to be served</u> in Helga Croner. <u>National Directory of Private Social Agencies</u>. Queen's Village, New York: Croner Press, 1985; <u>social problem perspective</u> in Charles Zastrow. <u>Introduction to Social Welfare</u>. Homewood, Illinois: Dorsey Press, 1982.

11. The author is following the interpretation of social services and human services as suggested in Alfred Kahn. <u>Social Policy and Social Services</u>. New York, NY: Random House, 1973, p. 24.

12. This listing of the common characteristics of human service networks is a composite of characteristics described by a variety of authors, such as Alan Gartner and Frank Riessman. <u>Service Society and Consumer Vanguard</u>. New York, NY: Harper and Row, Inc., 1974; Joan Wright and William Burmeister, <u>Introduction to Human Services</u>. Columbus, OH: Grid, Inc. 1973; Evelyn Schulman, <u>Intervention in Human Services</u>, St. Louis, MO: L. B. Mosby Co., 1974; and Karen Erickson, <u>Human Services Today</u>, Reston Publishing Co., Reston, VA, 1981.

13. The author's definition of what is called social welfare is substantially different than most textbooks. The concept used here is one which enables the student to grasp the complexity and variability of the human services network, yet make distinctions between various parts of the network.

14. These implications of a service economy were adapted from Solomon Barkin, op cit.; George Stigler, op cit., and Victor Fuchs, op cit.

SUGGESTED READINGS

Victor Fuchs. The Service Economy. New York, NY: Columbia University Press, 1968. For the individual who is not well grounded in economics, this monograph provides an overview of the concept of a service economy and its development.

Alan Gartner and Frank Riessman. Service Society and Consumer Vanguard. New York, NY: Harper and Row, Inc., 1974. This book provides a philosophical and conceptual foundation for the role of the consumer as a participant in social services and a description of the personal social services.

Marvin Olsen. The Process of Social Organization. New York, NY: Holt, Rinehart and Winston, Inc., 1968. This book provides the conceptual foundation for reviewing social institutions as social networks. For the individual acquainted with sociological thought, it provides an excellent background for an understanding of social organization and structure.

Arthur Pearl. "The Human Society: An Ecological Perspective," pp. 39-68 in Alan Gartner, Russell Nixon and Frank Riessman. Public Service Employment: An Analysis of Its History, Problems and Prospects. New York, NY: Praeger Publishers, 1973. This article will introduce the individual who is unfamiliar with the concept of an ecologically oriented economy to this concept and help explain why this concept will take on greater meaning in the near future.

Robert Wicks. Human Services: New Careers and Roles in the Helping Professions. Springfield, IL: Charles C. Thomas Co., 1978. For a more traditional view of the human services, this book provides a general overview.

REFERENCES

Azarnoff, Roy and Jerome Seliger. Delivering Human Services, Englewood Cliffs, NJ: Prentice Hall, Inc., 1982.

Baker, Frank and John Northman. Helping: Human Services for the 80s. St. Louis, MO: L. V. Mosby Co., 1981.

Barkin, Solomon. Manpower Problems in the Service Sector. Paris, France: Organization for Economic Cooperation and Development, 1966.

Croner, Helga and Kurt Guggenheim. National Directory of Private Social Agencies 1986. Queens Village, NY: Croner Publications, Inc. 1986.

Dolgoff, Ralph and Donald Feldstein. Understanding Social Welfare 2nd Ed. New York: NY: Longman Inc., 1984.

Epstein, Charlotte. An Introduction to the Human Services. Englewood Cliffs, NJ: Prentice Hall, Inc., 1981.

Erickson, Karen. Human Services Today. Reston, VA: Reston Publishing Co., 1981.

Fink, Arthur, Jane Pfouts and Andrew Dobelstein. The Field of Social Work, 8th ed. Beverly Hills, CA: Sage Publications, Inc., 1986.

Fuchs, Victor. "The Growing Importance of Service Industries." Occasional Paper #96, New York, NY: National Bureau of Economic Research, 1965.

Fuchs, Victor. The Service Economy. New York, NY: Columbia University Press, 1968.

Galbraith, John. The New Industrial State, 3rd Ed. Boston Massachusetts: Haughton Mifflin Co., 1978.

Gartner, Alan and Frank Riessman. Service Society and Consumer Vanguard. New York, NY: Harper and Row, Inc., 1974.

Gersuny, Carl and William Rosengren. The Service Society. Cambridge, MA: Schenkman Publishing Co., 1973.

Gilbert, Neil and Harry Specht. Handbook of the Social Services. Englewood Cliffs, NJ: Prentice Hall, Inc., 1981.

Halmos, Paul. The Personal Service Society. New York, NY: Schocken Books, 1970.

Kahn, Alfred. Social Policy and Social Services. New York, NY: Random House Inc., 1973.

Kase, Donald. The Human Services. New York, NY: AMS Press, Inc., 1979.

Kleinberg, Benjamin. American Society in the Post Industrial Age. Columbus, OH: Charles E. Merrill Co., 1973.

Macarov, David. The Design of Social Welfare. New York, NY: Holt, Rinehart and Winston, Inc., 1978.

Mehr, Joseph. Human Services. Boston, MA: Allyn and Bacon, Inc., 1980.

Minahan, Anne (ed.). Encyclopedia of Social Work. Two volumes, 18th issue. Washington, DC: National Association of Social Workers, 1986.

Morris, Robert. Social Policy of the American Welfare State. New York, NY: Harper and Row Publishers, 1979.

Naisbitt, John. Megatrends. New York, NY: Random House, 1984.

Olsen, Marvin. The Process of Social Organization. New York, NY: Holt, Rinehart and Winston, Inc., 1968.

Pearl, Arthur. "The Human Society: An Ecological Perspective," pp. 39-68 in Alan Gartner, Russell Nixon and Frank Riessman, Public Service Employment: An Analysis of Its History, Problems and Prospects. New York, NY: Praeger Publishers, 1973.

Russo, Francis and George Willis. Human Services in America. Englewood Cliffs, NJ: Prentice-Hall, Inc., 1986.

Schmolling, Paul, Jr., Merrill Youkeles and William R. Burger. Human Services in Contemporary America. Monterey, CA: Brooks Cole Publishing Co., 1985.

Schulman, Evelyn. Intervention in Human Services. St. Louis, MO: L. B. Mosby Co., 1974.

Siegel, Sheldon. Social Service Manpower Needs: An Overview to 1980. New York, NY: Council on Social Work Education, 1975.

Stigler, George. Trends on Employment in the Service Industries. Princeton, NJ: Princeton University Press, 1956.

United States Department of Commerce. Bureau of the Census, <u>1980</u> <u>Census of Population: Classified Index of Industries and Occupations: Final Edition</u>, Washington, D.C.: U.S. Government Printing Office, 1982.

United States Department of Commerce, Bureau of the Census, <u>Statistical Abstract of the United States: 1986 (106th Edition)</u>, Washington, D.C.: U.S. Government Printing Office, 1985.

United States Department of Labor, <u>Occupational Outlook Handbook 1986-87 Edition</u>, Washington, D.C.: U.S. Government Printing Office, 1986.

Wicks, Robert. <u>Human Services: New Careers and Roles in the Helping Professions</u>. Springfield, IL: Charles C. Thomas Co., 1978.

Wright, Joan and William Burmeister. <u>Introduction to Human Services</u>. Columbus, OH: Grid, Inc., 1973.

Zastrow, Charles. <u>Introduction to Social Welfare Institutions</u>. Homewood, IL: Dorsey Press, 1982.

CHAPTER 2

HUMAN SERVICES and HELPING PROFESSIONS*

"For true quality of life, some basic conditions must be met, among which the very least would be: 1) security; 2) a measure of (but not too much) comfort; 3) congruency and meaning in life; and 4) opportunity for attaining a sense of belonging, competence and usefulness." (Pearl, 1973:60)

INTRODUCTION

The above statement, written by an economist, is arguing for a redefinition of what economics is or should be. Economics is not just big business but is involved with the totality of one's life style. The objectives stated above reflect a human service oriented economy. In the last chapter there was a discussion of service industries and the location of human services within the network of societal institutions and a distinction made between general human services and social welfare. This chapter focuses on what are the occupations and professions in the human service networks, which of them can be called helping professions, and their commonality and differences. A model is then presented of the commonalities and differences between the helping professions.

OCCUPATIONS and PROFESSIONS (PROFESSIONAL HELPERS)

Using the concept of a human service network discussed in chapter 1, the next logical question is; what are human service occupations and professions? A human service occupation or profession is one which has as its primary focus serving people and is employed by one of the human service networks. Another way of expressing this is to label them "professional helpers," (concern is people and their problems) as indicated in Chapter 1.

Figure 2-1 shows examples of human service occupations and professions involved in each societal network.[1]

CLASSIFICATION of PROFESSIONAL HELPER OCCUPATIONS and PROFESSIONS

The following listing of occupations and professions is not exhaustive since the number of occupational titles which are used in the human service network is voluminous. According to

41

Figure 2-1

Some Examples of Human Service Occupations
and Professions Employed in Each Societal Network

	Occupation Status	
	Profession (4 yr. BA, BS degree or above	Paraprofession (1-2 yr. cert. or AA degree or les
Aesthetic	Art, dance, music therapy, social work, psychology, psychiatry	Art, dance, music therapist aide
Corrections	Social work, criminal justice, nurse, dentist, physician, child care, sociology, psychology, human service, teacher, clergy	Correctional officer, child care worker, recreation specialist
Economic	Personnel manager, clergy, social work, psychologist, nurse, librarian	Clerk, personnel aide
Education	Teacher, guidance counselor, social work, psychology, nurse, librarian	Teacher aide, day care worker
Employment and Manpower	Vocational counselor, manpower specialist, social Work, teacher	Interviewer
Environment Protection	Home economics, consumer affairs, social work, physician, library science, nurse	Consumer complaint specialist
Housing	Housing specialist, housing manager urban planner, architect, social work	Housing aide, awareness counselor
Income Maintenance	Social work, social security, supervision, home economics, lawyer	Welfare aide, financial assistance worker, social security aide, interviewer, homemaker
Information and Referral	Library science and information science, social work	Library aide
Judicial	Judge, lawyer, court administrator, social Work, psychology, psychiatry, physician	Clerk of court, court stenographe
Legal	Lawyer, social work, psychology	Legal assistant, legal stenographe

42

Figure 2-1 (cont'd)

| | Occupation Status | |
| | Profession | Paraprofession |
	(4 yr. BA, BS degree or above	(1-2 yr. cert. or AA degree or less
ure and Recreation	Sociology, psychology, social work, therapeutic recreation	Leisure aide
al Health	Psychology, social work, psychiatry, nursing, library science	Mental health aide
tary	Physician, nurse, social work, psychology, psychiatry, library and information science, teacher	Technician, social service aide, psychiatric aide, medical aide, recreation specialist
al Support	Professional volunteer, social work	Volunteers
onal Social Service	Social work, psychology, psychiatry, human service generalist, home economics	Human service, social service aide, technician, welfare aide
ical Health	Physician, nursing, allied health, hospital adm., medical records, social work, dietician, public health	Paramedic, medical records, licensed practical nurse, midwife
tical	Psychology, social work, Lawyer, public relations	Volunteers
ective Service	Law enforcement, FBI, criminal justice, security specialist	Meter person, clerk, firefighter
bilitation	Rehabilitation counselor, social work, therapeutic recreation	Orderly, nursing aide
gious	Clergy, pastoral counselor, social work	Lay worker, volunteer

the Classified Index of Industries and Occupations (1982) there are over 2,000 occupational and professional titles which directly relate to employment of personnel in the human service networks. According to the 1980 Census of Population: Subject Reports: Occupation by Industry (1984) their were over 16 million people employed in occupations and professions which are in the human service networks. These occupational and professional titles are classified as: managerial and professional specialty occupations, technical sales and administrative support occupations, and service occupations.

MANAGERIAL and PROFESSIONAL SPECIALTY—This classification is subdivided into three categories: managerial, executive and legislative, and professional specialist. Some examples of managerial (administration) occupations and professions include the following: consumer affairs, corrections, courts, education, employment, health, hospital, housing, immigrant relocation, manpower, parks and recreation, personnel, police and fire, social security, social services, etc.

Some examples of executive and legislative occupations and professions include the following: alderman, assemblyman, congressman, delegate, legislator, tribal councilman, U.S. representative, U.S. senator, United Nations delegate, etc. Some examples of professional specialty occupations and professions include the following: anthropology, architect archivist/ curator, art therapy, chiropractor, clergy/nun, consumer affairs, counselor (college placement, education, employment, guidance, rehabilitation, veteran's, vocational), dentistry, dietectics, economist, genealogy, health diagnosing (acupuncture, hypnotherapy, etc.), historian, home economist, housing specialist, human service generalist, inhala- tion therapy, judge, lawyer, librarian (library and information science), manpower specialist, music therapy, occupational therapy, optometrist, physical therapy, physician (allopathic, homeopathic, osteopathic, psychiatry), personnel manager, physicians assistant, podiatrist, political scientist, psychology, public relations, recreation work, registered nurse, social security interviewer, sociology, social work, speech therapy and audiology, teacher (pre-kindergarten and kinder- garten, primary and secondary, college and university, special education, others), therapeutic recreation, urban planner, etc.

TECHNICAL, SALES and ADMINISTRATIVE SUPPORT—This classification is subdivided into three categories: technical, sales, and administrative support. Some examples of technical occupations include the following: clinical laboratory, dental hygiene, medical health records, medical technology, radiology, licensed practical nurse, health technician, legal assistant, etc. Some

examples of sales occupations include the following: demon-
strator, food counselor, goodwill representative, etc. Some
examples of administrative support occupations include the
following: child care, library clerk, medical clerk,
stenographer (court, legal, medical), teacher aide, etc.

PROTECTIVE SERVICES--This classification is subdivided into two
categories: protective service, and service occupations. Some
examples of protective service occupations include the following: corrections officer, Federal Bureau of Investigation
agents, firefighter, guards (public), guards (private), police
and detectives (public), police and detectives (private),
sheriffs and bailiff, human service generalist, etc. Some
examples of service occupations include the following: dental
assistant, child care, health aide, nursing aide, welfare
service aide, etc.

This listing of professional specialties and service occupations is similar to the classification system used by Hopke in
the Encyclopedia of Careers and Vocational Guidance (1978), but
is more extensive. The above listing of human service occupations and professions implicitly recognize some differences
between each of the major groupings of occupations and
professions.

DIFFERENCES BETWEEN PROFESSIONAL HELPER OCCUPATIONS and
PROFESSIONS

Ideally, professional helper occupations and professions
employed in the human service networks differ on a number of
attributes:

1. Focus of service - is it a specific problem or a general
    problem.

2. Type of interaction or relationship to the consumer - is it
    reactive (respond to situation), proactive (preventative to
    a situation), or interactive (mutual involvement in a
    situation).

3. Degree of professionalism - is there a low or a high
    development of educational and professional standards.

4. Intensity and timing of the relationship - is it minimal and
    a non-frequent involvement or an intense, frequent
    involvement.

5. Knowledge base - is it natural science, social science,
    philosophy or a combination.

For example, four professional helper occupations and professions employed in the human service network are fire fighter, library and information science, police/detective and social work. Each of these occupations vary on the attributes described above. Figure 2-2 shows an ideal model of how these occupations and professions would differ.

GENERAL DEVELOPMENT of PROFESSIONAL HELPER OCCUPATIONS and PROFESSIONS

Societies historically have had individuals or occupations and professions which helped individuals in need. Historically, the primary recognized professions have been clergy, lawyers and physicians. Until 1200-1300 A.D., it was common in Western society for a clergyman to be a lawyer as well as a physician. These three professions were the primary recognized ones until 1850, along with a series of other occupations including pharmacy, dentistry, overseers of the poor, male nurses, etc. In addition, there were professional problem-solvers such as engineers and architects.

1850-1925 - A period of rapid expansion of professional helpers was from 1850-1925, with the trend toward professionalization and specialization of occupations. This time period was one of rapid technological and social change in the United States, consisting of the Industrial Revolution, and the shift from a rural agrarian society to an urbanized technological society. It was a period of optimism (manifest destiny), new discoveries in medicine, natural science and the beginnings of social science. Along with these broad societal changes were specific problems of urban slums, public health, unemployment, limited education, immigration, etc. In order for society to cope with these problems, individuals and organizations began to utilize the new discoveries in natural and social science to develop programs and services to alleviate these problems.

As occupations utilized the findings of natural and social science, some previous occupations were striving for professionalization, and new occupations emerged which became professionalized. Some of the older occupations which became professionalized include dentists, historians, librarians, pharmacists, podiatrists and optometrists. Many newer occupations developed as society became specialized, performing tasks which were done previously by the family, kinship groups, or the clergy. Examples of the major occupations which developed between 1850-1925 include social work, nursing, teacher, home economics, police/detective, dietetics, chiropractors, recreational workers, vocational counselor, psychiatry, psychology, pastoral counselor, economist, anthropology,

Figure 2-2

Idealized Model of Some Differences Between Occupations and
Professions Employed in the Human Service Network on Selected Attributes

	Attribute				
Occupation and Profession	Focus of Service	Degree of Relation- ship	Degree of Profession- alization	Intensity & Timing	Knowledge Base
Fire Fighter	specific	low	low	low	natural science
Police/ Detective	specific	medium	medium	medium relations	law & human
Library and Information Science	specific	medium	medium	medium	resource information
Social Work	general/ specific	high	high	high	human relations & social science

sociology, political science, etc. In many cases, individuals involved in these occupations intially received in-service training, with educational programs for these occupations developing between 1900-1925. By 1950 all of the occupations listed above had achieved professional status.

1925-1960 — As the United States society became more tech-nological in its industrial orientation and social problems remained, the older and newer professions began to specialize. For example, in 1925 there were four to six specialties in medicine and nursing. Today, along with allied health there are over one hundred specialties. In social work in 1925, there were about four to six specialties, today there are over twenty-five. In addition to existing professions expanding and specializing, a series of other occupations emerged which eventually became recognized as professions.

Examples of occupations and professions which emerged since 1925 include hospital administrator, rehabilitation counselor, vocational (employment) counselor, occupational therapist, personnel manager, public relations expert, urban planner, osteopath, guidance counselor, physical therapist, speech pathologist, college placement officer, music therapist, etc.

1960 On - Newer occupational groups are still developing which are seeking professional status and recognition. Some examples of recent occupational groups seeking professional status include art and dance therapy, child care work, human service generalist, suicidologist, alcohol and drug specialist, sexual counselor, leisure counselor, consumer specialist, child placement specialist, therapeutic recreation, fire fighter, court administrator, housing manager, etc.

In this movement for professionalism there has also been an expansion of paraprofessional programs for corrections officers, paralegal aides, paramedics, paramental health aides, teacher aides, welfare aide, etc. In addition, there are specialized programs for professional volunteers.

"PROFESSIONAL HELPER" and "HELPING PROFESSION"

Not all professional helper occupations and professions employed in the human service network can be classified as a "helping profession." Although the occupations and professions listed on pages 44-45 are employed in the human service networks and are considered "professional helpers," not all of them can be considered to be a helping profession. A "professional helper" is one whose primary function is the delivery of a social service with no or a low degree of relationship with the client served. A "helping profession" is one whose primary function is the delivery of a social service with a high degree of relationship with the client served and uses knowledge of human behavior and skills in the formation of relationships in working with people.[2] In making distinctions between "professional helpers" and "helping profession," one relies on two concepts: the degree of professionalism and whether the focus of working with people is the establishment of some form of relationship.

PROFESSIONALISM

Major concepts used today in looking at occupations and professions are the concepts of para-professional and professional. The term paraprofessional usually connotes a technical training obtained either through in-service training or completion of a technical course (usually from 6 weeks to 2 years in duration. The term professional usually connotes university education (or recognized professional school) and a program of

48

3-plus years. Most professional programs require 4-6 years of post-secondary education.

Occupations which are considered a profession change over time, and not all occupations in their various aspects are equally professionalized. Prior to 1900 there were three main professions recognized (clergy, law and medicine), and many members of these professions did not obtain a university education. The concept of a university education and professional schools in the United States is primarily a development since 1900. A number of occupations which have been recognized as professions since 1900 include social work, psychology, nursing, education, etc., and the movement toward professionalism has increased dramatically since 1960. For example, prior to 1960 there was not a recognized profession of art therapy or child care, now there is. Police/detective occupations, although considered a profession, is not equally professionalized in all of its components. Some police/detective personnel have degrees (4 or more years) in Police Science or Criminal Justice, some have completed a technical (2-year degree) program in Police Science, others only in service training (a 2-6 month training program), and others may have learned on the job.

In addition to education and training, the term professional implies other characteristics such as mental activity and decision making. The term "profession" is usually assigned to an occupation which requires a high degree of mental activity with decision making functions, in addition to academic and experiential credentials. For example, a physician is expected to make a diagnosis and decide which treatment technique to use. A person becomes a physician after a period of academic training and internship. In contrast, a volunteer in a hospital is not expected to make major decisions and usually has not had a high level of academic training or a period of internship.

An acceptable way of viewing an occupation to determine whether it is a profession or not is to describe the general characteristics of a profession and then look at specific occupations to see whether they possess a number of these characteristics. In general, a profession has all or most of the following characteristics:

1. professional organization and culture.

2. a specialized body of knowledge.

3. an ethical code and a sense of altruism.

4. requires academic training, including an internship.

5.   is service oriented.

6.   a high degree of autonomy in making decisions.

7.   a system of self-regulation.

8.   a system of specialized techniques.

RELATIONSHIP

One of the attributes described earlier which creates distinctions between the various "professional helpers" is that of interaction or relationship (see figure 2-2 and definitions, page 45). A helping profession is expected to develop some form of interactive relationship (mutual involvement of both parties) with the person seeking service such as a family counselor or a teacher (primary, secondary and post secondary level). This relationship is expected to occur overtime and usually has a medium to high level of intensity.

For example, a teacher is expected to know each of their students and be able to discuss non-educational matters with the student which necessitates mutual involvement of both parties. A social worker is expected to explore feelings, emotions and perceptions of a person seeking or required to seek counseling which would necessitate mutual involvement of both parties. On the other hand, a clinical laboratory technician in preparing and analyzing tests may never see the patient. The medical records administrator may never see the patient, and the librarian may spend 1-2 (or more) minutes with the recipient of services.

HELPING PROFESSION

Using the concepts of profession and relationship one can look at those occupations and professions employed in the human service networks and listed on pages 44-45, and classify the following as a "helping profession": art therapy, clergy/nun, consumer affairs, counselor (college placement, education, employment, guidance, rehabilitation, veteran's, vocational, home economist, lawyer, judge, music therapy, occupational therapy, physical therapy, physician (allopathic, homeopathic, osteopathic, psychiatry), psychology, registered nurse, social work, speech therapy and audiology, teacher (pre-kindergarten, kindergarten, primary and secondary, college and university, special education, others), and therapeutic recreation. In effect, these professions are expected to provide some degree of individual and group counseling. Of the 53 professional specialty occupations listed on pages 44-45 as professional helpers, 30 can be included as a "helping profession."

The following technical and service occupations (paraprofessionals) striving for professional status listed on pages 44-45 because of changing concepts of their relative tasks can be considered as having "helping profession" functions: police/ detective, child care, human service generalist, and dance therapy amongst others.

COMMONALITY of the HELPING PROFESSIONS

If the "helping professions" are unique from the other "professional helpers," one should be able to identify some distinctive characteristics. One can look at characteristics which relate to the system of service, to the personnel implementing the service, and to a philosophical system.

SYSTEM of SERVICE

Ideally, some common elements of the "helping professions" as they relate to the system of service include:

1. A formalized and written commitment to provide service. Both the professional organization and the operational organization will have written policies or statements which indicate that providing service is their reason to be. For example, the code of ethics for the National Association of Social Workers contains a statement on "commitment to service" and the stated purpose of most correctional agencies is "protection of society and rehabilitation of the offender." Similar statements can be found in the code of ethics of the American Medical Association, American Bar Association, in hospitals courts, etc. [This characteristic may be true of all professional helpers, depending upon the degree of professionalization.]

2. A dependent clientele. When individuals, groups or larger social units come to the expert (voluntarily, or in some cases involuntarily) they usually depend upon the expert to make suggestions, recommendations or in some cases decisions. Therefore, the relationship between the provider or purveyor of a service and the person seeking service is usually one of dominance, and submission, or acceptance. A person normally accepts with resignation and compliance the diagnosis and recommendation of a physician and will normally submit to a warranted arrest by a police officer. In the educational system, children will usually accept the teacher as "the authority."

3. Institutionalized referral system. Most helping profession organizations do not heavily advertise to seek clients. Instead, clients come to them through other agencies, general knowledge, or informal resources. State prisons do not advertise their services nor use public relations techniques to attract inmates. Their clientele are sent to them by other agencies after having gone through a rather elaborate process, e.g., arrest, court hearing and conviction. With the development of private practice and a different orientation in the legal profession, this characteristic is becoming less visible.

4. Credentialing process. Most helping professions have a fairly rigid classification system of work activity based upon education and degrees, ranging from Ph.D. (doctoral degree) through M.S. (master's degree), B.S. (bachelor's degree), AA (associate of art degree), and high school education. See Figure 2-3 for examples of credentialism and specialization using the helping professions of medicine, law, theology and social work.

5. Specialization. The helping professions have a high degree of specialization (see Figure 2-3 for examples of specialization), partly as a consequence of the credentialing process, the variety of different tasks to be performed, and the breadth of knowledge needed. For example, there are at least thirty-two medical specialties and at least twenty-five social work specialties.

6. Generally operate through bureaucratic organizations. Many services are implemented through bureaucracies such as hospitals, mental institutions, public welfare departments, etc. Even when the service is provided through a smaller unit, there is still a well-organized and at times ritual-like atmosphere in obtaining services.

7. Role clusters. Helping professions find themselves filling certain role clusters, although the manner or mode they use to perform these roles will vary from profession to profession. Some common role clusters are: enabler, supporter, detection, broker, advocacy, mobilizer, instructor, behavior changer, restorative, information processor, administrator, care giver, consultant, rule maker, rule implementor, etc.

Figure 2-3

A Comparison Between Four Helping Professions
on Horizontal and Vertical Specialization*

Vertical Specialization by Degree of Professionalization or Training	Horizontal Specialization (speciality by problem or task) by Helping Profession			
	Medicine	Law	Theology	Social Work
Professional (Ph.D., M.S., or B.S. degrees depending upon profession)	Internist Neurologist Surgeon Obstetrics/ Gynecology Orthopedics Psychiatry	Corporate law Criminal law International law Maritime law Tax Law	Minister Priest Rabbi	Correctional Social Work Community Planner Psychiatric Social Work School Social Work
Paraprofessional (AA degrees, special training)	Laboratory Technician Paramedic Operating Room Assistant X-Ray Technician	Court Stenographer Legal Secretary Paralegal Aide	Lay Deacon Lay Sunday School Directors	Case Aide Child Care Worker Correctional Officer (guard) School Aide
Volunteer (No special training except orientation sessions)	Candy Striper Friendly Visitor Home Visitor	Intake Aide Research Aide	Advis. Brd. Members Sun. School Teachers Youth Activity Leaders	Hot lines Housecoping Volunteers in probation

Source: From Introduction to Social Welfare Institutions, revised edition, by Charles Zastrow, p. 79, Homewood, Illinois: Copyright (c) The Dorsey Press, 1978, 1982.

53

8. Parallel system. The helping professions in the United States primarily provide services through a public or private agency. In addition, one needs to recognize that many individuals bypass the helping professions and instead use an informal or folk system. The term "parallel system" means the simultaneous existence of a public, private and informal system to solve problems. Figure 2-4 shows the relationship of these three systems.[3]

PERSONNEL IMPLEMENTING the SERVICE

Some common characteristics of the helping professions who provide services are as follows:

1. Adherence to a problem-solving model. Depending upon different authors, the steps involved in the problem-solving model vary from five to seven. The basic steps in the problem-solving model are:

    a. Defining the problem situation.

    b. Determining the causes of or conditions associated with a specific problem.

    c. Determining the possible approaches or treatment plan to solving a specific problem.

    d. Determining the most feasible approach or treatment plan to solve a specific problem.

    e. Applying the selected approach or treatment plan to a specific problem.

    f. Evaluating the effectiveness of the approach or treatment plan in solving a specific problem.

2. Communication skills, both verbal and non-verbal. These skills involve those of observation, recording, reporting, speaking, writing and interviewing. The person should have an understanding of verbal and non-verbal communication as well as a sense of timing, affect and effect in talking with people.

3. Development of a relationship. The helping professions rely on person-to-person interaction and relationship skills in helping a person with a problem. A relationship with a client consists of three parts:

54

Figure 2-4

Examples of Parallel Systems of Human Service Networks

| Network | Parallel System | | |
	Public	Private	Folk (informal)
Education	Public Schools	Private Schools	Family Schools
Income Maintenance	Social Security Public Assistance	Pension plans Insurance plans	Parents, siblings
Medical Health	County/State Hospitals	Private Hospitals	Herbs, faith healing
Protective Service	State, County, Municipal Police	Merchants Police private security	Vigilante groups

a. Establishment of a relationship between the person seeking help and the person offering or providing help.

b. Use of the relationship as a medium of help which includes aspects of determination of reality, empathetic listening and talking, and provision for emotional support.

c. The process of a relationship which includes; mutual discussion, some unpleasantness, specific purpose of the relationship, offers something new, has an element of choice, is non-judgmental and occurs in the present, i.e., the interview situation.

4. Ethos and professional commitment. Professions have a code of ethics guiding their behavior and their sense of commitment in providing services to the client.[4]

PHILOSOPHICAL SYSTEM

Paul Halmos in The Personal Service Society (1970) ideally describes the philosophical assumptions underlying the helping professions which are more or less common to them. These assumptions are more typical of those professions having a social science knowlege base in comparison to those professions having a natural science base. He describes these commonalities as: ideology, values and knowledge base.

1. Examples of a common ideology which he calls the counseling ideology would include:

   a. Positive, caring, compassionate approach.

   b. Behavior is learned through intimate relationships.

   c. Behavior is changed through intimate relationships.

   d. Use of one's personality as part of behavior change.

   e. Generally a non-directive approach.

   f. Seek solution.

2. Examples of a common value base would include:

   a. Tolerance.

   b. Non-judgmentality.

   c. Honesty.

   d. Use of insight.

   e. Confidentiality.

3. Some examples of a common knowledge base would include:

   a. Human behavior is learned.

   b. Learning is developmental.

   c. Unconscious material.

   d. Use of mental defenses.

   e. All behavior is positive or negative.[5]

The above aspects of commonality were used in order to highlight the perspective that when one attempts to generally describe common factors of a complex system, one should have a clear concept of which part of the system one is describing and comparing.

Figure 2-5 compares the four helping professions of medicine, law, theology, and social work on some of the common characteristics. This model can be applied to other "helping professions" and "professional helpers."

DIFFERENCES BETWEEN the HELPING PROFESSIONS

Although there are some common characteristics which delineate "helping professions" from other "professional helpers," it is obvious there are differences between the helping professions. If there were no differences, between them, there would be no need for the multiplicity and proliferation of the "helping professions."

Undoubtedly, there are many ways in which one can compare and contrast helping professionals. The model presented here assumes six basic differences between the helping professions; knowledge base, value base, interventive repertoire, historical precedent, problem focus, and predominant role clustering.

KNOWLEDGE BASE

Depending upon the helping profession, the underlying knowledge base may be in social science, natural science, philosophy, or a combination. Within the knowledge base there again is a concentration on whether the emphasis is on techniques of working with people, a specialized area of social policy, or a specific social problem like acohol or drugs. For a helping profession only part of the knowledge base is learned in the university setting or through academic training. The remainder of one's knowledge is learned through internship programs, field training, and later, learning through experience.

VALUE BASE

Each helping profession has a code of ethics which articulates their values. The printed code of ethics for the helping professions sound remarkably the same, i.e., service oriented, client comes first, objectivity, etc. However, as one investigates the code of ethics and value base in more detail, one can detect differences in value assumptions regarding humankind, the role of the professional, and area of concern, such as whole person or specific problem.

Figure 2-5

A Comparison Between Four Helping Professions on the Common
Characteristics of Personnel Implementing a Service*

Common Elements	Helping Profession			
	Medicine	Law	Theology	Social Work
Problem Solving Process Model	a) Information b) Diagnosis c) Treatment plan d) Treatment e) Followup	a) Information b) Case or legal precedent c) Debate case d) Decision e) Followup	a) Information b) Theological or moral precedent c) Suggest alternatives d) Followup	a) Define Problem b) Find cause c) Treatment plan d) Treatment e) Evaluation
Communication Skills	Information Action/reaction and some interaction	Information Action/reaction and some interaction	Information and behavior modification type Transaction and interaction	Information and behavior modification type Transaction and interaction
Development of a Relationship	Specific, short-term, objective	Specific, short-term, objective	General, long-term, objective and specific, short-term, objective	Specific, long-term objective and spec short-term, object
Ethos and Professional Commitment	See American Medical Association Code of Ethics	See American Bar Association Code of Ethics	See specific denomina- of code of ethics	See National Associ of Social Workers of Ethics

*Source: From Introduction to Social Welfare Institutions, Revised Edition, by Charles Zastrow, p. 83, Homewood, Illinois: Copyright (c) The Dorsey Press, 1978, 1982.

INTERVENTIVE REPERTOIRE

All helping professions intervene in problems. Examples of interventive techniques include chemotherapy and surgery (medicine), legal precedent (law), moral advising and admonition (theology), and psychotherapy (social work). The style and range of intervention activities will vary, depending upon the profession's knowledge and value base.

HISTORICAL PRECEDENT

Most individuals have a perception that the helping professions which exist have been in existence for a long time. The actual fact is that only three helping professions were recognized prior to 1900. These were medicine, law, and theology. Each of these professions had been in existence since about 3000 B.C. or earlier. However, university training for medicine and law is rather recent (since 1850). Theology as a helping profession, to a limited extent, had some form of education at the university level or a separate professional school since the Middle Ages or about 1200 A.D.

PROBLEM FOCUS

This attribute is an intuitive one in the sense that we can classify the helping professions in terms of the specific concerns they concentrate on. For example, medicine-health problems, law-legal problems, theology-significance of self problems, and social work-social problems. There is some overlap of the problem focus for the helping professions, however, the problem focus clearly differentiates between certain helping professions.

PREDOMINANT ROLE CLUSTERING

Roles for specific helping professions will vary, depending upon the specialization within the profession. For example, in medicine a key role is that of restoration, in law advocate, in theology supporter, and in social work behavior changer. These role differences between the four exemplary helping professions are only examples of role differences. The reader cannot assume these are the only role differences nor that the other helping professions do not engage in these roles.

Figure 2-6, for exemplary purposes, compares and contrasts the helping professions of medicine, law, theology, and social work on the characteristics which delineate differences between the helping professions. This model can be applied to other "helping professions" and "professional helpers."[6]

Figure 2-6

A Comparison Between Four Helping Professions
on the Characteristic of Differences*

Difference Elements	Helping Profession			
	Medicine	Law	Theology	Social Work
Knowledge Base	Natural Science Physiology Anatomy Pathology	Philosophy/Social science/legal precedent Civil law Criminal law System of justice	Theology Philosophical principles Morality	Social Science Human Development Cultural variation Methods of interacti
Value Base	Man as a physical system contracts diseases. Concern is pathology and does not focus on the value of the individual.	Man as a social animal has conflicts over rights Basic concern is justice and does not focus on the value of the person.	Man is good but commits errors. Concern is the whole person.	Man is good. Individuality and understand whole person.
Interventive Repertoire	Surgery Drugs Advice	Case analysis Advice Information	Counseling Advice Information Prayer	Casework, which may include psychothera Group work Community organizati
Historical Precedent	Pre 3,000 B.C.	Pre 3,000 B.C.	Since mankind existed	Since 1900
Problem Focus	Physical problems	Legal problems	Moral problems	Social problems
Predominent Role Clustering	Restoration	Advocate	Supporter	Behavior changer

*Source: From Introduction to Social Welfare Institutions, Revised Edition, by Charles Zastrow, p. 84, Homewood, Illinois: Copyright (c) The Dorsey Press, 1978, 1982.

SUMMARY

This chapter focused on the broad range of occupations and professions responsible for the delivery of social services within the human service networks. There was a discussion of what is meant by the terms "occupation," "para-professional," and "professional." The general characteristics of a profession were described and a distinction made between "professional helpers" and "helping professions." A brief historical review showed the recent development of "professional helpers" and "helping professions" and indicated some of the emerging professions.

A model was then presented showing the commonality of the helping professions from the perspective of the system of service, personnel and philosophical system. A model showing the differences between the helping professions was developed. For expediency, the models of commonalities and differences of the helping professions was applied to four professions: medicine, law, theology and social work. The model could be applied to any of the "professional helpers" and "helping professions."

The format of the remainder of the book is to discuss each network in society, describe the social services offered within the network, occupations and professions involved in the network, the dominant occupations and professions in the network, and the role of social work in the network. Prior to beginning an analysis of each network, the following chapter focuses on one of the helping professions, social work. The model used to examine social work as one of the "helping professions" can be applied to any of the "professional helpers" and "helping professions."

FOOTNOTES

*This chapter was reviewed for comments by Donald Martin, Professor of Sociology, University of Wisconsin-Oshkosh, Oshkosh, Wisconsin.

1. Some standard references for someone who is interested in a thumb nail sketch of a variety of occupations and professions related to human services include the following: William Hopke. The Encyclopedia of Careers and Vocational Guidance. 2 vol., 4th Edition, Chicago, Illinois: J. G. Ferguson and Co, 1978; Arnold Walter. Career Opportunities in Community Service and Related Specialties. revised edition, Chicago, Illinois: J. H. Ferguson Co., 1974;

Robert Kensinger. Career Opportunities: Health Technicians, Revised Edition, Chicago, Illinois; J. G. Ferguson Co., 1974; Peter Vallitutte and Florence Christoplos (eds.) Interdisciplinary Approaches to Human Services. Baltimore, Maryland: University Park Press, 1977; United States Department of Defense, Military-Civilian Occupational Source Book, 2nd Edition, Fort Sheridan, Illinois: Department of Defense, 1978; United States Department of Labor, Criminal Justice Careers Guidebook, Washington, D.C.: U.S. Government Printing Office, 1982; United States Department of Labor, Career Opportunities in the Electric Power and Gas Utilities Industries, Washington, D.C.: U.S. Government Printing Office, 1978; United States Department of Labor, Occupational Outlook Handbook 1986-87 Edition, Washington, D.C.: U.S. Government Printing Office, 1986 and specific career and professional pamphlets as produced by AMS Press and various professional organizations.

2. The author's distinction between a "professional helper" and a "helping profession" relies heavily upon the work of Paul Halmos. The Personal Service Society, New York, NY: Schocken Books, 1970.

3. This material is an adaptation from the following resources: Carl Gersuny and William Rosengren. The Service Society. Cambridge, MA: Schenkman Publishing Co., 1973, and Paul Halmos. The Personal Service Society. New York, NY: Schocken Books, 1970, plus elaboration by the author.

4. This material is an adaptation from the following resources: Charlotte Epstein, An Introduction to the Human Services. Englewood Cliffs, NJ: Prentice-Hall, Inc., 1981; Evelyn Schulman. Intervention in Human Services. St. Louis, MO: L. B. Mosby Co., 1974, and Joseph Mehr. Human Services, Boston MA: Allyn and Bacon Co., 1980, plus elaboration by the author.

5. This material is an adaptation from Paul Halmos. The Faith of Counselors, New York, NY: Schocken Books, 1966, plus elaboration by the author.

6. The material on professions, commonality and differences between the helping professions is adapted from Charles Zastrow, Introduction to Social Welfare. Homewood Illinois: Copyright (c) The Dorsey Press, 1978, 1982, pp. 77-85 and is reproduced in part with the permission of Dorsey Press.

SUGGESTED READINGS

Neil Gilbert and Harry Specht. Handbook of the Social Services. Englewood Cliffs, NJ: Prentice Hall Inc., 1981. This book is an excellent overview of the social services having indepth chapters on specific areas which are only covered briefly in this book.

Everett Hughes. Education for the Professions of Medicine, Law, Theology and Social Welfare. New York, NY: McGraw Hill, Inc., 1973. For an individual who is unacquainted with the literature on occupations and professions this book provides an excellent overview as well as focussing on an indepth basis for four specific professions.

Francis Russo and Goerge Willis. Human Services in America. Englewood Cliffs, New Jersey: Prentice Hall, Inc., 1986. This recent book provides a brief but sound historical and sociological overview of the major six systems in the human services. These six systems are personal social service, health, education, housing, income transfer (income maintenance), and justice (law enforcement, courts, corrections).

Peter Vallitutte and Florence Christoplos (eds.). Interdisciplinary Approaches to Human Services. Baltimore, MD: University Park Press, 1977. This is one of the few books which has taken a broad approach to the human services. The book identifies a number of areas not usually covered, such as art therapy and has a comprehensive indepth chapter on each area.

REFERENCES

Arnold, Walter. Career Opportunities in Community Service and Related Specialties, revised edition, Chicago, IL: J. G. Ferguson Co., 1974.

Austin, Michael, Alex Shelding and Philip Smith. Delivering Human Services, New York, NY: Harper & Row Publishers, 1977.

Baker, Frank and John Northman. Helping: Human Services for the 80's. St. Louis, MO: C. V. Mosby Co., 1981.

Epstein, Charlotte. An Introduction to the Human Services. Englewood Cliffs, NJ: Prentice Hall, Inc., 1981.

Erikson, Karin. *Human Services Today*. Reston, VA: Reston Publishing Co., 1981.

Gilbert, Neil and Harry Specht. *Handbook of the Social Services*. Englewood Cliffs, NJ: Prentice Hall, Inc., 1981.

Gersuny, Carl and William Rosengren. *The Service Society*. Cambridge, MA: Schenkman Publishing Co., 1973.

Halmos, Paul. *The Personal Service Society*. New York, NY: Schocken Books, 1970.

Halmos, Paul. *The Faith of the Counselors*. New York, NY: Schocken Books, 1966.

Hopke, William. *The Encyclopedia of Careers and Vocational Guidance*. 2 vols. 4th ed., Chicago, IL: J. G. Ferguson and Company, 1978.

Hughes, Everett. *Education for the Professions of Medicine, Law, Theology, and Social Welfare*. New York, NY: McGraw Hill, Inc., 1973.

Kahn, Alfred. *Social Policy and Social Services*. New York, NY: Random House Press, 1973.

Kase, Ronald E. *The Human Services*. New York, NY: AMS Press, 1979.

Lyon, William and Bill Duke. *Introduction to Human Services*. Reston, VA: Reston Publishing Co., 1981.

Mehr, Joseph. *Human Services: Concepts and Intervention Strategies*. Boston, MA: Allyn and Bacon, Inc., 1980.

Minahan, Anne (ed.). *Encyclopedia of Social Work, 18th Issue*. Washington, DC: National Association of Social Workers, 1986.

Pearl, Arthur. "The Human Society: An Ecological Perspective," pp. 39-68 in Alan Gartner, Russell Nixon and Frank Riessman, *Public Service Employment: An Analysis of Its History, Problems and Prospects*. New York, NY: Praeger Publishers, 1973.

Russo, Francis and George Willis. *Human Services in America*. Englewood Cliffs, New Jersey: Prentice Hall, Inc., 1986.

Schmolling, Paul Jr., Merrill Youkeles and William R. Burger. Human Services in Contemporary America. Monterey, California: Brooks Cole Publishing Co., 1985.

Schulman, Evelyn. Intervention in Human Services. St. Louis, MO: L. B. Mosay Co., 1974.

Sugarman, Jule. Citizen's Guide to Changes in Human Services Programs. Washington, DC: Human Services Information Center, 1981.

United States Department of Commerce, Bureau of the Census. 1980 Census of Population: Classified Index of Industries and Occupations. Final Edition, Washington, D.C.: U.S. Government Printing Office, 1982.

United States Department of Commerce, Bureau of the Census, 1980 Census of Population: Volume 2 Subject Reports, Part 7C: Occupation by Industry. Washington, D.C.: U.S. Government Printing Office, 1984.

United States Department of Defense, Military-Civilian Occupational Source Book, 2nd Edition. Fort Sheridan, Illinois: Department of Defense, 1978.

United States Department of Labor. Criminal Justice Careers Guidebook. Washington, DC: U.S. Government Printing Office, 1982.

United States Department of Labor. Career Opportunities in the Electric Power and Gas Utilities Industries. Washington, DC: U.S. Government Printing Office, 1978.

United States Department of Labor. Occupational Outlook Handbook 1986-87 Edition. Washington, DC: U.S. Government Printing Office, 1986.

Vallitutte, Peter and Florence Christoplos (eds.). Inter-disciplinary Approaches to Human Services, Baltimore, MD: University Park Press, 1977.

Wicks, Robert. Human Services: New Careers and Roles in the Helping Professions. Springfield, IL: Charles C. Thomas Publishers, 1978.

Wright, Joan and William Burmeister. Introduction to Human Services, Columbus, OH: Grid, Inc., 1973.

Zastrow, Charles. Introduction to Social Welfare Institutions. Homewood, IL: Dorsey Press, 1982.

Chapter 3

SOCIAL WORK AS A HELPING PROFESSION*

"Until recently, social welfare and social
work were regarded as synonymous."
(Siporin, 1975:1)

INTRODUCTION

The profession of social work, like other professions
involved in the network of associations called human services,
social services and social welfare, is rapidly undergoing change
in its focus for practice, educational curriculum, and in
organizations delivering social services. The focus of this
chapter is to analyze social work as one example of a helping
profession involved in the delivery of human and social services.

WHAT is SOCIAL WORK as a PROFESSION?

Some common definitions of social work as a profession
include:

Walter Friedlander (1980:4) "Social work is a professional
service, based on scientific knowledge and skill in human
relations, which helps individuals, groups or communities
obtain social or personal satisfaction and independence."

Werner Boehm (1959:54) "Social work seeks to enhance the
social functioning of individuals, singly and in groups, by
activities focused upon their social relationships which
constitute the interaction between man and his environment. These activities can be grouped into three functions: restoration of impaired capacity; provision of
individual (and community) social resources; and prevention
of social dysfunctioning."

National Association of Social Workers (1976:4) "Social
work is the professional activity of helping individuals,
groups or communities enhance or restore their capacity for
social functioning and creating societal conditions favorable to this goal."

Numerous definitions of social work as a profession are
found in the literature. Regardless of the definition used,
common themes can be identified, such as relationship of

humankind to their total environment, the development of a more satisfying life style, and a multilevel approach (individual, group, community, and social institutions). In essence, social work as a profession attempts to view the client/consumer having varying levels of need and provides services where necessary.

WHAT is SOCIAL WORK as PRACTICE?

Depending upon the focus of a specific author, social work practice can be defined in a variety of ways for example:

National Association of Social Workers 1976:4-5) "Social work practice consists of the professional application of social work values, principles, and techniques to one or more of the following ends: helping people obtain tangible services; counseling and psychotherapy with individuals, families and groups; helping communities or groups provide or improve social and health services; and participating in relevant legislative processes."

Allen Pincus and Anne Minahan(1973:9) "Social work practice is to enhance the problem solving and coping capability of people, link people with systems that provide them with resources, services, and opportunities, promote the effective and humane operation of these systems, and contribute to the development and improvement of social policy."

Harriet Bartlett (1970:84) "Social work practice consists of the application of the knowledge, values, techniques of intervention to social problems."

Max Siporin (1975:6) "Social work practice in its entirety needs to be understood as expressing the social welfare policy of our society. Social welfare administration translates social policy into social programs and services. Social treatment or direct social services enact and actualize social policy."

As with the concept of social work as a profession, other definitions of social work practice exist. Regardless of the definition, common themes of social work practice can be identified, such as intervention at various levels and related techniques, knowledge base of human behavior, social service systems in a society and values of social work.

ELEMENTS of SOCIAL WORK PRACTICE

In reviewing the definitions of social work as a profession and social work as practice, some common elements emerge regarding social work practice. These common elements of practice are <u>intervention strategy</u>, <u>knowledge base</u> and <u>value system</u>.

INTERVENTION STRATEGY - There are two types of intervention strategy: level of intervention and knowledge of specific techniques. An ideal model of <u>levels</u> of <u>intervention</u> is shown in Figure 3-1 ranging from individual to societal.

<u>Intervention knowledge</u> is a combination of academic knowledge and its application through an internship or field experience program to develop skill within the individual in the practice of social work. This content area can be classified into three types:

1. Communication and interpersonal skills: Some examples of this area include; process of interviewing, understanding nonverbal communication, relating to people at their level, making individuals feel at ease in discussing sensitive issues, becoming aware of one's own biases, a professional use of self, recording, developing social histories, etc.

2. Intervention methods: Some examples of this area include: specific methods (casework, groupwork, community organization, etc.) and general methods (problem solving process).

3. Intervention strategies: Some examples of intervention strategies are shown in Figure 3-2.

KNOWLEDGE BASE - Social work practice utilizes two types of knowledge which can be classified as practice and social science.[1]

<u>Practice Knowledge</u> refers to experiential wisdom as a consequence of working in the field. While working with people, a person picks up cues on how to assess one's behavior, develops an intuitive sense of a problem, and learns how to interpret cultural behavior patterns. Some examples of this type of wisdom include: accurately assessing a person's propensity for aggressive behavior, knowing when someone is providing the worker with misleading information ("snow job"), developing a personal style in interviewing people, correctly interpreting the behavior and response patterns of a client from a different culture.

<u>Social science knowledge</u> refers to academic knowledge gleaned from a variety of social science disciplines, such as anthropology, economics, history, minority studies, political science, psychology, sociology, urban affairs, women's studies, etc. The range of knowledge a social worker should possess includes but is not exhaustive in the following content areas:

FIGURE 3-1

LEVELS OF INTERVENTION OF SOCIAL WORK PRACTICE
(Ideal Model)*

	Focus of Intervention	General Means of Intervention
Societal Level		
↑	Inter-Societal	Social Policy/Planning
	Societal/	Social Policy/Planning
	Inter-community	Community Organization/Planning/Policy
	Community	Community Organization/Planning
	Inter-Group	Group Work/Community Organization
	Group	Group Work
	Extended Family/Network	Casework/Counseling/Broker/Network Anal
↓	Family	Casework/Counseling/Broker
Individual Level	1 to 1	Casework/Counseling/Broker

* The depth of intervention is not outlined in this chart. For example, a casework relationship may range from concrete specific aid to a depth personality change focus depending upon a specific situation. Similarly, social policy intervention may occur in a group situation and is not limited to the highest level of abstraction on the above chart.

This model of levels of intervention would apply to other helping professions with modification of language to reflect a specific professional vocabulary and orientation.

70

FIGURE 3-2

TYPES OF STRATEGIES USED IN SOCIAL WORK BY
LEVEL OF INTERVENTION*

l of Intervention	Example of Strategy
Inter Societal	Relief programs, cooperative efforts
Societal	Lobbying on specific issues Planning programs
Intercommunity	Planning Coordination of activity Cooperative efforts
Community	Mediation Planning Coordination of activity Cooperative efforts
Inter group	Mediation Analysis of objectives
Group	Role Playing Confrontation of Individual
Extended Family/Network	Network Analysis
Family	Family Sculpturing Role Analysis
One to One	Reality/Confrontation Role Playing

ategies indicated are examples only and not exhaustive of the techniques used.

1. Social Policy: a. Dynamics of policy making--legislative processes
                      b. Policy implementation--organizational structure and administrative implementation
                      c. Social service programs and resources available
                      d. Historical and philosophical foundations of social policy and social welfare
                      e. Policy and program evaluation
                      f. Legal aspects of social service programs

2. Human Behavior: a. Development over the life span
                      b. Group dynamics
                      c. Organizational structure
                      d. Cultural variation
                      e. Disadvantaged conditions
                      f. Intergroup dynamics
                      g. Community dynamics
                      h. Social change
                      i. Abnormal and pathological behavior

3. Research methods: a. Design
                      b. Testing
                      c. Analysis and interpretation
                      d. Statistics and acquaintance with computer technology

VALUE BASE - Social work as a profession has a value system which is partially shared with other helping professions and partially unique. Some general values of social work as a profession include:

1. Conviction of the inherent worth, integrity and dignity of the individual.

2. The right of self-determination.

3. A firm belief in equal opportunity for all.

4. Social responsibility toward one's self, one's family, and one's society.

5. A belief that people can change.[2]

These general values are spelled out in almost any textbook on social work. In addition to these general values, the National Association of Social Workers has developed a code of ethics which is reproduced in summary form.

Code of Ethics

National Association of Social Workers

Summary of Major Principles

I. The Social Worker's Conduct and Comportment as a Social Worker

   A. Propriety. The social worker should maintain high standards of personal conduct in the capacity or identity as a social worker.
   B. Competence and Professional Development. The social worker should strive to become and remain proficient in professional practice and the performance of professional functions.
   C. Service. The social worker should regard as primary the service obligation of the social work profession.
   D. Integrity. The social worker should act in accordance with the highest standards of professional integrity.
   E. Scholarship and Research. The social worker engaged in study and research should be guided by the conventions of scholarly inquiry.

II. The Social Worker's Ethical Responsibility to Clients

   F. Primacy of Client's Interests. The social worker's primary responsibility is to clients.
   G. Rights and Prerogatives of Clients. The social worker should make every effort to foster maximum self-determination on the part of clients.
   H. Confidentiality and Privacy. The social worker should respect the privacy of clients and hold in confidence all information obtained in the course of professional service.
   I. Fees. When setting fees, the social worker should ensure that they are fair, reasonable, considerate, and commensurate with the service performed and with due regard for the client's ability to pay.

III. The Social Worker's Ethical Responsibility to Colleagues

   J. Respect, Fairness and Courtesy. The social worker should treat colleagues with respect, courtesy, fairness and good faith.

K. __Dealing with Colleagues' Clients__. The social worker has the responsibility to relate to the clients of colleagues with full professional consideration.

IV. The Social Worker's Ethical Responsibility to Employers and Employing Organizations

L. __Commitments to Employing Organizations__. The social worker should adhere to commitments made to the employing organizations.

V. The Social Worker's Ethical Responsibility to the Social Work Profession

M. __Maintaining the Integrity of the Profession__. The social worker should uphold and advance the values, ethics, knowledge and mission of the profession.
N. __Community Service__. The social worker should assist the profession in making social services available to the general public.
O. __Development of Knowledge__. The social worker should take responsibility for identifying, developing, and fully utilizing knowledge for professional practice.

VI. The Social Worker's Ethical Responsibility to Society

P. __Promoting the General Welfare__. The social worker should promote the general welfare of society.[3]

When one reviews value statements of other professions, a duplication of some values is apparent, such as dignity of the individual, confidentiality, knowing one's limits, and so on. Unique to social work, however, is the concern for the totality of the individual (holistic approach) and the linkage between an individual and societal problem.

HISTORICAL DEVELOPMENT

Social work as both an identifiable paid occupation and a profession is of rather recent origin, having developed since 1850. Prior to 1850 social work types of activities were carried out by family members, clergy/nuns, volunteers, and some paid public officials (overseers of the poor, county superintendents of the poor, etc). The development of a paid occupation which eventually was recognized as a profession, developed slowly since 1900 and from a variety of directions.

In describing the development of social work as a profession, one can look at the fields of practice, professional organizations and educational standards.

FIELDS of PRACTICE

The "roots" of social work as an occupation and profession are in the problem of poverty, and the attempt to develop a "scientific method" to dispense advice and assistance to needy people (Charity Organization movement), and attempts to mitigate the hardships of immigrants to a new community (Settlement House movement).

Charity Organization Societies originated in London, England (1869), and in the United States in Buffalo, New York (1877). Some of the underlying principles of the Charity Organization Societies include the following:

1. Problems are a consequence of the inherent weakness in the person.

2. Moral support and uplifting are more important than providing funds.

3. Investigate each case thoroughly to avoid fraud and duplication of services.

4. Friendly visitors with some training are necessary and utilize extensively volunteer workers.

5. Central registration of clients is essential, and cooperation between agencies is necessary to reduce fraud and dependency.

The Charity Organization Society movement reflected the prevailing social and philosophical principles of Social Darwinism, individualism, a coordinating agency, and a reliance on private philanthropy. In essence, it was a response of the upper classes to benignly help the poor.

The Settlement House movement also originated in London, England (1884), with the first one in the United States in New York City (1887). The Settlement House movement had as its underlying principles the following:

1. Society has problems and individuals are caught up in them.

2. Basic services are necessary to help people cope with problems.

75

3. Reeducation is necessary to help clients, especially those who have migrated from other countries.

4. Advocacy and community organization are helpful in solving problems.

The Settlement House movement reflected the social and philosophical principles of the social gospel movement of 1870-1900 (social consciousness) with linkages to the progressive movement and political reform of the late 1800s and early 1900s.[4]

Both of the above humanitarian movements focussed on the problem of poverty, were forms of private charity, and a reaction to the public welfare system of that time period. Public welfare in the 1870's consisted of providing "help" to the poor primarily through almshouses, and secondarily, relief in the home. These private systems of "help" for the needy relied on moral exhortation and advice to solve problems rather than the disbursing of financial assistance. Individuals operating the public welfare system were appointees who had no training and had a limited awareness of the cause of the problem for which they were providing services.

More specifically, the Charity Organization Society movement was a reaction to the abuses of public welfare (indiscriminate relief-giving and lack of coordination), and attempted to develop a "scientific basis" for providing help and, later for providing financial assistance to the needy. The Settlement House movement attempted to improve social conditions, such as housing and became involved in social reform and preventative legislation. Together, these two humanitarian movements maintained the dominance of private philanthropy in the resolution of poverty until 1935 when, during the Great Depression, public welfare became the dominant means of focusing on poverty.

It was from these early beginnings in attempting to focus on poverty from a private philanthropic perspective that social work as an identifiable occupation and profession emerged. During the time period between 1900-1930 there was a rapid expansion of social work personnel and practice into many areas of endeavor, such as corrections, mental health, physical and public health, schools, etc. Figure 3-3 shows examples of the historical development of the fields of practice in which social workers are employed.[5]

FIGURE 3-3

HISTORICAL TIME LINE OF SOCIAL WORK AS A PROFESSION

Period	Professional Component		
	Fields of Practice	Organization	Educational Standards
	-1867 Public Welfare (Poverty) -1869 Family Child Welfare -1873 Corrections	1874 Conference of State Boards of Charities (as a subgroup of the American Social Science Association) -1879 National Conference of Charities established (changed to National Conference of Charities and Corrections in 1884).	
	-1885 Groups 1887 Settlement Movement (Poverty) -1899 Children's Court 1905 Medical Health -1906 Mental Health/ Schools	 -1906 National Recreation Assoc.	-1898 1st Institute for training in New York (charity Organization Society) -1903 A one year graduate program- New York School of Philanthropy
	1912 Police/Law Enforcement -1928 Industrial / International - Rapid expansion of poverty/income maintencance programs - Research	-1917 National Conference on Social Work (see 1879) -1918 American Association of Medical Social Work -1919 National Association of School Social Workers -1921 National Social Workers Exchange (American Association of social workers) -1926 American Association of Psychiatric Social Workers -1936 American Association of Group Workers -1946 Association for study of Community Organization	-1910 A 2 year graduate program New York School of Philanthropy -1919 Association of Training Schools for Professional Social Work -1921 1 year of Graduate Education requirement -1927 American Association of Schools of Professional Social Work, Certification of programs -1932 1 yr. graduate program, the standard; certification procedure for 1 year graduate program -1937 2 hr. graduate program, the standard; certification for the 2 yr. program -1942 Association of Schools of Social Service Administration

FIGURE 3-3 (continued)

HISTORICAL TIME LINE OF SOCIAL WORK AS A PROFESSION

Time Period	Professional Component		
	Field of Practice	Organization	Educational Standards
1940			
	- Community Organization/ Military	-1949 Social Work Research Group -1950 National Conference on social welfare (see 1917)	one year graduate standard -1946 National Council on Social Work Education
1950	-Drugs/ Alcohol	-1955 National Association of Social Workers	-1952 Council on Social Work Education formed (2 year graduate education standard)
1960			
	-Political altruism Urban Planning Administration	-1961 Academy of Certified Social Workers	-1962 Constituent status, undergraduate -1967 Upgrade constituent status for undergraduates
1970	- Minority Women	-1970 Recognize Bachelor of Science degree (National Association of Social Workers) -1978 Clinical Social Work Registry	-1972 Approval status, Undergraduate -1974 Recognize Bachelor of Science degree and accredit as 1st professiona degree: graduate educatior a 2 year standard (advanced standing possible).
1980	-Retrenchment of traditional prog- rams, eg., income maintenance; ex- pansion of other areas, such as eating disorders, self-help groups, sexuality, etc.		-1984 Revised accreditation and curriculum standards for the baccalaureate and master's degree

78

PROFESSIONAL ORGANIZATIONS

One characteristic of an occupation becoming a profession is the development of professional organizations.6 In social work organizational development was occurring concurrently with the expansion of the fields of practice. Two types of professional groupings emerged: an agency organization (National Conference on Social Welfare) and a practitioner organization (National Association of Social Workers).

The first form of organization to develop represented primarily public welfare agencies, later private agencies became a participant. Initially called the Conference of State Boards of Charities, the group met as a subgroup of the American Social Science organization from 1874-1879. In 1879, the group separated from the social science organization, forming the National Conference on Charities and renamed the National Conference on Charities and Corrections in 1884, the National Conference on Social Work in 1917, and since 1950 has been known as the National Conference on Social Welfare. The focus of this organization is to respond to the needs of agencies and their personnel for information sharing, new developments in programming, new developments in funding and administrative concerns, etc. This organization does not have the task of ensuring professional practice standards or educational standards.

The organization responsible for professional practice standards is the National Association of Social Workers, formed in 1955 with the merger of the following specialized social work groups: American Association of Medical Social Work (1918), National Association of School Social Workers (1921), American Association of Psychiatric Social Workers (1926), American Association of Group Workers (1936), Association for the Study of Community Organization (1946), and Social Work Research Group (1949). Since its inception in 1955, the National Association of Social Workers developed a Code of Ethics (1960), recognized the bachelor's degree (1970), developed manpower and personnel standards (1976), and pioneered numerous other services (see Figure 3-3 for a summary of professional organizations). Figure 3-4 summarizes current standards for manpower and personnel, as endorsed by the National Association of Social Workers.

EDUCATIONAL STANDARDS

An important ingredient for an occupation to be considered a profession is the development of educational standards at a post-secondary level (beyond high school), with many professions requiring a minimum of a university education. The first

Figure 3-4

CURRENT MANPOWER STANDARDS OF THE
NATIONAL ASSOCIATION OF SOCIAL WORKERS*

PREPROFESSIONAL LEVEL

SOCIAL SERVICE AIDE

Qualifications

Life experiences and knowledge of the community or special groups are the primary abilities required.

Although high school graduation is not always required and may be irrelevant, basic skills in reading, writing, and computation are important. A high school diploma may be required for certain positions.

A concern for people and a willingness to learn on the job are essential attitudes.

SOCIAL SERVICE TECHNICIAN

Qualifications

Completion of an organized social welfare program leading to an associate of arts degree or a bachelor of arts degree in another field.

Motivation to help people.

PROFESSIONAL LEVEL

SOCIAL WORKER

Qualifications

Completion of a baccalaureate social work program accredited by the Council on Social Work Education.

GRADUATE SOCIAL WORKER

Qualifications

Completion of a master's of social work program in an institution accredited by the Council on Social Work Education.

Figure 3-4 (continued)

CERTIFIED SOCIAL WORKER

Qualifications

Completion of a master's degree program at an accredited school of social work and certification by the Academy of Certified Social Workers (ACSW).

SOCIAL WORK FELLOW

Qualifications

Completion of a doctoral program at an accredited school of social work or in a related discipline, with two years of specialization in an area of social work or certification by ACSW, and two years of social work experience in the field of specialization.

*Source: Adapted from National Association of Social Workers. Standards for Social Service Manpower. Washington, DC: National Association of Social Workers, 1976, pp. 14-19.

training provided for social workers (outside of in-service training in the agency) was a six--week summer institute developed by the New York Charity Organization Society in 1898. This program was expanded to one year in 1903 and was called the New York School of Philanthropy. By 1910 a second year of education was added to the curriculum. The New York School of Philanthropy became the New York School of Social Work in 1940, affiliating with Columbia University, and in 1962 became the Columbia University School of Social Work.

In the early development of social work education, three patterns of organization emerged: independent schools were formed with agency staff engaging in the teaching, such as the New York School of Philanthropy (1903), independent schools affiliating with a university, such as Chicago (1903), and college and university departments, such as Indiana and Ohio (1914-1918). Early social work education had no specific standards, consequently, programs varied in degrees offered, from an undergraduate degree to a one-year graduate degree to a two-year graduate degree. In order to develop a common educational standard, the Association of Training Schools for Professional Social Work was established in 1919, representing 19 schools. The purpose of the organization was to discuss educational standards and was renamed the American Association of

Schools of Professional Social Work (1927). The association developed a procedure for certification of programs and established a one year graduate level educational requirement as minimal standards for the practice of professional social work (1932).

The unrest of the 1930s was reflected in education. Undergraduate programs began to expand in numbers, and demands were pressed for a two year graduate education standard. Two organizations competed for prominence in establishing and monitoring educational standards: the existing American Association of Schools of Professional Social Work, and the newly organized Association of Schools of Social Service Administration (1942). The American Association of Schools of Professional Social Work adopted the 2-year graduate degree as the minimal educational requirement for the practice of social work in 1937. The Association of Schools of Social Service Administration adopted a 1-year graduate degree as the minimal educational requirement for the practice of professional social work in 1942. The conflict over minimal educational standards was resolved in 1952 with the creation of the Council on Social Work Education, which endorsed a two-year graduate degree as a minimal educational standard. The Council on Social Work Education as an organization was a result of merging the two existing educational organizations. Since 1952 the Council on Social Work Education has been the accrediting agency for graduate programs, and more recently, beginning in 1974, for undergraduate programs.

The Council on Social Work Education only accredits two-year graduate and four-year baccalaureate social work programs which have "a professional practice oriented degree." Other programs with social work type courses exist in the United States, such as a two year Associate of Arts degree program, a generalized human service program, and a multitude of schools which offer social work courses.[7] Educational standards are periodically reviewed for their relevance and appropriateness for professional social workers. (See figure 3-3 for a summary of educational standards.)

HOW MANY SOCIAL WORKERS are THERE?

The number of individuals employed under the designation of social work has increased dramatically between 1960 and 1980. In 1960 there were an estimated 95,153 social workers, in 1970 an estimated 216,623, and in 1980 an estimated 442,970. These figures represent an increase of 127 percent from 1960-1970, and 104 percent from 1970-1980 (Siegal: 1975:6 and Bureau of the Census: 1984:295-664).

Figure 3-5 shows the number of social workers employed by industrial classification in 1980. The vast majority of social workers are employed in service producing industries, 99.76 percent, and .24 percent in goods producing industries (see Chapter 1 for a discussion of industrial classifications). Within the service industries classification, the classification of service and public administration account for 98.67 percent of all employed social workers. An important trend is emerging when one compares 1970 and 1980 figures for social workers employed in goods producing and service producing industries which are nonsocial service industries. In 1970, 2,981 or 1.37 percent of social workers were employed in an industrial setting. In 1980 by combining numbers from Figure 3-5, social workers employed outside of the service and public administration industrial classifications and Figure 3-6, social workers employed in non-human service industrial classifications, there are an estimated 10,479 social workers employed in an industrial setting, which is 2.37 percent of all social workers, and an increase of 251 percent in ten years.

Figure 3-6 shows a detailed classification of the professional and related and public administration industrial classifications and the number of social workers employed. This figure shows social workers are employed as follows: <u>15.71 percent in health areas</u>, <u>.25 percent in legal firms</u>, <u>4.91 percent in education</u>, <u>42.24 percent in social services</u>, <u>1.70 percent in related professions</u>, and <u>34.13 percent in public administration</u>. The remaining 1.06 percent are employed in non-human service classifications of the service industries.

Of particular interest in Figure 3-6, is the detailed tabulation of social workers employed in the industrial classification of public administration. Figure 3-6 shows .23 percent of social workers employed in an executive or legislative office, 20.12 percent in administration, .21 percent in national security and international programs, 5.48 percent in general government, 7.88 percent in justice, public order and safety, and .21 percent in public finances. The significance of these figures is the percent of social workers employed in executive and legislative offices and administration. From this detailed breakdown of employment, one can readily visualize the variety of places in which social workers are employed. Neither Figure 3-5 nor Figure 3-6 shows the ratio between men and women in social work. In 1980, of the 442,970 social workers, 155,393 or 35.08 percent, were male, and 287,577 or 64.92 percent were female. This distribution between males and females in social

Figure 3-5

NUMBER AND PERCENT OF SOCIAL WORKERS EMPLOYED BY INDUSTRIAL

CLASSIFICATION IN 1980*

	Number	Percent
INDUSTRIAL CLASSIFICATION		
Goods Production		
Agriculture/Forestry and Fisheries	126	.03
Mining		
Construction	160	.04
Manufacturing	770	.17
Total	1,056	.24
Services Production		
Transportation, Communication and Public Utilities	583	.13
Wholesale Trade	323	.08
Retail Trade	830	.19
Finance, Insurance, Real Estate	3,073	.69
Services	287,914	64.99
Public Administration	149,191	33.68
Total	441,914	99.76
Grand Total	442,970	100.00

*Source: Adapted from: United States Department of Commerce, Bureau of the Census, 1980 Census of Population Volume 2: Subject Reports Part 7C: Occupation by Industry, Washington, DC: U.S. Government Printing Office, 1984, pages 295-664.

The term social worker as used in the census is the occupational designation of a social worker and does not mean the individuals graduated from either a baccalaureate or graduate program in social work which is accredited by the Council on Social Work Education.

84

Figure 3-6

NUMBER AND PERCENT OF SOCIAL WORKERS EMPLOYED

IN THE SERVICE AND PUBLIC ADMINISTRATION CLASSIFICATIONS

OF SERVICE INDUSTRIES IN 1980*

	Number	Percent
SERVICE INDUSTRY CLASSIFICATION		
PROFESSIONAL AND RELATED TOTAL	283,300	64.810
Health total	68,655	15.710
Office of Physician	1,033	.230
Dentist	13	.002
Chiropracter	7	.001
Optometrist	72	.030
Health Practitioner	415	.090
Hospital	37,606	8.600
Nursing Home	11,949	2.740
Nonspecified Health	17,560	4.017
Legal Total	1,106	.250
Education Total	21,466	4.910
Elementary/Secondary	16,626	3.820
College/University	2,747	.620
Business/Trade School	195	.040
Library	114	.020
Nonspecifeed	1,784	.410
Social Services Total	184,647	42.240
Job Training/Vocational Rehabilitation	6,551	1.490
Child Day Care	4,152	.950
Residential Care (Group Homes)	20,054	4.590
Nonspecified	153,890	35.210

85

Figure 3-6 (continued)

Related Professional Total	7,426	1.700
Religious Organization	3,690	.850
Museum/Art Gallery	138	.030
Membership Organization	2,013	.460
Engineering/Architecture/Survey	95	.020
Accounting	63	.010
Research	1,183	.270
Miscellaneous	244	.060
PUBLIC ADMINISTRATION TOTAL	149,191	34.130
Executive/Legislative Office	1,007	.230
General Government	23,984	5.480
Justice/Public Order (includes Law		
Enforcement/Courts/Corrections)	34,414	7.880
Public Finance	913	.210
Administration–Human Resource Program	85,064	19.470
Administration–Environmental Quality		
and Housing	1,052	.240
Administration–Economic Program	1,789	.410
National Security and International	898	.210
BUSINESS and REPAIR	2,634	.600
PERSONAL SERVICE	987	.230
ENTERTAINMENT and RECREATION	993	.230
Grand Total	437,105	100.000

*Source: Adapted from United States Department of Commerce, Bureau of the Census 1980 Census of Population Volume 2 Subject Reports 7C; Occupation by Industry Washington, DC: U.S. Government Printing Office, 1984, pages 295–664. See footnote on Figure 3-5.

Figure 3-7

SOCIAL WORK PRACTICE SETTINGS and NETWORKS OF ASSOCIATIONS

NETWORK OF ASSOCIATION   EXAMPLES OF SOCIAL WORK PRACTICE SETTINGS

Aesthetic   Various therapeutic aspects (art, music,
                                          dance)
Corrections   Juvenile Court/Probation, Parole
Economic   Employee Assistance Programs
Education   School Social Work
Employment and Manpower   Employment/Unemployment Counseling
Environment Protection   Financial Management/Child Development,
                                          Family Planning, Consumer Advocacy
Housing   Relocation/Tenant Advocacy/Housing Project
                                          Services
Income Maintenance   Public Assistance Programs/Social Security
Information and Referral   Libraries/Helplines
Judicial   Courts
Legal   Legal Aid/Private Attorney's Office
Leisure and Recreation   Group Work/Settlement Houses
Mental Health   Psychiatric Social Work
Military   Veteran's Administration/Military
                                          Establishment
Mutual Support   Various Volunteer Efforts for Specific
                                          Problems
Personal Social Service   Family
                                          Private Practice
                                          Child Welfare/Day Care
                                          Specific Problem areas—Alcohol/Drugs/
                                          Suicide
Protective Service   Police Social Work
Physical Health   Medical Social Work/Public Health/Nursing
                                          Homes
Political   Lobbyist/Planning/Community Organization
                                          International
Rehabilitation   Physically and Emotionally Disabled
Religious   Pastoral Counseling/Community Outreach
Special Groups   Minority Groups/Women

work is consistent with the 1970 figures, where 37.3 percent
were males and 62.7 percent were females and with earlier
figures on the ratio between male and female.

    Of future significance for the development of social work in
a service economy is its growing importance in areas, such as
industry, private practice, information careers, and related

professional services. As the United States moves further into a service economy, more social workers will be employed in private practice, in providing consultation to various groups, and in attempting to enhance the general quality of life.

FIELDS of PRACTICE WHICH EMPLOY SOCIAL WORKERS

Social work as a profession is represented in a vast array of employment settings: federal, state and local governments; private industry; private practice, etc. One way to graphically portray the variety of the fields of social work practice is to identify the major societal networks of associations (institutions) and the related area of social work practice. Figure 3-7 ideally shows examples of the role of social work in each societal network. This listing is not exhaustive of practice areas for social work but rather a representative listing.

In addition to the areas or fields of social work practice, one can describe social work activities by the type of services provided. Figure 3-8 is a representative listing of the services provided by social work personnel. Obviously, social services overlap with the fields of practice, since one field of practice would offer multiple services. For example, county social service departments which were designed to implement income maintenance programs also provide homemaking, foster care, adoptions, protective services, family counseling, etc.

The particular emphasis on a specific field of practice will vary with the economic and social needs of a society at a particular point in time. In the 1950s the concern of social work was individual casework, in the 1960s a shift was made to poverty programs and community organization, in the 1970s the concern was legal advocacy and criminal justice, and in the 1980s the concern is family violence, child and spouse abuse, sexual assault, employee assistance programs, and a continued interest in minority groups. These specific problem areas, along with traditional fields of practice such as child welfare, alcohol, drugs, etc., are commonly referred to as the personal social services. Consequently, the employment market expands and contracts depending upon the needs of society at a particular period time.

PERSONAL SOCIAL SERVICES

In England implementation of services and programs within the personal social service network is predominantly the role of social work. In the United States, social workers are heavily involved in implementation of the personal social service network which includes the following: protective services, utilitarian service, developmental and socialization services,

Figure 3-8

EXAMPLES OF SOCIAL SERVICES AFFILIATED WITH SOCIAL WORK PRACTICE*

PROTECTIVE SERVICES
Child Care
Chid Welfare and Protection (abuse, adoption, foster care, neglect)
Assessment for Courts, Schools, Camps
Family Violence (spouse abuse)
Sexual Violence (rape)
Probation and Parole Services
Consumer Protection for the Aged, and other groups

UTILITARIAN SERVICES
Advocacy and Legal Services
Community Coordination, Planning and Organizing
Day Care Facilities
Financial Assistance (Social Security, Supplemental Security Income, Public
   Assistance)
Food Stamps, Surplus Commodities
Homemakers
Information and Referral
Personnel Work
Institutional Services (medical, mental, corrections, mentally retarded, etc.)

DEVELOPMENTAL and SOCIALIZATION SERVICES
Volunteer and self-help program development
Child Development
Community Centers for Youth, Families and the Aged
Family and Marital Counseling
Family Planning
Divorce and Bereavement Counseling
Immigrant Services
Services to Minorities and Women
Program Evaluation and Research

REHABILITATIVE and THERAPEUTIC SERVICES
Personal Counseling and Therapy
Alcohol, Drugs, Sexual Assault
Mutual Support Groups
Rehabilitation (physical, vocational)
Employment Counseling, Evaluation and Placement

*Source: This list of services are examples drawn from a variety of resources
including the following: Alfred Kahn. Social Policy and Social Services, New
York, New York: Random House Inc., 1973, pp. 13, 28-30; Ralph Dolgoff and Donald
Feldstein. Understanding Social Welfare. New York, New York: Harper Row and
Publishers, 1980, pp. 216-222; and David Macarov. The Design of Social Welfare,
New York, New York: Holt, Rinehart and Winston, Inc., 1978, pp. 7-15.

and rehabilitative and therapeutic services (see Chapter 22 Personal Social Services). Some examples of social work involvement in the personal social service network include the following:

PROTECTIVE SERVICES

Child welfare, family violence (spouse abuse, child abuse, parent abuse), the elderly, including alternate care, such as nursing homes, etc.

UTILITARIAN SERVICES

Day care, homemaking, advocacy (both legal and consumer focussed), information and referral, hot lines, etc.

DEVELOPMENTAL and SOCIALIZATION SERVICES

Family and marital counseling, services for unwed mother, services for youth, etc.

REHABILITATIVE and THERAPEUTIC SERVICES

Alcohol abuse, drug addiction, suicide prevention and counseling, sexual problems and dysfunctioning, assaultive/ abusive behavior, aberrant behavior, etc.

SPECIAL POPULATIONS

One historic role of social work has been involvement with the disadvantaged populations. This tradition still continues with numerous individuals working directly or indirectly with minority groups and women (see Chapter 25 Special Populations and Chapter 24 Rehabilitation). Some examples of social work involvement with special populations include the following:

ASIAN

Vietnam and Cambodian Refugee Centers, Chinese associations, Japanese associations, Filipino associations, Asian Social Work Association, etc.

BLACK

Inner-city development projects, Black awareness centers, Black Social Work Association, etc.

EUROPEAN ETHNIC

International Social Service Centers, Travelers Aid Associations, etc.

NATIVE AMERICAN

Native American centers, Native American Social Workers, etc.

SAME SEX PREFERENCE

Gay Awareness centers, information and referral, Gay Social Workers Union, etc.

SPANISH-SPEAKING

Cuban refugee centers, Spanish centers, Puerto Rican centers, Migrant Services, Spanish Social Workers Association, etc.

WOMEN

Women's Crisis Line, Women's Assault Centers, Women Social Workers Association, etc.

ISSUES

Social Work, like other professions, is a reflection of the broader society, responding to economic, political and social needs. As a profession, some of the current issues are: accountability, changing fields of practice, redefinition of social work practice, and a changing emphasis in education.

ACCOUNTABILITY

Social work accountability takes two forms: licensing and enforceable ethical codes or self-regulation. Skidmore (1976: 400-403) indicated that one of the current issues for social work as a profession is registration and licensing. Licensing or registration is one mechanism in society to ensure a degree of professional accountability since provisions for licensing include penalties or negative sanctions for violations. In 1970 there were eight states which regulated social workers, by 1984 there were thirty one states and a number of other states were considering licensure.

A second vehicle for upgrading professional standards is a stronger code of ethics which addresses ethical issues as they relate to a professional group. The revision of the Code of Ethics by the National Association of Social Workers in November

91

1979 is a step in this direction. It is interesting to note that legal cases are both <u>limiting</u> professional discretion, as in the case of confidentiality, and <u>enforcing</u> aspects of ethical codes, such as continued professional development. For many years, courts would not review cases of professional ethics, however, the 1970s and 1980s has seen a rapid increase in the number of court cases involving professional ethics.

FIELDS of PRACTICE

Societal demands and needs are in flux. Today there is a high degree of concern about employee assistance programs, family violence, sexual assault, sexism, ecology, recreation and leisure, etc. These concerns are above and beyond the rapid increase in rising medical costs and problems, such as an aging population, intransigent poverty, racism, urban blight and other social problems in which social workers were traditionally involved.

Many of the services provided by social workers from 1935-1975 were sponsored and implemented by public agencies and public funds. The last decade (1976-1986), has seen an increase in the use of private agencies and an emerging private practice using a combination of public and private funding. The trend toward private practice in social work will continue, with further development of social services in the recently recognized problem areas. Consequently, one would expect more social workers to become involved in industry and specialized problem areas, such as family violence, sexual assault, etc. The provision of concrete services at an international level, such as aiding refugees from various foreign countries, could be expanded as a practice area. Of interest is whether social work will become a participant in the ecology movement as the United States attempts to cope with the limitations of its natural resources. With dwindling resources one has to become concerned about fiscal management and the wise use of resources. It is ironic that the ecology problem is arising at the same time that the American worker will have more leisure time. Enabling individuals to wisely use leisure time with limited resources may become a significant aspect of social work practice.

REDEFINITION of SOCIAL WORK PRACTICE

In Chapter 2, there was a discussion of the commonalities of the human service and helping professions. All of the human service professions use some form of counseling techniques in completing their tasks. Social work as a professional group will need to clearly define what is unique about social work which differentiates the profession from other helping professions. Relying on old definitions based upon an individual counseling perspective will be insufficient. It would seem that social work has a distinct knowledge base with its emphasis on social science disciplines, its understanding of social service systems and programs, and its ability to relate to social problems on a micro (small system), mezzo (middle system), and macro (large system) level. Figure 3-9 shows the relationship of social work as a profession to society in general and the major social networks.

EDUCATION

Social work educational standards for professional practice underwent rapid transformation in the 1970s with the acceptance of baccalaureate education and a shift away from a psycho-analytical psychological perspective to a more general or eclectic social science orientation.

Schools of social work will have to respond to the needs of American society, including content on family violence, sexual assault, women's issues, minority groups and, in a wider context, private practice and occupational/industrial social work. The trend toward having the bachelor's degree program form the base of social work practice will continue with graduate programs providing enrichment and specialized programs.

Other areas in which social work education needs to expand and enrich curriculum content include: program evaluation and implementation, styles of administrative management, and computerized diagnostic techniques. In essence, the structure of social work education already has changed, now the changes need to be in specific content areas and the emphasis of the curriculum. Educational content should be modified to meet the demands of a service economy, e.g., managing small-scale programs with numerous part-time employees and more participation by the recipient of services in the management of service programs.

SUMMARY

Social work as a profession and as a field of professional practice was described. The elements of social work practice which include interventive strategies, knowledge base, and a value system, were outlined to provide a broad perspective on what constitutes social work practice.

A brief history of the development of social work since 1850 from the perspective of fields of practice, professional organizations and professional education was presented. All three of these developments occurred simultaneously but represented different concerns. The "roots" of social work as a

Figure 3-9

Relationship of the Social Work Profession to the
Overall Society and the Networks of Associations

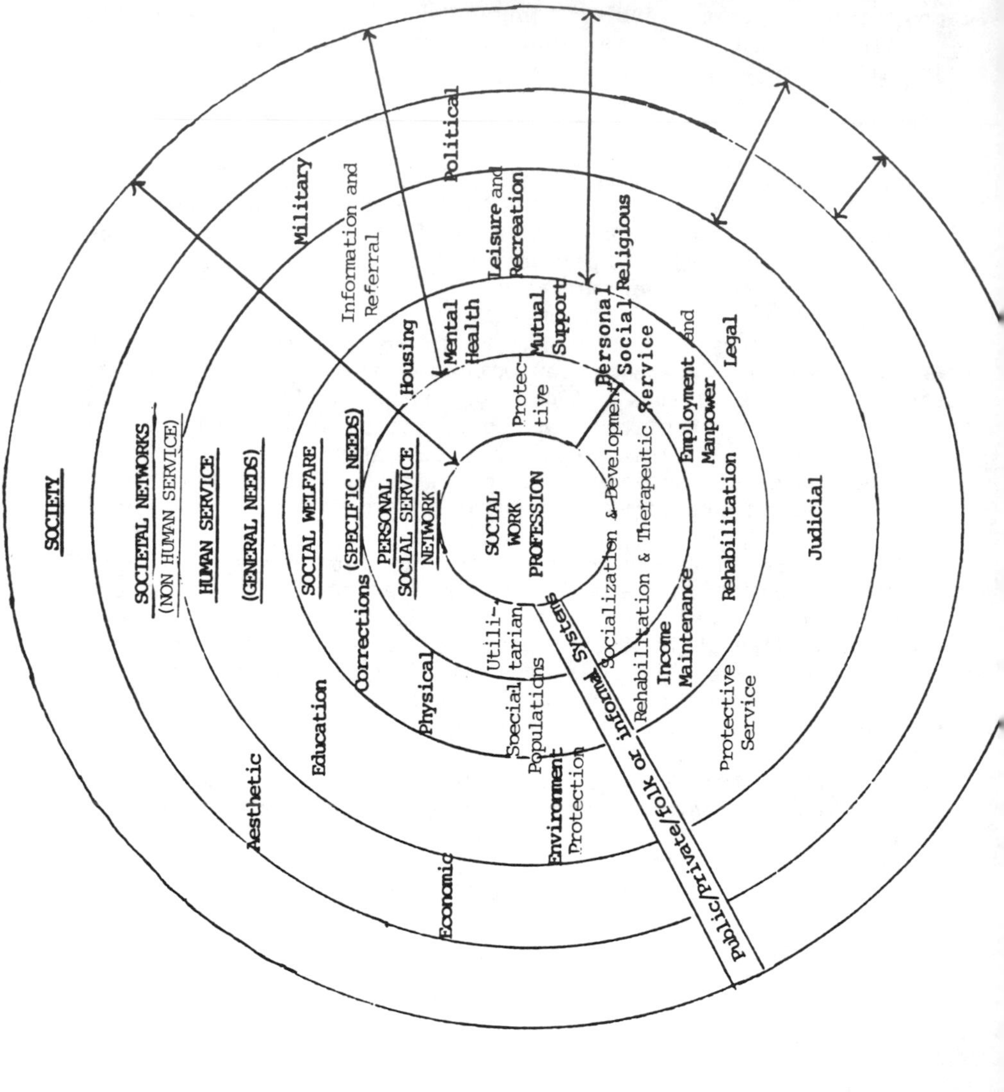

94

profession was the problem of poverty and attempts to "scientifically" manage it, mainly through the Charity Organization Society movement and the Settlement House movement. From 1900-1970 there was a rapid expansion of social work activities into numerous fields, with continued expansion into the 1980s, although at a slower pace.

The variety of the fields of practice for social work were identified by presenting a model of the major networks of associations (institutions) in society and the related social work activities. In addition to fields of practice, a representative listing of social services which social workers implement was presented. Statistical data on employment of social workers showed a trend of rapid growth between 1970-1980 and a high representation of women in the field.

Social work, like other professions, is a reflection of and a response to the changing needs of society. Some issues for social work as a profession were discussed including professional accountability, changing fields of practice, redefinition of social work practice, and a changing emphasis in social work education.

FOOTNOTES

*This chapter was reviewed for comments by Professor Walter Trattner, Department of History (specialty area, History of Social Welfare), University of Wisconsin-Milwaukee, Milwaukee, Wisconsin.

1. This classification of a knowledge base for social work is an adaptation from an article by Robert Scheurell, "Expectations of a Baccalaureate Social Worker," Iowa Journal of Social Work, Spring 1972 Vol. V No. 2, (Spring 1972), pp. 3-7.

2. The listing of the value base for social work is adapted from Walter Friedlander, Concepts and Methods of Social Work, Englewood Cliffs, New Jersey: Prentice Hall, Inc., 1976, pp. 2-6.

3. The Code of Ethics by the National Association of Social Workers was adopted by the Delegate Assembly on October 13, 1960, revised in April, 1967 and November 1979. The Code of Ethics has been reproduced with the permission of the National Association of Social Workers.

4. Both the Charity Organization Society movement and Settlement House movement had close ties to the religious reform movements of the late 1800s. Therefore, both movements shared some common ideals in spite of the divergent approaches to solving social problems.

5. The movement for professionalism in social work was not an isolated event, since other occupations, such as teaching, nursing, home economics, amongst others, were organizing at the same time. The period between 1870-1900 was one of rapid urban growth, with subsequent problems of housing, unemployment and sanitation. Urban centers were becoming overwhelmed with immigrants from other countries who were having some difficulty in adjusting to the "American way of life." Political corruption was visible in many places, and the welfare system, both public and private, was overloaded. Within this context of societal unrest and upheaval, the various occupations needed a vehicle to communicate with their fellow colleagues on how to handle problems, what newer techniques were developing to provide services, and how to better coordinate and integrate efforts. This need for communication and coordination led to a rethinking of what tasks and functions ought to be accomplished, as well as a need for minimal standards of training and education.

6. Some form of organization is essential for occupations and professions to keep abreast of changes and current trends in a field, to develop a consistency and commonality to the approaches used to ameliorate problems, and in the development of consistent educational and practice standards. A professional organization further serves the purpose of a political interest group, as well as, a system for monitoring (self-regulating) the performance of professional colleagues. In addition to the formal organization and profession of social work, many individuals attempt to use the informal or folk network of social work. An individual has a problem but instead of going to an agency will call a friend, colleague or acquaintance who is a social worker for "off the record" advice and consultation.

7. There are two types of accreditation for colleges and universities: institutional, and professional. Institutional accreditation refers to an entire college or university and all of its programs, degrees and majors. This form of accreditation provides legitimacy for the institution to grant degrees. Almost all colleges and universities in the United States have received this form of accreditation which is routinely implemented through a regional accrediting body such as the North Central Regional Accrediting Association

(see Chapter 8 Education, footnote number 10). Some colleges and universities which offer courses in social work, may have a social work major, and a two-year college may offer a program in social service and have obtained institutional accreditation but not professional accreditation. Professional accreditation is in addition to institutional accreditation and refers to a specific program (in this case, social work) which meets standards for a "professionally practice-oriented program." The Council on Social Work Education is the organization responsible for professional accreditation of social work programs at the bachelor's (four-year degree) and master's level (two-year graduate degree).

8. For further information on the profession of social work one can contact the following organizations: The National Association of Social Workers, 7981 Eastern Avenue, Silver Spring, MD, 20910; The Council on Social Work Education, 1744 R Street, NW, Suite 400, Washington, DC 20009; the National Conference on Social Welfare, 1730 M Street N.W., Suite 911, Washington, D.C. 20036; or the National Association of Christians in Social Work, Box 90, St. David's, PA 19087.

The National Association of Social Workers has a chapter in each state. One can contact the state or regional chapter of the National Association of Social Workers or a local university which has a social work program.

SUGGESTED READINGS

Harriet Bartlett. The Common Base of Social Work Practice, New York, NY: National Association of Social Workers, 1970. This is an older but classic book which in a readable fashion explains the elements of social work as professional practice and would provide an overview for the individual not acquainted with social work.

David Macarov. The Design of Social Welfare, New York, NY: Holt, Rinehart and Winston, Inc., 1978. For the individual seeking general information on the development of social welfare in Western society, this book provides an excellent overview.

Anne Minahan (Ed.), Encyclopedia of Social Work. 2 Vols, 18th Issue, Washington, DC: National Association of Social Workers, 1986. This standard work is a compendium of information on all facets of social work. For an individual seeking immediate information on a specific topic this is a sound resource.

Walter Trattner. From Poor Law to Welfare State, 2nd ed., New York, NY: Free Press, 1979. For the individual seeking information on the general development of social welfare and social work in the United States, this book provides an excellent overview.

REFERENCES

Bartlett, Harriet. The Common Base of Social Work Practice. New York, NY: National Association of Social Workers, 1970.

Boehm, Werner. Objectives of the Social Work Curriculum of the Future, Vol. 1, Curriculum Study. New York, NY: Council on Social Work Education, 1959.

Cohen, Nathan. Social Work in the American Tradition. New York, NY: Holt, Rinehart and Winston, Inc., 1958.

Friedlander, Walter. Concepts and Methods of Social Work. Englewood Cliffs, NJ: Prentice Hall, Inc., 1976.

Friedlander, Walter and Robert Apte. Introduction to Social Welfare, 5th ed. Englewood Cliffs, NJ: Prentice Hall, Inc., 1980.

Goodman, James (ed.). Dynamics of Racism in Social Work Practice. Washington, DC: National Association of Social Workers, 1972.

Lubove, Roy. The Professional Altruist. New York, NY: Atheneum Press, 1969.

Macarov, David. The Design of Social Welfare. New York, NY: Holt, Rinehart and Winston, Inc., 1978.

Minahan, Anne (Ed.). Encyclopedia of Social Work, 2 vols., 18th Issue, Washington, DC: National Association of Social Workers, 1986.

National Association of Social Workers. Standards for Social Service Manpower. Washington, DC: National Association of Social Workers, 1976.

National Association of Social Workers. Code of Ethics. Washington, DC: National Association of Social Workers, 1980.

Pincus, Allen and Anne Minahan. Social Work Practice: Model and Methods. Itasca, IL: F.E. Peacock Publishers, Inc., 1973.

Salinsburg, Eric. The Personal Social Services. London, England: Pittman Publishing Co., 1977.

Scott, Carl, (Ed.). Ethnic Minorities in Social Work Education, New York, NY: Council on Social Work Education, 1970.

Siegel, Sheldon. Social Service Manpower Needs: An Overview to 1980, New York, NY: Council on Social Work Education, 1975.

Scheurell, Robert. "Expectations of a Baccalaureate Social Worker," Iowa Journal of Social Work, Vol. V No. 2 (Spring 1972), pp. 3-7.

Siporin, Max. Introduction to Social Work Practice, New York, NY: Macmillan Publishing Co., 1975.

Skidmore, Rex and Milton Thackeray. Introduction to Social Work, Englewood Cliffs, NJ: Prentice Hall, Inc., 1976.

Trattner, Walter. From Poor Law to Welfare State, 2nd ed., New York, NY: The Free Press, 1979.

United States Department of Commerce, Bureau of the Census, 1980 Census of Population: Volume 2, Subject Reports, Part 7C: Occupation by Industry, Washington, DC: U.S. Government Printing Office, 1984.

Woodroofe, Kathleen. From Charity to Social Work, London, England: Routledge and Kegan Paul, Inc., 1964.

Zastrow, Charles. The Practice of Social Work, Homewood, IL: Dorsey Press, 1981.

SECTION 2

NONHUMAN SERVICE NETWORKS

Nonhuman service networks are those which have as their primary function the total needs of a society for survival, such as political allocation of power, military defense, an economic system and a means of expression. That is, the focus of these networks is on something other than socialization of individuals in a society or a means to solve or ameliorate individual and group problems.

Chapter 4 describes the aesthetic network and the professions of art, dance and music therapy and the role of social work. Chapter 5 describes the economic network and the profession of personnel management and the role of industrial or occupational social work. Chapter 6 describes the military network and the profession of military officer and the role of social work both as part of the military network and as a civilian employee. Chapter 7 describes the political network and the profession of a politician and the role of social work at the international level, as well, as within the political network.

Chapter 4

AESTHETIC NETWORK*

"Many people think art is something special and apart from their daily lives, is a luxury, an occupation or hobby for impractical individuals. This is a mistake. Mankind cannot live without art. It is a necessity, as religion is. If mankind cannot communicate they die of loneliness. Art is communication on the deepest and most lasting level. . . All of us need to tell what is in our hearts." (DeMille:1963:7).

INTRODUCTION

The above quotation from DeMille indicates the necessity for people to communicate and express their deepest emotions and thoughts. The broad interpretation of the aesthetic network in this chapter refers to the arts: painting/drawing, sculpture, literature, music, poetry, dancing, acting, film-making, photography, graphics, etc. From the perspective of the network approach, all of the arts have a unity in that all of them are mediums through which individuals or groups of individuals seek to express feelings and perceptions. In addition, the arts are a means for people to enjoy creativity (within oneself). Most individuals enjoy the arts from a consumer perspective, meaning they experience aesthetics through going to places to be entertained (commercialism of music, dance, painting and film-making, etc.). The consumer perspective is not the focus of this chapter, but one must recognize that the more commercial components of the arts are part of the aesthetic network.

The arts are a reflection of the following: one's inner feelings, thoughts, and perceptions, a technical expertise in the use of one of the mediums of art, a specific historical time period and its prevailing attitudes, and what is considered to be aesthetically pleasing (beautiful) at a given point in time. Beauty, or an aesthetically pleasing quality, depends upon the viewer or consumer of the product. What one person sees and feels as pleasing may have no impact on another individual. The aesthetically pleasing aspect of the arts is a secondary quality for the product of the artist, since the artist's primary concern is expression and creativity.

103

Although the arts are known to express emotions, feelings, and to alleviate loneliness or a feeling of emptiness, it was not until the 1920s when formal specialties using some form of the arts as a medium were utilized for therapeutic purposes. This chapter describes the role of art, dance, and music therapy and the role of social work.

SIZE

All cultures and societies have some form of aesthetic network, including commercialized forms, organized public forms of aesthetic experience, individual expression and private expression. The size of the aesthetic network in the United States is rather extensive and estimates will vary, depending upon how broadly or narrowly one defines the network. For our purposes, the aesthetic network consists of places of employment for those who practice one of the arts, or places where a consumer is entertained by one of the arts, and the various schools and individuals who engage in the arts.

An estimate on the size of the aesthetic network is shown in Figure 4-1. In 1982 there were an estimated 16,375 establishments in the United States focusing on the arts, with expenditures of 7.3 billion dollars, employing an estimated 153,731 individuals and having an attendance of over 390.3 million individuals. These figures on employees do not distinguish between professionals and amateurs in an area nor do they count the thousands of people who are providing private music, dance or art lessons.[1]

HISTORICAL DEVELOPMENT

The three major specializations of the aesthetic network which are involved in human services are art, dance and music therapy. There are other specializations, such as poetry therapy, drama therapy, photo therapy, psychodrama, bibliotherapy, etc. However, these specializations are of a much smaller dimension than art, dance or music therapy. The major focus of this historical review is on general themes or styles of art, dance and music in Western society. Figure 4-2 shows the generalized historical development of art, dance and music as a reflection of society.

ART

Art as a meaningful expression of emotion reflects the prevailing attitudes or themes of a society, as well as the innermost thoughts of the artist. The use of art as a medium of expression dates to the earliest times of mankind. There is a

Figure 4-1

Estimated Size of the Aesthetic Network in 1984*

ted Criteria	Selected Elements of the Aesthetic Network		
	Dance, Theater, Music etc.[1]	Museum and Art Gallery[1]	Total
r of blishments	11,967	4,408	16,375
ditures lars)	4,667,434,000	2,662,283,000	7,329,717,000
r of oyees	116,198	37,533	153,731
dance endance)	42,500,000 plus[2]	347,800,000[2]	390,300,000[2]

ces: Adapted from United States Department of Commerce, Bureau of the Census, 1982 ensus of Service Industries, United States: Geographic Series, Washington, D.C.: U.S. overnment Printing Office, 1984, pp. 5-7; United States Department of Commerce, Bureau of the Census, Statistical Abstract of the United States: 1986 (106th Ed.), Washington, .C. U.S. Government Printing Office, 1985, pp. 234-236.

 Census of Service Industries Op Cit, pp. 5, 7. The dance, theater and music lassification includes the following: producers, orchestra, entertainer, dance group, rtists, symphony, opera company, chamber music, other musical entertainment, legitimate heater, dance halls, studios and schools. This figure does not include craftsmen, herapists, and individuals employed in other networks like social service, religious rganizations, etc.

istical Abstract of the United States: 1986 (106th Ed.), Op Cit, pp. 234, 236. his figure is estimated for the year 1984 and only includes play, opera and symphony. he count is a multiple count since most individuals attend more than one event.

105

Figure 4-2

HISTORICAL TIME LINE OF THE AESTHETIC NETWORK*

Historical Time Period	General Themes	Examples of Specific Medium		
		Art	Dance	Music
Prehistoric Pre 10,000 BC	Nature oriented/ Religious Motivation	Cave painting pottery painting	Circular imitation of animals or symbolic rites	Drums, early flutes unison singing (chants)
Classical Greek and Roman 500 BC – 450 AD	Rationalism, harmony of creation and world. Practical, utilitarian organization	Appollodorus Attalus Architecture, used painting and frieze	Choral, Pyrrhiche Emmeleia Pantomine Exhibitionist	Seikolas, Aristophanes, Pythagorus Achaneaus, mainly a performing art
Medieval 450 AD – 1400 AD	Mysticism, other worldly authoritarian, stylized (conformity). Heroic deeds, triumph of life over death, other world, stylized	Miniature and grand murals in churches, monastery. Giotto, El Greco, Cimabue	Spielmann (hand dance). Dance macabre Ilappaldie Religious Theme	Gregorian Chant Cassidorius Unison Singing Landini, Phillippe de Vitus Chanson de Geste
Renaissance 1400 AD – 1600 AD	Humanism, dignity, Individual expression	Raphael, Leonardo da Vinci, Michelangelo	Basse Dance, Branle de Marche Court Dance	Francesca, Josquin DesPerez, Orlando Lassus
Baroque and its synthesis 1600 – 1750	Action oriented but stylized (conformity). Nationalistic, Domestic, individualism with recognized styles refined	Van Dyck, Rembrandt, Jan Vermeer, Rubens, David, Goya, Chardon	Galliard, Brando Bassadanza Baroque Synthesis Minuet, Ballet, Contredance Round Dance	Handel, Humphrey, Bach Beethoven, CPE Bach Mozart
Revolutionary and Romantic 1750 – 1900	naturalistic, truth, passion	Van Gogh Lautrec	Waltz, Polka, Can Can, Cakewalk	Wagner, Brahms, Chopin Mozart
Contemporary, Surrealism 1900 – on	Individual expression, symbolism, mechanistic, inner feeling	Picasso, Dali Use as therapy	Duncan, Charleston Swing, Disco, Break Use as therapy	Mahler, Schoenberg, Strauss, Gershwin, Presley, Beatles Use as therapy

*Note: The general themes relate to overall styles of art accepted by the elite and society, and does not reflect upper class art or folk traditions. From the 11th through the 18th Century, there was a clear distinction between upper class art forms and those of the peasant class.

functional component to art known as crafts. This functional or practical, utilitarian approach to art includes clothing styles, decorating residences and pottery. One can identify major periods in the styles of art which reflect the prevailing themes in society. General historical themes in art are as follows:

CLASSICAL, 500 B.C. to 450 A.D. - This time period includes the period of Greek and Roman styles. The general themes reflected in art were of a worldly orientation, i.e., humanism, harmony of mankind with the world, individualism, and utilitarianism. Examples of this time period include Appollodarus (440 B.C.), Attalus and Pergamon.

MEDIEVAL, 450 to 1400 - This time period includes the Romanesque and Gothic styles. Generalizable societal themes are: other-world oriented (spirituality), authoritarianism, mysticism, and heroic deeds. Examples of this period include the Bayeaux tapestries, and artists like El Greco, Giotto and Cimabue.

RENAISSANCE, 1400-1600 - This time period includes the Italian, Florentine and Spanish stages. General societal themes were humanism, individual dignity and worldliness. It is a conflicting, tumultuous period, with the break-up of feudalism, the development of the nation state, a changing economic system to small cottage factories, a changing political system from monarchy to thoughts of democracy, and the religious reformation. In response to these conflicts in society, expression of the artists became extremely repressive and moody, or optimistic, with a humanistic (this world) quality. Examples of this time period include Leonardo da Vinci (1452-1519), Raphael (1483-1520) and Michelangelo (1475-1564).

BAROQUE and its SYNTHESIS, 1600-1750 - This time period includes both the aristocratic and popular styles. General societal themes were domesticity, nationalism and individualism. Examples of this period include Peter Rubens (1577-1640), Rembrandt (1609-1669), Van Dyck, Davids (1748-1845), Goya 1746-1828) and Chardon.

REVOLUTIONARY and ROMANTIC, 1750-1900 - This time period includes styles which were naturalistic in nature, and political. General societal themes were mixed; on one hand there was the concept of unrest, turmoil, and a tempestuous society, and on the other hand a back-to-nature movement. Examples of this time period include Van Gogh and Lautrec.

IMPRESSIONISM and CONTEMPORARY, 1900 on - This time period includes cubism, abstractionism and realism and other related schools of artistic expression. Artists rebelled against the conformity of society and developed different means of expression. General societal themes are interpretation of one's experiences and using symbolism in order to interpret this reality. Some examples of this time period include Picasso (1881-1961) and Salvadore Dali (1904-1956).

It is with this latter trend in art, i.e., a form of individual expression and creativity, there developed a utilization of art as a therapeutic medium.

DANCE

Dancing as a form of religious or social expression is considered to be the oldest of the aesthetic mediums by some authors (DeMille, 1973). Dancing, like other forms of aesthetic expression, is a reflection of the broader social themes of a particular historical period. General historical themes in dance are as follows:

CLASSICAL, 450 B.C. to 450 A.D. - This time period includes the Greek and Roman civilizations. There was an emphasis in dancing, upon harmony, the unitary nature of mankind with their environment and a rational discipline. The discipline in dance is consistent with the generalized themes of rationality. Dancing at this time was highly stylized, with very little individual creativity. The Romans added a utilitarian or practical component to dancing in that they danced for enjoyment, entertainment, as well as sensationalism. The disciplined, rational harmony of the Greek dances was lost in the Roman period. Examples of the dance in this time period include pantomime, exhibitionist and choral dancing.

MEDIEVAL - 450-1400 - This time period had two different forms of expression. In the early Medieval period (450-1200) folk dancing was allowed, which conveyed a high degree of expression of emotion by individuals. On the other hand, there was the emergence of a heavy religious theme to dancing, and these dances tended to become more stylized in performance. In the later Medieval period (1200-1400) there was a deemphasis on social dancing in an attempt to prescribe a religious element, i.e., a high degree of conformity to all dancing. This is the period of time which had an extremely somber emotional expression in its dancing, such as dances of death, to ward off disease and to ensure the future of the world. Society at this time was rebounding from the bubonic plague and there was an obsession about survival. This is reflected in dances, such as St. Vitas, dance of death, etc.

RENAISSANCE, 1400-1600 - This time period reflected the changing concerns of society, i.e., the dignity of man, humanism, worldly orientation, and individualism. In contrast to the late Medieval period, there was an influx of folk dancing and the early development of stylized court dancing.

BAROQUE and its SYNTHESIS - 1600-1750 - This time period was known for its stylized forms of dance with the rapid expansion of the ballet and the minuet. There was further development of some of the more popular types of folk dancing, such as circle dancing and round dancing, which were more popular than couple dancing.

REVOLUTIONARY and ROMANTIC - 1750-1900 - This time period was known for the development of many modern-day dances, such as the polka and waltz, which became extremely popular. These were forms of couple dancing, which indicated a return to individual expression and expression of emotion for couples. Both the waltz and the polka during this time period were not stylized dancing as we know them today.

IMPRESSIONISM and CONTEMPORARY - 1900 on - This was a period of time when dancers rebelled against the conformity of society and sought different means of expression. Dancing today is highly individualized. We have the disco, break and the older generation the charleston, swing (jitterbug), and ball room dancing. Dancing today is both couple and individual dancing, with a high degree of individual expression involved. It is with the development of individualized expression in dancing that use of dance as a therapeutic medium developed.

MUSIC

The use of musical instruments, like some of the other means of aesthetic expression, dates back to prehistoric times and probably developed as an accompaniment to dance. Like the other arts, music is also a reflection of the societal attitudes of a prevailing period of time. General historical themes in music are as follows:

CLASSICAL, 500 B.C. to 450 A.D. - This time period includes both the Greek and Roman styles. The Greek style of music expressed the unitary nature of mankind and rationality. The Roman style of music stressed the performing art for entertainment. Examples of this time period include: Aristophanes (444 B.C.) Athaneaus (200 B.C.), Pythagorus (497 B.C.) and Seikolas.

MEDIEVAL, 450 to 1400 - This time period with its religious orientation was in contrast to the unitary style of the Greeks or the performing sensationalist music of the Romans. An example of music in this period of time include the Gregorian chant as used in churches, as well as, congregational, polyphonic and unison singing.

RENAISSANCE, 1400-1600 - This time period was one of contrasts, with extremely oppressive, somber music reflecting the turmoil in society, as well as, an expression of lighter styles referring to expression of individuality. Examples of this time period include; Josquin Des Pres (1445), Arlando Lassus and Francesca.

BAROQUE and its SYNTHESIS, 1600-1750 - Music of this time period expressed both the highly stylized forms of music, as well as, some of the folk music which was of a more individual nature. Chamber music which was the stylized variety of music was extremely popular along with the development of string quartets, wind ensembles and opera. Examples of this time period include Johann Sebastian Bach (1685-1750), George Handel (1759-1865), Ludwig van Beethoven (1700-1827), C. P. E. Bach (1714-1788) and Humphry.

REVOLUTIONARY and ROMANTIC, 1750-1900 - This time period again reflected the turmoil occuring in society, with oppressive, somber music as well as the lighter varieties. Examples of this period include Mozart (1756-1791), Chopin (1809-1849), Brahms (1833-1897) and Wagner (1813-1883).

IMPRESSIONISM and CONTEMPORARY - 1900 on - Musicians during this time period rebelled against the conformity of society and sought different means of expression. In addition to the stylized chamber music of the Baroque and Revolutionary period, there was the development of many popular forms of singing, i.e., folk songs, semi-classical, jazz, hard rock, etc. Examples of this time period include Mahter, Schoenberg, Strauss (1864-1899), Gershwin (1898-1957) and groups, such as the Beatles (1960's) or individuals like Elvis Presley (1935-1979) and electronic music. Music therapy as an ancillary to psychiatric therapy had to wait until the development of music with highly individualized expression.

STRUCTURE

Unlike other fields in the human services, the aesthetic network does not have a strong overall identification with government organization, since a large proportion of the aesthetic services are implemented through individuals, small private groups, and local governments. Although the structure is not as clear as in other networks, one can still look at the structure of the network from its organizational context, services provided, occupations and professions, and dominant occupations and professions.

ORGANIZATIONAL CONTEXT

The overall network of aesthetics is rather loosely defined, consisting of many individual entrepreneurs, small local private facilities, local and regional, public and private organized activities, and institutional activities. The aesthetic network goes beyond state and national boundaries, with many organized activities at the international level. The government structure does provide grants and various endowments to a multiplicity of public and private foundations. Figure 4-3 shows an idealized government structure for the aesthetic network.[2]

SERVICES PROVIDED

Regardless of whether one is in art, dance or music therapy, similar services are provided to clientele. A sampling of the services provided by these therapies are as follows:

- Psychological assessment

- Activity for individuals and groups

- Development of a relationship with individuals and groups

- Providing a sense of well-being to the client and diminishing their feelings of isolation and loneliness

- Individual and group therapy

- Team support groups in human services, i.e., working in conjunction with social workers, psychologists, psychiatrists and psychiatric nurses.

OCCUPATIONS and PROFESSIONS

In 1980 of the estimated 443,048 individuals represented in six aesthetic occupations and professions (actor, author, dancer, musician, painter/sculptor, etc., and not specified), 140,293, or 32.4 percent,were employed in the industrial classifications of professional-related and public administration, 133,709, or 30.9 percent, were employed in the industrial classifications of entertainment and recreation, and the remaining 159, 046 or 36.7 percent, were employed in a variety of industrial classifications in the goods-producing and service-producing industries. Figure 4-4 shows the employment of selected aesthetic occupations in the United States in 1980.

Figure 4-3

Idealized Organization of the Aesthetic Network
Showing the Location of the Human Service Components*

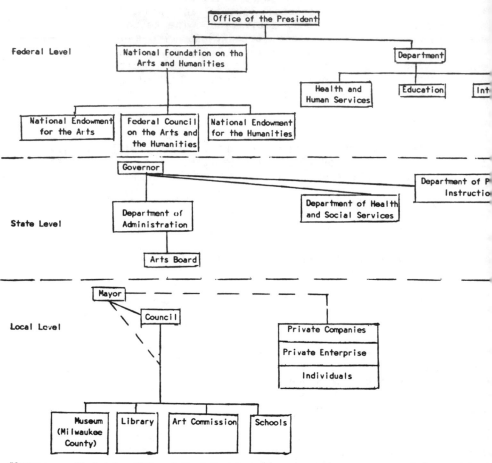

Federal Level

Office of the President

National Foundation on the
Arts and Humanities

Department

Health and
Human Services

Education

Int

National Endowment
for the Arts

Federal Council
on the Arts and
the Humanities

National Endowment
for the Humanities

State Level

Governor

Department of
Administration

Department of Health
and Social Services

Department of P
Instructio

Arts Board

Local Level

Mayor

Council

Private Companies

Private Enterprise

Individuals

Museum
(Milwaukee
County)

Library

Art Commission

Schools

*Sources: Adapted from Office of the Federal Register, United States Government Manual 1985-86,
Washington, D.C.: U.S. Government Printing Office, 1985, pp. 840, 842, 844, 861, Wisconsi
Legislative Reference Bureau, Wisconsin Blue book, 1985-86. Madison, Wisconsin; Departmen
Administration, 1985, pp. 468, 512, 562; Office of the City Clerk. Milwaukee Report,
Milwaukee, Wisconsin: Office of the City Clerk, 1976.

112

Figure 4-4

Number and Percent of Selected Aesthetic Occupations
and Professions Employed by Industrial Classification in 1980*

ected thetic upations and fession	Industrial Classification				
	Goods Producing	Entertainment/ Recreation	Professional/ Related	Public Administration	Other Service Producing
or/Director	935	29,092	2,669	877	23,117
hor	4,197	1,659	33,734	995	3,447
cer	78	8,063	318	70	3,023
ician/ mposer etc.	1,624	72,538	35,261	810	18,576
nter/Sculpter/ aftman/etc.	37,396	2,516	54,062	3,717	48,453
c.	5,688	19,841	6,804	976	12,512
tal	49,918	133,709	132,848	7,445	109,128
cent of tal Industries	11.5	30.9	30.7	1.7	25.2

rce: Adapted from United States Department of Commerce, Bureau of the Census, 1980 Census of
lation: Volume 2 Subject Reports. Part 7C: Occupation by Industry, Washington, DC: U.S. Government
ting Office, 1984, pp. 295-664.

113

Our concern are those individuals who are employed in human service related industrial classifications. Figure 4-5 shows the estimated number of aesthetic occupations employed in human service related industries. Of the 140,293 individuals employed in the professional/related and public administration industrial classification, 56,445, or 40.2 percent, are employees in human service related industries, and the remaining 83,848, or 59.8 percent, are employed in non-human service industries, or are listed as non-specified. Another way of looking at the figures for employment of selected aesthetic occupations in human service related industries is that 56,445 individuals, or 13.0 percent, of selected aesthetic occupations and professions are employed in human service related industries, and the remaining 376,603, or 87 percent, are not employed in human service related agencies.

DOMINANT OCCUPATIONS and PROFESSIONS

The focus of our concern in the aesthetic network is those specialties which have become involved in therapeutic relation-ships with individuals, specifically, art, dance and music therapy. Figure 4-6 shows an idealized range of aesthetic personnel and other human service professions operating on a team basis.[3]

Although a formalized occupation and profession did not develop in the three therapies until after 1940, aesthetics had been used informally to help individuals organize their thought processes, provide direction, provide a leisure and recreation activity, and in religious institutions working with the elderly and the sick to provide them with some comfort and enjoyment. From this perspective, aesthetic occupations can be viewed as part of the human services since about 400 B.C.

Since our major concern is the newly emerging aesthetic therapies, such as art, music and dance, estimates of the number of individuals who are employed and registered with appropriate professional organizations in these therapies are as follows: 1,324 art therapists; 1,050 dance therapists; 2,200 music therapists. Registration with a professional association is not mandatory.

ART THERAPY

The use of art as a therapeutic treatment dates back to the late 1920's and early 1930's with the use of art as a medium of expression and as an adjuvant to psychotherapy in mental insti-tutions and veterans hospitals. One of the early examples of the use of art as a therapeutic device was at the Menninger Clinic in 1925. Art therapy uses graphic communication for purposes of psychological assessment, development of a

In Selected Industrial Classifications of Professional and Related
and Public Administration in 1980*

Selected Industrial Classification	Occupational Classification						
	Actor/Director	Author	Dancer	Musician Composer	Painter/sculpture etc.	Not specified artistic, etc.	Total
Health	116	119	20	183	1,132	601	2,171
Legal	135	50	-	12	116	7	320
Education	1,283	1,048	133	3,832	4,652	2,892	13,840
Library	102	32	-	-	200	39	373
Museum and Art Gallery	85	44	19	90	1,435	503	2,176
Religious Organizations	455	170	20	27,530	407	328	28,910
Social Service	223	127	13	256	383	208	1,210
Public Administration	877	995	70	810	3,717	976	7,445
Total	3,276	2,585	275	32,713	12,042	5,554	56,445
Percent of Total in Human Services	5.8	4.6	.5	57.9	21.3	9.9	100.0
Total Number in each Occupational Group	56,690	44,032	11,552	128,809	146,144	45,821	433,048
Percent of Occupational Group in Human Services	5.8	5.9	2.4	25.4	8.2	12.1	13.0

*Source: Adapted from United States Department of Commerce, Bureau of the Census, 1980 Census of Population, Volume 2 Subject Reports, Part 7C: Occupation by Industry, Washington, D.C.: U.S. Government Printing Office, 1984, pp. 295-664.

[1] These figures exclude employment in engineering/architecture/surveying, membership organization, accounting, research and miscellaneous components of the professional/related and public administration industrial classification and employment of miscellaneous artists etc.

115

Figure 4-6

SAMPLE RANGE OF AESTHETIC AND HUMAN SERVICE OCCUPATIONS
PARTICIPATING IN A TEAM THERAPEUTIC EFFORT*

*Mental health is used as an example for illustrative purposes. These
occupations and professions are used in a variety of settings, such as
corrections, nursing homes, schools, veteran's administration, etc.

relationship with an individual and to enable people to express their emotions and feelings. Hopefully through this medium individuals will be able to transform or change some of their behaviors and their attitudes towards themselves and others.

In the 1960's art therapy developed a more specialized theoretical orientation and a professional association known as the American Art Therapy Association (1969). The Art Therapy Association has established certification procedures for individuals and an accreditation process for art therapy programs. The current standards for art therapy are a Masters degree in art therapy from an accredited program offered at educational institutions and special schools. Today art therapy is used in many locations, such as mental institutions, correctional institutions, and nursing homes, as part of a team treatment program.

The major functions of an art therapist include the following:

- Psychological assessment

- Developing close relations with the client

- Developing empathy with the client

- Enable individuals and groups to express their feelings and work through emotions and memories.

Painting, drawing, and sculpture as activities are used to express feelings and to enable an individual or group to work through these feelings. The use of these mediums aid the process of socialization and the development of other coping skills individuals need in our society. The art therapist usually operates as a team member with other human service professions, such as social work, psychiatry, psychology, and psychiatric nursing. Primary therapy is usually the domain of the other team members, and art therapy is usually an adjuvant to the therapeutic process.[4]

DANCE THERAPY

One of the earlier users of dance as an ancillary activity to therapy was the Menninger Clinic in 1925. Like the other forms of aesthetic therapies, dance therapy has become a specialization rather recently with the development of a National Dance Therapy Association (1966) which has developed an accreditation process for specialized degrees in dance therapy. Dance therapy programs are offered at both educational institutions and special schools.

The major functions of a dance therapist include the following:

- Development of a positive body image in the client

- Self-concept

- Expression of nonverbal communication

- Awareness of the continuity between inner and physiological states and psychological behavior

- Increased use of the physical body to reduce anxiety and in selected individuals, to force physical movement.

Dancing is used as a medium for expression, as well as, to provide a structured experience in time and space for individuals and groups who lack structure in their thought processes or in their physical behavior. The dance therapist usually operates as a team member with other human service professions, such as social work, psychiatry, psychology, and psychiatric nursing. Primary therapy is usually the domain of the other team members and dance therapy is usually an adjuvant to the therapeutic process.[5]

MUSIC THERAPY

Music and its calming influence on disturbed minds was a well-known phenomenon to the Egyptians and Greeks. The aesculapean temples of healing (400 B.C.) in Greece, used music to help calm individuals. No formal professionalization of music therapy occurred until 1925 when music was used in the Menninger Clinic as an adjunct to therapy. By the 1940s music was used in several mental institutions, correctional institutions and in nursing and veterans' homes. In 1950 some music therapy programs were established with the development of the National Association of Music Therapy. There currently are established schools of music, both educational institutions and special schools, with bachelor's degree and other programs including the Ph.D. level which stress different components of music education. There is a process for credentialing of a music therapist which has been in existence since 1950 and a process of accreditation for educational programs.

Music as a medium of expression can be viewed as having a passive and active phase. The passive phase is when one is listening to music and receiving psychic and emotional impressions. The active phase is when one is playing an instrument or singing, and expressing themselves. Whether the client is

118

passive or active in the use of music, the functions of a music therapist include the following:

- Provide structure for a thought process

- Channel feelings and emotions

- Enhance one's sensory motor development, either individually or in groups.

The major goals of music therapy are: increasing movement of handicapped limbs, improving memory, i.e., recall and retention of material, enhancing self-esteem, increasing one's attention span, and generally providing a vehicle for increased socialization skills and verbal interaction (Ludwig, 1977:142). The music therapist operates as a team member with other human service professions, such as social work, psychiatry, psychology, and psychiatric nursing. Primary therapy is usually the domain of other members of the human service professions and music therapy is an adjuvant to the therapeutic process.[6]

SOCIAL WORK

The aesthetic network is predominantly oriented toward individual creativity and expression with a social service component implemented through specialists in one of the aesthetic therapies but employed in a non-aesthetic network, such as psychiatric hospital, geriatric hospital, etc. Most social workers, on the other hand, are employed in the human service networks such as physical health, mental health, corrections, etc. A small number of social workers in 1980 were employed in the industrial classification of entertainment and recreation (993) and in museum and art galleries (38) (see figure 3-6, pp.85-86, Chapter 3 Social Work as a Helping Profession). The role of a social worker would vary, depending upon which one of the human service networks in which they are employed. For example, the role of a social worker in a mental health institution would be somewhat different than the role of a social worker employed in a school or a corrections setting. The example used here is that of a social worker employed in the area of mental health since many of the aesthetic therapists are also employed in the same area.

A social worker uses personal interaction, both verbal and nonverbal and the development of a relationship, as the medium for therapy, which is in contrast to the activity focus of art, dance and music therapy. The social worker is generally part of a team consisting of a psychologist, psychiatrist, psychiatric nurse, and the adjuvant aesthetic therapies. A social worker may be assigned primary therapy to individuals and groups, develop social histories and assessments of behavior, as well as contacting family members and arranging for a continued therapy program after a person is released from a mental institution.

A social worker's tasks include individual case work, group work, community organization, staff development, consultation and research.

INDIVIDUAL CASEWORK

An example of the individual casework approach would be when a person is spending time with an individual exploring their emotions, thought processes, and aiding that person in gaining insight into their problems and to enable them to cope better with their environment.

GROUP WORK

An example of the group work approach would be a number of individuals discussing their problems and reflecting on various solutions to those problems.

COMMUNITY ORGANIZATION

An example of the community organization approach would be lobbying for funding for mental hospitals or legislation which would enhance the ability of the mental health services to provide better service for their clientele.[7]

CONSULTATION and RESEARCH

Consultation could be program evaluation, redesign agency structure and functioning or the development of staff in-service training programs. Research could consist of program evaluation, testing of techniques and outcomes, etc.

PERSONAL SOCIAL SERVICES

The aesthetic network to a large extent is a commercialized network which has an impact on all individuals in the United States. This network, like other networks, has linkages with the personal social service network (see Chapter 22 Personal Social Service). Some examples of the personal social services in the aesthetic network include the following:

PROTECTIVE SERVICES

Programs for abused elderly and mental health patients. Movies and films focussing on abuse, such as Violence in the Homes: An American Nightmare (1980), On the Brink (1980), A

120

Conversation with Helen (1977) and In Need of Special Attention (1981).

UTILITARIAN SERVICES

Day care or homemaking services for clients and films, such as Day Care in America (1979) and In Support of Mothers (1980).

DEVELOPMENTAL and SOCIALIZATION SERVICES

Marital counseling, specifically films, plays etc. on family and marital problems, such as Chillysmith Farm (1981), Family Living Styles: Legal Rights and Responsibilities (1977), Susan's New Job (1979) and Daddy Doesn't Live Here Anymore (1981).

REHABILITATIVE and THERAPEUTIC SERVICES:

Alcohol and drug programs, for example films and workshops on addictive problems ,such as Living with an Alcoholic (1981), Lisa, The Legacy of Sandra Blain (1979), Feeling Good (1979), Sexual Abuse of Children: America's Secret Shame (1980) and Incest the Hidden Crime (1979).

SPECIAL POPULATIONS

Since the United States is a country of diverse cultures and traditions, it is appropriate for the aesthetic network to reflect this diversity through programs for special populations. (See Chapter 25 Special Populations, and Chapter 24 Rehabilitation). Examples of programs for special populations in the aesthetic network include the following:

ASIAN

Music programs on Vietnam, China, Japan, etc. Dance Groups and cultural events, such as the "Ten Ten" parade for Chinese in Chicago, Illinois and art forms of the Hmong of Southeast Asia in Milwaukee, Wisconsin. Some cultural films include Chinese Americans (1973) and Japanese Americans (1974).

BLACK

Dance groups and theater groups on black culture. For example, the Jean Baptiste Point Du Sable museum in Chicago, Illinois and the Ko-Thi Dance Company and People's Theater in Milwaukee, Wisconsin. Some films include Black Like Me (1964) and the Poets TV Series.

EUROPEAN ETHNICS

Ethnic, oriental shows, festivals, dance, music groups, such as the annual Folk Festival in Milwaukee and specific events such as Polish Fest, German Fest, Irish Fest, etc. Some films include the Pascuks of Chicago (1977), A Village in Baltimore (1981).

NATIVE AMERICAN

Dance groups, tribal historical museums, Pow Wows which are open to the public. Cultural awareness groups have been formed, such as Uptown in Chicago, Illinois and the United Indians of Milwaukee, Wisconsin. Some examples of films include Growing Up Indian (1980) and Indian Legends-Ojibway (1980).

SAME SEX PREFERENCE

Art displays and films showing the works and/or life experiences of homosexuals, such as the "Torch Song Trilogy" (1984) and Pink Triangles (1982).

SPANISH SPEAKING

Dance, music groups and films on Spanish culture, such as Climate of the Street (1973) and Portrait of a Minority Group (1978).

WOMEN

Art displays by women artists, films, books, etc., which focus on the perception of women, such as the famous artists Imogene Cunningham and Romaine Brooks. Some examples of films include The Life and Times of Rosie the Riviter (1980), ERA: The War Between Women (1977) and The Artist was a Woman (1977).

ISSUES

Since the aesthetic network does not have as its primary function the provision of social services, some issues relate to the education of aesthetic therapists and social work.

EDUCATION of AESTHETIC THERAPISTS

The issues for art therapy and dance therapy as newer professions are quite similar. A significant issue is; should these mediums be adjunct or adjuvant to a therapeutic relationship with other professions having primary resonsibility for therapy, or should these mediums be a therapy in their own right. Music therapy is a more established profession and does not have the identity problem nor lack of recognition that the newly emerging aesthetic therapies are facing.

Since most of the aesthetic therapies have recently begun the process of professionalization, there is still debate on which forms of credentials are necessary to be certified as a therapist and what kind of curriculum is most appropriate. This issue has been generally resolved for music therapy. An issue which does relate to all aesthetic therapies is the role of private practice and how to monitor the performance of individuals in private practice.

EDUCATION of SOCIAL WORKERS

For social work one of the issues is the awareness that aesthetic therapies are specialties and to recognize these specialties as part of a team approach. Social work needs to clarify its use of techniques of intervention to avoid repetition or duplication of effort when working in a team situation.

SUMMARY

The aesthetic network in the United States is rather large and complex, and in contrast to other networks, such as the political and education networks, does not have a well-defined government organization structure. Many of the services provided in this network are through individuals or small groups and local communities. The function of the aesthetic network is primarily the expression of an individual's feelings, thoughts and perceptions and not social services. The aesthetic network has formally developed a series of specializations, such as art, dance and music therapy (amongst others) since 1924.

A brief discussion of the historical development of art, dance and music therapy has indicated some of the major trends in these areas since the arts of a given period of time will reflect the predominant societal attitudes and values. The aesthetic therapies have developed as an occupation in 1925 and as professions since 1940. Prior to the twentieth century, many of the arts were highly stylized and conformist. Although they did express the views of individuals, the manner of their presentation was highly structured and inflexible. Consequently, when one talks about using one of the art mediums as a therapy, there has to be a concept of individual creativity and expression, which was a product of the twentieth century. There are numerous occupations involved in the aesthetic network, with the major therapies consisting of art, dance and music. A generalized description of the functions of these therapies was described and then contrasted with the role of a social worker.

An issue that relates to the aesthetic therapies is their relationship to other human service professions. In particular, this is an issue for the newer therapies like art and dance. Music therapy has been recognized since the 1940s, and they have generally resolved this issue of identification and relationship to other professions. There are educational and curricular matters for these professions to resolve. For social work a major issue is to incorporate materials into the educational program on the aesthetic therapies, since the team approach (multiple disciplines) is an expanding concept in treatment.

FOOTNOTES

*This chapter was reviewed for comments by Rolf Hickman, Professor, Fine Arts-Art, Leo Muskatevc, Professor, Fine Arts-Music, University of Wisconsin-Milwaukee; and Peter Baim, Professor of Music, Wisconsin Conservatory of Music, Milwaukee, WI.

1. Basic statistics on the size of the aesthetic network are taken from the following publications: United States Department of Commerce, Bureau of the Census, 1982 Census of Service Industries United States: Geographic Series, Washington, D.C.: U.S. Government Printing Office, 1984; United States Department of Commerce, Bureau of the Census, Statistical Abstract of the United States: 1986 (106th Ed.) edition), Washington, D.C.: U.S. Government Printing Office, 1985' and United States Department of Commerce, Bureau of the Census, 1980 Census of the Population: Volume 2 Subject Reports, Part 7C: Occupation by Industry, Washington, D.C.: U.S. Government Printing Office, 1984. These figures on occupations do not distinguish between professionals and amateurs within a specific occupation.

2. In addition to the loosely structured aesthetic network an individual uses an informal folk system for aesthetic purposes. An individual may work with family members, relatives, friends and colleagues for their benefit and appreciation. These informal aesthetic works may be never seen by anyone else (public exposure).

3. For a review of the therapies in the aesthetic network, the reader is referred to Peter Vallitutte and Florence Christoplos, Interdisciplinary Approachs to Human Services, Baltimore, MD: University Park Press, 1977.

4. For information on art therapy as a profession, contact the American Art Therapy Association, P.O. Box 11604, Pittsburgh, PA 15228.

5. For information on dance therapy as a profession, contact the American Dance Therapy Association, 2000 Century Plaza, Columbia, MD 21044

6. For information on music therapy as a profession, contact the National Association for Music Therapy, P.O. Box 610, Lawrence, KS 66044.

7. For information on social work as a profession, contact the National Association of Social Workers, 7981 Eastern Avenue, Silver Spring, Maryland 20901.

SUGGESTED READINGS

William Fleming. Arts and Ideas. New York, NY: Holt Rinehart Winston, Inc., 1963. This is a classic book describing from a historical perspective, the shifting focus of the arts.

Helen Gardener. Art Through the Ages, 7th Ed. New York, NY: Harcourt, Brace, Jovanovich, 1980. This is a classic reference on the history of art and relates art as a medium to the prevailing social, religious and political context of specific time periods.

Helene Lefco. Dance Therapy. Chicago, Illinois: Nelson Hall Press, 1974. This book provides a nontechnical overview of dance therapy.

Peter Vallitutte and Florence Christoplos. Interdisciplinary Approaches to Human Services. Baltimore, Maryland: University Park Press, 1977. This book contains articles on art, dance and music therapy which provides an overview for each of these professions as well as related professions like nursing, education, etc.

REFERENCES

Artz, Frederick. From the Renaissance to Romanticism: Trends in Style in Art, Literature and Music, 1300-1830. Chicago, IL: University of Chicago Press, 1962.

Bunney, Judith. "Dance Therapy," pp. 49-59 in Vallitutte, Peter and Florence Christoplos, Interdisciplinary Approaches to Human Services. Baltimore, MD: University Park Press, 1977.

DeMille, Agnes. The Book of Dance. New York, NY: Golden Press, 1963.

Department of Health, Education and Welfare, Health Resources Statistics: 1976-1977 Edition. Washington, D.C.: U.S. Government Printing Office, 1978.

Fleming, William. Arts and Ideas. New York, NY: Holt, Rinehart Winston, Inc., 1963.

Gardener, Helen. Art Through the Ages. 7th Ed. New York, New York: Harcourt, Brace, Jovanovich, 1980.

Headington, Christopher. The Brodly Head History of Western Music. London, England: Brodly Head, Ltd., 1974.

Isaacs, Leslie. "Art Therapy Group for Latency Age Children," Social Work, Vol. 22,1 (January 1977), pp. 57-59.

Jacobs, Jay. The Color Encyclopedia of World Art. New York, New York: Crown Publishing, 1975.

Kwiatkowska, Hanna. Family Therapy and Evaluation Through Art. Springfield, IL: Charles C. Thomas Co., 1978.

Lefco, Helene. Dance Therapy. Chicago, IL: Nelson Hall Press, 1974.

Lerner, Arthur. Poetry in the Therapeutic Experience. New York, NY: Pergamon Press, 1978.

Ludwig, Alice. "Music Therapy," pp. 135-154 in Vallitutte, Peter and Florence Christoplos, Interdisciplinary Approaches to Human Services. Baltimore, MD: University Park Press, 1977.

Menninger Clinic. "Activity Therapy and Psychiatric Treatment," Bulletin of the Menninger Clinic, Vol. 35, #1 (January, 1975), pp. 47-100.

Minahan, Anne (Ed.). Encyclopedia of Social Work, 18th Issue, Washington, D.C.: National Association of Social Workers, 1986.

Office of the City Clerk, Milwaukee Report, Milwaukee, Wisconsin: Office of the City Clerk, 1976.

Office of the Federal Register, United States Government Manual, 1985/86. Washington, D.C.: U.S. Government Printing Office, 1985.

Roberts, Vera. On Stage: The History of the Theater, 2nd Edition. New York, NY: Harper and Row Publishers, 1974.

Rubin, Rhea. Using Bibliotherapy: A Guide to Theory and Practice. Phoenix, AZ: Aryx Press, 1978.

Sachs, Kirk. World History of the Dance. New York, NY: W. W. Norton and Co., 1937.

Sargent, Lois. "Poetry in Therapy," Social Work, vol. 24,2 (March 1979), pp. 157-159.

Ulman, Elinor, Edith Kramer and Hanna Kwiatkowska. "Art Therapy," pp. 13-47, in Vallitutte, Peter and Florence Christoplos, Interdisciplinary Approaches to Human Services. Baltimore, MD: University Park Press, 1977.

United States Department of Commerce, Bureau of the Census, 1980 Census of Population: Volume 2 Subject Reports, Part 7C: Occupation by Industry, Washington, D.C.: U.S. Government Printing Office, 1984.

United States Department of Commerce, Bureau of the Census, 1982 Census of Service Industries, United States: Geographic Series, Washington, D.C.: U.S. Government Printing Office, 1984.

United States Department of Commerce, Bureau of the Census, Statistical Abstract of the United States: 1986 (106th Ed.), Washington, D.C.: U.S. Government Printing Office, 1985.

Wisconsin Legislative Reference Bureau, Wisconsin Blue Book 1985/86, Madison, Wisconsin: Department of Administration, 1985.

Wolman, Benjamin (ed.). International Encyclopedia of Psychiatry, Psychology, Psychoanalysis and Neurology, vol. 2. New York, NY: Aesculapius Publishers, Inc., 1977.

CHAPTER 5

ECONOMIC NETWORK*

"Industry-centered health and security plans
which bulk ever larger on the voluntary
welfare scene have so far not been thought
of as 'philanthropic,' but they fit the
criteria of Social Welfare used here. These
programs, it should be noted, are not
'industrial social work' in the European
tradition of workers offering family and
other services from an outpost in the
plant. The latter development, hailed for
the past twenty years as a 'new frontier in
social work,' simply has not materialized in
America." (Wilensky and Le Beaux, 1965:162.

INTRODUCTION

The above statement by Wilensky and Le Beaux still holds
true in the United States in 1986, since a small fraction of
social work activities occurs within the economic network. The
economic network in the United States is large, complex and
diverse, consisting of large, multi-company corporations
(national and international), small companies, individual ownership of companies, individual and corporate farms, large trade
unions and employee associations, and their local chapters.

As the United States becomes more immersed in a service-
oriented economy and more concern is expressed about the quality
of life, along with production, there will be a slow but imper-
ceptable trend for the provision of social services within the
economic network. The older term for social services in the
economic network was industrial social services. The current
trend is to refer to social services in the occupational workplace, or occupational social services, which incorporates the
broadened concept of the economic network described above.

This chapter briefly describes the economic network, the
profession of personnel management and the role of social work.

SIZE

In 1982 there were an estimated 14,546,000 business establishments (including individual farm ownership) with estimated
expenditures of 7.7 trillion dollars. In 1984 the estimated

129

number of employed individuals in the work force was estimated at 106,702,000 individuals including the industrial classification of public administration (government and military). Of these 106.7 million individuals employed in the work force, 31,938,000 or 29.9 percent were employed in goods producing industries (agriculture, mining, construction and manufacturing), and 74,764,000 or 70.1 percent were employed in service-producing industries (transportation and public utilities, wholesale and retail trade, finance, insurance and real estate, services, and government including military).[1]

In 1982 there were an estimated 82,973 unions and employee associations (collective bargaining units). Expenditures in 1979 were estimated at 6.6 billion dollars and having a membership of 24.4 million members or about 28.5 percent of the work force. Figure 5-1 shows the estimated size of the economic network.[2]

HISTORICAL DEVELOPMENT

The organization of the economic network in the United States consists of the following: business and farm establishments, labor unions and employee associations, and employee benefits.

BUSINESS and FARM ESTABLISHMENTS

ANCIENT CIVILIZATION (3000 B.C. 450 A.D.) - The ancient civilizations of Greece and Rome had agriculture as the primary economic activity, with specialized craftsmen involved in manufacturing goods and merchants/traders distributing the products.

Greek agriculture was organized on a system of serfs (helots) and slaves working the land owned by a landed aristocracy in the south and east (Thessalia, Laconica, Messenia) and of individual ownership by the farmers in the north and west (Epirus and Eubola). The city/state developed regulations for trade and commerce, with the urban centers (cities) becoming the main center for specialized craftsmen (in small shops) who produced products using slaves under their supervision. Trade flourished through independent traders and merchants, guided by the regulations of a city/state, such as Athens.

Roman agriculture in the early days of the Republic (509-264 B.C.) was organized predominantly under the ownership of the individual farmer. During the later stages of the Republic (264 B.C.-27 A.D.) many of the small landowners lost their land, and agriculture became dominated by a landed aristocracy who developed large estates (latifundia), with slaves working the land. Many of the dispossessed farmers joined the plebian class

Figure 5-1

Estimated Size of the Economic Network 1982-84*

| | Aspect of Economic Network | |
	Business Enterprise	Unions and Employee Associations
Number of establishments	14,546,000[1]	82,973[2]
Expenditures (dollars)	7,755,000,000,000	6,618,000,000
Number in Workforce (employees)	105,005,000[3]	24,400,000
Population served (number)	238,816,000[4]	24,400,000

*Source: Adapted from United States Department of Commerce, Bureau of the Census, Statistical Abstract of the United States: 1986 (106th Ed.), Washington, DC: U.S. Government Printing Office, 1985, pp. 390, 404, 423, 425, 517; and United States Department of Labor, Directory of National Unions and Employee Associations, 1979, Washington, DC: U.S. Government Printing Office, 1980, pp. 55, 73.

[1]These figures exclude government (public administration and military) as an industrial classification.

[2]Figures include national organizations and local chapters (number of bargaining units).

[3]Statistical Abstract of the United States: 1986 Op Cit., p. 390, 1984 estimate.

[4]A 1985 estimate from Statistical Abstract of the United States: 1986 (106th Ed.), Op Cit., p. 32.

(lower class) in the cities or became soldiers. A shortage of slaves developed, and in order to maintain the agricultural system, between 27 A.D. and 450 A.D. individual farmers were allowed to work on the latifundia as coloni (tenant farmers). Emperor Diocletion (284-305) decreed that the farmer was attached to the land and could not leave it, and Emperor Constantine (306-337) decreed that the farmer (peasant) was

131

attached to the land as a serf. Roman society had a concentration of skilled craftsmen (artisans) working in small shops in the cities and had a trade and commercial class. In contrast to Greece, many of the policy discussions on economics were made by the central government in Rome or by the central government of each province.[3]

FEUDALISM, 450-1600 A.D. - This economic system was based on agriculture and a lord/serf relationship. Like the preceding ancient civilization, the feudalistic economy was based on agriculture. The feudalistic period can be divided into early and late. The early Medieval period (450-1200 A.D.) was one of a transition from Roman central government to small self-contained manors (local lord) and continuation of a landed aristocracy. After the decline of the Roman Empire, central authority literally collapsed, and each village was left on its own and many serfs left the land and became freemen. Slowly the feudal economy took hold with the lord (landowner) having almost absolute control over the peasant (agricultural worker). A system of rights and duties between the lord and the serf developed. The serf, in producing agricultural products for the lord, had the right to be defended by the lord and to be fed during times of famine. The artisan (craftsman) gravitated to the small cities, along with freemen and traders. Most of the economic activity centered on the manor and not the small cities.

In the late Middle Ages (1200-1600 A.D.) the feudal agricultural economy, with serfdom for the peasant, was fully developed in Western Europe. England, although having a feudal economy, did not develop the absolute forms of monarchy as existed in France and the German city states. By 1300, trade with other countries was beginning to expand and as a consequence a mercantile (merchant/middle class) was emerging. This mercantile group needed goods to trade, consequently, artisans (craftsmen) began to expand their production, and other products, such as clothes were made in the home for trading purposes (domestic manufacturing). Large trading companies and banks were established, like Genoa, Italy, 1346. The economic network was essentially locally controlled in the manor, village, or the free city/state.

MERCANTILISM, 1600-1700 A.D. - This economic system was based on agriculture, but the concept was to export more goods than one imports. There was further expansion of domestic manufacturing (in one's home), trading companies and entrepreneurial landlords. The landlords could make more money by raising sheep and having the laborers make clothes in their own homes than by raising crops. Consequently, much of the land in England was enclosed (for raising sheep) and the dispossessed laborer moved to the city seeking employment. The artisan (craftsman) continued his activities in small shops. This form of economy was controlled by the emerging nation/state. Wealth was measured from a nationalistic perspective, not an individual perspective.

PHYSIOCRATIC, 1700-1800 A.D. - This economic system was based on agriculture, with free trade and unrestrained governmental interference. Agriculture was the main economic activity, however, the mercantile class needed expanding markets in order to make more money. To accomplish this, the mercantile class needed few restraints from government regulations and a more efficient means of producing goods than the domestic (in home manufacturing) system. Early development of the factory system was taking place by 1714 and accelerated with the beginning of the Industrial Revolution by 1750. The Industrial Revolution consisted of technological innovations in energy use (steam engine, 1698), techniques of making goods (spinning jenny and flying shuttle, 1750), which allowed for faster production of goods and a concentration of laborers and resources for production in one place. Ownership of the emerging industrial businesses was concentrated into the hands of the already wealthy landowner or merchant. The older system of serfdom was declining with the rapid rise of an unemployed proletariat (worker).

LAISSEZ FAIRE/CAPITALIST, 1800-1935 A.D. - This economic system was based upon the production of industrial products and a factory system. Although agriculture remained the dominant economic activity until 1900, there was a rapid increase and expansion of industrial or manufacturing products. Land ownership in many places became decentralized with individual farm owners. Industrial production was concentrated into the hands of wealthy families or individuals. This was the period of classical economics (laissez faire), meaning minimum government interference, with individual competition as the guide to economic development. The Industrial Revolution was in full swing, with many technological changes, resulting in mass production and large factories. England and Western Europe felt the impact of industrialization before the United States, and these countries were already moving into a welfare capitalist system by 1900-1910, and in some cases, socialism. Since 1900, the production of goods (manufacturing) was the predominant economic activity.

WELFARE CAPITALIST, 1935 - 1980 - The United States' economic system has variously been labeled welfare capitalist, military/industrial complex, or service/industrial complex. Essentially, the economy is a compromise between free reign, laissez faire capitalism and socialism. The key issue is that government interference has developed to assure a basic minimum of financial support which may or may not be above the poverty level for

133

the worker. The term "military/industrial complex" refers to the development of military products as a basic part of goods production, and the term "service/industrial complex" or information/service complex refers to the service industries as a basic part of production and employment.

With the emphasis on both the production of goods and services, there has been a shift from family-owned businesses to large corporations, with decisions made on a national and international level. With certain service programs, such as Public Assistance and Social Security, decisions made at the federal level of government will directly impact on employment.

SERVICE/INFORMATION ECONOMY, 1980-on - The period of time since 1980 is one of seemingly incompatible trends. On one hand, the economy is moving more toward the direction of a service economy and specifically toward information and computerized systems. On the other hand, Reaganomics is decreasing the amount of assured minimum financial support for agriculture and lower income groups and increasing support for goods production industries. If these two trends are incompatible, one can expect a period of transition and dislocation within the economic network. It appears the trend toward a service economy will continue and pressure will build up politically to alter some of the policies of Reaganomics to assure basic financial support for the dispossessed or dislocated individuals who for a variety of reasons will find themselves unemployed. One can speculate that we are economically in a state of transition like the United States was in 1900.

LABOR/UNION and EMPLOYEE ASSOCIATIONS

ANCIENT CIVILIZATION, 3000 B.C. - 450 A.D. - The agricultural worker was relegated to the position of either a slave, tennant farmer, or serf who was managed by a landed aristocracy. The slaves and serfs did not develop organizations, however, they did periodically revolt against their low status, such as Eunus (134 B.C.), Tryphan (104 B.C.) and Spartacus (73 B.C.). Artisan guilds (craftsman organizations) were developed early in Greece (600 B.C.) and Rome (715 B.C.). These guilds were primarily organized as regulatory and friendly societies for specific crafts.

FEUDALISM, 450 - 1600 - Like the ancient civilizations, the agricultural worker was in the status of a serf and did not develop organizations to enhance their status. This does not mean the serfs did not attempt to change their posi- tion. There were periodic peasant revolts to gain freedom, such as 1251, 1358 and 1524. All of these revolts were brutally put down, and after the revolt of 1524 in Germany, the next major next major challenge to serfdom in Western Europe did not occur until the French Revolution in 1789 (excluding England which by 1650 was already granting some social and political rights to peasants and the fledgling middle class).

The major organization for craftsmen in the feudal economy was the guild. In the early Medieval period (450-1200 A.D.) the craft guilds were organized for reasons of protection and providing mutual aid. In the later Medieval period (1200-1600 A.D.) the guilds expanded numerically and into economic and political functions including: regulation of trade, goods production, wages and quality of the product. Some examples of these guilds include the Weavers' Guild (1099), Merchant Guild (1000) and Painters' Guild (1303). The guild became the major organization for craftsmen and provided financial, social welfare and protective services for their members. The guilds were generally based in a local area and were not regional or nationwide.

MERCANTILISM, 1600-1700 A.D. - With the developing domestic system of manufacturing, the expansion of the mercantile class, and the entrepreneurial landlord, the influence of the guild as the organizing force began to decline. Discussions on wages and the settling of labor disputes were handled by the central government or the employer. Some wage associations were formed to present labor's case to the central government or employer. There were periodic riots by laborers for various reasons, such as London, England (1661).

PHYSIOCRATIC ECONOMY, 1700-1800 - A number of friendly and benevolent societies were formed in England and other countries to aid the laborer, such as The Ancient Society of Gardeners (1716), Goldsmith Friendly Society (1712) and Brotherhood of Glassmakers (1755). Other combinations or groups of workers organized and went on strike, which led ultimately to the Combinations Acts of 1799-1824. The government in England discouraged labor organizations based upon the philosophy of the employer and employee established an individual labor contract. As laborers went on strike the government response was to ban labor organizations with the Combinations Acts.

LAISSEZ FAIRE CAPITALIST, 1800-1935 - With the development of the industrial economy and the shift from a domestic system of production to a factory system of production, labor, both agricultural and industrial, organized. In the early period from 1800-1870 a number of cooperative societies and unions developed to press demands for better wages, prices and working conditions from employers. Examples of organizations from this early period include the New York and Connecticut Dairying Cooperative (1810), New York Cooperative Cheese Factories

(1850), Mechanics Union (1827), Journeymen Cordweavers' Union (1805), United Tailoresses Union (1825) and the Typographical Union (1852). The trade union movement was received negatively by employers, and in some cases union officials were tried and convicted for conspiracy (Journeymen Cordweavers in 1806).

In the period from 1870 to 1935 there was a rapid increase in the union movement and periodic violence and attempts by employers to destroy or negate the union movement. Some examples of major unions which developed include the following: Knights of Labor (1869), American Federation of Labor (AFL) (1886), Industrial Workers of America (1905), Committee of Industrial Organizations (1935), which became the Congress of Industrial Organizations in 1938 (CIO). Some examples of labor disturbances which occurred were: Haymarket riot (1886), Pullman strike (1894) and the copper workers' strike (1917), in Bisbee, Arizona. The general objective was to organize specific trades as well as mass production workers. Some of the issues for the union movement included collective bargaining/wages, the right to organize, pension plans and safety conditions. Companies, in response to the union movement, developed welfare paternalism (a series of company-supplied and controlled benefits) and discouraged union organization through activities, such as hired strike breakers, injunctions, yellow-dog contracts and discrimination against union employees.

WELFARE CAPITALIST, 1935 TO 1980 - The process of organizing trades, specific occupations and mass production industrial workers continued. As union activity and collective bargaining were accepted by companies as well as the courts, the forces of collective bargaining shifted to consolidation of fringe benefits, grievance arbitration, and in some cases, development of new fringe benefits, such as legal advice and employee counseling. Consolidation of the union movement developed with the merger of the AFL-CIO in 1955.

With the focus of industrial production shifting from goods production to service production industries, the current trend is to organize white-collar workers (clerical, government, professional) and pink-collar workers (women), either as a union or employee association. Some examples of these organizations include the following: American Postal Workers (1971), American Federation of State, County, Municipal Employees (1975), American Association of Classified School Employees, American Association of University Professors and American Nurses Association.

SERVICE/INFORMATION ECONOMY, 1980-on - The period since 1980 has seen union activity developing in two directions which is a reflection of the transition in the economy and Reaganomics. On one hand the push toward unionizing white and pink collar workers is continuing. This is a vital move for unions, since in 1979 unions represented only about 28.5 percent of the work force. On the other hand, the traditional blue collar union is being forced to give up some long fought for benefits and accustomed wage increases in order to preserve their jobs. In some cases, business leaders are clearly giving out the message of attempting to nullify the power of the union. These seemingly incompatible trends are a sign that our economic network is in transition.

EMPLOYEE BENEFITS

ANCIENT CIVILIZATION, 3000 B.C. - 450 A.D. - The landed aristocracy provided minimal benefits for employees, outside of minimal care to keep them physically able-bodied. The artisan and craft guilds provided social and recreational programs and helped individuals in the guilds when they had financial or social needs.

FEUDALISM, 450 A.D. - 1600 A.D. - The landed aristocracy provided minimal benefits for the serf (agricultural worker) but did have obligations to provide protection from famine, physical harm, and to provide social and recreational activities. The craftsmen and merchants, as they organized into guilds, provided mutual protection, financial assistance, supportive emotional assistance, and social and recreational activities.

MERCANTILISM, 1600-1700 - With the decline of guilds for the craftsmen and the enclosure movement resulting in a large number of dispossessed farmers, the laborer was left on his own to contract for wages or to develop wage associations to plead and argue their case. This was a period of individualism and competition, and employers provided minimal benefits.

PHYSIOCRATIC, 1700-1800 - The laborers found themselves in a developing factory system and began to organize friendly societies as mutual support groups to provide financial support and social and recreational activities. The employer was not bound to provide other services beyond minimal wages.

LAISSEZ FAIRE CAPITALIST, 1800-1935 - As the industrial revolution continued and laborers were left at the mercy of the employer for wages and benefits, conflict erupted between the laborer and the employer. Laborers organized into trade unions. In the conflict between the company and unions, two patterns emerged in the provision of employee benefits: company/management programs and union programs.

Company/Management Programs - In this phase of the development of human service programs in the economic network the term "Welfare Capitalism" or "Welfare Paternalism" is applicable. In response to the demands of labor, companies developed a series of fringe benefits to placate the laborer and to prevent or minimize the impact of unionization. Programs developed by companies were an attempt to humanize the industrial revolution but at the price of a laborer's loyalty to a company. Welfare capitalism can be described as:

"Any service provided for the comfort or improvement of employees which was neither a necessity of the industry or required by law. Welfare capitalism constituted one solution offered by American businessmen to the crisis of labor management relations. "[4]

The major development of company programs or welfare capitalism was from 1850-1940. Some examples of programs sponsored by companies include the following: housing and company stores (by 1916, 1000 companies had a system of housing and company stores), educational programs (nursery school and through eighth grade), religious programs, 1926, recreation programs, 1851, medical and pension programs, 1860s, libraries, 1910, employee representatives (company unions, 1886, 1898) and social work services (individual casework 1875). These programs were established to enhance the quality of life of the employee and were paid for by the company. The "company town" had many advantages in providing security for employees, but under misperceived or misguided management, became tools to control the employee and to delay or negate the development of employee unions. That is, a loyal employee received the company benefits, and a disagreeable employee was fired and lost all benefits.[5]

Union Programs - In response to the company-controlled programs, unions developed their own autonomous system of benefits. Examples of benefits available from some unions for the worker include the following:

- Training and retraining - International Brotherhood of Electrical Workers, United Auto Workers Union

- Employment referral - International Brotherhood of Electrical Workers

- Pensions - Teamsters Union

- Housing - International Union of Electrical and Machine Workers

138

- Financial services - Teamsters Union

- Social and recreational facilities - Teamsters Union

- Life and health insurances - International Brotherhood of Electrical Workers, Teamsters Union

- Medical facilities - International Ladies Garment Workers Union, United Mine Workers Union.

WELFARE CAPITALIST, 1935 TO 1980 - Over time, the position of the American worker improved because of company and union programs and the shifting focus of labor/management negotiation. The focal concern for negotiation between labor and management from 1860-1945 was wages, rights to collective bargaining and the right to organize. The focal concern for negotiation between labor and management from 1945-80 was fringe benefits. As fringe benefits became part of labor contracts, the significance of company controlled programs declined. Other additional factors involved in the decline of company programs include the following: the automobile (a worker was no longer immobile), development of mandatory legislated programs (social security, disability), and resentment of the worker toward the older paternalistic measures of the company. Today, all companies provide all or some of the following benefits which can be classified as:

- Legally required - social security, disability, unemployment compensation, workmen's compensation, Medicare hospitalization, etc.

- Private security and welfare - pension, life insurance, hospital, surgical and medical plans, etc.

- Employee services - employee counseling, social recreation plans, tuition aid, purchase discounts, industrial health facilities, etc.

- Payment for non-work time - holidays, vacations, sick leave, rest periods, etc.

- Special and extra compensation - profit sharing, thrift plans, bonuses, etc.

It is estimated that employer expenses for the above programs were 420 billion dollars in 1979. The trade union movement expanded its own programs to include counseling (International Ladies Garment Workers Union and American Federation of Labor), hiring of professional community organizers (AFL-CIO, 1945) and have what is commonly called a welfare counselor. In 1964 there were an estimated 40,000 welfare counselors working for a union.[6]

SERVICE/INFORMATION ECONOMY, 1980 ON

With an emphasis in the late 1970s and 1980s on problems, such as alcohol and drugs and their impact on productivity, two new concepts emerged in the delivery of employee services: joint company/union programs and contract-out programs. Some companies and unions have joined together in a cooperative endeavor to provide alcohol, drug and family counseling to employees, such as the Illinois Central Gulf Railroad.[7] Other companies have a contract with a private agency to provide employee assistance in alcohol and drug counseling, such as the Pabst Brewing Company in Milwaukee, Wisconsin.

Both unions and business recognize that employees may have problems, such as alcoholism, drugs, family, etc. In a survey of 204 companies completed by the Bureau of National Affairs in 1971, 158 or 78 percent of the companies had an informal system of focusing on employee problems (supervisor, personnel relations department), 41 or 20 percent used both informal and formal systems (in-house counseling or referral), and 5 or 2 percent used a formal system (in-house counseling or referral). Of the 204 companies, 92 or 45 percent used in-house counseling, and 112 or 50 percent used a referral system to other agencies.

Of the 92 companies having an in-house counseling program, 24 or 36 percent used outside expertise, such as a psychologist, psychiatrist, social worker, or clergy, and 68 or 74 percent used the personnel department. In general, employee counseling of an in-house nature is a small component of employee counseling. Many companies are recognizing the problems of employees, since 57 or 28 percent had programs for alcoholism, 51 or 25 percent had programs for mental illness, 48 or 24 percent had programs for personal problems, and 40 or 20 percent had programs for drug addiction. With the broadening of concern for the social and psychological needs of the employees, there emerged the concept of employee counseling and assistance programs and a shift in perceptual language to programs for human resources. Concurrent with this growing awareness of the problems of employees is the awareness of the role of other helping professions, including social work in providing social services in the economic network. Figure 5-2 shows a historical time line and overall development of the economic network.

STRUCTURE

In developing an overview of the structure of the economic network one can look at its organizational context, services

140

provided, occupations and professions and dominant occupations and professions.

ORGANIZATIONAL CONTEXT

Governmental units as they impact on the economic network are shown in Figure 5-3. Few, if any, industries have an organizational unit known as social services. The more usual pattern is to have services placed in the personnel area either under health and safety or benefits and services. Figure 5-4 is an idealized model of a corporate structure highlighting the personnel section.

In smaller companies one person may occupy multiple positions including those of production and personnel management. Within larger companies there has been specialization of functions as shown in Figure 5-4.

Trade unions have developed a series of their own programs, and the structure of the AFL-CIO is shown in Figure 5-5.

Like other societal networks there is a folk or informal system to alleviate economic problems, such as colleagues, family members, relative, friends, etc. Some individuals are reverting to a barter system for goods and services. For example, a painter may agree to paint the house of a dentist and in return receive free dental care.

SERVICES PROVIDED

In taking a broad view of services (employee benefits) provided by industry and unions, they can be classified into: employee financial security programs, counseling programs, social programs and supportive or ancillary programs. Examples of programs offered within the economic network include the following:

-Employee Financial
 Security: Accident/disability insurance
                           Medical/hospital insurance
                           Pensions
                           Profit-sharing plans
                           Home financing/credit unions
                           Welfare funds

-Counseling Programs: Mental health services
                           Alcohol/drug services
                           Child development services
                           Family/marital counseling services
                           Legal aid/income tax

Figure 5-2

Historical Time Line of the Economic Network

Economic Network	Component of Network	Focus
Ancient Civilization 3000 B.C.-450 A.D.	Business/Farm	Agriculture Small Shop Craftsman
	Labor Union and Employee Associations	No organization (some small guilds for craftsman) Artisan Guilds 600 B.C. Greece, 715 B.C. slave revolts
	Employee Benefits	Craft Guilds provide social, recreation and financial services
Feudalism 450 A.D.-1600 A.D.	Business/Farm	Agriculture Small Shop Craftsman
	Labor Union and Employee Associations	Rise of craft guilds and trade associations 925, Craft Guilds 1200 Freeman Guilds 1000 Merchant Guilds
	Employee Benefits	Craft guilds provide social, recreation and financial services
Mercantilism 1600-1700	Business/Farm	Agriculture/Developing Merchant Class and Trade
	Labor Union and Employee Associations	Wage Associations Decline of guilds
	Employee Benefits	Few benefits/employer had minimal responsibility

Figure 5-2 (continued)

Physiocratic 1700-1800	Business/Farm	Agriculture/Large farms/ Home Manufacturing
	Labor Union and Employee Associations	Friendly and benevolent societies (trade unions banned) 1712 Goldsmith 1716 Gardners, 1755 Glassmakers
	Employee Benefits	Friendly societies provide social, recreational and financial assistance
Laissez Faire Capitalist 1800-1935	Business/Farm	Transition from Agriculture to Goods producing industry and industrial revolution
	Labor Union and Employee Associations	Trade unions/collective bargaining 1869 Knights of Labor, 1886 American Federation of Labor 1905 Industrial Workers of America 1935 Congress of Industrial Organization
	Employee Benefits	Company programs-housing, education, medical, etc. Union programs-housing, medical, etc.

Figure 5-2 (continued)

Welfare Capitalism
(continued)

Welfare Capitalist 1935-1980	Business/Farm	Goods producing industries/emergence of service industries
	Labor Union and Employee Associations	Trade unions/blue collar Beginning development employee associations - 1955 AFL-CIO 1971 American Postal Workers 1975 American Federation of State, County, Municipal Employees; Teachers Unions and Associations
	Employee Benefits	Medical, financial, legal sick leave, profit sharing, etc. Beginning of counseling programs
Service Information 1980 on	Business/Farm	Service industries predominate. Emphasis emerging on information
	Labor Union and Employee Associations	Trade unions/white collar Increase in Employee Associations. Some anti-union sentiment
	Employee Benefits	Employee Assistance Programs. Decrease in some benefits such as salary in order to maintain jobs

Figure 5-3

Abbreviated Government Organization and the Economic Network*

Federal Level

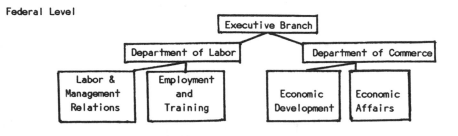

State Level

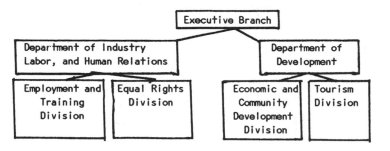

Local Level

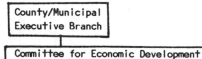

*   Sources: Adapted from Office of the Federal Register, United States
     Government Manual 1985–86, Washington, D.C.: U.S. Government Printing
     Office, 1985, p. 835, 846, Wisconsin Legislative Reference Bureau,
     Wisconsin Blue Book 1985–86. Madison, Wisconsin: Department of
     Administration, 1985, pp. 437, 531; Annual Reports City and County of
     Milwaukee, 1984.

145

Figure 5-4
Model of A Typical Business Structure Showing the Location
Personnel Relations and Employee Assistance Programs.*

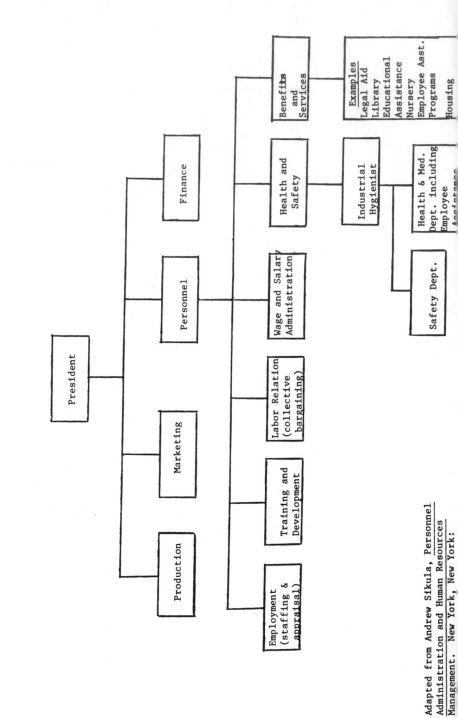

Adapted from Andrew Sikula, Personnel
Administration and Human Resources
Management. New York, New York:

Figure 5-5

Organization of the AFL-CIO*

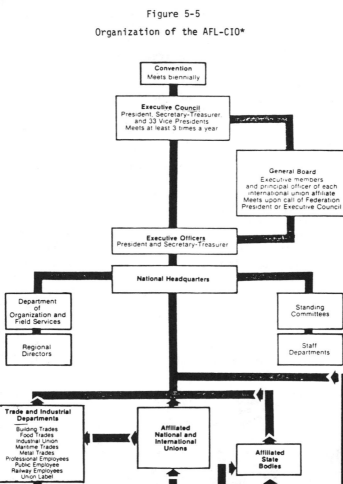

rce: Adapted from: United States Department of Labor, <u>Directory of National Unions and</u> <u>oyee Associations 1979</u> Washington, D.C.: U.S. Government Printing Office, 1980, 2.

147

Social Programs:	Athletic teams
	Dances
	Picnics
	Club memberships
	Literary groups

Supportive Programs:	Housing
	Cafeteria
	Beauty shops
	Store
	Nursery/Day care
	Medical examinations, pharmacy[8]

OCCUPATIONS and PROFESSIONS

A large business, such as American Motors Corporation, Boeing Corporation, etc., is in effect a small community. Subsequently, in addition to the direct labor force a wide variety of human service occupations and professions are employed. Figure 5-6 shows a variety of selected human service occupations and professions employed in the economic network in 1980. Some of the larger occupations and professions numerically include protective service, guards and watchmen, personnel and labor relations, physicians, and related, etc. The dominant occupation and profession is that of personnel relations.

DOMINANT OCCUPATIONS and PROFESSIONS

In an industrial setting the dominant occupation and profession is that of personnel relations or personnel administration. Figure 5-7 shows the occupation of personnel managers/relations and where they are employed by industrial classification in 1980. Of the 625,115 personnel/relations managers, 139,587 or 22.33 percent are employed in manufacturing, 110,709 or 17.71 percent are employed in public administration, 88,298 or 14.125 are employed in wholesale/retail trade, and the remaining 286,521 or 45.835 percent are employed in a variety of industrial classifications.

In many companies, the counseling of individuals is done by the personnel relations or management department. Early attempts to increase work productivity was through the scientific management school or Taylorism of the 1920s. Scientific management had as its aim the increase of productivity through a more efficient means of production accomplished by reducing the productive process into small elements and

Figure 5-6

Number and Percent of Selected Human Service Occupations and Professions
Employed in all Industrial Classifications Except
Professional and Related and Public Administration in 1980*

Occupation/Profession	Number and Percent	
	Number	Percent
Personnel, Labor Relations	435,441	24.60
Public Relations	71,953	4.10
Social Work	10,549	.59
Recreation Work	7,415	.42
Clergy and Religious	2,775	.16
Psychologist	2,486	.14
Sociologist	373	.02
Urban Planner	1,279	.07
Child Care Worker	143,035	8.10
Economist	76,698	4.30
Guards/Security (Private)	432,777	24.50
Fire fighters/Prevention	21,018	1.18
Lawyers	43,833	2.50
Legal Assistant	35,487	2.00
Teacher	142,461	8.10
Counselor (Education, Vocational)	5,039	.28
Librarian	10,838	.60
Archivist	3,281	.19
Physician	5,564	.30
Registered Nurse	52,232	3.00
Licensed Practical Nurse	24,034	1.40
Pharmacist	105,243	5.90
Health Aide/Orderly	84,280	4.77
Health Records	466	.03
Dentist	959	.05
Dietician	3,579	.20
Therapist	3,878	.22
Physician's Assistant	5,340	.30
TOTAL	1,767,797	100.00

*Source: Adapted from United States Department of Commerce, Bureau of the Census, 1980 Census of Population Volume 2 Subject Reports Part 7C: Occupation by Industry, Washington, DC: U.S. Government Printing Office, 1984, pp. 295-664.
These figures exclude the industrial classifications of professional and related and public administration since these two industrial classifications employ the vast majority of human service personnel.

149

Figure 5-7

Number and Percent of Personnel Managers/Relations
Employed by Industrial Classification in 1980*

Industry	Number	Percent
Agriculture/Forestry/Fishing	4,190	.670
Mining	6,519	1.043
Construction	13,282	2.123
Manufacturing	139,587	22.330
Transportation, Communications		
Public Utility	48,967	7.833
Wholesale/Retail Trade	88,298	14.125
Finance, Insurance, Real Estate	47,107	7.536
Business and Repair	77,938	12.468
Personal Services	7,809	1.250
Entertainment and Recreation	4,744	.759
Professional and Related	75,965	12.153
Public Administration	110,709	17.710
TOTAL	625,115	100.000

*Source: Adapted from United States Department of Commerce, Bureau of the Census, 1980 Census of Population Volume 2 Subject Reports Part 7C: Occupation by Industry, Washington, DC: U.S. Government Printing Office, 1984, pp. 295-664.

developing a quota system for production. When workers surpassed the quotas of production, they were given a wage incentive. Subsequently, industry began to employ individuals who understood scientific management, i.e., industrial engineers. The scientific management school of thought led to many conflicts since it led to a dehumanizing work environment and did not take into consideration the psychology of work.

The Hawthorne studies at the Western Electric Company in Illinois from 1927-1932 were the beginning of a movement toward human relations in industry. The focus of human relations was on communication with employees and development of a more satisfactory psychological work environment. It is from the human relations or industrial relations approach that personnel management developed as a field of practice. Companies in the 1930s and 1940s hired individuals to screen potential employees, act as a labor relations mediator, counsel employees, etc. The research works of Elton Mayo and Fritz Roethlisberger in human relations corresponded with this time period from 1930-1950. By the late 1970's a human resource model was emerging in personnel management. An assumption of the human resource model is that employees should be a participant in parts of the decisionmaking process in a company which affects them (participation and consultative management).

The human resource model views the worker as an individual who has psychological and social needs (Abraham Maslow), and a function of administration is to have an individual employee make optimum use of their abilities and resources. Personnel departments (and the company) become concerned when the human resource (employee) cannot be used to their full potential because of personal problems, such as alcohol, drugs, etc.

Personnel administration is rapidly developing from an eclectic occupation to achieving professional status. Professional organizations have been developed, such as the American Society for Personnel Administration which has encouraged development of the following: specialized training programs, professional certification (through the American Society of Personnel Administrators-Accreditation Institute) and a clarification of tasks and roles.

The personnel administrator needs knowledge in data processing, production, industrial psychology, business organization, unions, etc. Educationally, the general standard for personnel administration is that of a bachelor's degree; however, some companies may require an advanced degree.

Certification standards in the area of personnel administration are rapidly changing. An individual can be certified as a

151

specialist or generalist. For the certification exams one needs either a B.S. or an M.A. degree plus 6-10 years' experience, depending upon the area of certification. For example, those who <u>specialize</u> in education or consultation can be certified as an accredited Personnel Specialist (must possess B.S. or M.S. degree and six years experience) or as a Personnel Diplomat (must possess B.S. or M.S. and ten years experience or both). A <u>generalist</u> is one working in the field. They can become certified as an Accredited Personnel Manager or an Accredited Executive Manager, or both. In this case the individual must possess a degree, have five years experience, and pass exams in the following six functional areas: employment (placement, personnel and planning), training and development, compensation and benefits, health, safety and security, employee and labor relations and personnel records.

According to Sikula (1976:58-60), the major roles of a personnel administrator include the following: social conscience (humanize the work place), mediator, general problem-solver, counselor, company spokesman, change agent and a host of miscellaneous unspecified tasks.

Another way of viewing the task of a personnel administrator is to describe the job function. Job functions can be classified as:

- Staffing

- Personnel maintenance

- Labor relations

- Training and development

- Employee compensation

- Employee communication

- Organization

- Administration

- Personnel policies and planning

- Review, audit and research of specific items

- Employee services (which may involve some counseling and referral).

Most of the work of a personnel administrator is not directly with people and their problems but in other tasks of relevance to the company. It frequently occurs, however, that when individuals have a problem, they seek out the personnel administration individual. The personnel administrator is not a personal administrator (Sikula:1976, 41).[9]

Although numerous services are provided by industry and unions, personnel relations individuals are not welfare workers. Andrew Sikula (1976:39) clearly articulates that only a small fraction of a personnel relations person's time is spent on welfare concerns, therefore, to implement specific programs other types of professional personnel are needed.

SOCIAL WORK

The concept of employee counseling is an extension of the concept of employee benefits, which has a history dating back to the middle 1850s under welfare capitalism and union programs. Social workers were employed in some industries by 1875 with a dual function; help individuals with problems and to "spy" on the workers. This situation led to an extreme distrust of social workers by employees, and ultimately led to few social workers working in industry. It has been only since 1960 that the use of social workers in industry has increased.

Figure 5-8 shows the number of social workers employed by major industrial grouping in 1980. Social workers in the economic network account for 2.4 percent of the total number of social workers in the United States. Of the 10,594 social workers employed in the economic network in 1980, 1,061 or 10 percent were in goods-producing industries, and 9,533 or 90 percent were in service-producing industries. Although a small percentage of social workers are employed in the economic network, the number almost tripled between 1970-1980, increasing from 2,981 in 1970 to 10,594 in 1980, or a 255 percent increase.[10]

The general functions of a social worker in the economic network are varied, including individual and group services and community organization.

INDIVIDUAL CASEWORK and GROUP WORK

Individual and group type activities have focused on employee assistance programs for alcohol and drug use, family counseling, and general mental health problems. An example of this type of activity is the Employee Assistance Program at the Illinois Central Gulf Railroad which was established in 1974.

153

The Illinois Central Gulf Railroad Employee Assistance Program is a joint labor-management sponsored program administratively responsible to the Board of Directors of the company.[11] The program provides individual and group counseling to Illinois Central Gulf employees and their families. The program began initially to provide services to problem drinkers, but has been expanded to provide services for depression, attempted suicide, sexual problems, parent-child relationships, marital problems, unwanted pregnancies, other drug problems, financial problems and legal problems.[12]

The employee assistant program for drinking problems provides a diagnostic evaluation (medical, psychological and social work evaluation), a period of treatment and an ongoing evaluation and support system for the employee. The ongoing support system is seen as an important aspect of the program since the drinking problem is not necessarily resolved but under control. The support system may be the employee assistance staff, an outside agency, an outside mutual support group such as Alcoholics Anonymous, or any combination.

COMMUNITY ORGANIZATION

Organizing activities would include staff development, in-service training, working with other social welfare groups to enhance the delivery of services, lobbying for particular issues at a local level or a higher level in the political network. Leo Perlis (1978) describes some of the issues and concerns about social work in the economic network:

"It is in the promotion and implementation of the human contract in the workplace that social workers can play a most important role in fulfilling their functions as caseworkers, group workers, and community organizers and contribute to the development of social policy in industry and the community."[13]

Theodore Walden (1978) is more explicit about the potential role of social work in an organizing capacity by referring to activities, such as a third party to negotiate differences between labor and management, lobbying for a humanized workplace, and lobbying for social policies in industry which would enhance the quality of life for the employee. Although the emphasis today in social work and the economic network is employee assistance and personal services, it is clear an important task should be that of a mediator and bargainer.

154

Figure 5-8

Number and Percent of Social Workers Employed in Other Than
Professional and Related and Public Administration
Industrial Classifications in 1980*

Industrial Classification	Number	Percent
Goods Producing - Total	1,061	10.0
Agriculture/Forestry and Related	126	1.2
Mining	--	--
Construction	165	1.6
Manufacturing	770	7.2
Service Producing - Total	9,533	90.0
Transportation	253	2.4
Communication	101	1.0
Utilities	229	2.2
Wholesale/Retail Trade	1,150	10.8
Finance, Insurance	3,183	30.0
Business/Repair	2,634	24.9
Personal Services	987	9.3
Entertainment/Recreation	993	9.4
Total	10,594	100.0

*Source: Adapted from United States Department of Commerce, Bureau of the Census, 1980 Census of Population. Volume 2 Subject Reports Part 7C: Occupation by Industry, Washington, DC: U.S. Government Printing Office, 1984, pp. 295-664.

These figures exclude the industrial classifications of professional and related and public administration, since these classifications are where the majority of social workers, 432,376 or 97.6 percent are employed and the remaining 2.4 percent in the industrial classifications listed above.

PERSONAL SOCIAL SERVICES

The personal social services, as a network, have programs directly linked into the economic network (see Chapter 22 Personal Social Service). Some examples of personal social service programs in the economic network include the following:

155

PROTECTIVE SERVICES

Counseling spouses and child abuse, such as the Milwaukee County Employee Assistance program, Milwaukee, Wisconsin.

UTILITARIAN SERVICES

Day care, legal advice, financial management counseling such as the 3M Corporation, Minneapolis, Minnesota.

DEVELOPMENTAL and SOCIALIZATION SERVICES

Family and marital counseling, such as the 3M Corporation, Minneapolis, Minnesota.

REHABILITATIVE and THERAPEUTIC SERVICES

Alcohol and drug counseling, such as the Illinois Central Gulf Railroad, Chicago, Illinois.

SPECIAL POPULATIONS

Since the work force is a diverse population, special populations are directly involved. (See Chapter 25 Special Populations and Chapter 24 Rehabilitation). Some examples of programs for special populations in the economic network include the following:

ASIAN

Affirmative action and non-discrimination programs and organizations, such as Asian American National Business Alliance, Los Angeles, California; Asian American Chamber of Commerce Association, Washington, D.C. and Asian American Legal Defense and Education Fund, New York, New York.

BLACK

Affirmative action and non-discrimination programs and organizations, such as the National Urban League, New York, New York; Chicago Economic Development Corporation, Chicago, Illinois and Legal Defense Fund, National Association for the Advancement of Colored People, New York, New York.

EUROPEAN ETHNIC

Affirmative action and non-discrimination programs and organizations, such as National Confederation of American Ethnic Groups, Washington, D.C. and (EMPAC) Ethnic Millions Political Action Committee), Bayville, New York.

NATIVE AMERICAN

Affirmative action and non-discrimination programs and organizations, such as the AKBAR Fund, Sante Fe, New Mexico; American Indian Resources and Development Service Inc., Muskegon Heights, Michigan.

SAME SEX PREFERENCE

Affirmative action and non-discrimination programs and organizations, such as the Lesbian Resource Center, Minneapolis, Minnesota and Homosexual Information Center, Hollywood, California.

SPANISH-SPEAKING

Affirmative action and non-discrimination programs and organizations, such as the AKBAR Fund, Sante Fe, New Mexico, National Economic Development Association, Washington, D.C. and Chicano Legal Defense Fund, Austin, Texas.

WOMEN

Affirmative action and non-discrimination programs and organizations, such as Advocates for Women, San Francisco, California; Flexible Careers, Chicago, Illinois and Equal Rights Division, Department of Justice, Washington, D.C.

ISSUES

Social work in the early 1920s became identified as a profession which was the handmaiden of the company and in the 1960s as a profession which sought numerous social changes in society and in the workplace. Consequently, a social worker today is viewed from a suspicious and cautious perspective by both labor and management. Major issues which confront social work practice in the economic network can be classified as organizational and knowledge.

ORGANIZATIONAL

A major issue is who employs the social worker and therefore who is the social worker responsible to: the company, the union, or jointly. Perlis (1978) argues that the company or union-controlled employee assistance programs have built-in problems, therefore, the most feasible model is a joint labor and management program.

Administration of the program is an issue since the concerns are the degree of autonomy of the social worker in making policy, maintenance of confidentiality, development of a team-work approach with other professions, and development of community linkages and alternate programs for employees. Should the social worker be located under personnel, medical, occupational safety, benefits and services, or as a semi-independent unit in the corporate structure. Confidentiality is a key to employee assistance programs since the employees do not desire to have reprisals taken against them for admitting to either the company or the union they have a problem.

A related issue rapidly developing is the forced examinations of employees at nonrandom times for traces of drugs which raises legal and ethical questions. In 1986 the issue of forced examinations is highlighted in the newspapers quite frequently.

KNOWLEDGE

In addition to the usual content in social work, a person should have a background in business and corporate structure and operations. A business perspective is different than a social service perspective. Information on business and unions, their development and operation is necessary. Material on labor relations and industrial psychology would be invaluable.

Since the economic network is organized around labor and management as different groups, it is necessary to obtain a knowledge base in both areas as well as an exploration of how social work ethics may be implemented or constrained in the economic network. One should avoid employer and union paternalism, but create a balance where employer and employee participation are paramount.

SUMMARY

The concept of social services in the economic network is not new since social workers, psychologists, physicians, etc., have been employed in industry since the late 1800's. There has been a resurgence of social services in the economic network since 1960 in response to problems of employee alienation, alcohol and drug problems, and general employee/employer dissatisfaction.

A general historical overview showed that social services in the economic network have developed in a series of phases with a different organizational emphasis. Organizationally four patterns emerged in the economic network in the provision of employee assistance programs. From 1900-1940, company controlled programs were developed, from 1940-1960 union controlled programs were developed, and since 1960 joint programs and contracting out programs were developed.

The dominant occupation in the economic network is that of the personnel/relations manager. The function of personnel work is changing to a human resources management concept as companies are hiring other human service professions for the personal social services and for handling personal problems of the employees.

Social work, as one of the helping professions, is a minority of the human service personnel employed in the economic network, as only 2.4 percent of all social workers in the United States were employed in the economic network in 1980. A general description of social work tasks provided in the economic network shows a need for a full range of casework, group work, and community organization skills. Some issues for social workers in the economic network were described as organizational problems and a modified knowledge base to enable the social worker to understand the business and union perspective of the workplace.[14]

FOOTNOTES

*This chapter was reviewed for comments by Alan Meyer, Assistant Professor, School of Business, Robert Holzhauer, Professor Emeritus, School of Social Welfare, and Dennis Staral, Education Services Assistant I (ASPA certified), from the University of Wisconsin-Milwaukee and Joseph DeRosa, Director, Employee Assistance Program, Illinois Central Gulf Railroad Company, Chicago, Illinois.

1. The military and government, although crucial to the development of the economic network, are described separately in Chapter 6, Military Network, and Chapter 7, Political Network.

2. Figures on the size of the economic network (excluding military and government) are adapted from the following sources: United States Department of Commerce, Bureau of the Census, Statistical Abstract of the United States: 1986 (106th edition), Washington, D.C.: U.S. Government Printing Office, 1985, pp. 32, 390, 404, 423, 425, 517; United States Department of Labor, Occupational Outlook Handbook, 1986-87, Washington, D.C.: U.S. Government Printing Office, 1986, pp 13-22; and United States Department of Labor, Directory of National Unions and Employee Associations, 1979, Washington, D.C.: U.S. Government Printing Office, 1980, pp. 55, 73.

3. This detailed history of the dispossession of the individual farmholder and the development of a landed aristocracy with the agricultural worker becoming a serf, is developed to indicate that serfdom developed before the feudalistic era. The agricultural worker in Greece suffered similar dispossession of his land. For example, the Spartans (700 B.C.) conquered Messenia and made helots (serfs) out of the dispossessed landowners. The economic situation today in the United States has some similarities since individual ownership of farm land is decreasing rapidly in comparison to corporate ownership.

4. Stuart Brandes, American Welfare Capitalism: 1880-1940, Chicago, IL: University of Illinois Press, 1976, p. 5. This book is an excellent review of the development of company programs, their ultimate difficulties, and the rise of Taylorism in personnel work.

5. Numerous books have been written about company towns and how they controlled the employee, especially the sharecropper farmer and the company store. Examples of two cities which developed as company towns and are predominately company towns today are Kohler, Wisconsin (Kohler Plumbing, Inc.) and Marathon, Ontario, Canada (Marathon Paper Company).

6. The term 'welfare counselor' does not necessarily mean a paid social service position or a professional helping person. The welfare counselor may be a person who is paid by the union but is an employee who primarily acts as a broker for individuals seeking social services. It is rather rare for the welfare counselor to provide social services themselves.

7. The Illinois Central Gulf Railroad has a substantial program of employee assistance for alcohol and drug use under the direction of Joseph De Rosa. Knowledge of the Illinois Central Gulf Railroad program is through personal conversations with Mr. De Rosa and their program in 1979. For a description of the Kennecot Copper Company program, see Andrew Weisman, "A Social Service Strategy in Industry," Social Work (September 1975), Vol. 25, pp. 401-403.

8. This list of examples of programs offered by industry and unions is adapted from Andrew Sikula, Personnel Administration and Human Resources Management, New York, NY: John Wiley and Sons, Inc., 1976, pp. 319, 328-330. Not all companies or unions offer all of the services provided. Some organizations may have a minimum of services while others offer a range of services. More recent publications in the personnel management field such as William Werther

and Keith Davis. Personnel Management and Human Services. New York, New York: McGraw Hill Book Company, 1985, organizationally place employee assistance programs within the personnel department, either in the employee benefits and services or health and safety subdivisions.

9. Examples of some organizations which focus on personnel relations include the following: American Society for Personnel Administration, 30 Park Drive, Berea, OH, 44017; American Association for Counseling and Development, 5999 Stevenson Ave., Alexandria, Virginia 22304; American Personnel and Guidance Association, Two Skyline Place, Suite 400, 5203 Leesburg Pike, Falls Church, VA, 22041; American Society for Training and Development, P.O. Box 5307, Madison, WI, 53705; Association of Labor Management Administration and Consultants on Alcoholism, Inc., Suite 907, 1800 N. Kent Street, Arlington, VA, 22207; and Administrative Management Society, AMS Building, Maryland Road, Willow Grove, PA, 19090. For information on certification as a personnel relations manager, contact the Personnel Management Institute (ASPA Accreditation Institute), P.O. Box F, Berea, OH 44017. This organization also provides materials and information on accreditation of personnel relations programs.

Many unions hire personnel relations professionals and provide employee counseling programs. An example of a union organization is the American Federation of Labor and Congress of Industrial Organization, 815- 16th Street N.W., Washington, DC 20000 and American Federation of State, County and Municipal Employees (AFSCME), 1625 L Street N.W., Washington, DC 20036.

10. The term 'social worker' refers to the title of the worker, according to the 1980 census and does not imply that all of these individuals have a bachelor's or master's degree in social work.

11. This pattern of a joint labor management program and administration not under the personnel section is not typical of many employee assistance programs. In most of the cases, programs are either offered by the company and administratively are under the personnel section, or are offered by the union. Information on the Illinois Central Gulf program is taken from a conversation with Joseph De Rosa, Director of the program, in July 1979.

12. The listing of problem areas in which the employee assistance program became involved is taken from the Annual Report 1978 of the Illinois Central Gulf Railroad Employee Assistance Program, p. 10, as prepared by Joseph De Rosa, ACSW.

13. Leo Perlis. "Industrial Social Work: Problems and Prospects," Newsletter. National Association of Social Workers, May 1978.

14. The increasing awareness of the role of social work in industry is indicated by: the development of a joint National Association of Social Workers/ Council on Social Work Education Committee, the publication of the proceedings of the first Industrial Social Work Conference in 1978 (Ababas, Kurzman and Kolben, 1979), the development of an Employee Assistance Program Digest which began in 1981, and establishment of state contacts for industrial social workers, such as Social Work in Industry Committee, Illinois Chapter of the National Association of Social Workers, 220 South State Street, Chicago, IL 60604. For more information on social work in industry, the reader is referred to: Industrial Social Welfare Center, Columbia University, School of Social Work, 622 West 113th Street, New York, NY 10025; the National Association of Social Workers, 7981 Eastern Avenue, Silver Spring, Maryland 20910; or the Council on Social Work Education, 1744 R St., NW., Suite 400, Washington, DC 20009.

SUGGESTED READINGS

Sheila Abbas and Paul Kurzman. Work, Workers and Work Organizations. Englewood Cliffs, NJ: Prentice Hall, Inc., 1982. this is one of the few books written on social work and social services in the work place in the past ten years.

Stuart Brandes. American Welfare Capitalism: 1880-1940. Chicago, IL: University of Chicago Press, 1976. This book provides an excellent overview of the development and decline of company programs.

Joseph Fallman, Jr. Helping the Troubled Employee. New York, NY: Amacom, 1978. This book provides a general overview of employee assistance programs.

Andrew Sikula. Personnel Administration and Human Resources
Management. New York, NY: John Wiley and Sons, Inc.,
1976. This book provides a nonsophisticated overview of the
development, organization and functions of personnel
administration.

Dale Yoder and Herbert Henneman. ASPA Handbook of Personnel and
Industrial Relations. Washington, DC: Bureau of National
Affairs, 1979. This book consists of a series of chapters
on different aspects of personnel relations, including
employee assistance programs. This is an excellent resource
book since each chapter is an indepth analysis of each
subject and contains numerous references.

REFERENCES

Ababas, Sheila and Paul Kurzman. Work, Workers and Work
Organizations. Englewood Cliffs, NJ: Prentice Hall, Inc.,
1982.

Ababas, Sheila, Paul Kurzman and Nancy Kolben. Labor and
Industrial Settings: Sites for Social Work Practice. New
York, NY: Council on Social Work Education, 1979.

Abbott, William. Effective Union Administration. Honolulu,
Hawaii: University of Hawaii, 1967.

Asma, Fern et al. "Twenty-five Years of Rehabilitation of
Employees with Drinking Problems." Journal of Occupational
Medicine. Vol. 22, No. 4 pp. 241-244.

Bakalinsky, Rosalie. "People Vs. Profits: Social Work in
Industry." Social Work, Vol. 25, No. 6 (November 1980), pp.
471-475.

Balsam, Daniel and Otto Jones. "Social Work Practice in
Industry." Social Work (May 1974), Vol. 19, No. 3, pp.
280-286.

Barbash, Jack. Labor's Grass Roots: A Study of the Local
Union. Westport, CT: Greenwood Press Publishers, 1961.

Beach, Dale. Personnel: The Management of People at Work. New
York, New York: Macmillan Publishing Co., 1980.

Berg, Norbert and John Mal. "Assistance for Troubled Employees." In Yoder, Dale and Herbert Henneman, ASPA Handbook of Personnel and Industrial Relations. Washington, DC: Bureau of National Affairs, 1979.

Brandes, Stuart. American Welfare Capitalism: 1880-1940. Chicago, IL: University of Chicago Press, 1976.

Bureau of Labor Statistics, Department of Labor, Brief History of the American Labor Movement, Washington, DC: U.S. Government Printing Office, 1976.

Bureau of National Affairs. Services for Employees: PPF Survey 105. Washington, DC: Bureau of National Affairs, 1974.

_____. Employee Health and Welfare Benefits, PPS Survey 107. Washington, DC: Bureau of National Affairs, 1974.

_____. Social, Recreational and Holiday Programs, PPF Survey 109. Washington, DC: Bureau of National Affairs, 1975.

_____. Bureau of National Affairs. ASPA-BNA Survey 34, Counseling Policies and Programs for Employees with Problems. Washington, DC: Bureau of National Affairs, 1978.

Cummings, Scott. Self Help in Urban America: Patterns of Minority Business Enterprise. Port Washington, NY: Kennekat Press, 1980.

Fallman, Joseph Jr. Helping the Troubled Employee. New York, NY: Amacom, 1978.

Filipowicz, Christine. "The Troubled Employee: Whose Responsibility?" The Personnel Administrator, (June 1979), pp. 17-22.

Friedlander, Walter and Robert Apte. Introduction to Social Welfare, Fifth Edition. Englewood Cliffs, NJ: Prentice Hall, Inc., 1980.

Heyman, Margaret. "Employer Sponsored Programs for Problem Drinkers," Social Casework Vol. 52, (November 1971), p. 548.

Kay, M. Jane. "Employee Counseling," pp. 75-104 in Yoder, Dale and Herbert Henneman ASPA Handbook of Personnel and Industrial Relations. Washington, DC: Bureau of National Affairs, 1979.

Kropotkin, Peter. Mutual Aid. New York, NY: Alfred M. Knopf, Inc., 1921.

Kurzman, Paul and Sheila Ababas. "Industrial Social Work As an Arena for Practice." Social Work, Vol. 26, No. 1 (January 1981), pp. 52-59.

Lindsey, Fred. "Employee Benefits Hit New High." National Business, Vol. 68, No. 10 (October 1980), pp. 82-84.

Lockwood, Howard. "Equal Employment Opportunities," pp. 245-296 in Yoder, Dale and Herbert Henneman, ASAP Handbook of Personnel and Industrial Relations. Washington, DC: Bureau of National Affairs, 1979.

Minahan, Anne (Ed.) Encyclopedia of Social Work, 18th Issue. Washington, DC: National Association of Social Workers, 1986.

"More Help for Emotionally Troubled Employees." Business Week, March 12, 1979, pp. 97-102.

Noland, Robert. Industrial Mental Health and Employee Counseling. New York, NY: Behavioral Publication, 1973.

Office of the Federal Register. United States Government Manual 1985-86, Washington, DC: U.S. Government Printing Office, 1985.

Ozawa, Martha. "Development of Social Services in Industry: Why and How?" Social Work, Vol. 25, No. 6 (November 1980), pp. 464-469.

Perlis, Leo. "Industrial Social Work: Problems and Prospects." Newsletter, National Association of Social Workers, May 1978.

Queen, Stuart. Social Work in the Light of History. Philadelphia, PA: J.B. Lippincott Company, 1922, pp. 90-102.

Reagan, Michael. Politics, Economics and the General Welfare. Glenview, IL: Scott, Foresman and Co., 1965.

Sikula, Andrew. Personnel Administration and Human Resources Management. New York, NY: John Wiley and Sons, Inc., 1976.

Slotkin, Elizabeth, Leo Levy, Edwin Wetmore and Ferdinand Rank. Mental Health Related Activities of Companies and Unions: A Survey Based on the Metropolitan Chicago Area. New York, NY: Behavioral Publications, Inc., 1971.

United States Department of Commerce, Bureau of the Census.
    1980 Census of Population Volume 2 Subject Reports Part 7C:
    Occupation by Industry. Washington, DC: U.S. Government
    Printing Office, 1984.

United States Department of Commerce, Bureau of the Census,
    Statistical Abstract of the United States: 1986 (106th
    Edition). Washington, DC: U.S. Government Printing Office,
    1985.

United States Department of Labor, Employee Benefits in Medium
    and Large Firms. Washington, DC: U.S. Government Printing
    Office, 1984.

United States Department of Labor, Occupational Outlook
    Handbook. 1986-87 edition, Washington, DC: U.S. Government
    Printing Office, 1986.

Walden, Theodore. "Industrial Social Work: A Conflict in
    Definitions." Newsletter. National Association of Social
    Workers, September 1978.

Weisman, Andrew. " A Social Service Strategy in Industry."
    Social Work (September 1975), Vol. 20. No. 5, pp. 401-403.

Werther, William and Keith Davis. Personnel Management and
    Human Resources. New York, New York: McGraw Hill Book Co.,
    1985.

Wilensky, Harold and Charles Le Beaux. Industrial Society and
    Social Welfare. New York, NY: Free Press, 1965.

Wisconsin Legislative Reference Bureau. Wisconsin Blue Book
    1985-86. Madison, WI: Department of Administration, 1985.

CHAPTER 6

MILITARY NETWORK*

"The military profession cannot escape from its
primary purpose, the killing business, or, as
scholars prefer to call it, management of
violence in the service of the state. Yet few
military men seriously view their profession in
terms of killing alone. Over the past
generation, the profession has become
increasingly similar to civilian professions.
Military skills, values and attitudes closely
parallel those of a federal civil service."
(Sarkesian: 1975:5).

INTRODUCTION

The military network in the United States has been undergoing rapid change since 1960 with the development of the
following: highly sophisticated weapon systems, career and
professional ladders for officers and enlisted personnel,
specialization of functions to the point of where only 14
percent of military personnel are used in combat, a volunteer
professional army and aggressive recruitment of women. The
military network of 1986 is far different than the military
network of 1960.

Along with these technological and occupational changes,
there has been a growing concern over the military lifestyle,
with its built-in tensions for families, and a concern over
human relations, i.e., social adjustment. Consequently, there
is a growing awareness of the need for human service programs
and professionals in the military network. The military network
consists of the following: active forces, inactive forces
(Army, Navy and Air Force Reserves and the National Guard) and
programs for veterans through the Veterans Administration and
various state programs. Human services personnel and social
workers have been regularly used in veterans' programs since the
early 1920's, in comparison to the use of human services
personnel (excluding physicians and nurses) in the active armed
forces, which has emerged since 1945. This chapter focuses on
the development of the military network, the military officer
and the role of social work.

SIZE

The military network in the United States is rather extensive, with expenditures increasing rather rapidly. In 1977 estimated expenditures were $126.5 billion dollars, and in 1985 an estimated $280.7 billion dollars, for an increase of 122 percent in eight years. Although expenditures for the military increased sharply, the percentage of the total United States Governmental budget allocated to the military network remained relatively stable, consisting of 27.4 percent of the budget in 1977 and 29.3 percent of the budget in 1985.

The number of employees directly involved in the military network was over five million in 1985. In addition, there are at least six million civilians who have employment through the manufacturing of supplies and equipment (directly or indirectly) for the military through the defense industries.[1] Some estimates on the size of the military network are shown in Figure 6-1.

ACTIVE and INACTIVE ARMED FORCES

In 1985 the active armed forces consisted of 2,152,000 personnel, and expenditures for this component of the military network totalled $239.5 billion dollars. The number of military installations was approximately 1,400. In addition to active duty personnel, the active armed forces employed 1,044,000 civilian employees in 1985. One normally does not think about the military personnel's family as part of the network. In 1985 there were an estimated 1.9 million dependents of individuals who were on active duty.

In 1985 the inactive armed forces consisted of 2,295,000 personnel, with expenditures of 14.3 billion dollars. Inactive armed forces include the National Guard and the Army, Navy and Air Force Reserve units. The inactive armed forces had 4,500 facilities throughout the United States.[2]

VETERANS ADMINISTRATION and PROGRAMS

Programs for veterans consist of both federal and state programs. Since a small number of states have special programs for veterans (seventeen), this discussion will focus on the Veterans Administration at the federal level of government.[3]

In 1985 the Veterans Admininstration had expenditures of $26.9 billion dollars. The Veterans Administration operated 517 facilities and employed 199,000 individuals. There were an estimated 28.1 million veterans in the United States in 1984,

Figure 6-1

ESTIMATED SIZE OF the MILITARY NETWORK in 1985*

Selected Criteria	Component of the Military Network	
	Active & Inactive Reserve Forces	Veterans Administration
Expenditures (Billion)	253.8 billion	26.9 billion
Number of Facilities	5,900	517
Number of Employees (military and civilian personnel)	5,491,000	199,000
Population Served (Million)	238.6 (population of the United States)	28.1

Sources: Adapted from Installation Directory Service. United States Military and Government Installation Directory. LaJolla, California: Organization Chart Service, 1983, pp. 14-500; United States Department of Commerce, Bureau of the Census, Statistical Abstract of the United States: 1986 (106th Ed.). Washington, D.C.: U.S. Government Printing Office, 1985, pp. 331, 333, 340, 341, 343, 345-350.

which is about 42 percent of the male population. The facilities of the Veterans Administration are heavily used by veterans
and their dependents. In 1984 there were 18.6 million visits to
the outpatient units, 1.4 million veterans were hospitalized on
an inpatient basis and 4.1 million veterans were receiving
pensions. Other benefits included education, loans, insurance,
etc., which had expenditure of about 28.8 billion dollars in
1984.[4]

It is interesting to note that the United States maintained
no large permanent military establishment until the Korean
Conflict of 1950. The network has grown steadily since 1950,
and some individuals refer to the economy of the United States
as a military industrial complex.

HISTORICAL DEVELOPMENT

Usually a historical perspective is developed chrono-
logically in sequential time periods. Since military history is
closely intertwined with political history, it is impractical to
discuss these developments in detail. Consequently, this
historical review will look at broad themes in military history.

When one reviews military and political history, a number of
broad themes emerge: the significance of military figures in
history, the broadened base of population for military strategy,
technological development, utilization of human service professions, programs for veterans, emergence of a large permanent
professional army, role of women, and more recently, nuclear war
and star war capability.

MILITARY HISTORICAL FIGURES

One perspective of history is that of identifying significant military and political events and figures. As one engages
in this process, one finds numerous examples of military figures
who are of historical importance. Some examples of important
military and political figures include the following: Leonidas,
Greek and Persian Wars (480 B.C.); Philip of Macedonia and his
son, Alexander the Great, Greek and Persian Wars (390 B.C.);
Hannibal, Punic Wars (218 B.C.); Julius Caesar, Roman Empire
(44 B.C.); Attila the Hun, Mongol Invasion, (453 A.D.);
Charlemagne, Frankish-Moor Wars (800 A.D.); Genghis Khan, Mongol
Invasion (1237 A.D.); Ivan the Terrible, and Peter the Great,
Russian Turkish Wars (1547 A.D., 1682); Frederick the Great, War
of Succession (1750 A.D.); George Washington, American Revolu-
tion (1776); Napolean Bonaparte, Napoleonic Wars (1805 A.D.);
Andrew Jackson, War of 1812 (1813); Tecumsah, Midwest Indian
Wars (1811); Osceola, Seminole Wars (1818); Winfield Scott,
Mexican War (1846); Robert E. Lee and Ulysses S. Grant, Civil

War (1861-1865); Theodore Roosevelt, Spanish-American War (1898); John Pershing, World War I (1918); Dwight Eisenhower and Douglas MacArthur, World War II and Korean Conflict (1944 and 1953) and William Westmoreland, Vietnam Conflict (1970). These historical examples clearly indicate the significance of military figures in helping determine political and historical events and concurrently show the chronic nature of warfare amongst humankind.

BROADENED BASE of POPULATION for MILITARY STRATEGY

Most societies have a system of self-defense where all able-bodied males are expected to provide military functions on an emergency basis known as the militia or home guard.[5] As societies increased in numbers, the militia became a back-up emergency or support system for a regular mercenary or professional army. The empires of Carthage, Rome and Greece relied on professional regular armies supplemented through the use of mercenaries and backed up by a militia. As the Roman Empire declined and Medieval Europe developed a feudal system, the militia again assumed a major role in self-defense, such as Switzerland (1271) and the German states. By 1400, small professional armies were emerging for military functions and were generally staffed by nobility, supplemented with mercenaries. With the rise of the professional army since 1400, there was a corresponding declining role for the militia, and in many circumstances the ordinary citizen no longer had weapons for self-defense purposes (especially in Europe).

The major military strategy with the use of a professional army in ancient, medieval, and early modern times was the engagement of one's army with the opposing army, with the objective of defeating the opposing army. The ordinary citizen (non-military) many times was left untouched by military activities, and there was limited destruction of property which was not of military significance. That is, battles were fought with opposing armies, there was destruction where the battles were fought, and outside of those localized areas there was limited destruction to property and harm to the citizens.[6]

During the period of the Reformation (1500-1600), there was the emergence of an army based upon conscription or the draft of able-bodied males for military purposes to supplement the regular armies. An example of early conscription was Sweden in the Thirty Years War (1618-1648) under King Gustavus Adolphus. It was after 1700 that the concept of small professional armies engaging each other in combat began to merge with large armies, and later into mass citizen armies. The size of armies began to increase, and by the late 1700's there was a use of massive national armies based upon conscription, such as France (1792) and Prussia (1805). The French Revolution and the Napoleonic Era (1789-1815) was one of the first times a nation's total resources were organized around warfare.

Those individuals who were not in the military were expected to provide other services for the military, such as making clothes, taking care of the wounded, etc. In essence, the distinction between citizen and military personnel was becoming blurred.

Experiences in the American Revolution (1776) and the French Revolution (1789) signaled a shift from a reliance on small professional armies for military purposes to a citizen army.[7] During the American Revolution of 1776-1783, approximately 60 percent of the military forces of the American government were state militia, of either a short term or long term basis. The short term basis ranged from a specific engagement to ninety days, and long term basis usually meant the duration of the war. The military objective was the defeat of the opposing army, however, more and more citizens became involved in military activities. During the Civil War (1861-1865) military strategy shifted to negating the supportive economic resources available to the opposing military operation. That is, the means of producing food, ammunition, supplies, etc., should be diminished in order to weaken the military operation. Part of the concept of this military strategy was to weaken the will or spirit of the citizens to support a war effort through destruction of their livelihood and support for the war effort. An extension of this concept was applied in both World War I and World War II, which were total wars where the distinction between the civilian and the military became obscured, and the military strategy was both the defeat of the opposing army, as well as, decreasing the capacity of the civilians to support the war effort. The population base for warfare now was the entire population and not small professional armies defeating small professional armies. Because of the massive disruption and destruction of both World War I and World War II, the focus today has again shifted to the development of professional armies engaging in limited and self-containing actions with the potential for total societal and world destruction.[8]

TECHNOLOGICAL DEVELOPMENT

Technological advances in weaponry have been accelerating since 1914. From early historical times to about 1300, the mainstay of weaponry was swords, spears, lances, etc. With the introduction of gunpowder in the 1300s, the rifle, pistol, and cannon quickly became the mainstay of weaponry. Further acceleration of these weapons continued until 1914. These weapons relied heavily on foot soldiers or infantry and horse cavalry for implementation during a battle. Since 1914 there has been the development of tanks, machine guns, airplanes, radar, missiles, rockets, guidance systems, lasar rays, nuclear arms, chemical and biological weapons, "Darth Vader helmets" and now the possibility of space warfare. Consequently, the modern military relies on numerous specialists in weaponry and less on combat infantry. For example, in 1977, 14 percent of the United States military personnel were designated as combat infantry, whereas in the Civil War (1861-1865) 70 percent of military personnel were designated as combat infantry.

HUMAN SERVICES PROFESSIONS

Military forces have always used the professions of medicine, theology and nursing for support services. What has emerged since 1860 was the broadened use of social services for military personnel, and consequently the use of other human service professions. The development of social service programs for military personnel had its beginnings with the Crimean War (1853-1856), the Austro-Sardinian War (1858-1860) and the American Civil War (1861-1865). Part of the reason for the development of social services at this time was the use of massive armies in a wide geographical range of territory. This meant that the sufferings of soldiers was no longer isolated and unseen (limited to battle ground areas), but was openly viewed by the public, who became incensed over the lack of social and medical services.[9] Jean Henri Dumont became concerned about the lack of medical attention for soldiers in the Austro-Sardinian War (Battle of Salferino, 1859) and consequently helped organize the International Red Cross in 1864, which provides medical and social services. Florence Nightingale, an English nurse, worked in the hospital at Scutari during the Crimean War (1853-56), and reformed the military hospital. Clara Barton, in the United States, was also concerned about the needs of military men and worked at various hospitals during the Civil War (1861-1865). Later she established the American Red Cross in 1882. During the Civil War extensive use was made of nurses, social recreation programs offered by the Young Men's Christian Association and other groups who volunteered their efforts to ease the life of the common soldier.

The Red Cross, both International and American, was the prime provider of social services for military personnel until World War II. The Red Cross, in addition to providing medical services, was expected to provide social recreational programs, personal and group counseling, emergency relief programs, etc. Although the armed forces had built medical care into their network, social services prior to World War II were peripheral to the military network. In World War II, with the conscription of many helping professionals for military service, such as

173

social workers and psychologists, the military network informally began to provide personal counseling for military
personnel. The armed forces realized the significance of these
programs and in 1943 the military network officially recognized
a social service function and organized a social service section
within the Surgeon General's office. There was a rapid expansion of the use of social workers and psychologists in the
military during the Korean and Vietnam Conflicts. Currently,
human service professions are used by all branches of the armed
forces, Army, Air Force, and Navy. The armed forces have two
types of positions for human service professions: civilian
employee hired to provide personal social services, and career
personnel, as an officer within the military network. In this
second position of employment, a person with a professional
background, such as medicine, law, and social work, automatically became an officer within the military structure.

PROGRAMS for VETERANS

The primary employer of human service professions in the
military network is the Veterans Administration, which provides
medical, psychiatric, social service, and other programs for
veterans.

Since at least 1400, most countries in Western Europe had
some form of program for veterans. For example, France allowed
blind and disabled veterans to use hospices (hospitals) at state
expense, and England (1569) allowed veterans to officially beg
for aid and paid a small pension for disabled veterans. The
United States early provided small pensions for disabled
veterans (1636), gave land bounty rights to individuals in lieu
of a pension (1753), and during the Revolutionary War
(1776-1783) added pensions for disability, death, needy and
widows through federal legislation of 1792, 1818 and 1828.
Although the Revolutionary War seems to be ancient history, it
is a curious note that the last Revolutionary War pension
benefit payment was made in 1906. Bounty land rights and
pensions were granted to veterans of the War of 1812, Mexican
War, and Indian Wars. The first home for veterans by the
federal government was established in Washington, D.C. (1851).
With the Civil War, veterans' benefits were expanded to include
the concept of nursing homes and Soldiers' Homes, both federal
and state,such as the state home in King, Wisconsin (1889) and
federal hospitals, such as Wood Veterans Hospital Milwaukee,
Wisconsin (1866), now named the Clement J. Zablocki Medical
Center.

A massive reorganization of veterans' programs occurred in
1917 to handle the problems of servicemen returning from
Europe. Prior to 1917 a Bureau of Pensions for military

174

veterans was established in 1792 under the War Department. In 1914 this bureau was transferred to the Treasury Department. In addition to the earlier programs of pensions, there was added the concept of vocational rehabilitation, medical rehabilitation, family allowances, insurance compensation for death, disability, burial funds, etc. With the expansion of benefits in 1921, the Veterans' Bureau became an independent agency. The current Veterans Administration, as an independent agency, was developed in 1931.

The Veterans Administration, because of its responsibility for medical and rehabilitation programs, has been a prime employer of human service personnel. The general activities of the Veterans Administration include psychiatric services, substitute care facilities, individual and group counseling, alcohol and drug programs and a full range of medical programs. After World War II there was a rapid expansion of services offered by the Veterans Administration with benefits to include educational allowances under the Veterans Readjustment Act of 1944 (G.I. Bill) and subsequent amendments for the Korean and Vietnam Conflicts. The G.I. Bill has been extremely significant in helping individuals obtain and change employment in the United States. In general, the United States since 1917 has developed a comprehensive program of benefits for veterans which is totally different than giving out land bounty warrants and/or widow allowances, as used in 1776.[10]

EMERGENCE of a LARGE PERMANENT PROFESSIONAL ARMED FORCE

The United States, prior to the end of the Korean Conflict in 1953, did not maintain a large permanent professional armed force. The military network consisted of a small core of professionals, and when warfare erupted, the army was supplemented entirely by militia, then volunteers and then conscription. After each period of warfare ended, there was a rapid demobilization of the military forces.

The first United States Army was organized by the Continental Congress in 1775 for service in the Revolutionary War. The peak strength of the army during the Revolutionary War was about 20,000 troops. Shortly after the war (1783-1790), the regular army was reduced to 800 troops.

During the War of 1812, the peak strength of the army was 38,000 troops, and was reduced to 10,000 troops by 1818. The Mexican War (1846) had a peak strength of 115,000, and this force was reduced to 16,000 troops by 1860.

The Civil War (1861-1865) was a war with massive armies. The North had a peak strength of about 1.5 million troops, the

South about 900,000 troops. By 1875 the army was reduced to 25,000 troops, and the army of the South was disbanded. In the Spanish-American War, about 105,000 troops were involved, and about 100,000 Guardsmen were mobilized. At the beginning of World War I in 1914, the regular army consisted of 200,000 troops and was increased to four million troops by 1918. In 1920 the army was reduced to 265,000, and by 1930 to 174,000 troops. World War II and its mobilization resulted in an army of six million troops, which was demobilized and reduced to 554,000 by 1948. In 1950 at the outbreak of the Korean Conflict, 583,000 troops were in the army and reached a peak strength of 1,596,000 by June, 1952. After the Korean Conflict the army maintained a strength of about one million troops. It was after the Korean Conflict when a permanent peace-time army was established, and by 1960 politicians were talking about the Military Industrial complex. Similar periods of expansion and contraction occurred in the Navy, Air Force, Marines, etc.

ROLE of WOMEN

The official or formal role of women in the armed forces is dramatically changing. Women were used for nursing services in most wars. In the Civil War, there were groups of women who provided social recreation programs. During World War I, many women worked with private agencies like the Red Cross in providing social services.

In World War II the role of women expanded from the traditional nursing to include non-combatant positions, such as file clerks, typists, stenographers, public relations, etc. During and after the Vietnam Conflict, 1953-1973, there has been a steady movement to provide equal opportunity for women in the armed forces. Attitudes of the traditional male-oriented professional armed forces are ambivalent and cautious. Some officers think that women should remain in non-combatant roles, and others think women should be placed in a limited variety of combatant roles.

NUCLEAR and SPACE WAR

The past ten years (1976-1986) have seen a sizeable anti-nuclear war movement in the United States and in other parts of the world. The movie, "The Day After," in 1984 depicted the results of a nuclear war and its aftermath. Similar movies were shown in Japan and Europe.

The immediate concern of the mass population was the thought of survival in a radioactive world with most means of production and transportation destroyed and massive destruction of basic necessities, such as food, shelter and medical facilities.

Scientists have now turned their attention to a phenomenon called "Nuclear Winter," when the aftermath of a nuclear war would destroy living conditions on this planet. The recent nuclear accident of a reactor in Chernobyl, Russia (1986) where at least 30 people died shows how little society can really protect itself from the aftermath of a nuclear war.

A concern is now expressed about the possibility of war in space, using killer satellites, space stations, space shuttles, laser beams, etc. Space war, until 1970, was viewed as science fiction, and movies such as the trilogy, "Star Wars," "The Empire Strikes Back," and "The Return of the Jedi," and "Battleship Galactica," were perceived as science fiction. With the rapidly developing space technology (and medicine), the differences between the world of science fiction and the world of reality is decreasing. Within ten years technology will have developed to a point where space war or star war is feasible. The spector of star wars has been used politically by the Reagan Administration as a bargaining point with the Soviet Union in arms reduction talks in 1984-86. Figure 6-2 summarizes the historical themes in the military network.

STRUCTURE

The structure of the military network can be described from its organizational context, services provided, occupations and professions and dominant occupations and professions.

ORGANIZATIONAL CONTEXT

The predominant organizational unit for the active and inactive armed forces is the Department of Defense at the federal level, with parallel state organizations for national guard units. The predominant organizational unit for programs for veterans is the Veterans Administration at the federal level, with some parallel state organizations. Figures 6-3, 6-4, 6-5 and 6-6 show the organization of the military network at the federal and state level.

Social services are part of the Surgeon General's office in the Department of Defense and are usually linked with medical services. Social services, as part of the medical complex, are a consequence of social services developing as a byproduct and extension of medical care. In the Veterans Administration, social services are an independent unit, responsible to a Chief of Staff. Figures 6-7 and 6-8 show the organization of the Clement J. Zablocki Medical Center, Veteran's Administration Milwaukee, Wisconsin.

Figure 6-2

HISTORICAL THEMES IN THE DEVELOPMENT OF THE MILITARY NETWORK

SIGNIFICANT MILITARY and POLITICAL FIGURES		THEMES
Leonidas	480 BC	Small professional armies, supplemented with use of mercenaries. Use of physicians and nurse.
Phillip and Alexander the Great	390	
Hannibal	218	
Julius Caeser	44	
Attila the Hun	453 AD	Militia and self-defense groups.
Charlemagne	800	
Ghengis Khan	1237	Some minimal privileges for veterans (begging); small professional armies, supplemented with use of mercenaries and militia. Use of gunpowder.
Ivan the Terrible	1547	
Peter the Great	1682	Conscription of civilians. Bounty land for veterans.
Frederick the Great	1750	
George Washington	1776	
Napolean Bonaparte	1805	Pensions and disability for veterans. Massive civilian armies with a core of professionals.
Andrew Jackson	1813	
Tecumsah	1811	
Osceala	1818	
Winifield Scott	1846	

(Figure 6-2 continued)

SIGNIFICANT MILITARY and POLITICAL FIGURES		THEMES
Robert E. Lee Ulysses Grant	1861-1865	Development of the Red Cross, some social recreation programs. Strategy to weaken civilian support for a war. Multi shot weapons. Medical programs, pensions and special homes for veterans.
Theodore Roosevelt John Pershing	1898 1918	Blurring of the distinction between civilian and military. Technology – airplane, tank, machine gun, gas, etc. Use of psychology and psychiatry. Vocational rehabilitation and loans for veterans.
Dwight Eisenhower Douglas MacArthur	1941-1945	Technology – atomic weapons, biological weapons. Use of social workers. Maintain large professional army. Educational and training programs for veterans.
William Westmoreland	1970	Professional armies, in some cases volunteer. Technology – laser beams, death ray, missles, space satellites, nuclear weapons, etc.
	1984	Recruitment of women. Threat of nuclear and space war.

179

Figure 6-3

Abbreviated Organization of the Department of
Defense, United States Government *

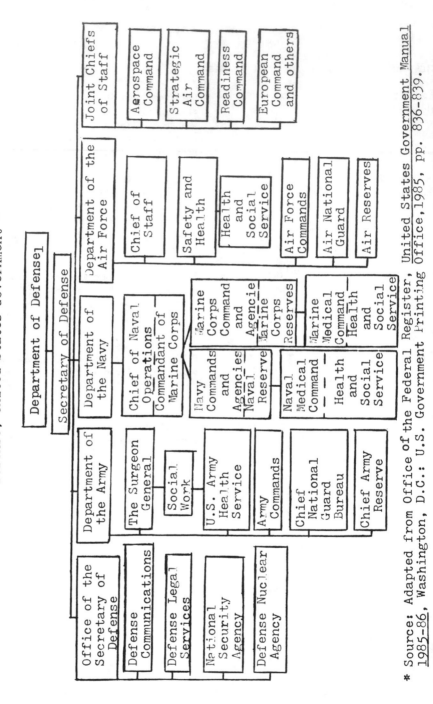

* Source: Adapted from Office of the Federal Register, United States Government Manual 1985-86, Washington, D.C.: U.S. Government Printing Office, 1985, pp. 836-839.

180

ORGANIZATION OF THE VETERAN'S ADMINISTRATION, UNITED STATES*

VETERANS ADMINISTRATION

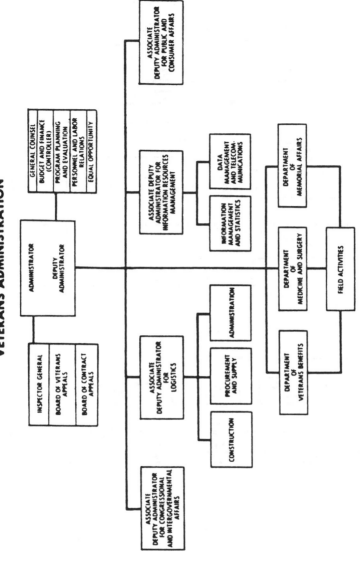

*Source: Adapted from Office of the Federal Register, United States Government Manual 1985–86, Washington, D.C.: U.S. Government Printing Office, 1985, p. 874.

FIGURE 6-5

Organization of the Department of Military Affairs, State of Wisconsi

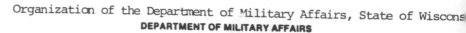

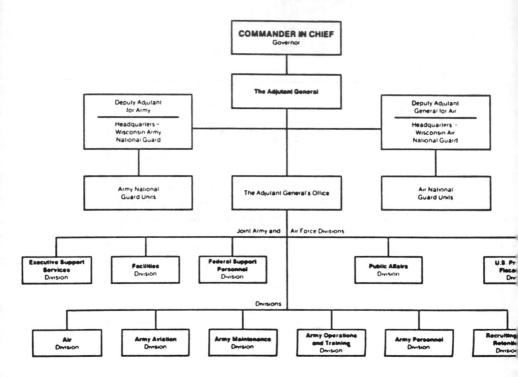

* Source: Adapted from Wisconsin Legislative Reference Bureau
  Wisconsin Blue Book 1985-86, Madison, Wisconsin: Department
  of Administration, 1985, p. 542. Reprinted with permission.

FIGURE 6-6

Organization of the Department of Veteran's Affairs, State of Wisconsin*

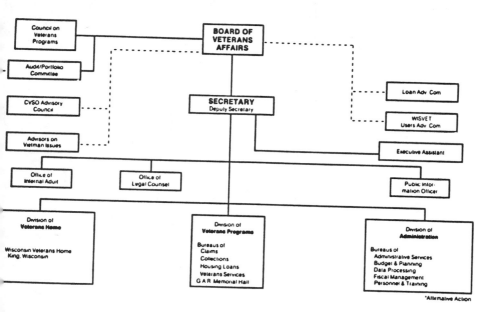

DEPARTMENT OF VETERANS AFFAIRS

Source: Adapted from Wisconsin Legislative Reference Bureau,
Wisconsin Blue Book 1985-86, Madison, Wisconsin: Department
of Administration , 1985, p. 549. Reprinted with permission.

Figure 6-7
Organization of the Clement J. Zablocki Medical Center, Veteran's Administration
Milwaukee, Wisconsin*

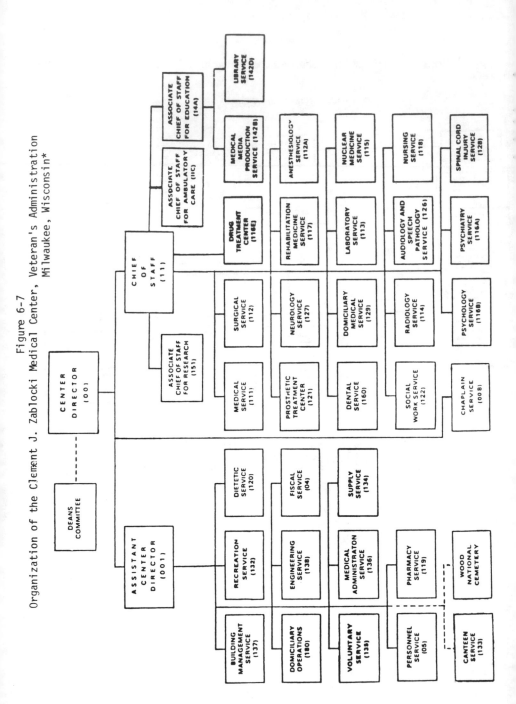

184

Figure 6-8

Organization of Social Work Services
Clement J. Zablocki Medical Center
Veterans Administration, Milwaukee, Wisconsin*

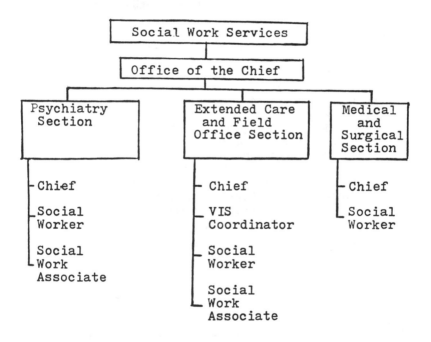

* Source: Adapted from the organizational chart
Clement J. Zablocki Medical Center, Veterans
Administration, Milwaukee, Wisconsin, 1985.

In addition to the formal military network, there are examples of informal paramilitary networks, such as the Minute Men, who are an organized group for maintaining guerilla warfare in case of an invasion of the United States and Civilian Material Assistance group in Alabama. If one views some of the smaller groups which are designed for self-defense purposes, such as the Jewish Defense League and the Posse Comitatus, as an informal military organization, there exists a folk network of self-defense.[11]

SERVICES PROVIDED

The military network has a comprehensive program for the provision of social services for active armed forces personnel and veterans. Some examples of the types of services and programs available to military personnel and veterans include the following:

- Medical care (both inpatient and outpatient
- Pensions
- Domiciliaries
- Psychiatric and psychological services
- Legal advice
- Educational benefits
- Educational training
- Specialized libraries
- Insurance and loan programs
- Financial relief programs
- Individual, family and group counseling
- Community service programs
- Social recreational programs
- Psychological testing
- Vocational rehabilitation programs
- Volunteer programs (for community involvement)
- Vocational counseling
- Religious counseling
- Day care programs
- Alcohol and drug abuse programs.

OCCUPATIONS and PROFESSIONS

Contrary to popular opinion, only about 14 percent of military personnel are in combat positions, and there is a close relationship between civilian occupational categories and military occupational categories. Figure 6-9 shows selected examples of human service occupations and professions employed as civilians in the active armed forces in 1979.

The Veterans Administration has a larger number of human service occupations and professions employed as civilians than

Figure 6-9

NUMBER AND PERCENT OF SELECTED HUMAN SERVICE OCCUPATIONS AND PROFESSIONS
EMPLOYED AS CIVILIANS BY THE ACTIVE ARMED FORCES IN 1979*

Selected Occupation and Profession	Number	Percent
Therapist (occupational, physical, corrective, art, music, dance, manual arts, education, rehabilitation)	49	.079
Social work and aide	321	.512
Psychology and aide	915	1.480
Clergy	4	.006
Recreation and parks	3,244	5.274
Environment protection	140	.217
Fire prevention/fighting	10,227	16.631
Protective services (police, guards, investigators)	9,073	14.854
Community planning	137	.212
Personnel, employee, labor relations	4,330	7.041
Pharmacist and aide	472	7.67
Physician and aide	868	1.411
Registered nurse	3,887	6.321
Dietician	17	.017
Dentist and aide	1,387	2.255
Housing manager	1,153	1.875
Lawyers, clerks and paralegals	492	.800
Librarians and aide	1,977	3.215
Educator	17,495	28.440
Vocational rehabilitation	4	.006
Music specialist	34	.045
Art specialist	162	.253
Public health nurse and others	53	.086
Nursing assistant	3,373	5.485
Medical records and others	923	1.501
Architect	755	1.217
Total	61,492	100.000

*Source: Adapted from United States Civil Service Commission, Occupations of
Federal White Collar Workers: 1979, Washington, DC: U.S. Government Printing
Office, 1981, pp. 112-123.

the active armed forces. Selected human service occupations and professions employed as civilians by the Veterans Administration are shown in Figure 6-10.

The above figures are not exhaustive of all human service occupations and professions represented within the military network. There are numerous other human service professions, and in some cases there is a range of specialties within one area. For example, there are approximately 45 different medical specialties and at least five different social work specialties.

DOMINANT OCCUPATIONS and PROFESSIONS

The primary profession of the military network is that of the military officer. In 1985 the number of personnel in the active armed forces was estimated at 2,152,000, of which 307,736 or 14.3 percent were officers, and 1,844,264 or 85.7 percent were enlisted personnel. The number of women in the active armed forces has increased from 32,000 in 1960 to 200,800 in 1985, and comprises 9.3 percent of the active armed forces personnel and 9.3 percent of officers, or 28,600 individuals.[12]

There are four ways an individual can become an officer in the armed forces: pre-service training, in-service training, experience plus in-service training and a direct commission.

PRE-SERVICE TRAINING - This form of training refers to training prior to becoming a member of the active armed forces and can be achieved by attending a military academy or enrollment in the Reserve Officer Training Corps Program. This type of training developed in the late 1700s, such as the military academy at St. Cyr, France; Prussia (1806); the Royal Military Academy in England, and in the United States, the Military Academy at West Point, 1802. As technology began to reform military strategies, the old system of in-service training and experience was found to be inadequate. Consequently, specialty schools were developed. Today an individual can become an officer in one of the branches of the United States military by attending one of the following academies: Naval Academy in Annapolis, Maryland, (1845); Air Force Academy, Denver, Colorado (1955); Military Academy at West Point, New York (1802); Coast Guard Academy at New London, Connecticut (1910); and the Merchant Marine Academy, Kings Point, New York (1942).

A second form of pre-service training is completion of a Reserve Officer Training Corps (ROTC) program (1916) while attending college. Once an individual has completed the pre-service education and is on active duty, they could participate in the more advanced levels of in-service training.

Figure 6-10

NUMBER AND PERCENT OF SELECTED HUMAN SERVICE OCCUPATIONS AND PROFESSIONS
EMPLOYED AS CIVILIANS BY THE VETERAN'S ADMINISTRATION IN 1979*

Selected Occupation and Profession	Number	Percent
Therapist (occupational, physical, corrective, art, music, dance, manual arts, education, rehabilitation)	2,914	3.400
Social work and aide	3,139	3.652
Psychology and aide	1,920	2.234
Clergy	410	.477
Recreation and parks	629	.731
Environment protection	---	---
Fire prevention/fighting	510	.593
Protective services (police, guards, investigators)	1,767	2.056
Community planning	2	.002
Personnel, employee, labor relations	1,807	2.102
Pharmacist and aide	3,105	3.612
Physician and aide	6,337	7.373
Registered nurse	26,597	30.947
Dietician	1,076	1.252
Dentist and aide	1,865	2.170
Housing manager	8	.009
Lawyers, clerks and paralegals	108	.125
Librarians and aide	2,450	2.850
Educator	740	.861
Vocational rehabilitation	284	.330
Music Specialist	1	.001
Art Specialist	1	.001
Public health nurse and others	...	---
Nursing assistant	29,432	34.246
Medical records and others	755	.878
Architect	85	.098
Total	85,942	100.000

*Source: Adapted from United States Civil Service Commission, Occupations of Federal White Collar Workers: 1979. Washington, DC: U.S. Government Printing Office, 1981, pp. 112-123.

IN-SERVICE TRAINING - This form of training refers to training while actively on duty with the armed forces. This type of training for military professionals was the major, if not the only, form of training until the establishment of the pre-service specialty schools in the early 1800s.

An individual would begin their military training by completion of basic training, "boot camp," and if selected for officers' training, would attend the Officer Candidate School (OCS). Upon completion of OCS, the individual would be commissioned as a second lieutenant. After the initial commision, an individual could participate in more advanced training if selected. The general levels of military in-service training programs are as follows:

1. Officer Candidate School-<u>second lieutenant</u>. Each branch of the military conducts its own program. An individual who has completed a pre-service program or obtains a direct commission would enter the military service at this level.

2. Advanced Officers' Schools-<u>captain</u>. Each branch of the military conducts its own program. An example is the squadron officer school and other specialized programs.

3. Command and Staff Colleges-<u>major and lieutenant colonel</u>. An example is the Air Command and Staff College, Montgomery, Alabama; Army Command and Staff College at Fort Leavenworth, Kansas; and Navy Command and Staff College at Newport, Rhode Island.

4. War College-lieutenant colonel, colonel, and above. Each branch of the military has a war college; however, personnel in each of the branches may participate in any of the war colleges when selected. Examples of the war colleges are: Air War College, Montgomery, Alabama (1946); Army War College, Carlisle Barracks, Pennsylvania (1901); and the Naval War College at Newport, Rhode Island (1884). In addition to the specific war colleges, joint military colleges include: the National War College in Washington, D.C. (1946); Air University, Montgomery, Alabama (1946); Armed Forces Staff College, Norfolk, Virginia (1946); and the Industrial College of the Armed Forces in Washington, D.C. (1924).

EXPERIENCE - Some individuals show leadership qualities and move up the ranks to officers' training school and then continue on with different levels of in-service training as identified above.

DIRECT COMMISSION - The military network has a policy of providing professionals, such as doctors, lawyers, and social workers with a commission upon entrance into military service. That is, the professional individual automatically becomes an officer by the nature of their profession and then would continue on with in-service training while in service.

Regardless of the route taken in becoming an officer, there are some basic themes in military professionalism. These themes are as follows: integrity, obedience, loyalty, commitment, trust, honor and service.[13] Trust and honor are central aspects of military professionalism and are usually summarized in the West Point tradition of "Duty, honor and country." In general, the officer would have the following functions:

- Command decisions
- Disciplinary measures
- Military strategy
- Informal counseling.

Although an officer is the military professional, there has been a significant change in the career development of enlisted personnel. Until the close of World War II, most enlisted personnel were unspecialized and did not have a clear career occupational pattern in the military. More importantly, there was a minimal linkage between military and civilian occupations. Currently, there are approximately 530 military occupational specialties, and most of these have some form of equivalency with civilian occupations. The current operating procedure in the military network is to design within the military services an occupational career plan for enlisted personnel, which provides flexibility for moving up through the ranks within a particular military occupation. The concept of a career ladder is consistent with the development of a volunteer professional active armed forces. Many of these specializations and career patterns have developed as a consequence of new technology in weapons, therefore individuals are experts in high tech areas, such as electronics, missiles, radar, etc., which are also skills needed in the nonmilitary occupational ranks.

The military network since World War II has taken on a number of characteristics of civilian employment such as working eight-hour days, management expertise, hiring of civilian specialists, military specialists used in civilian occupations, and a growing emphasis on human relations and social adjustment.[14]

SOCIAL WORK

The social work professional can be employed in the military network as a civilian employee, or as a commissioned officer. The number of social workers employed as civilians by the active armed forces in 1982 was 321, and by the Veterans Administration 3,139.

The task of the social worker, either in the active armed forces or in veterans' programs, is similar to other social workers who are employed in medical, psychiatric and family settings. That is, the individual is expected to provide case work and group counseling, marital counseling, and acting as a broker and resource person for individuals with particular problems.

The situation of a military family where the oldest son committed suicide in order to save the family money was reported in the newspapers in September, 1984. The child felt the family would have one less mouth to feed. This crisis situation of one family indicates the need for a coordinated social service system and highlights the fact that military families are in need of social services.

Some examples of functions social workers in the military network would engage in are as follows:

INDIVIDUAL COUNSELING

If a person has an alcohol problem, they may seek advice and consultation from the social worker in solving this problem.

GROUP WORK

This would range from a marital counseling situation where the husband and wife and/or family are involved, to a psychiatric group, or a group with alcohol/drug problems.

COMMUNITY ORGANIZATION

Some examples of community tasks would be: acting as a broker for an individual and referral to other agencies; providing a concrete service in finding housing and clarifying for non-military personnel some specific needs of military personnel.

Although the general tasks of the social worker would be similar to those of a social worker in other networks, some differences occur based upon the specific setting within the military network. Some of the differences for social work in the military network include the following: decision making, certain restrictions would be placed upon the type of decisions which could be made, resources may be more limited than in some other areas, education, the social worker would need to understand and be aware of the military network, its structure and development.[15]

PERSONAL SOCIAL SERVICES

The military network has a variety of personal social services provided for its employees through the personal social service network. (See Chapter 22 Personal Social Service.) Some examples of the personal social services and the military network include the following:

PROTECTIVE SERVICES

Child and spouse abuse programs, family and marital counseling, such as the National Military Family Association, Arlington, Virginia and Air Force Aid Society, Arlington, Virginia.

UTILITARIAN SERVICES

Financial and legal advice, such as a United States Army Service Center for the Armed Forces and Housing Department, Department of Defense, Alexandria, Virginia.

DEVELOPMENTAL and SOCIALIZATION SERVICES

Family and marital counseling, such as Community and Family Support, Army Department, Alexandria, Virginia and United Service Organization (USO), Washington, D.C.

REHABILITATIVE and THERAPEUTIC SERVICES

Alcohol and drug counseling, such as Surgeon General, Army Department, Falls Church, Virginia; Drug/Alcohol and Abuse Control, Air Force Department, Washington, D.C. and Navy (Marines) Drug and Alcohol Abuse Prevention and Control, Washington, D.C.

SPECIAL POPULATIONS

Many minority groups are employed by the military network, consequently, efforts have been made to meet the needs of these groups. (See Chapter 25, Special Populations and Chapter 24, Rehabilitation.) Some examples of programs for special populations in the military network include the following:

ASIAN

Cultural awareness and sensitivity programs, such as Equal Opportunity Programs, Department of Defense, Washington, D.C. and a small number of veterans groups.

BLACK

Cultural awareness and sensitivity programs and veterans groups, such as Equal Opportunity Programs, Department of Defense, Washington, D.C.; Black Veterans Inc., Brooklyn, New York, and National Black Veteran's Organization, Washington, D.C.

EUROPEAN ETHNIC

Cultural awareness and sensitivity programs and veterans groups, such as Equal Opportunity Programs, Department of Defense, Washington, D.C.; Association of Byelorussian American Veterans, Highland Park, New Jersey and Polish Legion of American Veterans, Chicago, Illinois.

NATIVE AMERICAN

Cultural awareness and sensitivity programs and veterans groups, such as Equal Opportunity Programs, Department of Defense, Washington, D.C.; Navajo Code Talkers Association, Window Rock, Arizona and Vietnam Era Inter-Tribal Association, Oklahoma City, Oklahoma.

SAME SEX PREFERENCE

Cultural awareness and sensitivity programs, such as those sponsored by Tangent Group, Hollywood, California and their Committee to Fight Exclusion of Homosexuals from the Armed Forces. A high degree of tension and conflict has developed within the military network as to whether homosexuality should be condoned or condemned, with the individual automatically given a discharge. It is probable the Equal Opportunity Programs, Department of Defense, Washington, D.C. receives inquiries on this special population group.

SPANISH-SPEAKING

Cultural awareness and sensitivity programs and veterans groups, such as Equal Opportunity Programs, Department of Defense, Washington, D.C.; National Congress of Puerto Rican Veterans, New York, New York; American G.I. Forum, Washington, D.C. and Hispanic American Veterans Association, New York, New York.

WOMEN

Cultural awareness and sensitivity programs and veterans groups, such as Equal Opportunity Programs, Department of Defense, Washington, D.C.; Army Distaff Foundation, Washington,

194

D.C.; Women's Equity Action League, Washington, D.C. and Women's Army Corps Veterans Association, Cleveland, Ohio.

ISSUES

The military network as it undergoes changes has a number of built-in tensions and concerns which have an impact on the provision of social services. These issues can be divided into two categories: the military network as an organization, and education and training of social workers.

ORGANIZATION ISSUES

As the military network becomes more civilianized, the role of the military in the political process is shifting, as well as the perceived appropriate role of the military professional. Historically, the United States has viewed the military professional as an isolated, non-political unit under the authority of the Congress and the president. As the military became more civilianized, this concept of an isolated military professional with minimal political input is rapidly changing. Military personnel are now becoming more involved in the political processes, and as a consequence, will be more involved in the policy-making processes of society. The broader issue is two-fold:

1) Should civilians control the military, of military organizations or the military control the politicians. The traditional American response has been civilian control over the military. As the military becomes more involved in the political process, this distinction of civilian versus military control becomes blurred. The release of General Douglas MacArthur as Commander-in-Chief during the Korean Conflict is an example of this tension between the political and the military. Some individuals would argue that it was the civilians, i.e., politicians, who were the ones which led the United States to involvement in Vietnam, and not the military. The broader concern is militarism. In the United States, whether we have a military or a civilian form of militarism is inconsequential. What is important is that militarism not be abused or used for entirely political purposes.

2) A concern for equity within the military network. That is, instead of relying on a military hierarchy for rigid decision making and a limited concern for the individuals involved in the military, the military network should become more humanistic and more individualistic-oriented. This type of philosophy is consistent with the development of an all-volunteer and professional armed force.

With the development of the volunteer army and the rapid recruitment of women, it is difficult to ascertain concrete operational implications for the military network. It is known that personnel needed to maintain the active armed forces at a sufficiently high level of experience and training are in short supply. There are major problems of re-enlistment of individuals after they have been in service for seven to ten years. The inclusion of women has eased, to a certain extent, the personnel situation, however, there are numerous problems in retaining officers and enlisted personnel, and in accepting women in the active armed forces.[16] The military network has had a significantly lower salary level than the non-military economic network, and consequently many of the experienced individuals are leaving military service in order to pursue more lucrative civilian careers.

SOCIAL WORK EDUCATION

Social work education has to recognize the military network as one of the major networks in the United States with provisions for the delivery of personal and other social services for individuals and families. Curriculum content should be modified to expose the students to the concept that social work as a profession is utilized within the military network and to provide background knowledge for understanding the military network.

One cannot discuss the military network without recognizing a great concern our society has about nuclear war, or in the near future, a space war. The United States, after active involvement in Vietnam, has had military operations in Grenada (1982) in Central America (Guatemala, El Salvador, Nicaragua, 1980-1986) and more recently Libya (1986). The fear of nuclear war or space war and its implications not only affect military and political decision making and action, but will affect the entire world. Some authors strongly feel that a nuclear war means the end of our society and world as we know it.

SUMMARY

Although the military network has defense as its primary function, there has been the emergence of social services within the network. The military network in the United States consists of two elements: the active and inactive armed forces, and veterans' programs. The military network in 1985 had expenditures estimated at 280.7 billion dollars, consisted of over 5,900 facilities, and employed approximately five million people directly and at least six million people indirectly in defense industries. These figures reflect the fact that the military network represents about eleven percent of all employed individuals in the United States.

A brief history of both the active armed forces and the Veterans Administration was provided to indicate the changing nature of the military network. Major changes in the active armed forces include: the use of small professional armies with limited objectives (defeating the opposing army) to massive citizen armies, sophisticated technology for weapons systems, management procedures, concept of total warfare, veterans' programs, changing role for women and the spector of space war or star war. Programs for veterans changed from bounty land rights to comprehensive medical, psychiatric, rehabilitative and educational services. Concurrent with these broad changes, there has emerged the use of human services personnel within the military network. The use of social workers, for example, is relatively recent, begining in World War II.

The dominant occupation and profession in the network is the military officer. The military network has a variety of educational and training facilities for its personnel. The theme of officer training has been summarized by the motto, "Duty, honor, and country." The roles of the military officer and the social worker were discussed.

Some major issues facing the military network include the following: the armed forces are becoming more civilian today in that military occupations have a closer relationship to non-military occupations, many individuals work eight-hour days, and military officers, etc., are becoming involved in the political process. As the military network becomes more civilianized, there are certain organizational issues involved, such as civilian versus military control, the use of an all-volunteer professional army, and the recruitment of women. There is a strong debate today on the role of women in the armed forces. It is clear that an all-volunteer professional military network will make more extensive use of women than the military network of the past. Societal issues include the spector of a nuclear or space war which could threaten the survival of our society and the world.

FOOTNOTES

*This chapter was reviewed for comments by David Miller, Jr., Professor (LTC), Commandant, Department of Military Science, University of Wisconsin-Milwaukee, Milwaukee, Wisconsin.

1. This estimate of expenditures of the military network does not include the costs of government contracts for defense spending which amounted to about $87.4 billion in 1983. These figures were adapted from the United States Bureau of

the Census, Statistical Abstract of the United States: 1986 (106th Ed.), Washington, D.C.: U.S. Government Printing Office, 1985, and United States and World Military and Government Installation Directory, La Jolla, CA: Organization Chart Service, 1983.

Yarmolinsky (1971) used the concept of military establishment to analyze the impact of the military network on American society. The concept of the military establishment, in addition to the active and inactive armed forces and veterans' programs, includes the Atomic Energy Commission, Selective Service System, defense contracts, and indirect employment as a consequence of defense contracts, which amounts to employing approximately six million individuals per year. Adding these estimates of expenditures and employment in the military establishment to the estimates on pp. 168-170, the total cost of the military establishment in 1985 would be over 368 billion dollars, and accounting for the employment of over eleven million individuals or 5.6 percent of the civilian work force in 1985. One related component of the military network which individuals do not usually consider is the Coast Guard, which has about 38,000 employees and becomes part of the military network during wartime.

2. These figures on personnel were adapted from the United States Department of Commerce, Bureau of the Census, Statistical Abstract of the United States: 1986, (106th Ed.), Washington, D.C.: U.S. Government Printing Office, 1985, pp. 340, 345.

3. Some examples of state programs include: Wisconsin (home for veterans, loans, and educational grants for Vietnam veterans, medical and subsistence grants); Louisiana (veterans' home, Vietnam bonus, educational assistance); Connecticut (soldiers', sailors', and marines' funds); and Florida (a National Guard retirement). For more details see: William Lawrence and Stephen Leeds, An Inventory of State and Local Income Transfer Programs, Fiscal Year 1977, White Plains, NY: Institute for Socioeconomic Studies, 1980.

4. These figures were adapted from United States Department of Commerce, Bureau of the Census, Statistical Abstract of the United States: 1986 (106th Ed.), Washington, D.C.: U.S. Government Printing Office, 1985, pp. 346-350.

5. The concept of a militia, or citizen support system, was used in Greece, Rome, Medieval Europe, and was the backbone of the American military system through the War of 1812. In the United States the militia was used for frontier defense

and for general defense purposes. For example, most of the American troops in King Phillip's War (1675-1678), the French-Indian Wars (1689-1763), The American Revolution (1776-1783) and the War of 1812 were militia. The modern day version of the militia in the United States is the National Guard.

6. In general, civilians (noncombatants) were not severely touched by warfare. However, there are numerous examples of mass destruction and harm to the citizens when warfare was a consequence of religious friction, such as Thirty Years War (1618-1648), or political freedom, Peasants' War or Revolt in Germany (1524-1525). On some occasions military leaders used a scorched earth strategy to defeat an army, and in that circumstance civilians suffered immeasureably (Hannibal, 218 B.C.).

7. The period from 1776 to 1861 was a significant period for the transformation of military strategy, from the use of small professional armies engaging small professional armies to massive citizen armies, blurring the distinction between military and civilian personnel. The United States, until the end of the Korean Conflict, maintained a small professional army and relied on a militia and/or citizen army in case of war. Since 1953 the United States has maintained a large professional and regular army as a consequence of the Cold War and its commitments overseas. The United States established the following military units: Army (1775), Navy (1775), Marine Corps (1775), Coast Guard (1790), Air Force (1907), Women's Units (1942), Reserves (1792), and National Guard (1903).

8. Although military strategy is to engage in limited and contained warfare, the experience of guerilla warfare in Vietnam (1957-1973) and El Salvador (1981-86) indicates the blurring of the distinction between civilian and military personnel. In guerrilla warfare citizens face tremendous danger, and the possibility of mass destruction exists.

9. For a brief review of the development of social services in the military network, the reader is referred to Anne Minahan (Ed.) Encyclopedia of Social Work, 18th Edition, Washington, D.C., National Association of Social Workers, 1986.

10. For a discussion of pension plans for veterans, see Chapter 19, Income Maintenance Network.

11. The Posse Comitatus is a civilian form of militia in Northern Wisconsin, which is organized for the protection of property and constitutional rights.

12. These figures were adapted from the United States Department of Commerce, Bureau of the Census, <u>Statistical Abstract of the United States: 1986 (106th Ed.)</u>, Washington, D.C.: U.S. Government Printing Office, 1985, pp. 340, 341.

13. For a discussion of military professionalism, the reader is referred to <u>American Behavioral Scientist</u>, (May/June) 1976, Vol. 19, No. 5, pp. 495-664, which is a special issue on military ethics and professionalism, and Samuel Sarkesian, <u>The Professional Army Officer in a Changing Society</u>. Chicago, IL: Nelson-Hall Publishing Co., 1975.

Some examples of organizations to contact for information on the active armed forces include: Department of the Air Force, Department of the Navy, Department of the Army, the Pentagon, Washington, D.C. 20330, or the local recruitment office. For information on the Reserves or National Guard contact the local office.

14. Veterans' programs were not discussed as having a dominant occupational and professional group, since a majority of the personnel in veterans' programs have a specific occupation or professional background other than a military profession. Some examples of organizations for veterans include: Amvets (American Veteran's of World War II, Korea and Vietnam), 4647 Forbes Blvd., Lanham, Maryland 20706; American Legion (AL), P.O. Box 1055, 700A Pennsylvania St., Indianapolis, Indiana 46204, or the local chapter of each group.

15. For further information on social work and the military network, the reader is referred to: The National Association of Social Workers, 7981 Eastern Avenue, Silver Spring, MD 20910, or Social Work Staff Office Headquarters, United States Army Health Services Command, Fort Sam Houston, TX 78234. Within the last decade (1975-85) the army has reorganized its medical areas and has recognized social work and social services as an independent staff unit.

16. The decades of 1960-80 were a period of rapid advancement in the rights of women. Debates still continue over the merits of the defunct Equal Rights Amendment and the drafting of women (in spite of the 1981 Supreme Court decision). Ironically, women have historically played a significant role in the military network. Many individuals perceive women as participating in the military as noncombatants. Yet in the United States women had an active role (although in small numbers) in most of the wars in which the United States participated. For example, during the Revolutionary War a group of women engaged a British squad in combat and

captured them, and the story of Molly Pitcher during the Revolutionary War is well-known. During the Civil War over 400 women fought in combat units for the Union. For a more detailed description of women and involvement in military affairs, the reader is referred to Chapter 24, Special Populations and for veterans programs see Chapter 19, Income Maintenance Network. During World War II the following specialized units were established for women: Women's Army Corp (1942), Women Accepted for Voluntary Emergency Service (1942), Women in the Air Force (1947), and United States Coast Guard Women's Reserve (1942). These women's units were initially separate from the active armed service, but by 1950 were integrated into the active armed service. These units were initially viewed as auxiliary units with a noncombatant role, but this has changed since 1950.

SUGGESTED READINGS

Dean Hummel. The Counselor and Military Service Opportunities. Boston, Massachusetts, Houghton Mifflin and Co., 1972. This book discusses the variety of counselor functions in the military organization.

Walter Mills. Arms and Men: A Study of American Military History New York, New York: Manpower Books, 1958. For the individual seeking a nonsophisticated military history, this book provides an excellent overview.

Samuel Sarkesian. The Professional Army Officer in a Changing Society Chicago, Illinois: Nelson Hall Publishing Co., 1975. This book provides an insight into the tensions, conflicts and stresses the professional military person is facing in a changing concept of the role of the military organization.

Adam Yarmolinsky. The Military Establishment: Its Impact on American Society New York, New York: Harper and Row Inc., 1971. For ·an individual who is seeking the impact of the military organization on the total society this book is a must.

REFERENCES

Dupey, Trevor, Col., Grace Hayes and Col. John Andrews. The Almanac of World Military Powers, 4th Edition. New York, NY: R. R. Bowker Co., 1983.

Fiorello, Thomas. "Consumer Education Needed" Social Work
  Vol. 18 No. 1 (January 1963), pp. 109-110.

Hummel, Dean L. The Counselor and Military Service
  Opportunities. Boston, MA: Houghton Mifflin and Co., 1972.

Installation Directory Services. United States Military and
  Government Installation Directory. La Jolla, CA:
  Organization Chart Service, 1983.

Janowitz, Morris. Sociology and the Military Establishment.
  New York, NY: Russell Sage Foundation, 1959.

Krause, Eliot. The Sociology of Occupations. Boston, MA:
  Little, Brown and Co., 1971.

Lawrence, William and Stephen Leeds. An Inventory of Federal
  Income Transfer Programs: Fiscal Year 1977. White Plains,
  NY: Institute for Socioeconomic Studies, 1978.

Lawrence, William and Stephen Leeds. An Inventory of State and
  Local Income Transfer Programs: Fiscal Year 1977. White
  Plains, NY: Institute for Socioeconomic Studies, 1980.

Levitan, Sar and Karen Cleary. Old Wars Remain Unfinished.
  Baltimore, Maryland: John Hopkins, University Press, 1973.

Office of the Federal Register, United States Government Manual
  1985-86, Washington, D.C.: U.S. Government Printing Office,
  1985.

Mills, Walter. Arms and Men: A Study of American Military
  History. New York, NY: Manpower Books, 1958.

Minahan, Anne (Ed.). Encyclopedia of Social Work, 18th
  Edition. Washington, DC: National Association of Social
  Workers, 1986.

Sarkesian, Samuel. The Professional Army Officer in a Changing
  Society. Chicago, IL: Nelson-Hall Publishing Co., 1975.

Simons, William. Liberal Education in the Service Academies.
  New York, NY: Institute of Higher Education, 1965.

Starr, Paul. Discarded Army. New York, New York: Charterhouse
  Co., 1974.

United States Department of Commerce, Bureau of the Census, 1980 Census of Population: Vol. 2 Subject Reports. Part 7C, Occupation by Industry, Washington, DC: U.S. Government Printing Office, 1984.

United States Department of Commerce, Bureau of the Census, Statistical Abstract of the United States: 1986 (106th Ed.), Washington, DC: U.S. Government Printing Office, 1985.

United States Civil Service Commission, Occupations of Federal White Collar Workers 1979, Washington, DC: U.S. Government Printing Office, 1981.

Yarmolinsky, Adam. The Military Establishment: Its Impact on American Society. New York, NY: Harper and Row, Inc., 1971.

Weber, Gustavus and Lawrence Schmeckebier. The Veterans Administration: Its History, Activities and Organization. Washington, DC: The Brookings Institute, 1934.

Weigley, Russell. Towards an American Army: Military Thought From Washington to Marshall. New York, NY: Columbia University Press, 1962.

Wisconsin Legislative Reference Bureau, Wisconsin Blue Book 1985-1986, Madison, Wisconsin: Department of Administration, 1985.

Wool, Harold. The Military Specialist: Skilled Manpower for the Armed Forces. Baltimore, MD: John Hopkins Press, 1963.

CHAPTER 7

POLITICAL NETWORK*

"Of the various functions imputed to
political parties in a democracy, two are
foremost: contesting and winning elections
and controlling and managing governments.
Electoral success is a prerequisite of the
political party's ability to play a role in
government.   The management of government
functions presumes that a party will fulfill
a third function of advancing and promoting
policies   for   the   public   welfare."
(Penniman:1952:12).

INTRODUCTION

When one thinks about politics one usually has in mind
politicians and government. In reality, the polity (political
network) consists of the following: government, political
parties, special interest (pressure) groups and citizen participation. The levels of governmental structure includes the
United Nations, federal, state, county, parish/township/ town,
city, and village governments, school districts and special
districts.

Generally, when individuals think of government they tend to
identify the federal or state, yet there is a vast array of
human service programs at the international level through the
United Nations and approximately 82,000 county, township, city,
school and special governmental districts in the United States.
Although most of the attention of the public focuses on the
federal/state government level, much of the political action in
the United States is at the sub-national level, i.e., city,
county, township, etc. This chapter describes the political
network and its various components, government, political
parties, special interest (pressure) groups, citizen participation, and the role of the politician and social work in the
network.

SIZE

When one looks at the political network it is important to
take a broad view of what comprises the network. For our
purposes, the political network consists of four major components: government, political parties, special interest groups
(pressure groups) and citizen participation.

GOVERNMENT

Most individuals when asked about the government, usually respond by referring to the United States federal government or state government. Yet, when one looks at government as part of the political network, the concept includes international, national, state, local and special units. Figure 7-1 shows the estimated size of the government component of the political network from 1980-1984.

INTERNATIONAL - The United Nations, which was established in 1945, is the major international form of government, although there are a number of other international organizations, such as the Organization of American States.

The United Nations, in 1980, had a budget of $1,339,151,200 and 23,044 employees. Both the budget and employees are distributed into two categories: the United Nations organization and related independent agencies. The United Nations Organization consists of six major organs, such as the General Assembly, the Economic and Security Council, the United Nations Educational, Scientific, and Cultural Organization (UNESCO), which is a subunit of the Economic and Security Council. The United Nations, in 1980, had 157 nation/state members, each with one vote and each maintains a mission of numerous individuals. Theoretically the number of people served by the United Nations is the world's population which was estimated at 5 billion in 1986. If one estimates conservatively that 20 percent of the world's population directly received services from the United Nations, that would mean at least 100 million people.

NATIONAL - The United States Federal government was formed in 1789. The size of this government has grown dramatically since 1935, and in particular, between 1960-1970. In 1984, the federal government had a budget of 851.8 billion dollars and employed 2,942,000 people. The federal government, in 1984, had 537 elected officials (.018 percent of the employees) and serves the entire 235.6 million people of the United States and various territories. The 1986 population estimate is 240 million.

STATE - Each of the 50 states in the United States has a government as well as the District of Columbia and various territories. In 1983, the 50 state governments had expenditures of 233.0 billion dollars and employed 3,898,000 individuals. State governments, in 1984, had 15,294 elected officials (.39 percent of the employees). The population served would vary from state to state depending upon its size. For example, the State of Colorado had a population of 5,889,644 in 1980, and New York had a population of 17,558,072.

206

Figure 7-1

SIZE OF THE GOVERNMENT COMPONENT OF THE POLITICAL NETWORK
ON SELECTED CHARACTERISTICS IN 1980-84*

| ected
teristics	Level of Government					
	United
Nations	Federal	State	County/
Municipal
Township | School
District | Special |
| of
ments | 1 | 1 | 50 | 38,851 | 14,851 | 28,588 |
| of
l/Appointed
als | 157
(Member nations
and missions
are appointed) | 537 | 15,294 | 316,905 | 87,062 | 72,377 |
| of
es^2 | 23,044 | 2,942,000 | 3,898,000 | 4,692,000 | 4,387,000 | 516,000 |
| tures
s)^3 | 1.3 billion | 851.8
billion | 233.0
billion | 199.6
billion | 122.1
billion | 34.8
billion |
| ion | 5.0 billion | 235.6
million | varies upon
size of state | varies upon
size of unit | varies upon
size of
district | varies upon
size of
district |

s: Adapted from National Associations of Counties. The County Yearbook 1976. Washington, DC: National
tion of Counties, 1976, p. 22; United States Department of Commerce, Bureau of the Census, Statistical
t of the United States: 1986 (106th Ed.), Washington, D.C.: U.S. Government Printing Office, 1985, pp.
2, 294, 286; United States Department of Commerce, Bureau of the Census. 1982 Census of Government; Vol.
rnment Organization, Washington, DC: U.S. Government Printing Office, 1983, pp. i-x and United Nations,
k of the United Nations 1980, Vol. 34, New York, NY: United Nations, 1983, pp. 1208, 1230.

States Department of Commerce, Bureau of the Census, 1977 Census of Government, Vol. I Government
ation, Washington, DC: U.S. Government Printing Office, 1979, p. 9.

ees in 1984 from Statistical Abstract of the United States: 1986 (106th Ed.) op cit., p. 294 and
States Department of Commerce, Bureau of the Census, Public Employment in 1984, Washington, D.C.: U.S.
ent Printing Office, 1985, p. V and I.

itures in 1983 from Statistical Abstract of the United States: 1986 (106th Ed.) op cit., pp. 262,
ederal expenditures are estimated from1984 from Statistical Abstract: 1986 op cit., p. 306.

LOCAL - This form of government is most numerous in the United States consisting of 38,851 separate governmental units classified as follows: county - (3,041); municipal - (19,076); and town or township - (16,734). These local units of government had expenditures of 199.6 billion dollars in 1983 and employed 4,692,000 individuals. These local units of government, in 1984, had 316,905 elected officials (6.7 percent of the employees). The population served would vary depending upon the type of government and population base. For example, Cedar Rapids Township in Rusk County, Wisconsin, had a population of 30 in 1980, in contrast to Queens County, New York which had a population of 1,891,825 in 1981 and Lockport Township in New York County, New York which had a population of 424,844.

SPECIAL DISTRICTS- This form of government consists of two types: school and special districts. Special districts refer to sanitation, electricity, natural resources, fire protection, housing and community development projects etc., which have powers of taxation.

School Districts were rather numerous in the United States in 1982, with 14,851 separate autonomous units. This form of government had expenditures of 122.1 billion dollars in 1983 and employed 4,387,000 individuals. Most school districts have a school board which is elected, therefore it should not be a surprise to find that the number of elected officials is large 87,062 (1.98 percent of employees). The population served by a specific school district will vary depending upon its location and size. For example, the City of Milwaukee in 1982 had a population of 636,210 and an enrollment of students in public schools of 86,312; Los Angeles City had a population of 2,966,850 and an enrollment of 540,903 students in public schools; and the City of Bellevue, Nebraska had a population of 21,813 and 8,337 students enrolled in public schools.

Special Units with taxation powers for sanitation, etc., are rather numerous consisting of approximately 28,588 units in 1982. This form of government had expenditures of 34.8 billion dollars in 1983 and employed 516,000 individuals in 1984. Many of these special units have a commissioner and other personnel who are elected as the management, therefore it is not surprising to find 72,377 elected officials (14.0 percent of its employees). The population served would vary depending upon the location of the unit and the population in the area. For example, the Milwaukee Metropolitan Sewage District had a population of 964,988 in 1980 and the Jackson County Water District in Kansas had a population of 270,269 in 1980.[1]

POLITICAL PARTIES

The two major, and oldest, political parties in the United States are the Democratic and Republican. One should not lose sight of the fact that other political parties are active in the United States. Political parties recognized in the United States, include the following:

Democratic Party - (1828)
Republican Party - (1854)
National Statesman (Prohibition) Party - (1869)
Socialist Labor Party - (1901)
Socialist Workers Party - (1938)
Communist Party - (1919)
American Party - (1968)
People Party - (1971)
Libertarian Party - (1971)
American Independent Party - (1972)
United States Labor Party - (1973)
National Unity Party - (1980 dissolved 1982)

Our major concern is with the two major political parties, Democratic and Republican. Both political parties are loosely structured with a national coordinating committee and state and local organizations. Estimates on the size of political parties are difficult to obtain, since individuals do not have to be a paid party member to vote for a member of a political party. Consequently, estimates on political party strength are inferred from figures on political party conventions and voting statistics.[2] In 1984, there were approximately 10,000 individuals who participated in the National Democratic and Republican Party Conventions as delegates or alternate delegates and approximately 30,000 visitors. It is further estimated that over 10.4 million individuals were active in the campaigns of the major and minor political parties.

Voting records for presidential elections provide an estimate of political strength. In 1984 there were 92.6 million votes cast in the presidental election. Of these 92.6 million votes, 54.5 million or 58.8 percent were cast for the Republican candidate, 37.6 million or 40.6 percent were cast for the Democratic candidate and the remaining .6 million votes or .6 percent were cast for other candidates, such as Libertarian, Independent, Socialist, etc. These figures indicate the relative strength of the Republican party currently and is a reflection of the time. In other elections the strength of the two parties has been reversed. The active and recurrent participation of individuals in political parties is estimated at 5 percent of the voting age population or about 8.2 million people and another 5 percent or 8.2 million people who attend rallies and meetings.[3]

For the 1984 presidential election, the estimated total expenditures for the election was 201.9 million dollars of which 82.6 million dollars or 40.9 percent was expended for the Republican candidate, 118.9 million dollars or 58.9 percent were expended for the Democratic candidates, and .4 million dollars or .2 percent for third party candidates. In addition to the presidential election, an additional 5.3 million dollars was expended on congressional races. One can readily see that running for a political office involves a tremendous monetary investment. Not all of this funding was the responsibility of the political party. Of the 207.2 million dollars expended on the presidential and congressional elections in 1984, 184.5 million dollars or 89 percent were from federal funds and 22.7 million dollars from independent sources. In addition, there was funding from political action committees (PAC's) or interest groups, individual contributiions, party contributions, etc. Of the 207.2 million dollars, 121.2 million dollars or 58.5 percent was expended for Democratic candidates, 85.5 million dollars or 41.3 percent for Republican candidates and .5 million dollars or .2 percent for third party candidates. These estimates on the cost of elections and expenditures does not take into account the thousands of local elections which are held each year.

SPECIAL INTEREST (PRESSURE) GROUPS

The United States political network has always had some form of special interest groups who hired lobbyists to influence legislators. The two decades from 1965-1985 has seen an expansion and growth of special interest or pressure groups which are now referred to as political action groups or committees. In 1974, there were an estimated 1.5 thousand special interest groups which spent about $13 million on congressional campaigns.

In 1980, there were an estimated 2.5 thousand special interest groups who contributed $60 million, or 46 percent, of their political expenditures directly to congressional campaigns, and $70.9 million, or 54 percent, to other political activities. In 1982, it was estimated there were over 3,000 special interest groups with at least 10,000 paid lobbyists serving at the federal, state and local levels of government. In 1984, political action committees contributed 77.4 million dollars to various individuals in congress. The major special interest groups can be classified as: corporate (business), labor, religious, health, ideological and a series of small groups. Some political scientists, such as Stephen Miller (1983) see the role or influence of special interest groups on legislators increasing as the financial cost of elections increase and as one or two parties are usually dominant in the political process of the United States.

CITIZEN PARTICIPATION

The extent of citizen participation varies from presidential to congressional and local elections. In the 1984 presidential election there were an estimated 173.4 million individuals of voting age or eligible voters of which 118.8. million or 68.5 percent were registered to vote, and 54.6 million or 31.5 percent were not registered to vote. Of the 118.8 million registered voters, 92.6 million or 77.9 percent actually voted in the 1984 election which represents 53.4 percent of eligible voters. Another way of looking at the 1984 election is that the Republican party had 54.4 million votes or 31.4 percent of the eligible voters, the Democratic party had 37.6 million votes or 21.7 percent of eligible voters, third parties had .6 million votes or .3 percent of the eligible voters with the remaining 80.8 million individuals or 46.6 percent of eligible voters not participating.

The percentage of citizens who participate in elections decreases as one analyzes congressional and local elections. In the 1982 congressional elections, 48.5 percent of registered voters participated and in 1984, 47.9 percent of registered voters participated. In a survey completed by the International City Management Association of 1.495 cities in 1978, it was found that about .01 percent of a city's population participated in open hearings and public meetings. This estimate was based on an average of 30 people attending meetings in cities of a large size.[4] In many municipal elections, the voter turn out is estimated at 25 percent.

The fact that citizen participation is not overwhelming is not a new phenomenon. Alice Tyler in Freedom's Ferment (1944:556) suggests that at the eve of the democratic republic in 1789, about 25-30 percent of the eligible voters actually participated in the election for President George Washington.

HISTORICAL DEVELOPMENT

Since the political network consists of government, political parties, special interest groups, and citizen participation, each of these will be discussed separately.

GOVERNMENT

As indicated earlier, the term government as used here refers to international, national, state and local.

INTERNATIONAL - The role of International government like the United Nations, is a cooperative effort by many nations with decisions made by this body not necessarily binding on other

nations. Prior to the development of the United Nations in
1945, there were other efforts of international cooperation,
primarily from private agencies.   For example, the Red Cross was
established in 1861 to provide emergency medical services, YMCAs
and YWCAs were established in 1894 in the area of recreation and
leisure, the International Social Welfare Conference was established in 1849, and numerous other religious groups had international efforts, such as Catholic Relief Services, Hebrew
Immigration Aid Societies and Church World Services.

On a governmental basis, the League of Nations (1919) was
the first attempt at an international form of government, since
the Roman Empire.   The League of Nations as part of its
structure had various committees which dealt with social welfare
concerns.   The League of Nations was powerless to stop the
invasions of China (1936), Poland (1939) and was abolished by
1941.

Although the United Nations was established in 1945, some
independent organizations were established earlier which were
incorporated into the United Nations.   For example, the United
Nations Relief and Rehabilitation Administration was formed in
1943 to handle the tremendous relief and displacement problems
as a consequence of World War II.   This organization was to
provide food, medical services, social services and housing to
the populations of war torn countries.   In 1946 the various
functions of the United Nations Relief and Rehabilitation
Organization were transferred to the World Health Organization
(WHO), International Labor Organization (ILO), International
Refugee Organization (IRO), Food and Agricultural Organization
(FAO), the Children's Emergency Fund (UNICEF), and one of the
six major units of the United Nations, the Economic and Social
Council and its subunit the Educational, Scientific and Cultural
Organization (UNESCO).   UNESCO is the major organ of the United
Nations which has primary responsibility for human service
programs in conjunction with the separate organizations listed
above.

NATIONAL - Figure 7-2 shows a generalized historical time
line of government.   In general, there has been a slow shift in
the various forms of government which includes the following:
tribal government (pre-4000 B.C.), God-Kings in Egypt and
Babylonia (4000 B.C. to 300 B.C.), an oligarchial republic in
Greece and early Rome (300 B.C. to 50 B.C.), divine emperors in
the Roman Empire (50 B.C. to 450 A.D.), church theocracy, (450
A.D. to 1400 A.D.), a feudal autocracy, i.e., lords and kings
(1400-1700), (divine right kings in Europe in terms of absolute
monarchy (1500 A.D. to 1800 A.D.), and in England the constitutional monarchy, by the 1600's) republics (citizen input) and
totalitarian states (dictatorships) since 1800.   In the general

Figure 7-2

HISTORICAL TIME LINE OF GOVERNMENT DEVELOPMENT*

4,000 BC	Tribal organization - Chief/Tribal leader

0 BC - 300 BC	Ancient Civilizations

Egypt
Babylonia   God/King
Sumeria

BC - 450 AD	Classical Civilizations

Greece - Democratic Oligarchy
Roman - Republic 30 BC - 50 BC
Empire - 50 BC - 450 AD
(God Emperor) and (Pax Romana)

- 1400	Medieval Theocracy - Papacy (Holy Roman Empire)
	Autocracy - small individual fiefdoms

- 1700	Nation/state-absolute monarchy - France - 1450

(Divine Right Kings)
Constitutional monarchy - England 1350-1600
(Limited male suffrage)

- 1900	Nation/State Republics - United States 1776
	France 1789

Development of political parties
Expansion of suffrage to include most white males

on	Nation/State - Social Democracy - United States 1960

Universal suffrage - England 1945

Military dictatorships - fascism - Germany 1933
Communistic Republics - Soviet Union - 1917

World Organization - 1919 League of Nations
1945 United Nations

tions listed are only examples of the type of Government organization, and is
an exhaustive listing of all types of government.

sweep of history, mass citizen participation of those governed, in the process of government, is rather recent, since around 1800. The nation state as we know it developed around 1500 to 1600 and the concept of world government since 1919.

STATE AND LOCAL. The sub-national forms of government, such as county, township/town/parish, city, are modern day versions of local autonomy which existed in early European times by 450 A.D. In the United States, initially there was county, township and provincial or colonial governments and after the revolution of 1776-1783, the Articles of Confederation and later in 1789 the Constitution of the United States, established state and federal government.

POLITICAL PARTIES

Political parties with extensive citizen participation such as Democratic, Republican, Socialist, etc., as we know them are products of the development of democratic republics in the late 1700's and early 1800's. There were political parties of a sort prior to that time since a group of people either supported or did not support those in power, however, there was a high degree of mistrust of mass citizen support in any organized fashion. The average citizen was seen as a potential threat to the established government. In the United States, political parties were established immediately after the close of the Revolutionary War in 1783 with the development of the Federalist, (Hamiltonian) and the Democratic/Republican (Jeffersonian) parties. These parties held dominance from 1783 to 1824. Later, the dominant political parties were the Whigs and Democrats (1824-1860), and Republicans and Democrats since 1860. In the United States there were numerous third parties, such as the Progressive Party, established in Wisconsin (1900-1944), Prohibitionist Party (1869), Populist Party (1891), American Party (1968), Socialist Party (1901), Communist Party (1919), etc. Depending upon the type of political network, a nation may allow more than one party on the ballot (democracy/republic) or allow only one party on the ballot (communism and facism).

SPECIAL INTEREST (PRESSURE) GROUPS

Various groups which attempt to influence those in power or minor government officials have been in existence since governments have been formed. Under a monarchy or absolutist rule the appeals were made directly to the top administrative officials or to their representative. In a democracy or a republic of elected officials, appeals are made to lower and high ranking government employees who can influence legislation, as well as, appeals made to legislative officials themselves (members of

214

Congress). In the United States, major special interest groups (political action committees) include: business, labor, military, education, agriculture, medicine, minority groups, religious groups and social services. Prior to 1975, special interest groups did not have to register with the local or federal government. Since 1975, there has been a system of registration in most states and at the federal level, in order to monitor the activities of political action committees and to reduce the possibility of improper conduct or tainted politics.

CITIZEN PARTICIPATION

Citizen participation in the political network occurs in all societies. The basic issue is the extent or degree of citizen participation and influence. In some societies citizen partici- pation is limited because of class, religion, sex, political structure, etc. In other societies, participation is limited to one political party and in other societies participation means free elections and multiple political parties. The notion of citizen participation is not new, but the concept of a repre- sentative participatory democracy with universal suffrage (vot- ing rights) is a product of the last 150 years.

In ancient Greek society (300 B.C.) a male citizen had voting rights and was expected to become a full participant in political affairs. Women, slaves and common laborers did not have the rights of suffrage. Roman society in its Republican stage (300 B.C.-50 B.C.) was similar to the Greeks in that male property owners had the right to vote and participate in the councils. From 50 B.C.-450 A.D., the Roman Empire became a monarchy with a god-king and suffrage became further restricted. Groups and individuals theoretically could appeal to the monarch and his delegates about their concerns.

Medieval Europe (450-1400 A.D.), continued with concepts of monarchy and god-kings (divine rights of monarchs). There were councils of the nobility (lords and knights) and of the clergy which were advisory to the monarch or the local lord. The common laborers (serf), tradesmen, merchant and women did not have the right of suffrage. These groups could appeal directly to the local authority about their concerns. Even in this period of time there were exceptions. When a person was a freeman or a free merchant living in a city, they generally had voting rights, but this was restricted based upon property ownership, religion and sex.

The beginnings of representative democracy as we think of it, began with the Magna Carta in England (1215 A.D.) when the lords or nobles gained political concessions from King John. One of these concessions was to grant political power to the

Great Council consisting of the higher ranking nobility. This Great Council ultimately became known as the House of Lords. In 1265, lesser nobility and some town merchants were invited to participate in the Great Council and were called the Small Council. This group ultimately became the House of Commons. From this beginning, suffrage was slowly expanded to include less wealthy property owners who could vote with periodic reforms, such as in 1689, 1867 and 1884-1885. Even in these reforms, suffrage was for males and based on property or income level. It was not until 1918 in England when all citizens, male and female, obtained rights of suffrage.

The United States followed a similar development in the granting of the rights of suffrage as England. Prior to the revolutionary War, each colony developed its own rules regarding rights of suffrage. Most colonies required a person to own property in order to have a right to vote, and this was restricted to men. For a short period of time, Virginia and New Jersey granted voting rights to women, but eventually these rules were changed. On a general basis, voting rights were restricted to property owners and excluded others. The equalitarian movement to expand voting rights occurred around the 1820's with Jacksonian Democracy. By 1850, most white males had voting rights. Theoretically, this was granted to blacks in 1866 (XIV Amendment), however, a variety of means were used to prevent blacks from voting, such as a poll tax, property ownership, literacy tests, white constitutions, etc.

Universal suffrage in the United States was expanded to women in 1920 (XIX Amendment). Further court action was necessary to make universal suffrage a reality in the United States. Native Americans were declared citizens in 1924, even though they were theoretically included under the XIV Amendment to the Constitution in 1866. The Civil Rights Act of 1965 prohibits the use of a fee or literacy test to deny voting rights and a 1975 amendment prohibits denial of voting rights to those individuals whose primary language is not English. The United States took almost 150 years to actually grant universal suffrage to all citizens of the country.

STRUCTURE

The structure of the political network can be viewed from its organizational context, services provided, occupations and professions, and the dominant occupations and professions.

ORGANIZATIONAL CONTEXT

GOVERNMENT - Government as part of the political network is rather complex. Most individuals tend to think of the federal

216

or state governments in the provision of social services, yet neglect the international government, the 38,000 plus county, municipal and townships governments and 40,000 special governmental taxation units.

International - In the United Nations, the primary structure concerned with human services is The Economic and Security Council (a related agency) with its standing committees and sub-organizations. Figure 7-3 shows the structure of the United Nations.

National - The United States government is organized on the basis of a judicial, legislative and executive branch. For human service functions, most of the programs that involve social services are organized and implemented through cabinet departments, such as the Departments of Education, Health and Human Services, Housing and Urban Development, Interior and Labor. Figure 7-4 shows the structure of the United States government.

State - Although the federal government allocates resources to state and counties in the area of human services, much of the decision-making and distribution of these resources is accomplished through the state, county, township and city governments. Figure 7-5 is a model of a state government showing those cabinet departments which normally have most jurisdiction over human services and the delivery of social services, such as the Departments of Industry Labor and Human Relations, Health and Social Service and Education.

Local - In many states, it is at the county level where implementation of numerous human service and social service programs occur. In the program areas of poverty and mental health, the county is the key governmental unit for implementation of programs. Figure 7-6 shows a model of a county/township government with the welfare department as one of the key units for social services.

Many cities and villages provide programs in the human services particularly through the educational, medical and park and recreation systems. Figure 7-7 shows a typical structure of a city/village government.[5]

POLITICAL PARTIES - Like government, political parties have a tiered or a hierarchy level of organization including a national committee, state organization, city ward and precinct level, and finally the individual citizen. Figure 7-8 shows a typical model of a political party organization in the United States. In contrast to the organization of the government, each

Figure 7-3
ORGANIZATION of the UNITED NATIONS:
EXAMPLE of a WORLD GOVERNMENT*

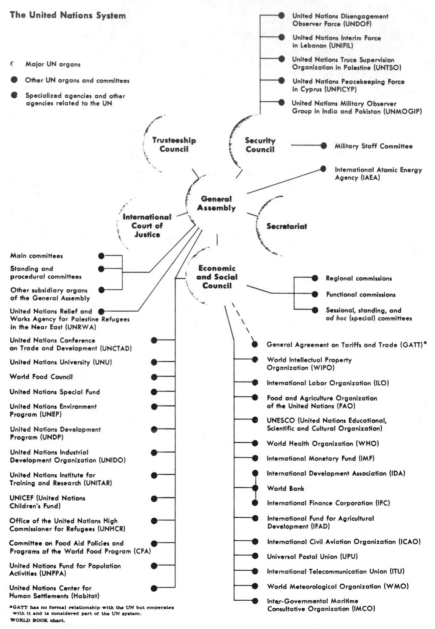

The United Nations System

(Major UN organs

● Other UN organs and committees

◖ Specialized agencies and other agencies related to the UN

United Nations Disengagement Observer Force (UNDOF)

United Nations Interim Force in Lebanon (UNIFIL)

United Nations Truce Supervision Organization in Palestine (UNTSO)

United Nations Peacekeeping Force in Cyprus (UNFICYP)

United Nations Military Observer Group in India and Pakistan (UNMOGIP)

Trusteeship Council

Security Council ——— Military Staff Committee

International Atomic Energy Agency (IAEA)

General Assembly

International Court of Justice

Secretariat

Economic and Social Council

Main committees

Standing and procedural committees

Other subsidiary organs of the General Assembly

United Nations Relief and Works Agency for Palestine Refugees in the Near East (UNRWA)

Regional commissions

Functional commissions

Sessional, standing, and ad hoc (special) committees

United Nations Conference on Trade and Development (UNCTAD)

United Nations University (UNU)

World Food Council

United Nations Special Fund

United Nations Environment Program (UNEP)

United Nations Development Program (UNDP)

United Nations Industrial Development Organization (UNIDO)

United Nations Institute for Training and Research (UNITAR)

UNICEF (United Nations Children's Fund)

Office of the United Nations High Commissioner for Refugees (UNHCR)

Committee on Food Aid Policies and Programs of the World Food Program (CFA)

United Nations Fund for Population Activities (UNFPA)

United Nations Center for Human Settlements (Habitat)

General Agreement on Tariffs and Trade (GATT)*

World Intellectual Property Organization (WIPO)

International Labor Organization (ILO)

Food and Agriculture Organization of the United Nations (FAO)

UNESCO (United Nations Educational, Scientific and Cultural Organization)

World Health Organization (WHO)

International Monetary Fund (IMF)

International Development Association (IDA)

World Bank

International Finance Corporation (IFC)

International Fund for Agricultural Development (IFAD)

International Civil Aviation Organization (ICAO)

Universal Postal Union (UPU)

International Telecommunication Union (ITU)

World Meteorological Organization (WMO)

Inter-Governmental Maritime Consultative Organization (IMCO)

*GATT has no formal relationship with the UN but cooperates with it and is considered part of the UN system.
WORLD BOOK chart.

* Source: From the <u>World Book Encyclopedia</u> © 1986 World Book, Inc., 27.

218

FIGURE 7-4

ORGANIZATION OF THE GOVERNMENT OF THE UNITED STATES

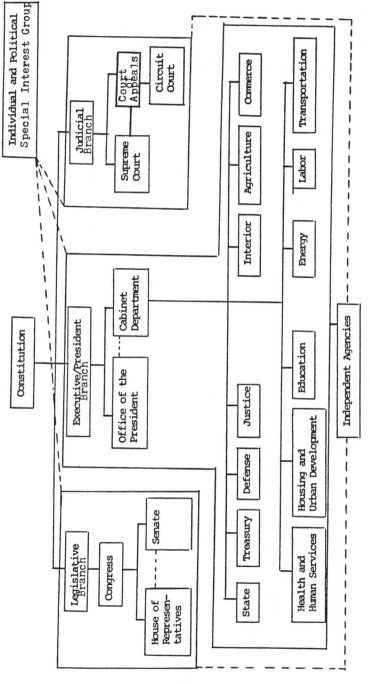

*Source: Adapted from Office of the Federal Register, United States Government Manual, 1985-86, Washington, D.C.: U.S. Government Printing Office, 1985, p. 827.

219

FIGURE 7-5

EXAMPLE OF A STATE GOVERNMENT ORGANIZATION*

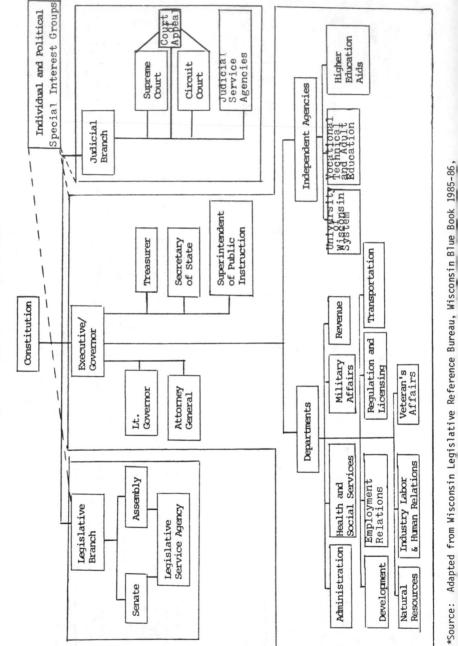

*Source: Adapted from Wisconsin Legislative Reference Bureau, Wisconsin Blue Book 1985-86,

FIGURE 7-6

EXAMPLE OF A LOCAL COUNTY/TOWNSHIP GOVERNMENT ORGANIZATION

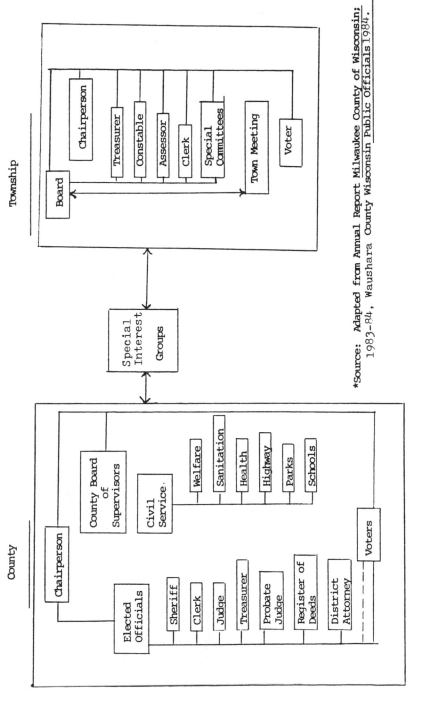

*Source: Adapted from Annual Report Milwaukee County of Wisconsin: 1983-84, Waushara County Wisconsin Public Officials 1984.

221

FIGURE 7-7

EXAMPLE OF A MUNICIPAL GOVERNMENT ORGANIZATION*

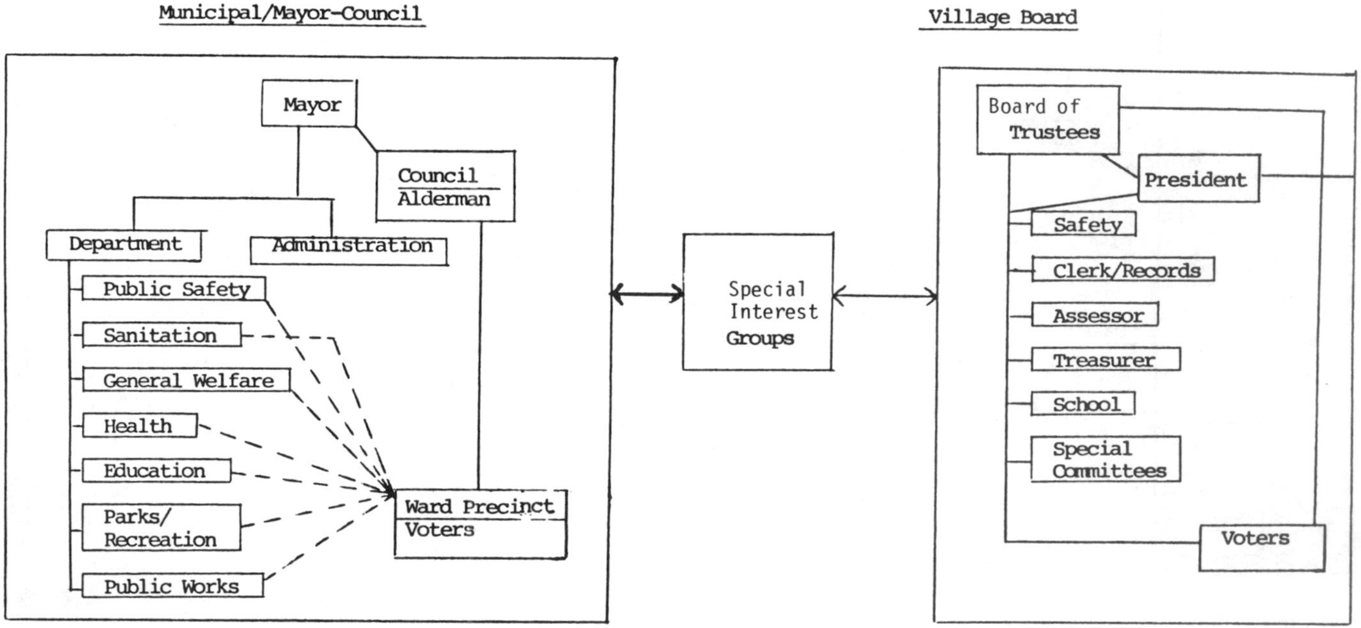

Village Board

Municipal/Mayor-Council

*Source: Adapted from City of Milwaukee, Wisconsin Annual Report, 1985 and Handbook for Wisconsin Municipal Officers, 1985.

FIGURE 7-8

GENERALIZED STRUCTURE OF POLITICAL PARTIES*

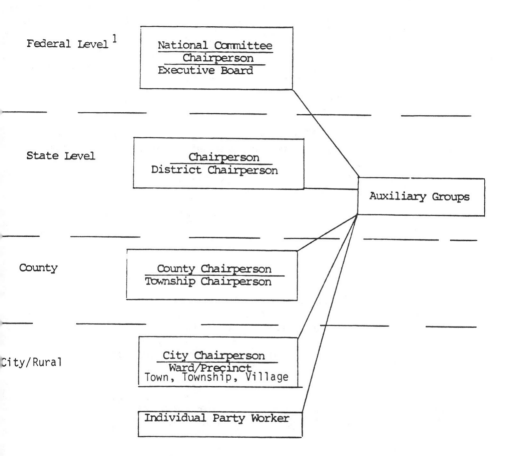

Federal Level [1]

National Committee
Chairperson
Executive Board

State Level

Chairperson
District Chairperson

Auxiliary Groups

County

County Chairperson
Township Chairperson

City/Rural

City Chairperson
Ward/Precinct
Town, Township, Village

Individual Party Worker

rce: Political Parties in America 2nd Edition by Robert J. Huckshorn.
right (c) 1984, 1980 by Wadsworth, Inc. Reprinted by permission of
ks/Cole Publishing Company, Monterey, California 93940.

[1] Although political parties have a hierarchial structure, each
level is autonomous from the others and is essentially operated
on a committee basis, in contrast to the hierarchial/and line
authority of a bureaucracy.

223

of the various levels of political parties are somewhat autonomous, having their own committees and power of decision-making. The lower levels of a political party are not mandated to follow the advice or policies of the next higher level although they are expected to follow suit.

SPECIAL INTEREST (PRESSURE) GROUPS - Depending upon the size of the group, there usually is an executive director, vice-president, and other officers with an executive advisory board. The group would hire a lobbyist or some other consultant to represent the organization in influencing legislators, or members of the group themselves would serve as informal lobbyists.

CITIZEN PARTICIPATION - Many citizens represent themselves as individuals by attendance at various meetings, participation in political parties, voting, or as members of interest groups. It is possible for individuals to become involved in neighborhood and community organization groups, as well as, to advocate political issues through the mail, telephone, etc. If there is a structure to citizen participation it is primarily based upon socio-economic status, education, religious background, political party and other group affiliation, etc.

SERVICES PROVIDED

The political network either directly through the various governmental units or indirectly through political parties, special interest groups and citizen participation is involved in the full range of human services in a society. The list of services and programs would be extremely lengthy and complicated. Figure 7-9 shows by level of governmental operation the type of service provided. In general, the major human service types of programs are implemented through state and county governments with the federal government developing overall policy and distribution of financial grants and program monies.

OCCUPATIONS and PROFESSIONS

In the political network, there is no one particular occupation and profession which is dominant. In the broadest sense, a person becomes an elected official because of their motivation and desire for the position and their ability to win elections. There are no specific educational, experiential, or certification requirements.[6]

Those individuals who become politicians are elected officials, who have a variety of backgrounds, including: medicine, law, education, engineering, theology, farming, pharmacy, real estate, insurance, manufacturing, military, etc. There

FIGURE 7-9

EXAMPLES OF MAJOR SERVICES PROVIDED BY LEVEL OF GOVERNMENT*

	Human Service Programs										
rment	Physical Health	Financial Welfare	Housing	Trans-portation	Employ-ment	Law En-forcement	Courts	Correc-tions	Schools	Mental Health	Family
d ns	X	X	X			X	X			X	
al rment	X	X	X	X	X	X	X	X	X	X	X
	X	X	X	X	X	X	X	X	X	X	X
y	X	X	X	X		X	X	X	X	X	X
hip	X			X		X					
ge	X		X	X		X	X		X		

	Human Service Programs									
ment	Child Welfare	Attorney	Leisure/Parks	Library	Sanitation	Civil Defense	Planning	Conservation	Public Health	Vital Records
d ns	X	X		X			X	X	X	
al rment	X	X	X	X		X	X	X	X	X
e	X	X	X	X		X	X	X	X	X
y	X	X	X	X		X	X	X	X	X
hip			X		X		X	X	X	X
ge		X	X	X	X	X	X	X	X	X

*Sources: Adapted from League of Wisconsin Municipalities. Handbook for Wisconsin Municipal Officers, Madison, Wisconsin: League of Wisconsin Municipalities, 1976; Lemay, Michael, Wisconsin Towns. Madison, Wisconsin; Institute of Governmental Affairs, U. of Wisconsin Extension, 1975; Freidlander, Walter: International Social Welfare Englewood Cliffs, New Jersey: Prentice Hall Inc. 1975, and Office of the Federal Register. United States Government Manual 1978-79. Washington D.C.: Government Printing Office, 1978.

seems to be a larger proportion of individuals with legal and financial backgrounds in the political process than other groups. At the higher level of the political network (state and federal government), there is a tendency for individuals to have a college degree, law or financial backgrounds. At the lower level of the political network (local parties, neighborhood groups), there is a representation of the general population of the United States. Consequently, the variety of occupations and professions represented by individuals participating in the political process would approximate the variety of occupations and professions in the United States.

In addition to occupations and professions represented in the political process, one can look at employees of the political network which is partially represented in the industrial classification of executive and legislative officials. Figure 7-10 shows a selected number of human service occupations and professions which are employed in the executive and legislative officials category of public administration. Some of these individuals may be elected officials, some may be appointed officials and some may be regular employees.

DOMINANT OCCUPATIONS and PROFESSIONS

As indicated earlier, no specific occupation and profession dominates the political network, although we use the term politician. A politician is any individual who runs for public office or is otherwise active in political affairs.[7]

The absence of a specific degree or background for a politician does not mean an individual receives no training. Once a person is elected, there are two types of training programs: on the job, and in-service. On the job training refers to learning the specific position for which one was elected and using that position as the groundwork for a higher level position. For example, a person with a legal background works in a district attorney's office, and becomes a candidate for a district attorney's position. Later, the same person may become a candidate for the state legislature, governor or federal congress. In-service training refers to seminars, institutes and other educational opportunities related to a specific position. Some individuals engage in the political network by assuming various tasks for a party or special interest group and eventually perform higher level tasks in the party or special interest group. Eventually, these individuals, through experience, may choose to run for an elected position. The process is sometimes called "political socialization," which is different than academic training which is required for most other professions.

Figure 7-10

NUMBER and PERCENT OF SELECTED HUMAN SERVICE OCCUPATIONS and
PROFESSIONS EMPLOYED IN THE EXECUTIVE AND LEGISLATIVE OFFICIALS
INDUSTRIAL CLASSIFICATION IN 1980*

ation and Profession[1]	Number	Percent
r	48	.76
er/Judge	3,497	53.81
al Work	1,077	16.57
ation	94	1.45
gy	37	.57
selor (Education/Vocational)	46	.70
omist	360	5.54
hologist	14	.21
r Social Science	70	1.03
n Planner	152	2.34
ician	24	.37
stered Nurse	76	1.17
ician	24	.37
apist (occupational, physical, etc.)	7	.11
itect	32	.49
nistrators (education, health)	35	.54
onnel and Labor Relations	686	10.56
cian, etc.	66	1.01
st, Painter, Dancer	117	1.81
r Health Fields	38	.59
L	6,500	100.00

rce: Adapted from United States Department of Commerce, Bureau of the
us, 1980 Census of Population: Volume 2 Subject Reports. Part 7C:
ation by Industry, Washington, DC: U.S. Government Printing Office,
, pp. 295-664.

industrial classification of executives and legislative officials
udes the following: city government: alderman, commissioner, Indian
al council, manager, mayor, prosecuting attorney, register of deeds, etc;
an tribal council; state government: assembly, commissioner, House of
asentatives, Legislature, Senate, etc.; United States government:
ress, Senate, House of Representatives, Office of the President, etc. In
, there were approximately 490,000 elected officials at all levels of
rnment in the United States. The occupations and professions listed may
ay not be elected positions.

227

The politician has various functions depending upon the specific position, they were elected for. In general, a legislative politician has the following functions:

- Attends committee and legislative meetings
- Reviews bills for passage
- Communicates with representatives from the district
- Holds open hearings on special issues
- Communicates with local citizens
- Keeps abreast of socioeconomic issues
- Influence other legislators toward particular viewpoints
- Acts as an advocate for individual citizens and groups.

A non-legislative politician is a person elected for a specific position, such as treasurer, clerk, etc. They are expected to perform the specific tasks of that particular office. In addition to elected officials there are numerous appointed delegates to various government units which represent a specific nation/state and these tasks may be similar to those of a legislator, such as the United Nations.

The politician in a political party generally has a dual representation: they represent the viewpoints of a specific party, and the interest of the constituency in their electoral district. In addition, the individual politician should vote on legislation which is best for the nation/state according to their individual conscience.

The lobbyist for a special interest group is expected to keep abreast of legislation which impacts on their interest group, make reports and presentations to various groups in order to influence legislation, and discuss the issues with various appointed and elected officials. The lobbyist's basic concern can be described as one of "mutual interest" since they have a specific group, and a specific interest for which they are working.

The individual citizen participates in all levels of the political network and is really an interest group of one, since the person represents an individualized view.[8]

SOCIAL WORK

No exact figures are known of the number of social workers who are involved in the political network. Since many social workers are employed directly for a governmental unit, they are employed for a specific function, such as child welfare, corrections, etc. In addition the social worker can assume other roles, such as politician, community organizer, and lobbyist in issues related to their employment. As individual citizens,

228

many are involved in political parties and other special interest groups.

GOVERNMENT EMPLOYMENT

In governmental units, social workers, are involved in social service programs at all levels (United Nations through city government). At the international level social workers are employed in staff positions for UNESCO, UNICEF, Refugee works, etc. In addition, numerous individuals are consultants to various countries and specific groups. Many private organizations have utilized social workers in their international programs, such as Catholic Charities, World Wide Adoptions, Red Cross, etc.

At the federal level, many social workers are employed to implement the various social service programs. Occasionally there have been social workers involved at the policy and decision making level for social services. For example, Wilbur Cohen was instrumental in the development of the Social Security Act, of 1935, and Lillian Rankin as a legislator from a western state in 1914 was a key figure for women's rights and protective legislation.

At the state level, social workers are involved at both the administrative staff level and as employees of the governmental unit in implementing programs. Some social workers have become professional politicians and are elected members of a state legislature. Social workers may be employed as planners or organizers, and in some states they have been employed as an ombudsmen to act as a mediator between the administration and the local population.

At the county/town level, social workers are employed in the welfare or social service departments and other human service agencies. Some social workers take an active part in the political process and become members of county or town boards. At this level a person can organize small groups and neighborhoods over specific issues and enable the citizens to have input into the political process. Some counties have employed social workers as an ombudsmen to act as a mediator between the county government and its citizens.

At the city level it is more common for social workers to have positions related to community organization, planning, recreation, neighborhood groups and other community groups. In some cases, the social worker may become a professional politician and become elected as an alderman. Some of the larger cities employ social workers as an ombudsmen to act as a mediator between the local government and the citizens.

229

POLITICAL PARTY and LOBBYIST

When a social worker becomes involved in a political party, it is extremely difficult to make a distinction between whether they are acting as an individual citizen, or as a professional social worker. There are indications that the various political parties use social workers informally as ombudsmen, organizers, and brokers (people who can act as an information referral system). Some social workers are directly employed as a lobbyist for a special interest group related to social services.

INDIVIDUAL CITIZEN

Obviously the social worker, as an individual citizen, can become involved in the political process by advocating their own viewpoints as well as viewpoints for some group.[9]

PERSONAL SOCIAL SERVICES

The political network, like other networks utilizes the personal social services for specific problems which involve members of the political network. (See Chapter 22, Personal Social Service.) Some examples of the personal social services in the political network include the following:

PROTECTIVE SERVICES

Referral for problems of family violence through the Physicians Office for members of Congress in Washington, D.C. and specific groups, such as the Senior Political Action Committee, Senate Children's Caucus and Senate Caucus on the Family in Washington, D.C.

UTILITARIAN SERVICES

Day care services available during large political rallies of the Democratic and Republican parties, programs to aid drought victims in Ethiopia through the United Nations, the House Placement Office and Legal Counsel of the Senate, Washington, D.C.

DEVELOPMENTAL and SOCIALIZATION

Family and marital counseling services available for members of the legislature both federal and state, the American Youth Work Center and the Youth Project, Washington, D.C.

REHABILITATIVE and THERAPEUTIC SERVICES

Alcohol/drug programs for members of Congress in Washington, D.C. at Walter Reed Hospital, the Office of Personnel Management, Employee Health Services, Attending Physician and Senate Drug Enforcement Caucus, Washington, D.C.

SPECIAL POPULATIONS

After a lengthy period of benign neglect, the political network is intermittently responding to the needs of special populations. (See Chapter 25, Special Populations, and Chapter 24 Rehabilitation). Some examples of programs and services for special populations in the political network include the following:

ASIAN

Asian Forum, Chicago, Illinois; Japanese American Citizens League and Organization of Chinese Americans, Washington, D.C.

BLACK

Black National Political Convention; Congressional Black Caucus and Joint Center for Political Studies, Washington, D.C.

EUROPEAN ETHNIC

Irish American Conference, Gaithersburg, Maryland; American Council for Nationalities and National Italian American Foundation, Washington, D.C.

NATIVE AMERICAN

Americans for Indian Opportunity, Albuquerque, New Mexico; National Congress of Native Americans and National Tribal Chairmen's Association, Washington, D.C.

SAME SEX PREFERENCE

Gay People's Union, Milwaukee, Wisconsin; Human Rights Compaign Fund, Rainbow Lobby and Gay Activists Alliance, Washington, D.C.

SPANISH SPEAKING

Association for the Advancement of Mexican Americans; National Association of Latino Elected and Appointed Officials and the Congressional Hispanic Caucus, Washington, D.C.

WOMEN

Astrea Foundation, Bronx, New York; Rainbow Lobby, Capital Hill Women's Political Caucus and Congressional Caucus for Women's Issues, Washington, D.C.

ISSUES

The political network has a series of significant issues relating to citizen participation, role of special interest groups, responding to the needs of its citizens, responding to international politics, etc. Of all of the variety of issues in the political network, only a few have been selected for further elaboration which include citizen participation, role of special interest groups, finances and issues related to social work.

CITIZEN PARTICIPATION

As indicated earlier, citizen participation in federal elections averages about 50 percent of all eligible voters and in state and local elections this percentage decreases to as low as 20 percent. If citizens indeed believe in the concept of a representative democracy and desire to have more influence in the political process, citizen participation needs to be expanded. It is not only in the electoral process where citizen participation should be increased, but also in the workings of political parties, community meetings and involvement and individually contacting their political representatives.

SPECIAL INTEREST GROUPS

As the cost of elections increases and as the general citizen is not organized, the role of special interest groups is becoming more influential at all levels of government. The major concern about special interest groups and their influence is whether the politicians will respond to the issues based upon the needs of their constituency, region or country or upon the needs of special interest groups which might contradict the needs of their constituency. In 1986, the Congress endorsed legislation restricting the amount of money a political action committee can contribute to a politician's campaign fund.

FINANCES

Government finances and ability to maintain a balanced budget at all levels of government have been a problem as services expected by the society or community increase. In particular, the financial problems are exaggerated in times of recession like 1978-82 and with shifting priorities for expenditures. Many state governments have had to reduce expenditures in the 1980's yet at the same time receive less monies from the federal government. A unique approach to achieving a balanced budget is the Gramm-Rudman bill of 1985 which mandates a balanced budget at the federal level by 1991. The Gramm-Rudman bill specifies a percentage reduction in federal spending for each budgetary period. The Supreme Court in 1986 has ruled part of the Gramm-Rudman bill unconstitutional and has reserved the right of making budget cuts to the United States Congress and not the General Accounting Office (the federal bureaucracy).

SOCIAL WORK

Two primary issues for social work are funding of programs and educational content. Many social service programs are funded by the federal and state governments and only for a short period of term. As a consequence it is possible to start a program to fill a specific need, and after two or three years the program is disbanded because of the unavailability or shortage of funding. In social work education there should be an orientation to the political network, with more stress on the sub-national aspect of decision making. There should be an awareness of the variety of roles a social worker fills in the full range of governmental activity, and not just a concentration on planning or consultation. The social worker needs to have a knowledge of politics, and how the political process works in order to gain access to various local groups, and how to initiate and influence legislation.

SUMMARY

The political network consists of government, political parties, special interest (pressure) groups, and citizen participation. When individuals normally think about the political network they tend to think of the federal government, yet there is a full range of governmental activities from the United Nations to the local county, township and city level. The political network is extremely diverse and complex. For example, in the United States there are approximately 38,000 county townships and city governments, with an additional 42,000 special governmental tax units, like sewer districts, school districts, etc. It is estimated that less than five percent of the population actively and consistently belong to political parties and only a few more become involved at specific times and issues for rallies and meetings and public hearings. Voting records indicate that about 53 percent of the eligible voting population participates in presidential elections. A brief historical analysis showed that the rise of government (nation/state), with the concept of citizen participation, and the utilization of political parties as we know it, is the product of the last 200 years. Prior to 1800 there was minimal citizen participation and political parties consisted of the elite who either supported or were opposed to the established government.

The dominant profession in the political network is that of the politician. The criteria for becoming a politician include motivation, interest, and capacity to run for and be elected for public office. It is estimated there are 2.3 politicians per 1000 individuals in the United States. A politician can have any occupational and professional background. There is no formalized educational and training program for becoming a politician, but there are processes of "political socialization" through in-service training and staff development. There was a brief description of the role of a social worker at the various levels of government ranging from the United Nations to the county township government level, as well as, the role of a social worker as a politician in political parties and as a consultant for special interest groups.

FOOTNOTES

*This chapter was reviewed for comments by Clarke Hagensick, Professor, Department of Political Science and Department of Governmental Affairs, University of Wisconsin Extension, University of Wisconsin-Milwaukee, Milwaukee, Wisconsin.

1. Expenditures for the federal government have increased 500 percent from 1950 to 1972. Expenditures for local govern- ment have increased by 700 percent in the same time period. The number of federal employees has increased 10 percent from 1963 to 1972, however, the number of local government employees has increased 60 percent in the same time period. The reader is referred to George Berkley and Douglas Cox, Eighty Thousand Governments; The Politics of Sub-national America, Boston, Massachusetts: Allyn and Bacon Inc., 1978.

Sources used for estimating the size of the political network include the following: Herbert Alexander, Financing the 1980 Election. Lexington, MA: D.C. Heath Co., 1983, pp. 111-126; John Andriot, Population Abstract of the United States, McLean, VA: Andriot Associates, 1983, pp. 68, 92, 284, 486, 556, 558, 881, 883; Stephen Miller, Special Interest Groups in American Politics, New Brunswick, NJ: Transaction Books, 1983, pp. 2, 140; Marquis Academic Media, Directory of Registered Lobbyists and Lobbyist Legislation, 2nd ed., Chicago, IL: Marquis Who's Who Inc., 1975, pp. 451-645; United States Department of Commerce, Bureau of the

Census, <u>Statistical Abstract of the United States: 1986</u> <u>(106th Ed.),</u> Washington, DC: U.S. Government Printing Office, 1985, pp. 262, 286, 294, 306; <u>1977 Census of Government Vol. 1 Part 2 Popularly Elected Officials</u>, 1979, p. 2; <u>1982 Census of Government</u>, <u>Finances of Special Districts,</u> <u>Vol. 4 Number 2,</u> 1984, p. 9; <u>1982 Census of Government, Vol.</u> <u>1; Governmental Organization</u>, 1983, pp. x-xix; <u>1982 Census</u> <u>of Government, Vol. 4 Number 1; Finances of Public School</u> <u>Systems</u>, 1984, pp. 6-7, 25, 80, 139; <u>Public Employment in</u> <u>1984,</u> 1985, p. V, 1 and United Nations <u>Yearbook of the</u> <u>United Nations 1980 Vol. 34,</u> New York, NY: United Nations, 1983, pp. 1208, 1230.

2. The author infers that all elected officials in the United States, of which there are about 490,265 are politicians to some degree. Consequently the term politician is loosely used to describe an individual who is a candidate in an election for a public office whether they are a senator, a representative, a county clerk or sheriff. Other sources for estimating the size of the political network are indicated in footnote 1.

3. Based on a survey of 2,255 people by the Michigan Social Science Survey Unit. Other sources for estimating the size of the political network are indicated in footnote 1.

4. International City Managers Association. <u>The Municipal</u> <u>Yearbook 1980</u>. Washington, D.C.: International City Managers Association, 1980. Other sources for estimating citizen participation are indicated in footnote 1.

5. In addition to the formal organization of government, there is an informal network in operation where many decisions are made. A quasi-government which is illegal but which has a means to enforce rules, collect money, etc., is organized crime or the Cosa Nostra (Mafia).

6. For example, the elected official of a treasurer at the county level. The issue of a lack of formalized education or specific requirements for an elected official can, at times, be embarrassing and inefficient. For example, in one election for county treasurer, the winner of the election, not having any background and experience, was obligated to hire a full-time person to handle the functions of a treasurer. In this case, the county in effect had two treasurers: the elected official, and a new full-time position for someone to perform the functions of a treasurer.

7. In 1977, there were an estimated 2.3 politicians i.e. public officials per 1000 population. (Milwaukee Journal:July 1980).

8. For information on becoming a politician as a career one should contact the political parties in ones local area, such as Democratic, Republican, Libertarion, etc.

9. For information on social work as a career, contact the National Association of Social Workers 7981 Eastern Ave. Silver Spring, Maryland 20910 or the local National Association of Social Workers office.

SUGGESTED READINGS

George Berkley and Douglas Fox. Eighty Thousand Governments: Politics of Sub-National America. Boston, MA: Allyn and Bacon Inc., 1978. For an individual who is unacquainted with the role of local government in the United States, this book provides an excellent overview.

David Botter. Politicians and What They Do. New York, NY: Franklin Watts, Inc., 1970. For an individual seeking a nonsophisticated discussion of the role of the politician, this book is a solid introduction.

David Coyle. The United Nations and How It Works. New York, NY: Columbia University Press, 1969. For a brief introduction to the United Nations, this book is an excellent resource.

Walter Friedlander. International Social Welfare. Englewood Cliffs, NJ: Prentice Hall, Inc., 1975. This is one of the few textbooks which in one volume addresses the issue of international social welfare programs instead of a country by country analysis.

Stephen Miller. Special Interest Groups in American Politics. New Brunswick, NJ: Transaction Books, 1983. This book is an excellent source for understanding the development of special interest groups (political action committees) and their growing influence in the legislative process.

Anne Minahan (Ed.). Encyclopedia of Social Work, 18th Issue. Washington, DC: National Association of Social Workers, 1986. For a general description of the role of social work in the political process, the specific article in this encyclopedia will provide the reader with a general overview and some reference sources for further reading.

REFERENCES

Alexander, Herbert. Financing the 1980 Election. Lexington, MA: D.C. Heath and Co., 1983.

Andriot, John. Population Abstract of the United States. McLean, VA: Andriot Associates, 1983.

Berki, R.N. The History of Political Thought. Tatowa, New Jersey: Rowman and Little Field Publishers, 1977.

Berkley, George and Douglas Fox. Eighty Thousand Governments: Politics of Sub-National America. Boston, Massachusetts: Allyn and Bacon Inc., 1978.

Bloomfield, Lincoln. "United Nations" Vol. 20 U-V. The World Book Encyclopedia. Chicago, Illinois: Field Enterprises Educational Corporation, 1973.

Botter, David. Politicians and What They Do. New York, NY: Franklin Watts Inc., 1970.

Clements, John. Taylors Encyclopedia of Government Officials: Federal and State, Vol. 10, 1985-86. Dallas, Texas: Political Research Inc., 1985.

Cohen, Wilbur. "What Every Social Worker Should Know About Political Action," Social Work, Vol. 11, No. 3 (July 1966), pp. 3-12.

Coyle, David. The United Nations and How It Works. New York, NY: Columbia University Press, 1969.

Council of State Governments. Book of the States: 1984-85 Vol. 27. Lexington, Kentucky: Council of State Governments, 1984.

Department of Administration. Annual Financial Report. County of Milwaukee, Wisconsin. Milwaukee, Wisconsin: Department of Administration, 1979.

Friedlander, Walter. International Social Welfare. Englewood
    Cliffs, New Jersey: Prentice Hall Inc., 1975.

Hajnal, Peter. Guide to the United Nations: Organization,
    Documentation and Publishing. Dobb's Ferry, New York:
    Oceana Publications Inc., 1978.

Huckshorn, Robert. Political Parties in America. North
    Scituate, Massachsuetts: Duxbury Press, 1980.

International City Management Association. Municipal Yearbook,
    1980. Washington D.C.: International City Management
    Association, 1980.

Kahn, Alfred and Sheilia Kamerman. Social Services in
    International Perspective. Washington D.C.:   U.S.
    Department of Health, Education and Welfare, 1976.

Laufer, Armand. Social Planning at the Community Level.
    Englewood Cliffs, New Jersey: Prentice Hall Inc., 1978.

League of Wisconsin Municipalities. Handbook for Wisconsin
    Municipal Officers. Madison, WI: League of Wisconsin
    Municipalities, 1976.

Lemay, Michael. Wisconsin Towns, Madison WI: Institute of
    Governmental Affairs, University of Wisconsin-Extension,
    1975.

Marquis Academic Media. Directory of Registered Lobbyists and
    Lobbyist Legislation, 2nd Ed. Chicago, IL: Marquis Who's
    Who Inc., 1975.

Miller, Stephen. Special Interest Groups in American Politics.
    New Brunswick, NJ: Transaction Books, 1983.

Minahan, Anne (Ed.). Encyclopedia of Social Work, 18th Issue,
    Washington D.C.: National Association of Social Workers,
    1986.

Office of the Federal Register, United States Government
    Manual, 1985-86. Washington D.C.: U.S. Government Printing
    Office, 1985.

Ornstein, Norman and Shirley Elder. Interest Groups, Lobbying
    and Policy Making. Washington D.C.: Congressional
    Quarterly Press, 1978.

Peltason, J.W. and James M. Burns. Functions and Policies of American Government. Second edition, Englewood Cliffs, New Jersey: Prentice Hall Inc., 1962.

Penniman, Howard. Sait's American Parties and Elections, Fifth Edition, New York, NY: Appleton Century Crofts Inc., 1982.

Russalto, Patricia. National Party Conventions: 1831-1980. Washington, DC: Congressional Quarterly Press, 1983.

Smith, Virginia. "How Interest Groups Influence Legislators," Social Work, Vol. 24, No. 3 (May, 1979), pp. 234-240.

Taylor, James and Jerry Randolph. Community Workers. New York, NY: Jason Aronson, Inc., 1975.

United Nations. Yearbook of the United Nations, 1980, Vol. 34. New York, NY: United Nations, 1983.

United States Department of Commerce, Bureau of the Census. Statistical Abstract of the United States: 1986 (106th Ed), Washington, D.C.: U.S. Government Printing Office, 1985.

United States Department of Commerce, Bureau of the Census. 1982 Census of Government: Vol. 1, Governmental Organization, Washington, DC: U.S. Government Printing Office, 1983.

_____, 1982 Census of Government: Vol. 4, Finances of Public School Districts, Washington, DC: U.S. Government Printing Office, 1984.

_____, 1982 Census of Government: Vol. 4, Number 2, Finances of Special Districts, Washington, DC: U.S. Government Printing Office, 1984.

_____, 1977 Census of Government: Volume 1 Number 2 Popularly Elected Officials, Washington, D.C.: U.S. Government Printing Office, 1979.

_____, Public Employment in 1984, Washington, D.C.: U.S. Government Printing Office, 1985.

_____, 1980 Census of Population: Volume 2 Subject Reports Part 7C: Occupation by Industry. Washington, DC: U.S. Government Printing Office, 1984.

Wade, Allen. "The Social Worker in the Political Process," Social Welfare Forum 1966, pp. 52-67.

Wisconsin Legislative Reference Bureau, <u>Wisconsin Blue Book,</u> <u>1985-86</u>. Madison, WI: Department of Administration, 1985.

Zwlig, Franklin. "The Social Worker as Legislative Ombudsmen," (pp. 152-162) in Anthony Tripodi, Phillip Fellin, and Irving Epstein <u>Social Workers at Work</u>, Ithasca, Ill.: Peacock Publishing Co., 1972.

SECTION 3

GENERAL HUMAN SERVICE NETWORKS

General human service networks are those organized around a societal problem which affects individuals and groups but do not have a specific social service program as their primary function.

Chapter 8 describes the education network and the professions of teaching, guidance counselor, and the role of a school social worker. Chapter 9 describes the environment protection network and the professions of home economics, consumer affairs and the role of social work in the physical environment (energy, pollution, etc.) and the population environment (family planning and consumerism). Chapter 10 describes the information and referral network and the profession of library and information science and the role of social work. Chapter 11 describes the judicial network and the professions of judge, prosecuting attorney, public defender, court administrator and the role of social work. Chapter 12 describes the protective service network and the professions of law enforcement, private security and the role of a police social worker. Chapter 13 describes the legal network and the profession of law, the occupation of paralegal aid, and the role of social work. Chapter 14 describes the leisure and recreation network and the professions of recreation, recreation therapist and the role of social work. Chapter 15 describes the religious network and the professions of clergy, pastoral counselor and the role of social work.

CHAPTER 8

EDUCATION NETWORK*

"The educator knows, too, that the secret of a
discipline he imparts is not the final secret of
existence. The world is not to become perfect,
even with the best education for everybody.
Education does not pose as insurance against
error or sin. There will continue to be plenty
of both in the universe which man did not create,
and which he inhabits as a more or less refrac-
tory citizen." Van Doren:1959:8.

INTRODUCTION

Mass public education has been a major contribution of the
United States to Western society. Americans have tended to view
the education network as one which would solve most social
problems and is essential for a democracy to survive. It is not
surprising, then, to find some form of education has become a
standard response to any social problem. The above statement by
Van Doren is a cautious one, but clearly indicates that education is not a panacea for solving all of society's problems.

The United States has used the education network for:
academic, vocational, and professional training; general
socialization of students; and attempts to alleviate major
social problems, such as institutional and individual racism.
This chapter briefly describes the nature and extent of the
education network and the variety of human service occupations
and professions employed within the network. The role of the
dominant professions of a teacher and guidance counselor are
compared with that of a school social worker.

SIZE

The education network in the United States is extremely
diverse and complex, consisting of preschool programs, public
school system (primary and secondary), private school system
(primary and secondary), vocational technical system, higher
education system (both public and private) and continuing
education. Each of these components of the education network
have their own autonomy, with school boards or other groups
having administrative and policy accountability. With the
diversity and complexity of the education network, one should

not be astonished at the expenditures for this multilevel network. Figure 8-1 shows the estimated size of the education network from 1982 to 1985. Figures on primary and secondary education, vocational and technical education, and higher education were used to estimate the size of the education network.

PRIMARY and SECONDARY EDUCATION

The largest component of the education network is the primary and secondary education system which in 1984 had expenditures of approximately 139.0 billion dollars, employed an estimated 5.7 million individuals, and had an estimated enrollment of 56.9 million students in 1985. The number of schools at this level of education was estimated at 105,504.

PUBLIC PRIMARY and SECONDARY EDUCATION--The public primary and secondary school education component of the education network in 1984 consisted of approximately 15,786 school districts, each with its own autonomy and authority, and having responsibility for an estimated 84,740 schools. The public primary and secondary education component in 1985 had estimated expenditures of 127.5 billion dollars, employed an estimated 1.9 million teachers, and in 1985 had an estimated student enrollment of 38.9 million.

PRIVATE PRIMARY and SECONDARY EDUCATION--The private primary and secondary school component of the education network in 1982 consisted of 20,764 schools, had estimated expenditures in 1984 of 11.5 billion dollars, employed approximately one million teachers and in 1985 had an estimated enrollment of 5.7 million students.

VOCATIONAL and TECHNICAL EDUCATION--In 1982 the vocational and technical school component of the education network consisted of approximately 7,296 schools, employed approximately 98,000+ individuals, had expenditures of approximately 6.8 billion dollars, and an estimated enrollment of 8.9 million students. This estimate of students is for post secondary education programs in the vocational technical system and for continuing ·education. The vocational and technical system can be subdivided into those schools which offer only non-collegiate courses and programs (6,000 schools) and those schools which also offer college parallel courses (1,296 schools).

HIGHER EDUCATION

The higher education component of the education network consists of both public and private schools, of which there were approximately 3,284 in 1983. Of these schools, 2,013 were four-year or more institutions offering degrees from the

Figure 8-I

Estimated Size of the Education Network 1982-1985*

	TYPE OF EDUCATION NETWORK		
Selected Characteristics	Primary and Secondary (public and private)	Vocational Technical (includes public & private & noncollegiate programs)	Higher Education (Both 4 yr. & 2 yr. public and private)
Number of Schools (Institutions)	105,504	7,296	3,284
Number of Employees	5,761,252[1]	98,000+[1]	3,299,000
Expenditures (Billion)	139.0 Billion	6.8 Billion[2]	90.1 Billion [1]
Enrollment (Number)	56,924,000	8,963,000	12,247,000

Sources: Adapted from United States Department of Commerce, Bureau of the Census, Statistical Abstract of the United States: 1986 (106th Ed.), Washington, D.C.: U.S. Government Printing Office, 1985, pp. 127, 128, 130, 154, 158, 161.

[1]United States Department of Commerce, Bureau of the Census, 1980 Census of Population: Volume 2 Subject Reports Part 7C: Occupation by Industry, Washington, D.C.: U.S. Government Printing Office, 1984, pp. 295-664, and United States, Department of Commerce, Bureau of the Census, Public Employment in 1984, Washington, D.C.: U.S. Government Printing Office, 1985, p. viii.

[2]United States Department of Commerce, Bureau of the Census, Statistical Abstract of the United States: 1984 (104th Ed.), Washington, D.C.: U.S. Government Printing Office, 1983, pp. 161.

In addition to the estimates shown, there are 5.9 million children attending nursery school and kindergarten and approximately 21.2 million individuals classified as attending adult continuing education programs.

245

bachelor level through the Ph.D. level, and 1,271 schools were two-year community colleges. This component of the education network in 1984 had expenditures estimated at 90.1 billion dollars, employed approximately 3.2 million individuals, and had a student enrollment of approximately 12.2 million.

PUBLIC HIGHER EDUCATION--This component of the education network in 1983 consisted of 1,497 schools. In 1984 expenditures were estimated at 59.7 billion dollars with a full time instructional staff of 684,000 and 1,285,000 other employees. The estimated enrollment for 1985 was 9.6 million students.

PRIVATE HIGHER EDUCATION--This component of the education network consisted of 1,787 schools. In 1984 expenditures were estimated at 30.4 billion dollars with a full time faculty of 98,851 in 1983. The estimated enrollment for 1985 was 2.7 million students.

One can readily see the extensive size of the education network in the United States. Total direct expenditures for the education network in 1985 were estimated at 235.9 billion dollars. These figures do not include the expenditures for approximately 21.2 million individuals who enrolled in adult education programs, or 5.9 million children who were attending pre-kindergarten programs.[1]

HISTORICAL DEVELOPMENT

The major components of the education network include primary and secondary education, vocational and technical education and higher education. Each of these components of the education network represents different philosophies and have different historical precedents. Subsequently, each of these components of the education network will be discussed separately.

PRIMARY and SECONDARY EDUCATION

CLASSICAL CIVILIZATION--PRE 450 A.D.--For many years the educational experience for individuals consisted of learning from the tribal or clan elders, the elders in one's family, or in one's own home by their parents. In early classical societies like Greece and Rome (1100 BC-450 AD), there was a two-track system of education: the socio-economic elite went to some form of primary school, usually private and religious-orientated, and then to the gymnasium, which is equivalent to our secondary school; the common people became an apprentice to an individual to learn a trade or learned their parent's occupation. Both the Greeks and the Romans developed a secular teacher who was distinctly different from the clergy-teacher.

This secular teacher at the primary level was called a ludus, and at the secondary level a grammaticus.

MEDIEVAL EUROPE (400 AD-1500 AD)--This period of time was dominated by the church, consequently, one would expect the education network to be under the control of the church. The clergy operated parish and catechism schools where the catechism was taught in order to have individuals understand and know their major religious beliefs. Formal education for most individuals stopped at this level. Only those who were in training as a cleric, priest, monk or nun received any formal education, and they attended the cathedral and monastery schools. A common person either learned their parents' trade or became an apprentice in a guild in order to learn a trade. In some guilds a rudimentary level of reading and writing was taught.[2]

REFORMATION and RENAISSANCE (1500 - 1600)--This time period was significant in the development of primary and secondary education since an emphasis was placed upon reading for religious purposes, i.e., to understand the Bible, consequently there was an upsurge in interest to provide a minimum education for the common person. In addition to the religious rationale for some education, there was a growing concern and demand for education by the developing merchant and middle classes for specific skills. A vernacular school was developed in many parts of Protestant Europe which functioned as a form of primary school. The vernacular school which was developed in this time period, and the earlier parish and catechism schools were the forerunners of the primary education system as we know it today. During this time period there was the development at the secondary level of the gymnasium and the latin secondary school for the gifted, nobility, and training for the priesthood. This advanced form of education system was the forerunner of the secondary school system. Teachers in both the vernacular and gymnasium schools were a combination of clergy teachers, with a very few secular or lay teachers.

UNITED STATES--The United States, in its Colonial days (1620-1783), followed the pattern of its European heritage by establishing catechism and vernacular schools, called the common school, for the basic rudiments of reading, writing and arithmetic. The wealthy classes either hired an individual as a private tutor or sent their children to a secondary and gymnasium school in Europe. The first grammar school (boys' preparatory school for college) was established in Boston, Massachusetts (in 1635). Although the education system followed the earlier pattern of Europe, modifications were made between 1783 and 1850, which would make the United States' education

network distinctly different and unique from the European education model. Some of these modifications included free public
primary education, free public secondary education, compulsory
attendance and local control of educational policy and programs.

Free public Primary Education existed as a concept in the
United States in Colonial days. A rudimentary form of primary
level education was taking place in a variety of forms. For
example, individuals were taught at home, in church schools, a
private dame (a widow would teach a small group of children),
the apprentice system and the common or vernacular school. A
parent was not compelled to send their children to the vernacular or common school, however, there were early laws in some
colonies requiring the parent to have their children learn to
read and write through one means or another. In 1642, a
Massachusetts law stipulated that parents were responsible for
having their children learn to read and write. In 1647,
Massachusetts required each town of fifty families to establish
a primary or common school. Other colonies developed a primary
school in cities, townships, etc. The post-Revolutionary War
period was one of expansion and recognition of the public common
school, with the concept of a common or primary school written
into the Northwest Ordinance Act of 1787. This act required
each township to set aside a plot of land for the purpose of
education. The Northwest Ordinance Act of 1787 covered the
current states of Ohio, Indiana, Illinois, Michigan, Wisconsin
and Minnesota. Article 3 of the Northwest Ordinance Act states
in part:

"Religion, morality and knowledge is necessary to
good government and the happiness of mankind,
schools as a means of education shall forever be
encouraged."[3]

Although the establishment of a public common or primary
school was widely accepted in the United States, these schools
were not initially free public education, since a tuition fee
was charged or the parents provided in-kind services, such as
bringing firewood, coal, and other supplies. In some jurisdictions a tax rate bill which was a daily fee per child in school
was assessed against the parent like any other tax. The movement for a free public primary school system developed in 1849
in New York State under the leadership of Christopher Morgen and
Samuel Young. The free public primary school movement spread
rapidly, and by 1875 the notion of free public primary schools
was accepted. Parents still had the option of sending their
children to a private or parochial school.

Free public secondary education had an earlier precedent in
the Colonial period which used the European model of the latin

grammar school. The first latin grammar school in the United States was established in Boston, Massachusetts (1635). The latin grammar school prepared individuals for college and usually were schools for the elite and wealthy of society.[4] These schools were usually a tuition-based school, although Massachusetts in 1647 did require each town of one hundred families to establish a latin grammar school. An alternative to the traditional rote memorization of the latin grammar school was the development of the academy concept in 1751 under the influence of Benjamin Franklin in Philadelphia, Pennsylvania, and a similar movement in Andover, Massachusetts in 1782. The academy was a private school which was more practical oriented than the latin grammar school. A practical orientation meant bookkeeping, auditing, and other practical skills related to the needs of the rapidly expanding merchant class or business sector of the economy.

The latin grammar school declined in significance after 1780 with the rise of the academy. In 1821, Boston, Massachusetts established the first public secondary (high) school. Like the early common schools, the public secondary school was not initially free since the parents were charged a tuition. The secondary school movement spread slowly, with the establishment of separate schools for males and females. A significant event in the emergence of the secondary school as free public educa-tion was the Supreme Court decision involving Kalamazoo, Michigan in 1874. This court decision declared that tax monies could be used for supporting secondary schools. After this court decision, the free public secondary school movement spread rapidly, with the concurrent decline of the academy. The free public secondary school by 1900 became the established system for secondary-level education.

With the establishment of free public secondary education, the focus of the secondary school changed from preparation for college to the concept of a comprehensive school with multiple functions. These multiple functions include general education, vocational education, preparation for college, preparation for specific occupations and preparation for general citizenship.

Compulsory Attendance as a concept was contained in the Massachusetts law of 1642 which required parents to teach their children to read and write. Although this law was on the books, it was not particularly enforced. The first state to require compulsory primary school attendance was Massachusetts in 1853. The movement for compulsory education at the primary level spread rapidly through the states, such as Vermont (1867), Wisconsin (1879), and by 1918 all states had some form of compulsory attendance laws. Compulsory attendance laws in most states also apply to secondary education.

During the 1960s three states repealed the compulsory attendance laws at the secondary level and developed a system of local options. The intent of these laws was to avoid desegregation of the school system.

Local Control and States' Rights in the United States, at the primary and secondary levels of education is a constitutional issue. The United States Constitution of 1789, under Article 10 of the Bill of Rights, specifies the following:

"The powers not delegated to the United States by the Constitution, nor prohibited by it to the States, are reserved to the States respectively or to the people."[5]

Education is one of these functions which has been reserved to the states. Since each state is responsible for education, there is some variation in compulsory attendance laws, curriculum, policies, school desegregation policies, etc. Although the state has responsibility for education, the local town, city or county initially was the central focus of educational policy and administration until the mid-1800s. The first state Superintendent of Schools was in New York (1812) and the first state Board of Education was in Massachusetts (1832). By 1900 administration of primary and secondary education became a joint local and state responsibility, with the local school board or district controlling specific curricula and day-to-day implementation of education. The state had the responsibility to provide general guidelines for education, approving general and specific programs and certifying teachers. Beginning with World War II, states have developed minimal guidelines and curriculum for all schools.

Although education is a state responsibility, there is a complex system of local, state and federal level of participation in the funding of programs. The federal government early took an interest in education, as indicated by the establishment of the Office of Education in the Department of the Interior in 1867. This department was transferred to the federal security agency in 1939, then to the Department of Health, Education and Welfare in 1953. In 1980, a separate Department of Education was established.

Financial involvement at the federal level of government has been a consequence of a series of acts which provided financial support for educational institutions, such as The Smith-Hughes Act of 1917 (vocational and technical education), the Johnson-O'Malley Act of 1934 (Indian education), the Economic Opportunity Act of 1964 (War on Poverty), the Elementary and Secondary Education Act of 1965, the Education Amendments Act of

1972, the Concentrated Employment Act of 1974 and the Education for All Handicapped Children's Act of 1975.[6] In addition to finances, other federal legislation has had an impact on primary and secondary school education, such as the court decision of Brown vs. Board of Education (1954), which was the Supreme Court case, declaring school segregation unconstitutional, the Civil Rights Act of 1964, and more recently, the reaffirmation of the ban on school prayers in 1984.[7] In 1983 the President's Task Force on Primary and Secondary School education made a number of recommendations which could have an impact on the primary and secondary level of education including topics, such as curriculum, salaries, competency of students and teachers and discipline.

VOCATIONAL and TECHNICAL EDUCATION

For many years a person learned a trade by becoming an apprentice to a master craftsman for a specified period of time, such as seven years to become a master carpenter (1700). The system of apprenticeship was also a means for a local community to take care of orphans and other children who were homeless. Most individuals learned their occupation or trade from their parents' or other relatives.

During the early Industrial Revolution from 1800 to 1900, it was recognized that specialty training was needed to meet the needs of the changing industrial and economic network from an agricultural system to a factory and machine system. Specialty schools were developed to train individuals for specific occupations, and these early schools were called manual arts, industrial or trade schools. The first of these specialty schools was developed in St. Louis, Missouri (1880). Initially, these trade schools were operated by a city, such as Baltimore, Maryland (1884) and were few in number. The trade school movement developed slowly, with Wisconsin becoming the first state in 1911 to authorize a state-wide vocational and technical education system.

From an early emphasis on manual and industrial arts, the vocational technical schools have shifted their focus and programs over time to include adult high school education in the 1930s, associate of arts degrees in specialized areas (one or two-year programs) which developed in the 1930s, adult education or continuing education in hobbies or crafts in the 1940s, general education (two-year college programs) in the 1950s, and more recently, to relate to the changing technology, by adding courses in high-technology training in computer programming and computer science in the 1970s and 1980's.

Vocational technical education, like other parts of the education network, has been influenced by federal legislation and Supreme Court decisions. The Smith-Hughes Act of 1917 provided federal funding for technical education, and the G.I. Bill of 1944 (Veterans Education) resulted in a large influx of students. Other legislation which has had an impact on the vocational technical system include the 1954 Supreme Court decision on desegregation, the 1964 Civil Rights Act, the Higher Education Facilities Act of 1963 and the Education Amendment Act of 1973, amongst others.

HIGHER EDUCATION

The post-secondary level of education consists of universities and colleges which offer bachelor degrees through Ph.D. programs and a system of junior colleges.

UNIVERSITY AND COLLEGE--The university or college system is an outgrowth of the Medieval university of approximately 1200 A.D. The early universities developed out of cathedral (affiliated with a church) and monastery (affiliated with a monastery) schools and were essentially a training institution for clergy. The curriculum emphasis was on the liberal arts known as the Trivium (grammar, rhetoric, and logic including theology), and the Quadrivium (arithmetic, geometry, astronomy, and music).

The guild (collegial organization) was the dominant organizing element of the university system, with two patterns emerging: the teacher guild and the student guild. The teacher guild was where the teacher or faculty controlled the university and generally was associated with those universities which emerged from the cathedral schools, such as the University of Paris (1200). The student guild, where students controlled the university, developed in Italy, such as the University of Bologna (1000). Eventually, both patterns merged into the current system where ideally faculty are responsible and accountable for making policy decisions as well as development and implementation of curriculum, with input from students and other interested parties.

Until 1800 a university or college education was primarily for the clergy or the elite of society with a classical orientation or focus. The classical orientation refers to the study of the arts: language, literature, arts, philosophy, etc. Initially, the United States followed the European model of establishing private schools and universities in a classical tradition, such as Harvard University in Connecticut (1636), William and Mary College in Virginia (1693), Yale University in Connecticut (1701), Princeton University in New Jersey (1746) and Dartmouth College in New Hampshire (1769). These early universities enrolled males only. In addition to the private schools, some states began to develop state-funded universities, such as Georgia (1785), North Carolina (1795) and Virginia (1819). An impetus for the development of public-supported universities and colleges was the Supreme Court decision of 1819 and the Morrill Land Grant Act of 1862. The Supreme Court in the Dartmouth College vs. Woodward case (1819), ruled that a state could not co-opt (take over) a private college and transform it into a state college or university. This meant that the state, in order to develop a public university system, would have to establish its own independent schools. The 1862 Morrill Act provided for the selling of public lands in each state, with the proceeds designated for the development of public universities or colleges which would focus its curriculum on agriculture, mechanical arts, domestic and military science. As a consequence of this act, thirty states established a university. Eighteen states distributed the money collected to already-existing universities, such as Wisconsin (University of Wisconsin established in 1848), three states distributed the money to private universities and nine states established a separate university.

In addition to the financial aspect of the Morrill Land Grant Act, this act reinforced a shifting focus of university education and was partly a response to the educational controversies of the time. Some of these educational controversies included the following: education for women, a practical focus for higher education, type of curriculum (liberal arts or classical), and type of institution (public, private, college or university). Higher educational institutions in the 1800s were generally divided into male and female institutions. The first college to admit women, therefore becoming co-educational, was Oberlin College in Ohio (1833). The coeducational movement spread slowly, with many of the public universities becoming coeducational by 1900. Many private schools did not become coeducational until well in the twentieth century, meaning 1970, and some special schools for men and women exist in 1986.

Many early universities were primarily institutions to train religious personnel, consequently the curriculum was heavy on the liberal arts or classical tradition of philosophy, logic, literature and culture. As knowledge expanded in many areas and the role of higher education shifted to prepare individuals for multiple occupations, the focus of higher education became more pragmatic, providing course work for specific occupations and professions. Subsequently, most institutions of higher education adopted a liberal arts model or curriculum which consisted of a general broad base of courses and was known as liberal arts and then a concentration in a specific area. Currently, there is some tension between the objective of the university as preparing general citizens, i.e., liberal arts, or preparing people for specific professions, such as engineering, education, social work, etc.

A parallel development, with the shifting focus in higher education, was the debate over the pragmatic issues of what type of curriculum and institution was needed. Should a curriculum be relatively rigid (mostly required courses) or relatively open (mostly elective courses)? The expanding knowledge base in many professional areas resulted in most schools adopting a curriculum consisting of both required and elective courses. In the 1960s the trend was to decrease requirements and to increase electives and in the late 1970s and mid-1980s to increase requirements and reduce electives. In effect, there was a high degree of concern over whether the university system was adequately preparing students in content areas, such as mathematics, English, computer science, etc. A report by the President's Task Force on Post Secondary Education in 1985 indicated concern about the laxity of content in these areas. As the above changes occurred in higher education, institutions began to specialize in their educational focus, such as becoming schools of agriculture, education, commerce, military, research, etc. Examples of this trend are the Massachusetts Institute of Technology and the Military Academy at Annapolis. The United States in general has developed a system of higher education which was a compromise on many of these issues.

Like primary and secondary education, higher education is controlled either by the state or by a private board of directors. The federal government had an influence on higher education through various acts, beginning with the Morrill Land Act of 1862. Federal involvement has been primarily one of providing financial support for educational institutions for training specific types of professionals through financial grants for research and student support. Some examples of significant legislation which had an impact on higher education include the following: G.I. Bill of 1944 (veterans' education), Mental Health Act of 1946, (funds to train mental health professionals), Rehabilitation Act of 1954 (funds to train rehabilitation counselors), Public Health Amendment of 1956 (funds to train public health personnel), Nurse Training Act of 1964 (funds to train nurses), and the Indian Education Act of 1980 (funds to develop programs and curriculum on the Indian reservations). Some legislation provided funding to train disadvantaged citizens, such as the Economic Opportunity Act (1964) and the Concentrated Employment Act (1974). Some legislation provided funds for facilities, such as the Higher Education Facilities Act (1963) and the Education Amendment Act (1972). All of the decisions by the courts which have had an impact on higher education are those which are related to civil rights and desegregation and faculty governance. For example, the Supreme Court decision of 1954 on desegregation, the Civil Rights Act of 1964 and the Supreme Court decision in 1980 on faculty in private schools. The 1980 court decision concluded that since faculty are part of the management of the institution, the labor laws referring to the right to organize do not necessarily apply.

JUNIOR COLLEGES--The two-year system of college education or junior college, is of recent origin. The first two-year college in the United States was located at Joliet, Illinois (1901). The general intent of the junior college is to provide the first two years of a university education (general education) to students in their local communities. This provides an opportunity for individuals to attend a university or college at a lower cost and to provide time for testing so an individual could decide whether they wanted to continue on in their education.

The junior college movement expanded rapidly, and in 1983 consisted of 38.7 percent of higher education institutions. Some of the vocational and technical schools (see prior section) have also developed two-year college parallel programs and those students can transfer to a university, such as the Madison and Milwaukee, Wisconsin Area Technical Colleges.

RELATED EDUCATION PROGRAMS

Two related educational developments of significance are those of pre-school and continuing adult education.

PRE-SCHOOL EDUCATION--This component of the education network consists of nursery schools (see Chapter 22--Personal Social Service for discussion of nursery schools) and kinder-garten. In the United States the kindergarten movement began in 1856 at Watertown, Wisconsin, as a private school. The first public kindergarten was in St. Louis, Missouri (1873). Kinder-garten is usually for one year and on a part-time basis, with the goal to allow the child to make the transition from spending the majority of their time at home to spending the majority of their time in school.

CONTINUING ADULT EDUCATION--In the United States this component of the education network initially consisted of the following: lectures, lyceums (a series of lectures), traveling educational programs and courses. A historically popular approach to continuing adult education was the Chautauqua movement of 1874 in New York which consisted of summer courses and correspondence courses for adults. In addition to the Chautauqua home-based program, the movement developed a travel-ing educational system called the "Tent Chataugua" of 1903 to

1930, which was a traveling lyceum and lecture series. A further impetus for adult education was the Smith Lever Act (agricultural extension act) and the Smith Hughes Act (vocational training) of 1917. Continuing adult education is currently emphasized through: short courses, institutes, attendance in institutions of higher education, attendance in other post secondary programs and seminars. Seminars are sometimes offered for academic credit through vocational, technical, and higher education systems or for continuing education credit called CEUs. Continuing education credit is used by many employers for promotional and merit consideration in one's employment. Figure 8-2 shows a historical time line with important dates in the development of the education network.

STRUCTURE

The education network of the United States is essentially controlled locally (city, county, state) and is a collection of public and private institutions. The structure of the education network can be described from its organizational context, services provided, occupations and professions and dominant occupations and professions.

ORGANIZATIONAL CONTEXT

The education network in the United States consists of a sequential series of separate but interrelated educational experiences and levels generally based upon chronological age. Ideally, the entry level for education is nursery school at ages 3 and 4, and kindergarten, ages 4 through six, and the ideal ending level is post-doctoral study and continuing education for individuals for the remainder of one's life. An idealized sequential arrangement of educational experiences is shown in Figure 8-3.

Both public and private educational facilities provide educational experiences identified in Figure 8-3. As indicated in the historical section, education in the United States is controlled at the local level, with the federal government providing supplemental funding for special projects, research, facility construction, student grants, loans, etc. Faculty and school administrators are responsible for curriculum development and day-to-day operations, and a school board or board of trustees, legislature, etc., is responsible for the overall budget and development of policy direction.

Figure 8-2

Historical Time Line of the Education Network*

	Component of the Education Network		
Time Period	Primary and Secondary	Vocational and Technical	Higher Education
eece 1100-300 BC	Parents/private and religious schools/ gymnasium	Apprenticeship	Academy 387 BC and Lyceum 330 BC (advanced gymnasium)
ome 100 BC-450 AD	Parents/Ludus and grammaticus teachers	Apprenticeship	Schools of Rhetoric
dieval Europe 400-1500 AD	Parents/clergy Parish schools Cathedral/ Monastery school Guild school	Apprenticeship Guilds	University 1200 Trivium (grammar, rhetoric, logic) quadrivruim (arithmetic, geometry, astronomy, music)
naissance-formation 1500-1600	Parents/clergy Vernacular schools Gymnasium Latin secondary school	Apprenticeship Guilds	University—Classical Education
lonial 1600-ited States 1783	Parents/tutor Elementary education Academy	Apprenticeship Friendly society and Mutual societies	University—Classical Education
st Colonial 1783 ited States to the Present	Common school 1787 Academy school Elementary school Secondary school Nursery school 1837 Kindergarten 1854 Multipurpose 1920 education Desegregation 1954	Apprenticeship Private societies technical institutes Lyceums Technical schools Certificate programs Desegregation	Education for women Liberal Arts Education Professional schools (law, medicine, education, etc.) Morrill Act 1862 Junior College University—professional education etc. Continuing Education Desegregation

257

Figure 8-3

Idealized Model of the Organizational Context of the Education Network*

AGE LEVEL	PROGRAM	GRADE LEVEL
3	Nursery School	--
4-6	Kindergarten	--
6-12 or 14	Primary (Elementary) Education	1-6 or 8
12 or 14 to 17-18	Secondary Education[1]	6 or 8-12
18-20+	Associate Degree Community College	Freshman/Sophomore
18-26+	Bachelor's Degree (4 or 5 year degree)	Freshman through senior
26+	Master's Degree (1-3 year program)	Graduate 1 or 2 - 3
26+	Doctoral Degree (2-3 year program)	Graduate 2 or 3 - 6
26+	Post Doctoral Study and Research	Graduate 3 - 6+
26+	Continuing Education[2]	--

*Source: Adapted from United States Department of Health, Education and Welfare, Educa in the United States of America, Washington, D.C.: U.S. Government Prii Office, 1960 p. 5.

[1] Some schools organize the primary and secondary level on different patterns, example, some school districts have junior high (grades 7-8) then high school (g 9-12), others have high school as grades 9-12, and others have a combined junior senior high school, grades 7-12.

[2] The author added the concept of continuing education.

In primary and secondary education, the local school district or board is responsible for overall direction, and the state generally provides certification of programs and teachers. In vocational technical adult education, a local school district or board is responsible for overall direction with a state agency providing certification of programs and teachers. At the higher education level, a board of trustees, board of regents, or a board of directors for each institution is responsible for overall policy direction and budgets. In some states like Wisconsin and California, there is a statewide university and college education system under one administration. Figures 8-4, 8-5, and 8-6 show the governmental context of the education network at the federal, state and local levels.[8]

SERVICES PROVIDED

Depending upon the specific component of the education network and the level of educational experience, the following services may or may not be provided:

- Free lunches and hot meals

- Medical care

- Financial assistance (books and/or student support)

- Psychiatric and psychological testing and diagnosis

- Aptitude and career testing

- Individual guidance and counseling

- Library resources and services

- Day care

- Recreation activities

- Social activities

- Counseling

- Employment and career counseling

- Placement services

- General academic programs

Figure 8-4

Organizational Context of the Education Network Federal Level in 1983*

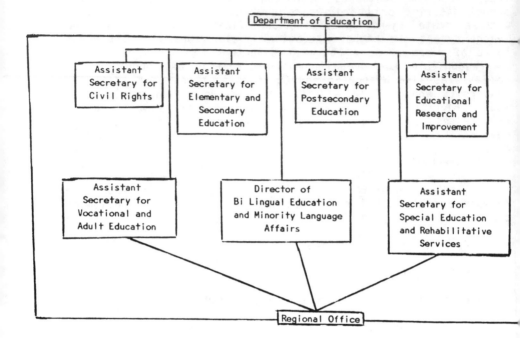

Source: Adapted from Office of Federal Register, <u>United States Government Manual</u> <u>1985-86</u>, Washington, D.C.: U.S. Government Printing Office, 1985, p. 840.

Figure 8-5

Organizational Context of the Education Network
State Level in 1985*

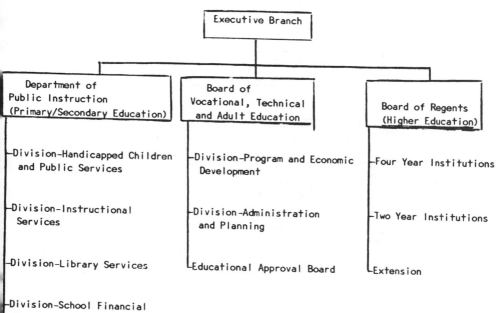

Source: Adapted from Wisconsin Legislative Reference Bureau, <u>Wisconsin Blue Book</u>
         <u>1985-86</u>, Madison Wisconsin: Department of Administration, 1985 p. 448, 471, 487.

FIGURE 8-6

ORGANIZATION of the PUBLIC EDUCATION
NETWORK at the LOCAL LEVEL (PRIMARY/
SECONDARY EDUCATION)*

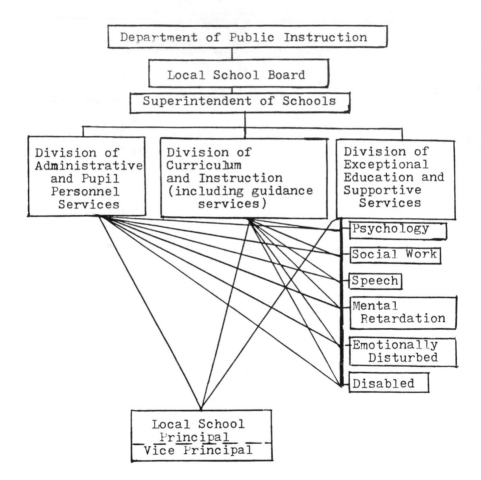

* Source: Adapted from organizational charts
Milwaukee Public Schools: 1986-87. Milwaukee,
Wisconsin: Milwaukee Public Schools, 1986.

Figure 8-6 Continued

ORGANIZATION of the PUBLIC EDUCATION
NETWORK at the LOCAL LEVEL (VOCATIONAL,
TECHNICAL, ADULT EDUCATION)*

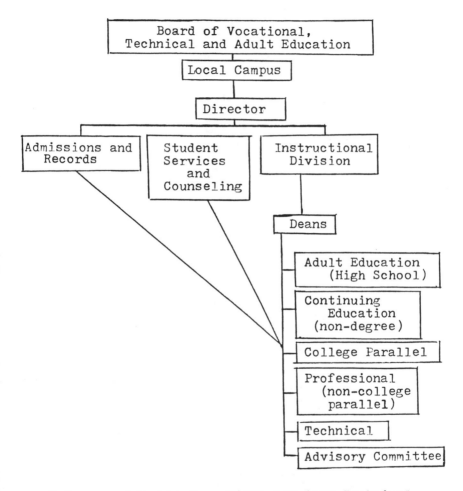

* Source: Adapted from Milwaukee Area Technical
College. Occupational Advisory Committee Handbook.
Milwaukee, Wisconsin: Milwaukee Area Technical
College, 1986.

FIGURE 8-6 CONTINUED

ORGANIZATION of the PUBLIC EDUCATION
NETWORK at the LOCAL LEVEL (HIGHER EDUCATION)*

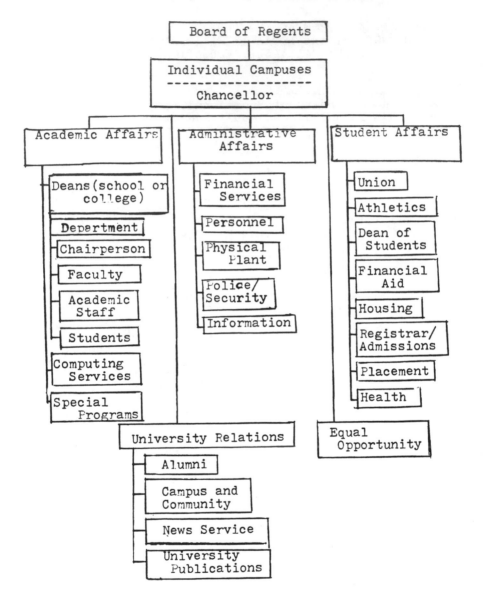

* Source: Adapted from organizational chart. University
of Wisconsin-Milwaukee: 1986-87 . Milwaukee, Wisconsin:
University of Wisconsin-Milwaukee, 1986.

- Special academic programs for women, disabled, minority groups, special education, adult and continuing education

- Legal advice and counseling (particularly in higher education)

- Veterans advice and counseling (particularly in higher education)

- Protective and security services.

OCCUPATIONS and PROFESSIONS

The education network employs a variety of human service professions, of which approximately 87.5 percent are teachers, administrators, counselors and teacher aides. Figure 8-7 shows a selected number of human service occupations and professions employed in the industrial classification of educational services (education network) in 1980. One will note the range of occupations employed in the education network, such as social work, child care, clergy, personnel and labor relations, therapists, medical records, etc.

DOMINANT OCCUPATIONS and PROFESSIONS

Although a variety of human service occupations and professions are employed in the education network, the major professional groups of the selected human service occupations are those of a teacher, 72.5 percent, education/vocational counselor, 2.6 percent, school administrator, 8.7 percent, and teacher aides, 3.5 percent. The teacher is the largest profession represented in the network, however, the education and vocational counselor, or guidance counselor, is included in this discussion since this group represents a social service component of the education network.

Figure 8-8 shows the employment of teachers and counselors by industrial classification in 1980. As expected, the vast majority of teachers, 92.41 percent and counselors, 76.1 percent are employed in educational services. The other major industrial classifications of employment for both groups is professional and related and public administration.

TEACHER--As indicated in the section on history, up until the 1800s, the teaching profession was dominated by clergy/ teachers, and standards for teachers were highly variable depending upon the level of teaching and the location. The clergy/teacher generally had some academic background based upon theological study or attended an institution of higher education. Some lay teachers attended an institution of higher

Figure 8-7

Number and Percent of Selected Human Service Occupations and Professions
Employed in the Industrial Classification of Educational Services
(Education Network) in 1980*

OCCUPATION and PROFESSION	NUMBER	PERCENT
Administrator-Education	477,218	8.746
Teacher[1] Post Secondary	614,254	11.257
Pre Kindergarten/Kindergarten	44,151	.808
Elementary/Secondary	3,134,907	57.453
Special Education	18,074	.331
Not Specified	146,340	2.682
Teacher Aide	192,917	3.536
Counselor-Education/Vocational[1]	146,798	2.691
Social Work[1]	21,352	.391
Welfare Aide	2,574	.047
Child Care	233,263	4.274
Clergy and Religious Workers	4,188	.076
Librarian/Archivist and Aides	171,055	3.134
Lawyer and legal Assistant	3,115	.057
Guards and Fire Fighter	59,792	1.095
Personnel and labor Relations	7,811	.143
Psychologist	22,652	.415
Other Social Science and Architect	5,572	.102
Authors, Musicians, Painters, Dance, etc.	13,840	.253
Therapist (Physical, Occupational, etc.)	34,265	.627
Registered Nurse	43,238	.792
Dietician	4,527	.082
Recreation	1,655	.030
Physician	11,055	.202
Health Aides (Nurse, Health, Dental)	21,284	.390
Medical Records	194	.003
Other Health	20,363	.383
TOTAL	5,456,464	100.000

*Source: Adapted from United States Department of Commerce, Bureau of the Census, 19
Census of Population, Volume 2 Subject Reports Part 7C: Occupation
Industry, Washington, D.C.: U.S. Government Printing Office, 1984,
295-664.

[1]These figures exclude the classification of library services.

Figure 8-8

Number and Percent of Teachers and Counselors (Education, Vocational Rehabilitation)
Employed by Industrial Classification in 1980*

USTRIAL CLASSIFICATION	TEACHERS		COUNSELORS	
	Number	Percent	Number	Percent
iculture/Fishing/Forestry	1,164	.03	76	.039
ing	452	.01	9	.005
struction	737	.02	104	.054
ufacturing	17,285	.40	932	.482
nsportation/Communication/				
blic Utilities	9,126	.21	295	.153
lesale/Retail Trade	17,072	.40	412	.213
ances/Real Estate	2,726	.06	811	.419
iness/Repair	5,188	.12	1,779	.920
tertainment/Recreation	52,158	1.22	285	.147
sonal Services	14,113	.33	336	.174
fessional and Related	182,734	4.27	22,918	11.846
cational Services[1]	3,958,673	92.41	147,131[1]	76.054
lic Administration	22,440	.52	18,368	9.494
TOTAL	4,284,868	100.00	193,456	100.000

urce: Adapted from United States Department of Commerce Bureau of the Census, 1980
Census of Population Volume 2 Subject Reports. Part 7C: Occupation by
Industry, Washington, D.C.: U.S. Government printing Office, 1984, pp. 295-664.

 occupation counselor consisted of education, vocational and rehabilitation
nselors. Those counselors listed under educational services are more than likely
ool and guidance counselors. The 22,918 counselors listed under professional and
ated are probably rehabilitation counselors and the 18,368 counselors listed under
lic administration are probably vocational or guidance counselors in the employment
work.

ese figures exclude the classification of library services.

education, and others completed a program in the academy, grammar school, or in some situations, only just a common school program. There was little consistency established for certification of teachers. Each school district, and sometimes a specific school, hired teachers and certified teachers. Generally, certification consisted of a local board or district which reviewed a person's education or learning, moral character and ability. Upon successful completion of this review, a certificate was then granted to teach in a specific school in a specific town.[9]

Primary and secondary level teacher education programs in the United States began with a movement called "normal schools" which were established at Lexington, Massachusetts (1839). By 1860 there were only twelve schools in the United States having teacher education programs. During the post-Civil War period, there was a development of normal chairs (a teaching professorship at the university level) at Indiana (1852), Wisconsin (1855) and Iowa (1873). The more common development in higher education was to have specialized schools for the teaching of teachers at a one or two-year teacher-training "normal schools." For example, a normal teachers' college was established in Platteville, Wisconsin (1863). Concurrent with training programs there was the development of professional organizations, such as the National Education Association (1857) which merged with the American Normal School Association and National Association of School Superintendents to form the National Education Association in 1870. Teachers also organized in their own behalf with the establishment of the American Federation of Teachers in 1916 and its various local chapters.

The "normal college" system in Wisconsin in 1863 initially granted a teacher's certificate at the completion of a one-year program. The required length of training to obtain a teacher's certificate in Wisconsin was expanded to two years in 1911, and by 1927 a four-year degree. At the completion of the required training program, an individual was then granted a certificate to teach. Since the required amount of training changed over time, it was possible to have teachers with different educational requirements teaching at the same time. For example, up until the late 1950s in Wisconsin, some individuals would have graduated from a two-year educational program, others from a three-year program, and others from a four-year program. The educational background of the teachers varied, since certification procedures applied to teachers as they entered the field. By the 1960s, those teachers who had less than a four-year degree were retiring and replaced by those having a four-year degree or even a master's degree.

Concurrent with lengthening the degree requirement for a teacher's certificate, there was a shift in who was responsible for certifying a person for teaching. Initially, pre-1861, the specific city, school or town certified one for teaching in a specific school in a specific town. In Wisconsin the county began certifying teachers in 1861, and by 1939 the state certified teachers. Other states followed a similar pattern as Wisconsin, with initially school or town certification procedures, then moving to county and state certification by 1945.

In addition to state certification procedures for teachers, the training schools for teachers changed from one and two-year normal schools to four-year university and college programs and in some cases Ph.D. granting programs. Professional schools of education became the norm for teacher education programs. At the college and university level, teacher training programs obtain accreditation of the professional teacher program by the National Council for Accreditation of Teacher Education (NCATE) which was established in 1919 as a subdivision of the Natinal Education Association. The accreditation of a professional education program in teaching is in addition to the usual accreditation of a college or university.[10]

Vocational technical education teacher programs paralleled the growth and changes in training programs for the primary and secondary level of education. The vocational technical education system has a similar process for the training and certification of teachers as the secondary and primary level.[11]

Higher Education programs have a different pattern for certification and employability than the procedures used at the primary and secondary level and vocational and technical level of education. Instead of certification through teacher education programs, most university or college faculty obtain certification by the nature of the degree and the area of specialization. The standard qualification for a teacher at the higher education level is a Ph.D. degree or equivalent in a specific or allied area in which the individual has a teaching, research or administrative assignment. A division exists in higher education with most major universities requiring a Ph.D. and many of the smaller universities or colleges desiring Ph.Ds but because of the lack of Ph.D.'s in specialty areas, would hire individuals with a master's degree. Many academic and professional disciplines require that the specialty area be approved or recognized by an appropriate professional organization.[12]

The tasks of a teacher, regardless of level, are generally the following:

- Develop curriculum

- Prepare lecture notes

- Prepare study plans

- Prepare examinations

- Evaluate student performance

- Evaluate student social adjustment

- Enhance learning of the student

- Advise and counsel student

- Participate in faculty committees and other faculty governing bodies

- Develop policies

- Review curriculum

- Participate in the community through talks, lectures, public relations, etc.

In institutions of higher education, other tasks include:

- Research

- Writing

- Publication

- Seeking financial grants

- Consultation

- Staff development by organizing specialized institutes and other forms of continuing education.

University professors, like their counterpart, elementary and secondary teachers established professional organizations, such as the American Association of University Professors (1917) and National Association of Professors (1967) which has been renamed the National Education Association - Higher Education Council (1974).

GUIDANCE COUNSELOR--Since many teachers develop a close relationship with the student, they often shift from a teaching function into that of a counseling function. In recognition of this added expectation of a teacher, the education network has developed a subspecialty in teaching known variously as a guidance counselor, vocational counselor, educational counselor or school counselor. In reviewing Figure 8-7, it should be noted that 2.6 percent of the selected human service personnel employed in the education network are vocational, educational or school counselors.

Guidance counseling as a subspecialty in education is an outgrowth of the vocational counseling movement which was established in 1908 in Boston, Massachusetts. Secondary schools, recognizing the need for career and guidance counseling for their students, developed a vocational guidance specialty in 1915. Later, post 1945, it was recognized that vocational counselors continually became involved in the social and emotional problems of the students, consequently there was a broadening of the vocational counselor's role to that of guidance and counseling. With this shift in role functioning from a vocational counselor to a guidance counselor, some schools initially would use a teacher with no particular train- ing as a guidance counselor or school counselor, but other schools would utilize a teacher who had developed some expertise and credentials in the area.

A major piece of legislation which encouraged the develop- ment of specific training in guidance and counseling was the National Defense Act of 1958 which provided federal funding for the upgrading of guidance programs. The preferred educational standard recommended by the American Association for Counseling and Development for guidance counselors is a bachelor's degree in education and a master's degree in guidance and counseling. Like their professional counterpart, the teacher, guidance and counseling programs obtain professional accreditation through the Association for Counselor Education and Supervision which is a subdivision of the American Personnel and Guidance Associa- tion, which was established in 1952 and has been renamed the American Association for Counseling and Development (1984). In addition to professional accreditation, an individual is usually certified by the State Board of Education.[13]

The guidance counselor. regardless of the school, usually is engaged in the following tasks:

- Provides educational counseling

- Provides individual counseling

- Checks course, program and graduation requirements

271

- Confers with parents

- Contacts parents of students in difficult situations

- Supervises tests

- Followup on students

- Referral to social service agencies, including referral to
  the school social worker.

The primary functions of both the teacher and the guidance counselor relate more to the educational process and needs of the student rather than the students' specific social and emotional development. There is some potential overlapping between the interests of teachers, guidance counselors and school social workers as they relate to students and their specific problems.

SOCIAL WORK

Figure 8-7 shows approximately 21,352 social workers and 2,574 welfare aides employed in the education network in 1980. The social workers employed in the education network were primarily at the primary and secondary level of education. Of the social workers employed in the education network, 16,626 or 77.9 percent were employed at the primary and secondary level, 195 or 9.0 percent at the vocational technical education level, 2,747 or 12.9 percent at the higher education level, and the remaining 1,784 or 8.3 percent did not have the education level specified on the United States Census in 1980.

School social work developed early in the twentieth century with programs in Boston, Massachusetts and Hartford, Connecticut (1906) and New York City (1907). Initially, the school social worker was called the "visiting teacher," and a professional organization was developed in 1916 which eventually merged with the National Association of Social Workers in 1955.

In a survey of school social workers compiled by the National Association of Social Workers in 1974, it was found that all states employed school social workers, although only six states required or mandated their use[14]. Thirty-two of the states surveyed required certification as a school social worker, however, the requirements for certification varied, depending upon the state. For example, sixteen states required a master's degree in social work, six required any master's degree, eight required a bachelor's degree, and seven required either teaching experience or a teaching certificate. The 1974 survey further concluded that the school social worker used their working time as follows: 37.8 percent on casework activity, 7.5 percent on group activity and 1.8 percent on community activities. The remaining 52.9 percent of the time was spent on miscellaneous school tasks and activities.

The functions of a school social worker varies from school district to school district. In some cases, the school social worker has become a glorified truant and attendance officer, in other cases they have become treatment and facilitators in M teams (multiple education teams), and in other cases are involved in a team approach with psychologists, psychiatrists, and guidance counselors in preparing a specific program for a specific student. Regardless of the educational program, the generalized tasks of a school social worker are as follows:

INDIVIDUAL LEVEL

The school social worker, based upon a referral from teachers or from general observation of a particular student, would engage the student in individual counseling. In this situation, the attempt is to enhance the student's performance at school and to determine whether there are major difficulties at home which create a social or emotional problem which may need further counseling. In addition to the individual counseling of the student, the school social worker would normally contact the parents of a particular student, indicating what problems there were and ways in which these problems could be handled or managed.

GROUP LEVEL

In some situations the school social worker may gather together a number of individuals with a particular problem, or a particular interest, and develop either an information, activity or counseling group. The intent of the group is to use the group process and peer influence as a mechanism in order to increase the student's ability to cope with either the school situation or their external environment.

COMMUNITY LEVEL

The school social worker should be involved in public relations in the community, explaining the school's programs to the neighboring community, as well as coordinating activities and efforts for a specific school function. In this capacity as a community organizer, it is also possible for the school social worker to organize citizens in the neighborhood in regard to particular policies which may relate to a specific school, which eventually needs the approval of a broader school district or board.

As indicated earlier, about half of the time of the school social worker is related to school tasks such as inservice training, staff development, conferring with students, welfare tasks, etc. Although there is some relationship between the counseling role of the guidance counselor and the casework role of the school social worker, the school social worker should focus on the individual and their problems on a more indepth psychological level.[15] Figure 8-9 compares ideally the typical tasks of a guidance counselor with that of a school social worker.

PERSONAL SOCIAL SERVICES

The personal social services have many direct service programs and linkages with the education network. (See Chapter 22 - Personal Social Service). Some examples of the personal social services in the education network include the following:

PROTECTIVE SERVICES

Mandatory programs for referring suspected cases of child abuse, both physical and sexual. A latchkey program, such as Milwaukee, Wisconsin to provide care for children in one's home after school.

UTILITARIAN SERVICES

Examples would be day care programs which are sponsored by the local school, such as those offered in Minneapolis, Minnesota.

DEVELOPMENTAL and SOCIALIZATION SERVICES

Programs for individual counseling, group counseling, and a variety of recreation activities, such as municipal school district sponsored activities. Milwaukee, Wisconsin has a rather extensive recreational program.

REHABILITATIVE and THERAPEUTIC SERVICES

Specialized programs for alcohol and drug counseling. This type of service would also include student organizations which are involved in attempting to deal with the problems of abuse, such as Students Against Drunken Driving (SADD).

SPECIAL POPULATIONS

Since the education network has as two of its functions the transmission of culture and socialization of the individual,

Figure 8-9

Comparison Between a Guidance Counselor
and a School Social Worker*

Selected Attribute	Profession	
	Guidance Counselor	School Social Worker
Credentials	Education	Social Work
Main Roles	Conduct interviews with students	Casework service
	Plan and administer testing programs	Consultation with teachers and family members
	Career, school and employment guidance	Use other social service agencies
	Assist in planning curriculum and registration	In service education
	Consult with Teachers on problem individuals	Coordination of school and community services
	Assist faculty members	Planning needs for students

*Source: Adapted from Leslie Moser and Ruth Moser. Counseling and Guidance: An Exploration. Englewood Cliffs, New Jersey: Prentice Hall Inc. 1963, pp. 169-170 and 175-176, and Donald Mortenson and Alan Schmuller, Guidance in Today's Schools, 3rd ed. New York, NY: John Wiley and Sons Inc., 1976, pp. 15, 190-191.

there are a wide variety of programs for special populations in most schools. (See Chapter 25 - Special Populations, and Chapter 24 - Rehabilitation). Some examples of programs and organizations which have special populations and education as a major concern and have an impact on the education network include the following:

ASIAN

Asian American Bi Lingual Center, Berkeley, California; Asian American Communities for Education, San Francisco,

275

California and Asian American Resource Center, St. Paul, Minnesota.

BLACK

Afro American Cultural and Historical Society, Cleveland Ohio; Alabama Center for Higher Education, Birmingham, Alabama and Black Educators of Pontiac Michigan.

EUROPEAN ETHNIC

Lectures, displays and awareness days sponsored by groups, such as Irish American Heritage Center, Chicago, Illinois; German Society of Pennsylvania, Philadelphia, Pennsylvania; Comhaltas Ceoltoiri Erieinn, Lake Grove, New York and Goethe House, Milwaukee, Wisconsin.

NATIVE AMERICAN

American Indian Cultural and Resource Center, St. Paul, Minnesota; American Indian Bi Lingual Center, Albuquerque, New Mexico and Ahmium Education Incorporated, San Jacento, California.

SAME SEX PREFERENCE

Specialized curriculum content, awareness days and weeks, and informational displays as developed by the Lesbian Resource Center, Minneapolis, Minnesota and the Homosexual Information Center, Hollywood, California.

SPANISH SPEAKING

Mexican American Cultural Center, San Antonio, Texas and Oklahoma City, Oklahoma; Bilingual Educational Services Incorporated, South Pasadena, California.

WOMEN

Specialized curriculum content, awareness days and weeks, and informational displays sponsored by, such groups as Change for Women, San Francisco, California; Lollipop Power Inc., Chapel Hill, North Carolina and Feminist Resource for Equal Education, Framingham, Massachusetts.

ISSUES

The education network in the United States has a series of problems which can be categorized as: issues of discrimination and accessibility, focus of education, quality of the educational experience, accountability to the public and social work curriculum.

DISCRIMINATION and ACCESSIBILITY

Since the Brown vs. Board of Education Supreme Court decision (1954), the primary, secondary, vocational technical, and higher education systems, whether public or private, have been under court guidelines to insure accessibility of their educational programs to various minority groups and to develop relevant curricula for these particular groups. The Civil Rights Act (1964) has added further legal weight to have programs become relevant for minority groups, including women, and to assure equal accessibility to various aspects of the educational program. Numerous articles and books have been written on the process of desegregation (one aspect of discrimination and accessibility as an issue) discussing whether desegregation should be voluntary or mandatory, and whether busing is an adequate solution to the problem or not. The bottom line or root of the desegregation issue is the recognition and sanctioning of different cultures in the United States, and the fact that segregation by race or ethnicity is unconstitutional. The problem of accessibility of minority students to educational programs is an educational and ethical concern regardless of the level and system of education.

Issues of discrimination and accessibility have expanded beyond the concept of minority group status to other areas. For example, bilingual education is now a significant issue. In some areas of the United States there are a high percentage of students who speak a foreign language, such as Spanish, Vietnamese, French and Native American (Menominee in Wisconsin, Dakota Sioux, South Dakota, etc.). The issue is, should bilingual education programs be taught in those areas of the country where there are significant numbers of individuals who speak a different language. From 1964 to 1984 the federal government has encouraged bilingual education, but since 1984 there has been a decrease in the amount of funding available and a slow retreat from the concept of bilingual education.

A noneducational issue which could have a significant impact on the accessibility of individuals to educational programs is the current debate (1986) on whether to allow victims of AIDS (acquired immune deficiency syndrome) to attend school and to socially mix with other students. School boards in New York City, Chicago, San Francisco and others are struggling with this issue. Related to AIDS is the potential discrimination against teachers (and students) who are homosexual or have homosexual tendencies. The issue of homosexuality and teaching has always been a touchy one, but with the current debate about AIDS, the issue could become rather explosive.

FOCUS of EDUCATION

The utility of the broad base of liberal arts education is currently under attack since many individuals today feel that the education network, both primary and secondary and higher education levels, should be preparing the individual for some specific occupation or profession within the economic network. Therefore, there is a tension between the more traditional liberal arts curriculum and the vocational and professional-oriented curriculum of today. This debate is very similar to the debate and problems experienced in the 1850-1860 and 1930-1940 time periods. This conflict is resulting in a division amongst faculty, legislators, the public and students about the focus and objective of the education network.

At the primary and secondary level public and legislative concern is moving more toward teaching the basics (reading, writing, arithmetic) instead of stressing the socio-emotional aspect of the child's development. The university, which has been more concerned about liberal arts, is under increasing demands to have more vocational and professional education programs. Yet, at the same time higher education is to establish more rigorous general education requirements including competency examinations. Partly as a consequence of this tension, as well as, potential costs, enrollment at vocational technical schools is rapidly increasing since these schools meet a specific need of the general population for a technical or job oriented education.

QUALITY of the EDUCATIONAL EXPERIENCE

Reading scores at both the primary and secondary and at the higher education levels indicate that students in general have a lower reading level in 1986 than was the case in 1960. The same trend appears to be true regarding the comprehension of material that students have read. Consequently, there is a growing concern about the quality of the American educational experience and how well it is preparing students for the immediate future. At both levels of education national reports have been published in 1983 and 1985 from committees established by the President's Office recommending a number of changes in the education network.[16]

An issue related to the quality of the educational experience, especially at the primary and secondary level of education is that of student discipline. For many teachers in large metropolitan communities, such as New York City, Chicago, and

278

Los Angeles, the key problem at the later primary and secondary level is that of student discipline. If teachers have to be more concerned with student conduct and behavior, disarming students, then the quality of the educational experience will decrease.

ACCOUNTABILITY to the PUBLIC

During the decade of the 1970s a high degree of concern was expressed by legislatures, professional organizations and the general public about abuses of the tenure system regardless of the education component (primary and secondary, vocational and technical or higher education). The tenure system in the United States grants an individual a semipermanent position after a specified period of time of satisfactory performance, as defined by a specific system. The time period for a probationary employee is usually two to five years in the primary and secondary system, and seven years in the vocational and technical and higher education system.

The purpose of tenure is to protect and insure academic freedom of expression and speech guaranteed by the Bill of Rights, Article 1, of the United States Constitution. To encourage freedom of speech and to protect the individual, the granting of tenure reduces the risk of losing one's position and reduces the risk of reprisal and avoids constant jobhunting as a consequence of one's unpopular, or at times ideological, viewpoints. The popular misconception is that once a person obtains tenure, they no longer remain productive. This is clearly not the case for the vast majority of teachers. In any event, as a consequence of potential, and at times real abuses of the tenure system, legislators are seeking to find ways to minimize the impact of granting tenure to an individual.

A side, but related issue to that of tenure is the movement toward collective bargaining for teachers and the unionization of teachers. The vast majority of teachers are government employees and strikes or walk-offs are banned. Yet, every year there are more strikes and walk-offs as teachers attempt to organize in their own behalf. Teachers have strong organizations in the primary and secondary and vocational and technical systems. The movement toward unionization in the higher education system varies from state to state and type of institution.

An issue related to accountability is the definition of the "public." There is a high degree of concern about the teaching of "secular humanism" in social science classes. Some school districts are censoring reading lists and textbooks which are not espousing traditional values. There are two court cases in 1986 in the states of Tennessee and Alabama by groups "public" which are challenging the concept of "secular humanism," "humanism" and are seeking ways to have textbooks espouse more traditional Christian values.

SOCIAL WORK CURRICULUM

Social work education in its training of social workers should stress the relationship of school social work to the education network, with the curriculum providing specialized content about the education network. In addition to specialized content regarding the education network, individuals who are interested in the area of school social work should in addition have field work or an internship program under adequate supervision in a school system.

SUMMARY

The education network in the United States is an extremely diverse network which includes public and private primary and secondary education, vocational and technical education, and higher education (college and university). Each of these components of the education network has its own autonomy, and sometimes the relationship between these systems is not clearly visible. The education network in 1982 consisted of approximately 116,000 schools, and in 1985 had an estimated enrollment of 78 million students. Estimated expenditures in 1984 were 235.9 billion dollars and in 1983 employed over 9.6 million individuals. These figures do not include an estimated 5.9 children in preschool programs and 21.2 million individuals involved in adult continuing education programs.

A history of the development of the three main components of the education network, primary and secondary, vocational and technical, and higher education, was presented in order to show the differences in philosophy, historical perspective, and certification procedures of teachers in each of the components of the education network. Teaching is the predominant occupation within the education network, with about 72.4 percent of selected human service employees in the education network, and employs a variety of other human service professions, such as social work, psychiatry, psychology, nursing, etc. The role of the teacher and the guidance counselor was discussed and compared to the role of the school social worker. Some issues relating to the education network were discussed, such as desegregation and discrimination, accessibility, the focus of education, quality of the educational experience for the student, accountability of teachers to the legislature and the public and social work curriculum.

*This chapter was reviewed for comments by Richard Cummings, Professor, Department of Cultural Foundations, School of Education, University of Wisconsin-Milwaukee, Milwaukee, WI.

1. Estimates on the size of the education network are adapted from the United States Department of Commerce, Bureau of the Census, Statistical Abstract of the United States: 1986 (106th Edition), Washington, D.C.: U.S. Government Printing Office, 1985, pp. 127, 128, 130, 154, 158, 161; United States Department of Commerce, Bureau of the Census, Statistical Abstract of the United States 1984 (104th Ed.), Washington, D.C.: U.S. Government Printing Office, 1983, p. 161; United States Department of Commerce, Bureau of the Census, 1982 Census of Government, Volume 4, Finances of Public School Districts. Washington, D.C.: U.S. Government Printing Office, 1984, pp. 2-9; United States Department of Commerce, Bureau of the Census, 1980 Census of Population. Volume 2 Subject Reports, Part 7C: Occupation by Industry, Washington, D.C.: U.S. Government Printing Office, 1984. pp. 295-664; and Public Employment in 1984, Washington, D.C.: U.S. Government Printing Office, 1985, p. 3.

2. For a more detailed description of the Medieval guild, see Chapter 5, Economic Network, and Chapter 21, Mutual Support Network.

3. The source for the Northwest Ordinance Act of 1787 is Henry Good and James Feller, A History of American Education, 3rd edition, New York, NY: Macmillan and Company, 1973.

4. Generally, when one thinks of primary, secondary, and post-secondary education, one has in mind a sequential arrangement of educational experiences. In colonial days, although a primary or common school existed along with the latin grammar and academy schools, there was no concept of a sequential educational experience. A person could be admitted into a university without having attended a common school, latin grammar school, or academy school. Individuals may have gained the prerequisite knowledge through an individual tutor or some other system. The latin grammar and academy schools did not depend upon a person attending a primary school first, but having knowledge of material which had been taught in the primary schools.

5. For a more detailed discussion, see Thomas Norton. Constitution of the United States, New York, NY: Committee for Constitutional Government, 1956, p. 280.

6. The Economic Opportunity Act of 1964 established a number of programs which directly impacted on the education network at all levels. Some examples of these programs include the following: primary and secondary system--Project Headstart, Project Upward Bound, day care centers, migrant worker programs and work study programs; higher education system, work study programs; vocational technical system, work training and work study programs.

   The Concentrated Employment Act of 1974 allowed for employment of individuals as teachers and other forms of temporary limited-term employment in the education network. All three components of the education network have used CETA employees.

7. The discussion in this section and succeeding sections focuses on public education. Private education, such as church schools (Catholic, Lutheran, etc.) and private universities, have equally been subject to the guidelines of federal legislation particularly if they are recipients of federal monies.

8. Like other networks, there is an informal folk system of providing an education. Some of these are rather informal, such as home education, and others more structured, such as the Amish religious group or the White Citizens Movement. Some states, like Wisconsin, have specific legislation which exempts some groups from the compulsory attendance laws.

9. This brief review of the history of teacher certification programs is adapted from Wisconsin Educational Association, A Handbook for Wisconsin Teachers, Madison, Wisconsin George Banta Publishing Company, 1954, p. 21-22. Moral character in 1872, for example, referred to non-drinking, nonsmoking and limited courting. Example of a rule for teachers was: "A male teacher who was single could go courting one night a week unless he was a good church member, then he could go courting twice a week." (Rules for Teachers, 1872).

10. Examples of professional organizations focusing on primary and secondary education include the following: National Education Association, 1201 16th Street, N.W., Washington, D.C., 20036; American Federation of Teachers, 11 Du Pont Circle, Washington, D.C., 20036; National Career Information Center, Two Skyline Place, Suite 400, 5203 Leesburg Pike, Falls Church, VA, 22041; Council for American Private Education, 1625 Eye Street, N.W., Washington, D.C., 20006; and the National Catholic Education Association, Washington, D.C. Accreditation for teacher education programs is through the National Council for Accreditation of Teacher

Education (NCATE), 1919 Pennsylvania Avenue, N.W., Washington, D.C., 20006. Accreditation for secondary school programs is through the Regional Accrediting Body and the local state Department of Instruction. There are six Regional Accrediting Bodies; North Central Association of Colleges and Schools, New England Association of Schools and Colleges, Northwest Association of Schools and Colleges, Middle States Association of Schools and Colleges, Western Association of Schools and Colleges and the Southern Association of Schools and Colleges. Certification of teachers at both the primary and secondary levels is through the local state Department of Instruction.

11. Examples of professional organizations focusing on vocational and technical education include the following: American Technical Education Association, North Dakota State School of Science, Wahpeton, North Dakota, 58075; National Association of Industrial and Technical Teacher Education, Department of Practical Arts and Vocational Technical Education, University of Missouri, Columbia, Missouri, 65211 and American Vocational Association, 2220 North 14th Street, Arlington, VA 22201. Accreditation of vocational and technical programs including post-secondary programs, whether associate degree or general education, is through one of the six regional accrediting bodies (see Footnote 10) and the local state board of vocational, technical and adult education. Teachers in the vocational, technical and adult system are certified by a local state department of instruction unless it involves post-secondary programs (see Footnote 12). In addition to accreditation of a general program, there is further accreditation of a specific occupational or professional program, such as licensed practical nurse, nursing, occupational therapist etc., by their respective professional accrediting bodies.

12. Some examples of organizations focusing on higher education include the following: American Association of University Professors (AAUP), One Du Pont Circle, Washington, D.C., 20036; American Association of State Colleges and Universities (same address as AAUP); Council on Post-Secondary Education (same address as AAUP); American Association of Community and Junior Colleges National Center for Higher Education, One Dupont Circle #410, Washington, D.C., 20036 and National Association of Independent Colleges and Universities, 1717 Massachusetts Ave., NW, Suite 503, Washington, D.C. 20036. Some junior colleges, including vocational and technical schools, offer associate degree programs in human services, and some four-year programs offer degrees in human services. Two organizations which reflect these programs include the

National Organization of Human Services, P.O. Box 999, Loretta Station, Denver, CO 80236 and the National Association of Human Service Technology, 1127 11th Street, Main Floor, Sacramento, CA 95814.

General accreditation of higher education programs, two year or four year, is through one of the six regional accrediting bodies. (See Footnote 10.) In addition, there are specific accreditation requirements for professional programs through specialized accrediting bodies, such as education, social work, etc. Certification of teachers at the higher education level is through the attainment of an advanced degree in a specialized area. Most four-year programs prefer, if not require, a Ph.D. in a subject area, and most two-year programs prefer, if not require, an advanced degree, master's or Ph.D., in a specific subject area.

13. A professional organization focusing on guidance and counseling is the American Association for Counseling and Development, 5999 Stevenson Avenue, Alexandria, Virginia 22340 (formerly the American Personnel and Guidance Association) and its subdivision, the American School Counselor Association. The American Association for Counseling and Development has twelve subdivisions which include the following: American College Personnel Association; Association for Counselor Education and Supervision; National Vocational Guidance Association; American School Counselor Association; American Rehabilitation Counseling Association; Association for Measurement and Evaluation in Counseling and Development; National Employment Counseling Association; Association for Non-White Concerns in Personnel and Guidance; Association for Religious and Value Issues in Counseling; Association for Specialists in Group Work; Public Offender Counselor Association and American Mental Health Counselors Association.

Guidance and counseling programs are accredited by the Association for Counselor Education and Supervision. In addition to accreditation of guidance and counseling programs, an individual is usually certified as a school or guidance counselor, by the local state Department of Instruction in the primary and secondary system. In the higher education system, one becomes certified through the attainment of an advanced degree which is usually a master's degree or above.

14. National Association of Social Workers, A Survey of Social Workers in the Schools, Washington, D.C., National Association of Social Workers, 1976.

15. The professional organizations focusing on social work include the National Association of Social Workers, 7981 Eastern Avenue, Silver Spring, MD 20918, and the Council on Social Work Education, 1744 "R" Street, N.W., Suite 400, Washington, D.C. 20009. Programs in social work at both the bachelor's and master's level are accredited by the Council on Social Work Education. Certification of the school social worker is through the local state Department of Instruction after completion of a designated sequence of courses in education and social work.

16. An example of program accountability are the recent figures produced by the Department of Commerce, Bureau of the Census. It is estimated that 13 percent of adults in the United States were illiterate, which was defined as a reading level of 5th grade. Of those involved in the sample of 3,400 individuals, 34.3 percent had 6-8 years of schooling, 18.6 percent had some high school education, 6 percent had finished high school and 8 percent had some college education. Milwaukee Journal, April 21, 1986.

SUGGESTED READINGS

David Fellman. The Supreme Court and Education, 3rd ed. New York, NY: Teachers College Press, 1976. Many individuals are not aware of it, but there are many legal issues involved in the education network. This book provides an excellent overview of these issues and interprets case decisions.

Walter Friedlander and Robert Apte. Introduction to Social Welfare, 5th ed. Englewood Cliffs, NJ: Prentice Hall, 1980. Although this book focuses on a variety of fields of practice for social work, the chapter on "School Social Work" provides an adequate background for the individual seeking a basic source material in the area.

S.E. Frost and Kenneth Bailey. Historical and Philosophical Foundations of Western Education, 2nd ed. Columbus, OH: Merrill Publishing Co., 1973. This book provides an excellent historical perspective on the development of education and is a good reference source.

Donald Mortensen and Alan Schmuller. Guidance in Today's Schools, 3rd ed. New York, NY: John Wiley and Sons, Inc., 1976. This book provides a background on the development of guidance counseling, the functions of guidance counseling and describes some of the major issues of the field.

United States Department of Health, Education and Welfare, Education in the United States of America, Washington, DC: U.S. Government Printing Office, 1960. This handbook on education in the United States is dated, but succinctly and in nonsophisticated language provides an excellent history of education. For the individual seeking basic information, this book is highly recommended.

REFERENCES

Arbuckle, David. Counseling Philosophy, Theory and Practice. Boston, MA: Allan Bacon, Inc., 1969.

Coleman, James. Equality of Educational Opportunity. Washington, D.C.: U.S. Government Printing Office, 1966.

Cook, T. G. Education and the Professions. London, England: Methuen Company, Inc., 1973.

Cremim, Lawrence. The Transformation of a School. New York, NY: Knopf, Inc., 1961.

Crow, Lester and Alice Crow. An Introduction to Guidance: Basic Principles and Practices in Education. New York, NY: American Book Company, 1960.

Deighton, Lee, editor. The Encyclopedia of Education (10 volumes). New York, NY: Crowell Collier Educational Corp., 1971.

Dye, Thomas. Understanding Public Policy. 5th edition, Englewood Cliffs, NJ: Prentice Hall, Inc., 1984.

Edwards, Harry and Virginia Nordin. Higher Education and the Law. Cambridge, Massachusetts: Institute for Educational Management, Harvard University, 1979.

Eiden, Leo. Education in the United States: Statistical Highlights Through 1979-80. Washington, D.C.: National Center for Education Statistics, 1981.

Fellman, David. The Supreme Court and Education. 3rd edition, New York, NY: Teachers College Press, 1976.

Ferguson, Elizabeth. Social Work: An Introduction. 3rd edition, Philadelphia, PA: J. B. Lippincott Co., 1975.

French, William. America's Educational Tradition. Boston, MA: D. C. Heath and Company, 1964.

Friedlander, Walter and Robert Apte. Introduction to Social Welfare, 5th edition. Englewood Cliffs, NJ: Prentice Hall, Inc., 1980.

Frost, S. E. and Kenneth Bailey. Historical and Philosophical Foundations of Western Education, 2nd edition. Columbus, OH: Merrill Publishing Company, Inc., 1973.

Good, Henry and James Feller. A History of American Education, 3rd edition. New York, NY: Macmillan and Company, 1973.

Hummel, Dean and S. J. Bonham, Jr. Pupil Personnel Services in Schools: Organization and Coordination. Chicago, IL: Rand McNally Company, 1968.

Kay, Evelyn. Enrollment and Programs in Non-Collegiate Post-Secondary Programs, 1978. Washington, D.C., National Center for Educational Statistics, 1979.

Kazamies, Andres and Byron Massidas. Tradition and Change in Education: A Comparative Study. Englewood Cliffs, NJ: Prentice Hall, Inc., 1965.

Minahan, Anne (Ed.). Encyclopedia of Social Work, 18th Issue. Washington, D.C.: National Association of Social Workers, 1986.

Mortenson, Donald and Alan Schmuller. Guidance in Today's Schools. 3rd edition, New York, NY: John Wiley & Sons, Inc., 1976.

National Association of School Counselors. Counselor Certification Requirements. Washington, D.C., National Association of School Counselors, 1977.

National Association of Social Workers. Social Workers in the Schools. Washington, D.C., National Association of Social Workers, 1976.

Norton, Thomas. The Constitution of the United States. New York, NY: Committee for Constitutional Government, Inc., 1956.

Office of the Federal Register, United States Government Manual, 1985-86. Washington, D.C.: U.S. Government Printing Office, 1985.

Pedley, F. H. Education of Social Workers. London, England:
    Pergamon Press, 1967.

United States Department of Commerce, Bureau of the Census,
    1980 Census of Population Volume 2 Subject Reports, Part
    7C: Occupation by Industry, Washington, D.C.:   U.S.
    Government Printing Office, 1984.

United States Department of Commerce, Bureau of the Census, 1982
    Census of Government, Volume 4 Number 1, Finances of Public
    School   Districts, Washington,   D.C.:   U.S.   Government
    Printing Office, 1984.

United States Department of Commerce, Bureau of the Census,
    Statistical Abstract of the United States, 1986 (106th
    Edition), Washington, D.C.:   U.S.   Government   Printing
    Office, 1985.

United States Department of Commerce, Bureau of the Census,
    Statistical Abstract of the United States: 1984 (104th
    Ed.), Washington, D.C.:   U.S. Government Printing Office,
    1983.

United States Department of Commerce, Bureau of the Census,
    Public Employment in 1984, Washington,   D.C.:   U.S.
    Government Printing Office, 1985.

United States Department of Health, Education and Welfare.
    Education in the United States of America, Washington,
    D.C.: U.S. Government Printing Office, 1960.

Van Doren, Mark. Liberal Education, 2nd edition. Boston, MA:
    Beacon Press, 1959.

Wilcox, Claire. Towards Social Welfare. Homewood, IL: Richard
    D. Irwin, Inc., 1969.

Williamson, John. Strategies Against Poverty in America. New
    York, NY: John Wiley & Sons, Inc., 1975.

Wisconsin Legislative Reference Bureau, Wisconsin Blue Book,
    1985-86. Madison, WI: Department of Administration, 1985.

Woellner, Elizabeth. Requirements for Certification for
    Elementary Schools, Secondary Schools, Junior Colleges, 46th
    edition, 1981-82. Chicago, IL: University of Chicago Press,
    1981.

CHAPTER 9

ENVIRONMENT PROTECTION NETWORK*

"In the past few years the space program has dramatically illustrated to men how finite and precious the earth's life-support system is. It has helped men to see how vital it is that resources be conserved and recycled. The challenge is survival . . . on the personal level, this handbook seeks to demonstrate that there is an alternative to the consumptive rat race. In rational, palatable steps you, the consumer, can modify your lifestyle to bring it more into balance with your ecosystem. Here, too, the benefits to the individual go beyond self preservation." (Swatek:1970:20)

INTRODUCTION

Since the late 1960's there has been a growing concern over the relationship of the use of world and national resources to the supply of world and national resources. Terms, such as ecology, eco-system, conservation, consumer ecology are now common place. This concern over one's environment has been slowly growing since 1960, but has been heightened by events in other parts of the world, such as the oil crisis in Iran (1974, 1978, 1980) and the famine in Ethiopia (1986.) Our modern technology has led people to assume that resources would always be there, yet many of our resources are finite in amount.

The environment and its resources can be divided into two broad categories: natural resources and human resources. Natural resources include energy resources and land, water and air resources. Major problems in this area include limited supply and use of resources and pollution. Energy and its use is a growing national and world problem. Energy and its use for heating homes, businesses and factories is a survival issue. The use of oil and its refined products like gasoline and diesel fuel used for transportation is no more a luxury item, but a survival problem. Human resources are the people. Major problems in this area are overpopulation and wise consumer use of resources.

This chapter provides an overview of the environment protection network (both natural and human resources) with an emphasis on problem areas instead of the total network. The potential and emerging roles of social work in the natural resource component are explored and the more traditional roles of home economics and social work in the population component, such as family planning and consumerism are described.

SIZE

As defined in this chapter the environment protection network includes natural resources (energy, air, land and water) and human resources (family planning and consumerism). The focus of the description of this network relates to estimates of its size in terms of problem areas, such as resource use, pollution, overpopulation and consumerism. The United States, in 1983, had 4.2 percent of the worlds population, used 25.5 percent of the energy resources and produced 21.7 percent of the world's energy resources. In essence, the United States used five times the energy resources in proportion to its population. In other words, 4.2 percent of the world's population used 25.5 of the energy resources and 95.8 percent of the world's population used 74.5 percent of the energy resources. Figure 9-1 shows some estimates on the size of the environment protection network.[1]

NATURAL RESOURCES

ENERGY - The major issues surrounding energy resources are; is there a sufficient supply and how are we using it. In 1982 the amount of expenditures for energy use (excluding transportation) was estimated at 246.4 billion dollars. The number of people employed by energy establishments was estimated at 410,000+, and the number of establishments specializing in the supply of energy resources was estimated at 600+.

TRANSPORTATION - One of the larger uses of energy in the United States is our transportation system which relies on oil. In 1982, of the 419.6 billion dollars expended for energy use, 173.2 billion dollars or 37.6 percent was spent on transportation. Of the 173.2 billion dollars spent on transportation, 129.9 billion dollars or 75 percent was spent on gasoline. In effect, 30.9 percent of energy expenditures was used for transporation using gasoline. Transportation and travel expenditures in 1984 were estimated at 713.3 billion dollars, of which 385 billion dollars or 53.9 percent was spent on the private automobile.[2] The number of employees in the transportation and travel industry was estimated at 7.9 million in 1984 with at least 346.5 thousand establishments in 1982.

Figure 9-1

ESTIMATED SIZE OF THE ENVIRONMENT PROTECTION NETWORK

IN 1976-1984

Selected Criteria	Environment Resource					
	NATURAL				HUMAN	
	Energy and Its Uses		Air, Land, Water - Use and Control			
	Resources	Transportation (Travel)	Use of Resource (Fed/State Parks)	Pollution Control of Resource	Family Planning	Consumerism
Number of Establishments	600+	346,452	100,000	18,554	4,660	17,000+
Expenditures (Billion)	246.4 Billion	713.3 Billion	$5.0 Billion	62.5 Billion	$25 Billion	$100 Billion
Number of Employees	410,000+	7,960,300	514,000	194,400	43,674	100,000+
Population Served	236.6 Million	236.6 Million	998 Million Visits	236.6 Million	5.1 Million	236.6 Million

Sources adapted from: United States Environmental Protection Agency, Resources and Pollution Control, Washington, D.C.: U.S. Government Printing Office, 1979; United States Department of Commerce, Bureau of the Census, Statistical Abstract of the United States: 1986 (106th Ed.), Washington, D.C.: U.S. Government Printing Office, 1985; United States Department of Commerce, Bureau of the Census, Public Employment in 1984, Washington, D.C.: U.S. Government Printing Office, 1985 and United States Department of Health, Education and Welfare, Health: The United States 1978, Washington, D.C.: U.S. Government Printing Office, 1978.

AIR, LAND, WATER USE - This component of the environment protection network had about 100,000 establishments, expenditures of about 5 billion dollars, and employed about 500,000 individuals in 1982. For the federal and state part systems, there were an estimated 998.0 million visits in 1984.

AIR, LAND, WATER POLLUTION CONTROL - This component of the natural resources component as distinct from resource use had expenditures estimated at 62.5 billion dollars in 1983. The number of establishments was estimated at 18.5 thousand with 194.4 thousand employees in 1982.

HUMAN RESOURCES

FAMILY PLANNING - The formal system of family planning consists of medical clinics, independent or attached to an agency. In 1976 there were an estimated 4,660 family planning clinics, with expenditures estimated at 25 billion dollars, employed an estimated 43,674 individuals, and served an estimated 5.1 million individuals. In 1982, it was estimated that 54,099,000 or 45.3 pecent of women between the ages of 15-44 years used some form of contraceptive. Of these 54,099,000 women, 35.4 percent were never married, 52.2 percent were married, and 12.4 percent were formerly married. It was further estimated that the rate of visits to family planning services in one year was 1,079 per 1,000 women aged 15-44. This rate of visitation means a percentage of women made multiple visits. The estimated number of legal abortions in 1982 was estimated at 1,573,900 or 28.8 abortions per 1,000 women and a ratio between abortions and live births of 426:1,000. The rate of abortions for white women was 24.3 per 1,000 and black women was 55.9 per 1,000 women.

CONSUMERISM - Estimates on the consumer system are at least 898 national and state organizations, and about 16,000+ other organizations which focus on consumerism. Expenditures for consumer oriented programs were estimated at 100 billion dollars and these organizations employed about 100,000 individuals.

HISTORICAL DEVELOPMENT

Concern with the environment, and the role of the individual in protecting the environment (ecology and ecosystems) is primarily the product of the 20th century, especially since 1930. There were other time periods when society has been concerned about the environment, however, few programs were developed which focused on the problem. History has some prime examples of the consequences of not paying attention to environmental issues, such as the deteriotion of the Central American Mayan empire (800 A.D.), the bubonic plague and other health problems of Western Europe (1300-1400), and the 1843-1848 Irish famine.[3]

NATURAL RESOURCES

The attitude of the American population toward the environment was one of exploitation until late in the 1800s, when some individuals and groups expressed concern over the exploitation of resources and developed the conservation movement (see Chapter 14 Leisure and Recreation). The general assumption was one of unlimited natural resources and plenty of opportunity and space for an expanding population. Figure 9-2 shows a historical time line of the development of programs related to protection of the environment.

ENERGY - For a large portion of historical time, populations used the resources around them on a self sufficient basis. In the United States forests were burned to clear the ground for farming, and there appeared to be an unlimited source of timber, coal, and water for energy purposes. In the United States land as a major resource was literally given away at a minimal cost to encourage settlement in various areas through legislation, such as land grants (1787), bounty lands for veterans (1814), Homestead Act (1862), and later giving lands to railroad companies to encourage the building of railroads i.e. Railroad Rights. Similar rights were given to mining companies for coal, iron etc. With the development of the oil industry, oil and gas rights were given to companies to encourage exploration and development.

The first major piece of federal legislation to focus on energy use occurred after the Iranian Imbargo of petroleum in 1973 and more recently after the 1979 Iranian embargo on petroleum. The Department of Energy was created in 1978 and a comprehensive energy bill passed in 1979. The political climate of the 1980's slowed the trend toward protection of energy resources. A symbol of this trend was the curtailing of the budget and functions of the Department of Energy, with the ultimate purpose of potentially disbanding this agency. The focus of current legislation is to encourage new sources of energy, such as solar, nuclear, geothermal, wind etc. and to encourage energy conservation to develop a self-reliant nation in the use of energy by the year 2000.

Figure 9-2

HISTORICAL TIME LINE OF THE ENVIRONMENT PROTECTION NETWORK

Time Period	NATURAL				HUMAN	
	Type of Resource					
	Energy	Transportation	Land, Air, Water		Family Planning	Consumerism
	Use		Use	Pollution		
1200	Self Sufficient Exploitation Wood, Water	Little Concern	Plazas	Exploitation	Little Concern Used Infanticide	Little Concern
1600	Self Sufficient Exploitation Wood, Water	Little Concern	Village Parks	Exploitation	Little Concern Used Infanticide	Little Concern
1800	Exploitation Coal, Steam, Gas/Oil	Little Concern	Conservation Movement 1855	Exploitation 1891 – Refuse Act	Malthus 1793 Drysdale 1854 Besant 1877	1862 Morrill Act Domestic Science
1900	Electricity Gas/Oil	Little Concern	State, City and National Parks	1902 Reclamation Act 1920 Water Power Act	Margaret Sanger 1916 Planned Parenthood 1921	1909 Home Ec. Association 1915 Dept. of Agriculture 1923 Bureau of Home Economics
Today	Nuclear/Gas/Oil/solar/Electricity Legislation on energy use 1973	1953 Highway Act 1963 Pollution Act 1978 Air Quality Act	Outdoor Recreation Resource Commission 1969 Environmental Policy	1963 Clean Air Act, 1965 Water and Solid Waste Act, 1969 Environmental Policy	1965 Legalized Birth Control 1973 and 1986 Court Decision Abortion Acts Modified	1961 Nutrition Research, 1965 Consumer Affairs Office

294

TRANSPORTATION - The primary mode of transportation in the United States consists of passenger vehicles, buses and airplanes, which accounts for 30.9 percent of energy use in the United States. Prior to the development of the gasoline engine, the primary mode of transportation was shipping (sailing ships either wood or coal burning), railroad (wood or coalburning), use of animals (horse, donkey), or walking.

When the gasoline engine was invented it was hailed as an asset to the enviroment since it would decrease the pollution of cities occuring as a consequence of the horse, coalburning stoves, railroads, ships, and factories. Early legislation for regulating the use of automobiles and airplanes was left up to the various local and state governments including commerical transportation which developed in the early 1920s. Until the 1960s the primary concern of transportation legislation was the development of roads and highways, such as the highway bill of 1953, and safety measures for commerical transportation. A shift to an energy and antipollution focus did not occur until 1963 when the pollution problems of some cities became apparent, such as Donara, Pennsylvania (1948-fatalities from respiratory illness) Los Angeles, California (1961-smog), and New York City (1963-smog). As a consequence of the growing recognition of pollution by cars, clean air acts were passed in 1963, 1967 and 1975 to control lead and carbondioxide pollution from automobiles.

Concurrent with the growing concern over pollution caused by the gasoline engine, legislation aimed at energy conservation, and a more efficient means of mass transportation was encouraged. A Department of Transportation was created at the federal level in 1978, and its functions include monitoring safety provisions, pollution control and a practical means to develop a mass transportation system for the larger cities.

AIR, LAND, WATER USE and POLLUTION CONTROL- Pollution of land, air and water resources continues at a steady rate through both chemical and waste pollutants. Since 1964, this problem of pollution has become almost epidemic especially as one recognizes the consequences of acid rain which is affecting large parts of the United States and Canada in 1986. The conservation movement focussing on land use and abuse rapidly incorporated pollution of these resources by chemical and waste pollutants as a major concern and a political issue.[4]

National attention was focused on the environment and ecology by 1964 when it was learned that Lake Erie was a dying lake because of pollution and that pollution could spread to the rest of the Great Lakes. Three other events focused attention on the environment: the Cuyahoga river in Pittsburg, Pennsylvania caught on fire in 1969; the Buffalo River in Buffalo, New York caught on fire three times and the 1980 incident in Love Canal, New York.

Early attempts to control air, water and land pollution were part of the overall conservation movement. Early federal legislation on pollution centered on timber and watersheds such as the 1891 Forest Reserve Act (to prevent erosion), the Refuse Act of 1899 which was the first legislation dealing with water pollution and in 1902 the Land Reclamation Act. Other legislation included the Federal Water Power Act, in 1920, a Soil Erosion Service was established in the Agriculture Department and by 1936 there were Flood Control Acts. Every state had established some form of conservation department by 1936. The largest overall push for antipollution standards developed in the 1960s, such as the 1963 Clean Air Act, 1964 Wilderness Act, 1965 Water Quality and Solid Waste Disposal Act, and in 1969 the National Environmental Policy Act. These antipollution policies are implemented through a maze of local, state and federal agencies. Within a 25 year period of time (1961-1986) the seriousness of the imbalance of the environment and pollution problem has been recognized by a larger number of people in the United States. The next ten years will see a growing concern in the Great Lakes states over use of the fresh water of the great lakes (including Canada) and potential political conflicts between the United States and Canada on the use of water from the Great Lakes and the problem of acid rain.

HUMAN RESOURCES

As with natural resources, little attention was paid to problems of human resources, such as family planning and consumerism, until the mid twentieth century. The general attitude was that people needed large families in order to economically survive. The growing children added significantly to the overall family income, or a large family was necessary since it was expected that a large percentage of children would die before reaching the age of maturity. The attitude on consumerism prior to 1960 was "let the buyer beware," or "caveat emptor".

FAMILY PLANNING - An early classical writer on population problems was Thomas Robert Malthus (1766-1834) and his classic "Essay on the Principal of Population" (1793) where he postulated that a population would double itself every generation, unless checked by preventative techniques i.e. moral restraint, war, famine and pestilence. Malthus saw overpopulation in comparison to resources as a major cause of poverty.[5] Although Malthus recognized the consequence of over population, his general response to birth control techniques was moral restraint.

Historically individuals had a variety of mechanisms which were used to control (if desired) the size of families, such as infanticide (killing newborn babies), abortion, moral restraint, late marriages, bear grease, lithosperm, and a variety of other greases, oils etc. The family planning movement had early advocates, such as Francis Place who published "Illustrations and Proofs of the Principal of Population," (1822), George Drysdale who published "Elements of Social Science" (1854), and Robert Owen in the United States who published "Moral Physiology" (1830). Initially, advocates of birth control were ignored or harassed and the movement remained in obscurity until the trial of Charles Bradlaugh and Annie Besant in 1877 in England. Birth control and family planning was viewed as a moral issue, and in many jurisdictions the selling, mailing, or advertising of contraceptives was illegal. In the United States the Comstock Bill of 1873 prohibited the mailing and advertising of obscene materials, including contraceptives.[6] The first birth control clinic in the world was established in Holland in 1878.

The family planning movement in the United States was largely the work of Margaret Sanger a visiting nurse. She established a clinic in Brooklyn, New York in 1916 that was promptly closed down and she was arrested. It was through her efforts that the National Birth Control Association was formed in 1921 which changed its name to Planned Parenthood in 1942. After initial opposition to the planned parenthood movement, states began to modify legislation to allow physicians to mail material in 1933, and by 1939 Planned Parenthood clinics could legally operate in the United States.

The decade of rapid increase in the planned parenthood movement in the United States was the 1960s when the Office of Economic Opportunity in 1964 encouraged family planning as one of the strategies to combat the problem of poverty, and the development of the birth control pill. In 1965, the Supreme Court in Griswald vs. Connecticut, legalized birth control methods as an individual right. In 1967 federal grants were made available to finance family planning clinics and in 1968 family planning was to be a service provided to AFDC populations. Abortion laws were modified and in most states were legalized under certain circumstances by 1973 which was reinforced by the Supreme Court decision of Roe v. Wade. In general, the Planned Parenthood movement has been primarily one of voluntary and private efforts with minimal involvement of the government. Currently there are over 4,000 family planning clinics, however, legal and moral issues involved in family

planning are still unsettled. The extent of these issues is
indicated by the interest taken in the 1984 presidential
election on this issue, and the fact the Reagan Administration
in 1985 is refusing to grant certain forms of aid to countries
which are pro abortion or to countries of a different ideological orientation, such as China. The issue of abortion has
created an emotional climate in the United States which has
resulted in attempted bombings and boycotts of abortion clinics
in 1986. The Supreme Court reviewed an abortion law from
Pennsylvania in 1986, which reaffirmed the 1973 decision.

CONSUMERISM - An organized consumer movement of rights,
protections and advocacy is a product of the 1960s, however,
consumer issues and the optimal use of resources has been a
standard concern of the home economics profession and its
various specialities since the development of home economics as
a profession (see section on Home Economics).

The importance of home economics as a field of practice is
indicated by the development of an Office of Home Economics in
the Department of Agriculture in 1915, which became the Bureau
of Home Economics in 1923.

By the 1930's, the United States entered the period of mass
produced clothes, quick foods and prepared foods. As more and
more people purchased their goods already made or partially
prepared, a shift toward consumerism, financial management, and
family relations was developing within the home economics
profession. By 1961 the Federal Government established the
institute on Nutrition and Consumer Use Research Bureau and in
1965 changed its title to the Consumer and Food Economic
Research Bureau. The consumer orientation and specializations
within the broad field of home economics is only one phase of
the consumer movement. Two other phases of the consumer movement which are independent but overlap with home economics are:
consumer rights and protection, and advocacy. Both of these
areas of consumerism are a product of the 1930s but gained
national significance in the 1960s. Under the influence of
Ralph Nader a Consumers Affairs Office was created in 1965 and
the Office of Economic Opportunity in 1964 developed a comprehensive consumer oriented program. During the 1960s, there was
the development of consumer organizations, such as the Alliance
for Consumer Protection in North Carolina, and the Concerned
Consumers League in Milwaukee, Wisconsin, among other organizations. Today, there are well over 2000 agencies specializing in
consumer issues.

STRUCTURE

Like other networks, the environment protection network can be described from its organizational context, services provided, occupations and professions, and dominant occupations and professions.

ORGANIZATIONAL CONTEXT

The environment protection network consists of a variety of federal, state, local and private agencies which provide a myriad of technical, consultative and social services. Consequently an organizational chart for each component of the network is shown in Figures 9-3 through 9-7.

NATURAL RESOURCES

ENERGY--Figure 9-3 shows a typical federal, state and local organizational context for energy concerns.

TRANSPORTATION--Figure 9-4 shows a typical federal, state and local organizational context for transportation problems.

AIR, LAND, WATER USE and POLLUTION CONTROL- Figure 9-5 shows a typical federal, state and local organizational context for air, water, and land resources and concerns over chemical and solid waste pollution problems.

HUMAN RESOURCES

FAMILY PLANNING--Figure 9-6 shows a typical federal, state and local organizational context for family planning.

CONSUMERISM--Figure 9-7 shows a typical federal, state and local organizational context for consumer problems.[7]

SERVICES PROVIDED

The service services provided in each component of the environment protection network varies, however there are some forms of social service provided in each component of the environment protection network.

Figure 9-3

IDEALIZED GOVERNMENT ORGANIZATION
FOR ENERGY USE*

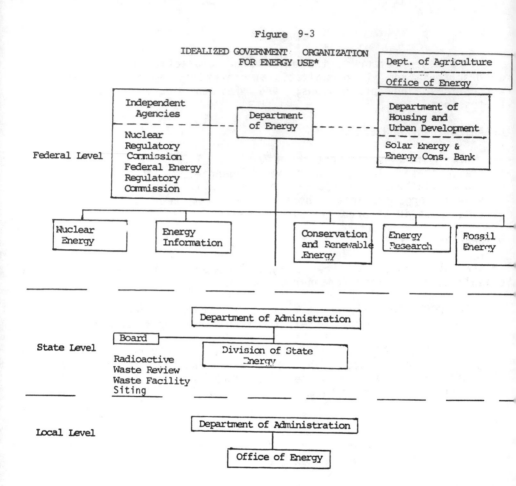

*Sources: Adapted from Office of the Federal Register, <u>United
State■ Government Manual 1985-86</u>, Washington, D.C.:
U.S. Government Printing Office, 1985, pp. 834,841,
843,863 and Wisconsin Legislative Reference Bureau,
<u>Wisconsin Blue Book 1985-86</u>, Madison, Wisconsin:
Department of Administration,1985,p. 553.

Figure 9-4

IDEALIZED GOVERNMENT ORGANIZATION
FOR TRANSPORTATION USE*

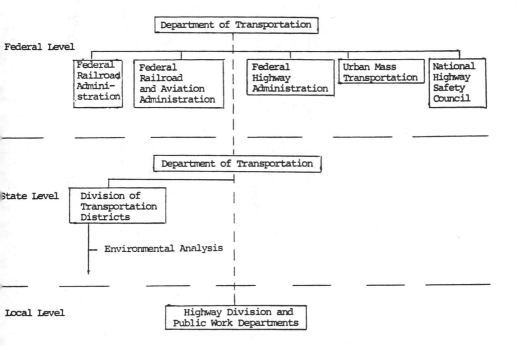

Source: Adapted from Office of the Federal Register, United States Government
          Manual 1985-86, Washington, D.C.: U.S. Government Printing Office,
          1985, p. 848, and Wisconsin Legislative Reference Bureau, Wisconsin
          Blue Book 1985-1986, Madison, Wisconsin: Department of Administration,
          1985, p. 501.

Figure 9-5

IDEALIZED GOVERNMENT ORGANIZATION FOR
AIR, LAND and WATER RESOURCES*

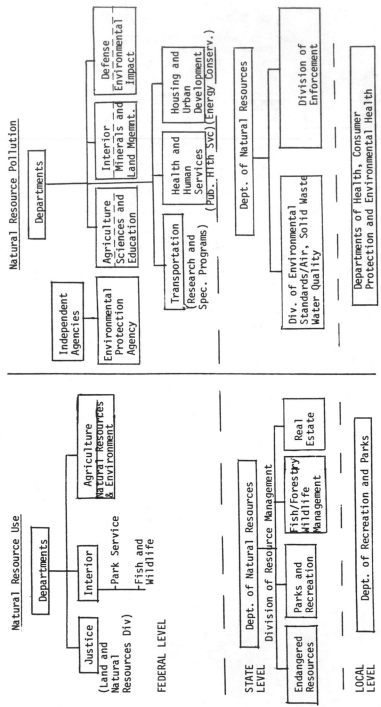

*Source: Adapted from Office of the Federal Register, United States Government Manual 1985-86, Washington, D.C.:
           U.S. Government Printing Office, 1985, pp. 834, 842, 843, 844, 845, 851, 836-839, 868; Wisconsin

Figure 9-6

IDEALIZED GOVERNMENT ORGANIZATION
FOR FAMILY PLANNING *

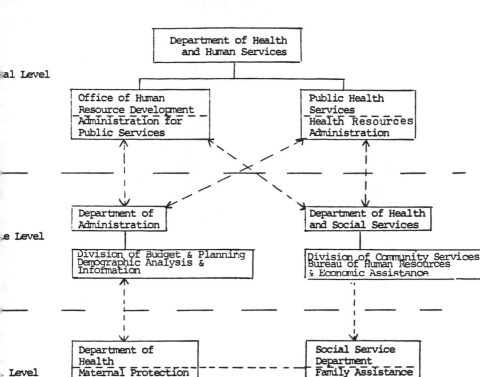

al Level

Department of Health
and Human Services

Office of Human
Resource Development
Administration for
Public Services

Public Health
Services
Health Resources
Administration

e Level

Department of
Administration

Division of Budget & Planning
Demographic Analysis &
Information

Department of Health
and Social Services

Division of Community Services
Bureau Of Human Resources
& Economic Assistance

Level

Department of
Health
Maternal Protection
and Information

Social Service
Department
Family Assistance
Programs

ources: Adapted from Office of the Federal Register, United States Government
Manual 1985-86, Washington, D.C.: U.S. Government Printing Office,
1985, p. 842; and Wisconsin Legislative Reference Bureau, Wisconsin
Blue Book, 1985-1986, Madison, Wisconsin Department of Administration,
1985, pp. 512, 553.

303

Figure 9-7

IDEALIZED GOVERNMENT ORGANIZATION
FOR CONSUMERISM*

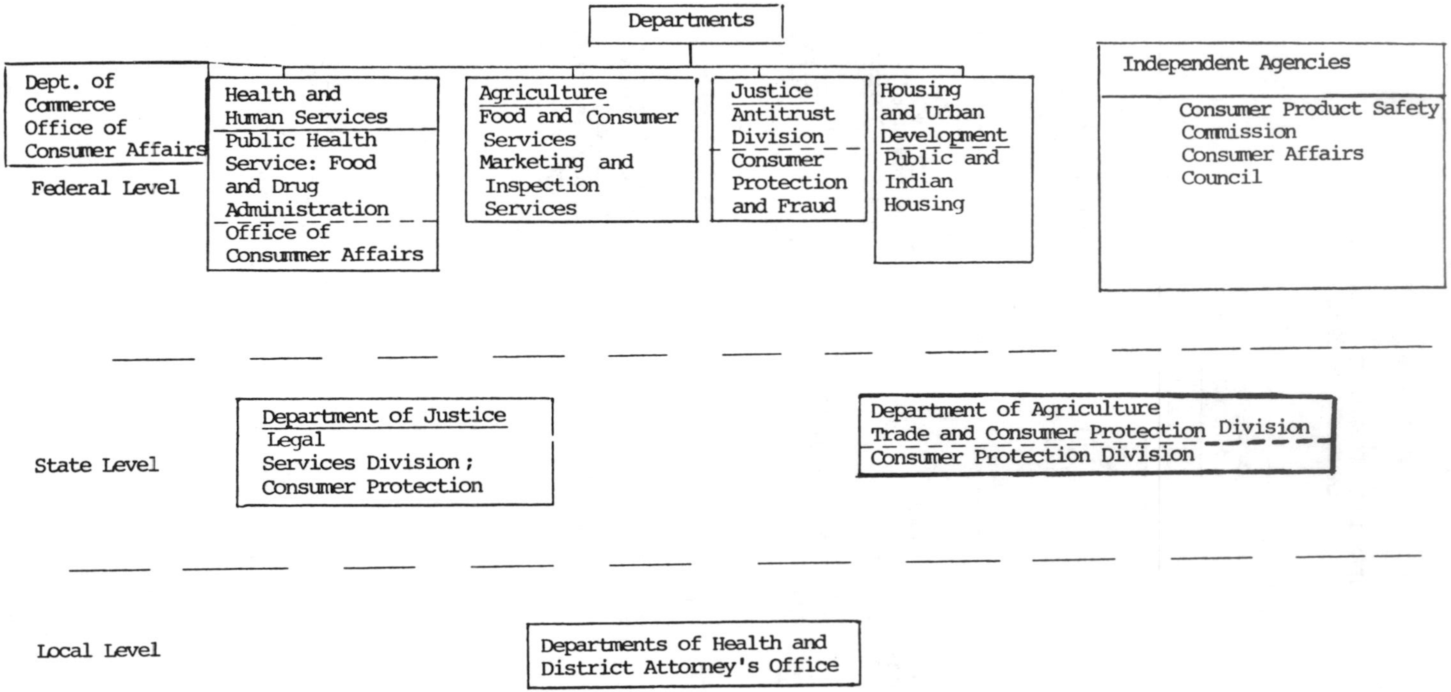

Independent Agencies

Consumer Product Safety
Commission
Consumer Affairs
Council

Departments

Federal Level

Dept. of
Commerce
Office of
Consumer Affairs

Health and
Human Services
Public Health
Service: Food
and Drug
Administration
Office of
Consumer Affairs

Agriculture
Food and Consumer
Services
Marketing and
Inspection
Services

Justice
Antitrust
Division
Consumer
Protection
and Fraud

Housing
and Urban
Development
Public and
Indian
Housing

State Level

Department of Justice
Legal
Services Division;
Consumer Protection

Department of Agriculture
Trade and Consumer Protection Division
Consumer Protection Division

Local Level

Departments of Health and
District Attorney's Office

*Sources: Adapted from Office of the Office of the Federal Register, United States Government Manual 1985-86, Washington, D.C.:
U.S. Government Printing Office, 1985, pp. 824, 825, 842, 843, 845; and Wisconsin Legislative

304

NATURAL RESOURCES

ENERGY - Some services provided include:

- Legal consultation
- Information retrieval
- Minimal health and safety standards
- Public education
- Financial aid for the poor.

TRANSPORTATION - Some services provided include:

- Personal safety
- Planning
- Information
- Public education.

AIR, LAND, WATER USE and POLLUTION CONTROL - Some services provided include:

- Planning
- Education
- Legal advice
- Counseling.

HUMAN RESOURCES

FAMILY PLANNING - Some services provided include:

- Medical histories
- Medical diagnosis
- Information
- Legal advice
- Education
- Abortion information, referral, and implementation
- Individual and group counseling.

CONSUMERISM - Some services provided include:

- Family financial management
- Consumer decision making
- Legal advice
- Education
- Advocacy
- Policy making
- Research and fact finding
- Organization of community groups.

OCCUPATIONS and PROFESSIONS

Of all of the components of the environment protection network, the two which have the most relevance for the human service professions are family planning and consumerism. Human service professions are minimally involved in the natural resource areas of energy, transportation, air, land and water use and pollution control. These areas primarily employ engineers, natural scientists, and related occupations. An exception to the use of natural science oriented professions are the varied sub-specialities of home economics. Figure 9-8 is a summary of selected human service occupations and professions employed in the industrial classifications of forestry, fishing/hunting, mining, pulp/paper production, drugs and agriculture chemicals, industrial and miscellaneous chemicals, petroleum refining, miscellaneous petroleum and coal, logging, sawmills, transportation, utilities and administration of environmental and housing programs. A larger variety of human service professions are employed in family planning and consumerism than in the natural resource area. The family planning component is dominated by nurses and physicians and the consumer movement has a significant number of home economists and lawyers. Figure 9-9 shows some estimates of selected human service professions in family planning and consumerism.

DOMINANT OCCUPATIONS and PROFESSIONS

Many of the programs in the environment protection network are relatively new (last 25 years) and are not specifically human services oriented. All of the components of the environment protection network have a potential or an active role for human service professions.

NATURAL RESOURCES

ENERGY--An example of a human service professions' interest in energy is the Spring/Winter 1979 issue of the Journal of Home Economics which discusses eco-systems and energy problems. The role of human service professions outside of research activity and public relations is unclear, however, there are lawyers, physicians, nurses, and social workers, etc., who play an active role in the energy area. Home economics as a profession has specialities in consumerism, and many of these individuals are employed in energy related agencies. The primary employees of the energy system are engineers, chemists, and allied natural sciences. The role of the physician and nurse would relate to health problems as it relates to the physical impact of utilizing particular energy resources.

Figure 9-8

Number and Percent of Selected Human Service Occupations
and Professions Employed in Industries Which Reflect the
Natural Resource Component of the Environment Protection Network in 1980*

Occupation	Number[1]	Percent
Teachers[2]	10,755	9.602
Social Work	1,669	1.489
Lawyer	10,576	9.442
Health, Technical Fields	10,400	9.284
Medical Records	50	.045
Therapist	205	.183
Dietician	273	.244
Physician	1,259	1.124
Physican Assistant	4,404	3.933
Nurse	3,217	2.872
Counselor	403	.359
Librarian	2,385	2.129
Psychologist	257	.229
Urban Planner	1,304	1.164
Clergy/Religious Work	190	.169
Recreation Work	1,813	1.618
Author, Musician, Painter, Actor, Dancer	2,854	2.548
Guards and Supervisors	52,345	46.729
Child Care	2,833	2.529
Miscellaneous Health	4,826	4.308
TOTAL	112,018	100.000

Source: Adapted from United States Department of Commerce, Bureau of the Census, 1980 Census of Population. Volume 2 Subject Reports. Part 7C: Occupation by Industry, Washington, D.C.: U.S. Government Printing Office, 1984, pp. 295-664.

1 Figures on the environment protection network include the following industrial classifications: forestry, fishing/hunting, mining, pulp/paper production, drugs and agriculture chemicals, industrial and miscellaneous chemicals, petroleum refining, miscellaneous petroleum and coal, logging, sawmills, transportation, utilities, and administration of environmental and housing programs.

2 On the census, home economics is listed as part of teachers non-specified.

Figure 9-9

SELECTED HUMAN SERVICE OCCUPATIONS
PROFESSIONS IN THE HUMAN RESOURCE COMPONENT
OF THE ENVIRONMENT PROTECTION NETWORK*

Family Planning		Consumerism
Physicians and Assistants	11,289	Home Economics
Nurse	10,750	Consumer Affairs
Health Education	950	Financial Specialist
Nutritionist	567	Social Work
Outreach Worker	2,959	Lawyers
Social Work	1,784	Psychology
Other	5,375	Personnel Manager
Total	43,674	Physician
		Librarian
		Education

*Source: Adapted from United States Department of Health, Education and Welfare, Health Resources Statistics:1976, Washington, D.C.: U Government Printing Office,1976 , United States Civil Service Commission, Occupations of Federal White Collar Workers, 1979, Washington, D.C.: U.S. Government Printing Office, 1981.

TRANSPORTATION--Employees in the transportation area are generally non-human service personnel, such as engineers or professions tangential to human services, such as architecture, planning, etc. Professional journals in home economics and social work, such as the Family Economic Review of 1979 and Social Work carry articles on transportation problems and the potential role of these professions.

AIR, LAND, WATER USE and POLLUTION CONTROL--Most employees in this area are natural scientists, conservationist, agricultural agents, forestry, and related fields. There are established roles for medical specialties, such as environmental medicine, legal problems, general education, planning, etc. The role for other professions like home economists and social work, would be research, planning and public relations.

HUMAN RESOURCES

FAMILY PLANNING--The dominance of the health professions in family planning is clearly indicated in Figure 9-9 where 50.5 percent of employees in clinics are almost equally split between physicians and nurses, 1.3 percent nutritionists (home economics), and 4.1 percent social workers. For social work there is an overlapping with the function of a medical social worker (see Chapter 23, Physical Health Network). Some home economists with a family life speciality are employed in some family planning agencies as counselors.

CONSUMERISM--Figure 9-9 shows a potential distribution of human service occupations and professions which are involved in the consumer movement.

HOME ECONOMICS as a PROFESSION--Figure 9-10 shows employment of dieticians and home economists by industrial classification in 1980. The industrial classifications which have the highest percentages of dieticians and home economists as employees are wholesale and retail trade, 22.832 percent, health, 18.881 percent education, 13.479 percent, and the remaining 44.808 percent in a variety of industrial classifications. As one reviews Figure 9-10, it is apparent that home economists are employed in a variety of industrial classifications and many if not most of these industrial classifications involve consumer related activities.

Specialty areas or divisions within home economics include; design, housing, nutrition and foods, clothing and textiles, child development and family relations, business and industry, financial management, consumerism and institutional management. It is the specialties of child development and family relations

Figure 9–10

Number and Percent of Home Economists including Dieticians Employed
in the United States by Industrial Classification in 1980*

Industrial Classification	Dietician	Number Other Home Economists & Related Areas	Total	Percent
Agriculture/Forestry/ Fishery	116	33,376[1]	33,492	5.794
Mining/Construction/ Manufacturing	756	51,453	52,203	9.029
Transportation/Communica- tion Utilities	74	16,104	16,178	2.798
Entertainment/Recreation	192	3,680	3,872	.670
Wholesale/Retail Trade	1,440	130,565	132,005	22.832
Personal Services	433	58,380	58,813	10.172
Finance/Insurance/Real Estate	128	8,260	8,388	1.451
Business and Repair	43	6,927	6,970	1.206
Health	51,127	58,035	109,162	18.881
Legal	--	--	--	
Education	4,532	73,394	77,926	13.479
Social Services	2,307	17,593	19,900	3.442
Other Professional/ Related	784	42,407	43,191	7.471
Public Administration	3,295	12,750	16,045	2.775
TOTAL	65,221	512,924	578,145	100.000

1   This figure represents the estimated number of individuals involved in
agricultural extension services.

*Source: Adapted from United States Department of Commerce, Bureau of the
Census, 1980 Census of Population. Volume 2 Subject Reports Part
7C: Occupation by Industry. Washington, D.C.: U.S. Government
Printing Office, 1984, pp. 295–664 and communication of 3/26/85 with
the home economics program at the University of Wisconsin–Stevens
Point, Stevens Point, Wisconsin. The estimates on other home
economists and related areas are derived from various occupational
groupings and where they would primarily be employed by industrial
classification using the OES national census based matrix data.

(1930) and financial management (1960) of the American Home Economics Association where home economics has the clearest relationship with other helping professions.

Home economics as a profession had an earlier predecessor movement in the teaching and education of women known as "Domestic Science," such as sewing classes in Boston, Massachusetts (1798), household arts at the Troy Female Seminary (1821), private girls school in Hartford, Connecticut under Katherine Beecher (1822), the Winthrop Girls School in Boston, Massachusetts under Mary Hemenaway (1863) and the scientific study of household problems under the leadership of Benjamin Thompson (Count Rumford-1853), Brillat Savarin and his work "Physiology of Taste" (1825), Caleb Tickner who wrote the "Philosophy of Living" (1836) and Edward Youmans who wrote "Household Science" (1857).[8]

The movement toward a domestic science was a response to the health and nutrition problems experienced in the urban slums of the 1880s in cities, such as New York, Boston, and in areas of the South (Alabama). Juliet Carson on a voluntary basis developed a cooking school for women (Boston Cooking School), and other cities followed suit. The cooking school movement was known variously as the Kitchen Garden Association and the Rumfords Kitchen movement which was attached primarily to private agencies, such as the Settlement Houses of the 1870s. This movement spread rapidly under the influence of Mary Henman Abel in 1890. The Kitchen Garden Movement, as a direct approach to the problems of consumerism and nutrition, was unpopular with many people and failed to enlist the support of many women. An active supporter and participant in this movement was Ellen Richards who later became a leader in the profesionalization of home economics. Richards urged that home economics be a part of the curriculum in public schools to enhance the ability of people to make better use of their resources. As Richards encouraged the fledgling home economics movement, she also clearly made a distinction between home economics and domestic science. Home economics was a much broader term which referred to consumptive economics and family living. By 1888 home economics became a curricular area in the New York public schools. This direct educational method to meet the needs of the public for domestic science and the emerging profession of home economics was reinforced by the Morrill Act of 1862 which authorized training in domestic science and home economics as part of the   curriculum of Land Grant colleges. Examples of home economics programs established as a consequence of the Morrill Act include University of Illinois under Lou Allen (1871), University of Iowa under Mary Welch (1896), University of Kansas (1873), and the University of Wisconsin in 1903 under

Abbey Marlott. By 1908, home economics was taught in seven universities and most agricultural colleges.

A National Household Economic Association was established in 1893, which was superceded by the Lake Placid Conference of 1902-1909, which consisted of meetings of various home economics and domestic science teachers, out of which developed the American Home Economics Association in 1909 with Ellen Richards as the first president. The initial focus of the home economics movement was to create a distinction between the earlier domestic science and the broader concern of home economics.

An impetus for the development of home economics as a profession was the Smith-Hughes Act of 1921 which authorized funding for home economics services.[9] Other federal acts which provided funding for home economics services include the Purnell Act of 1925 (agricultural experimental stations), George Reid Act of 1927, George Dean Act of 1937 (teaching home economics), and more recently, the Vocational Educational Act of 1963 and the Elementary and Secondary Education Act of 1965.

Since home economics had a close alliance with elementary and secondary education, many individuals became certified through teacher training programs by 1940. Individuals who were interested in other aspects of home economics obtained general accreditation from the university or college they attended. Accreditation of home economics programs at the bachelors level is rather recent, beginning in 1971, and professional standards are a minimum of a bachelors degree from an accredited program.[10] In addition to the major specialties accepted by the American Home Economics Association, home economists are employed in a wide diversity of agencies including agricultural extension programs, consumer education offices, consumer programs, energy programs, public health departments, social service departments, rehabilitation agencies, research agencies, family planning agencies, international agencies, and in various projects and programs which combine home economics and counseling, such as VISTA (Volunteers in Service to America) and Upward Bound.

The role of the home economist will vary depending upon the specific setting in which a person is employed, such as teaching, business and industry, etc. The two practice settings which are more heavily involved in consumer issues are social service departments and consumer programs.[11]

Social service departments employ an estimated 11,000 home economists. The specific tasks they engage in include the following:

- Homemaking units (administer and supervise)
- Family financial management planning
- Budget status and evaluation
- Budget interpretation
- Staff development
- General family counseling
- Consumer information
- Education.

The homemaking units in social service departments mainly consist of nonprofessional homemakers (women who have no degree or special training and are considered paraprofessionals) who help welfare clients with the day-to-day operation of a home. An estimated 70,000 homemaker aides are employed by social service departments. One description of the role of a homemaker is contained in an article by Mirriam Shamas, "Use of Homemaker Service in Families that Neglect Their Children" Social Work, Vol. 9, No. 1 (January 1964) pp. 12-18.

Consumer programs employ an estimated 5,600 home economists who are employed by the cooperative extension service which involves consumer education and an additional 1,000 home economists are employed by consumer agencies. General tasks of home economists employed in consumer oriented programs include the following:

- Individual information/advising on decision making for specific products

- General information/advising on consumer goods

- Demonstration of products

- Public relations

- Referral to other consumer agencies and organizations

- Information on consumer rights and protection and advocacy

- Information on family management, budgets, etc.

CONSUMERISM as a PROFESSION

In the past 20 years, a variety of professions have become involved in a consumer issues, such as urban affairs, consumer affairs, social work, psychology, law, business, etc. There is no specific profession on consumerism although some educational programs have developed specialities in this area, such as Syracuse University, Syracuse, New York; Cornell University, Ithaca, New York and Auburn University, Auburn, Alabama.

The individual involved in consumer related issues may be employed by a variety of organizations, such as Concerned Consumer Leagues, lobby groups, energy companies, landlord tenant groups, etc. The general functions of the individual employed in consumer oriented agencies would include the following:

- Legal Advice
- Information on consumer rights and protection
- Public Relations
- Advocacy on grievances
- Referral to other agencies and organizations
- Attendance at public meetings
- Lobbying for consumer legislation
- Organizing a community around specific issues, etc.[12]

SOCIAL WORK

In 1980, there were an estimated 51 social workers employed in the agricultural, forestry, and fishery industry, 123 in the utility industry, 72 in the transportation industry, and in 1976, 1,784 in family planning clinics and about 2,000 in consumer oriented agencies. The specific roles social workers are performing in the above industries is unclear, however social work skills can be used in each of the components of the environment protection network. On a general basis, planning, research and organizational skills can be utilized within the natural resource component and direct services along with indirect services can be used in the human resource component of the environment protection network.

NATURAL RESOURCES

ENERGY--Potential roles for social workers include planning, organizing and public relations. (The author is aware of at least one social worker who is employed by an energy company to perform functions related to public relations.)

TRANSPORTATION--Potential roles for social workers include planning, organizing and public relations.

AIR, LAND, WATER USE and POLLUTION CONTROL--Potential roles for social workers include planning, organizing, public relations, information and referral services, and information on the rights and protection of individuals who own property and/or resources.

HUMAN RESOURCES

FAMILY PLANNING--A report by Lydia Rapoport (1970) describes some direct roles of the social worker in a family planning clinic which includes screening, intake, counseling, referral, followup, and outreach. Indirect roles for social workers would include administration, consultation, health education, staff development and in-service training. Both Rapoport (1970) and Haselkorn (1970) describe the role of a social worker in a family planning clinic.

CONSUMERISM--An article by Orlin (1973) and Fiorello (1963) describe the role of a social worker in a consumer program. In general, a social worker can become involved in the following direct services; consumer education, i.e. the rights of a consumer, laws, what are the best buys for limited financial resources, consumer advocacy, such as informal settlement of disputes, direct action at various stores or industries by boycott/pickets, and enlisting of law enforcement personnel to monitor current consumer laws. Social workers could also refer an individual to other agencies which have more expertise in consumer areas. Indirect services for the social worker include lobbying for various policies, monitoring enforcement of laws, research, and acting as liaison between business and consumers. The article by Fiorelo (1963) describes the Fort Carson Community Center Program sponsored by the Department of the Army in family management, debt and budget counseling.[13]

PERSONAL SOCIAL SERVICES

Like other networks the personal social services are utilized within the environment protection network (see Chapter 22, Personal Social Service). Some examples of the personal social services in the environment protection network include the following:

PROTECTIVE SERVICES

Programs for the aged sponsored by utility companies, such as the Wisconsin Power and Electric Company, Milwaukee, Wisconsin.

UTILITARIAN SERVICES

Day care, homemaking programs sponsored by the Concerned Consumer League, Milwaukee, Wisconsin.

315

DEVELOPMENTAL and SOCIALIZATION SERVICES

Family and marital counseling and financial counseling, such as Family Social Service of Milwaukee, Wisconsin

REHABILITATIVE and THERAPEUTIC SERVICES

Alcohol and drug programs along with financial counseling, such as Family Social Service of Milwaukee, Wisconsin.

SPECIAL POPULATIONS

The environment protection network has an impact upon all individuals in the United States. In the area of consumer problems there is a greater impact on special populations than the general population. (See Chapter 25, Special Populations, and Chapter 24, Rehabilitation.) Some examples of organizations and programs which focus on the concerns of special populations in the environment protection network include the following:

ASIAN

Consumer rights and protection, such as the Asian American Counseling Center, Chicago, Illinois; family planning, such as Asian Health Project, Los Angeles, California.

BLACK

Consumer rights and protection, such as the Associated Black Consumers Foundation, Berkely, California; East Harlem Food Buying Cooperative, New York, New York; energy, such as the American Association of Blacks in Energy, Denver, Colorado; and family planning, such as the Martin Luther King Center, Bronx, New York.

EUROPEAN ETHNIC

Consumer rights and protection, such as the International Institutes of Minneapolis, Minnesota and Milwaukee, Wisconsin; and family planning, such as Family Social Services of Milwaukee, Wisconsin

NATIVE AMERICAN

Consumer rights and protection, such as Acoma Pueblo, San Fidel, New Mexico and Boston Indian Council, Boston, Massachusetts or environment protection groups such as the Black Hills Alliance, Rapid City, South Dakota and the Mole Lake Indian Reservation, Crandon, Wisconsin, and family planning agencies, such as the American Indian Center, Dallas, Texas.

SAME SEX PREFERENCE

Consumer rights and protection, such as the Homosexual Information Center, Hollywood, California and the Lesbian Resource Center, Minneapolis, Minnesota.

SPANISH SPEAKING

Consumer rights and protection, such as Centro Cultural, Cornelius, Oregon, HELP, Albuquerque, New Mexico; environment protection, such as the Southwest Research and Information Center, Albuquerque, New Mexico, and family planning, such as the La Clinica Familiar De Barrio, Los Angeles, California.

WOMEN

Consumer rights and protection, such as the Women's Center, Waukesha, Wisconsin; and family planning, such as Bread and Roses, Milwaukee, Wisconsin.

ISSUES

Issues can be described from a societal perspective and the impact on the professions of home economics and social work.

SOCIETAL CONCERNS

General trends and issues in the environment protection network on a societal basis would be the recognition by the majority of the American population that there is, in fact, an environment and energy problem. Much of the population of the United States, although reading materials on energy and environment, are not convinced there is a problem. Consequently, a greater emphasis has to be placed upon public education and public relations, to adequately portray to the public the seriousness of the environment problem. Recognizing the problem means a change in the life style of many Americans, and will raise some conflicts between the rights of an individual versus the good of society.

There needs to be a greater recognition by corporations and industry that their use of resources may have to be monitored and curtailed even though it may mean lower production and higher cost. The eventual result, if resources are not used wisely, is that production will decline anyway for the lack of resources.

An issue which overlaps with the economic network is that of product and occupational safety. With the deregulation of some transportation industries, like the airlines, there has been a

317

growing problem of airplane safety as companies are cutting corners financially in order to reduce costs. It has been suggested that the increase in airplane crashes in 1985 is partly a consequence of cost saving measures by airlines. Some companies which specialize in the use of chemicals have not provided adequate protection for the employee (special clothes, ventilation, storage of waste materials, etc.) which has resulted in death (Chicago, Illinois, 1985) and in an increase of work related accidents and illnesses.

The health issues related to pollution are already clear. The use of certain chemicals in various factories are extremely dangerous to the employee, inadequate and illegal storage and disposal of waste materials has led to many individuals and communities developing illnesses. The United States population has to recognize that ecology and environment issues are not fancy terms to be used in academics to describe something, but on a practical level, may eventually result in the nonsurvival of the human race. Some authors have strongly suggested that the United States has about 40-50 years left to solve the problems of pollution and energy, or the consequences are irreversible.

HOME ECONOMICS as a PROFESSION

Home economics is currently a field undergoing rapid trans-formation and has a degree of intra-professional fragmentation. Some of the issues in home economics are: should there be a generalist or specialist?; should there be training for the traditional roles or new roles?; should the background be natural science or social science? and what is the relationship of those individuals who are trained in the family relations area of home economics to other helping professions. In a sense, the home economics profession has become fragmented because of the diversity of areas in home economics such as nutrition, foods, and dietetics, which rely on a natural science base versus those specializations, such as family relations, child development, and consumerism, which rely on a social science base.

SOCIAL WORK as a PROFESSION

There is a role for a social worker in each of the compo-nents of the environment protection network. These roles would normally be those which utilize skills in research, community organization, planning and public relations. Most individuals who enter social work indicate an interest in direct services and treatment. For those individuals interested in the natural resource area, they need a firm foundation in the natural sciences, specifically the biological and environmental sciences. For those individuals interested in the human resource area of family planning or consumerism, there is a need for medical knowledge and the legalities of consumer rights and protection. Additional knowledge a social worker in family planning needs includes family structure, how it changes, and the psychological and physiological aspects of sexuality. In consumerism, there should be content in schools of social work on family financial management, and consumer oriented legislation.

SUMMARY

Problems with the environment and ecology in the United States have only recently been recognized as a major social problem. The environment protection network consists of two components: <u>natural resources</u> (energy, air, land, water), with related problems of transportation, and pollution; and <u>human resources</u> with related problems of over population and consumerism.

A brief historical review of the environment protection network indicated the recency of the establishment of most programs. Prior to 1850 there were no programs in any of the environment protection areas. Early predecessor movements in the natural resource component include, the conservation movement of the 1860's and 1870's, and in the human resource component the family planning movement of 1910. The full recognition of environment protection as a problem developed in the 1960s when various cities began to experience smog and pollution, and there was medical evidence of diseases which were caused as a consequence of the pollution of natural resources. Since 1960 there has been a variety of legislation, federal, state and local, on issues related to the enviroment, as well as, the establishment of numerous agencies which focus on this problem. The recognition of a problem with human resources (over population and consumerism) followed a similar pattern with that of natural resources with most of the programs we have today having been established since 1960.

In the natural resource component of the environment protection network, most employees are natural scientists, or professional problem solvers like, engineers, architects, etc. There are roles for home economists and their varied specialities and social workers in this network in tasks related to, public relations, planning and some community organization. Human services personnel are more heavily employed in the human resource component of the environment protection network and its problem areas of overpopulation and consumerism. Employees of family planning agencies are predominately health professions, but a significant number of social workers are employed by these agencies, and some home economists with a speciality in life development. Consumerism early had members of the home economics and social work professions as active participants. The development of home economics as a profession and the emerging profession of consumerism was described. The role of social work in providing direct services in the environment protection network was described.

Issues in the environment protection network were described from three perspectives: societal basis, profession of home economics and the profession of social work. On a general societal basis, there has to be a recognition by the population that the issues of the environment are very serious and programs must be developed in order to deal with these problems. Along with the development of programs, the potentiality exists for forced curtailment of individual perogatives and rights as it relates to resource use, which could raise some legal questions which have to be resolved. There are problems emerging in product and occupational safety, as well as, health related problems due to pollution. In the profession of home economics there currently is a professional fragmentation of the field between those who rely on natural science as a knowledge base, such as food, nutrition, dietetics and those which rely on a social science knowledge base, such as child development, behavior, and family financial management counseling. In social work there has to be more of an emphasis on organization and planning skills as they relate to the environment protection network. Social workers must recognize that the environment and its use is a serious problem and that wise use of natural and human resources are a question of survival of the human race.

FOOTNOTES

*This chapter was reviewed for comments by Virginia Langrehr, Associate Professor, University of Utah, Logan, Utah.

1. Estimates on energy use in the United States in 1982 are as follows: residential, 18.8 percent; commercial, 13.4 percent; industrial, 21.3 percent; transportation, 37.6 percent; and electric utilities, 8.9 percent. The sources of energy include gasoline, 30.9 percent; natural gas, 16.1 percent; coal, 6.3 percent; electricity, 30.3 percent; and other, 16.4 percent. These estimates are adapted from United States Department of Commerce, Bureau of the Census, Statistical Abstract of the United States: 1986 (106th Edition), Washington, D.C.: U.S. Government Printing Office, 1985, pp. 559, 560.

2. Although mass transportation is more efficient and less costly than the private automobile, the United States population heavily relies upon the private automobile for transportation purposes. In 1984, Americans traveled 1.4 billion passenger miles using the automobile which is 83 percent of the estimated passenger miles. The reamining 17 percent of passenger miles were traveled on airplanes, busses, railroads or other mass transit systems. These estimates are adapted from United States Department of Commerce, Bureau of the Census, Statistical Abstract of the United States: 1986 (106th Edition), op. cit., p. 591.

3. Amos Turk and Janet Wittes, in Ecology Pollution, and Environment, Philadelphia, PA: J. & B Saunders Co., 1972, discuss these historical instances of not paying attention to the natural environment. In many areas of the world the land level is sinking as underground water is pumped out for irrigation, such as the State of Nevada, and there is historical evidence indicating a large portion of the Sahara Desert was at one time a fertile valley, along with the Indus River Valley and Tigris and Euphrates River Valley.

A major ecological and environmental crisis may be developing with the use of chloroflurocarbons and the "greenhouse effect." Chloroflurocarbons accumulate in the atmosphere causing the earth's temperature to slowly increase (1-2 degrees since 1958) and damage to the ozone layer. In 1986, scientists reported a hole in the ozone layer in Antarctica and predicted a temperature increase of 2 degrees in the next 20 years. The result of this trend is possibly farmlands becoming desert and glacial ice melting resulting in the oceans rising and submerging the current coastlines. Some scientists have predicted the end of human habitation in 500 to 1,000 years if the accumulation of chloroflurocarbons continues at the current rate.

4. For a more detailed historical development of the conservation movement the reader is referred to Chapter 14 Leisure and Recreation Network.

5. Malthus wrote his pesimistic view of population growth as a polemic against the positive and utopian thinking of the time which thought that technology would solve all problems i.e. William Goodwin and Adam Smith. Historically there were other figures who philosophically recognized there was a vague optimal population level, like Plato (340 B.C.), Confucious (500 B.C.), Cantillon (1620), and Frederick List (1709).

6. A detailed historical development of the planned parenthood movement is beyond the scope of this chapter. However the reader should be aware, there are legal and moral issues involved in the use of contraceptives and abortion. Both of these issues are in the headlines of newspapers and popular journals almost every day. If one followed the Equal Rights Amendment one would have noticed there are many arguments regarding abortion and the right to control or not control the size of families.

7. In addition to the formal structure and organizations for consumer services, many individuals use an informal or folk system for advice and services. This folk system usually consists of relatives, friends, colleagues etc. to whom a person can go to for consumer advice.

8. In the history of home economics it is interesting to note that early leadership positions were held by men until 1860, at which time the education movement and practice movement became dominated by women.

9. Examples of professional associations in home economics include the American Home Economics Association, 2210 Massachusetts Ave., NW Washington, D.C. 20036; The American Institute of Nutrition, 9639 Rockville Pike, Bethesada, Maryland 20014; and the American Dietetic Association, 430 N. Michigan Ave., Chicago, Illinois 60611.

10. In addition to accreditation at the baccalaureate level certain specialities in home economics require further certification, such as dietetics and nutrition.

11. Some home economists with a speciality in family life are employed as counselors in family planning agencies.

12. Some examples of consumer oriented organizations include the following: Concerned Consumer's League, 614 W. National Ave., Milwaukee, Wisconsin 53204 and Center for Consumer Affairs, 929 N. 6th St., Milwaukee, Wisconsin 53203.

13. Figures for the employment of social workers in 1980 are found in Chapter 3, Social Work as a Helping Profession. For information on social work as a profession the reader is referred to the National Association of Social Workers, 7981 Eastern Ave., Silver Spring, Maryland 20910 or the local chapter of the National Association of Social Workers.

SUGGESTED READINGS

Florence Haselkorn, "Family Planning: Implications for Social
Work Education," Journal of Education for Social Work, Vol.
6, No. 2 (Fall 1970), pp. 13-20. This article briefly
describes the family planning movement and role of social
work in family planning clinics.

Gilbert Masters. Introduction to Environmental Science and
Technology. New York, NY: John Wiley and Sons, Inc.,
1974. Although somewhat dated, this book provides a sound
overview of environmental problems and is a good reference
source.

Malinda Orlin. "A Role for Social Workers in the Consumer
Movement," Social Work, Vol. 18, No. 1 (January 1973),
pp. 60-65. This brief article describes the historical
involvement and roles of social work in the consumer
movement.

Joseph Petulla. American Environmental History. San Francisco,
CA: Boyd and Fraser Publishing Co., 1977. For the
individual seeking a nonsophisticated historical approach to
the problems of the environment, this book is excellent.

Eileen Quigley. Introduction to Home Economics. New York, NY:
Macmillan Publishing Co., 1974. Although somewhat dated,
this book provides a concise history of home economics and
describes the various sub-specialties and issues facing home
economics as a profession.

Paul Wasserman and Rita Siegman. Consumer Sourcebook 4th Ed.
Detroit, MI: Gale Research Co., 1983. For the individual
looking for basic reference material, this book is highly
recommended.

REFERENCES

Baldwin, Keturah. The American Home Economics Association Saga,
Washington D.C.: American Home Economics Association 1949.

Career Information Center. Consumer, Homemaking and Personal
Services, Hew York, New York: Butterick Publishing Co., 1979.

Fiorello, Thomas. "Consumer Education Needed," Social Work Vol.
18, No. 1 (January 1963) pp. 109-110.

Friedlander, Walter and Robert Apte. Introduction to Social Welfare, 5th Edition. Englewood Cliffs, NJ: Prentice-Hall, Inc., 1980.

Goodwin, Mary and Bonnie Liebman. "Nutrition and Foods," pp. 173-211 in Peter Vallitutte and Florence Christoplos Interdisciplinary Approaches to Human Services, Baltimore, Maryland: University Park Press, 1977.

Haselkorn, Florence. "Family Planning: Implications for Social Work Education," Journal of Education for Social Work Vol. 6, No. 2 (Fall 1970) pp. 13-20.

Macarov, David. The Design of Social Welfare, New York, NY: Rhinehart and Winston Co., 1978.

Masters Gilbert. Introduction to Environmental Science and Technology, New York, NY: John Wiley and Sons Inc., 1974.

Minahan, Anne. (Ed.). Encyclopedia of Social Work 18th Issue, Washington, D.C.: National association of Social Workers, 1986.

Office of the Federal Register, United States Government Manual 1985-86, Washington, D.C.: U.S. Government Printing Office, 1985.

Orlin, Malinda. "A Role for Social Workers in the Consumer Movement," Social Work Vol. 18, No. 1 (January 1973) pp. 60-65.

Percivall, Julia and Pixie Burger. Household Ecology, Englewood Cliffs, NJ: Prentice Hall, Inc., 1971.

Petulla, Joseph. American Environmental History San Francisco, CA: Boyd and Fraser Publishing Co., 1977.

Quigley, Eileen. Introduction to Home Economics, New York, NY: Macmillan Publishing Co., 1974.

Rapoport, Lydia. "Education and Training of Social Workers for Roles and Functions in Family Planning." Journal of Education for Social Work, Vol. 6, No. 2 (Fall 1970), pp. 27-38.

Rosenbloom, Joseph. Consumer Protection Guide 1977, New York, New York: Macmillan Publishing Co., 1976.

Shamas, Mirriam. "Use of Homemaker Service in Families that Neglect Their Children," Social Work Vol. 9, No. 1 (January 1964) pp. 12-18.

Swatek, Paul. The Users Guide to the Protection of the Environment New York, NY: Ballentine Books Inc. 1970.

Turk, Amos and Janet Wittes. Ecology, Pollution and Environment, Philadelphia, Pennsylvania: W.B. Saunders Co. 1972.

United States Civil Service Commission, Occupations of Federal White Collar Workers 1979, Washington, DC: U.S. Government Printing Office, 1981.

United States Department of Commerce, Bureau of the Census, 1980 Census of Population. Volume 2 Subject Reports Part 7C: Occupation by Industry, Washington, D.C.: U.S. Government Printing Office, 1984.

United States Department of Commerce, Bureau of the Census, Statistical Abstract of the United States: 1986 (106th Ed.), Washington, D.C.: U.S. Government Printing Office, 1985.

United States Department of Commerce, Directory of Consumer Agencies, Washington, D.C.: U.S. Government Printing Office, 1979.

United States Department of Labor, Employment and Training Administration, Environmental Protection Careers Guidebook, Washington, D.C.: U.S. Government Printing Office, 1980.

United States Department of Labor, Employment and Training Administration, Occuptional Outlook Handbook 1986-87, Ed., Washington, D.C.: U.S. Government Printing Office, 1986.

United States Environmental Protection Agency, Resources and Pollution Control, Washington, D.C.: U.S. Government Printing Office, 1979.

United States Department of Health, Education and Welfare, Resource Health Statistics, 1978, Washington D.C.: U.S. Government Printing Office, 1978.

United States Office of Economic Opportunity, Consumer Protection Agency, Washington, D.C.: U.S. Government Printing Office, 1965.

United States Department of Commerce, Bureau of the Census,
Public Employment in 1984, Washington, D.C.: U.S.
Government Printing Office, 1985.

Wald, Patricia. Law and Poverty 1965. Washington, D.C.:
U.S. Government Printing Office, 1965.

Wasserman, Paul and Rita Siegman, Consumer Sourcebook 4th
Edition. Detroit, Michigan: Gale Research Co., 1983.

Wilcox, Claire. Towards Social Welfare. Homewood, IL: Richard
D. Irvin Co., 1969.

Wisconsin Legislative Bureau. Wisconsin Bluebook 1985-86,
Madison, WI: Department of Administration, 1985.

CHAPTER 10

INFORMATION and REFERRAL NETWORK*

"The concept of information and referral services
is fairly new in human history. The very
proliferation of social services available to the
average citizen today for housing, health,
family, planning, recreation, legal aid, drug
information, etc. has created the necessity for a
system to alleviate the confusion and frustration
of trying to get the services and persons who
need it together. Social agencies themselves
have seen the need and created some information
referral services....and now the public library
....has accepted the challenge in an increasing
number of cities." (Becker:174:1)

INTRODUCTION

A societal network which will become more significant in the
delivery of social services in an economic network oriented
toward services and high technology is the information and
referral network. The number of agencies providing information
and referral services have been proliferating at a rapid pace
and becoming more specialized in their area of expertise. The
average citizen does not always know where to turn when confronted with a personal or family crisis. Many times a crisis
occurs when most if not all of the standard human service agencies are closed, i.e., midnight to 7:00 a.m. and a person does
not know where to seek help.

The information and referral network in human services consists of the following components: library services, traditional social welfare agencies and emergency telephone information
and referral agencies. This chapter briefly explores the
information and referral network as providing social services in
conjunction with libraries, traditional social welfare agencies,
and telephone hotlines. The role of library and information
science and social work in the information and referral network
is discussed.

SIZE

The largest component of this network is library services
and the smaller parts of the network are the traditional social

welfare agencies, and telephone hotlines for counseling and referral of individuals.[1]

LIBRARY SERVICES

The library network in the United States is large and complex, consisting of four major types: academic, public, school and special libraries. In total this network in 1984 consisted of 100,437 libraries, employed 305,291 individuals, had expenditures of at least 4.826 billion dollars and served a potential population base of over 295 million individuals (multiple counts since individuals use more than one library system).[2] Figure 10-1 shows the estimated size of the library network in 1982.

ACADEMIC LIBRARIES - This component of the library network in 1984 consisted of approximately 4,989 libraries, employed 58,421 individuals, had expenditures of 1.941 billion dollars and served a population of 13 million students and faculty.

PUBLIC LIBRARIES - This component of the library network in 1984 consisted of 15,055 libraries (including branch libraries), employed 112,527+ individuals, had expenditures of 1.5 billion dollars and served a potential population of 236 million people.

SCHOOL LIBRARIES - These figures represent elementary and secondary schools. In 1984 this component of the library network consisted of 70,854 schools, employed 117,700 individuals, had expenditures of 1.3 billion dollars and served a population of 46 million students and faculty.

SPECIAL LIBRARIES - This component of the library network in 1984 consisted of approximately 9,539 libraries, and employed 47,410 individuals. Adequate estimates on the expenditures of special libraries and the population served were not available.

TRADITIONAL SOCIAL WELFARE AGENCIES

There are an estimated 3,000 plus traditional social welfare agency and information referral services.

EMERGENCY TELEPHONE INFORMATION and REFERRAL AGENCIES

There are an estimated 2,000 plus telephone and emergency information and referral agencies.

HISTORICAL DEVELOPMENT

Each of the components of the information referral network is discussed separately with the major emphasis on library services.

Figure 10-1

Estimated Size of the Library Service Component of the
Information and Referral Network in 1984*

| Selected Criteria | Type of Library Service | | | |
	Academic	Public	Public School	Special and Other
Number of Libraries	4,989	15,055	70,854	9,539
Number of Employees	58,421	112,527	117,750	46,410
Expenditures (Billion)	1.941 billion	1.5 billion	1.385 billion	(1)
Population served (Million)	13 million	236 million	46 million	(1)

*Sources. Adapted from United States Government Department of Commerce Bureau of the Census, Statistical Abstract of the United States: 1986 (106th Edition). Washington, DC: U.S. Government Printing Office, 1985, pp. 155, 160, 161, 299, 325, 402 and United States Department of Commerce, Bureau of the Census, Public Employment in 1984, Washington, D.C.: U.S. Government Printing Office, 1985, p. 3.

(1) Phone conversation with the Information Office of the Special Library Association, October 1984, indicated a lack of adequate statistical reporting to estimate the expenditures of special libraries and the population served.

LIBRARY SERVICES

The concept of a library has shifted over time from a depository of information to dissemination of information, and from academic libraries to other forms of libraries.

ACADEMIC LIBRARIES - Some form of academic library has been in existence since early classical civilization, however, the function and focus of these libraries has changed.

Classical Civilizations (2700 B.C.-450 A.D.) maintained libraries as early as 2700 B.C. These libraries were primarily collections and depositories of information which were used by scholars, clergy and nobility. The most famous library was that of Alexandria which was destroyed by fire in 47 B.C. In addition to libraries attached to the temples, there were individual and private libraries, such as Aristotle's (350 B.C.), but these were not open to the public.

Libraries during the Roman Empire (47 B.C.-450 A.D.) followed the model of Greece with a number of them attached to temples and the use of individual and private libraries. Two innovations during this time period were public libraries and Christian community libraries. A public library for the use of the citizen was to be developed in the major city of each province, such as Hadrian's Library in Rome (120 A.D.). The growing Christian community after about 100 A.D. developed their own libraries. Both of these innovations were short lived due to political and military events.

From 284-305 A.D. Emperor Diocletian had many of the Christian libraries destroyed in the conflicts between the Roman Empire and the Christians. As the Roman empire declined politically and militarily, the periodic invasions of the barbarians (Goths 410 A.D., Vandals 455 A.D.) took its toll in the destruction of cities and libraries, with the looting and plundering of Rome in 457 A.D. This periodic destruction of the libraries as a by-product of warfare and invasion continued up until almost 1600. For example, the famous library in Constantinople was destroyed in 1204 A.D. and the few remaining libraries in Rome were destroyed in 1527 A.D. Those libraries which remained were individual private libraries, church libraries, or remnents of libraries which were carried away to other locations like monasteries.

Medieval Libraries (450-1500 A.D.) consisted of two major types, monastic libraries and university libraries. Monastic libraries (450-1200 A.D.) were the depositories for various collections during the period when public libraries were being destroyed as a by product of warfare and invasion. The church would collect what works were available and deposit them in monasteries, such as Cluny in France (800 A.D.); Monte Cassino in Italy (529 A.D.); Vivarium in Italy (540 A.D.) and St. Martins in France (782 A.D.). One of the centers for monastic libraries was Ireland about 470 A.D. (after the death of St. Patrick in

461 A.D.). Monasteries, such as Clonard, Durrow and Armagh in Ireland became centers of learning and expanded their influence into places like Scotland in 565 A.D. and Bobbio France in 614 A.D. where they established monastic libraries. The monastic library was used primarily by scholars, clergy and nobility.

During the later Medieval period the university library was established. The university as a system of higher education was emerging with the establishment of a university in Paris, France (1300) and Bologna, Italy (1200). As the university developed, many of the monastic libraries were shifted to the university. The use of library materials was primarily for scholars and clergy. Students had books they could use for courses but were generally denied or had limited access to library resources. Books for student use were so rare at this time, that books were chained to benches so they would not be stolen.

National and Private Libraries (1500-1745) were an asset to the university since scholars had access to these collections, although students generally did not. National libraries were established in France (1622), the French Royal Academy; Oxford, England (1598); Berlin, Germany (1659); Scotland (1682) and the Vatican in Italy.

Since 1745 many private libraries have been donated to a university which through the 1850's relied heavily on these donations of individuals for acquisitions of material. The concept of the general student population instead of only faculty and scholars having use of the academic library is a product of 1875-1900. Today, the perception is that academic libraries are there to serve students and faculty. Expansion of many academic libraries was possible through the Higher Education Act of 1965.

PUBLIC LIBRARIES - There were three early precedents for a public library system where material was available to the general public with a small fee or no cost: Romans (47 B.C.), Reformation (1517), and Commercial and Social Libraries (1727) in the United States.

The Romans from 47 B.C.-450 A.D. developed a system of public libraries in major cities which were usually attached to a temple. Almost all of these libraries were destroyed during the time period of 30-457 A.D. and the decline of the Roman Empire. Materials that did remain were deposited in monastic libraries.

The Reformation of 1517 and its political and cultural aftermath stressed an individual interpretation of the Bible which led to a movement to teach common people to read. In

331

Germany, for example, there developed a series of municipal church and private libraries which were made available to the common person for their use.

The United States initially had church libraries, academic libraries and individual private collections. With the Reformation as a social and religious background, and the political ideals of democracy, reading was seen as a responsibility of all citizens. To fill this need the Commercial and Social Library movement of 1727-1850 developed. The Commercial Library was a system where an individual could borrow books for a fee from churches, bookstores and the general store. The Social Library was a reading club which one joined for a fee like the Junto Club in Philadelphia in 1727. Social libraries became specialized by areas of interest, such as business, apprenticeship, merchants, etc. The commercial library represented more the interests of the common person and the social library the interests of the middle class.[3]

The Free Public Library movement was consistent with the ideals of democracy and began in Boston, Massachusetts in 1848. An impetus for the development of the Boston Public library was an act passed in Massachusetts in 1835 allowing the use of taxes to support a library in each school district. Through this precedent, George Tickner and Edward Everett advocated for a free public library system. The public library movement spread rapidly and by 1900 most major communities had a public library with reading rooms and free circulation of materials. The public library movement spread rapidly partially as a consequence of the aid and influence of Andrew Carnegie, a philanthropist, who by 1898 had provided funds to establish over 1,600 libraries.[4]

The public library has been undergoing fundamental changes since the 1930's. Two of these major changes are social responsibility and community outreach and referral. Social responsibility refers to using library resources for meetings, lectures and forums to inform citizens. These activities have led to occasional conflicts with the law, and occasional demands for censorship of material. For example, Zaia Horn in 1971 was jailed for contempt of court for refusing to provide information on individuals using specific library resources in the Lewisburg Seven Case in Pennsylvania. Some cities are pushing censorship for some well known books like Mark Twain's Huckleberry Finn.[5]

Community Outreach and Information Referral programs have been established in a number of public libraries beginning in the early 1960's. Community outreach programs are an effort to attract special population groups such as the aged, minorities, disabled, etc. to use the library. Programs, such as book-mobiles, special programs for youth, minority, etc. have been developed by many libraries.

Some communities use the public library as a central source for information and referral. Baltimore, Maryland in the 1960's experimented with a community information referral system. For a variety of reasons, this experiment was unsuccessful. Detroit Michigan in 1971 established TIP (The Information Place), as a community referral project and was successful. By 1977, there were at least 196 public libraries having a community informa-tion referral system including Milwaukee, Wisconsin (TAP-The Answer Place). Some individuals have anticipated a greater need for social workers in the public library system to help imple-ment community information referral systems and to work with "problem patrons."[6] Further expansion of the public library system was encouraged through the Library Services and Construc-tion Acts of 1956 and 1964.

SCHOOL LIBRARIES - These libraries serve the elementary and secondary levels of the education network, both public and pri-vate. The school library movement paralleled the development of the elementary and secondary schools in the 1800's. In 1827 the state of New York encouraged all schools to develop a library, but Massachusetts in 1835 was the first state to stipulate that each school district shall have a library and allocated tax funds for this purpose. Other states quickly followed the example of Massachusetts and established school libraries. New York was the first state in 1892 to require a school librarian.

Although school libraries developed rapidly, the period of greatest growth was after 1958 as a consequence of federal fund-ing through the National Defense Education Act of 1958 and the Elementary and Secondary School Education Act of 1965.

SPECIAL LIBRARIES - This is a collection of miscellaneous libraries, such as corporate, special interest (history, gene-alogy, medicine, law, defense etc.). The special libraries have a small but well defined clientele and have detailed information on a specific topic. The special library developed to fulfill the needs of an industrial society for detailed information on specific topics. The earliest special library was developed in New York City prior to 1850 through the Chamber of Commerce. The Silk Association of America established a special library in 1872. By 1880, there were about 12 corporations which had a special library and by 1909 about 114 corporations had special libraries.

The special library movement continues to expand with
specialization not restricted to corporations. Special libraries now exist in many historical societies, part of a general
library, in hospitals, law firms, government agencies, correctional and mental institutions, etc.[7]

TRADITIONAL SOCIAL WELFARE AGENCIES

The predecessor of an information referral service by traditional social welfare agencies was the Social Service Exchange
developed by the Charity Organization Movement of the 1870's.
The Social Service Exchange was rather specific in its function. The Social Service Exchange was to cross check the application of individuals applying for aid to determine whether or
not they were receiving aid from more than one agency. Its
function was to facilitate coordination between the agencies and
minimize duplication of effort and duplication of services by
agencies. For a variety of reasons, such as changing attitudes
toward clients, and full employment during World War II, social
service exchanges were generally not used after 1945.

Although the social service exchange concept declined, the
notion of information and referral services continued. In 1972,
the United Way of America listed over 60 information and referral services in operation under its auspices. Other information
and referral services operated by traditional agencies include,
Easter Seal, urban coalitions, labor unions, veterans information centers, etc.

TELEPHONE INFORMATION and REFERRAL AGENCIES

A product of the 1960's has been the rapid development of
independent agencies which provide emergency telephone counseling and information and referral services. These services
developed from three directions: suicide prevention programs,
juvenile runaway program, and free clinics and switchboards, as
a part of the counter-culture movement of the 1960's. A 24 hour
suicide prevention telephone service began in 1958 in Los
Angeles as a means to provide emergency psychiatric service. In
the same year, the Los Angeles Children's Hospital developed a
telephone counseling line, to provide emergency services to runaway youth. The counter-culture movement of the 1960's developed free medical clinics in Los Angeles (1967) and underground
switchboards (telephone information and referral) (1967) in San
Francisco. The use of these emergency hot lines was extensive,
and its use spread rapidly throughout the United States for
numerous problem areas, such as drugs, alcohol, parents anonymous, runaways, battered women, etc. These services are heavily
implemented through volunteers. For a summary of the historical

development of the information and referral network see Figure 10-2.

STRUCTURE

In looking at the structure of the information and referral network, one can look at its organizational context, services provided, occupations and professions, and dominant occupations and professions.

ORGANIZATIONAL CONTEXT

The information and referral network has three basic components: library services, traditional social welfare agencies and emergency telephone information referral.

LIBRARY SERVICES - The organizational context of the library service consists of government agencies and a network of the libraries. Figure 10-3 shows some of the government agencies involved with library srvices. There is a multi-tiered system of independent but cooperating libraries in a network including federal, state, local and special libraries. Figure 10-4 shows the layered, or tiered, network of the library system. Figure 10-5 shows a model of the internal organization of a major metropolitan library with its major divisions including community outreach and information and referral services.

The organization of a library will obviously vary depending upon its size, clientele, nature of collections, etc. For example, the university library may have a rare book department, microfilm department, archive department, special collections, etc., which many libraries do not have.

TRADITIONAL SOCIAL WELFARE AGENCIES - These agencies usually have a division or department which is given responsibility for development and implementation of information and referral services.

EMERGENCY TELEPHONE INFORMATION and REFERRAL - These agencies usually have a director, perhaps an assistant director, based upon agency size, and a staff of volunteers.

In addition to the information and referral systems discussed above, public and private, there is an extensive informal or folk system of relatives, friends neighbors, etc. which will provide information and referral services for each other.

Figure 10-2

HISTORICAL TIME LINE OF THE INFORMATION AND REFERRAL NETWORK

2,7000 BC—Sumeria library - Temple and Royal libraries

1,250 BC—Egypt - Temple libraries

384 BC—Greece - Temple libraries, Private Individuals and Nobility
owned libraries

332 BC—Alexandria library - Egypt

100 BC—450 AD - Rome develops public library system

450—1200 - Monastic and church libraries

1200—1500 - University, church, and individual libraries

Europe   1622—National library (France) and individual and church libraries

_____   1655—Parochial (church) or individual libraries

United   1727—Social library (Junto Club in Philadelphia)

States   1826—Commercial library movement

1835—School District library movement

1848—Public Library Movement - Boston, Massachusetts

1873—Professional Association Established - American Library
Association

1887—First library science school - Columbia College

1926—Minimal Education standards set by American Library
Association

1950s—Accreditation, 1 year Master's Degree Program in Library
Science;
Information Centers

1960s—Crisis Intervention and telephone hotlines

1970s—Community outreach, Information and Referral,
Fee Based Information Services

FIGURE 10-3

IDEALIZED GOVERNMENT ORGANIZATION
in the INFORMATION and REFERRAL NETWORK*

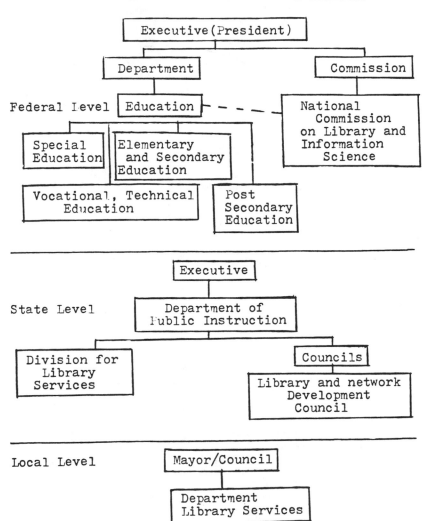

* Sources: Adapted from Office of the Federal Register,
Government Organization Manual: 1985-86,Washington
D.C.: U.S. Government Printing Office,1985,p.840;
Wisconsin Legislative Reference Bureau, Wisconsin
Blue Book 1985-1986, Madison, Wisconsin: Department
of Administration,1985,p. 468; City of Milwaukee
Annual Report:1984, Milwaukee, Wisconsin,1985.

Figure 10-4

IDEALIZED MODEL SHOWING THE LIBRARY NETWORK
IN THE UNITED STATES

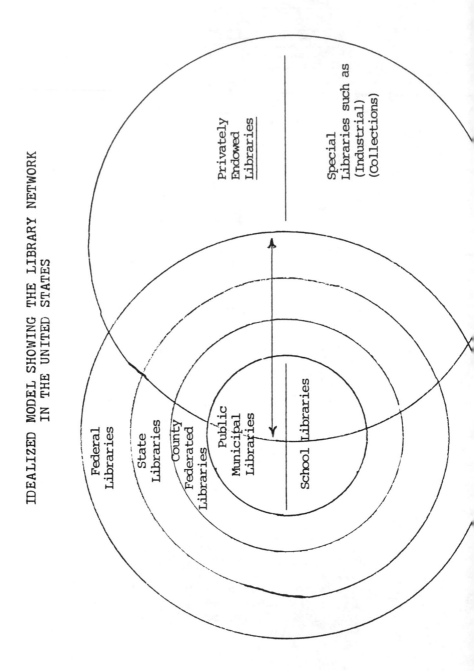

ORGANIZATION OF A TYPICAL LARGE METROPOLITAN LIBRARY*

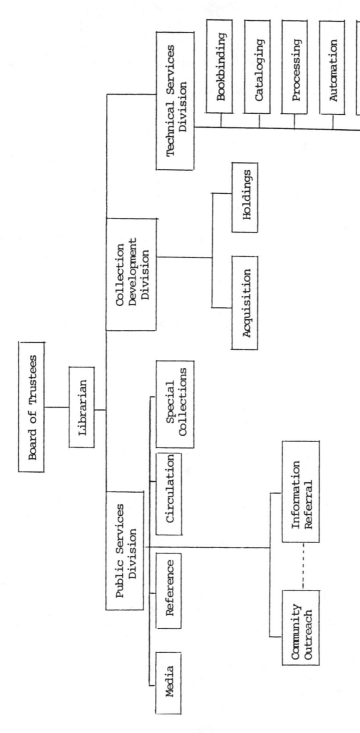

*Source: Adapted from organizational chart Milwaukee City
Public Library Milwaukee, Wisconsin, 1986.

SERVICES PROVIDED

A public library provides the following basic services:

- Circulation of materials
- Ready reference
- Assistance to patrons.

When a library has developed an extensive community outreach program, there would be special programs, such as films, slides, exhibits, shows, etc., for the following groups:

- Youth
- Elderly
- Disabled
- Special Populations (Asian, Black, European Ethnic, Native American, Same Sex Preference, Spanish, Women, etc.).

Other auxiliary services provided by a library include the following:

Information and Referral - operate a community wide service. A study by Thomas Childers (1984) of public libraries indicated that the following services were offered by some libraries:

- Advice on agencies
- Follow-up of referral
- Advocacy
- Feedback
- Counseling
- Transportation
- Escort services for women at night.

Mutual Support Groups - facilitate their development, and provide space for meetings.

Community Groups - provide facilities and publicity for meetings.

In other information and referral services where a traditional social welfare agency operates the service, or an emergency telephone information and referral agency is established as an independent agency, the following services would be provided:

- Information on various agencies and services
- Referral to specific agencies
- Emergency counseling

340

- Back up professional counseling
- Information about a specific problem
- Information about mutual support groups.

OCCUPATIONS and PROFESSIONS

Figure 10-6 shows selected examples of human service occupations and professions employed in the library services industrial classification in 1980 (public libraries).[8] The dominant profession and occupation in library services was that of a librarian of which there were 57,766 or 40.03 percent of the selected employees, library clerk of which there were 60,690 or 42.00 percent of the selected employees, and the remaining 25,843 or 17.97 percent of the selected employees included a variety of occupations and professions, such as social work, personel manager, registered nurse, physician, psychologist, lawyer, dietician, guards, etc.

When the information and referral system is operated within a traditional social welfare agency, personnel are usually that of the parent agency plus volunteers. For example, in a public welfare or a United Way information and referral service, social workers and volunteers implement the system, or in a psychiatric setting it would be a psychiatric social worker plus volunteers.

In emergency telephone information and referral agencies, there is usually a professional who is in charge of the agency or at least supervising the volunteers. Normally the professional staff would consist of a social worker, or a psychologist, a psychiatrist, etc. Volunteers usually are "street wise" individuals who receive staff development and in-service training from the professional in order to implement the service.

DOMINANT OCCUPATIONS and PROFESSIONS

Figure 10-7 shows the employment of the occupational classification of librarians in the United States in 1980. The largest percentage of librarians, 53.4 per cent are employed in schools (academic and elementary and secondary) and 30.9 per cent are employed in library services (public libraries). The remaining 15.7 percent are employed in a variety of special libraries in industrial classifications, such as mining, manufacturing, legal, wholesale and retail trade, health, social services, business and repair etc. Under the industrial classification of business and repair, there are librarians employed as information specialists and in fee based information services. In the business and repair industrial classification, 638 librarians were employed in computer and data processing, 587 in commerical research, development and testing, and 487 in business management and consultation.

341

Figure 10-6

NUMBER AND PERCENT OF SELECTED HUMAN SERVICE OCCUPATIONS AND PROFESSIONS
EMPLOYED IN THE LIBRARY SERVICE INDUSTRIAL CLASSIFICATION IN 1980*

Occupational Classification	Number	Percent
Librarian (public)[1]	57,766	40.030
Library Clerk	60,690	42.000
Teacher and Teacher Aide	1,065	.740
Counselor (Education and Vocational)	333	.230
Social Work	114	.080
Clergy and Religious Worker	8	.005
Administrator	4,515	3.230
Personnel & Labor Relations	17,441	12.010
Registered Nurse	29	.020
Dietician	5	.003
Therapist	9	.006
Psychologist	17	.020
Sociologist	14	.009
Social Science and Architect	248	.171
Lawyer and Legal Assistant	163	.130
Welfare Aide	44	.040
Child Care	370	.250
Guards	891	.620
Health Aide	26	.028
Nurse Aide	46	.031
Clinical Lab Technician	66	.045
Dental Hygiene	18	.020
Radiological Technician	34	.023
Health not specified	14	.009
Author, Musician, Painter, Dance, etc.	373	.250
Total	144,299	100.000

*Source: Adapted from United States Department of Commerce, Bureau of the
Census, 1980 Census of Population, Volume 2 Subject Reports Part 7C:
Occupation by Industry, Washington, DC: U.S. Government Printing Office,
1984, pp. 295-664. The term librarian as used here is an occupational title
and not the professional title.

[1]Includes librarians working in elementary, secondary, college, university
and business and vocational school industrial classifications.

Figure 10-7

NUMBER AND PERCENT OF LIBRARIANS EMPLOYED BY INDUSTRIAL

CLASSIFICATION IN 1980*

Industrial Classification	Number	Percent
Agriculture/Forestry/Fishery	78	.042
Mining	323	.174
Construction	231	.124
Manufacturing	4,060	2.190
Transportation/Communication/Public Utility	833	.449
Wholesale/Retail Trade	925	.499
Finance/Insurance	1,744	.940
Business/Repair	2,192[1]	1.182
Personal Service	74	.039
Entertainment/Recreation	378	.203
Legal	1,569	.845
Health	3,020	1.629
Education	99,131	53.492
Social Service	857	.462
Libraries	57,333[2]	30.932
Museum/Art Gallery/Zoo	6,268	3.381
Religious Organization	301	.162
Membership Organization	266	.143
Engineering/Architect/Survey	62	.033
Public Administration	5,706	3.079
Total	185,351	100.000

*Source: Adapted from United States Department of Commerce, Bureau of the
Census. 1980 Census of Population, Volume 2 Subject Reports Part 7C:
Occupation by Industry. Washington, DC: U.S. Government Printing
Office, 1984, pp. 295-664. The term librarian as used here is an
occupational title and not the professional title.

[1] In the business and repair service industrial classification, 638 librarians were in computer and data processing and 487 librarians in business
management and consultation, and 587 librarians in commercial/research
development and testing.

[2] See Figure 10-6 for a breakdown of librarians and other human service
personnel working in libraries.

343

In the information and referral network the librarian is the dominant profession. Prior to the development of the printing press, books were handcopied and relatively rare. The problems of the library system focused on the classification, indexing, storing and retrieval of information and materials which became a highly specialized position. As far back as 670 B.C., there were individuals assigned to libraries to organize and retrieve information. As books become more abundant and the amount of information collected became more voluminous, a need developed for individuals with special skills and a more sophisticated system of classification. By 1600, the profession of library science in the more modern use of the term was emerging. Three individuals which were noteworthy, in the fledgling days of library science include Nicolas Regaelt (1622), Gabriele Naudie (1627) and John Durie (1650).

Library science as a professional group organized the American Library Association in 1872. Like other professional groups the field of practice developed first, then professional organizations and lastly educational standards. Educational standards were initially developed in 1926, and in 1951 the American Library Association began to accredit one year master's degree programs. The current recognized professional degree is a graduate program accredited by the American Library Association.[9]

There are some specialty programs within library science, such as the training of teachers at the bachelor's level to work within a school library at the elementary and secondary level. Within the graduate programs there are specialities in information science, information specialists and information centers.

The professional librarian is responsible for the following:

- Administration and management of the library
- Selection and acquisition of materials
- Development of a system of classification and cataloging of material
- Provision for physical storage and accessibility of bibliographic and other recorded materials
- Long range planning for services provided for a specific or general clientele

In general, the professional librarian should be an administrator and a policy oriented individual. General day-to-day operations of managing a library, such as circulation, classification, book preparation, shelving, etc., is the responsibility of other occupational groups, such as library clerks, or to non-professionals and volunteers in smaller libraries. When a library does have an information and referral service, the task is primarily that of providing information and not advising or counseling.

The field of library science is expanding into a broader context, known as information science and information specialist. The librarian role is only one of many specialized roles in the area of library and information science. As <u>information science and information specialist</u> emerge as distinct professions, a sample range of functions would include:

- Abstractor - indexer
- Bibliographic searcher
- Data base manager
- Information broker
- Information center manager
- Data base researcher.

These newer specializations have as their primary mission, the service of disseminating knowledge and information to the consumer. In order to accomplish this task efficiently, knowledge and information resources must be centralized, and specialists developed to locate, retrieve, and disseminate information. Although, the traditional roles of library science may be absorbed into the broader concept of information science, it is the librarian's role, which will still have the most immediate impact on the consumer.

SOCIAL WORK

Figure 10-6 shows an estimated 114 social workers and 44 welfare aides employed in libraries in 1980. In addition to the industrial classification of library services, there were 79 social workers employed in the following subcategories of the business and repair industrial classification: computer and data processing, 79, commercial research, development and testing, 102 and business management and consultation, 470. These industrial classifications represent the newly emerging profession of information specialist. The role of the social worker in the information and referral network varies depending upon whether the individuals are participating in library services, in a traditional social welfare agency or in an emergency telephone information and referral agency.

LIBRARY SERVICES

Some of the functions of social workers in library services include the following:

345

- Handling problem patrons
- Directing information and referral services
- Staff development
- Consultation.

The social workers in performing various functions in library services would utilize the following methods:

INDIVIDUAL and GROUP WORK - Public libraries are becoming more concerned about problem patrons which the staff is not equipped to handle. Problem patrons refer to the following behaviors: unruly and antisocial behavior, individuals who may be mentally ill, and transient populations of vagrants, alcoholics, drug addicts, etc. Leo Fichtelberg and Janet Van Natten in the New Jersey Librarian, (1978-79), provide some examples of problematic behavior by their patrons, such as streaking, sexual harassment, and unruly behavior, which the staff was unable to handle. The only resource a librarian has for handling such problems is keeping a cool head, or calling the police. If libraries develop information and referral services using a social worker, a social worker could also handle a sizeable proportion of these problem patrons.

COMMUNITY ORGANIZATION - Ideally, a social worker knows community resources, therefore, would be a natural asset in the development and implementation of community information and referral services. This possibility is indicated in the Bureau of Labor Survey Report (1975), which projected the following:

"Community outreach personnel include librarians equipped with special skills for dealing with minorities and the disadvantaged; professional workers in related fields such as social work, sociology, and social psychology; the non- -professional level, assistants or aides who are familiar with the community and proficient in imparting basic information to individuals and groups.

The Bureau of Labor Survey results point to a strong demand for community outreach librarians; fully 44 percent of the public libraries hope to add community outreach workers to their staff during the decade of the 1970s (and later). One large library in the mid-west reported to the Bureau of Labor Survey interviewer that changing innercity service patterns will create a demand for new programs, and for specialty qualified training in social work as well as in librarianship; and a demonstrated ability to work with groups." (Bureau of Labor:pp. 39-40).

STAFF DEVELOPMENT and CONSULTATION - A social worker could provide in-service and staff development services to a library staff, in areas, such as understanding human behavior, and understanding different cultural and ethnic groups. There is a potential role for a social worker as a consultant and when community groups use library facilities. An example of a joint library/social work project is the article by Pat Dewdney "The Crouch Experiment."[10]

TRADITIONAL SOCIAL WELFARE AGENCIES

Social Welfare agency information and referral services usually involve a social worker as a coordinator or director of a program, as a supervisor and in direct intervention with the consumer of the service themselves.

EMERGENCY TELEPHONE INFORMATION and REFERRAL

These services usually have a social worker participating as a director or supervisor.[11] The social worker, in addition to staff development, and agency operations would more than likely become actively involved in telephone services and provide personal intervention in a certain proportion of cases. A social worker at a broader level, ideally could become involved in influencing policy favorable to filling the social needs of the clientele of information and referral services.[12]

PERSONAL SOCIAL SERVICES

The personal social services are found in all of the social networks including the information and referral network (See Chapter 22, Personal Social Services). Examples of the personal social services in the information and referral network include the following:

PROTECTIVE SERVICES

Special programs and counseling for the aged population; information on child welfare and, family violence programs; telephone counseling for family violence; special programs for youth, such as Milwaukee, Wisconsin.

UTILITARIAN SERVICES

Information on homemaking; use of facilities for day care centers and nursing schools, and day care computerized information and referral facilities, such as Minneapolis, Hennipin County and St. Paul, Ramsey County, Minnesota.

DEVELOPMENTAL and SOCIALIZATION SERVICES

Provide use of facilities for parenting groups; unwed mothers groups; information on family relations and parent child relations; telephone information referral and counseling, such as Project Adopt in Onondaga, New York; Detroit, Michigan; and Atlanta, Georgia.

REHABILITATIVE and THERAPEUTIC SERVICES

Films, slides and other presentations on specific problems like, alcohol, drugs, suicide, sexual harassment, etc. Telephone information and referral services, and emergency crisis counseling programs such as Atlanta, Georgia.

SPECIAL POPULATIONS

Programs for special populations are found in all of the networks of society (see Chapter 25, Special Populations and Chapter 24, Rehabilitation). Examples of programs for special populations in the information and referral network include the following:

ASIAN

Special language programs for recent refugees (Vietnamese, Cambodian); cultural awareness events (Chinese, Japanese, Filipino, etc.); emergency telephone intervention, such as Milwaukee, Wisconsin.

BLACK

Reading lists, films and slides for cultural awareness; Black studies and awareness series; telephone information and referral and emergency counseling, such as Atlanta, Georgia.

EUROPEAN ETHNIC

Special programs for bilingual writing, reading and speaking; cultural awareness events; telephone information and referral and emergency counseling, such as Milwaukee, Wisconsin.

NATIVE AMERICAN

Films, slides lectures for cultural awareness; facilities for dance groups and language classes; telephone information and referral, and emergency counseling, such as Chicago, Illinois.

SAME SEX PREFERENCE

Films, slides, lectures, etc., such as San Francisco, California.

SPANISH SPEAKING

Bilingual classes for writing, reading and speaking; special programs and information for migrants; telephone information and referral and emergency counseling, such as Houston and Dallas, Texas.

WOMEN

Lectures and presentations on women's rights and issues; telephone information and referral and emergency counseling such as Milwaukee, Wisconsin.

ISSUES

In the information and referral network, library and information science and social work have some issues that should be addressed.

LIBRARY and INFORMATION SCIENCE

Library services and training for library and information science should continue to reflect the concept of a social responsibility in meeting the needs of the community. Generally, some of the issues for training in library and information science include responding to the changes in the educational needs of the community; responding to the needs for community outreach, e.g., innovation of programs; grapple with the issues of problem patrons and to continuously re-evaluate the type and level of reading needed for both the general population and a professional/technical population. Since there is a movement to develop a broader information science profession based upon computer technology, new roles will have to be defined, and a reassessment of where the traditional role of the librarian, and library science, fits into the new movement.

There are other broader professional issues which have to be resolved, such as how many years of professional education are required at the graduate level (1 or 2), the adequacy of financial support for library services as budgets decline in the 1980's, should the focus be on the development of information and referral services or on maintenance and accessibility of literature, and to what extent can computer technology be used in many of the small libaries.

349

SOCIAL WORK

Social workers should be aware of information and referral services, and of the role public libraries can play in the delivery of these services. Social work should appreciate some of the dilemmas that libraries are currently involved in and provide some concrete suggestions for the solution of some problems such as the problem patron and understanding of different ethnic and cultural groups.

Information and referral services by traditional social welfare agencies like library services face certain problems. One of the problems is the specificity or focus for the problem area of services. Many service agencies will only provide information regarding a specific problem. There are further questions of duplication of effort, funding, and training of personnel.

Emergency telephone information and referral agencies face difficulties in the areas of funding, duplication of services, and the changing market for a particular service. Many telephone hot lines are developed in response to a specific clientele, with a specific problem, at a specific point in time. When that clientele shifts, like, the need for information on drugs in San Francisco in the late 1970s, the need for a particular service will change. Consequently, many of the current telephone hot lines may become short-term agencies, and unable to expand beyond a particular clientele. There are further managerial questions on telephone hot lines, such as will confidentiality be respected, the lack of follow-up services, and the extensive use of "street wise people." An issue is whether the "street wise people" have begun to establish some degree of professional identification and working with the clientele on a professional basis.

SUMMARY

The concept of information and referral services is rather recent in our society since 1960, however it is a consequence of the complexities, overlapping, and duplication of services in our society. In general, three types of information and referral networks are discussed: library services, traditional social welfare agencies and emergency telephone information and referral agencies, such as hot lines, and crisis centers.

Library services are rather extensive in the United States consisting of approximately 100,437 libraries, employing an estimated 305,291 individuals, having expenditures of an estimated 4.8 billion dollars annually, and servicing over 295 million individuals (double count of individuals since they use more than one type of library). Traditional social welfare agency information and referral services is a smaller part of the network consisting of approximately 3,000 agencies. In addition there are approximately 2,000 emergency telephone information and referral agencies like hot lines and crisis intervention centers.

There was a brief description of the historical development of libraries beginning in classical times in 2,700 B.C. and of other information and referral services. The concept of emergency telephone information and referral agencies is of rather recent, beginning in the late 1960s. The concept of emergency telephone information and referral agencies developed from three directions; suicide prevention centers in 1958, services for juvenile runaways in Los Angeles in 1958, and the counter-culture movement in Los Angeles and San Francisco, California, in the 1960s.

The structure of library services in the United States was described to show its complexity, as well as its diversity. The role of the public library was discussed with its growing emphasis on the importance of information and referral services and community outreach. The dominant profession in library services is that of library and information science. In traditional social welfare agencies and in emergency telephone information and referral agencies, a dominant profession has been that of social work with the use of volunteers. Potential roles of the social worker in the public library were discussed focussing on problem patrons, information and referral, consultation and staff development. Various issues involved in all three of these information and referral services were discussed, such as emerging and changing professional roles, impact of budget cutting in the provision of services, and coordination of effort between the different parts of the information and referral net-work.

FOOTNOTES

*This chapter was reviewed for comments by Paul Tutwiler, Assistant Dean, School of Library and Information Science, University of Wisconsin-Milwaukee, Milwaukee, Wisconsin.

[1]Currently, there is a redefinition occurring in the United States of the profession of library science. A broader concept of information science is emerging with library science as one specialization within information science. According to the

Occupational Survey of Information Professionals (University of Pittsburgh Press, 1980), the following professional roles are listed under information science: computer, education (training), financial, information services, library, management support, research, statistics, and technical publications. Although the field of information science is expanding, the focus in this chapter is on libraries, library science and librarians since it is these areas that have a majority of contact with the general public in the provision of services and information and referral. John Naisbitt in Megatrends. New York, New York: Warner Books, 1984, pp. 4-5, describes the post-industrial economic system as the information society. He recognizes the service economy, but sees information areas and careers as a significant element in the service economy.

2Figures on the size of the library network are compiled from the following resources: United States Department of Commerce, Bureau of the Census, Statistical Abstract of the United States: 1986, 106th Edition, Washington, D.C.: U.S. Government Printing Office, 1985; United States Department of Commerce, Bureau of the Census, 1980; Census of Population, Volume 2 Subject Reports: Part 7C: Occupation by Industry, Washington, D.C.: U.S. Government Printing Office, 1984; Boyd Ladd National Inventory of Library Needs, 1975, Washington, D.C.: U.S. Government Printing Office, 1977; United States Department of Labor, Bureau of Labor Statistics, Library Manpower: A Study of Demand and Supply, Washington, D.C.: U.S. Government Printing Office, 1975 and United States Department of Commerce, Bureau of the Cenus, Public Employment in 1984, Washington, D.C.: U.S. Government Printing Office, 1985, p. 3.

No attempt was made to calculate the number of private collections in the United States since these collections are normally for individual use and not for public use.

3Not discussed in this section, but of extreme importance, is the development of national and state historical libraries, such as the Library of Congress, Washington, D.C. (1800), New York (1804), Massachusetts (1791), and Wisconsin (1843).

4Not discussed in this section, but of extreme importance, is the utilization of privately endowed libraries, such as Newberry in Chicago (1878), and special libraries in industry.

5For a review of the concept of social responsibility and library science, the reader is referred to Patricia Schuman Social Responsibilities and Libraries, New York, New York: R.R. Bower and Co., 1976, pp. 7-11. Mark Twain's The Adventures of Huckleberry Finn (1885) has recently (1984-1986) come under scrutiny and potential censoring of the book in Waukegan, Illinois. The problem of potential censorship is particularly acute in school libraries. Other recent examples of attempted censorship include Abington, Virginia and Mukwonago, Wisconsin (1980) and West Allis, Wisconsin (1986) and their concern over secular humanism in sociology and psychology textbooks.

[6]This trend is discussed in United States Bureau of Labor, Statistics, Department of Labor. Library Manpower: A Study of Supply and Demand, Washington, DC: U.S. Government Printing Office, 1975, pp. 39-40.

[7]Two recent developments in information science not discussed in this section are the concepts of the information center and fee based information services. The information center is a facility where the staff does the investigation for a client and presents a detailed report. The report provides detailed information on a subject including supportive documentation. Depending upon the facility there may or may not be a fee for this services. There has been a rapid growth of specialized information centers since 1945.

Fee based information services consists of a private practitioner in information science who for a fee will search various data bases for specific information. This person is an information specialist who knows the different computerized data banks and the information they hold. For a fee, an individual can have the data banks checked for a specific topic. Fee based information services developed in the late 1960s and has had a rapid growth since the late 1970s. In 1980 it was estimated there were over 300 private fee based information services in the United States. Some examples of a fee based information service include Badger Infosearch in Milwaukee, Wisconsin; Information Yield in Syracuse, New York and Information on Demand in Berkeley, California.

[8]This classification does not include all librarians, since the industrial classification reviewed was under professional and related services and specifically libraries under educational services. Many librarians are working in special industrial libraries, such as agriculture, mining, construction, manufacturing, transportation, commerce, utilities, trade, finances, etc. The reader is also referred to United States Bureau of Labor Statistics, Library Manpower: A Study of Demand and Supply, 1975, for details.

[9]For specific details on library and information science as a career, the reader is referred to the American Library Association, 50 East Huron Street, Chicago, Illinois 60611 and the American Society for Information Science, 1010 Sixteenth Street, NW, Washington, DC 20036.

[10]The Crouch Experiment was the development of a comprehensive neighborhood and community information center in London, England, combining the resources of social agencies and the library (Canadian Library Journal, February-April, 1979).

[11]Hot lines and crisis information centers refer to walk-in clinics, crisis information centers, runaway programs, switchboards, parent-to-parent programs, abuse-neglect programs, battered women programs, parents helpline, drug, suicide, etc. Local and regional directories of these agencies are generally found in most public or university libraries.

[12]For further information on the profession of social work, contact the National Association of Social Workers, 7981 Eastern Avenue, Silver Spring, Maryland 20910 or the local state chapter.

SUGGESTED READINGS

Thomas Childers. Information and Referral: Public Libraries: Norwood, New Jersey: Ablex Publishing Co., 1984. This book provides an excellent overview of information and referral services as they are implemented in the public library system.

Anthony Debens et al. The Informational Professional: Survey of an Emerging Field. New York, New York: Marcel Dekker: Inc. 1981. This book provides a history and overview of the developing fields of information specialist and fee based information services.

Pat Dewdney. "The Crouch Experience: An Inter Agency Approach to Neighborhood Services". Canadian Library Journal. Vol. 36, Nos. 1 and 2 (February/April 1979, pp. 5-14. This article describes the role of a social worker in the library service system.

Sydney Jackson. Libraries and Librarianship in the West. New York, New York: McGraw-Hill Book Co., 1974. For a general historical review of the development of libraries and library science as a profession, this book provides a concise overview.

Alan Lincoln. Crime in the Library. New York, New York: R.R.
    Bowker Co., 1984. This book looks at a problem most of our
    society does not even know exists, that is the types of
    crimes which are committed in libraries.

Bruce Schuman. The River Bend Casebook: Problems in the Public
    Library Service. Phoenix, Arizona: Oryx Press, 1981. This
    book provides an insight into the human and social problems
    facing the public library system.

REFERENCES

American Library Association. World Encyclopedia of Library and
    Information Services. Chicago, IL: American Library Assoc-
    iation, 1980.

Becker, Carol. Community Information Service: A Directory of
    Public Library Involvement. Baltimore, MD: University of
    Maryland, 1974.

Bowler, Roberta. Local Public Library Administration. Chicago,
    IL: International City Managers' Association, 1964.

Childers, Thomas. Information and Referral: Public Libraries.
    Norwood, NJ: Ablex Publishing Co., 1984.

Debons, Anthony et al. The Informational Professional: Survey
    of an Emerging Field. New York, NY: Marcel Dekker, Inc.,
    1981.

Dewdney, Pat. "The Crouch Experience: An Inter-Agency Approach
    to Neighborhood Services." Canadian Library Journal,
    Vol. 36, Nos. 1 & 2 (February/April, 1979), pp. 5-14.

Estabrook, Leigh. "Emerging Trends in Community Library
    Services." Library Trends, Vol. 28, No. 2, Fall, 1977.

Fichtelberg, Leo. "Coping With Problem Patrons," New Jersey
    Libraries, Vol. 7, No. 9, (February 1979), pp. 10-11.

Forsman, Carolyn. Crisis Information Centers: A Research
    Guide. Minneapolis, MN: Exchange, 1973.

Gates, Gene. Introduction to Librarianship. New York, NY:
    McGraw-Hill Book Co., 1976.

355

Jackson, Sydney. Libraries and Librarianship in the West. New
York, NY: McGraw-Hill Book, Co., 1974.

Johnson, Robert and Roscoe Rouse. Organizational Charts of
Selected Libraries: School, Special, Public, and Academic.
Ann Arbor, MI: University of Michigan Microfilms, 1973.

King Research Inc. Library Human Resources: A Study of Supply
and Demand. Chicago, IL: American Library Association,
1983.
Kochen, Manfred and Joseph Donahue. Information for the
Community. Chicago, IL: American Library Association, 1976.

Ladd, Boyd. National Inventory of Library Needs, 1975.
Washington, D.C.: U.S. Government Printing Office, 1977.

Lincoln, Alan. Crime in the Library. New York, NY: R.R.
Bowker Co., 1984.

Maranjian, Lory and Richard Boss. Fee Based Information
Services. New York, NY: R.R. Bowker, Co., 1980.

Minahan, Anne (Ed.). Encyclopedia of Social Work 18th Issue.
Washington, D.C.: National Association of Social Workers,
1986.

Mount, Ellis. Special Libraries and Information Centers: An
Introductory Text. New York, NY: Special Libraries Association, 1983.

Naisbitt, John. Megatrends. New York: Warner Books, Inc., 1984.

Office of the Federal Register, Government Organization Manual
1985-86. Washington, D.C.: U.S. Government Printing
Office, 1985.

Potter, Gus. "Hot Lines for Troubled Youth," Federal Probation,
Vol. 35, No. 4, (December 1971), pp. 39-45.

School of Library Science. Occupational Survey of Information
Professionals. Pittsburgh, PA: University of Pittsburgh
Press, 1980.

Schuman, Bruce. The River Bend Casebook: Problems in the
Public Library Service. Phoenix, AZ: Oryz Press, 1981.

Schuman, Patricia. Social Responsibilities and Libraries. New
York, NY: R.R. Bowker Co., 1976.

United States Department of Commerce, Bureau of the Census, 1980
Census of Population: Volume 2 Subject Reports: Part 7C:
Occupation by Industry. Washington, D.C.: U.S. Government
Printing Office, 1984.

United States Department of Commerce, Bureau of the Census,
Statistical Abstract of the United States: 1986, (106th
Ed.). Washington, D.C.: U.S. Government Printing Office,
1985.

United States Department of Commerce, Bureau of the Census,
Public Employment in 1984, Washington, D.C.: U.S. Government Printing Office, 1985.

United States Department of Labor, Bureau of Labor Statistics,
Library Manpower: A Study of Demand and Supply, Washington,
D.C.: U.S. Government Printing Office, 1975.

Van Natten, Janet. "Coping With the Problem Patron," New Jersey
Libraries, Vols. 7 and 8, (December/January 1978-79),
pp. 3-4.

Wilkin, Lynne. "Mother's Discussion Groups in Public Libraries," Social Work, Vol. 21, No. 6 (November 1976) pp. 525-
527.

Wisconsin Legislative Reference Bureau, Wisconsin Blue Book
1985-1986, Madison, Wisconsin: Department of Administration, 1985.

Chapter 11

JUDICIAL NETWORK*

"As the selected arbiter in social, economic and
political confrontations courts have spoken out
on such issues as the rights of the poor, the
shelter deprived, the young, the student, the
activist, the debtor, the consumer, the conscien-
tious objector, and discrimination against non-
whites." (Tucker, 1971: III)

INTRODUCTION

The judicial network (courts) in the United States is a
highly complex network consisting of civil, criminal, probate
(estate), juvenile, and special courts (traffic, police, etc.),
at varied levels of governmental jurisdiction, (federal, state,
county and municipal). The judicial network, ideally is a
system of checks and balances with appeal procedures. The judicial network has been used to champion social causes and
social justice, as well as to impede social causes and social
justice depending upon the prevailing attitudes of society and
legal procedure. For example, at the Federal Supreme Court
level, the Brown vs. Board of Education case of 1954, declared
racial segregation unconstitutional (illegal), whereas the
Plessy vs. Ferguson case of 1896, declared racial segregation
constitutional (legal).

The judicial network like other organized aspects of society
is undergoing reorganization, specialization of role function,
and attempting to ameliorate problems of delays, long trials,
etc. This chapter describes the judicial network (emphasis on
criminal courts), and compares and contrasts the role of a
judge, prosecutor, indigent defense, and court administrator,
with that of a social worker.

SIZE

The judicial network consists of four interrelated
components: courts, prosecution and legal services, indigent
defense services, e.g., public defender and court appointed
attorneys and private defense attorneys, (the role of the
private defense attorney is discussed in Chapter 13, Legal
Network).

COURTS

In 1979 there were an estimated 17,057 courts in the United States at the federal, state and local level consisting of 14,745 judicial systems. Expenditures of the court system for criminal justice cases in 1982 were estimated at 2.2 billion dollars with at least an equal if not a higher expenditure for civil cases. The number of employees in the court system was estimated at 156,000. In 1983 there were an estimated 11,687,768 criminal and juvenile cases.

PROSECUTION and LEGAL SERVICES

In 1979 there were an estimated 10,300 agencies providing prosecution and legal services. In 1982, prosecution and legal services employed an estimated 73,000 individuals and had estimated expenditures of 1.5 billion dollars for criminal justice cases.

INDIGENT DEFENSE SERVICES

Defense services to the indigent, e.g., public defenders, and court appointed attorneys is the smallest part of the judicial network with an estimated 1,832 units in 1982. The indigent defense services in 1982 employed an estimated 25,294 individuals and had estimated expenditures of 942,188,000 dollars for criminal justice cases. These estimates include public defender services and legal aid services.

The number of individuals involved as the accused or accuser, in the judicial network is difficult to estimate since national court statistics have only recently become available. It is estimated that 11.6 million criminal and juvenile cases were brought to court in 1983 (10.5 million criminal cases and 1.1 million juvenile cases). If one case involves at least two people, that means at least 23.2 million people per year are involved in the judicial network and this is a conservative estimate, since the majority of cases involve more than two people. Figure 11-1, graphically shows the estimated size of the judicial network.

HISTORICAL DEVELOPMENT

Development of the judicial network in the United States has been relatively uneven with, courts having a long history, and separate prosecution and legal services, and defense services for the indigent (poor), having a more recent origin, since about 1850.

FIGURE II-I

Estimated Size of the Judicial Network in 1979-1983*

Selected Aspect	Components of the Judicial Network		
	Courts	Prosecution and Legal Services	Defense Services (Includes Legal Aid)
Number of facilities	17,057	10,300	1,832+
Number of Employees	156,000	73,000	25,294+
Expenditures (Billion)	2.2 Billion	1.5 Billion	942,188+
Number of Criminal Cases in 1981-82	11,687.768[1]	2	2

*Source: Adapted from United States Department of Justice, Bureau of Justice Statistics, Sourcebook of Criminal Justice Statistics-1984. Washington, DC: U.S. Government Printing Office, 1985, pp. 6, 9, 24, 28, 544, 562; United States Department of Commerce, Bureau of the Census, Statistical Abstract of the United States: 1986 (106th Edition).,Washington, D.C.: U.S. Government Printing Office, 1985, pp. 175, 176, 182, 183, 184, 185, 186, and United States Department of Commerce, Bureau of the Census, 1982 Census of Service Industries. Washington, D.C.: U.S. Government Printing Office, 1984, pp. 6, 7.

1 Figures include criminal and juvenile cases. There were an additional 29,914,000 child-related cases in the court system in 1982, which were not delinquency related.

2 The assumption made by the author is that all court cases would have prosecution and defense services. Therefore, the number of cases in these two categories would be the same as the number of court cases.

COURTS

The court system of the United States is an adaptation of the English system with modifications, such as special courts (family, traffic, etc.), a system of local predominance, check and balance system (federal, state, local administration), and an appeal process.

CLASSICAL SOCIETY - PRE-450 AD - The concept of a hearing before a third party (tribunal, court, king etc), in order to resolve differences between parties or to prosecute a person accused of a crime, is of ancient origin. In earlier periods of time, differences between two parties were resolved through battle or a blood feud. The criminal was punished by the tribal leaders or the god/king. In these earlier days the tribal leader, or a god/king, or a priest/judge would hear cases and dispense justice. In Egypt (1500 BC) for example, the Pharaoh (God/King) was responsible for hearing cases and delegated many cases to the vizier or first minister of government. In Babylonia (1700 BC) the God/King was responsible for justice, and amongst the Hebrews (1000 BC) the priest/judge was responsible for justice. Both the Greek (700 BC) and Roman societies (100 BC) had a tribunal to hear cases through the senate and local governmental officials.

EARLY and MEDIEVAL ENGLAND - 450-1485 - The court system in the United States as we know it is an adaptation of the English system and common law traditions (precedent), instead of the civil law traditions (statutory) of Rome and continental Europe. The English system is a combination of Anglo/Saxon courts, with modifications after the Norman invasion of 1066. In Anglo Saxon England (450-1066 AD), the court system primarily consisted of local courts with no centralized system, nor an appeal process to a higher court. Examples of these courts in Anglo Saxon England include: the Witan (King's Council); Shire Court (county); the Hundred Court (district within a Shire); Borough Court (large village); and private courts (manor and ecclesiastical church courts). With the Norman invasion of 1066, there was a movement to centralize the court system and decrease the power of the local courts. From 1066-1307, there was the development of the Kings Council (Curia Regis) and Exchequer Court under Henry II (1154-1189); the Magna Carta in 1215, which guaranteed specific court procedures (jury trials and bail); the King's Court (bench) under Henry III (1216-1272), and the Court of Common Pleas under Edward I (1272-1307). These newer courts were centralizing the court system in England with government control instead of local control. In addition to the newer courts of government, private courts continued (ecclesiastical, church and manor or seignorial courts). From 1307-1485, the three centralized courts of common law further defined their functions, such as Common Pleas (civil cases), Excheqeur (financial cases) and Assize (criminal cases). The Assize Court was an expansion of the King's Bench and was implemented through royal judges who traveled to different parts of England and were known as itinerant judges. During this period of time, there was a decrease in the influence and jurisdiction of the older Anglo Saxon courts, eg. the shire, hundred and borough courts.

ENGLISH NATION STATE - 1485 ON - From 1485-1637, there were further modifications in England, increasing the power of the centralized courts, and further decline of the older Anglo Saxon system, and the ecclesiastical and manor courts. From 1637 on further specialized courts were developed, such as juvenile, probate, etc.

UNITED STATES - The court system initially followed the English pattern of the court of common pleas, a county court and a colonial court. With the adoption of the Constitution in 1789, the United States developed a dual system of courts, federal, state and local, with an appeal procedure through both federal and state courts. The Constitution of 1789 and the Judiciary Act of 1790 provided rights to a jury trial and to bail (Article 3, and the 6th and 8th Amendment of the Constitution of the United States).

PROSECUTION and LEGAL SERVICES

Responsibility for prosecution of cases historically was located within the court itself consequently there was no distinction made between the court and prosecution and legal services.

CLASSICAL SOCIETY - PRE 450 AD - The tribal leader, God/King or Priest/Judge would hear a case as well as prosecute a case.

MEDIEVAL and ENGLISH NATION STATE 450 AD ON - In England both in Anglo Saxon times and after the Norman invasion of 1066, prosecution of a case was the responsibility of the judge, and their assistants, or local law enforcement officials.

UNITED STATES - One of the modifications of the English system in the United States was the development of the office of the District Attorney, which is responsible for prosecution of cases as well as providing other legal services for a governmental unit. The movement for a separate office for the prosecution of cases, independent of the judge, developed after 1850. The intent in developing a separate administrative unit for the prosecution of cases was to create a more balanced judicial network and to avoid a conflict of interest both politically and financially. Politically the conflict could be overzealous prosecution of a case without adequate grounds for a variety of reasons, and financially the conflict could be in providing better quality legal services because one is wealthy or important in the community. In large jurisdictions, the office of the district attorney has become specialized, and has subunits for: investigation, witness support service, sexual assault units, pre-trial diversion, etc.

INDIGENT DEFENSE SERVICES

One would assume an individual always had a right to legal counsel or an attorney to represent their case. Historically individuals were expected to plead their own defense.

CLASSICAL SOCIETY - PRE 450 AD - In Greece (700 BC), the individual was expected to plead their own case, however, one could ask a friend or a relative to assist them. By 400 BC, some individuals became professional advocates and would plead the case (early lawyers). In Rome (200 BC), a person was again expected to plead their own case, but could ask an advocate to supplement their case.

MEDIEVAL and ENGLISH NATION STATE 450 ON - The individual was expected to plead their own case, however, by 1268 a person could ask for a substitute to represent them in court, and by 1292, the right to legal counsel was established. Ironically, individuals accused of misdemeanors could have separate legal counsel, and felons could not. It was not until the legal and court reforms in England in 1836, that a felon was allowed separate legal counsel.

UNITED STATES - Initially the United States followed a similar pattern as England's with the individual pleading their own case. In addition, some of the colonies recognized a right to separate legal counsel, and prior to 1776, five colonies had these rights built into their constitution. The United States Constitution of 1789, guaranteed the right of separate legal counsel (6th Amendment), and the Judiciary Act of 1790 included the right of separate legal counsel assigned by the court. The retaining of a private attorney for one's defense is costly, consequently if a person had money, they would hire an attorney, and if one was poor, one did not have an attorney or the court appointed an attorney for the case. Currently there are three means through which a poor person can obtain separate legal counsel: Legal Aid and Legal Services, Public Defender's Office, and a court appointed attorney.

Legal Aid for the indigent movement began in the United States in 1876, when the German Society of New York provided legal services for new immigrants. Legal Aid was established as an independent private organization, sponsored through private foundations and donations. By 1900, there were only six cities in the United States with a legal aid office, and by 1917 only 41 cities. The Legal Aid movement rapidly spread after 1919 under the efforts of Reginald Heber Smith, and today most large cities have a Legal Aid Society. A related development to Legal Aid as a form of assistance is legal services for the poor, sponsored by the federal government under the Economic Opportunity Act of 1964. The name of the program was changed to the Legal Service Corporation in 1974. This federally funded program of legal services is expected to be deleted from the federal budget by 1988.

The paid public defender movement for providing legal services, developed in Los Angles, California 1914, followed by a number of states and cities like Milwaukee, Wisconsin in 1916. The public defender is a full time attorney hired by the governmental unit to provide legal counsel for the indigent. There was a slow movement in the development of a public defender system until 1963, and the Supreme Court decision of Gideon vs. Wainright. This court decision, mandated that a person accused of a felony must have legal counsel. This principle was further applied to misdemeanants in 1972 in the Argersinger vs. Hamlin case. The Constitution of the United States, as indicated earlier, granted individuals the right to legal counsel, however local and state courts were slow in guaranteeing legal counsel.

The court appointed attorney is the most common method for providing legal services for the indigent and was a common practice prior to 1940. At least 2,700 counties in the United States will appoint an attorney from an existing list of attorneys' for a specific fee to represent an indigent individual. Most courts, have a listing of attorneys they can use if an individual is indigent and requests an attorney instead of using the public defender's office.

Figure 11-2 is a historical time line for the judicial network.

STRUCTURE

The judicial network, like other societal networks, can be described from its organizational context, services provided, occupations and professions and dominant occupations and professions.

ORGANIZATIONAL CONTEXT

As indicated earlier, the judicial network consists of courts, prosecution and legal services, and indigent defense services.

COURTS - The court component of the judicial network in the United States is a dual system of federal and state (including

365

FIGURE 11-2

Historical Time Line of the Judicial Network
(England and United States)

	Court System	Prosecution and Legal Services	Defense Services
450 AD England	Witan (King's Court) Shire (County Court) Hundred (Subsection of a county) Borough (Large Village) Private (Seignorial or manor or church Courts)	Judge heard, prosecuted and developed cases	Accused expected to defend themself
1066- 1300 England	Court of Common Pleas 1178 Court of Exchequer Court of King's Bench (pre-1178)	Judge and staff or law enforcement official heard cases	Magna Carta 1215 Jury trial, Bail Accused could have someone plead for them (Barrister) or take their place (Attorney)
1300- 1750 England	Further centralization of the court system	Judge and staff or local law enforcement official heard cases	Rights to defense services for mis- demeanors, but not felons
1750- 1900 United States	Dual system of Courts 1789 and in 1790 an appeal procedure	Prosecution services separated from Judge (1850's)	Right to Bail and Right to Attorney 1789-1790 Legal Aid Movement 18
1900- on United States	Court reorganization Specialized Courts Court Administrator developed as a profession in 1937	Right to speedy trial Specialization of services in prosecu- tion to include diver- sion and support services	Public Defender 1916 Wainwright & Gideon 1963—counsel for fe cases Argersinger vs. Haml 1972—counsel for misdemeanant cases

*Sources: Adapted from M.M. Knappen, Constitutional and Legal History of England. N York, NY: Harcourt, Brace, and Co., 1942; and David Neubauer. America's Courts and Criminal Justice System. North Scituate, MA: Duxbury Press, 1979.

local) courts. Courts are organized on a hierarchial (lower to higher courts), geographical, and a regional basis. Hierarchially, courts are organized at the following levels:

Lower Court - (Inferior Court or Courts of Limited Jurisdiction). These courts are trial courts, whose legal jurisdiction covers only a particular type of case, eg., probate, juvenile, traffic, family, misdemeanor, small claims, etc. These courts may have a judge who is presiding, or in some cases, there may be a justice of the peace, court commissioner, or magistrate. It is at this level of the court system, where 90 percent of the individuals involved in the judicial network have their initial contact, and in many cases their only contact.

Major Court - (Court of General Jurisdiction). These courts are trial courts of unlimited jurisdiction and usually dispose of serious (felony) criminal cases. This court may be called a circuit court or county court, and hear cases not delegated to the lower courts, or in some cases share concurrently, jurisdiction with the lower court. In the federal system these courts are the District Courts.

Appellate - Court (Intermediate Appeal Court). These courts have jurisdiction of appeal and reviewing cases from the lower or major court. In exceptional cases, they may become a court of original jurisdiction or initial trial. The court usually has a panel of three judges. In the federal system, these courts are the court of appeals. This type of court is found in about 50 percent of the states.

Supreme Court - (Court of Last Resort). This court has jurisdiction of appeal and reviewing cases from the lower, major or appellate court, and is the highest court in the state (State Supreme Court), or in the United States (the United States Supreme Court.)

Geographically, the federal system consists of: 89 district courts, plus Puerto Rico, District of Columbia, Canal Zone, Guam, Virgin Islands and the Northern Mariana Islands; 11 courts of appeals, plus Puerto Rico and the District of Columbia; and the Supreme Court. The state court system will vary depending upon the state. Wisconsin for example has 133 municipal courts, 71 county courts, 26 circuit courts (71 locations), 5 appellate courts and one supreme court.[2]

PROSECUTION and LEGAL SERVICES - The prosecution and legal services component of the judicial network has as its primary function the prosecution of alleged criminal offenders, and the legal representation of the governmental unit in civil matters. In some large metropolitan areas, the prosecutor's office

(District Attorney), has become responsible for legal services which contribute to prosecution of a case, such as witness support, victim support, special investigating units on white collar crime, sensitive crimes (rape, sexual assault) and offender diversion programs.

INDIGENT DEFENSE SERVICES - It has been estimated that 65 percent of felony defendants are too poor to pay for a private attorney, consequently, defense services are necessary. The indigent defense services component of the judicial network consists of a public funded system (public defender office or a court appointed attorney). Figures 11-3 and 11-4 show an idealized organization of the judicial network and Figure 11-5 an idealized organization of the courts of a large metropolitan community.

In addition to the formal judicial network, a private system of courts has recently been established in New York, 1978, mediation centers established in 1980, and an informal system of extra legal groups exist, which attempt to impose justice, such as the Klu Klux Klan, Posse Comitatus, etc.

SERVICES PROVIDED

Most court systems are small with 23 percent having less than 9 employees, and 26 percent with 10-24 employees. Consequently the following listing of services is idealized, since only the largest of the judicial networks would be in a position to provide these services. Some of the services available in the judicial network include the following:

- Alcohol counseling

- Psychiatric and psychological counseling

- Diversionary and alternative programs

- Bail/bond procedures

- Sexual assault units

- Offender evaluation projects

- Probation services (see Chapter 16, Corrections Network for details).

Figure 11-3

Idealized Organization of the
Judicial Network

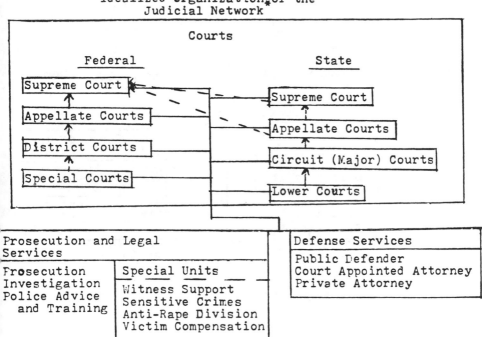

369

FIGURE 11-4

IDEALIZED GOVERNMENT ORGANIZATION of the JUDICIAL NETWORK*

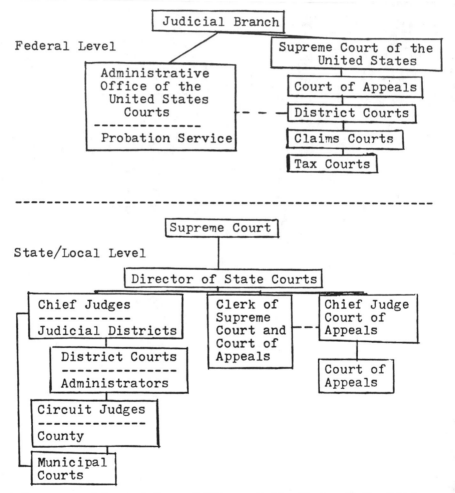

* Sources: Adapted from Office of the Federal Register, Government Organization Manual 1985-86,Washington D.C.: U.S. Government Printing Office,1985, p. 816 and Wiscons: Legislative Reference Bureau, Blue Book 1985-1986, Madis(Wisconsin: Department of Administration, 1985,p.623.

Figure 11-3

Idealized Organization of a Typical Large
Metropolitan Judicial Network*

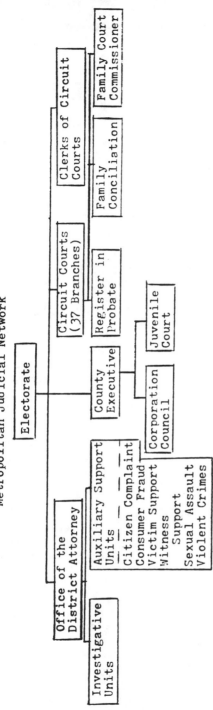

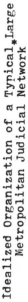

*Source: Adapted from: Milwaukee County Wisconsin Organizational Charts for the
Court System and District Attorney's Office, 1985.

- Family and marital counseling

- Witness support units

- Single parent services

- Child welfare legal services.

OCCUPATIONS and PROFESSIONS

The judicial network employs a wide variety of human service professions. Figure 11-6 shows a sample variety of employees in the judicial network in 1980. Judges, lawyers and bailiffs are the main occupations.

The key occupation in the judicial network is that of the judge, of which there are an estimated 27,576 in the United States (including magistrates, commissioners, justices of the peace, etc.) of which 22,139 or 80.3 percent are employed in the industrial classification of justice, public order and safety (a subcategory of the industrial classification of public administration and the remaining 5,437 or 19.7 percent are employed in other subcategories of the industrial classi- fication of public administration. In a survey of courts of general jurisdiction, (major trial courts), judges account for only 10 percent of the total employees of the courts as one component of the judicial network. Other occupations employed in the courts include the following:

Other officials exercising judicial authority (8.2 per- cent). This group includes magistrates, justices of the peace, court commissioners, etc. These are individuals who can hear cases and make decisions.

Clerks, deputy clerks, and court administrators (21.9 per- cent). Responsibilities of the clerk include maintaining the docket (calendar) for judges, selecting the names for a jury, maintaining records, collecting and managing court costs, non-support payments, etc.

Bailiffs (10.8 percent). This person is responsible for an orderly court, transporting accused individuals to and from court and generally is the courts security officer.

Court reporters (8.7 percent). This person is responsible for accurate transcripts of court proceedings.

FIGURE 11-6

Number and Percent of Selected Human Service Occupations and
Professions Employed in the Justice, Public Order and Safety
Industrial Classification (emphasis Judicial Network) in 1980*

Selected Occupation and Profession	Number	Percent
Judges	22,139	22.27
Lawyers	35,292	35.49
Social Work	16,861	16.95
Legal Assistant	2,258	2.37
Personnel Relations & Training	1,910	1.93
Psychologist	514	.51
Clergy & Religious Worker	281	.29
Physician	100 ¹	.10
Dentist	20 ¹	.02
Painter/Sculpter	62	.06
Bailiffs and Others	20,000	20.11
TOTAL	99,437	100.00

*Source: Adapted from United States Department of Commerce, Bureau of the
Census, 1980 Census of Population; Vol. 2 Subject Reports Part 7C: Occupation
by Industry. Washington, DC: U.S. Government Printing Office, 1984, pp.
295-664. The industrial classification of justice, public order and safety
represents the protective service, judicial and corrections networks. The
Subject Report is not detailed enough to clearly identify the judicial
network. Some occupations are clearly in the judicial network like judges,
others are clearly corrections like correctional guard, and others clearly
protective service like police and detectives. The above listing of occupations represents an attempt to identify those which were working in the
judicial network. This list is obviously representative and not exhaustive.

¹ These figures are estimates only based upon the probable distribution
between the protective service, judicial and corrections networks.

Probation officers (15.2 percent). In some jurisdictions,
probation officers are attached to the court instead of an
independent agency. Many of these probation officers are
social workers. (For a description of probation and parole see
Chapter 16, Corrections Network.)

Law clerks (2 percent). These individuals assist the judge in preparing legal decisions, looking up legal materials and generally engaging in legal research.

Staff attorneys (1.3 percent). These individuals may perform tasks similar to the law clerk, and generally assist the judge if investigations or legal research is necessary.

Other professional and technical (3.0 percent). This group includes, social workers (in addition to probation staff), psychiatrists, psychologists, etc., who may be needed as expert witnesses in some cases or provide ongoing consultation.

Clerical/secretarial (13.6 percent). This group provides secretarial services for the clerk of court.

Other (5.2 percent). A miscellaneous group of people, ranging from custodians to other maintenance personnel.[3]

The prosecution and legal services offices which are separate from the courts, are generally staffed by attorneys. Overall employment in the United States in prosecution and legal services, was estimated at 73,000 of which 35,770 or 49 percent were attorneys in the positions of Chief, and Assistant Chief Prosecutors, and Assistant Prosecutors. Fifty-one percent or 37,230 of the employees held other positions, such as investigators 8 percent, paralegals, 4 percent, administrative and supervisory personnel 3 percent, other, 1 percent which includes specialists, such as caseworkers, interpreters, consultants, social workers, etc. The remaining 35 percent of the employees were secretaries, stenographer's, etc.[4]

Services for the defense of the indigent (Office of the Public Defender) had a similar occupational distribution to that of the office of prosecution and legal services. Of the estimated 9,000 employees, 4,950 or 55 percent were attorneys distributed as follows: 9.33 percent Chief, and Assistant Chief Defenders, and 45.67 percent were Assistant Defenders. Of the remaining 4,050 employees or 45 percent of employees, 12 percent were investigators, 2.5 percent paralegals, 7 percent a combination of other occupations including administrators, and the remaining 23.5 percent of the employees were secretaries, etc.[5]

DOMINANT OCCUPATIONS and PROFESSIONS

Figure 11-6 indicates the predominate position of judges and lawyers in the judicial network. Figure 11-7 shows employment of judges and lawyers employed in the industrial classification of public administration in 1980.

The major area of employment for judges was in the industrial classification of justice, public order and safety with 22,139 or 80.283 percent of the total and the remaining 5,437 or 19.717 percent employed in other industrial classifications within public administration. Lawyers, on the other hand, were more widely distributed in the industrial classification of public administration with 35,292 or 52.285 percent employed in the industrial classification of justice, public order and safety, and the remaining 32,207 or 47.715 percent employed in other industrial classifications within public administration. Those occupations which will be discussed in more detail are those of a judge, lawyer (prosecution and defense) and court administrator.

JUDGE – Contrary to popular opinion, few individuals who become judges, have any training or background in the role of a judge, outside of their general legal background. In some jurisdictions, one does not need a legal background nor legal certification to become a judge. Since, most judges are elected or appointed, the selection criteria for judges varies widely from state to state and within courts within a state.

Except for an occasional circumstance, judges have a law degree or a legal background, consequently minimal standards of education have not posed a particular problem. The educational concern about the position of a judge is understanding the deliberating role of the judge as distinct from the adversary role of the lawyer, in implementing a court system.[6]

The President's Task Force on Law Enforcement had recommended that judges be required to participate in continuing education programs, and each state, develop a system of continuing education through institutes, or a special academy.[7] As of 1975, only 24 of the 50 states provided initial training for an individual who recently became a judge, however 47 states had some formal mechanism for in service training. Content of the in-service training sessions would vary, but examples of topics include: court management, hearing procedures, rules of evidence, waivers, supreme court decisions, news and media relations, etc. Further content of the in-service training sessions would vary depending upon whether the judge was operating in civil court, criminal court, probate court, family court, juvenile court, etc.

FIGURE II-7

Number and percent of Judges and Lawyers,
Employed in the Industrial Classification
of Public Administration in 1980*

Industrial Classification of Public Administration	Judges		Lawyers	
	Number	Percent	Number	Percent
Executive and Legislative Office	146	.529	3,351	4.965
Government (General)	2,044	7.413	11,707	17.344
Justice/Public Order and Safety[1]	22,139	80.283	35,292	52.285
Finance Administration	144	.523	2,790	4.134
Human Resource Administration	1,753	6.356	4,077	6.041
Environment Administration	136	.494	1,494	2.187
Economic Program Administration	875	3.173	7,133	10.567
National Security Administration	339	1.229	1,671	2.475
TOTAL	27,576	100.000	67,499	100.000

*Source: Adapted from United States Department of Commerce, Bureau of the Census, 1980 Census of Population. Vol. 2. Subject Reports Part 7C: Occupation by Industry, Washington, DC: U.S. Government Printing Office, 1984, pp. 295-664.

[1] The industrial classification of justice/public order and safety represents the protective service, judicial and corrections networks. The occupations of judges and lawyer primarily represent the judicial network. The Subject Report is not detailed enough to categorize other human service occupations whether they are employed in judicial or corrections.

Regardless of the specific court, some of the tasks of a judge include the following:

- Hears testimony, and reviews affidavits
- Conducts preliminary hearings
- Conducts and mediates conferences in chambers
- Rules on requests and motions
- Negotiates a plea bargaining charge if appropriate
- Researches and writes legal opinions
- Analyzes and evaluates evidence
- Conducts regular court hearings and bench or jury trials
- Manages the court calendar
- Sentences, the convicted offender.

LAWYER

The lawyer or attorney performs similar functions but for different purposes depending upon whether they are involved in prosecution services or defense services.

Prosecution services are performed through the appropriate governmental district attorney's office. As indicated earlier 49 percent of the employees in prosecution and legal services are attorneys. The prosecutor's office, in addition to the prosecution of cases depending upon the size of the court system can be highly involved in pre-trial diversion programs, such as alcohol, drugs, mental health, first offender programs, etc. The range of potential services include referring individuals for job training, employment, rehabilitative services, counseling, etc. Most attorneys in the prosecutor's office have received limited training for their role, consequently, in-service training programs have been developed to better enable the individual to perform the functions of that office. Some of the tasks of the prosecutors office include:

- Interview witnesses, police officers and victims of a crime
- Obtain and collect legal evidence
- Screen cases and advise citizens of appropriate courses of action
- Negotiate a plea bargain (reduction of a specific charge)
- Provide testimony at court hearings
- Review and evaluate evidence
- Conduct legal research[8].

Defense Services performed by a lawyer whether employed as a public defender, or as a court appointed attorney usually include the following tasks:

- Act as a legal advocate for the accused
- Negotiate a plea bargain (reduction of specific charge)

- Protect the legal rights of the accused
- Advise clients of their legal rights
- Manage multiple cases
- Prepare a case for court
- Interview and cross examine witnesses in court.

COURT ADMINISTRATOR

A developing profession in the judicial network is that of a court administrator. A court system needs individuals for the following tasks:

- Prepare the court calendar (docket)
- Maintain records
- Prepare reports
- Collect court fees, restitution and financial judgments
- Oversee jury selection.

In some jurisdictions these tasks are performed by an elected official, known as a Clerk of Court, in others by the Chief Judge (who also assigns judges to a specific court), and in others by a professional court administrator. The first court administrator was hired in Connecticut in 1937. By 1978, all states except one had a court administrator. Some larger cities have court administrators, but in most jurisdictions the Clerk of Court is responsible for the above tasks. In 1974, there were at least 455 court administrators with 66 percent of appellate courts and 15 percent of the courts of general juris-diction having a professional administrator. There is no agree-ment on educational qualifications for a court administrator. That is, should the court administrator have, a law degree, a bachelor's degree in court administration, or some other degree. An Institute for Court Management was developed in 1970 to provide training for court administrators. In addition to the court administrator, a newly formed occupational group is that of a paralegal clerk which in 1974 were used by 50 percent of the appellate courts and 79 percent of the courts of general jurisdiction.[9]

SOCIAL WORK

The number of social workers involved in the judicial network is difficult to ascertain, since many of them are involved either in support functions e.g., providing testimony, advocating for their client, or, in working directly for the court, e.g. as probation officers, in special units, and in diversion programs. According to the 1980 Census of Population, there were 16,861 social workers employed by local government in the industrial classification of justice, public order and safety. Presumably the vast majority of these individuals are

378

working in the judicial network as probation officers (see Figure 11-6). The social workers function would vary depending upon whether their task is: support, probation, special units, or diversion.

SUPPORT

Any social worker, in any employment situation could eventually participate in a court hearing. In many of these situations, the social worker is not an employee of the court, but of another agency, in which legal issues are involved. The tasks will vary depending upon whether a person is in child welfare, public assistance, education, psychiatric, medical settings, etc. Generally the role of a social worker in a supportive capacity would be as follows:

- Petitioner - The individual who alleges child neglect or abuse and files a petition to have the children removed from a parental home.

- Defendant - The individual who has to answer charges that the agency is not providing expected services, or may have made the wrong decision on a case.

- Client advocate - The individual would speak in behalf of their client, whom they are serving in a different capacity.

- Expert witness - The individual may be asked to appear in court to testify because of their knowledge of a subject matter, such as child abuse, sexual assault, etc.

- Corroborative testimony - The individual may be asked to provide testimony since they are employed by a companion public agency, eg., Social Services Department and has detailed knowledge of a specific situation.[10]

PROBATION

In some court systems a probation officer is an agent and employee of the court. The function of a probation officer is similar to those functions of probation and parole discussed in Chapter 16 Corrections Network. The main tasks of the probation officer include:

- Prepare pre-sentence investigation reports - A social history of an individual and their family to ascertain probable causes for the antisocial behavior, and a recommended rehabilitation program.

379

- Supervise probationers - Overseeing a person's adjustment while under supervision.

- Casework/group work services - Engage an individual in a personal relationship to enable the person to cope with problems they may be having.

- Client advocacy - In some situations advocating for the individual in seeking employment, redressing adverse minor situations.

- Miscellaneous - Special reports, public relations, etc.

SPECIAL UNIT

Depending upon the judicial network, specialized units, such as sexual assault, battered wives, anti-rape, witness support etc. will be established. Normally, these special units would be attached to the prosecutor's and legal services section (District Attorneys Office) of the judicial network. The social worker's tasks would vary depending upon the special unit, but would include the following:

- Counseling - Emergency counseling since an individual may have been a victim of a crime, such as rape, sexual assault etc. Follow up counseling is usually provided, and a referral to another agency for continuing counseling if needed.

- Judicial network advise - Explaining to an individual what the judicial network is, the process for seeking redress for a criminal act through the system, or generally being supportive with individuals who are serving as witnesses.

- Referral and broker agent - If an individual is not aware of a community's social service agencies, to provide sufficient information to obtain needed services.[11]

DIVERSION

Diversion refers to a process of having an individual avoid entry into the criminal justice system (pre-trial) or minimizing the impact of entry into the criminal justice system (post-trial). Specifically an assessment is made whether a criminal record, would be more destructive or constructive for a person's future as a first time offender. The type of tasks the social worker would be engaged in include:

- Evaluation - An assessment of the person's sense of responsibility to society, any mitigating circumstances of the specific offense, and an assessment of one's overall potential for non-repetition of the offense and for a positive or negative adjustment in society.

- Alternate program - Develop an alternate program to incarceration which could vary from volunteer work, required employment, educational program, treatment program, and restitution.

- Bail/bond evaluation - An assessment of the person's probability of not committing another crime or absconding (running away) and to enable a judge to set a reasonable bail (for a more detailed discussion of bail/bond see Chapter 16, Corrections).[12]

PERSONAL SOCIAL SERVICES

The judicial network, like other networks, has a personal social service component (see Chapter 22, Personal Social Service). Some examples of the personal social services in the judicial network include the following:

PROTECTIVE SERVICES

Services and legal rights of children, rights of parents, services and rights to the aged, and legal issues regarding transfer of custody and guardianship in child welfare such as Legal Advocacy for Older Adults and Legal Action of Milwaukee, Wisconsin.

UTILITARIAN SERVICES

Rights and services to landlords and tenants' and consumer fraud and rights of a consumer, such as Legal Action of Wisconsin and Tenants' Union of Milwaukee, Wisconsin.

DEVELOPMENTAL and SOCIALIZATION SERVICES

Rights of marital partners, emancipation of children, paternity issues in cases of unwed mothers, divorce procedures etc., such as Legal Action of Wisconsin and Divorce Pro Se of Milwaukee, Wisconsin.

REHABILITATIVE and THERAPEUTIC SERVICES

Counseling for alcohol and drug abusers, provision of social services to both groups, and legal rights in sexual assault cases, such as Milwaukee Council on Alcoholism and Legal Action of Wisconsin.

SPECIAL POPULATIONS

The judicial network has had both a negative and a positive impact on special populations (see Chapter 25, Special Populations and Chapter 24, Rehabilitation). Some examples of the involvement of the judicial network and special populations and organizations focussing on the judicial network include the following:

ASIAN

Issues of discrimination in housing, employment, education, and consumer fraud. Legal services offered through Asian Community Centers, such as the Asian Community Center, San Francisco, California and Asian American Legal Defense Fund, New York, New York.

BLACK

Issues of discrimination in housing, employment and education, special programs through the District Attorneys Office in selected large cities. The National Urban League and National Association for the Advancement of Colored People, New York, New York.

EUROPEAN ETHNIC

Issues of consumer fraud and discrimination in employment, such as the International Institutes of St. Paul Minnesota and Milwaukee, Wisconsin.

NATIVE AMERICAN

Issues of discrimination in housing, employment and education. Indian Community Centers and Indian Legal Aid, such as the Native American Rights Fund, Boulder, Colorado and the Native American Center of Oklahoma city, Oklahoma.

SAME SEX PREFERENCE

Issues of discrimination in housing, employment, legal rights of same sex marriages, child custody cases etc. For example the Homosexual Information Center of Hollywood, California.

SPANISH

Issues of discrimination in housing, employment and education. Spanish and Migrant Community Centers, such as La Casa de

Esperanza, Waukesha, Wisconsin and the Mexican American Legal Defense Fund of San Francisco, California.

WOMEN

Issues of credit equality, marital equality, discrimination in employment, etc. Feminist Centers and groups like Project Equality in Milwaukee, Wisconsin offer numerous programs, and the National Organization of Women and its local chapters.

ISSUES

The judicial network like other networks involved in human services is undergoing rapid change. Specifically, there are: expectations of continuing education, development of specialized units to address special needs, and the awareness that the judicial network needs expertise in management eg., court administration, as a distinct occupational professional group. In general, issues facing the judicial network as it relates to social services are of two main types: general operational concerns and educational concerns.

OPERATIONAL CONCERNS

The judicial network, depending upon the specific court setting, has certain operational problems. These include, but are not limited to: bail/bond, delay in hearings, plea bargaining, continuing education, and court administration.

BAIL/BOND - Recently, with the reported increase of assaultive crimes, the issue of bail/bond is becoming a political and legal football. Bail is the monetary amount set by the judge for one's release and bond is a percentage one pays to a bondsman for providing the money for bail. Specifically, some individuals with an assaultive record, have received a low bail monetarily, were released and then committed new offenses. Some jurisdictions, are arguing for the abolition of bail/bond procedures on certain offenses, and others for more specific guidelines. Some states now bypass the bondsman, allowing families to use personal and real estate property values as a means to provide money for bail. Contrary to popular opinion, studies on bail/bond have indicated only a small percentage of individuals released on bail, commit new offenses while on bail. In the Manhattan Bail Project, of 3,505 individuals released on recognizance (released by a judge without bail), only 56 or 6 percent would have spent time in jail for a new offense. Other studies on bail/bond procedures have indicated that if one is in jail at the time of the trial, there is a higher probability of conviction. The Vera Institute of Justice in New York has done studies on bail/bond and has developed a system for assessing, whether an individual is a high, or low risk potential for bail. The outcome of the bail/bond issue will have an impact on the type and extent of services to be offered by offender evaluation and diversion projects.[13]

DELAY in HEARINGS - It is quite common for cases of a criminal action to be in process for 1 to 2 years, and in civil action 1 to 7 years. The backlog of cases for judges runs into the thousands. This backlog of cases is due to the sheer number of cases to be processed with limited court resources and difficulties of court administration. An added factor is the time and cost involved in the development of a jury trial, eg. witnesses, attorneys, victims, and jury selection, even though jury trials represent a small percentage of cases (3-5 percent).

PLEA BARGAINING - The combination of the backlog of cases, and attempts to secure adjudication of cases, has led to the expedient system of plea bargaining in many criminal cases. That is, a specific legal charge would be reduced, because of the uncertainty of the evidence, or because of the expediency of getting the case into court. Plea bargaining is a problem, since it occasionally allows a dangerous individual to obtain a light sentence for a serious crime, or may cause someone who is innocent, to plead guilty to a lesser offense. In other words, an individual could be bribed into pleading guilty, when they are innocent. It has been estimated that 85-90 percent of criminal cases involve plea bargaining. Although, as many as 90 percent of the criminal court cases may involve plea bargaining, this does not mean the prosecutor or the judge has total discretion. Some jurisdictions limit plea bargaining to reduction of a legal charge to a specific offense, reduction of a charge within a specific offense, or in some cases to certain types of crimes. Plea bargaining is widespread and the concerns are twofold: leniency for serious offenses, and bribing or coercing an individual to plead guilty without having a trial.

CONTINUING EDUCATION - The issue of continuing education was previously discussed in relationship to both judges and prosecutor's. The fact, that many individual's occupy these positions without prior or concurrent training is rapidly changing. Court administration as a consequence of specialization within the judicial network is becoming more complex which has led to a need for court administrators with specialized training.

EDUCATIONAL CONCERNS

The development of specialized units which focus on problems of sexual assault, offender evaluation and diversion programs has resulted in the judicial network utilizing human service professions, including social work to a greater extent.

For social work education, there should be interdisciplinary courses to provide content on the judicial network, alternative programs to incarceration, and an introduction to law. Social workers generally should have some background in court procedures, since most of them will appear in court at some time either as a paid employee of the court or as a support service for another agency.

Conversely, lawyers should have content on human service networks, and the role of social work. The assumption is that both professions (social work and law) will be working more closely together in the future in a team environment, consequently an interprofessional perspective is desirable.

SUMMARY

The judicial network in the United States is decentralized with a check and balance system consisting of approximately 17,057 courts with different jurisdictions, (county, municipal, circuit, state, federal), 10,300 Prosecution and Legal Services agencies, and 530 Defense Service agencies (Public Defender).

A brief history of the development of the judicial network showed the United States has been predominantly responsible for the development of specialized prosecution and legal services, and indigent defense (public defender) services. It is interesting to note that the Constitution of 1789 provides a guarantee of legal counsel, yet it was necessary to have this principle reaffirmed by the Supreme Court in 1963 (felony cases) and 1972 (misdemeanant cases).

The predominate occupation/profession in the judicial network is that of a judge, lawyer, (prosecutor, or public defender), followed by clerks of court; and court administrators.

The role of social work was discussed within the judicial network depending upon whether the individual was: a paid court employee, eg., probation officer, or in a special unit, diversion program, or in a supportive role in a court hearing.

Some general issues of the judicial network were discussed, such as bail/bond, backlog of cases, plea bargaining, continuing education, court administration, and educational issues relating to the education of social workers and lawyers.

FOOTNOTES

1. Statistical information on the judicial network is adapted from the following resources produced by the United States Department of Justice, National Survey of Court Organization, Washington, D.C.: U.S. Government Printing Office, 1973; National Manpower Survey of the Criminal Justice System, Washington, D.C.: U.S. Government Printing Office, 1978; State and Local Prosecution and Civil Attorney Systems, Washington, D.C.: U.S. Government Printing Office, 1976; State Court Caseload Statistics: Annual Report, Washington, D.C.: U.S. Government Printing Office, 1975; and United States Department of Justice, Bureau of Justice Statistics, Sourcebook of Criminal Justice Statistics-1984, Washington, D.C.: U.S. Government Printing Office, 1985. Other government doucments include United States Department of Commerce, Bureau of the Census, Statistical Abstract of the United States: 1986 (106th Edition), Washington, D.C.: U.S. Government Printing Office, 1985, and Public Employment in 1984, Washington, D.C.: U.S. Government Printing Office, 1985. The emphasis in this chapter, has been on the criminal justice activities of the judicial network, since the vast majority of human service related activities occur in juvenile court and in criminal justice types of cases, and not civil court.

2. The geographic breakdown of the federal and state court systems is adapted from the Office of the Federal Register, Government Organization Manual 1985-86, Washington, D.C.: U.S. Government Printing Office, 1985 and Wisconsin Legislative Reference Bureau, Wisconsin Blue Book 1985-86, Madison, Wisconsin: Department of Administration, 1985.

3. Figures on employment in state and local courts are adapted from the National Institute of Law Enforcement and Criminal Justice, National Manpower Survey of the Criminal Justice System: Vol. 4 Courts, Washington, D.C.: U.S. Government Printing Office, 1978, pp.12-13; United States Department of Justice, Bureau of Justice Statistics, Sourcebook of Criminal Justice Statistics: 1984. Washington, D.C.: U.S. Government Printing Office, 1985 and United States Department of Commerce, Bureau of the Census, Public Employment in 1984, Washington, D.C.: U.S. Government Printing Office, 1985. These figures differ from the 1980 Census Occupation by Industry report, primarily because the 1980 census material was not categorized using the same occupational classifications.

4. Figures on employment in the legal service system (prosecu-
    tion and legal services) are adapted from the National
    Institute of Law Enforcement and Criminal Justice, National
    Manpower Survey of the Criminal Justice System: Vol. 4
    Courts, Washington D.C.: U.S. Government Printing Office,
    1978, p.14, and United States Department of Justice, Bureau
    of Justice Statistics, Sourcebook of Criminal Justice
    Statistics: 1984, Washington, D.C.: U.S. Government
    Printing Office, 1985.

5. Figures on employment in the Public Defenders office are
    adapted from the National Institute of Law Enforcement and
    Criminal Justice, National Manpower Survey of the Criminal
    Justice System: Vol. 4 Courts, Washington, D.C.: Govern-
    ment Printing Office, 1978, p.15 and United States Depart-
    ment of Justice, Bureau of Justice Statistics. Sourcebook
    of Criminal Justice Statistics, 1984. Washington, D.C.:
    U.S. Government Printing Office, 1985.

6. For information regarding educational training for various
    positions in the judicial network, the reader is referred
    to the following organizations: National Judicial College,
    Judicial College Building, University of Nevada, Reno,
    Nevada, 89557; National District Attorney's Association, 666
    North Lake Shore Drive, Suite 1432, Chicago, Illinois,
    60611; Conference of State Court Administrators, National
    Center for State Courts, 300 Newport Ave., Williamsburg,
    Virginia, 23185; and the National Legal Aid and Defender's
    Association, 2100 M. Street N.W., Washington, D.C., 20037.

7. National Institute of Law Enforcement and Criminal Justice.
    National Manpower Survey of the Criminal Justice System:
    Vol. 4 Courts, Washington, D.C.: U.S. Government Printing
    Office, 1978, p.47. In addition the American Bar Associa-
    tion has taken the concept of continuing education further,
    by recommending that all lawyers including, judges and
    prosecutors, be actively involved in continuing education
    programs.

8. These examples of tasks performed by judges and prosecutors
    are a shortened and adapted version of tasks outlined in the
    National Institute of Law Enforcement and Criminal Justice,
    National Manpower Survey of the Criminal Justice System:
    Volume 4: Courts, Washington, D.C.: U.S. Government
    Printing Office, 1978, pp.49-50.

9. Other professional associations representative of the judicial network include the following: American Judges Association, P.O. Box 1399, 188 Chestnut Street, Holghoke, Maryland 01040; American Judicature Society, 200 W. Monroe Street, Suite 1606, Chicago, Illinois 60606; the National Council of Juvenile and Family Court Judges, P.O. Box 8978, University of Nevada, Reno, Nevada, 89507; and the National Association of Paralegals Personnel, 188, W. Randolph Street, Chicago, Illinois 60601.

10. These various roles of the social worker participating in support tasks are adapted from Donald Brieland and John Lemmon. Social Work and the Law, St. Paul, Minnesota: West Publishing Co., 1977, p. 12. For further information on the profession of social work and the judicial network, the reader is referred to: The National Association of Social Workers, 7981 Eastern Avenue, Silver Spring, Maryland 20910 or the local National Association of Social Workers Office.

11. Some examples of special units in a District Attorneys office include: citizen complaint, legal and counseling services for battered women and family violence, consumer fraud-legal services for complaints, sexual assault-legal and counseling services for victims of sexual assault, victim-witness support-legal and counseling services for individuals involved in court cases including victim compensation.

12. Some examples of diversion programs include: volunteer work, (Outagamie County, Wisconsin) holding a case open for a specified period of time, and placement in a rehabilitation program (Rock County, Wisconsin).

13. A small number of cases become sensationalized in the community because an individual was released on bail and then committed another offense. Two cases of sexual assault and murder, occurred in Wisconsin in 1980. As a consequence of these cases, a state referendum was passed in 1981, directing the legislature to modify the bail/bond procedures to disallow the practice for certain crimes and offenders.

SUGGESTED READINGS

Donald Brieland and John Lemmon. Social Work and the Law. St. Paul, Minnesota; West Publishing Co., 1977. For the individual who is interested in a basic understanding of the law as it relates to social work practice, this book is invaluable.

Edward Farnsworth. An Introduction to the Legal System of the United States. New York, New York: Oceana Publications, 1975. For a general overview of the legal system this book would provide an excellent background as well as further references.

M.M. Knappen. Constitutional and Legal History of England. New York, New York: Harcourt, Brace and Co., 1942. For the individual interested in history, this book provides an excellent overview of the early development of the judicial network.

David Neubauer. America's Courts and the Criminal Justice System. North Scituate, Massachusetts: Duxbury Press, 1979. This is a general overview of the criminal justice system which will provide the reader with information on the interrelationship of the judicial network with other parts of the criminal justice system.

Edwin Tucker. Adjudication of Social Issues: Text, Cases and Problems. St. Paul, Minnesota: West Publishing Co., 1971. This book consists of a series of case studies which are relevant to the field of social welfare, such as welfare law, abortion, euthanasia, etc.

United States Department of Justice, Law Enforcement Assistance Administration, Two Hunderd Years of American Justice. Washington, D.C.: U.S. Government Printing Office, 1976. This monograph is a nonsophisticated history of the judicial network in the United States.

REFERENCES

Abadinsky, Howard. Social Services in Criminal Justice. Englewood Cliffs, New Jersey: Prentice Hall, Inc., 1979.

Brieland, Donald and John Lemmon. Social Work and the Law. St. Paul,Minnesota: West Publishing Co., 1977.

Chamblis, Rollin. Social Thought from Hammurabi to Comte. New York, New York: Holt and Company, Inc., 1954.

Council for Public Interest Law. Balancing the Scale of Justice: Financing Public Interest Law in America. Washington, D.C.: Council for Public Interest Law, 1976.

Farnsworth, Edward. An Introduction to the Legal System of the
    United States. New York, New York: Oceana Publications,
    1975.

Gottesman, Roberta. The Child and the Law. St. Paul,
    Minnesota: West Publishing Co., 1981.

Hall, James. Criminal Justice Administration: The American
    Plan. Dubuque, Iowa: Kendall/Hunt Publishing Co., 1976.

Karlen, Delmar. Anglo-American Criminal Justice. New York, New
    York: Oxford University Press, 1967.

Knappen, M.M. Constitutional and Legal History of England. New
    York, New York: Harcourt, Brace and Co., 1942.

Lewis, Merlin, Warren Bundy and James Haque. An Introduction to
    the Courts and Judicial Process. Englewood Cliffs, New
    Jersey: Prentice Hall, Inc., 1978.

McNeely, Roger and Carl Pope. Race, Crime and Criminal
    Justice. Beverly Hills, California: Sage Publications,
    1981.

National Criminal Justice Information and Statistics Service,
    State and Local Prosecution and Civil Attorney Systems,
    Washington, D.C.: U.S. Government Printing Office, 1976.

National Institute of Law Enforcement and Criminal Justice.
    National Manpower Survey of the Criminal Justice System,
    Volume 4, Courts. Washington, D.C.: U.S. Government
    Printing Office, 1978.

Neubauer, David. America's Courts and the Criminal Justice
    System. North Scituate, Massachusetts: Duxbury Press, 1979.

Minahan, Anne. (Ed.) Encyclopedia of Social Work 18th Issue.
    Washington, D.C.: National Association of Social Workers,
    1986.

Office of the Federal Register, Government Organization Manual
    1985-86. Washington, DC: U.S. Government Printing Office,
    1985.

Presidents Commission on Law Enforcement and Administration of
    Justice, Task Force Report: Courts, Washington, D.C.: U.S.
    Government Printing Office, 1967.

Tucker, Edwin. Adjudication of Social Issues: Text, Cases and
    Problems. St. Paul, Minnesota: West Publishing Co., 1971.

United States Department of Commerce, Bureau of the Census, Statistical Abstract of the United States: 1986 (106th Ed.), Washington, DC: U.S. Government Printing Office, 1985.

United States Department of Commerce, Bureau of the Census, 1980 Census of Population, Volume 2 Subject Reports: Part 7C, Occupation by Industry, Washington, DC: U.S. Government Printing Office, 1984.

United States Department of Commerce, Bureau of the Census, Public Employment in 1984, Washington, D.C.: U.S. Government Printing Office, 1985.

United States Department of Commerce, Bureau of the Census, 1982 Census of Service Industries: Summary, Washington, D.C.: U.S. Government Printing Office, 1984.

United States Department of Justice, National Survey of Court Organization, Washington, D.C.: U.S. Government Printing Office, 1973.

United States Department of Justice, Bureau of Justice Statistics, Sourcebook of Criminal Justice Statistics 1984. Washington, DC: U.S. Government Printing Office, 1985.

United States Department of Justice, State Court Caseload Statistics: Annual Report 1975, Washington, D.C.: U.S. Government Printing Office, 1979.

United States Department of Justice, Law Enforcement Assistance Administration, Two Hundred Years of American Justice. Washington, D.C.: U.S. Government Printing Office, 1976.

Waldron, Donald, et.al. The Criminal Justice System: An Introduction. Boston, Massachusetts: Houghton Mifflin Co., 1976.

Walker, Peter. The Courts of Law. Devon England: David and Charles Co., 1970.

Way, H. Frank. Criminal Justice and the American Constitution. North Scituate, Massachusetts: Duxbury Press, 1980.

Wisconsin Legislative Reference Bureau, Wisconsin Blue Book 1985-86, Madison, Wisconsin: Department of Administration, 1985.

CHAPTER 12

PROTECTIVE SERVICE NETWORK*

"In fact, police officers now spend much of their time
in "social work" roles. They attempt to settle disputes between spouses and between neighbors, counsel
children about attending school and obeying their
parents, and decide when to make arrests for non-
serious offenses, partially on the basis of whether
apprehension of the criminal will be likely to help
the individual or society." (Roberts, 1976:297).

INTRODUCTION

The decade of the 1960's and 70's has had a profound impact
upon the protective service network (law enforcement and private
security), its agencies and personnel from a legalistic,
educational and operational perspective. There was an increased
awareness of the community service and social service aspect of
law enforcement and an expanding need for private security personnel. The stimulus for these profound changes were: the
social consciousness of the 1960's, the President's Commission
on Law Enforcement and Administration of Justice, the rising
crime rate, and federal funding through the Law Enforcement
Assistance Administration.

The full impact of these changes cannot be fully measured as
yet, however, the process of change is expected to continue.
This chapter briefly explores the history of public law enforcement, the community and social service aspects of public law
enforcement, the growing importance of private security and the
role of social work in the protective service network.

SIZE

Community and individual protection is a major concern in
the United States. Generally, one thinks of public law enforcement as the major component in protective services, since they
are most visible, and rarely think about private protective
agencies and employees.

LAW ENFORCEMENT (PUBLIC)

In 1982 there were an estimated 40,000 public law enforcement agencies, with expenditures of about 18.6 billion dollars

and employing an estimated 749,000 individuals. The public law enforcement network serves the entire population of the United States which is approximately 236 million people. In 1984 the public law enforcement network arrested 8.9 million individuals and there were an estimated 11.8 million reported offenses.

The majority of the public law enforcement employees are at the local level (county and municipal) 79.8 percent, with 11.7 percent at the state level and 8.5 percent at the federal level of government. The distribution of public law enforcement agencies is similar to the distribution of employees with approximately 36,700 municipal agencies (91.7 percent), 3,050 county agencies (7.7 percent), 200 state agencies (.5 percent), and 50 federal agencies (1 percent). The sheer size, diversity and decentralization of the public law enforcement network has led to problems of coordination and service integration.

PRIVATE SECURITY

The Bureau of the Census in the 1982 Census of Service Industries estimated there were approximately 9,326 private security agencies, with expenditures of about 5.4 billion dollars, employing an estimated 775,051 individuals and serving an estimated 1 million plus individuals and agencies. The National Advisory Committee and its report on Private Security, in 1974 had a higher estimate of expenditures of about 6 billion dollars and employees of 1 million plus. Private security expanded rapidly in the United States with an estimated 300 percent increase since 1965. The private security network in the United States is at least as large as the public law enforcement network and some estimates are double the size of public law enforcement.[1] Figure 12-1 shows the estimated size of the protective service network.

HISTORICAL DEVELOPMENT

LAW ENFORCEMENT (PUBLIC)

All societies have systems of social control, some informal and others more formalized. Law enforcement in the United States followed some of the patterns of the English system, adding its uniqueness of a decentralized system, municipal, county, state, and federal jurisdictions. This pattern of development was markedly different from continental Europe where an association between military and law enforcement still exists with the concept of a centralized system.[2]

Early precedents for law enforcement consisted of using military forces, palace guards, self policing and the frankpledge

Figure 12-1

Estimated Size of the Protective Service
Network in 1982-1984*

Selected Attribute	Public Law-Enforcement	Non Public Police and Detectives & Private Protective Services
Number of Agencies	40,000	9,326
Expenditures (Number)	18,642,000,000	5,391,439,000
Number of Employees	749,000	775,051
Population Served (Number)	236,000,000	1,000,000+

*   Sources: Adapted from United States Department of Justice, Bureau of Justice Statistics, <u>Sourcebook of Criminal Justice-Statistics 1984</u>, Washington, D.C.: U.S. Government Printing Office, 1985, pp, 6, 9, 15, 24, 27, 28; United States Department of Commerce, Bureau of the Census, <u>1982 Census of Service Industries</u>, Washington, D.C.: U.S. Government Printing Office, 1984, pg. 5; United States Department of Commerce, Bureau of the Census, <u>Statistical Abstract of the United States: 1986 (106th Edition)</u>, Washing- ton, D.C.: U.S. Government Printing Office, 1985, pg. 173, 175; United States Department of Commerce, Bureau of the Census, <u>1980 Census of Population.   Vol. 2, Subject Reports, Part 7C: Occupation by Industry</u>, Washington, D.C.: U.S. Government Printing Office, 1984, pg. 294-665 and United Sates Department of Commerce, Bureau of the Census, <u>Public Employ- ment in 1984</u>, Washington, D.C.: U.S. Government Printing Office, 1985, pg. I.

system in England. The frankpledge system in England consisted of every free man over age 12 belonging to a group of 10 families and one person was selected as a tithingman who had law enforcement duties. Every 10 tithings (100 families) was called a hundred and elected a reeve who had law enforcement duties. Several hundred families formed a shire and selected a shire reeve (sheriff) who had law enforcement duties and represented the interests of the king.

The shire reeve system was in operation in early Medieval England, pre 1000 A.D. After the Norman invasion of 1066 a series of successive changes occurred with the development of a constable (1066) who was to assist the shire reeve, development of a night watchman (bailiff) in 1285, a justice of the peace in the reign of Edward the III and the first paid constable (as a special unit) in 1748. This system of voluntary law enforcement, night watchman, etc., proved inadequate to handle the rising crime rates in England. Subsequently, a Metropolitan Police Department was established in London, England (1829) under the urging of Sir Robert Peel. This was the first organized and paid police department in the world.

In the United States, the English pattern of constable (urban area) and sheriff (rural area) supplemented by watchman (day and night) was adopted. The first formally organized police department (combined day and night watchman) with paid employees was in New York City (1844). As indicated earlier, the United States added its uniqueness of decentralization of different jurisdictions, such as the federal marshall (1789), state jurisdiction (1836) with the Texas Rangers and state police in Pennsylvania. From the 1840's to 1900, there was a rapid development of law enforcement agencies so that most municipalities, and states had law enforcement officials. The rapid development of law enforcement agencies in the United States reflected the time period of 1850-1900 when other services were beginning to be developed by public or private agencies. This was a period of rapid urban expansion, immigration from other countries and migration to the "west" meaning the midwest and points beyond. It was a period of social unrest and as communities changed from a small community where everybody knew everybody to communities of subgroups and strangers, there was an increased need for more law enforcement personnel.

Since 1900 significant changes occurred in the training and expectations of law enforcement. Between 1900-1930 police departments have had some form of staff development and in-service training for their personnel. This form of training focused on technical skills needed to perform the functions of investigation of crime and apprehension of the suspected criminal. Police departments became specialized into various units, such as detective, traffic, patrol, etc. Between 1930 and 1960 some law enforcement agencies made use of more specialized training, such as the FBI Academy in Washington, D.C., and others took advantage of associate of arts degree programs (2 year degree) in Police Science. Since 1967, there has been a major rethinking of the role of law enforcement which now includes the concepts of human relations, crisis intervention and social services. With this newer emphasis in law enforcement many police departments are now encouraging their officers to obtain a bachelor's degree, such as criminal justice, police administration or police science. Other law enforcement units had already required the bachelor's degree of a specific type for an entry position, such as the Federal Bureau of Investigation. During the 1970's and 80's there has been a concerted effort to recruit minorities and women into law enforcement.

PRIVATE SECURITY

The development of private security organizations in the United States was a consequence of the inadequacies of the watchman system and numerical lack of public law enforcement officials. The primary emphasis of private security was to protect industrial property. The first private security agency was the North West Police Agency in 1855 under Allan Pinkerton which became the Pinkerton Protection Agency in 1857. The Brink's Protection agency was one of the early ones, developed in 1859. The growth of private security was not rapid until World War I, when there was a high increase in demands for protection services, as a consequence of potential sabotage. Another period of rapid growth was World War II and more recently in the 1970's. In the 1950's, it was estimated that the number of private security personnel was less than public law enforcement, whereas by 1975, it is estimated that the number of private security personnel are at least the same or perhaps double that of public law enforcement. The decade of the 1980's with an increase in world wide terrorism and the hijacking of airplanes has led to a rapid increase in private protection employees and systems. Individuals in the United States are much more aware of world terrorism since the raid on Libya in 1986. Figure 12-2 shows a brief historical time line of the development of the protective service network.

STRUCTURE

With the diversity and complexity of the protective service network one can look at its structure from the perspective of its organizational context, services provided, occupations and professions, and dominant occupations and professions.

397

Figure 12-2

Historical Time Line of the Protective Service Network

800 A.D.   Tithing man-one person in ten families had law-enforcement
                 functions.
                 Hundred man reeve - one person in one hundred families had
                 law enforcement functions.
                 Shire-reeve-law enforcement official for a shire (county).

1000 A.D.   Constable

1200   Night Watchman (bailiff)
                 Day Watchman
                 A hue and cry system-when a crime was committed a hue and
                   cry was raised and able bodied males formed a posse.

1789   Federal Marshall-United States
                 Other federal law enforcement

1836   State Police (Texas Rangers)

1829   Metropolitan Police Department-London, England

1844   Organization of Municipal Police Department-New York

1855   Northwest Police Agency (Pinkerton's)
                 Development of In-service training programs for law
                   enforcement

1859   Brink's Protection Agency

1912   Police social work units
                 Beginning specialization in law-enforcement
                 Development of police science programs as a supplement to
                 in-service

1967   Law Enforcement Assistance Administration
                 Recommend college education
                 Development of Criminal Justice Programs
                 Expansion of private security

1980's   Efforts to attract minorities and women
                 Increased concern over world wide terrorism and airplane
                 hijacking

ORGANIZATIONAL CONTEXT

Figure 12-3 is an idealized model of the organization of the public law enforcement network. Figure 12-4 shows an idealized organization of a municipal police department. Generally, if a police department has a social service area like police social work, the unit is attached to community relations, or personnel training. In addition to the formal organization of public law enforcement there are a number of para-military organizations which can be considered a folk system or self-help system of law enforcement, such as vigilante groups, Klu Klux Klan and Posse Comitatus.[3]

SERVICES PROVIDED

The prime stated function of public law enforcement is the detection and apprehension of criminals. The reality is that the police officer spends more time on community and social services. Examples of services provided by law enforcement agencies include the following:

- Psychiatric Consultation and Testing
- Employee Assistance Programs
- Youth Activities/Recreational Activities
- Volunteer Services
- Community Relations
- Crisis Intervention
- Family Crisis Intervention
- General Counseling.

OCCUPATIONS and PROFESSIONS

Contrary to popular perceptions, law enforcement and private security agencies employ more than police officers. Smaller police departments may not have other professions outside of the police officer and larger departments may hire a range of other professions.

Figure 12-5 shows a selected number of human service occupations and professions which participate in public law enforcement and private security agencies. Many departments will hire other professions on an as needed basis and not on a full time basis.

DOMINANT OCCUPATIONS and PROFESSIONS

The major occupation and profession in law enforcement is the police officer, either those with patrol or investigative functions. Figure 12-6 shows the employment of police, detectives and guards in 1980 in both public Administration (law

Figure 12-3

Idealized Model of Government Organization of the Public Law
Enforcement Component of the Protective Service Network*

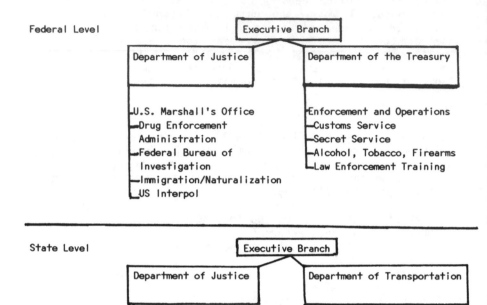

Federal Level

Executive Branch

Department of Justice

Department of the Treasury

⌐U.S. Marshall's Office
⊢Drug Enforcement
 Administration
⊢Federal Bureau of
 Investigation
⊢Immigration/Naturalization
⌊US Interpol

⌐Enforcement and Operations
⊢Customs Service
⊢Secret Service
⊢Alcohol, Tobacco, Firearms
⌊Law Enforcement Training

State Level

Executive Branch

Department of Justice

Department of Transportation

⊢Criminal Investigation
⊢Law Enforcement Services
⊢Legal Services
⊢Administrative Services
⌊Law Enforcement Standards
 Board

⊢Division of State Patrol
⊢Communcations
⊢District Operations
⊢Inspection
⌊Support Services

Local Level   Municipal/County Police/Detectives

*Source: Adapted from Office of the Federal Register, <u>United States Government
Manual 1985/86</u>, Washington, DC: U.S. Government Printing Office,
1985, pp. 845,849 and Wisconsin Legislature Reference Bureau, <u>Wisconsin Blue Book 1985/86</u>, Madison, Wisconsin: Department of Administration, 1985, pp. 501, 537.

400

Idealized Organization of a Municipal Police Department*

Chief

Field Operations
- Preventive
- Patrol
- Traffic
- Special

Investigation Unit
- Youth Services
- Special Investigation
- Detectives

Intelligence Unit

Administrative Services
- Fiscal
- Planning
- Community Relations
- Personnel Training
- Police Social Work Team

Technical Services
- Records
- Communications
- Identification
- Property
- Transportation

* **Source:** Paul Weston. Police Organization and Management. Pacific Palisades; California: Goodyear Publishing Co., 1976, p. 44.

401

Figure 12-5
Number and Percent of Selected Human Service
Occupations and Professions Employed in the Justice, Public
Order and Safety Industrial Classification (Both Public and Private) and
the Industrial Classification of Detective and Protective Services in 1980*

Selected Occupation/ and Profession	Industrial Classification			
	Justice, Public Order, Safety (Public & Private)		Detective & Protective Services (Business & Repair) [1]	
	Number	Percent	Number	Percent
Police/detectives Public	409,782	83.929	--	--
Sheriff, Bailiff & Others	61,482	12.442	--	--
Guards/police non public	11,814	2.391	157,376	98.126
Lawyers	6,000	1.214	632	.394
Counselor (Education Vocational/ Rehabilitation)	200 [2]	.041	22	.014
Health (Nurses, Therapist, Physician Asst., other)	1,500 [2]	.303	211	.133
Social Work	500 [2]	.101	233	.145
Psychologist	100 [2]	.020	11	.007
Physician	100 [2]	.020	12	.008
Clergy, Religious Worker	251 [2]	.051	10	.006
Personnel Relations & training	1,910 [2]	.387	1,661	1.035
Authors, Artists, Painters, etc.	100 [2]	.020	189	.117
Teachers	400 [2]	.081	24	.015
TOTAL	494,149	100.000	160,381	100.000

*Source: Adapted from Department of Commerce, Bureau of the Census, 1980 Census of Population: Vol. 2 Subject Reports Part 7C: Occupation by Industry, Washington, D.C.: U.S. Government Printing Office, 1984, pp. 295-664. The industrial classification of justice, public order and safety represents the protective service, judicial and corrections networks. The subject report is not detailed enough to clearly identify the protective service network. Some occupations are clearly in protective services like police, detectives, others are clearly in the judicial network like judges, and others are clearly in the corrections network like correctional guards. The above listing of occupations represents an attempt to identify those which were employed in the protective service network. This list is obviously representative and not exhaustive.

[1] Under the industrial classification of business and repair of service industries there is a subcategory called detectives and protective services. This classification does not include private guards and police which may be listed under the industrial classification of justice, public order and safety.

[2] These figures are estimates only, based upon the probable distribution between the protective service, judicial and corrections networks which are included under the industrial classification of justice, public order and safety.

Figure 12-6
Number and Percent of Public Police/Detectives and Sheriffs/ Bailiffs and Non Public Police/Detectives and Protective Service Workers Employed by Industrial Classification in 1980*

Occupation Classification

Industrial Classification	Public Police/Detectives, Sheriff and Bailiff		Non Public Guards and Police & Detective & Protective Service Worker	
	Number	Percent	Number	Percent
Agriculture	--	--	9,806	1.722
Construction	--	--	7,223	1.268
Mining	--	--	4,321	.758
Manufacturing	--	--	88,590	15.556
Transportaion/ Communication/ Public Utilities	--	--	31,038	5.451
Wholesale Trade	--	--	6,837	1.201
Retail Trade	--	--	42,389	7.444
Finance/Insurance/ Real Estate	--	--	33,449	5.873
Business/Repair	--	--	166,752	29.282
Personal Services	--	--	12,672	2.225
Entertainment/ Recreation	--	--	19,601	3.442
Professional and Related	--	--	92,131	16.177
Public Administration	471,274	100.00	54,674	9.601
TOTAL	471,274	100.00	569,484	100.000

Source: Adapted from United States Department of Commerce, Bureau of the Census, 1980 Census of Population. Vol. 2 Subject Reports Part 7C: Occupation by Industry, Washington, D.C.: U.S. Government Printing Office, 1984 pp. 294-665.

403

enforcement) and private security. One can easily see the differences between public law enforcement and private protective
services. All public law enforcement personnel are employed in
the industrial classification of public administration, whereas
in the private protective services, police, detectives and
guards are distributed throughout the industrial classifications
with the largest numbers employed in business and repair services, (detective and protective services), manufacturing and
professional and related (guards).

Another way of looking at where police, detectives and
guards are employed is a classification of protective service
agencies by public and private and level of governmental jurisdiction. Figure 12-7 shows a classification of protective
service agencies.

The predominate educational requirement for public law
enforcement in 1978 was a high school education, 81 percent of
law enforcement agencies, with 11 percent of law enforcement
agencies having no educational requirement and the remaining 8
percent having a requirement of less than a high school education.[4]

Currently law enforcement is undergoing rapid change and
various groups have recommended a college degree as the minimum
educational requirement. Since most law enforcement officials
do not have a college degree, there is a heavy emphasis on staff
development/in service training (police academies) and an
increasing emphasis on associate of arts degrees in police
science (2 year degree) or a bachelor's degree (4 year degree)
in criminal justice. Generally police officers, obtain course
content in the following areas: criminal justice system and
process, law, patrol and investigation procedures, human
relations/criminology, police proficiency, administration, etc.

Traditional Role--The traditional tasks of a law enforcement
official will vary depending upon whether the individual is
assigned as a patrol officer, investigator, special services or
assigned to a public service, like traffic control. In general,
the traditional tasks of a general police officer are as follows:

Patrol: - Observe a general vicinity for possible
                   law violations

                 - Observe a general vicinity for out of
                   the ordinary or suspicious circumstances

                 - Apprehend law violators

404

Figure 12-7
A CLASSIFICATION OF PUBLIC AND PRIVATE SECURITY FORCES AND ORGANIZATIONS
*

THE PUBLIC SECTOR

LAW ENFORCEMENT AGENCIES

Local Government
  Regular local police (municipalities, counties, townships,
    special districts)
  Reserve local police
  Special local law-enforcement agencies
    Park police (municipal, county)
    Transit police
    Public-housing police
    Building-department police
    Sanitation-department police
    Airport Police

State Government
  State police and/or state highway patrol
  Special state law-enforcement agencies
    State park police or forest rangers
    Narcotics agents and other investigators in state bureaus
    Fish and game wardens
    Police in state universities or colleges
    Etc.

Federal Government
  Department of Justice
    Federal Bureau of Investigation
    Immigration and Naturalization Service
    United States Marshals
    Border patrol
    Bureau of Narcotics and Dangerous Drugs
  Treasury Department
    Secret Service
    White House police
    Customs Bureau (ports investigators, customs agents)
    Internal Revenue Service
      Alcohol, tobacco, and firearms special investigators
      Intelligence special agents
      Internal security inspectors
  Department of the Interior
    United States Park rangers
    United States Park police
    Bureau of Indian Affairs investigators
    Sport fisheries and wildlife game management agents

Figure 12-7 (Continued)

Post Office Department
  Postal inspectors
Department of State
  Security agents
Zoo Police, Smithsonian
Etc.

GUARDS AND WATCHMEN

  Local Government

  State Government

  Federal Government
    General Services Administration guards
    Etc.

THE PRIVATE SECTOR

PURCHASED OR CONTRACT PRIVATE SECURITY SERVICES[a]

  Guards and watchmen employed by detective agencies and protective-service
    establishments
  Detectives, investigators, and undercover agents employed by detective
    agencies and protective-service establishments
  Patrolmen employed in private patrol establishments
  Guards employed in armored-car-service establishments
  Guards, respondents employed in central station alarm services establishments

IN-HOUSE OR PROPRIETARY PRIVATE SECURITY SERVICES

  Guards and watchmen employed by industries, businesses, institutions,
    and individuals
  Detectives, investigators and undercover agents employed by industries,
    businesses, institutions, and individuals

---

[a]Each class of private security service can be subcategorized by type
of client or user, e.g., by broad industry, business, and institutional
categories.

*Source: Reprinted with permission of the Rand Corporation from James
Kakalik and Sorrel Wildhorn The Private Police Industry: Its Nature and
Extent. Santa Monica, California: Rand Corporation, 1971, pg. 5.

                        - Respond to emergency calls, including
                          marital conflicts

Traffic: - Control of traffic flow

                        - Accident investigation

                        - Traffic law enforcement

Investigation: - Obtain evidence on specific crimes
                        - Analyze evidence

    Social Service Role--It is estimated that 50-70 percent of
a police officer's time is spent on community and social
service functions or other functions than that of detection and
apprehension of suspected criminals. The law enforcement
person can be viewed as a "gatekeeper" for social and individual problems. A gatekeeper is one who first becomes exposed
or alerted to problems and makes decisions on what to do about
the problems observed. In the case of law enforcement personnel, one of the first decisions is to arrest or not arrest.
After this initial decision, then other decisions have to be
made in many situations which may include referral to a medical
setting, mental health setting, alcohol detoxification center,
drug program, emergency shelter, etc.

    Law enforcement personnel are continuously providing the
following services:

    - Counseling juveniles and runaways
    - Providing advice for older citizens
    - Child abuse and neglect
    - Family and marital problems
    - Alcohol problems
    - Mental health problems.

Law enforcement personnel today need to know about mental illness and its symptomology, alcoholism, and have a sensitivity
to the perceptions and needs of minority groups and women. All
of these roles involve human relations and interviewing skills
in order to provide services. Although law enforcement is
deeply involved in the provision of social services, the role
of a police social worker is distinctly different than that of
a police officer.[5]

                            SOCIAL WORK

    Social workers employed in law enforcement is not a new
concept since the first police social worker was hired in 1912

                               407

in Los Angeles, California. The movement of employing police social workers continued until 1940 when changes in police training and social work education resulted in these two professions to develop divergent and at times incompatible viewpoints.

There is a difference between the older police social work movement and the current movement to hire social workers in police departments. The older image of a police social worker was that of a woman who was employed as a police officer who happened to have training as a social worker. The policewomen, in addition to regular police work were given responsibility for prevention and protective services in working with juveniles. Eventually the policewomen were placed in a separate section of the police department known as a Women's Bureau or Children's Bureau and primarily worked in that area and not traditional police work.

This separation and isolation of the police women (social worker), instead of leading to an integration of social work into police work, had the opposite effect of creating strain between the two professions. This strain was further enhanced when social work accepted the medical model of behavior, and in particular, the psychological theories of Sigmund Freud.

There has been a reemergence of social work in a police department since the late 1960's.[6] Figure 12-5 shows an estimated 733 social workers employed in the protective service net work. Part of the reason for the reemergence of police social work was the social consciousness of the 1960's and the recognition that law enforcement personnel are involved in the delivery of social services. This more current police social work movement differs from the earlier movement in two important aspects: the social worker is not hired as a police officer/social worker, but as a social worker, and the concept of a team. The team consists of the police officer and social worker cooperating in a specific situation. The police officer performs the social service tasks they currently are doing and the social worker performs their tasks in conjunction with the police officer. The tasks performed by a social worker, working in a police department, include the following:

- Social assessment
- Crisis intervention (on call 24 hours)
- Short term and some long term individual and marital counseling, family group therapy and group service
- Referral of individuals to community agencies
- Staff development functions in police training
- Employee assistance programs for police personnel
- Involvement in community relations.[7]

One of the states which has experimented heavily with the police social work team concept is that of Illinois. There are approximately 21 police social work units in that state.

Many of the police social work units which were established in the 1960's were partly a consequence of monies available from the Law Enforcement Assistance Administration. Since 1978 there has been a drastic reduction in federal monies available for these programs. The assumption was that federal money was seed money to begin a program and after a period of time (usually 3-6 years), the local community was expected to fund the program. Unfortunately in many communities, the police social work units became defunct as federal money decreased. In spite of the budgetary restraints many communities have maintained the police social work unit, such as Brookfield, Wisconsin.

With the varied tasks the social worker can perform in conjunction with law enforcement, social work skills at the individual, group and community level are used.

INDIVIDUAL LEVEL

The social worker can provide marital counseling to families, counseling to juveniles, referring individuals to other community resources, counseling minor adult offenders including problems, such as alcoholism and drugs.

An example is the case of Mrs. R. "Mrs. R is about forty years old. She is an alcoholic. Her husband was in the hospital for cancer surgery. Neighbors complained about Mrs. R's knocking on their door in a drunken stupor when asking for money. The social worker went to her home with an officer for an initial interview. At first they were refused admittance but the authority of the officer's position induced her to open the door. Mrs. R received aid and support from the social service department until her husband returned from the hospital."[8]

GROUP LEVEL

The social worker can become involved with youth groups, specialized support groups for problems, such as alcohol, drugs, family violence, etc. In specific communities where juvenile gangs are a problem, there may be a need to act as a mediator between groups.

COMMUNITY LEVEL

The social worker could act in a public relations manner describing the police social work concept, describing the police function and in general becoming involved in community relations. It is necessary to become aware of the power groups in the community to develop support for programming, to help coordinate resources and prevent, where possible, duplication of services.[9]

PERSONAL SOCIAL SERVICES

The protective service network like other networks, utilizes social services offered through the personal social service network. (See Chapter 22, Personal Social Service.) Some examples of the personal social services in the protective service network include the following:

PROTECTIVE SERVICES

Referral to child protective agencies in cases of abuse and neglect, specialized training for rape cases, such as the Sexual Assualt Treatment Center and Task Force on Battered Women in Milwaukee, Wisconsin.

UTILITARIAN SERVICES

Referral to legal services, day care and homemaking, such as local Legal Aid societies and Department of Social Services.

DEVELOPMENTAL and SOCIALIZATION SERVICES

Specialized training for family crisis intervention, such as the police social work unit in Jefferson County, Jefferson, Wisconsin and Youth Aid Bureau, Milwukee, Wisconsin.

REHABILITATIVE and THERAPEUTIC SERVICES

Hiring of social workers for emergency assessment and counseling, such as the police social work unit in Zion, Illinois.

SPECIAL POPULATIONS

Many of the clientele of the protective service network come from special populations (see Chapter 25, Special Populations and Chapter 24, Rehabilitation). Some examples of programs or services for special populations in the protective service network include the following:

410

ASIAN

Sensitivity training, liaison with the community and public relations and referral to an organization, such as the Asian Community Center, San Francisco, California.

BLACK

Public relations programs, sensitivity training, liaison with the community. Some examples of organizations include The Afro-American Patrolmen's League of Chicago, Illinois and the National Black Police Officer Association of Newark, New Jersey.

EUROPEAN ETHNICS

Having bi-lingual personnel on the staff, human relations training, and referral to agencies like the International Institutes in St. Paul, Minnesota and Milwaukee, Wisconsin.

NATIVE AMERICAN

Public relations programs, sensitivity training, liaison with the community. An example of an organization is the Indian Justice Commission of Nevada, Carson City, Nevada.

SAME SEX PREFERENCE

Liaison with the community, sensitivity training programs and referral to an organization, such as the Gay Community Counseling Center, San Francisco, California.

SPANISH SPEAKING

Having bi-lingual personnel on the staff, human relations training, liaison with the community. An example of an organization is the Latino Peace Officers Association, Oakland, California.

WOMEN

Specialized training for and awareness of the needs and creation of sensitivity for battered women and sexual assault cases and referral to organizations like the Sexual Assault Treatment Center and Task Force for Battered Women in Milwaukee, Wisconsin.

411

ISSUES

In the development of human service functions in law enforcement agencies, a number of stresses will occur for law enforcement as well as for social work.

LAW ENFORCEMENT

MODIFICATION of the POLICE FUNCTION--The police officer currently has multiple functions of: combating violation of the traditional law, (murder, rape, robbery, arson, etc.) combating violation of convenience norms (traffic and health regulations, etc.) and performing a miscellaneous group of service functions which account for 50-70 percent of their time. Since much of the police officer's duties are performing service functions a redefinition of tasks is necessary to avoid conflict with their major role.

UNDERSTANDING of HELPING PROFESSIONS--Generally police officers have been suspicious or indifferent to the helping professions and vice versa. Adequate information must be presented to dispel myths and open communication is necessary to maintain interdisciplinary cooperation.

UNDERSTANDING SOCIAL SERVICE SYSTEMS--Police officer's must be aware of the social service system in their community in order to have alternatives for action if needed in working with people.

ACCEPTANCE of WOMEN--Law enforcement traditionally has been a male dominated and oriented occupation. As social services develop in police departments the likelihood of women employees as social workers or as police officers increases.

SOCIAL WORK

ATTITUDE--Many social workers have a negative image of law enforcement. This is partly due to misinformation and partly due to lack of adequate understanding of the law enforcement function.

CONTENT KNOWLEDGE--A social worker as one of the helping professions, needs content about the specific system in which they are working. In this case, it is knowledge about police functioning, organization and management, legal parameters of police activity and conversely legal parameters of working in a police department and a legalistic system.

412

ASSESSMENT of ETHICAL PRINCIPLES--Legal and ethical principles for the human service professions, such as confidentiality can be easily breeched legally. Numerous discussions must be held on ethical issues to clearly identify the operational specifics.

ORGANIZATIONAL CONTROL--A major issue in a police department is where to locate a police social work unit. Should it be located in the chief's office, in a special unit, or in personnel? The explicit issues are who has authority or autonomy in the specifics of operation. Is the police social worker a combined police officer/social worker or a social worker in a police setting? The outcome of this issue heavily influences the degree of autonomy the social worker has and is a potential factor in the acceptance of the police social worker amongst law enforcement personnel as well as in the overall community.

SUMMARY

This chapter explored the complexity, diversity and size of the protective service network. The number of employees in public law enforcement is approximately 749,000 with the private security system having about 775,000+ employees. Between 1960 and 1976 the number of public employees increased 100%, however private security increased by 300%. The size of the network is also reflected in the fact there are over 40,000 public law enforcement units in the United States in autonomous jurisdictions at the federal, state, county and municipal level of government.

A brief history of public law enforcement and private security was presented to show the relative historical recency of these occupations since 1844. Although the dominant occupation in law enforcement and private security are those of a police officer, guard and watchmen, it was noted that a number of other helping professions were employed in the protective service network.

Most recently there has been a resurgence of the police social work concept, receiving a high degree of emphasis in the state of Illinois. The concept of a police social worker is not new, since numerous social workers were hired in the early 1900's, however by 1940 this movement faltered with a resurgence in the late 1960's. Some of the tasks of a police social worker were described as well as some of the issues facing law enforcement and social work as they develop a team approach. Some of the issues raised were: understanding of respective roles, having a sufficient knowledge base, inappropriate attitudes, organizational control and autonomy and ethical considerations.

FOOTNOTES

*   This chapter was reviewed for comments by John Conley,
    Associate Professor, Criminal Justice, School of Social
    Welfare, University of Wisconsin-Milwaukee, Milwaukee,
    Wisconsin.

1. These figures for estimates on the size of the public law
    enforcement and protective security network were taken from
    United States Department of Justice, Bureau of Justice
    Statistics, Sourcebook of Criminal Justice Statistics-1984,
    Washington, D.C.: U.S. Government Printing Office, 1985;
    United States Department of Commerce, Bureau of the Census,
    1982 Census of Service Industries, Washington D.C.: U.S.
    Government Printing Office, 1984; The National Advisory
    Committee on Criminal Justice Standards and Goals, Private
    Security: Report of the Task Force on Private Security,
    Washington, D.C.: U.S. Government Printing Office, 1976;
    United Stated Department of Commerce, Bureau of the Census,
    Statistical Abstract of the United States: 1986 (106th
    Ed.), Washington, D.C.: U.S. Government Printing Office,
    1985; United States Department of Commerce, Bureau of the
    Census, 1980 Census of Population, Vol. 2, Subject Reports,
    Part 7C: Occupation by Industry, Washington, D.C.: U.S.
    Government Printing Office, 1984, and Public Employment in
    1984, Washington, D.C.: U.S. Government Printing Office,
    1985, p. 1.

    Although this chapter discusses both public law-enforcement
    and private security, the emphasis of the chapter is on
    public law enforcement.

2. For a brief review of the history of law enforcement the
    reader is referred to Ronald, Waldron, et.al. The Criminal
    Justice System: An Introduction. Boston, Massachusetts:
    Houghton, Mifflin Co., 1976; United States Department of
    Justice, Law Enforcement Assistance Administration, Two
    Hundred Years of American Justice, Washington, D.C.: U.S.
    Government Printing Office, 1976, and James Richardson
    Urban Police in the United States, Port Washington, New
    York: Kennikat Press, 1974.

3. These groups are considered part of the folk system in that
    they operate outside the formal legal system. These organ-
    izations are influential in there respective communities in
    the enforcement of certain laws and intimidating certain
    groups.

4. National Institute of Law Enforcement and Criminal Justice, National Manpower Survey of the Criminal Justice System Vol. 2. Law Enforcement, Washington, D.C.: U.S. Government Printing Office, 1978 p. 17.

5. Some examples of professional organizations in law enforcement and private security include the following: American Academy for Professional Law Enforcement, 444 W. 50th St. Suite 5122, New York, New York 10019; International Association of Chiefs of Police, 13 Fairfield Road, Gaithersburg, Maryland 20878; National Council of Investigation and Security Services, 1133 15th St., NW Suite 620, Washington, D.C. 20005 and American Federation of Police, 1000 Conneticut Avenue NW, Suite 9, Washington, D.C. 20026. One can also contact local colleges with programs in criminal justice and law enforcement agencies.

6. For a brief historical review of police social work see Albert Roberts, "Training Police Social Workers: A Neglected Area of Social Work Education." Journal of Education for Social Work, Vol. 14, No. 2. (Spring 1978). pp. 98-110; Albert Roberts, "Police Social Work: A History". Social Work Vol. 2, No. 4 (July 1976), pp. 294-299; and Samual Walker. A Critical History of Police Reform: The Emergence of Professionalism Lexington, Massachusetts: Lexington Books, 1977.

7. These tasks for a police social worker were identified from Roy Roberg. The Changing Police Role, San Jose, California: Justice System Development, 1976, p. 264.

8. Roy Roberg, op. cit. p. 260.

9. For information on social work as a profession the reader is referred to the National Association of Social Workers, 7981 Eastern Avenue, Silver Spring, Maryland 20910 or the local office of the National Association of Social Workers.

SUGGESTED READINGS

National Advisory Committee on Criminal Justice Standards and Goals, Private Security: Report of the Task Force on Private Security, Washington, D.C.: U.S. Government Printing Office, 1976. This report by the National Advisory Committee is comprehensive in its analysis of private security in the United States.

D. D. Peel. The Story of Private Security. Springfield,
Illinois: Charles C. Thomas Co., 1971. For the individual
interested in the history of private security, this book is
an excellent reference.

Albert Roberts. "Police Social Work: A History." Social Work,
Vol. 2, No. 4, (July 1976), pp. 294-299. This short article provides a concise history of the police social work
movement and contains many useful references.

Roy Roberg. The Changing Police Role. San Jose, California:
Justice System Development, Inc., 1976. This book is a
must for the individual seeking to gain a perspective on
the shifting role of police officers from the traditional
concept to a social service concept.

Harvey Treger. The Police Social Work Team. Springfield,
Illinois: Carles C. Thomas Publishers, 1975. This is one
of the few books available on the subject. Most materials
are journal articles. This book is an excellent resource
for the individual who seeks more information on the
subject.

Samuel Walker. A Critical History of Police Reform: The
Emergence of Professionalism. Lexington, Massachusetts:
Lexington Books, 1977. For the individual seeking information on the history of law enforcement and an analysis of
emerging trends, this book is highly recomended.

REFERENCES

Henderson, Howard. "Helping Families in Crisis: Police and
Social Work Intervention." Social Work, Vol. 21, No. 4
(July 1976), pp. 314-315.

Kakalik, James and Sorrel Wildhorn. The Private Police
Industry: Its Nature and Extent. Santa Monica,
California: Rand Corporation, 1971.

Karlen, Delmar. Anglo-American Criminal Justice. New York,
New York: Oxford University Press, 1967.

Lane, Roger. Policing the City: Boston 1822-1885 Cambridge,
Massachusetts: Harvard University Press, 1967.

Miller, Wilbur. Cops and Bobbies: Police Authority in New York
and London 1830-1870, Chicago, Illinois: University of
Chicago Press, 1977.

Minahan, Anne (Ed.). Encyclopedia of Social Work 18th Issue. Washington, D.C.: National Association of Social Workers, 1986.

National Advisory Committee on Criminal Justice Standards and Goals, Private Security: Report of the Task Force on Private Security, Washington, D.C.: U.S. States Government Printing Office, 1976.

National Institute of Law Enforcement and Criminal Justice, National Manpower Survey of the Criminal Justice System, Vol. 2, Law Enforcement, Washington, D.C.: U.S. Government Printing Office, 1978.

Niederhaffer, Arthur and Abraham Blumberg. The Ambivalent Force: Perspective on the Police. 2nd. ed. Hinsdale, Illinois: The Dryden Press, 1976.

Office of the Federal Register, United States Government Manual 1985/86, Washington, D.C.: U.S. Government Printing Office, 1985.

Peel, D.D. The Story of Private Security. Springfield, Illinois: Charles C. Thomas Publishers, 1971.

Presidents Commission on Law Enforcement and Administration of Justice, Task Force Report: Law Enforcement, Washington, D.C.: U.S. Government Printing Office, 1967.

Richardson, James. Urban Police in the United States Port Washington, New York: Kennikat Press, 1974.

Roberg, Roy. The Changing Police Role. San Jose, California: Justice System Development, Inc., 1976.

Roberts, Albert. "Police Social Work: A History." Social Work, Vol. 2., No. 4, (July 1976), pp. 294-299.

Roberts, Albert. "Training Police Social Workers: A Neglected Area of Social Work Education." Journal of Education for Social Work, Vol. 14, No. 2 (Spring 1978), pp. 98-110.

Treger, Harvey. The Police Social Work Team. Springfield, Illinois: Charles C Thomas Publishers, 1975.

United States Department of Justice. Bureau of Justice Statistics, Sourcebook of Criminal Justice Statistics-1984, Washington, D.C.: U.S. Government Printing Office, 1985

United States Department of Commerce, Bureau of the Census, 1982 Census of Service Industries, Washington, D.C.: U.S. Government Printing Office, 1984.

United States Department of Commerce, Bureau of the Census, 1980 Census of Population, Vol. 2, . Subject Reports, Part 7C: Occupation by Industry, Washington, D.C.: U.S. Government Printing Office, 1984.

United States Department of Justice, Law Enforcement Assistance Administration, Two Hundred Years of American Justice, Washington, D.C.: U.S. Government Printing Office, 1976.

United States Department of Commerce, Bureau of the Census, Statistical Abstract of the United States: 1986 (106th Ed.), Washington, D.C.: U.S. Government Printing Office, 1985.

United States Department of Commerce, Bureau of the Census, Public Employment in 1984, Washington, D.C.: U.S. Government Printing Office, 1985.

Waldron, Ronald, et.al. The Criminal Justice System: An Introduction. Boston, Massachusetts: Houghton, Mifflin Co., 1976.

Walker, Samuel. A Critical History of Police Reform: The Emergence of Professionalism, Lexington, Massachusetts: Lexington Books, 1977.

Webster, John. The Realities of Police Work, Dubuque, Iowa: Kendall Hunt Publishing Co., 1973.

Weston, Paul. Police Organization and Management. Pacific Palisades, California: Goodyear Publishing Co., 1976.

Wisconsin Legislative Reference Bureau, Wisconsin Blue Book 1985/86, Madison, Wisconsin: Department of Administration, 1985.

CHAPTER 13

LEGAL NETWORK*

"Lawyer efforts run the alphabetical gamut from argument to
zeal, dealing with matters ranging from abandonment to zoning. A complete list of the activities and services offered
by the genus attorney is impossible, in fact, it might even
be easier to itemize the things lawyers do not do."
(Blaustein and Porter 1954:41)

INTRODUCTION

Although the legal network within the United States overlaps
with the judicial network (courts, prosecutors and legal services, and indigent defense services, see Chapter 11), it is
discussed separately, since a significant proportion of legal
services are provided outside of the courtroom setting and criminal justice related networks. A large proportion of a lawyer's services occurs within the confines of the office, at
meetings, in professional consultations, and in some cases in
the client's home. The legal profession, historically has concentrated its efforts on property matters, labor management disputes, tax matters, etc., and more recently, since 1960 has
taken a more active role in legal matters involving civil
rights, consumer affairs, social issues, criminal justice and
social welfare. The focus of this chapter is to provide an
overview of the legal network as it relates to criminal law
cases and the potential role of social work within the legal
network.

SIZE

In 1982 there were an estimated 167,896 legal establishments
in the United States. These legal establishments had expend-
itures/receipts of $34,325,371,000 and employed an estimated
751,790 individuals. In 1983 there were an estimated 80.5
million cases commenced in the federal and state judicial
system. Of these 80.5 million cases, 15.5 percent were civil,
13.0 percent were criminal, 1.4 percent were juvenile and 70.1
percent were traffic cases. This means at least 80.5 million
individuals had contact with attorneys. The number of individuals who have contact with attorneys is obviously greater since
numerous individuals see attorneys for non-court cases like
wills, property purchases and transfers, etc. Figure 13-1 shows
an estimated size of the legal network.[1]

419

Figure 13-1

Estimated Size of the Legal Network on
Selected Attributes*

Selected Attribute	Number
Number of Establishments	167,896
Expenditure/receipts (Dollars)	34,325,371,000
Number of Employees	751,790 [1]
Number of Population served	80,580,851 plus[2]

*Source: Adapted from United States Department of Commerce, Bureau of the Census, 1982 Census of Service Industries, Washington, D.C.: U.S. Government Printing Office, 1984, pp. 6, 7.

[1] Adapted from United States Department of Commerce, Bureau of the Census, 1980 Census of Population. Vol. 2 Subject Reports. Part 7C: Occupation by Industry, Washington, D.C.: U.S. Government Printing Office, 1984, pp. 295-664. The number of employees in legal services includes lawyers, clerical staff, legal stenographer, human service, personnel, etc.

[2] United States Department of Commerce, Bureau of the Census, Statistical Abstract of the United States: 1986 (106th Ed.). Washington, D.C.: U.S. Government Printing Office, 1985, pp 178, 179, 180 and United States Department of Justice, Bureau of Justice Statistics, Sourcebook of Criminal Justice Statistics - 1984, Washington, D.C.: U.S. Government Print- ing Office, 1985, p. 544. This figure is the number of civil, criminal, juvenile and traffic cases commenced in 1983 in the federal and state judicial systems. It is obvious that many individuals see lawyers and are not involved in court cases. Therefore the number of indivi- duals who see lawyers per year is well above the 80.5 million figure.

A study conducted by the American Bar Association through the National Opinion Research Center in 1974 provides some insight into the utilization of legal services by the general population.[2] The study was of a national sample of 2,064 individuals. This study indicated that 1,362 individuals or 66 percent of the sample had used legal services for a specific problem, and 702 individuals or 34 percent of the sample had never used legal services. Of those 1,362 individuals which had used a legal service, 395 or 29 percent used these legal services only once, and 967 or 71 percent had used legal services more than once. Generalization from this study would indicate that at least 60 percent of the adult population of the United States would use some form of legal services once in their lives, which means about 90-100 million individuals. The major reason individuals consult legal services is for property matters, including wills, which accounts for 58 percent of a lawyer's time.

HISTORICAL DEVELOPMENT

The legal profession and the provision of some form of legal services has had a long history dating back to at least the time of Hammurabi, 1700 B.C. and earlier.

CLASSICAL SOCIETY PRE 450 A.D.

In most earlier societies there were clergy/lawyers who heard cases, made decisions, and argued the fine points of the law. The accused person (litigant) was expected to defend themself, but could bring along a friend or relative as an advocate. This system of a friendly advocate was used in Greece before 700 B.C.. By 400 B.C. a professional advocate began to emerge, which was the early beginnings of a secular legal profession. In Roman society by 200 B.C., the secular advocate, as distinct from the priestly advocate, was well established.

MEDIEVAL EUROPE, 450-1500

In early Medieval Europe lawyers were primarily trained in theology and law and assumed roles of judges and magistrates. The accused individual was expected to defend themself against legal charges. Secular lawyers were trained through an apprentice system. During the later stages of Medieval Europe (1300-1400), the clergy/lawyers' role in England was diminished in ecclesiastical (church) courts, and a secular lawyer class quickly emerged. Under Henry II of England (1154-1159), a person could have an attorney physically represent them in court and provide advice, however, the pleader of a case for the King or the accused was called a barrister. When Edward I of England

(1272-1307) established one central location for the Court of Common Pleas, the professors of law gathered together and established an independent private school for the study of law called the Inns of Court. The barrister or pleader of a case was trained in the Inns of Court where they learned common law (law based upon precedent), in contrast to canon law (law based upon statutory provision). In the Inns of Court the future barrister learned court operations, the precedents of common law, and how to conduct a trial.

ENGLAND 1500 ON

In England the attorney could represent an individual in court and provide legal advice, but in comparison to the barrister was trained through an apprentice system. By 1400 some attorneys were trained in the Inns of Court.

Under the English system, both the barrister and the attorney needed the approval of a specific court in order to practice. In addition to the barrister and attorney, a third type of legal occupation developed by 1400 known as a solicitor. The solicitor could provide legal advice but not practice in court. It was not until 1873 that the functions of an attorney and solicitor were merged into a lawyer. The distinction between a barrister and attorney (solicitor) still exists in England in 1986. In felony cases it is common for the defendent to hire both a barrister for pleading a case in court and an attorney (solicitor) to provide advice and do necessary paper work. In 1986 the attorney (solicitor) was granted permission to read cases (present facts) in court for criminal cases, if the case was not contested. In England the dominant form of education was the Inns of Court until 1922, when law schools were established.

UNITED STATES

In the United States the legal profession and the provision of legal services initially followed the English model of training either in the Inns of Court in England or an apprentice style system. Two patterns emerged in the United States in the use of lawyers. New England states distrusted lawyers, consequently limited their activity and in some colonies (like Massachusetts, 1641) temporarily banned the lawyer from representing a person in court. The assumption was that each person could represent themself in court. In the Southern states, the English tradition of training in the Inns of Court continued. From this early period of low esteem for the legal profession, the period of 1730-1776 saw a rapid increase in the status and recognition of the legal profession. As more lawyers obtained

some degree of training, became involved in politics, and supported the growing discontent with English rule, the profession
increased in social status.

After the American Revolution of 1776-1783 there was a decline in the social status of lawyers, concurrent with a deprofessionalization of the profession. Many lawyers had remained
loyal to the British and were mistrusted by the general population. After the revolution few individuals went to England for
training, consequently there was a shortage of both trained lawyers and training facilities and faculty. "Jacksonian Democracy" became rampant from 1825 to 1850 and one of the main
ideologies was that "Any person could represent themselves."
There were minimal standards for admission into the then existing law schools, and loose and vague standards for professional
practice existed. This deprofessionalization of the legal profession was reflected in some state statutes like Indiana, which
from 1851 to 1933 allowed anyone to practice law who could pass
the bar examination, without prior educational experience. Many
lawyers in the United States had little or no training, and one
essentially became a lawyer by serving as an apprentice with a
practitioner.

Development of legal training in the United States began
with two competing systems: the independent private law school
and a law school attached to a university. An example of the
independent law school is the Litchfield Law School (1784-1883)
which emerged out of a private attorney's office. An example of
the university law school is the Harvard University Law School
which was established in 1829. The Harvard University Law
School, although attached to the university, was a separate
professional school and not part of the liberal arts program.

With the formation of the American Bar Association in 1878,
there was a rapid increase in educational standards for the
practice of law and development of specific admissions standards
for entrance into law schools. By 1905 three years of law
school were required to become a lawyer, however, there were no
prerequisite conditions to be admitted into many law schools.
In 1923 one year of college became a prerequisite to be admitted
into law school, in 1925 two years of college, 1952 three years
of college, and most schools currently require a bachelor's
degree as a prerequisite for admission. Since 1900 there has
been a rapid reprofessionalization of the legal profession with
specialization of legal practice (tax, labor, corporate law
etc.), an increase in status (social, economic and political),
and an increasing reliance of individuals to seek out legal
services for property, civil, criminal, family, civil rights,
and consumer protection concerns. Figure 13-2 summarizes the
historical development of the legal network.

Figure 13-2

Historical Time Line of the Legal Network

Classical Society   700 B.C.   Clergy/Lawyer
pre 450 A.D.   700 B.C.   Friendly Advocate–Greece
                           400 B.C.   Professional Advocate–Rome
                           200 B.C.   Secular Advocate–Rome

Medieval Europe
450–1500 A.D.   400 A.D.   Clergy/Lawyer
                          1150 A.D.   Pleader/Barrister
                                      Apprentice training–Attorney
                          1200 A.D.   Inns of Court Training–Barrister
                          1400 A.D.   Inns of Court Training–Attorney

England 1500–1600   Development of the Solicitor

England 1873   Combining of the roles of the attorney
                                          and solicitor into that of a lawyer
United States
1600–1800   New England States–early mistrust of
                                          lawyers–each person to plead their own
                                          case (lawyers were recognized by 1760)
                                      Southern states–recognized as
                                          professionals

1800–1900   Early 1800–mistrust of lawyers–each
                                          person to plead their own case
                                      Litchfield Law School 1784
                                          (Independent School)
                                      Harvard University Law School 1829
                                          (University Education)
                                      American Bar Association 1878

1900 on   Increased educational standards
                                      Specialization into various areas
                                          of law–such as taxation, corporate,
                                          etc.

424

STRUCTURE

The structure of the legal network can be described from its organizational context, services provided, occupations and professions, and dominant occupations and professions.

ORGANIZATIONAL CONTEXT

The legal network, in contrast to most of the other human services networks, is practiced largely through the confines of the lawyer's office and is predominantly private practice. Consequently, in describing the organizational context of the legal network, one essentially is referring to where lawyers are employed. Since a large percentage of lawyers, about 34 percent, work for a law firm, a typical organizational structure of a law firm is shown in Figure 13-3.

In addition to the public system of legal services for prosecution and defense, etc. (discussed in Chapter 11, Judicial Network) and the private system of legal services (corporate, education, private industry, etc.), there is in addition an informal network where individuals engage in their own legal defense, such as "jail house" lawyers, or individuals will use friends who provide "free legal advice" or individuals will read "how to defend yourself" manuals, etc.[3]

SERVICES PROVIDED

When one attempts to describe the services provided by the legal network, one usually describes the service, depending upon the specialty or knowledge needed for a specific problem. In general, services of the legal network can be classified according to an area of expertise which includes but is not limited to the following:

- International Law
- Tax Law
- Corporate Law
- Anti-Trust Law
- Real Estate/Inheritance Law
- Contract Law
- Military Law
- Criminal Law
- Labor Law
- Personal Injury Law
- Family/Divorce Law
- Maritime Law
- Welfare Law
- Commercial Law

Figure 13-3

Idealized Organization of a Large
New York Law Firm*

Senior Partners
(Executive Committee)

Tax Law Specialization	Corporate Law Specialization	Real Estate Law Specialization	Estate Law Specialization	Other Specialization
Senior Partner	Senior Partner	Senior Partner	Senior Partner	Senior Partner
Junior Partner	Junior Partner	Junior Partner	Junior Partner	Junior Partner
Associates	Associates	Associates	Associates	Associates
Other Staff Paralegals Stenographers Typists Receptionist Other	Other Staff Paralegals Stenographers Typists Receptionist Other	Other Staff Paralegals Stenographers Typists Receptionist Other	Other Staff Paralegals Stenographers Typists Receptionist Other	Other Staff Paralegals Stenographers Typists Receptionist Other

*Source: Adapted from Erwin Smegel, The Wall Street Lawyer New York, New York: Free Press of Glencoe, 1964 pp. 204-205.

426

        -       Constitution/Civil Rights Law
        -       Trade Regulation/Licensing Law
        -       Administrative Law.

Although some lawyers have one of the specialty areas described above, most lawyers are general practitioners, handling a
variety of legal problems and in addition, providing counseling
for individuals on personal matters.

OCCUPATIONS and PROFESSIONS

Contrary to popular belief, a variety of other human service
occupations and professions are involved in the legal network,
in addition to the lawyer. Figure 13-4 shows a variety of human
service occupations and professions involved in the legal network. Lawyers and legal assistants account for 97.1 percent of
the human service employees of the legal network. The remaining
2.9 percent of the employees were distributed amongst other
human service occupations and professions including social work.

DOMINANT OCCUPATIONS and PROFESSIONS

Of the 751,790 individuals employed in the legal network in
1980 (total employees not selected human service employees as
shown in Figure 13-4), 370,948 or 49.34 percent were lawyers.
One can then ask, where are lawyers employed? Figure 13-5 shows
the employment of lawyers by industrial classification in 1980.

The vast majority of lawyers are employed in the industrial
classification of legal services, 370,948 or 75.107 percent. An
additional 14,950 lawyers or 3.027 percent are employed in the
industrial classification of professional and related, 67,499 or
13.666 percent in public administration and the remaining 40.501
or 8.2 percent are distributed amongst a variety of industrial
classifications. Another way of asking the same question is by
practice area. Figure 13-6 shows the number of lawyers involved
in legal services in 1977 and the areas of practice. The vast
majority of lawyers were involved in general practice which is
presumably individual proprietorship or ownership of a law
office.

Earlier the development of legal education was discussed,
indicating an increasing professionalization of the legal profession at the university and college level since 1900. With
the changing character of legal education, one would expect a
higher percentage of lawyers having a law degree. In 1948, 60
per cent of all lawyers had a law degree, whereas in 1970, 92.7
per cent of lawyers had a law degree.[4] Since the early
1970's, most law schools require a college degree as a prerequisite for admissions, and all have a three year legal training

Figure 13-4

Number and Percent of Selected Human Service Occupations and
Professions Employed in the Legal Services
Industrial Classification of Professional and Related Services
(Legal Network) in 1980*

Occupation/Profession	Number	Percent
Lawyers	370,948	91.178
Legal Assistant (Paralegal)	26,791	6.584
Stenographer	2,125	.523
Social Work	1,106	.272
Welfare Aide	45	.012
Child Care	26	.006
Physician	367	.091
Registered Nurse	136	.033
Therapist (Health)	37	.009
Teacher-Post Secondary	122	.029
Teacher (Exceptional Ed, and not specified)	78	.004
Teacher Aide	20	.004
Librarian	1,569	.385
Library Clerk	528	.129
Personnel Relations	842	.206
Counselor Education/Vocational	60	.014
Psychologist	54	.013
Clergy	68	.016
Author	50	.012
Health Technician	99	.024
Licensed Practical Nurse	24	.005
Guards	1,474	.362
Firefighters	28	.006
Other Health	133	.032
Architect	121	.029
Urban Planner	29	.007
TOTAL	406,880	100.000

*Source: Adapted from United States Department of Commerce, Bureau of the Census, 1980 Census of Population, Vol. 2 Subject Reports Part 7C: Occupation by Industry, Washington D.C.: U.S. Government Printing Office, 1984 pp. 295-664

The industrial classification of professional and related includes areas such as education, social services, health, library and legal services amongst others. Legal services includes the industrial classifications of office of attorney, law firm, lawyers office, law office, legal aid agency, etc. Those attorneys employed in the judicial network are under the classification of public administration-government general or justice/public order and safety.

Figure 13-5

Number and Percent of
Lawyers Employed by Industrial
Classification in 1980*

Industrial Classification	Number	Percent
Agriculture/Forestry/Fishery	165	.033
Mining	31	.006
Construction	1,214	.245
Manufacturing	11,756	2.381
Transportation/Communication/ Public Utilities	5,648	1.143
Wholesale Trade	99	.121
Retail Trade	1,787	.362
Finances/Insurance/Real Estate	16,159	3.273
Business and Repair	2,807	.568
Personal Services	276	.055
Entertainment/Recreation	554	.113
Professional and Related[1]	14,950	3.027
Legal Services	370,948	75.107
Public Administration	67,499	13.666
TOTAL	493,893	100.000

*Source: Adapted from United States Department of Commerce,
Bureau of the Census, 1980 Census of Population, Vol. 2 Sub-
ject Reports, Part 7C: Occupation by Industry, Washington,
D.C.: U.S. Government Printing Office, 1984 pp. 295-664.

[1]The industrial classification of professional and related
services includes areas, such as education, health, legal
services, etc. Legal services includes office of attorney,
law firm, lawyers office, law office, legal aid office,
legal aid agency, etc. Those attorneys employed in the
judicial network are under the classification of public
administration-government general or justice/public order
and safety.

Figure 13-6

Distribution of Lawyers by Practice Area in 1977*

Practice Area	Lawyers Number	Percent
General Practice	147,067	58.0
Corporation	14,707	5.8
Criminal	4,818	1.9
Domestic Relations	4,311	1.7
Insurance Law	5,325	2.1
Negligence/Defendant	9,382	3.7
Negligence/Plaintiff	8,368	3.3
Patent Trademark, Copyright	4,057	1.6
Real Estate	11,664	4.6
Taxation	7,100	2.8
Wills, Estate Planning, Probate	11,410	4.5
Other	25,356	10.0
TOTAL	253,565	100.0

*Source: Adapted from United States Department of Commerce, Bureau of the Census, 1977 Census of Service Industries, Washington, D.C.: U.S. Government Printing Office, 1979, p. 5-6.

program.[5] Within the legal network, like many other human services, a major issue is continuing education. Many lawyers are trained as general lawyers, therefore are not equipped to handle specialty cases. Consequently, there has been an increasing awareness and demand for continuing education, based upon specialty needs. In general the functions of a lawyer are as follows:

- Counselor--Provide legal advice on a variety of legal problems.

- Advocate--Represent a client to obtain the optimum decision in light of current law in both civil and criminal cases. (For a discussion of a defense lawyer in criminal cases, see Chapter 11, Judicial network).

- Investigator--Provide legal research on cases, as well as, obtain the facts on a current problem.

- Clarify legal issues--In many cases the legal issues are unclear and the lawyer must clarify what the specific issues are.

- Mediator--In some situations, the lawyer is expected to be an arbitrator or mediator, between third parties.

In addition to the lawyer, other developing professions in the legal network are those of a paralegal aide (also called a legal assistant), legal stenographer and court reporter. A paralegal aide is an individual who has obtained an associate of arts degree (2 year degree and in some cases a 4 year degree), and works as a lawyer's aide. A legal stenographer is one who records and transcribes informal hearings and a court reporter transcribes court proceedings.[6]

SOCIAL WORK

The role of social work in the judicial network was previously discussed (see Chapter 11 Judicial Network), consequently this discussion is restricted to the small number of social workers employed in the legal network and their potential roles.

As previously indicated (Figure 13-4), there were 1,106 social workers employed in the legal services industrial classification in 1980. This represents an increase of 586 percent from 1970 when 161 social workers were employed in legal services. The role of a social worker in a legal firm would vary, depending upon whether the specialty was criminal law, family law, welfare law, etc. The general functions performed by a social worker in the legal network include the following:

INVESTIGATION

In some situations, the lawyer would need social histories of a family or of an individual as an aid in providing legal advice. For example, prior to taking on a criminal case where the person admits their complicity, the lawyer may need further information in order to take on the case and present a defense.

BROKER

In some cases, the lawyer may not be aware of social services or alternate programs for pre-trial diversion in the community, therefore would need a social worker to provide needed information.

CONSULTATION

In cases involving commitment for mental illness, a social worker could be instrumental in enabling the lawyer to adequately give advice to the client, their family or the court.

MEDIATION

In some cases, the difficulty between two grieved parties, may be a lack of communication, or a misunderstanding. In this situation a legal agreement or action may not be necessary but only a talking through of the situation.

FAMILY COUNSELING

Since close to 1.7 percent of a lawyer's specialty cases involve divorce actions or family actions, the social worker could provide invaluable assistance in an assessment of the families problem's or provide crisis counseling to avoid additional problems.

RESEARCH

The social worker should have a knowledge of specific social policies and legislation, therefore should be able to provide research support on specific issues, which would enable the lawyer to more adequately provide advice to the clients or the court.

In the absence of concrete facts on what tasks the 1,106 social workers employed in legal services in 1980 actually perform, the tasks outlined above are somewhat idealized, but certainly within the realm of reality. Since there has been a long history of the interrelatedness between the professions of law and social work, it is somewhat inconsistent that more social workers are not utilized within the legal network.[7]

PERSONAL SOCIAL SERVICES

The legal network is highly involved in the personal social service network through establishing legal guidelines and boundaries, consultation, and clarifying legal issues (see Chapter 22 Personal Social Services). Some examples of the personal social services in the legal network are as follows:

PROTECTIVE SERVICES

Child welfare services, child abuse and neglect services, legal social service, family violence services, and rights and services to the aged and disabled. Some examples of organizations or programs include Legal Advocacy for Older Adults, and the Human Element, Milwaukee, Wisconsin.

UTILITARIAN SERVICES

Day care centers, responsibility of individuals involved in homecare and homemaking, consumer advocacy and rights, landlord and tenant relations, and financial and debt counseling. The need for legal services in Day Care Centers is indicated by the McMartin PreSchool case in Manhattan Beach, California in 1984-85. Some examples of organizations and programs include Legal Action of Wisconsin and Legal Aid Society, Milwaukee, Wisconsin.

DEVELOPMENTAL and SOCIALIZATION SERVICES

Services and legal rights of children and parents, services to families and legal rights of respective marital partners and responsibility of youth recreation centers and camps. Some examples of programs and organizations include Wisconsin Institute on Divorce and You're Not Alone Inc., Milwaukee, Wisconsin and Family Hotline, Milwaukee, Wisconsin.

REHABILITATIVE and THERAPEUTIC SERVICES

Services and legal rights for alcoholics and drug addicts, responsibilities of suicide prevention centers, and specialized services for sexual assault and child exploitation. Some examples of organizations or programs include American Civil Liberties Union local chapter and Milwaukee Council on Alchololism, Milwaukee, Wisconsin.

SPECIAL POPULATIONS

The legal network, since 1960, has had a significant impact on the treatment of special populations in society (see Chapter 25, Special Populations and Chapter 24, Rehabilitation). Some examples of the legal network and programs for special populations are as follows:

ASIAN

Problems of discrimination in housing, property ownership, special programs for current refugees, e.g., Vietnam, Cambodia. Some examples of organizations and programs include the Asian American Committee for Human Rights in New Jersey, Asian Community Center, San Francisco, California and Asian American Legal Services, Los Angeles, California.

BLACK

Problems of discrimination in housing, employment, fair labor practices, and consumer rights. For example the National Association for the Advancement of Colored People Legal Defense and Education Fund and the National Urban League, New York, New York (and local chapters) .

EUROPEAN ETHNIC

The International Institutes of Milwaukee, Wisconsin and St. Paul, Minnesota which provides legal advice for immigrants.

NATIVE AMERICAN

Legal problems relating to treaties, social services for urban Indians, property rights of individuals versus tribal ownership, special programs for foster care, discrimination in housing and employment. For example the California Indian Legal Services, Berkeley, California, Native American Rights Fund, Boulder, Colorado and the National Native American Center, Oklahoma City, Oklahoma.

SAME SEX PREFERENCE

Gay Rights Union Milwaukee, Wisconsin which provides legal advice and the Homosexual Information Center in Hollywood, California.

SPANISH SPEAKING

Spanish Centers, such as Milwaukee, Wisconsin provides legal services and LaRaza Centro Legal, San Francisco, California; Mexican American Legal Defense and Education Fund, San Francisco, California and La Casa de Esperanza, Waukesha, Wisconsin.

WOMEN

National Organization for Women local chapters and Women Pro Se in Milwaukee, Wisconsin which provides legal advice.

ISSUES

The legal network is extremely diverse and oriented toward individualistic legal problems which may have broader social implications. Many of the issues of the legal network are societal, related to one's individual access to, or understanding of a specific situation as having legal implications, and educational concerns.

SOCIETAL ISSUES

The Supreme Court based upon decisions of the past 30 years has immersed itself in a series of broad social and political issues. Examples include: Brown vs. Board of Education case in 1954 on segregation, the Gideon vs. Wainwright decision in 1963 on legal counsel for adult felons who are indigent, the Roe vs. Wade decision on abortion in 1973 and more recently decisions to reaffirm abortion rights 1986, reaffirming the ban on prayer 1984, ending mandatory bussing in Virginia (1986) and the Baby Jane Doe case of 1986 regarding the right of parents to make life/death decisions on infants who are physically deformed. The issues involved in these cases are significant social issues.

ACCESS ISSUES

Historically the following adage was true, "if a person had money, they had access to quality legal services. If they did not have money, they relied on no services or poor services." To a great extent, this is still true today. However, the development of specialized programs, such as a public legal aid service, specialized landlord and tenant groups, and public defenders, has somewhat ameliorated the access problem. In spite of the development of the above services, there is a significant cost factor for those who seek and receive legal services.

In addition to the cost factor, other related concerns of accessibility, relate to minority groups and other specialized legal concerns, such as gay rights, student rights, abortion, etc. The number of lawyers from minority groups is relatively small, and efforts have been made through affirmative action to increase minority and women's perspectives in legal education and practice. Accessibility also refers to the type of cases lawyers will handle. As seen from Figure 13-6, the dominant area of practice for a lawyer is general practice, 58.0 percent and property concerns, 11.9 percent. On the other hand, civil rights, welfare rights, individual rights, etc., are extremely important types of cases and are included in the 10.0 percent of other practice areas.

EDUCATIONAL ISSUES

Legal education has been primarily in the classroom and has emphasized property, personal injury, or constitutional types of cases. Since lawyers work with people, more attention should be paid to the people aspect of their practice. This part of a lawyers training should involve psychology, basic interviewing,

435

cultural awareness, and an internship program in practice, either concurrent with, or after completion of the basic curriculum.

Social work on the other hand, has neglected the area of law in their curriculum. Social workers should have a knowledge of general legal issues as they affect social work practice, as well as, specific laws, as they relate to family, juveniles, corrections, etc. The trend today is toward a more legalistic society, consequently, social workers should be more prepared to practice within the legal network.

SUMMARY

The legal network is extremely diverse and consists primarily of lawyers in private practice, individual or group, (66 percent of all lawyers). The estimated number of lawyers in the United States in 1980 was 493,893. Data on the utilization of legal services by the United States population is inadequate, however, one study indicated that 66 percent of a sample of 2,064 individuals (1974), used lawyers at least once, and the primary reason for seeking legal advice related to property matters including wills.

A brief history of the legal profession indicated that the profession has had periods of high social status and low social status. Legal training outside of the clergy, began about 1200-1300 in the Inns of Court in England. Initially, training was primarily for individuals who became barristers and practiced in court. Later, an apprentice system developed for solicitors (general attorney's). The United States in its development of the legal profession further developed the role of the attorney at law, in contrast to the English model of the barrister and solicitor. Formal legal training at a university level was recognized in the United States in 1829 with the establishment of the Law School at Harvard University, and slowly expanded into the present system of law schools and mandatory legal education.

Contrary to popular public opinion, numerous human service occupations and professions are employed in the legal network, such as 1,106 Social Workers. The legal profession is dominant in the network comprising 49.34 percent of all employees. The potential role for social work in the legal network was discussed, as well as, some issues relating to social issues, accessibility of legal services for individual clients, and educational concerns for both lawyers and social work.

FOOTNOTES

*This chapter was reviewed for comments by Ellen Hochstedler, Associate Professor, Criminal Justice, School of Social Welfare, University of Wisconsin-Milwaukee, Milwaukee, Wisconsin.

1. Sources for estimating the size of the legal network include the following: United States Department of Commerce, Bureau of the Census. Statistical Abstract of the United States 1986 (106th Ed.), Washington, D.C.: U.S. Government Printing Office, 1985, pp. 177, 180, 181; United States Department of Commerce, Bureau of the Census, 1980 Census of Population Volume 2 Subject Reports. Part 7C: Occupation by Industry, Washington, DC: U.S. Government Printing Office, 1984, pp. 295-664 and United States Department of Commerce, Bureau of the Census, 1982 Census of Service Industries, Washington, D.C.: U.S. Government Printing Office, 1984, pp. 6,7.

2. The reader is referred to Barbara Curran and Francis Spalding. The Legal Needs of the Public. Chicago, Illinois: American Bar Association, 1974, for further details.

3. For a discussion of legal aid as a movement and a program for the delivery of legal services, the reader is referred to Chapter 11, Judicial Network.

4. American Bar Association. Report of the Task Force on Professional Utilization. Chicago, IL: American Bar Association, 1973, p. 29.

5. For information on the legal profession and educational standards, the reader is referred to the Association of American Law Schools, One Dupont Circle N.W., Suite 370, Washington, D.C., and the American Bar Association, 1155 E. 60th St., Chicago, IL 60637.

6. Some examples of professional organizations in the legal network include the following: American Bar Association (see footnote No. 5); National Association of Paralegal Personnel, 188 W. Randolph Street, Chicago, IL 60601; Center on Social Welfare Policy and the Law, 95 Madison Avenue, New York, NY 10016; and the American Academy of Matrimonial Lawyers, John Hancock Center, Suite 8504, 175 E. Delaware Place, Chicago, IL 60611.

7. For further information on the profession of social work as it relates to the legal network, the reader is referred to The National Association of Social Workers, 7981 Eastern Avenue, Silver Spring, Maryland 20910, and the National

Conference on Lawyers and Social Workers, in care of the National Association of Social Workers or contact the local office of the National Association of Social Workers.

SUGGESTED READINGS

Donald Brieland and John Lemmon. Social Work and the Law, St. Paul, Minnesota: West Publishing co., 1977. This is a classic book on the relationship of law and social work and in addition provides the social worker with a needed legal background.

Alan Farnsworth. An Introduction to the Legal System of the United States. New York, New York: Oceana Publications Inc., 1975. This book provides a general overview of the legal system and contains numerous useful references.

M.M. Knappen. Constitutional and Legal History of England. New York, New York: Harcourt, Brace and Co., 1942. Although an old book, this book provides an excellent history of the legal profession and shows how the profession changes as the concept of the court and legal rights changed.

Elliott Krause. The Sociology of Occupations . Boston, Massachusetts: Little Brown and Co., 1971. This book analyzes four professions, one of which is law. For the individual who is interested in a sociological approach to the profession of law, this is a sound reference book.

Roscoe Pound. The Lawyer from Antiquity to Modern Times. St. Paul, Minnesota: West Publishing Co., 1953. This is a classic book describing the historical development of the legal profession. For those interested in history this book is highly recommended.

Edwin Tucker. Adjudication of Social Issues: Text, Cases and Problems. St. Paul, Minnesota: West Publishing Co., 1971. This book describes some problem areas related to social issues in which both lawyers and social workers become involved.

REFERENCES

American Bar Association. Report of the Task Force on Professional Utilization.Chicago, Illinois: American Bar Association, 1973.

Association of American Law Schools. <u>Pre Law Handbook 1978-79</u>.
Washington, D.C.: Association of American Law Schools and
the Law School Admission Council Inc., 1978.

Auman, Francis. <u>The Changing American Legal System: Some
Selected Phases</u>. Columbus, Ohio: Ohio State University,
1940.
Association of American Law Schools. <u>Selected Readings on the
Legal Profession</u>. St. Paul, MN: West Publishing Co., 1962.

Blaustein, Albert and Charles Porter. <u>The American Lawyer</u>.
Chicago, Illinois: University of Chicago Press, 1954.

Brieland, Donald and John Lemmon. <u>Social Work and the Law</u>. St.
Paul, Minnesota: West Publishing Co., 1977.

Council for Public Interest Law. <u>Balancing the Scale of
Justice: Financing Public Interest Law in America</u>.
Washington, D.C.: Council for Public Interest Law, 1976.

Curran, Barbara and Francis Spalding. <u>The Legal Needs of the
Public</u>. Chicago, Illinois: American Bar Foundation, 1974.

Farnsworth, Alan. <u>An Introduction to the Legal Systems of the
United States</u>. New York, New York: Oceana Publications
Inc., 1975.

Gottesman, Roberta. <u>The Child and the Law</u>. St. Paul, MN: West
Publishing Co., 1981.

Hall, James. <u>Criminal Justice Administration: The American
Plan</u>. Dubuque, Iowa: Kendall/Hunt Publishing Co., 1976.

Knappen, M.M. <u>Constitutional and Legal History of England</u>. New
York, NY: Harcourt, Brace and Co., 1942.

Krause, Elliott. <u>The Sociology of Occupations</u>. Boston,
Massachusetts: Little Brown & Co., 1971.

McNeely, R.L. and Carl Pope. <u>Race, Crime and Criminal Justice</u>.
Beverly Hills, CA: Sage Publications, 1981.

Minahan, Anne (Ed). <u>Encyclopedia of Social Work 18th Issue</u>.
Washington, D.C.: National Association of Social Workers,
1986.

National Criminal Justice Information and Statistics Service,
<u>State and Local Prosecution and Civil Attorney Systems</u>,
Washington, D.C.: U.S. Government Printing Office, 1976.

Pound, Roscoe. The Lawyer from Antiquity to Modern Times. St. Paul, Minnesota: West Publishing Co., 1953.

Scherrer, James. "How Social Workers Help Lawyers." Social Work, Vol. 21, No. 4 (July 1976) pp. 279-284.

Smegel, Erwin. The Wall Street Lawyer. New York, NY: Free Press of Glenco, Illinois, 1964.

Tucker, Edwin. Adjudication of Social Issues: Text, Cases, and Problems. St. Paul, MN: West Publishing Co., 1971.

United States Department of Commerce, Bureau of the Census, 1980 Census of Population Vol. 2 Subject Reports: Part 7C: Occupation by Industry, Washington, D.C.: U.S. Government Printing Office, 1984.

United States Department of Commerce, Bureau of the Census, Statistical Abstract of the United States: 1986 (106th Ed.), Washington, D.C.: U.S. Government Printing Office, 1985.

United States Department of Commerce, Bureau of the Census, 1982 Census of Service Industries, Washington, DC: U.S. Government Printing Office, 1984.

United States Department of Justice, Bureau of Justice Statistics, Sourcebook of Criminal Justice Statistics--1984, Washington, D.C.: U.S. Government Printing Office, 1985.

United States Department of Commerce, Bureau of the Census, 1977 Census of Service Industries, Washington, D.C.: U.S. Government Printing Office, 1979.

Wald, Patricia. Law and Poverty: 1965. Washington, D.C.: U.S. Government Printing Office, 1965.

Waldron, Ronald, et.al. The Criminal Justice System: An Introduction. Boston, Massachusetts: Houghton, Mifflin Co., 1976.

Chapter 14

LEISURE and RECREATION*

"It has been said that the final test of a
civilization is its ability to use free time wisely
and profitably, and leisure has been described as
the main content of a free life and the nurse of
civilization. The amount and quality of a society's
leisure activities set the tone of its civilization
and define its vision of a good life." (Jensen:
1976:1)

INTRODUCTION

In 1982 an article in the United States News and World
Report (7/6/82) indicated that Americans spent approximately
262 billion dollars in 1982 for selected leisure and recreation
activities, and is one of the nations largest industries. In
essence leisure and recreation activity is big business and in
tourist states like Wisconsin, is one of the largest industries.

The variety of leisure and recreation activities include
individualized activities, such as reading, watching television,
drinking at home, drinking at bars etc., mass and group activities, such as commercial amusements, sports events, cultural
events, and active participation in sports activities, such as
bowling, baseball, hiking etc. Leisure and recreation activities are either highly individualized or commercialized, consequently human service personnel are minimally involved in large
parts of this network. Some aspects of leisure and recreation,
such as participant sports, hobbies and crafts, and outdoor
recreation activities utilize human service professions more
than other parts of the network. This chapter generally
describes leisure and recreation as a network, but focuses on
outdoor recreation and participant recreation, since these two
areas employ most of the human service occupations and professions. A related specialty in the leisure and recreation network is that of a recreation therapist, and the role of this
profession is compared with that of social work in the leisure
and recreation network.

SIZE

With the decline of the average work week from approximately
60 hours per week in 1900 to 40 hours per week in 1957 and in
many cases to 35 hours per week in 1986, the average American
worker has more time for leisure and recreation activities.
Many articles have been written attempting to define leisure and

441

to differentiate the concept of leisure and recreation. In general, leisure refers to time not related to survival activity i.e. working for income, and recreation refers to specific activities one becomes involved in during one's leisure time.[1]

The size of the leisure and recreation network is enormous with a variety of measures of classifying this network and determining its size. Figure 14-1 is one way of attempting to ascertain an estimated size of this network. Major categories in leisure and recreation shown in Figure 14-1 include: hotels, motels and other lodging; spectator sports; amusement and recreation services; museums, art galleries, botanical and zoological gardens; outdoor recreation; theatre performance; motion pictures; and bowling and billiards. Many leisure and recreation activities are not included in Figure 14-1, such as listening to the radio, writing letters and books, watching TV, reading, jogging etc. Figure 14-1 shows a minimum number of establishments in 1982 at 302, 993, with expenditures of 139 billion dollars. In 1985 it was estimated that personal expenditures for recreation activities was 157 billion dollars which is in addition to the expenditures of the recreation and leisure establishments. The leisure and recreation network employs at least 4,869,470 individuals and the population use (multiple count) is at least 9.8 billion individual visits and participants in leisure and recreation activities.[2]

Figure 14-2 shows estimates of individuals involved in various activities, such as hobbies and miscellaneous activities, participant sports, spectator sports, and cultural events. Although spectator sports and miscellaneous activities are not the main object of our concern, the figures provide some estimate of the proportion of people involved in participant sports versus spectator sports as well as hobbies versus cultural events.[3]

HISTORICAL DEVELOPMENT

The development of organized outdoor recreation activity and organized municipal recreation activity as we know them, are products of the last 125 years. These two areas of leisure and recreation are what Jensen (1976) labels recreational resources and recreational services, and these activities represent the more professionalized component of the leisure and recreation network, in comparison to what Jensen labels tourism, amusements, entertainment and commercialism.

442

Figure 14-1

Estimated Size of the Leisure and
Recreation Network on Selected Activities 1982*

Activity	Number of Establishments	(Dollars) Expenditures	Number of Employees	Population Use (Number)
Hotels, Motels and other Lodging	147,061	94,703,174,000	3,382,151	1,396,000,000
Spectator Sports[1]	2,360	3,418,467,000	62,447	246,660,000
Amusement and Recreation Services[2]	33,515	10,438,668,000	344,917	6,500,000,000
Museums, art gallery, botanical and Zoological Gardens	2,607	2,662,283,000	63,301	245,000,000
Outdoor Recreation[3]	84,500	8,500,000,000	328,661	998,024,000
Theatre Performance and Orchestras, symphony	8,322	4,399,200,000	98,414	402,202,000
Theatre/Motion picture	17,249	13,692,771,000	230,670	
Bowling and Billards	7,379	2,263,967,000	108,909	17,000,000
Total	302,993	139,978,530,000	4,869,470	9,804,886,000[4]

*Sources: Adapted from United States Department of Commerce, Bureau of the Census, Statistical Abstract of the United States: 1986 (106th Ed.), Washington D.C.: U.S. Government Printing Office 1985, pp. 222, 223, 225, 229, 230, 233, 234; United States Department of Commerce, Bureau of the Census, 1982 Census of Service Industries, Washington D.C.: U.S. Government Printing Office, 1984, pp. 4-7; Public Employment in 1984, Washington D.C.: U.S. Government Printing Office, 1985, p. 3.

[1]Instead of attempting to estimate the size of the entire leisure and recreation network, only a few activities are used to show the relative size of the network. Spectator sports refers to commercial sports i.e. professional clubs or racing.

[2]Includes dance halls and schools, amusement parks and fairs, carnivals, golf, private clubs etc.

[3]Includes the National Park Service and state park and recreation lands.

[4]The total equals more than the population of the United States, since individuals are involved in more than one activity and usually engage in this activity more than once.

Figure 14-2

ESTIMATED NUMBER OF INDIVIDUALS PARTICIPATING
IN SELECTED LEISURE AND RECREATION ACTIVITIES*

Estimated Number of Individuals Participating in Millions			
Other Activity	Participant (Individuals Sports Participating)	Spectator Sports Attendance)	Cultural Events (Attend at least once
No. of families (millions)			
Gardening 40.0	Swimming 35.0	Horse Race 74.0	Museum
C B Radio 20.0	Bicycle 28.0	Auto Race 50.0	Visit 78.0
Stamp	Fishing 26.0	Baseball 45.2	
Collecting 16.0	Camping 20.0	(Major)	Theater
Bridge	Bowling 67.0	Baseball	(Live) 62.0
Playing 10.0	Boating 35.2	(Minor) 11.3	
Chess 10.0	Table Tennis 32.0	Football 13.6	Popular
Genealogy 10.0	Tennis 25.4	(College)	Music
Photography 3.0	Softball 35.0	Football	Concert 54.0
Coin	Basketball 11.0	(Professional) 14.0	
Collecting 1.0	Ice Skate 25.8	Harness Race 30.7	Classical
	Hunting 11.0	Basketball	Music
(Number of Individuals)	Golf 14.5	(Professional) 11.1	Concert 27.0
Education 18.0	Baseball 15.7	Basketball	
Volunteer	Football 14.9	(College) 31.1	Ballet/
Service 60.0	Water ski 14.7	Greyhound Race 22.0	Other 24.0
Pleasure	Snow ski 11.0	Hockey (Major) 12.4	
Driving 118.3	Motorbike 9.9		
Visit Parks	Snowmobile 9.2		
Zoo, etc. 123.6	Jogging 19.0		
Picnic 123.8	Sailing 7.3		
Sightsee 106.5	Archery 5.5	Wrestling 5.0	
	Handball 5.3	Boxing 3.2	
	Racquetball 2.7	Soccer 1.1	
	Horseback Riding 25.2	Golf	
	Hiking 48.1	(Professional) 2.3	
		Tennis	
		(Professional) 2.2	

*Source: Adapted from United States News and World Report "How Americans Pursue
Happiness," Vol. 82 #20, 5-23-77, pp. 60, 76 and United States Department
of Commerce, Bureau of the Census, Statistical Abstract of the United
States 1986 (106th Ed.), Washington, D.C.: U.S. Government Printing Office,
1985, pp. 229, 230.

GENERAL DEVELOPMENT

From a historical perspective, at least four major themes can be identified relating to leisure and recreation activities: 1) social economic distinctions between the leisure activities of the wealthy and the masses; 2) a slow but progressive trend toward popularization of leisure and recreation activities; 3) the recency of the development of outdoor and organized recreation activity for the general population, and 4) the development of recreation professions.

SOCIAL CLASS and POPULARIZATION of RECREATION ACTIVITIES

The wealthy i.e. nobility, engaged in leisure and recreation activities, such as hunting, falconry, the arts, tournaments (mock battles), horse racing, drinking, etc., whereas the masses attended fairs, had holidays (holy days), drinking, physical activity (boxing, wrestling) and mass spectator sports (cock fighting, bull fighting, etc.). The wealthy tended to gravitate toward the non-physical and cultural activities whereas, the masses gravitated toward amusements, spectator sports and physical activities. This distinction between the social classes in recreation activity became blurred with popularization of recreation activity since 1800, with both the wealthy and the masses engaging in similar activities. The social class differences today are differences in style and conspicuous consumption, i.e., masses go to the beach or a public swimming pool, the wealthy have their own pool or join a private club. Figure 14-3 shows a historical time line in leisure and recreation, and specifically the trends in outdoor recreation and organized recreation activities.

OUTDOOR RECREATION

Gardens and parks were known to exist in Sumeria (2,400 B.C.), Babylonia (1,000 B.C.), and in Greece and Rome. However, these gardens and parks were normally the property of the wealthy who would allow the public into these areas for visits. Public parks set aside for the use of the common people were developed around 1400 in Italy and in England. These public grounds were used for fairs and people walked for miles to attend these events.

These early parks, and the city commons, such as Boston, Massachussetts (1682), were not developed with the idea of organized recreation activities. Organized recreation as a concept and the setting aside of specific land areas for visitation and site seeing was a consequence of the conservation movement and the park movement of the middle to late 1800s. The conservation movement developed as a response to attempt to

445

Figure 14-3

Historical Time Line of the Leisure and Recreation Network

Time Period	General Development	Outdoor Recreation	Organized Municipal Recreation	Voluntary and Fraternal Organization
Classical Civilization pre 450 A.D.	Class distinction wealthy—arts, theater, gambling common person — spectator sports	not organized	not organized	crafts organization
Medieval Europe 450–1500	class distinction wealthy — arts, hunting, tourna-ments common person — holiday (Holy day) fairs, physical activity, bowling	not organized	not organized	Guilds
Renaissance/ Reformation 1500–1700 and Enlightenment 1700–1800	class distinction wealthy—arts, hunting, theater, coffee house, horse racing, gambling common person — fairs, festivals, physical activity, cockfights, golf	development of city commons or greens used for social/ recreational activities	not organized	Friendly societies Private self improvement clubs
Early Industrial 1800–1900 (United States)	Popularization of recreation activity Class distinction-conspicuous consumption Beginning Develop-ment of spectator sports-baseball 1839, football 1869+	1864–Yosemite State Park 1872–Yellowstone Natl' Park 1891–U.S. Forest Preserves	1820s–Outdoor gymnasiums 1853–Central Park–New York 1887–children's playgrounds 1889–City Parks	1843–B'Nai B'rith 1851–YMCA; 1866–YMCA 1851–Employer programs 1882–Knights of Columbus 1889–Hull House 1892–Sierra Club 1898–Eagles Club

446

Figure 14-3 Continued

Time Period	General Development	Outdoor Recreation	Organized Municipal	Voluntary and Fraternal
Late Industrial 1900-1980 (United States)	Development of Commercial Recreation - amusement parks, tourism, parks, zoos, cultural events 1960 Outdoor Recreation Resources Act	1916-National Park Service State, municipal parks Private Parks 1966-Historic Preservation sites	Continued Development of parks and structured recreation activities to include school recreation programs	1906-Boy's clubs 1910-Boy scouts 1912-Girl Scouts 1922-Izaak Walton 1915-Kiwanis Club 1905-Rotary Club
Service Economy 1980 on (United States)	Concern developing over appropriate use of leisure development of leisure specialties and recreation therapists	Continued Development	Continued Development	Some fraternal organizations having financial and membership difficulties

preserve natural resources. The park movement had as its specific objective the setting aside of locations for visitation and preservation of resources with early parks established in Chicago, Illinois (1839) and New York City (1853 Central Park).

Those individuals in the park movement who were concerned about resource preservation i.e. outdoor recreation, became part of the conservation movement. Parks were established by all levels of government, such as state recreation areas, Yosemite State Park (1864), Adirondack State Park in New York (1885); federal recreation areas were developed, such as Yellowstone Park (1872), United States Forest Preserves (1891), and the National Park Service (1916), and county/township recreation areas were developed after the 1900s. The initial concern of the development of these recreation areas was the preservation of natural resources and not organized recreation activities, such as campgrounds, picnic areas, hotels, swimming areas, hiking or bicycle trails, etc. The development of organized activities in the federal and state park systems slowly developed since 1930. Currently there is a variety of organized activities in outdoor recreation areas including campgrounds with counselors, organized camps, etc.

447

ORGANIZED MUNICIPAL and VOLUNTARY RECREATION

Those individuals in the park movement who were concerned about resource use or services (recreation activity) became involved in the development of municipal recreation systems, along with a variety of voluntary agencies which stressed recreation activities. In both cases the motivation was to provide a wholesome environment for the laboring classes and the poor, who had little opportunity or access to "wholesome recreation activities and opportunities."

MUNICIPAL RECREATION - organized recreation activities had its early beginnings in 1821, in Salem, Massachusettes with outdoor gymnasiums and Central Park in New York City in 1853. Urban problems, such as overcrowding, lack of sanitation and the large in-flux of immigrants to the United States led to a concern about adequate recreation facilities and space. The municipal playground movement developed in Boston, Massachusettes in 1885, utilizing volunteers, and in 1887, utilized paid professional employees. The municipal playground movement spread rapidly in the United States. By 1900, fourteen cities had municipal playgrounds, such as Milwaukee, Wisconsin; New York, New York; Boston, Massachusetts; Minneapolis, Minnesota, and Cleveland, Ohio. The primary focus of this movement was on activity i.e. playgrounds, swimming, golf, baseball, hiking trails, bicycle trails, etc.

VOLUNTARY RECREATION - Private agencies had a multiple motivation in their interest in the development of recreation programs: spiritual uplifting, immigrant adaptation and mutual interest societies attempting to provide wholesome activity. Examples of the Spiritual uplifting agencies include the Young Mens Christian Association (1851), Young Womans Christian Association (1866), Boys Club (1906), Boy Scouts (1910), and Girl Scouts (1912). These agencies relied on individuals with a general college degree and interest in people for providing leadership in organized recreation activities and for individual counseling.

Examples of the immigrant adaptation agency was the Settlement House and Neighborhood Center, such as Hull House in Chicago (1889), and the Neighborhood Center in New York (1886), which employed numerous group workers from a social work background. Examples of the mutual interest group agency include the B'nai B'rith (1843), Knights of Columbus (1882), Eagles Club (1888), Kiwannis Club (1915), Rotary Club (1905), employer recreation programs (1851), Union recreation programs (1886), Sierra Club (1892) and Isaac Walton League (1922). These agencies made extensive use of volunteers, and some have employed a variety of recreation professions and specialists.

448

All of the above agencies, municipal and voluntary, have broadened and modified their leisure and recreation services since their early development to include counseling and social services.

RECREATION PROFESSIONS

Concurrent with the development of organized activities in outdoor recreation areas there was the slow development of a recreation profession which initially focused on content and training in areas of park administration, management and utilization of resources. Later, recreation programs included social service activities, such as counseling and working with the disabled.

STRUCTURE

As indicated earlier, of the variety of leisure and recreation activities, only outdoor recreation and organized recreation activity are discussed further, since it is in these two areas where human service professions are more routinely employed. The structure of the leisure and recreation network can be viewed from its organizational context, services provided, occupations and professions, and dominant occupations and professions.

ORGANIZATIONAL CONTEXT

The vast majority of outdoor recreation areas are owned by federal, state, county and township, governments. Consequently, the structure of outdoor recreation as a specialized area of recreation closely parallels government structure. Figure 14-4 shows a model of federal and state government organization and outdoor recreation.

Many organized recreation activities are sponsored by a municipal government or by a voluntary agency. Figure 14-5 shows a model of a county and municipal recreation department and Figure 14-6 a typical neighborhood community center.[4]

SERVICES PROVIDED

The services provided by the leisure and recreation network are varied depending upon whether the focus is on outdoor recreation, organized public community recreation or voluntary private agencies and clubs. In general, the following are examples of services provided in the leisure and recreation network:

Figure 14-4

IDEALIZED MODEL OF THE FEDERAL AND STATE GOVERNMENT ORGANIZATION
IN THE LEISURE AND RECREATION NETWORK (OUTDOOR RECREATION)*

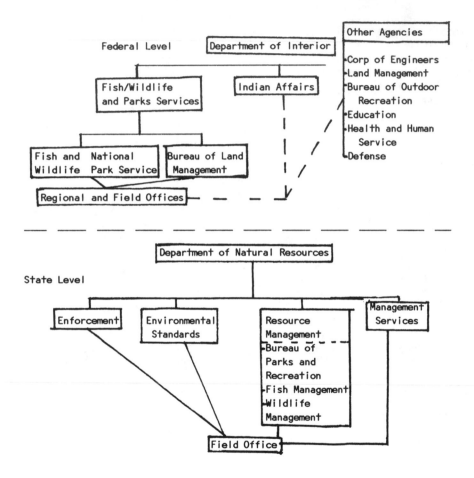

*Sources: Adapted from Office of Federal Register, United States Government
Manual 1985-86, Washington D.C. U.S. Government Printing Office, 1985, pp.
844, 840, 843, 836; and Wisconsin Legislative Reference Bureau, Wisconsin Blue
Book 1985-86, Madison Wisconsin: Department of Administration, 1985, p. 493.

Figure 14-5

IDEALIZED MODEL OF A LOCAL GOVERNMENT ORGANIZATION
IN THE LEISURE AND RECREATION NETWORK (OUTDOOR RECREATION)*
AND ORGANIZED MUNICIPAL RECREATION

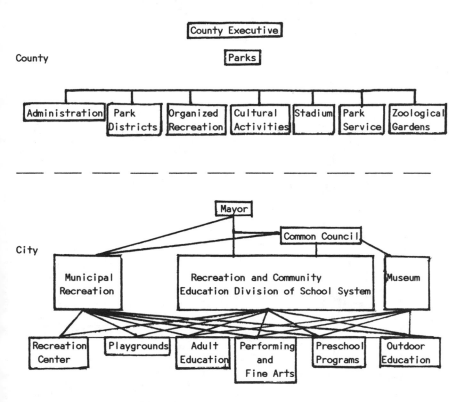

*Sources: Adapted from Fiscal Affairs Division Annual Financial Report:
County of Milwaukee, Wisconsin, 1984, Milwaukee, Wisconsin: Department of
Administration, 1985, and Annual Report City of Milwaukee 1984.

Figure 14-6

IDEALIZED MODEL OF THE ORGANIZATION OF
A NEIGHBORHOOD SETTLEMENT HOUSE
(PRIVATE VOLUNTARY AGENCY)*

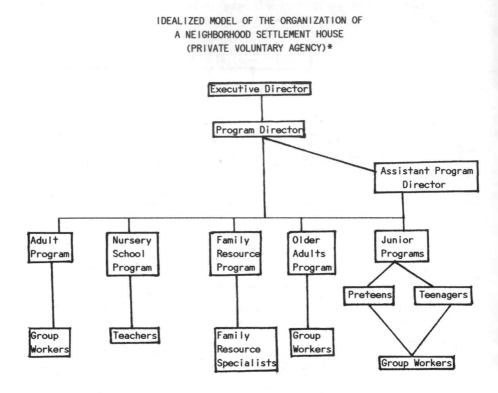

*Source: Adapted from Neighborhood House Program Activities 1982, Milwaukee, Wisconsin. Reprinted with permission of the Neighborhood House of Milwaukee, Wisconsin.

Outdoor recreation:

- Organized camping (with counselors and social workers
    and others as employees and volunteers)
- Individual camping
- Horseback riding, hiking and bicycle trails
- Picnic and tourist sites
- Educational displays and lectures
- Consultation and public relations
- Swimming and boating areas (hunting in selected areas).

Organized community outdoor recreation activities:

- Camping, camps, picnics, hikes, etc.
- Games and sports, such as baseball, archery, basketball,
    etc.
- Water sports
- Winter sports
- Crafts and arts
- Fine arts
- Performing arts
- Special programs for the disabled, aging etc.

Voluntary agencies and clubs, such as a Neighborhood House:

- Nursery school
- Child care
- Arts and crafts
- Sports and games
- Camping (organized and short-term)
- Group counseling
- Individual counseling
- Financial management counseling
- Community advocacy and action
- Educational resources
- Organized clubs.

OCCUPATIONS and PROFESSIONS

In contrast to many of the other human service networks, the recreation worker and recreation therapist as professions are not the dominant group numerically in the industrial classifications of entertainment and recreation, eating , drinking places, hotel/motel/lodging, museums and art galleries and administration of environmental programs, which represent part of the leisure and recreation network.[5] Figure 14-7 shows a selected number of human service occupations and professions in the leisure and recreation network.

453

Figure 14-7

Number and Percent of Selected Human Service Occupations and Professions
Employed in the Industrial Classifications of Entertainment/Recreation,
Eating/Drinking Places, Hotel/Motel/Lodging, Museums and Art
Galleries, and Administration of Environmental and Housing Resources
(Leisure and Recreation Network) in 1980*

Selected Occupation and Profession	Number	Percent
Recreation Work	1,339	.305
Therapist (includes Recreation, Art, Dance, Music)	571	.130
Architect	71	.016
Social Work	2,129	.485
Counselor	723	.165
Personnel and Labor Relations	11,068+	2.519
Teacher	58,314+	13.274
Librarian	1,956	.445
Lawyer	1,732	.394
Clergy/Religious Worker	967	.220
Psychologist	161	.037
Urban Planner	539	.123
Child Care	129,274	29.427
Physician and Assistant	404	.092
Dietician	1,092	.249
Registered Nurse	993	.226
Licensed Practical Nurse	243	.055
Health Aide	1,581	.360
Nurse Aide	3,825	.871
Guards/Watchmen	222,323	50.607
Total	439,305	100.000

*Source: Adapted from United States Department of Commerce, Bureau of the
Census, 1980 Census of Population Vol. 2 Subject Reports Part 7C: Occupation
by Industry, Washington D.C.: U.S. Government Printing Office, 1984,
pp. 295-664.

Figure 14-7 (continued)

The industrial classification of entertainment and recreation includes bowling alleys, billard and pool halls, commercial amusements, spectator sports, dance halls and studios, etc. The industrial classification of museums and art galleries includes zoological and botanical gardens and parks. Estimates on the human service occupations and professions from the industrial classification of administration of environmental and housing resources was based on a distribution of 46 percent to recreation and leisure, 18 percent to housing and 26 percent to energy and environment.

Numerically the largest human service occupations and professions in the leisure and recreation network are guards and watchmen, 50.6 percent, child care workers, 29.4 percent, and teachers, 13.2 percent. Although recreation workers and recreation therapists do not dominate the leisure and recreation network numerically, these two groups represent the developing professionalism within the leisure and recreation network.

DOMINANT OCCUPATIONS and PROFESSIONS

The occupation grouping of recreation worker and recreation therapist account for .435 percent of the selected human service occupations and professions employed in the leisure and recreation network as shown in Figure 14-7. Figure 14-8 shows the occupational classification of recreation work and where they were employed by industrial classification in 1980. The industrial classification where recreation workers were primarily employed include health 36.193 percent, membership organizations 14.502 percent, entertainment and recreation 14.147 percent, and social services 8.689 percent. The remaining 26.469 percent of recreation workers are distributed amongst a variety of industrial classifications.

One of the reasons for the lack of one profession to dominate the leisure and recreation network is the recency of professionalism within the network i.e. since 1940. The current movement toward professionalism is derived from two sources: the park and playground movement of the late 1800s (recreation major), and the hospital recreation movement of the 1940s (therapeutic recreation).

RECREATION MAJOR--During the late 1800's with the dual concerns in the United States over the conservation of natural resources and the problems of urban slums, a number of individuals and groups became concerned about recreation issues. Two types of groups were forming; those who were concerned about resource

Figure 14-8

Number and Percent of Recreation Workers
Employed by Industrial Classification in 1980*

Industrial Classification	Number	Percent
Agriculture/Forestry/Fishery	110	.325
Mining	24	.072
Construction	28	.083
Manufacturing	287	.849
Transportation, Communication, Public Utility	122	.361
Wholesale/Retail Trade	232	.686
Finances/Real estate, Insurance	304	.899
Business/repair	219	.648
Personal Service	1,307	3.867
Entertainment/Recreation	4,782+	14.147
Health	12,234	36.193
Legal	68	.201
Education	1,655	4.896
Social Service	2,937	8.689
Membership Organization	4,902	14.502
Other Professional and Related	261	.772
Religious Organizations	624	1.846
Administration of Environment/Housing	1,595	4.719
General Government	968	2.863
Administration of Human Resources	469	1.388
Justice, Safety Public order	337	.997
Other Public Administration	337	.997
Total	33,802	100.000

*Source: Adapted from United States Department of Commerce, Bureau of the Census, 1980 Census of Population Vol. 2 Subject Reports Part 7C: Occupation by Industry, Washington D.C.: U.S. Government Printing Office, 1984 pp 295-664

[1]The above figures do not include recreation therapists which are partially listed under the occupational classification of therapist along with other therapists like art, dance, corrective, etc.

preservation and conservation and those who were concerned about recreation. The first group formed the nucleus of the park movement and the second group formed the nucleus of the play-ground movement. The park movement at the state level was established in California in 1864 (Yosemite Park) and at the federal level in 1872 with the first national park (Yellowstone National Park). A series of professional associations developed which focused on resource preservation and management, such as the American Forestry Association, National Association of Park Management, and the Soil Conservation Association. An emphasis of this movement was on resource management with some college courses established in forestry by 1873 and later park management at Syracuse University. By 1910 there were 19 colleges offering forestry and conservation programs. Some of the organizations participating in the resource management movement merged with some of the organizations participating in the playground movement in 1965 to form the National Recreation and Park Association.

The focus of the playground movement was to provide an opportunity for recreation activities, and to enhance the quality of life for the laboring and poor classes in the developing urban centers. The impetus for the development of the playground movement was from three directions: social work through Settlement Houses and Community Centers (1886, 1889) using early individual and group work techniques; education through its interest in physical education (1905-1912), and moral uplifting agencies, such as the Young Men's Christian Association (1851) and Young Women's Christian Association (1866). Playgrounds and recreation centers were established rapidly after 1885. The Playground Association was established in 1906, which changed its name to the National Recreation Association in 1917.

Educational programs were established by 1911 in Chicago for playground directors (later a part of Northwestern University), in New York for community centers and settlement houses (later a part of Columbia University), and by 1930, 25 colleges offered physical education programs with an emphasis on recreation. The American Association of Health, Physical Education, and Recreation was formed as part of the National Education Association in 1937. Over time the need for individuals with a clear focus on recreation was needed, and these programs were primarily placed in schools of education or allied health programs.[7] In 1965, there was a merger of the playground associations (National Recreation Association, and American Recreation Society) with the previously discussed park movement (National Recreation Park Association) to form an umbrella professional association known as the National Recreation and Park Association.[8]

In contrast to most other human service professions, there is no formal accreditation process in the broad area of leisure and recreation but there is in specific areas, such as forestry, conservation, park management etc. Two recent developments which indicate a movement toward certification and potential accreditation are: some states like New Jersey (1966) have developed certification procedures for individuals who are employed as recreation professionals, and the National Recreation and Park Association has developed some general guidelines for curriculum and a system of specialization based upon degree. In general, the National Recreation and Park Association has recommended a bachelors degree with a recreation major or a related field as an entry level degree, and the Masters degree in recreation would be a specialty or advanced level degree for a particular area in the leisure and recreation network.

Recreation majors are developing with the following 9 feasible concentrations:

- Outdoor recreation and resource management
- Community, school, and education recreation
- Industrial recreation
- College union management
- Municipal recreation and park management
- Tourism and commercial recreation
- Recreation in correctional institutions[9]
- Volunteer youth agency work[9]
- Therapeutic recreation.[9]

Since the above recommendations have been formulated in 1965, there has developed a sizable number of associate of art degree programs in recreation. Their role in the overall development of a professional group in leisure and recreation, is not clearly defined at this time. In general, the functions of the recreation major in the leisure and recreation network include the following:

- Administration--planning, organizing and providing leadership for recreation and park programs. This includes the management of facilities, public relations, hiring and releasing personnel.

- Supervision--a large organization, such as the United States Department of Interior or a State Natural Resources Department which administers a geographical region or district. In smaller programs one would administer a specific phase of the overall program and personnel in that program.

- Director of a center or facility--a specific site or recreation location in a large recreation program. This person would have administrative responsibility for the program, as well as, become involved in direct relationship roles with individuals or groups.

- Direct leader--organize and direct the specific activities, as these relate to individuals participating in a program, and provide when necessary an appropriate amount of general counseling.

THERAPEUTIC RECREATION--In contrast to the park and playground movement which developed in response to the growing concerns of resource preservation and use, and the problems of urban slums, the therapeutic recreation movement developed out of the needs of hospital patients for physical activity to enhance a persons recovery and in adapting to any permanent physical conditions which would affect one's functioning.

Early development of therapeutic recreation was in the late 1800s and early 1900s from individuals who were involved in social group work, and realized the potential of using recreation activity as a form of a therapeutic endeavor. The first course in the subject was at Case Western Reserve University in 1923. In 1925, the Menninger Clinic used recreation therapy as one of the adjuvant activities to therapy. The use of recreation therapy expanded to other institutions, such as correctional institutions and the general hospital. The first college preparatory course for therapeutic recreation was developed in the 1940s, and the first masters degree program was developed at West Virginia in 1951. The Veterans Administration, was one of the first large physical and mental health networks, which established a recreation section (1945), in order to enhance the recovery of many of the veterans who were returning from World War II.

Three professional associations were developed which reflected the needs of therapeutic recreation: Hospital Recreation Section of the American Hospital Association (1949), National Association of Recreation Therapists (1952) and the Recreation Therapy Section of the American Association of Health, Physical Education and Recreation (1952). The close relationship of therapeutic recreation to both the mental and physical health networks continued until 1965 when a merger occurred between the National Recreation and Park Association and the Therapeutic Recreation Association. With the merger of the National Recreation and Park Association in 1965, the National Therapeutic Recreation Society was formed with responsibility for development of a suggested model or curriculum and a certification process for recreation therapists. Currently, there are accreditation procedures for therapeutic recreation, however, there is only a voluntary registration with the National Therapeutic Recreation Society. The National Therapeutic Recreation Society has recommended a sequence of training and classification for therapeutic recreation ranging from a Therapeutic Recreation Assistant--2 years previous experience to

459

a Master Therapeutic Recreation Specialist--Masters Degree and at least two years experience.

As of 1980, there were about 9,000 therapeutic recreationists registered with the National Society. Of these, 65 percent were employed in hospitals, and 35 percent in special schools, corrections agencies, etc.

The tasks of the therapeutic recreationist would vary depending upon whether one is in administration, supervision, consultation, research, education or direct service. Responsibilities for administration and supervision would be very similar to responsibilities of other human service professions involved in these tasks.

The therapeutic recreationist in <u>direct service</u> would have the following objectives: to enhance a positive morale and positive thinking of individuals with debilitating conditions, encourage the formation of proper habits and attitudes toward recreation activities, channel aggressive drives into constructive outlets, and encourage individuals to overcome physical and mental barriers. Some of the specific functions of the therapeutic recreationist would enclude the following:

- Evaluation of an individual's capabilities
- Diagnostic program for an activity analysis
- Leisure counseling
- Individual and group counseling
- Leisure education
- Enable individuals to perform specific activities.

The role of the therapeutic recreationist has some aspects of counseling, however, the major emphasis is on the use of recreation activity and the therapeutic recreationist acting in an adjuvant role in the treatment process, along with psychologists, psychiatrists, and social workers. Areas of employment for therapeutic recreationists include facilities for the blind, disabled, cerebral palsy, multiple dystrophy, multiple sclerosis, heart patients, mental patients, nursing homes, rehabilitation centers, corrections, etc.[10]

SOCIAL WORK

Accurate figures on the number of social workers involved in the leisure and recreation network are difficult to ascertain, since social workers are employed in many voluntary welfare agencies, clubs, as well as, in the entertainment and recreation industry as such. Figure 14-7 indicates there were at least 2,129 social workers employed in the industrial classifications of entertainment/recreation, museum/art gallery, eating drinking places, hotel/motel/lodging, and administration of environmental and housing programs. This figure of social workers in the leisure and recreation network represents only a small percentage of social workers in the network, since they would be employed in other industrial classifications, such as social services, religious organizations or membership organizations. Social work was early involved in the area of leisure and recreation through the Settlement House movement and the Neighborhood Center movement of 1886 and 1889. These early movements had an emphasis on group work, with recreation activities as part of the intervention technique in order to enable individuals to better cope with urban life. There was an early use of recreation therapy in some of the mental hospitals which was essentially an outgrowth of the group work process.

In general, the roles of a social worker would vary depending upon whether they were involved in case work, group work, community organization, staff development, consultation, or research.

CASE WORK

The case worker in a leisure and recreation setting would focus on individual perceptions of ones surroundings and try to clarify ways in which the individual can cope with a frustrating environment. In this process there would be recommendations on recreational activities one could engage in during one's leisure time to either foster insight into problem areas or to channelize energies into a positive direction.

GROUP WORK

The use of group work would vary depending upon whether one was working with a youth club, activity group, or therapy group. The differences between these types of groups are the focus and direction of the group and the degree of involvement and expected leadership from the group worker. Generally, the group worker in a youth club acts as a moderator, and a mediator providing suggestions and directions, but does not take over leadership of the group. In the activity group the group worker would more than likely have a direct role in leading the activities, in enabling individuals to perform certain tasks and through this direct role develop a relationship with individuals in discussing various problems. In a therapy group the group worker would normally act as a mediator or moderator by allowing a range of topics to be discussed at the request and interest of the group. In addition, the worker may take a more direct role in leading the group.

461

COMMUNITY ORGANIZATION

In community organization the worker would represent the specific group, to provide direction on how to advocate for particular issues, give the group ideas on how to publicize their particular concerns, provide information on important individuals to see in influencing a policy, and provide resources for the group to meet. In essence the community organizer working in a neighborhood center would in effect perform the roles of broker, referral agent, educator, and a consultant.

STAFF DEVELOPMENT and CONSULTATION

In staff development and consultation, the social worker would provide information and insight on the dynamics of groups, the cultural differences between ethnic and minority groups, and how the group process would provide a better understanding of a situation, as well as, come to a resolution of problems[11].

PERSONAL SOCIAL SERVICES

The leisure and recreation network has numerous linkages with the personal social service network. (See chapter 22, Personal Social Service.) Some examples of the personal social services in the leisure and recreation network include the following:

PROTECTIVE SERVICES

Seminars on child abuse, family neglect, aging held in the local Young Men's and Young Women's Christian Association, such as Chicago, Illinois.

UTILITARIAN SERVICES

Day care and home making programs sponsored by a Neighborhood House, such as Milwaukee, Wisconsin.

DEVELOPMENTAL and SOCIALIZATION SERVICES

Marriage encounter groups, awareness programs for unwed mother's sponsored by the Young Women's or Young Men's Christian Association, such as Los Angeles, California or New York, New York. Services oriented toward youth, such as the Boys Clubs of America.

REHABILITATIVE and THERAPEUTIC SERVICES

Alcoholic Anonymous group, sponsored by the Young Men's Christian Association, special programs on suicide, sexual assault, pornography etc. sponsored by the Young Men's or Women's Christian Association.

SPECIAL POPULATIONS

The leisure and recreation network affects all individuals including special populations. (See Chapter 25, Special Populations, and Chapter 24, Rehabilitation). Some examples of programs and services for special populations in the leisure and recreation network include the following:

ASIAN

Japanese Community Youth Council, San Francisco, California and Korean Self Help Center, Los Angeles, California.

BLACK

Black and Non-White staffs, YMCA, Washington, D.C. and Martin Luther King Center, Milwaukee, Wisconsin.

EUROPEAN ETHNIC

Jewish Community Center, Milwaukee, Wisconsin and International Institutes of Milwaukee, Wisconsin and Minneapolis, Minnesota.

NATIVE AMERICANS

American Indian Scouting, Brunswick, New Jersey and Oneida Community Center, Oneida, Wisconsin.

SAME SEX PREFERENCE

Lesbian Resource Center, Minneapolis, Minnesota and Friends for Lesbian and Gay Concerns, Sumneytown, Pennsylvania.

SPANISH SPEAKING

Centro Cultural, Cornelius, Oregon and Concelio de Organizations Hispanos, Philadelphia, Pennsylvania.

WOMEN

Women, San Francisco, California and Young Women's Christian Association and its local organizations.

ISSUES

The leisure and recreation network has issues related to professionlization, duplication of services and for social work education a recognition of leisure and recreation as a significant area of practice.

PROFESSIONALIZATION

Since the leisure and recreation network does not have a dominant profession but a number of fledging professions there are a number of concerns about the future directions of these professions in the leisure and recreation network. Specifically, there is a current debate on whether the orientation in the outdoor recreation area should be on park management, maintenance and preservation, or whether the focus should be on resource use, i.e., activities. There is no agreement on whether a leisure and recreation profession should be in schools of education, allied health, social work, conservation, or whether a special program separate from other disciplines should be developed. Along with the issue of whether or not there should be a special independent profession, there are questions relating to accreditation standards, curriculum content and professional certification.

Therapeutic recreation has some of the same issues of professionalism as experienced in other parts of the leisure and recreation network. Although there is an accreditation process and voluntary registration of therapeutic recreationists, there is a changing concept of what is the content and focus of therapeutic recreation programs. In addition, there are some concerns about clearly defining the role of therapeutic recreation in relationship to other human service professions.

DUPLICATION of SERVICES

In addition to issues relating to professionalization within the leisure and recreation network there are other broader societal concerns. Should there be a duplication of public facilities and activities with commercial facilities? That is, should municipal recreation areas become involved in activities, such as bowling, cultural events, etc., when these are available in the commercial establishments. Should public facilities charge fees, if so to what extent? The major concern is whether the charging of fees in a public facility would defeat the basic purpose of having open facilities to the average citizen. At what price will citizen use decrease instead of increase because of fees. Should resources be used for preservation and conservation, or for use of individuals and groups? The debate in 1983-86 on whether to use national forest land for commercial development or for resource management is a good example of this issue. Most individuals adhere to the concept, that a balance must be developed between resource use and resource preservation. Should there be a focus on the individual need of a person involved in leisure and recreation, or should there be more of an emphasis on amusement and mass spectator sports?

SOCIAL WORK EDUCATION

In social work there are essentially two concerns, one is professional and the other is curriculum. Although social workers were heavily involved in leisure and recreation activities in the early development of the popular recreation movements of the late 1890s, social work today has not recognized the current or potential role of social workers in the leisure and recreation network. In most schools of social work there has been a deemphasis on leisure and recreation as a social problem and a deemphasis on group work as a methodology in the curriculum. Since leisure and recreation is becoming a major problem and is one of the largest industries in the United States, social work education should incorporate more material and content into its curriculum in this area. There are some other potential roles for social workers in the leisure and recreation network in addition to the traditional group and the neighborhood center movement. Specifically, social workers can provide functions of staff development, consultation, and preparation of counselors for organized camping as well as specialized programs. There are other potentialities for these tasks to be performed in private clubs, commercial establishments, and in college and university unions.

SUMMARY

The leisure and recreation network in the United States is extremely large and diverse. It is estimated that in 1982 at least 262 billion dollars was spent on leisure and recreation activities. Generally, leisure refers to time away from work and recreation refers to a specific activity which a person engages in during that time. The diversity of leisure and recreation is indicated by the fact that some people use activities such as reading, watching television, listening to radio, tape decks, and stereos for leisure and recreation; others engage in mass spectator sports i.e. watching football, baseball games; others will go to cultural events; others will become actively involved in recreation activities themselves, such as hiking, camping, baseball, etc.

There is no dominate occupation or profession in the area of leisure and recreation. There are a variety of leisure and recreation professions which have developed since the 1930's in schools of education, forestry/conservation, allied health amongst others. The movement toward professionalization of leisure and recreation occupations has stemmed from two sources: the park and playground movement, and hospital recreation movement. The park movement developed in the late 1860s in an attempt to preserve natural resources. The playground movement developed in the late 1800s in an attempt to provide recreation outlets and activities for the laboring class and poorer people in the urban centers. The recreation major developed in response to these needs. Professional organizations were developed in both areas, such as the American Forestry Association (focus on parks) and the American Recreation Society (focus on playgrounds) and it was not until 1965 when both of these movements merged into a joint Park and Recreation Association which has become a unified professional association for a leisure and recreation profession.

The second professional area of leisure and recreation was the hospital recreation movement which developed therapeutic recreation as a subspecialty. This subspecialty initially was developed in the mental and physical health networks in the late 1920s. It was one of the early adjuvant therapies which became recognized as an important function in rehabilitating mental and physical health patients. The movement toward professionalization of therapeutic recreation was rather rapid, with a professional organization established in 1949. Therapeutic recreation as a professional association merged with the National Park and Recreation Association in 1965 and is now part of the overall umbrella organization in leisure and recreation.

The role of the recreation major was compared with that of therapeutic recreation and both of these were than compared with the role of a social worker in the leisure and recreation network. Social work was early involved in leisure and recreation activities through the Settlement House and Neighborhood Center movement of the 1890s. The role of a social worker as traditionally defined has been that of a group worker in a neighborhood settlement house. There are other potentialities for the role of social work in the leisure and recreation network including staff development and consultation, and working in commercial leisure and recreation establishments.

Professional issues for both the recreation profession and social work were discussed. Some of the issues in the professional area of recreation are: determination of appropriate professional credentials, type of curriculum, its content and accreditation and certification. Social work should redefine its role in the leisure and recreation network and both professions have to look to the future in terms of some of the broader aspects of society as these are related to the leisure and recreation network.

*The general format of this chapter was discussed with Richard Schild, Associate Professor, Human Kinectics, University of Wisconsin-Milwaukee, Milwaukee, Wisconsin.

FOOTNOTES

1. For example, see James Charlesworth Leisure in America: Blessing or Curse, Philadelphia, Pennsylvania: American Academy of Political and Social Science, 1964.

2. Clayne Jensen Leisure and Recreation: An Introduction and Overview, Philadelphia, Pennsylvania: Lea and Feibiger, Inc., 1977. Since individuals participate in more than one leisure and recreation activity, the total is more than the population of the United States.

3. Attendance and participation estimates equal more than the 237 million estimated people in the United States in 1986, since many individuals participate in more than one activity, and many engage in certain activities on a rather frequent basis.

4. In addition to the more formalized aspect of leisure and recreation, most individuals use an informal or folk network for leisure and recreation, such as family, relatives, neighbors, friends, colleagues, acquaintances, etc.

5. Although cultural events are included as part of leisure and recreation, the human service aspect of culture i.e. art therapy, music therapy, dance therapy are discussed in Chapter 4 Aesthetic Network. Consequently, no further dis-cussion of cultural activities is developed in this chapter.

6. Child care workers are listed as part of the personal service occupations. Other occupations listed in the 1980 census as a personal service worker include the following: attendant (recreation and amusement), attendant (personal service), attendant (public transportation) baggage porter and bellhop, barber, boarding and lodging housekeepers, bootblack, guide, elevator operator, hairdresser and cosme-tologist, housekeeper, school monitor, usher and welfare service aide.

7. In 1982, of the 190 universities and colleges which offer a major in leisure and recreation, 60 percent are located in schools of education or combined schools of health, physical education or recreation, 15 percent in forestry and conservation programs, and 15 percent in the arts and sciences.

8. The National Association of Social Workers, was one of the organizations participating in the National Recreation Education Accreditation Project of 1963, but was not part of the merging process that occurred in 1965-1966.

9. Recreation workers in a corrections setting, voluntary youth agency work, and therapeutic recreation, have some overlap and potential duplication with social work.

10. Examples of professional associations in the area of leisure and recreation include: National Park and Recreation Associa- tion, 1601 N. Kent Street, Arlington, Virginia 22209; American Association of Museums, 2233 Wisconsin Avenue, N.W., Washington D.C. 20027; American Alliance for Health, Physical Education, and Recreation, 1201 16th Street, N.W., Washington D.C. 20036 and the National Therapeutic Recreation Society, 1601 N. Kent Street, Arlington, Virginia, 22209.

    For an Extensive listing of agencies related to leisure and recreation see Clayne Jensen, Leisure and Recreation: Introduction and Overview, Philadelphia, Pennsylvania: Lea and Feibiger, 1977.

11. For further information on social work as a profession the reader is referred to the National Association of Social Workers 7981 Eastern Avenue, Silver Spring, Maryland 20910 or the local chapter of the National Association of Social Workers.

SUGGESTED READINGS

John Armitage. Man at Play: Nine Centuries of Pleasure Making. Mew York, New York: Frederick Warner Company Limited, 1977. For an individual interested in a non-technical history of leisure and recreation this book is an excellent resource.

Neil Cheek and William Burch, Jr. Social Organization of Leisure in Human Society. New York, New York: Harper and Row Publishers, 1976. For the individual interested in a sociological approach to leisure and recreation this book is a good resource.

Virginia Frye and Martha Peters. Therapeutic Recreation: Theory Philosophy and Practice. Harrisburg, PA: Stackpole Co. 1972. This book provides an overview of the developing profession of therapeutic recreation.

Clayne Jensen. Recreation and Leisure Time Careers. Louisville, KY: Data Career, Inc. 1976. For the individual who is seeking a brief overview of careers, this book is an excellent resource.

Anne Minahan (Ed.) Encyclopedia of Social Work, 18th Issue. Washington, D.C.: National Association of Social Workers, 1986. This encyclopedia of social work has a variety of articles describing the role of social work in the leisure and recreation network and biographies of various individuals who were significant in the development of social work and leisure and recreation.

REFERENCES

Anderson, Nells. Work and Leisure. New York, New York. Free Press, 1961.

Armitage, John. Man at Play: Nine Centuries of Pleasure Making, New York, NY: Frederick Warner and Company Limited, 1977.

Carlson, Reynold, Theodore Deppe and Janet MacLean. Recreation in American Life, 2nd Ed., Belmont, California: Wadsworth Publishing Co., 1972.

Charlesworth, James (ed) Leisure in America: Blessing or Curse, Philadelphia, Pennsylvania: American Academy of Political and Social Sciences, 1964.

Cheek, Neil and William Burch, Jr. Social Organization of Leisure in Human Society, New York, NY: Harper and Row Publishers, 1976.

Croner, Helga and Kurt Guggenheim. National Directory of Private Social Agencies 1986. Queens Village, New York: Croner Publishing Co., 1986 (Updated annually).

DeGrazia, Sebastian. Of Time, Work and Leisure. New York, New York: Twentieth Century Fund, 1962.

469

Frye, Virginia and Martha Peters. Therapeutic Recreation: Theory, Philosophy and Practice, Harrisburg, Pennsylvania: Stackpole Co., 1972.

Jensen, Clayne. Recreation and Leisure Time Careers, Louisville, KY: Data Career, Inc., 1976.

Jensen, Clayne. Leisure and Recreation: Introduction and Overview, Philadelphia, Pennsylvania: Lea and Feibiger, Inc., 1977.

Hall, Helen. Unfinished Business in a Neighborhood and Nation, New York, NY: MacMillan and Co., 1971.

Kraus, Richard. Recreation and Leisure in Modern Society, New York, NY: Appleton Century Crofts, Inc., 1971.

Lerman, Paul. "Groupwork With Youth In Conflict," Social Work Vol. 3, No. 4 (October 1958) pp. 71-77.

Miller, Norman and Duane Robinson. The Leisure Age: Its Challenge to Recreation. Belmont, California: Wadsworth Publishing Co., 1963.

Minahan, Anne (Ed.). Encyclopedia of Social Work 18th Issue, Washington, D.C.: National Association of Social Workers, 1986.

Office of the Federal Register, United States Government Manual 1985-86, Washington, D.C.: U.S. Government Printing Office, 1985.

Park, David and Vicki Annand. "Therapeutic Recreation," pp. 415-432 in Vallitutte, Peter and Florence Christoplos An Interdisciplinary Approach to Human Services, Baltimore, MA: University Park Press, 1977.

Sessoms, H. Douglas. "Organized Recreation Resources for Youth: Past, Present and Future," New Designs for Youth Development Vol. 1, No. 3 (March/April 1980) pp. 1-6.

Shivers, J. and Hollis Fair. Therapeutic and Adaptive Recreational Services, Philadelphia, Pennsylvania: Lea and Feibiger Publishers, 1975.

United States Department of Commerce, Bureau of the Census, 1982 Census of Service Industries: Summary, Washington, D.C.: U.S. Government Printing Office, 1984.

United States Department of Commerce, Bureau of the Census,
     1980 Census of Population Vol. 2 Subject Reports Part 7C:
     Occupation by Industry, Washington D.C.:   U.S. Government
     Printing Office, 1984.

United States Department of Commerce, Bureau of the Census,
     Public   Employment   in   1984,   Washington,   D.C.:   U.S.
     Government Printing Office, 1985.

United States Department of Commerce, Bureau of the Census,
     Statistical Abstract of the United States: 1986 (106th
     Edition),   Washington,   D.C.:   U.S.   Government   Printing
     Office, 1985.

United States News and World Report. pp.60-76, Vol 82. No. 20,
     522-577 and Vol. 81 No. 7 pp. 40-42.

Wisconsin Legislative Reference Bureau, Wisconsin Bluebook,
     1985-86, Madison, WI: Department of Administration, 1985.

CHAPTER 15

RELIGIOUS NETWORK*

"Thus, it seems to be a fact that there is a deep rooted tendency in man which urges him to join with others in the worship of the numen (deity or god) and thus, to derive encouragement, strength and comfort from sharing what he has with others. Faith in the value of such communion all through the history of mankind has been so profound that some of the efficacious religious and sociological concepts and institutions have been created by it." (Wach: 1944:332-333).

INTRODUCTION

Religious expression of some kind is a given for all societies including the atheistic governments, such as the Soviet Union and China. The patterns or forms of religious expression are varied and complex depending upon specific cultures, and whether the religious expression is: highly individualized (Taoism); ritualized (Greek Orthodox); poly-theistic (multi-god-Hinduism); Monotheistic (one god-Judaism and Christianity); or nature oriented, (Native American). Regard-less of the system of religious belief, one common theme is to provide services, or provide help for ones fellow humankind.

Within the scope of this chapter, one cannot describe all of the varieties of religious expression, consequently, the focus will be on the two main religious bodies within the United States, which have been extremely influential in the development of Western culture, that is, Judaism and Christianity. These two religious groupings form the nucleus of the values for our society, and each has had a significant impact upon the delivery of social services within American society. Each of these groups has established a sub-specialty for their clergy as a pastoral counselor, and this role is then contrasted with the role of social work in the religious network.[1]

SIZE

In 1986, there were an estimated 219 religious groups in the United States with an estimated 344,410 churches. Expenditures for this network were estimated at $12,474,478,007 and this network employed an estimated 655,962 individuals in 1980. Reported church membership in 1986 was 142,172,138 individuals

Figure 15-1

Estimated Size of the Religious Network on Selected Attributes in 1986*

Selected Attribute	Number
Number of religious bodies	219
Number of churches	344,410
Expenditures[1] (Dollars)	$12,474,478,007
Number of Employees[2]	655,962
Membership (number)	142,172,138

*Source: From Yearbook of American and Canadian Churches, 1986, edited by Constant H. Jacquet, Jr. Copyright 1986 by the National Council of the Churches of Christ in the USA. Used by permission of the publisher, Abingdon Press, pp. 246, 254-255.

[1]Expenditures refers to the amount of expenses for operational and benevolent items of church spending. This amount is equal to the amount of contributions to the various church organizations, Constant H. Jacquet, Jr. op.cit. p. 254. In addition to the figures for church spending, an additional 23 billion dollars were contributed to religious organizations in 1984. Constant H. Jacquet, Jr. op.cit. p. 257.

[2]Adapted from United States Department of Commerce, Bureau of the Census, 1980 Census of Population Vol. 2 Subject Reports Part 7C: Occupation by Industry, Washington, DC: U.S. Government Printing Office 1984, pp. 635-636. Of the 655,962 employees in religious organizations in 1980, 263,172 or 40.1 percent were clergy, 23,842 or 6.5 percent were religious workers and the remaining 349,948 individuals or 53.4 percent were a variety of other occupations and professions.

which represents 60.0 percent of the estimated 237 million individuals in the United States. Figure 15-1 summarizes the estimated size of the religious network.

The diversity of religious groups in the United States is shown in Figure 15-2. The major religious groups in the United States in 1986 are Protestant with 78,701,677 members or 55.36 percent of reported church membership, followed by Roman Catholic with a membership of 52,286,043 or 36.78 percent, Jewish with a membership of 5,817,000 or 4.09 percent, Eastern churches and other Catholic with a membership of 5,077,250 or 3.57 percent, and other membership of 290,168 or .20 percent. In other words, the United States is a predominantly Christian country, 95.71 percent, with a number of other religious groups.[2]

HISTORICAL DEVELOPMENT

The two major religious groupings, e.g., Judaism and Christianity, are discussed, since together they represent the mainstream of thought in Western and American culture.[3] However, in order to maintain a perspective on the development and variety of the major religions of the world, a chronology of religious development is shown in Figure 15-3. This chronology begins about 4,000 B.C., or before, with Native American religions, Shintoism and Hinduism. Historically one can not separate the development of organized religion, from the development of an associated system, for the provision of social welfare needs. The Judaic and Christian religions have always had a provision for helping the needy and unfortunate. Initially, these systems were highly localized and implemented through a specific congregation, parish, or small local group. Later there was the development of a formalized social welfare system, under the auspices of religious groups. Since social welfare services were essentially private, e.g. religious in motivation until 1935, and primarily implemented by women, this historical sketch of the religious network will include the role of women.

JUDAISM

Judaism, as a religion was the first to stress the concept of one god, e.g. Yahweh, and the concept of monotheism. The origins of Judaism are obscure in early prehistoric times but tradition has Judaism developing in the middle east with the semitic tribes of Chaldea. As an identifiable religious group, tradition has Judaism emerging from the tribe of Abraham and his family about 2,000 B.C. Initial religious worship was in the temple. About 600 B.C., the Synagogue, such as the one in Xenephyris, Egypt (143 B.C.), began to replace the temple, as the central focus of religious life. About the same time period, the Bible (Torah and Talmud) became the authority on civil and religious matters.

Most individuals have heard about the movements of the Jewish population, such as Joseph in Egypt, the movement to Cannan now Palestine, (the exodus of Moses), the reigns of King Solomon and David, the Babylonian exile; and eventually the subjugation of Palestine by Greece and Rome. As a separate state, the Jewish state ceased to exist in 73 A.D. when the Jewish zealots were defeated and committed suicide at Massada. The Jewish population was then scattered throughout Palestine and other parts of the world, mainly in Western and Eastern

475

Figure 15-2

MAJOR RELIGIOUS GROUPS IN THE RELIGIOUS NETWORK

IN THE UNITED STATES 1986*

Type of Religious Groups	Number of Religious Groups	Number of Churches	Number of Members	Percent of Total Membership
Buddhist	1	100	100,000	.07
Eastern Churches	18	1,661	4,052,668	2.85
Jewish Congregation	1	3,416	5,817,000	4.09
Old Catholic, Polish National, Catholic American	7	427	1,024,582	.72
Protestant	186	313,411	78,701,677	55.36
Roman Catholic	1	24,275	52,286,043	36.78
Miscellaneous[1]	5	1,120	190,168	.13
Total	219	344,410	144,172,138[2]	100.00

*Source: From Yearbook of American and Canadian Churches, 1986, edited by Constant H. Jacquet, Jr. Copyright 1986 by the National Council of the Churches of Christ in the USA. Used by the permission of the publisher, Abingdon Press, p. 246.

[1]This category consists of a variety of religious groups which are officially non-Christian, such as Spiritualists, Ethical Culture Movement, Unitarian Universalists, and eastern philosophies. Figures are unreliable; however, there are an estimated 10,000 Hindus, 5,000 followers of Confucious, 10,000 followers of Taoism and 60,000 Moslems in the United States.

[2]Church membership in the United States represents 60.0 percent of the estimated 237 million individuals in 1986.

Figure 15-3

HISTORICAL TIME LINE OF THE MAJOR RELIGIOUS GROUPS

IN THE RELIGIOUS NETWORK*

4000 + BC	Native American Religions
4000 + BC	Shintoism Hinduism
2000 + BC	Judaism (Abraham) (monotheistic religion)
600 BC	Zoroastrianism (Zoroaster) Buddhism (Siddharata Guatama) Jainism (Natapulta Vardhamma) Confucianism (Ch'iu K'ung, Confucious) Taoism (Lao Tze)
33 AD	Christianity (Jesus of Nazareth) monotheistic religion Jerusalem 33 AD
44 AD	Roman Bishopric established (Peter)
622 AD	Islam or Moslem (Mohammed Ibn Abdullah)
1054 AD	Split between Roman Catholic Church and Greek Orthodox Church
1517 AD	Protestant Reformation (numerous denominations)
1900	Bahai Faith (Baha' a Ila'h) (oneness of mankind, unity of religions)

*Dates for religious groups prior to Christianity are approximations. Monotheistic religion means one God or Deity. The number of religious bodies including cults would run over 1,000, consequently only selected ones are included on this chart.

Europe, and later the United States. The periodic pogroms or periods of harassement and persecution of the Jewish population, are well documented in history in Medieval Europe, as well as, in the modern world. The most recent systematic pogrom against the Jewish population occurred in Nazi Germany during World War II, and in the Soviet Union since 1945. It was after World War II, that Israel became an independent state, and a significant number of the Jewish population of the world, moved to Israel.

Judaism, like other religions, has had its own internal conflicts, therefore, there are different factions within Judaism, such as the Orthodox, reformed, and the liberal. Regardless of the location of the Jewish population, there has always been a strong motivation based upon the Torah, to care for the needy, and to provide welfare services for individuals. As a consequence, the Jewish population has a strong commitment to philanthropy and to serving the social, emotional, and financial needs of their population.

CHRISTIANITY

Jesus of Nazareth had a short ministerial career, of about three years (30 33 A.D.), prior to his crucifixion. Initially, his disciples and followers, were a small cult within Judaism with the early church centered in Jerusalem in 34 A.D. Satellite churches slowly spread because of missionary work, and were established in Antioch (35 A.D.), Ephesus about 42 A.D., Rome about 40 A.D., Corinth about 45 A.D., and Athens (47 A.D.). These early churches were established by Peter, Paul and the other apostles. A significant council was held in 50 A.D. in Jerusalem, in which a decision was made, to allow non-Jewish individuals to become members of the religion. It was this decision which resulted, in a rapid expansion of the movement of Christianity, and resulted in the separation of a small cult within a Jewish sect, to a Gentile and universal religion. It is with the establishment of the church at Antioch (35 A.D.), that followers of the movement were called Christians.

The early church had no hierarchy, with the disciples becoming the first priests, and an individual being designated as a priest, when a disciple was not available. Each church or parish was essentially a religious community, and was autonomous from other religious communities. Local councils were held on a periodic basis, to have the clergy discuss various issues in order to develop a commonality between the various churches, like the Council of Jerusalem (50 A.D.). In this early period there were intermittent and local persecutions, such as Emperor Nero in Rome (64 A.D.). Within 70 years of the crucifixion of Christ, significant changes began to occur in the Christian movement. Part of these changes related to the fact the movement was spreading to Greece and Rome, which had a different philosophy and culture, than Palestine. The Christian movement was competing with Greek and Roman polytheistic, nature, and eastern mystic religions, like Zoroastrianism. Consequently, Christianity began to development sacramental rights, such as baptism, e.g. purification, a Christian meal, e.g. the mass, in order to attract individuals who were acquainted with these rituals in the other religions.

There was a slow but steady increase of the Christian movement in both the number of churches, and the number of individuals involved. As a consequence, it became impractical to have a "layman" clergy, as the individual, who ran local churches. Slowly, a distinction was made between the clergy and the general population, and concurrently the philosophy of one faith, one ritual, and one church organization was established. As the number of churches increased, there was a corresponding increase in the number of clergy. Initially, churches were established in urban centers. As satellite churches in outlying communities developed, the local clergy looked to the urban centers as their "mother church," and gave preeminence to the head of the urban clergy, as an overseer of the satellite churches. Slowly, this practice reinforced the preeminence of the head of urban churches which become institutionalized in the rank of a bishop. Subsequently, church councils became councils of bishops. As the church slowly expanded, the bishops of Rome and Constantinople became more preeminent, than rural priests and local bishops.

During the 4th century A.D., changes occurred both within the formalization of church structure, as well, as in the recognition of Christianity. After a series of persecutions by the Roman authorities, Christianity was accepted as the official state religion by Theodosius (395 A.D.). The Roman bishopric became the primary head of the western church (the Council of Sardica, 343 A.D.), which became institutionalized with the development of the Petrine theory in the Council of Chalcedon (451 A.D. - the papacy and Rome as the center of the church). Along with the preeminence of Rome, there was the development of monasteries (monastic revolt, 340 A.D.) and the establishment of a variety of religious orders. That is, by the end of the fourth century, a church hierarchy was developed in the west, with the preeminence of Rome, and a hierarchial order or various groupings of nuns, monks, priests, bishops, cardinals, and the head bishop, e.g., the Pope. Christianity was becoming a universal religion with extensive property which was partially used to establish welfare services for needy individuals, such as homes for the aged, unwanted children, almsgiving, parish relief, and monastery relief for the poor and sick.

479

Although in the west, Rome was considered the supreme bishopric, this view was not shared within the entire realm of Christianity. For a period of time, the bishop in Constantinople (the east) was viewed as a co-equal to the bishop in the west (Rome). There was an uneasy tension existing between the west and east branches of Christianity. In 1054 the east branch officially separated from the western branch, and became known as the Eastern Orthodox Church. Shortly after this split between the east and the west churches, western Christianity was shaken by the period of the Crusades to free the Holy Land from the Turks (1096 A.D. to 1267 A.D.). This period of unrest was followed by periodic inquisitions to stamp out heresy, beginning with Gregory the Ninth in 1233. There were a number of local crusades to stamp out heresy in the western church, focussing on specific groups, such as the Albigensian crusade (1208-1229) and the Hutterite crusade (1420-1434). Shortly thereafter, the western church was again split with the development of the Protestant Reformation under Martin Luther (1517), and the Counter-reformation ending with the Council of Trent in 1545. Subsequently, there was the establishment of a series of Protestant denominations, with the major ones consisting of: Lutheran (1521), Unitarian (1530), Church of England (Anglican) (1534), Bapist (1607), Congregrational (1620), Quakers (Society of Friends 1647), Presbyterian (1690), Methodist (1729), Episcopal (1789), Disciples of Christ (1800) and Latter Day Saints (Morman 1830). There are numerous other Christian denominations, some of which have changed little since the Counter-Reformation, such as the Amish (1690), and the Mennonites (1525), and others, which have changed considerably since their foundation, such as the Unitarians (1530).

Religious reforms and revivals, are an on going process, with organized religion today undergoing significant changes. Organized religion in the 1960's advocated for social and political ends, as well as a concern about developing a personal approach to spirituality through a process of pastoral counseling. In the 1980's organized religion is espousing both liberal causes (end institutional racism), as well as, conservative causes (censorship and the moral majority). The notion of the clergy becoming involved in social, political, and personal issues of the congregation or parish, is not new, since both Judaism and Christianity have a tradition of the clergy acting as a shepard for their flock (the parish or congregation). The clergy were traditionally used for providing spiritual and emotional advice, solace, and emotional support. What has developed in the twentieth century is a specialty within the clergy with training in pastoral counseling which combines the traditional role of the clergy, with knowledge from the social sciences, such as psychology, psychiatry, anthropology, etc.[4]

RELIGIOUS NETWORK and SOCIAL WELFARE

Both Judaism and Christianity as religious organizations, and as a social philosophy, have stressed charity and one's obligations to others. Religious sources, such as the Bible, Torah and Talmud contain numerous references to the obligation of caring for the poor and unfortunate. For example, Deuteronomy 15:11, "For the poor shall never cease out of the land: therefore I command thee saying, 'Thou shalt open thine hand wide unto thy brother, to thy poor and to thy needy, in thy land,'" or Matthew 19:21, "Jesus said unto him, 'If thou wilt be perfect, go and sell what thou hast, and give to the poor, and thou shalt have treasure in heaven.'"

JUDAIC TRADITION - Moses Maimonides (1135-1204) a philosopher of the Jewish Talmudic tradition, described eight degrees of charity for the needy ranging from providing employment, taking a person in as a partner, to reluctant giving. With this mandate to aid the poor and unfortunate, Judaism developed social welfare programs to care for or accept responsibility for the poor and unfortunate. In the early Jewish community, individuals were: obligated to tithe (10 percent of one's income) which was to be used for individuals who were needy; expected to use part of their harvest for use of the poor; and to contribute to both regular (Kuppah), and emergency (Tamchue) collections. In addition, individuals sought out the rabbi for religious and emotional guidance, e.g., loving kindness.

Initially, these services were provided by the local synagogue through a volunteer provider (Parnes) but with the movement of the Jewish population to various locations in Europe and the United States, and the development of numerous synagogues, there ultimately emerged the concept of the Jewish community, and Jewish community service programs (about 1800). For example, in the United States, although the synagogue initially was the center for Jewish social services, with the rapid immigration of Jewish populations after 1840, the local synagogues were unable to respond to the needs of this population. Consequently, the community center and social welfare agencies were established for the Jewish population which were independent of a specific synagogue. The community center was expected to provide recreational, social, educational, emotional, and financial support. This pattern of a community center and related social welfare agencies independent of the local synagogue, is a different approach, than that taken by the various denominations of Christianity. Jewish social services are extensive consisting of hospitals, nursing homes, social recreational facilities, marital counseling programs, family counseling programs, alcohol and drug programs, child welfare, etc.

CHRISTIAN TRADITION - The christian community formally responsed to needy individuals through an <u>institutional response</u> (Roman Catholic), or an <u>individual response</u> (Protestant).[5] In the Christian tradition an individual was expected to contribute to charity as an obligation. The formal Catholic response to the needy, was the establishment of hospitals, orphanages, parish relief, educational institutions, etc. In general, this response is an <u>institutional response</u> built into the Catholic hierarchy. Some Protestant denominations, such as Lutheran and Episcopal have also used this approach. Initially, each parish was responsible for its needy, sick, orphans, widows, etc. Later, because of financial resources, the diocese became the focal point for the establishment and maintenance of social welfare programs. For example, in the United States, each diocese was expected to develop a social welfare organization to oversee the provision of social services to its population. In the United States, the movement from parish responsibility to diocesan responsibility occurred after the mass immigration of Irish and Germans to the United States in the 1840's. Prior to that time, the number of Catholics in the United States was relatively small and the parish was generally able to respond to the needs of its population.

Protestant denominations also recognized an obligation of carrying for the unfortunate. The formal Protestant response generally was more of an <u>individualistic response</u>, e.g., an individual would become highly concerned about a specific problem and would develop a program in response to the problem, and then seek funding. In many cases, the agency was minimally attached to a specific denomination, although the agency, may have started from a particular denominational perspective. For example, the Salvation Army, (1880) was established by an individual who was a Methodist, however, it is nondenominational in its services. Similarly, the Young Men's Christian Association (1851), the Young Women's Christian Association, (1858), the Charity Organization Society, (1877), and the Children's Aid Society (1853), were motivated by Protestant organizations, but are nondenominational. Some of the protestant denominations have their own social welfare programs, for their populations, such as Lutheran Social Services, Baptist Social Services, Seventh Day Adventist, etc.

In the development of social welfare services, especially in the United States, one has to be aware that most social services were sponsored by the religious network prior to the twentieth century. From the establishment of the United States as a colony of England, and later as a separate republic, the private religious agency was more significant in the provision of social welfare services, than the public agency. Arnaud Marts (1966:129-131) estimated there were 480,000 private agencies in the Unites States of a nonsectarian nature. It is only since 1935, that the public agency has maintained a dominance in the provision of social services.[6] The 1980's, with its ideological conflicts, and governmental budget cutting, will see a shift of social services for individuals and groups, from government funded services to services sponsored by the religious network. The implication of this trend, is that the religious network will need to collect more money for social service programs, which may be difficult for individuals who currently use their money for nonreligious purposes and have not perceived charity as a priority.

RELIGIOUS NETWORK and the ROLE of WOMEN

In reviewing the history of religious social welfare agencies in the United States, as well as, other areas of the world, it should be noted that women have played a predominant role in the development, and implementation of social services. There are numerous examples of women who played a significant role in the development of social services. Only a few examples will be used to show the reliance of early social welfare programs in the religious network on women. In the United States, a significant individual in the establishment of social services, was Elizabeth Seton, also known as Mother Seton, who established the Sisters of Charity (1809). The Sisters of Charity were a Catholic order devoted to the establishment of poor relief programs, as well as, child welfare services. The Ursuline Sisters established one of the first homes for orphans in the United States (1729). Individuals of prominence in early social welfare programs include: Dorothea Dix (1841), who was an advocate for individuals who were mentally ill; Martha Falconer (1890), who was an advocate for individuals who became involved with violations of the law; Clara Barton who established the American Red Cross (1877), which provided social services for the military; Jane Adams who established Hull House (1889) which was a settlement house; and both Edith and Grace Abbott who established settlement houses. The Charity Organization Society, which was a predecessor for family social welfare services, had Mary Richmond (1891) as their front line reformer.

In addition to the religious network, women were highly significant in the establishment of other fields of practice in social work, such as Louisa Schuyler (1861) who helped establish the first state Charities Board; Ida and Mary Cannon (1906 and 1909) who were early medical social workers; Mary Follett (1900) was an early school social worker; Josephine Goldmare and

483

Pauline Goldmare (1902-1905) were early advocates for consumer concerns, child welfare and labor legislation. This brief excursion into the role of women only scratches the surface of the significance of women in the religious network and in early social welfare programs. As one investigates the historical development of many social welfare agencies, whether these agencies were established under Judaism, Roman Catholicism or Protestantism, women have played a key role in the development and establishment of social service programs, and are still a potent force.[7]

STRUCTURE

Like other social networks, the structure of the religious network can be described from its organizational context, services provided, occupations and professions, and dominant occupations and professions.

ORGANIZATIONAL CONTEXT

The clergy, including the pastoral counselor depending upon the religious denomination are a part of a hierarcy with limited local autonomy, or part of a loose federation with a higher degree of local autonomy. Figure 15-4 shows three abbreviated models of church organization: Papal hierarchy (Roman Catholic Model 1); Council/Synod hierarchy (Model 2) and general convention hierarchy (Model 3). All three models indicate the respective positions of the clergy, pastoral counselor and other social service agencies.

Since the United States has a separation of church and state, there is no official state religion "public religion." If one views some of the smaller cults or study movements as folk movements, there would be an informal religious network, such as the Church of Scientology, the United Spiritualist Church, and the Hope Light Movement. In any event, regardless of the model used the clergy becomes a focal point at the local parish or congregation level in responding to the problems of individuals.

SERVICES PROVIDED

The religious network provides a full range of social services from multi-purpose agencies, such as family services to specific agencies for adoptions, aging, etc. The range of services provided by the religious network include but are not limited to the following:

FIGURE 15-4

ORGANIZATIONAL MODEL for the RELIGIOUS
NETWORK in the UNITED STATES*

Model 1

Adapted Version of Roman
Catholic Organization

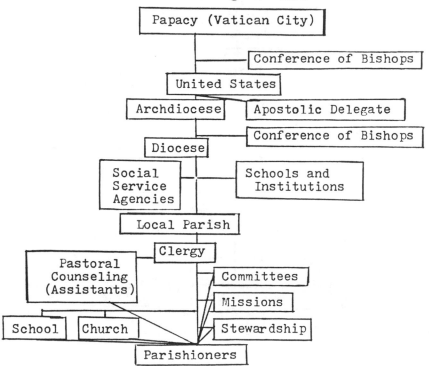

* Sources: This chart was developed after reviewing a
variety of materials including Constant H. Jacquet Jr.
(Ed) <u>Yearbook of American and Canadian Churches 1986</u>
Nashville, Tennessee: Abingdon Press, 1986,pp. 90-96.

FIGURE 15-4 CONTINUED

Model 2*

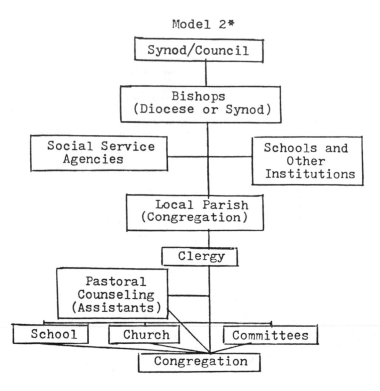

* Sources: This chart was developed after reviewing a
  variety of materials including Constant H. Jacquet Jr.
  (Ed) Yearbook of American and Canadian Churches 1986
  Nashville, Tennessee: Abingdon Press, 1986, pp. 71-73.

FIGURE 15-4 CONTINUED

Model 3

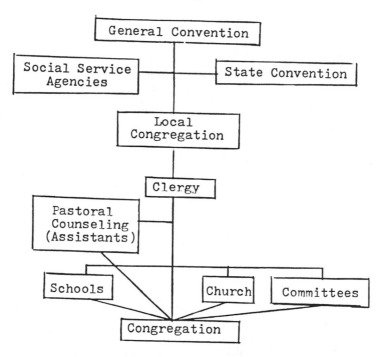

* Sources: This chart was developed after reviewing a
  variety of materials including Constant H. Jacquet Jr.
  (Ed) Yearbook of American and Canadian Churches 1986
  Nashville, Tennessee: Abingdon Press, 1986, pp. 54-56.

487

- Aging

- Child care

- Day care

- Pastoral counseling (individual group and marital counseling)

- Delinquency programs

- Medical programs

- Psychiatric programs

- Community relation programs

- Political advocacy

- Youth and recreational programs

- Alcohol and drug programs

- Educational programs

- Home and hospital visitation

- Social and recreational programs

- Study programs

- Foster care

- Adoptions

- Financial assistance

- Meals

- Housing

- Employment services.

OCCUPATIONS and PROFESSIONS

The religious network, as already indicated, in addition to the local clergy, operates a wide variety of social welfare agencies. Consequently, one should not be surprised to find a wide range of human service professions employed within religious organizations. Figure 15-5 shows a selected number of human service occupations and professions employed in the religious network.

Amongst the selected occupations and professions represented in Figure 15-5, the largest groups are clergy, 70.9 percent, religious workers 11.5 percent, musicians 7.4 percent, chid care work 3.8 percent, teacher 1.7 percent, social work .9 percent and lawyer .9 percent. The occupations represented in Figure 15-5 show the dominance of clergy and religious workers when one looks at human service occupations and professions participating in the religious network.

DOMINANT OCCUPATIONS and PROFESSIONS

The dominance of the clergy and religious workers in the religious network is shown in Figure 15-5. Figure 15-6 shows where clergy and religious workers are employed by industrial classification.

CLERGY - The vast majority of clergy are employed in the industrial classification of religious organizations in 1980, 93.6 percent, 5.0 percent are employed in the industrial classi- fication of professional and related, and the reamining 1.4 percent are employed in service positions in other industrial classifications.

Contrary to public opinion, many clergy are not trained as counselors for emotional and marital problems. It is recognized that the clergy have a multiple role including administrator, organizer, pastor, preacher, priest, teacher, and counselor. In a study on role expectations of clergy completed by Kenneth Bentz (1968), ministers expected they were to become involved in the counseling of individuals and families and in emotional problems. Yet, the primary roles performed by the clergy were those of administrator and organizer, and teacher/priest. It was concluded there was some degree of role disharmony between what the clergy desired to do, and what they were expected to do. Many clergy are involved in their profession because they have an interest in people, and would like to help individuals successfully cope with the various crises of living.

In reviewing the history of the education of the clergy one has to recognize, that historically individuals became part of the clergy through either an apprentice system of learning their position, or through a system of heredity. It was not until the early and middle Medieval period (400-1200) when the major clergy began to receive specialized training. In fact, in Medieval Europe, the rule of thumb was, members of the hierarchy, e.g. bishops and above, received some degree of university education, whereas the normal parish priest was

Figure 15-5

NUMBER AND PERCENT OF SELECTED HUMAN SERVICE OCCUPATIONS
AND PROFESSIONS EMPLOYED IN THE RELIGIOUS ORGANIZATION
INDUSTRIAL CLASSIFICATION OF PROFESSIONAL AND RELATED SERVICES
(RELIGIOUS NETWORK) IN 1980*

Occupation and Profession	Number	Percent
Clergy	263,172	70.924
Religious Worker	42,842	11.545
Social Worker	3,690	.994
Welfare Aide	191	.051
Recreation Work	624	.168
Child Care Work	14,223	3.843
Lawyer	3,471	.935
Physician	35	.009
Other Health Diagnosing	27	.007
Registered Nurse	621	.167
Dietician	225	.062
Therapist (Health)	168	.045
Other Health	252	.067
Licensed Practical Nurse	175	.047
Nurses Aide	1,396	.376
Teacher Post Secondary	494	.133
Teacher-Except Post Secondary	5,841	1.574
Teacher Aide	398	.107
Counselor Educational/Vocational	1,130	.304
Librarian	1,317	.354
Library Clerk	197	.053
Economist	384	.103
Psychologist	516	.139
Urban Planner	50	.013
Architect	198	.053
Author	50	.013

Figure 5 (continued)

Occupation and Profession	Number	Percent
Musician	27,530	7.419
Actor	455	.122
Painter/Sculpter	407	.109
Guards	973	.262
Firefighters	8	.002
Total	371,060	100.000

*Source: Adapted from United States Department of Commerce, Bureau of the Census. 1980 Census of Population Vol. 2 Subject Reports Part 7C: Occupation by Industry, Washington, DC: U.S. Government Printing Office, 1984, pp. 295-664.

[1]The occupational classification of religious worker includes nuns, monks, brothers, Sunday school teachers, etc.

usually a graduate of the local cathechism school.   In about the 1700's there was the establishment of specialized schools for the training of most clergy.   The general rule of thumb today, is that a rabbi would have between three to six years of seminary education in addition to a college degree, a Catholic priest would have about four years of theology in addition to a bachelor's degree and in the Protestant denominations it varies, as some denominations require two to three years of theological study beyond the bachelor's degree, and others do not.   When one talks about the clergy today they are generally a well educated population, however most of these individuals have not been specifically trained in pastoral counseling.[8]

Regardless of the religious denomination, the general functions of the clergy would include the following:

- Administration of a church, synagogue, or parish

- Organizer of social and religious events for their membership

- Counselor for personal problems and spiritual growth

- Teacher of moral values and appropriate and expected behavior

491

Figure 15-6

NUMBER AND PERCENT OF CLERGY AND RELIGIOUS WORKERS EMPLOYED BY
INDUSTRIAL CLASSIFICATION IN 1980*

Industrial Classification	Clergy		Religious Worker[1]	
	Number	Percent	Number	Percent
Agriculture/Fishery/Forestry	94	.033	13	.026
Mining	7	.003	--	--
Construction	55	.019	10	.021
Manufacturing	539	.192	150	.307
Transportation, Communication, Public Utility	115	.041	44	.091
Wholesale/Retail Trade	128	.045	181	.371
Finances, Insurance, Real Estate	205	.073	12	.024
Business and Repair	52	.018	38	.077
Personal Services	325	.115	93	.191
Entertainment/Recreation	540	.193	113	.232
Professional and Related	14,242	5.069	5,051	10.348
Religious Organization	263,172	93.683	42,842	87.769
Public Administration	1,448	.516	265	.543
Total	280,922	100.000	48,812	100.000

*Source: Adapted from United States Department of Commerce, Bureau of the Census, 1980 Census of Population. Vol 2 Subject Reports Part 7C: Occupation by Industry, Washington, DC: U.S. Government Printing Office, 1984, pp. 295-664.

[1]The occupation classification of religious workers includes nuns, monks, brothers, church school teachers, etc.

- Social advocate for consistency of societal attitudes and behaviors to religious and moral teaching

- Visitation to individuals in hospitals and homes because of illness or some other personal emergency or crisis

- Perform church services and rituals.

RELIGIOUS WORKERS - The distribution of employment of religious workers in Fugure 15-6 shows that 87.7 percent are employed in the industrial classification of religious organizations, 10.3 percent in the industrial classification of professional and related and the remaining 2.0 percent in service positions in other industrial classifications.[9] This category of religious personnel includes nuns, monks, brothers, lay ministers, trained volunteers, Sunday school teachers, etc. The education and training for this group would vary depending upon a specific denomination. For example, nuns, monks and brothers may have an education ranging from a bachelor's degree to a Ph.D. and volunteers may have no training or a series of seminars and institutes.

Religious workers perform a variety of functions which will vary depending upon the specifics of one's assignment. Some of the functions of the religious worker would include the following:

- Visitation to individuals in hospitals and homes because of illness or some other personal emergency or crisis

- Teaching in a parochial school system or post secondary system

- Teaching in Sunday School and adult education

- Missionary work and evangelism

- Administer a social service program

- Individual and group counseling.

PASTORAL COUNSELING - A subspecialty within theological education for pastoral counseling began in the early 1920's, with William Keller and Anton Boisen. These two individuals recognized a need for clergy to utilize the knowledge of social science in order to counsel their members about family, marital and personal problems. From these early beginnings, and the work of Keller and Boisen in 1923, the Clinical Pastoral Education movement spread, with the development of specialized schools or programs for clinical pastoral counseling training. The first specialized school in pastoral counseling was established in 1930. A national organization for clinical pastoral counseling was established in 1953 and standards for a clinical pastoral counselor were established in 1968. The clinical pastoral counseling education movement has primarily been non-denominational, although many of the clergy in the Roman Catholic church, and in Judaism receive specialized training in pastoral counseling from their own training units or by seeking

other degrees like social work. Currently, there is an association for clinical pastoral education which licenses individuals
for pastoral counseling.[10]

The role of the pastoral counselor can be described as
follows:

- The provision of case work and counseling services to
  parishoners

- Home, hospital, and other insitutional visitation to
  discuss individual problems

- Coordinating activities of other religious groups for fund
  raising.

The pastoral counselor today with specialized training,
departs from the more traditional perspective of the clergy.
Traditional clergy would listen to the problems of their
parishoners, and would utilize their theological background to
place the behavior of individuals into a religious perspective.
A pastoral counselor on the other hand may become involved in
some aspects of psychotherapy using social science techniques.
The pastoral counselor, would use the techniques of psychology
and psychiatry, but relate these to the theological under-
pinnings of human behavior.

SOCIAL WORK

The number of social workers involved in the religious
network will vary, depending upon the source used. Figure 15-5
shows 3,690 social workers employed in the industrial classification of religious organizations (an increase of 190 percent
from 1970). According to the Encyclopedia of Social Work, 1986,
15 percent of all social workers were involved in sectarian
settings, which would equal approximately 66,000 social
workers. In the 1980 census material, many of these social
workers would be classified in the industrial classification of
social services and not religious organization. Regardless of
the source used, it is obvious a significant number of social
workers are involved in the religious network.[11]

The role of the social worker will vary depending upon the
particular organization for whom they are employed and the tasks
to be performed. That is, if a person is involved with a
sectarian organization as a caseworker, group worker or a
community organizer, their functions would be similar to the
usual case work, group work, and community organization tasks of
any social worker. (See chapter 3, Social Work as a Profession)
There will be some variation in tasks and functions whether the

494

individual is employed by a traditional social welfare agency or a particular parish or congregation as a parish assistant.

TRADITIONAL SOCIAL WELFARE AGENCY

The social worker employed in a traditional social welfare agency sponsored by a religious denomination would utilize their skills in casework, groupwork, community organization and administration.

CASEWORK - At the individual level, the social worker would become involved in general counseling, family and marriage therapy and counseling, and counseling for specific problems like alcohol abuse, placing children in foster or adoptive homes, etc.

GROUPWORK - Many, if not most, agencies use groupwork services in working with specific populations, such as the aging, juvenile and youth groups, marriage and family sensitivity groups, expectant parents groups, etc.

COMMUNITY ORGANIZATION - Depending upon the agency, the social worker may become involved in fund raising, public relations, advocating for social policy changes within the agency or in government policy, etc.

ADMINISTRATION - Some social workers become involved in administration of an agency or program which involves program planning, budget, personnel hiring, firing, training and staff development. Depending upon the size of the agency, the administrator may supervise other staff or there may be staff with supervisory functions.

PARISH ASSISTANT

Instead of working in a traditional social welfare agency sponsored by a religious denomination, the social worker may be employed by a specific church, parish, or synagogue as a parish assistant. Alice Taggart (1962) describes the role of a social worker as a parish assistant. The employment situation Taggart described was an individual who was employed as a parish assistant with a Unitarian Church, and provided case work counseling, consultation, and community services. Taggert felt, that the role of the social worker varied from typical social work because of a total use of oneself. Since the worker knew people beyond the case work relationship, it was more difficult to maintain a confidential relationship. There was a more emotional aspect to the case work relationship, since the worker relates to the client on more than just a professional basis (they see each other socially at church functions), and that the counseling which is provided is tempered with the spirtual beliefs of the particular denomination. In general, when one discusses the role of the social worker in a parish setting, it is recognized they will provide many of the tasks which a typical social worker provides. The difference in perspective for the social worker as a parish assistant is a result of the expected adherence to the spiritual beliefs of the particular denomination by which one is employed.

PERSONAL SOCIAL SERVICES

The religious network has a variety of social welfare agencies and programs, which focus on the personal social services. (See Chapter 22, Personal Social Service.) In some areas of the personal social services, the religious network is predominant, like child welfare, and in other areas of the personal social services, public agencies are predominant, such as family planning. Some examples of the involvement of the religious network in the personal social services, include the following:

PROTECTIVE SERVICES

Child welfare agencies (Catholic, Luthern, Jewish, etc.), homes for the aged (Catholic, Luthern, Jewish, Episcopalian, Methodist, etc), child abuse and family violence agencies.

UTILITARIAN SERVICES

Luthern, Catholic, Jewish social services, Methodist Health and Welfare Ministry, Presbyterian Welfare etc.

DEVELOPMENTAL and SOCIALIZATION SERVICES

Family and marital counseling servies to unwed mothers; youth centers, Neighborhood Houses, Luthern, Episcopalian, Catholic, Jewish agencies, etc.

REHABILITATIVE and THERAPEUTIC SERVICES

St. Vincent DePaul Society, Salvation Army and other sectarion agencies.

SPECIAL POPULATIONS

The religious network, traditionally, has been concerned with the unfortunate and downtrodden in society including special populations, subsequently specialized programs have been developed for specific populations. (See Chapter 25, Special Populations, and Chapter 24, Rehabilitation.) Some examples of

the involvement of the religious network with special populations include the following:

ASIAN

Social service centers sponsored by specific religious
groups, such as Presbyterian, Methodist, Catholic, Lutheran, etc.

BLACK

Special programs through mission boards, and other sectarian
agencies etc.

EUROPEAN ETHNIC

Family service oriented agencies, such as Luthern social
services, Catholic Social Services, Jewish social services etc.

NATIVE AMERICAN

Special programs through mission boards of specific denominations, and other sectarion agencies.

SAME SEX PREFERENCE

Special programs for learning about and understanding
homosexuality.

SPANISH SPEAKING

Spanish centers, refugee centers, special programs through
mission boards and other sectarion agencies.

WOMEN

Homes for unwed mothers, awareness groups, and sensitivity
groups sponsored by specific denominations.

ISSUES

The percentage of individuals belonging to a church, and
those attending church in the United States has declined since
1950. Organized religion has undergone many changes since the
1960's, with further changes anticipated. Some of the major
issues related to human services and the religious network are
funding, duplication of services, changing focus of service,
shortage of personnel, curriculum content in social work and use
of volunteers.

FUNDING

Prior to 1960, most funds for religious supported social service programs were from private donations, either individual, organizational, or denominational. With the development of a system of subcontracting and grant related projects, through federal and state programs, many private agencies began to rely on public monies for their programs. There are two consequences of this reliance on public money: <u>instability</u> - as federal money becomes more difficult to obtain, a corresponding increase in private donations is needed; <u>guidelines and regulations</u> - a more fundamental and critical problem is the following of government guidelines which may be incompatible with the mission or purpose of the private agency. For example, the use of federal money cannot be discriminatory, based on religion, yet some agencies may wish to serve only their own population. An agency may be opposed to abortion and recognition of gay rights, yet acceptance of federal money may dictate a change in that policy. Subsequently, some private agencies are in a position where they must decide against the use of federal money in order to maintain their relgious integrity. With the federal and state governments cutting back on expenditures for human services in the 1980's, the problems of money, its collection and dissemination for human services programs, will continue to be a major problem.

DUPLICATION of SERVICES

With the rapid increase in public programs, there has developed a dual system for the provision of services (public and private agencies), such as child welfare (adoption, foster care). The concept of a dual system of services is compatible with United Sates values and social philosophy, however, severe questions develop around service coordination, integration, and program effectiveness. Those agencies which have a solid base of support (financial and clientele) will continue, others may not.

CHANGING FOCUS of SERVICE

As society's attitudes towards selected social problems change, and the population gets older, there are shifts in the major thrust of social services. Up until 1965, child welfare services (adoption, foster care, unwed mothers) were a major program for private agencies. With changing societal attitudes towards unwed mothers, more individuals are keeping their children, consequently the need for adoptive homes is declining, in spite of the demand for more prospective adoptive parents. Similarly, as the population gets older, more services are oriented toward the aging population.

SHORTAGE of PERSONNEL

The number of individuals participating on an ongoing basis with religious organizations has declined since 1950. There is a serious shortage of males who are entering the clergy, which could create change in some religious organizations to utilize women in religious ceremonies and rituals to a greater degree.

CURRICULUM CONTENT

Few schools of social work have courses on voluntary agencies although most schools incorporate some of this content in their courses. Since the private agency is a major provider of social services in the United States, information on this network should be included.

It is not expected that academic programs would have specialties in pastoral counseling, however, it is appropriate to include some material on the existence of the pastoral counseling speciality, and how it relates to social work.

USE of VOLUNTEERS

Traditionally, many private agencies have used a high percentage of volunteers to implement programs. No change is anticiated in this pattern of using volunteers, however, there will be an increased emphasis on in-service training for volunteers, and the provision of some incentives to engage in volunteer work, such as meals and transportation expenses.

SUMMARY

The religious network in the United States is rather extensive consisting of approximately 219 groups with about 263,000 clergy and about 344,410 churches in 1986. The estimated number of individuals who belong to religious organizations is approximately 60.0 percent of the population, or 142.2 million individuals. The amount of money contributed to the religious network per year is approximately 12.5 billion dollars, which does not include an additional 19.4 billion dollars of donations to religious organizations.

A brief history of both Judaism and Christianity as part of the religious network was presented, since these two religious groups represent the major thrust of social philosophy in Western culture. Along with a brief description of the historical development of Judaism from approximately 2,000 B.C., and Christianity from 33 A.D., a brief description of the role of the religious network in the provision of social welfare services until 1935 was provided. Until the great depression

(1929-1941), the religious network was the primary network for the delivery of social services.

Three patterns in the development of social services through the religious network were described: a community center response independent from the synagogue in Judaism, an institutional or hierarchial response through the Roman Catholic church and an individualistic response through some of the protestant denominations in addition to their own agencies.

A critical component in the development of social services through the religious network in Western Europe and in the United States has been the role of women. The Roman Catholic Church has had a variety of orders of nuns, such as the Sisters of Charity, Ursuline Sisters, which provided social services to various individuals and groups. Protestant denominations had key individuals who were leaders in their field, such as Dorthea Dix in mental illness, Martha Falconer in corrections, Josephine Goldmare in child welfare, Ida and Mary Cannon in medical social work, and so on. Judaism, in its doctrines relating to care of the needy, articulated a clear role for women, in the implementation of social services, as part of the practice of charity. The charitable role was seen as a positive virture and appropriate role for women.

The development of pastoral counseling as a subspeciality in the education of clergy was described, even though the role and background of a pastoral counselor will vary depending upon a specific denomination. Some denominations, such as Roman Catholicism have a hierarchal arrangement in which the parish priest and the pastoral counselor relate to a higher level of hierarchy, whereas in certain Protestant denominations the local clergy and the pastoral counselor are fairly autonomous. There was a brief discussion of the role of social work in comparison to that of a pastoral counselor. Some of the issues relating to human services and the religious network were described, such as funding, changing focus of service, shortage of personnel, curriculum content in social work and the use of volunteers.

FOOTNOTES

*This chapter was reviewed for comments by Paul Tutwiler, Assistant Dean, School of Library and Information Science, University of Wisconsin-Milwaukee, Milwaukee, Wisconsin, and a graduate of Gregorian University, Vatican City, Vatican.

1. Mankind has a variety of approaches and means to worship a numen (deity) ranging from animism and totemism, to poly-

theism, and monotheism. It is impractical to discuss all of the approaches and varieties of religious experience. Consequently the focus of this chapter is on Judaism and Christianity which are the dominant religions within the United States in terms of American social and philosophical foundations. In addition to the major religious groupings in the United States, there are an estimated 1,000 cults which does not include Native American religions.

2. Sources used for estimating the size of the religious network include the following: Constant J. Jacquet, Jr. Yearbook of American and Canadian Churches 1986, Nashville, Tennessee; Abingdon Press, 1986, pp. 246, 252-255 and United States Department of Commerce, Bureau of the Census. 1980 Census of Population. Vol 2. Subject Reports Part 7C: Occupation by Industry, Washington, DC: U.S. Government Printing Office, 1984, pp. 635-636.

3. A religious grouping not discussed is that of Native American. Since Native American religions represent a small percentage of membership in the United States, it was felt their religion did not represent the mainstream of American social philosophy as it affects United States institutions. One should recognize, that certain aspects of Native American philosophy could take on added significance, as the United States moves into the last decades of the 20th century. Native American religions stress the relationship or harmony between the individual and nature. That is, Native American religions stress a philosophy which is ecologically sound in terms of the balance between ones resources and their use, reverence for nature, and recongition of the limitations of natural resources. It is a pro-ecological perspective, in contrast to some other religious themes which in effect are anti-ecological. The protestant ethic partially based on Calvinism, equates godliness with success, and success is symbolized by prosperity, e.g. material wealth. To make money, one produces tangible goods which are resource consuming. The Native American religions also place a premium on the concept of toleration and acceptance, which has not been true of some of the other religious groupings.

4. There are numerous histories of religions of the world including those of the United States. For the development of religion in general, and Judaism and Christianity specifically, the reader is referred to Morton Enslin, Christian Beginnings, New York, NY: Harper and Row Publishers, 1958; Joseph Gaer, How the Great Religions Began, New York, NY: New American Library of World Literature, 1956 and Pocket Library, History of Israel Until

501

1880, Jerusalem, Israel, Keter Publishing House Limited, 1973.

5. The three different patterns of community, institutional, and individualistic responses to social welfare concerns, are generalizations. All three patterns of response are found in the various religious denominations, however, there tends to be a predominant response in each major religious group.

6. For a brief history of religion and social services the reader is referred to Marguerite Boylan, Catholic Church and Social Welfare, New York, NY: Greenwich Book Publishing Co., 1961; Arnaud Marts, The Generosity of Americans: Its Sources and Achievements, Englewood Cliffs, NJ: Prentice-Hall, Inc., 1966 and Robert Morris and Michael Freund, Trends and Issues in Jewish Social Welfare in the United States: 1899-1952, Philadelphia, PA: Jewish Publication Society, 1966. The history of income maintenance programs and the personal social services are generally related to the development of the religious network until the twentieth century. For a more detailed history, see Chapter 19, Income Maintenance Network, and Chapter 22 the Personal Social Service Network.

7. For a brief review of the role of women in social work see Anne Minahan, (ed.), Encyclopedia of Social Work, 18th Issue, Washington, D.C.: National Association of Social Workers, 1986.

8. For information on education for the clergy, the reader is referred to the major religious groupings for information, such as the Association of Theological schools, P.O. Box 30, Vandalia, Ohio, 45377; National Conference of Catholic Bishops, 1312 Massachusetts Ave. NW, Washington D.C., 20005; Synagogue Council of America, 432 Park Avenue, South, New York, NY, 10022; Episcopal Church Center, 815 Second Ave., New York, NY, 10017; Luthern Church of America, 2900 Queen Lane, Philadephia, PA, 19129; Missouri Synod Luthern Church, 500 N. Broadway Blvd., St. Louis, MO, 53102; United Methodist Church, P.O. Box 871, Nashville, TN, 37202 and the American Baptist Churches of America, Valley Forge, PA, 19481. Information on other religious groupings, can be found in Constant Jacquet Jr. Yearbook of American and Canadian Churches 1986. Nashville, TN: Abingdon Press, 1986.

9. The definition of religious organizations is that taken from the United States Department of Commerce, Bureau of the Census, 1980 Census of Population; Classified Index of Industries and Occupations: Final Report, Washington, DC:

U.S. Government Printing Office, 1982. It is recognized there is an overlap between the definition of religious organizations and other parts of the social service classification.

10. For information on training programs for clinical pastoral counseling, the reader is referred to the Association for Clinical Pastoral Education Inc., Interchurch Center, 475 Riverside Drive, New York, NY, 10027, or write to a specific religious group as indicated in footnote number 8.

11. Some examples of social service agencies within the religious network include the following: National Association of Christian Social Workers, P.O. Box 84, Wheaton, IL, 60187; National Conference of Catholic Charities, 1347 Connecticut Ave., NW, Washington, D.C., 20006; Council of Jewish Federations and Welfare Funds, 575 Lexington Ave., New york, NY, 10222; Luthern Church of America, Luthern Social Services, 2900 Queen Lane, Philadelphia, PA, 19129; United Methodist Church, Health and Welfare Ministry, 1200 Davis Street, Evanston, Il, 62001; Episcopal Church Center, 815 Second Ave., New York, NY, 10017 and United Presbyterian Health, Education and Welfare Association, 475 Riverside Dr., New York, NY, 10011.

There are literally, hundreds of other social service agencies within the religious network and the reader is referred to Nancy Yakes and Denise Akey Encyclopedia of Associations, Vol. 1, Detroit, MI: Gale Research Company, 1980. A review of the telephone book, or of a social welare resource guide, in ones own community, will provide an overview of the religous network and social services in a local community. For further information on the profession of social work, the reader should contact the National Association of Social Workers, 7981 Eastern Avenue, Silver Spring, Maryland 20910 or the local office of the National Association of Social Workers.

SUGGESTED READINGS

Joseph Gaer. How the Great Religions Began. New York, NY: American Library of World Literature, 1956. Although this book is somewhat dated, it does provide a brief overview of the development of the major religious groups.

Arthur Hands. <u>Charities and Social Aid In Greece and Rome</u>. Ithaca, NY: Cornell University Press, 1968. A sound historical treatment of the early programs for helping the poor and unfortunate is found in this book.

Elliott Krause. <u>Sociology of Occupations</u>. Boston, MA: Little Brown and Co., 1974. For the reader interested in a sociological analysis of the clergy as a profession, this is an excellent resource.

Alice Taggert. "The Caseworker as Parish Assistant," <u>Social Casework</u>, Vol. 43, No. 2 (February 1962) pp. 75-78. This brief article describes the functions of a social worker as a parish assistant and some of the difficulties.

Edward Thornton. <u>Professional Education for Ministers: A History of Clinical Pastoral Education</u>. Nashville, TN: Abingdon Press, 1970. This book describes the historical development of clinical pastoral education and analyzes the functions of a clinical pastoral counselor.

Joachim Wach. <u>Sociology of Religion</u>. Chicago, IL: University of Chicago Press, 1944. This book is dated, but is a classic in the application of sociological theory in analyzing religion as a social institution.

REFERENCES

Albanese, Catherine. <u>American Religions and Religion</u>. Florence, Kentucky: Wadsworth Publishing Co., 1977.

Association for Clinical Pastoral Education. <u>Standards and Procedures for Accreditation of CP Centers</u>. New York, NY: Association for Clinical Pastoral Education, 1977.

Baldwin, Marshall. <u>The Medieval Church</u>. Ithaca, NY: Cornell University Press, 1953.

Bedell, George and Leo Sandon, Jr., Charles T. Welborn. <u>Religion in America</u>. New York, New York: Macmillan Co., 1975.

Bentz, Kenneth. "Consensus Between Role Expectations and Role Behavior Among Ministers." <u>Community Mental Health Journal</u> Vol. 4, No. 4 (August 1968), pp. 301-306.

Biobakee. Saburi: <u>Sources of Yoruba History</u>, Oxford, England: Clarendon Press, 1973.

Boylan, Marguerite. The Catholic Church and Social Welfare. New York, NY: Greenwich Book Publishing Co., 1961.

Brodsky, Carrol. "Clergymen as Psychotherapists: Problems in Interrole Communication." Community Mental Health Journal, Vol. 4 No. 5 (December, 1968) pp. 482-491.

Croner, Helga and Kurt Guggenheim. National Directory of Private Social Agencies 1986. Queens Village, New York: Croner Publishing Co., 1986 (updated annually).

Durkheim, Emile. Elementary Forms of Religious Life. New York, NY: Collier Books, 1961.

Enslin, Morton. Christian Beginnings. New York, NY: Harper and Row Publishing Co., 1958.

Frisch, Ephraim. An Historical Survey of Jewish Philanthropy, New York, New York: Macmillan Company, 1924.

Gaer, Joseph. How the Great Religions Began. New York, NY: New American Library of World Literature, 1956.

Hands, Arthur. Charities and Social Aid in Greece and Rome. Ithaca, New York: Cornell University Press, 1968.

Hiltner, Seward. The Christian Shepard: Some Aspects of Pastoral Care. Nashville, TN: Abingdon Press, 1959.

The Holy Bible. New York, New York: World Publishing Co.

Israel, Richard "The Elusive Appeal to Authority in Rabbinic Counseling" Journal of Jewish Communal Service, Vol. 45, No. 4, pp. 303-312.

Jacquet, Constant, Jr. Yearbook of American and Canadian Churches, 1986. Nashville, TN: Abingdon Press, 1986.

Krause, Elliott. Sociology of Occupations. Boston, MA: Little Brown & Co., 1974.

Luce, Henry (ed.). The World's Great Religions. New York, NY: Time, Inc., 1957.

Marts, Arnaud. Generosity of Americans: Its Sources and Achievements. Englewood Cliffs, NJ: Prentice-Hall, Inc., 1956.

Minahan, Anne (ed.). Encyclopedia of Social Work, 18th Issue. Washington, D.C.: National Association of Social Workers, 1986.

Morris, Robert and Michael Freund. Trends and Issues in Jewish Social Welfare in the United States: 1899-1952. Philadelphia, PA: Jewish Publication Society, 1966.

O'Grady, John. Catholic Charities in the United States. Washington, D.C.: National Conference of Catholic Charities, 1930.

Pocket Library. History of Israel to 1880. Jerusalem, Israel: Keter Publishing House, Ltd., 1973.

Ritzenthaler, Robert and Pat Ritzenthaler. Woodland Indians of the Western Great Lakes. Garden City, NY: Natural History Press, 1970.

Spann, John. Pastoral Care. New York, NY: Abingdon-Cokesbury Press, 1951.

Taggart, Alice. "The Case Worker as Parish Assistant." Social Casework, Vol. 43, No. 2 (February, 1962) pp. 75-78.

Tawney, R.H.. Religion and the Rise of Capitalism. New York, NY: Harcourt Brace and Company Inc., 1926.

Thornton, Edward. Professional Education for Ministers: A History of Clinical Pastoral Education. Nashville, TN: Abingdon Press, 1970.

United States Department of Commerce, Bureau of the Census, 1980 Census of Population: Vol. 2 Subject Reports Part 7C: Occupation by Industry, Washington, D.C.: U.S. Government Printing Office, 1984.

United States Department of Commerce, Bureau of the Census, Statistical Abstract of the United States 1986 (106th Ed.), Washington, D.C.: U.S. Government Printing Office, 1985.

Vonhoff, Heinz. People Who Care: An Illustrated History of Human Compassion. Philadephia, PA: Fortress Press, 1971.

Wach, Joachim. Sociology of Religion. Chicago, IL: University of Chicago Press, 1944.

Westhues, Kenneth. "The Roman Catholic Church and the Field of Social Welfare." Social Work, Vol. 16, No. 1 (July, 1971) pp. 60-65.

SECTION 4

SPECIFIC HUMAN SERVICE NETWORKS (SOCIAL WELFARE)

Social Welfare in the context of this book refcrs to those societal networks (institutions) which have as their primary function the amelioration or resolution of specific problems which directly affect individuals and groups and their lack of functioning or to help individuals and groups cope better with problems.

Chapter 16 describes the corrections network and the occupations of corrections officer, child care worker, the profession of criminal justice and the role of social work. Chapter 17 describes the employment and manpower network and the profession of vocational counselor, the occupation of employment interviewer and the role of social work. Chapter 18 describes the housing network and the professions of architect, urban planner, housing manager and the role of social work. Chapter 19 describes the income maintenance network and the professions of social security administrator, social security claims examiner, unemployment claims examiner, veterans claims examiner, the occupations of financial aides and social welfare worker, and the role of social work. Chapter 20 describes the mental health network and the professions of psychiatry, psychology, psychiatric nursing, human service generalist and social work. Chapter 21 describes the mutual support network and the emerging professionalism of volunteerism and the role of social work. Chapter 22 describes the personal social service network from the perspective of target or problem groups and the role of social work. Chapter 23 describes the physical health network and the professions of medicine, nursing, public health, allied health and the role of social work. Chapter 24 describes the rehabilitation network and the profession of rehabilitation counseling and the role of social work.

Chapter 16

CORRECTIONS NETWORK*

"Corrections remains a world almost unknown
to most law abiding citizens, and there is a
tendency to think that imprisonment is the total
correctional process. However, this is a very
simplistic view of an extremely complex system
composed of a diverse amalgam of facilities,
theories, techniques and people." (Cull and
Hardy:1973:82)

INTRODUCTION

Corrections, like the other networks in the criminal justice
process, i.e., judicial, protective service and legal (see
Chapter 11, 12, 13) is undergoing change in its underlying
philosophy, strategies for social service and organizational
structure. The corrections network is a combination of institutional facilities (jails, prisons, detention centers, halfway
houses), field programs (probation, parole, community treatment), and other resources, such as private agencies, group
homes, etc. In order to understand the complexity of this
network one must relate it to other parts of the criminal
justice process as well as to the varied administrative units,
federal, state and local. This chapter provides an overview of
the corrections network and describes the occupations of a
corrections officer, child care work and the role of social work.

SIZE

The corrections network is large and diverse consisting of a
variety of public and private agencies. In 1984 the public
corrections network consisted of at least 6,431 agencies. This
estimate includes approximately 870 state and federal prisons,
3,338 jails, 1,023 juvenile institutions and 1,200 probation and
parole units. Estimated expenditures for public corrections
agencies was estimated at $8.9 billion, with 342,470 employees.
The majority of expenditures was for institutions, 72.3 percent
with a similar trend for employees with 66.8 percent employed in
institutions. In other words, 27.7 percent of expenditures and
33.2 percent of employees were in community programs like probation and parole, in institutional social services and related
programs. Of the 2,503,753 individuals under the jurisdiction
of the corrections network in 1984, 73.1 percent were on probation or parole and 26.9 percent were in institutions. That is,

the ratio between institutionalized individuals and those on probation or parole is close to 1:4.

In addition to the figures listed above private agencies are involved in the corrections network and there is an organization called the Correctional Service Federation of the United States. This organization consists of 25 private agencies which provide social services to individuals in the corrections network utilizing 1,400 related agencies and 5,000 institutions.[1] Figure 16-1 shows the estimated size of the public corrections network.

HISTORICAL DEVELOPMENT

The corrections network is actually a mixture of networks, each having developed autonomously at different periods of time. These major networks are: jails, House of Correction, prisons, reformatories, juvenile institutions, probation and parole services, and private agencies. This brief historical overview does not take into account jurisdictional levels, such as federal, state and local.

JAILS and HOUSE of CORRECTION

JAILS--The jail or goal was used as a detention facility since before 800 A.D., with some jurisdictions using the jail as a means of punishment instead of temporary detention.[2] The predominant function of the jail was as a temporary place of detention until an individual was found innocent or guilty of the charges against them. If the person was found guilty, the process of punishment consisted of one or more of the following: corporal punishment (whipping, stocks, etc.), capital punishment (execution), fines, transportation (to another country like the penal colony in Australia or as an indentured servant to the United States), and or forced labor, such as galley slaves . It was not until the 19th century that prisons were established as a means of punishment. Current jails house both individuals waiting for trial and those sentenced to short terms of normally less than one year.

Over time, the structure and daily operations of the jail were influenced by humanitarian reform movements and changed from a congregate system (one room for everybody) to a cell block system (one person per cell) and in addition provided food, clothing, medical care, etc. In early jails, the prisoners were kept in one large room (congregate system). The inmate supplemented their meager food diet by paying for extra food, having relatives bring in food, begging through the windows or having food smuggled in. Current jails provide minimum comforts of clothing, food, etc. Most jails still do not have adequate

Figure 16-1
Estimated Size of the Public Corrections Network in 1982-1985*

Selected Criteria	Major Components of the Public Corrections Network		
	Institutions (including juvenile custody and jails)	Probation/Parole/ Other	Total
Number of Agencies	5,231	1,200 [1]	6,431
Expenditures (Dollars)	7,156,000,000	1,800,000,000	8,956,000,000
Number of Employees	250,570	91,900	342,470
Population Served (Number)	713,853	1,789,900	2,503,753

* Source: Adapted from United States Department of Justice, Bureau of Justice Statistics, Sourcebook of Criminal Justice Statistics-1984. Washington, D.C.: U.S. Government Printing Office, 1985 pp. 6, 9, 15, 23, 24, 27, 28, 115, 614; United States Department of Commerce, Bureau of the Census. Statistical Abstract of the United States: 1986 (106th Ed.), Washington, D.C.: U.S. Government Printing Office, 1985, pp. 175, 176, 182, 183, 184, 185, 307, 325; United States, Department of Commerce, Bureau of the Census, Public Employment in 1984, Washington, D.C.: U.S. Government Printing Office, 1985, p. 3 and Diana Travisono (Ed.) American Correctional Association Directory - 1986. College Park, Maryland: American Correctional Association, 1986, pp. x-xxxvi.

[1] Estimated number of jurisdictions and probation/parole agencies which includes regional districts.

social, recreational, counseling, educational, or work programs to keep the inmates occupied.

The period of the early 1900's was a period of social reform in the United States. The Progressive Party and its platform for social legislation on women's rights, child welfare laws, employment protection plans, workmen's compensation, etc. also had an impact on programs for jail populations. Recognizing the social cost of a jail term for short term offenders (less than one year) Wisconsin in 1913 instituted the Huber Law which allowed an individual to be released from jail during the day time to continue one's employment. The purpose of this work release program was to reduce the impact of incarceration on one's family, to prevent families from going on welfare programs, to allow a person to continue employment and reduce the financial cost of jail time. The concept of a Huber Law is now used in all states and in other parts of the world and has been expanded to include educational release programs for high school and post secondary education.[3]

Another program which had an influence on the jail population is that of bail. The concept of bail (release from confinement prior to one's court date) is not a new reform, but a constitutional right which has operationally been guaranteed to meet the needs of the poor population. In recent times, the use of bail was motivated as much to ensure legal rights for the accused, as well as, an attempt to keep the jail population down. Bail means the payment of a specific financial amount (as set by the court) in lieu of confinement prior to one's court date. The function of bail is to prevent unnecessary confinement and to insure ones appearance in court. Bond is the payment of a percentage of the bail, usually to a bondsman, who then insures the court, the person will be present at the court hearing.

Bail was already in use during the time of Henry VI in 1444, when the English Parliament authorized an act allowing for individuals to be released from confinement prior to the court date upon providing a surety guarantee, (usually financial) that they would appear in court. This right to release based upon a surety bond was reconfirmed under the Declaration of Rights during the reign of William III and Mary (1689-1702). The Charter of William Penn in Pennsylvania (1682) contained a provision for bail. The United States Constitution of 1792, Article VIII, Bill of Rights refers to bail as a fundamental right and the amount of bail should not be excessive. (See Chapter 11, Judicial network, for a discussion of some of the criticisms and abuses of current bail and bond procedures.)

HOUSE of CORRECTION--as a separate local corrections facility, the House of Correction developed in the late 1500's and initially had a close relationship to the workhouse, poorhouse or almshouse. The Dutch in 1596 in Amsterdam established a workhouse in which the able bodied poor could be housed and put to work engaging in productive labor. The workhouse was a combination facility to house the able bodied poor, those in need of correction, the elderly and the sick. The concept of the workhouse quickly spread to other countries like England, France and later the United States. Ultimately, the function of the workhouse was to house the able bodied poor and the elderly. The English poor law of 1597 authorized the establishment of poorhouses and workhouses. Preceding the workhouse in Amsterdam by about 40 years was the development of the Bridewell in London in 1555. The Bridewell was an unused royal palace which was set aside to house idle people and people of bad character and put them to work. The Bridewell program to house people of bad character was the direct antecedent of a series of institutions called the house of correction.[4]

Eventually, most houses of corrections were replaced by the state corrections facilities. Some of the larger metropolitan areas or large counties, still retain a house of correction, such as Milwaukee, Wisconsin. The function of the house of correction has not changed, since their purpose is the incarceration of short term offenders, of less than one year. These institutions make extensive use of work release and study release programs. Houses of correction like their local counterpart, the jails, usually have a minimum of social, recreational, counseling, educational, or work programs to keep the inmates occupied.

PRISONS, REFORMATORIES and JUVENILE INSTITUTIONS

Correctional institutions, such as the penitentiary (prison), reformatories, and juvenile institutions are all products of the 19th century. The development of these institutions is closely related to humanitarian and religious movements of that time period and a changing shift from local community control to state control of programs for criminal and juvenile offenders.

PRISONS (PENITENTIARY)--Prior to 1800, an accused person was held in jail until convicted. Upon conviction the punishment consisted of one of the following: fine, corporal punishment (whipping, dunking, branding, pillary, stocks etc.), capital punishment (execution by a variety of means), or deportation and exile. With the humanitarian and religious reform movement of the late 1700's and early 1800's, a more "humane" system of punishment was developed known as the penitentiary (prison). The general concept behind the development of the prison was that instead of corporal punishment, the offender should be placed in a penitentiary as punishment and to spend time reflecting upon their evil ways and change their behavior. In effect the penitentiary (prison) was viewed as more humane since its function was to punish as well as to have a person repent and change their behavior (rehabilitation).

513

The first prison (as a place of punishment) was the Walnut Street Jail in Philadelphia in 1790. As part of its reforms, a section of the jail was set aside to house the convicted offender in an isolated cell to think, meditate and repent their errant ways. Two forms of a penitentiary developed: the Pennsylvania System and the Auburn System.

The Pennsylvania system modeled itself after the Walnut Street jail using the concepts of social isolation, individual cells, and no interaction at any time with other prisoners as the means to reform people. Each prisoner lived in their own cell and were not allowed out of the cell for eating, work or recreation. A prison was built in 1826 in western Pennsylvania based upon the above concepts. Ironically the Pennsylvania system of a prison was not extensively used in the United States, but did have a heavy influence on European prisons.

The Auburn system is named after the model of a prison built in Auburn, New York in 1819. This system used individual cells but allowed inmates to leave the cell for eating, working and recreation. This system was less expensive to build in comparison to the Pennsylvania system and was more economical, since it was easier to place prisoners in work situations. The idea of social isolation was maintained through rules of silence, such as no talking around others, not sitting face to face with others, wearing hoods over ones head, etc.

The prison or penitentiary system of a modified Auburn type quickly supplanted corporal punishment and capital punishment as the major means of punishment. The period of time from 1825-1950 has been called the "age of institutions" in the United States with the majority of prisons having been built between 1850-1925.

Many changes have been made to the Auburn system since 1819. The strict rules of silence, wearing hoods and not sitting face to face have been abolished. In most institutions today there is more than one person per cell, dormitory living with the following services available: psychological, psychiatric, and religious counseling, educational and training programs, work and recreational programs, medical programs, social service programs, and legal assistance.

In addition to the programatic changes indicated above, further significant changes in the prison system relate to classification procedures and programs for early release. Institutions are classified and designed (structurally and psychologically) as maximum, medium and minimum security. Maximum security is typical of an institution with individual cells and a high 20-30 foot wall surrounding the institution, with corrections officers manning the watchtowers. Medium security is typical of an institution with a cottage style living (each person has a room) with a wire fence surrounding the institution with guard towers which may or may not be manned with corrections officers. Minimum security is typical of an institution with dormitory living and there may or may not be a wire fence surrounding the institution.

The concept behind different types of institutions and programs within institutions is classification. Classification as a process reviews each offender as they enter an institution and assess the offender on the following: degree of danger to themselves and others; are their encounters with the law caused by psychological forces, sociological forces, a lack of education and training; is the individual assaultive and aggressive; is the individual an escape risk; or a combination of any of the above. A decision is then made by a parole board or other staff board whether a person should be placed in a maximum, medium or minimum type of institution. Institutions are further specialized for adult male and female, juvenile male and female, drug and alcohol problems, sexual problems etc.

Programs for early release include parole (see next section) and good time behavior. In most institutions an inmate is given time for good behavior which can be accumulated over a period of time. These accumulated days of good time are then reduced from ones release date from the institution.

REFORMATORY and JUVENILE INSTITUTIONS--These institutions are part of what is called the age of institutions from 1825-1950 in which the societal response to crime and mental illness was to institutionalize individuals. The reformatory movement was established in the United States in Elmira, New York in 1876. The reformatory as an institution was initially designed for the youthful offender ages 16-30. The emphasis was on reform and included educational and vocational training programs, library and recreational facilities, etc. Two innovations of correctional philosophy which had a significant impact on the reformatory movement were the indeterminate sentence and the mark system. (For a discussion of the mark system, see the section on parole.) An indeterminate sentence means a variable sentence indicating a minimum and a maximum period of time to serve in the institution. The concept behind a variable sentence is, if an inmate knows their own behavior has an impact upon one's release date, the inmate would have an incentive to modify their behavior. The system of an indeterminate sentence and some variation of a mark or point system has now been established in most juvenile and adult institutions. In the 1980's the philosophy of the indeterminate sentence has been challenged and some jurisdictions, such as Maine, Connecticut,

515

Indiana and California have adopted a modified "just deserts" model which is a variation of the determinate or fixed sentence. The original goals of the reformatory movement were fulfilled and by 1920, many reformatories became maximum security institutions for youthful offenders.

Specialized <u>institutions for juvenile delinquents</u> were developed in the United States after 1800. Prior to 1800 delinquent children were generally treated as adults or were placed in an almhouse as a dependent, neglected or delinquent child. The early institutions for delinquent children were modeled after the House of Refuge in New York City (1825), which was a private facility which housed dependent, neglected and delinquent youth. Many private institutions were built between 1825-1900 for wayward youth.

Public institutions were established in the late 1800's. Massachusetts developed a state school in 1854 and Ohio (1858) used the concept of cottage living. Ohio in 1866 established a county children's home. The most rapid increase in state schools occurred from 1870 on, such as Michigan (1874) and Wisconsin (1875). These earlier state schools were called by various names, such as vocational school, training school, and boys or girls school. These early institutions although designed for the handling of delinquents, also housed a proportion of youth who were dependent and neglected. These juvenile institutions by 1950 no longer cared for dependent and neglected youth. Many of the private institutions today have become treatment centers where they handle pre or early delinquent children with emotional problems.

PROBATION and PAROLE

The predominant form of community programs for individuals involved in the corrections network are probation (supervision of a person instead of incarceration), and parole (supervision of an individual after release from incarceration). Each of these programs has a distinct historical development.

PROBATION--These services were developed as a volunteer effort by John Augustus in Boston, Massachusetts and Matthew Hill in Birmingham, England in 1841. In both cases, the intent was to prevent the first offender from being sent to prison, and the individual's sentence was suspended by the court with custody remanded, i.e., granted, to the volunteer for a specified period of time who would then supervise the individual in the community. Although 1841 is the customary date for the beginning of probation, there were earlier precedents for the release of individuals to the community, such as their own recognizance (own right or having a responsible moral and personal character);

judicial reprieve (a judge holding a case open for a period of time instead of imposing a sentence), the right of sanctuary (a person could take sanctuary in a holy place, such as a church, and avoid prosecution), benefit of clergy (if a person could read certain psalms from the bible and agree to live by its principles the judge would release the person), and bail (posting of a financial amount as stipulated by the court for an individuals release).

From the voluntary beginnings of probation, there was a rapid movement toward a formalized probation system with Boston, Massachusetts establishing a volunteer agent in 1869, paid employees by 1878 and a statewide system for Massachusetts in 1891. Between 1890-1940 most states developed a system of probation, such as Wisconsin (1911) with the last state developing a system in 1956. Like other parts of the corrections network, probation departments exist on all jurisdictional levels; federal, state, county and municipal. In 1984, for adult cases, 41 states administered probation and parole as companion services, meaning the same office and personnel handle both probation and parole cases and in nine states these services are handled independently, either by different state agencies or a combination of state and local agencies. In juvenile cases, in 21 states the court or county has jurisdiction for probation instead of the state.

PAROLE--These services were initially part of the prison system and developed as a means to provide incentives for good behavior by making it possible to obtain an early release from prison. In the United States, parole as a formalized system developed in the Elmira Reformatory in New York in 1876 with the inception of a mark system. An individual was given a "mark" for good behavior for a specified period of time. After an accumulation of a predetermined number of marks, an individual was released early from prison. The mark system of Elmira New York, was modeled after the "ticket of leave" system developed by Alexander Maconochie in Australia (1840), and the "Irish" system developed by Walter Crofton in (1855). Crofton added the ingredient of supervision of the released individual by police officers in their local community. Some of the earlier precedents for early release were commutation laws (a shortening of one's sentence by executive order--usually a governor), the indeterminate sentence (a variable sentence indicating a minimum and maximum period of time), and good time behavior laws (a reduction of a sentence for a specified time for acceptable behavior).

Like probation, there was a rapid expansion of parole as a method of early release during the period of 1876-1930, such as Wisconsin (1907). By 1959 only one state did not have a parole system and by 1970 all states had a system of parole. In the 1980's with the adoption of a modified "just deserts" model of punishment, which is a variation of a determinate sentence (fixed sentence) some jurisdictions have reduced the discretionary powers of the parole board and in at least one instance abolished the use of parole. Some examples of states which have adopted a modified form of the "just deserts" model include Maine, Calfornia, Connecticut and Indiana. In 1986, some states which have adopted a modified "just deserts" model (between 1978-1984) are considering shifting back to the indeterminate sentence model. The jurisdiction for parole varies from federal, state and county agencies with most jurisdictions having an overall parole board which has authority over the entire system. In 1984, of the 52 paroling authorities, 46 were independent units and six were part of a broader unit, such as a department of corrections or public safety. In ten paroling authorities, field supervision of the parolee was through the paroling authority and in 42 paroling authorities, field supervision was handled by a broader unit, such as a division of corrections or public safety along with probation cases.

Probation and parole as community programs have been modified to include: psychiatric, psychological and social work counseling programs, specialized programs for problem areas, such as alcohol, drugs, sexual deviation; and have developed a wide range of treatment programs through purchase of service, i.e., title XX, other community resources and private agencies. There is a tendency today to develop more community type programs which links traditional community programs, such as probation and parole with halfway houses, pre-release centers and community treatment centers. In some jurisdictions, like the state of Wisconsin, part of the camp system was transferred to a Bureau of Community Corrections (Probation and Parole) to develop a centralized community treatment program.

PRIVATE AGENCIES

The period from 1850-1925 was one of preeminence of private agencies in private agencies for providing services to individuals involved in the corrections network. Although the public sector currently is predominant in providing services to the individual involved in the corrections process one can not neglect nor ignore the private sector. Early organizations focusing on individuals involved in the corrections process include: the John Howard Association of Massachusetts (1889), the Pennsylvania Prison Society (1865); the Women's Prison Association of New York (1845), and the Salvation Army (1846). A later development in private agency cooperation is the International Prisoners Aid Association (1950), representing 30 countries and 40 agencies. From 1950-1973, the International

Prisoners Aid Association had their office in Milwaukee, Wisconsin and currently (1986) is in Louisville, Kentucky.

The function of most private agencies involved in corrections has changed from direct service to consultation and research. An example of one private agency still involved in direct services is the Wisconsin Correctional Service, located in Milwaukee, Wisconsin, which has a full range of direct services focusing on individuals, such as probationers', parolees', those awaiting court trial, and those serving terms in the House of Correction. The trend since 1960 is for private agencies to secure funding from the federal government for specific projects and to secure money under Title XX or other legislation through the states for specific projects. Although the role of private agencies has been reduced since 1930, they are still a significant force in the corrections network and have developed in some states a variety of diversionary and alternative programs to incarceration.

A recent trend (1980-86) developing in the United States is the utilization of a prison built and maintained by private enterprise. The states of Tennessee and Texas for example have plans for new prisons to be built by private corporations. The Behavioral System Southwest Corporation in Pasadena, California and the Correctional Corporation of America in Houston, Texas are examples of private corporations becoming involved in the corrections system.

Figure 16-2 shows a historical time line in the development of the corrections network. Essentially, the figure shows a specialization of services since 1900, and a shifting from local and private facilities to state facilities.

STRUCTURE

The structure of the corrections network can be viewed from its organizational context, services provided, occupations and professions, and dominant occupations and professions.

ORGANIZATIONAL CONTEXT

The organizational context of corrections is complicated because of different jurisdictions, federal, state, county and local. Figure 16-3 schematically shows the varied parts of the corrections network. Figure 16-4 shows the bifurcation of the federal system (parole, and probation are housed in different departments) and the centralization of the system in the State of Wisconsin. As indicated earlier, in most states, juvenile and adult systems are organizationally implemented through different agencies and in some cases, probation and parole are

519

Figure 16-2
Historical Time Line of the Corrections Network

800 AD (and before)	Gaol (Jail) Fines, Capital and Corporal Punishment Galley Slaves
1200	Release on one's own recognizance Judicial Reprieve Benefit of Clergy Right of Sanctuary Bail
1500	1555 - Bridewell London, England 1596 - Workhouse Amsterdam, Holland House of corrections, England
1700's	1776 Prison Ships (Hulks) 1776 Deportation to Australia 1790 Walnut Street Jail, Philadelphia, Pennsylvania

1800's	1819 Auburn System—Auburn, New York
	1825 Training School for Delinquents, New York
	1826 Pennsylvania System—Western Pennsylvania
	1840 Ticket of Leave System—Machonochie in Australia
	1841 Voluntary Probation John Augustus, Boston,
	        Massachusetts
	1855 Irish System—Crofton in Ireland
	1876 Reformatory System—Elmira, New York
	        Mark System for Release —
	        Indeterminate Sentence
	1878 State Probation Service
	Development of Private Agencies (1850-1900)

1900's	1909 State Parole Services 1913 Huber Law, Wisconsin
1940's	Humanitarian Reforms of Institution Concept of Rehabilitation
1960's	Community Corrections Development of Professional Programs in Sociology, Psychology, Education, Social Work and Criminal Justi
1970's	Debate: rehabilitation versus incarceration Debate: determinate versus indeterminate sentence Debate: role of parole boards Debate: role of social services and rehabilitation Debate: role of capital punishment
1980's	Tendency toward institutionalization of offenders Private Corporations build and maintain prisons

handled by different agencies.[5] Figure 16-5 shows the organization of a private agency.

SERVICES PROVIDED

Although custody (incarceration) is the primary function of corrections, a significant number of services are available to individuals and groups in the corrections network. These services can be classified as: educational, health, vocational, recreational, religious, psychological and social services.

Educational services include:

- Elementary and secondary education
- Limited post secondary education
- Diagnostic testing/evaluation
- Libraries.

Health services include:

- Medical and dental care
- Occupational and physical therapy.

Vocational services include:

- Work study and training in a variety of specialized technical areas;
- Diagnostic testing and evaluation and rehabilitation counseling.

Religious services include:

- Individual and group counseling.

Psychological services include:

- Psychological and psychiatric diagnostic testing, individual and group treatment programs.

Recreational services include:

- Arts, crafts, physical education, music therapy

Social services include:

- Social history assessment
- Provision of concrete services (looking for a house, employment)
- Individual and group counseling
- Special therapy programs

Figure 16-3

Idealized Model of the Organization
of the Corrections Network

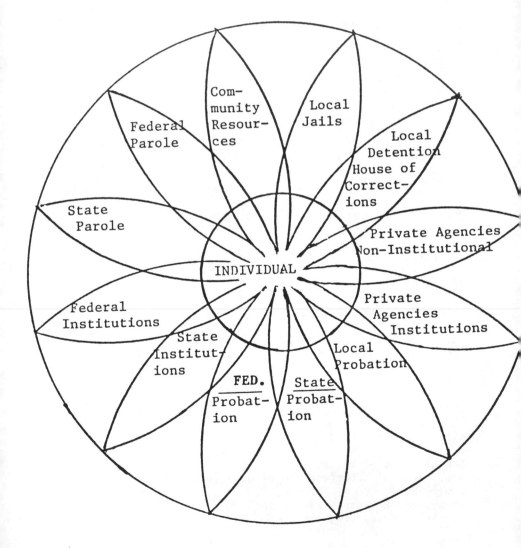

Figure 16-4
Idealized Organization of the Federal and the State of
Wisconsin Corrections Network*

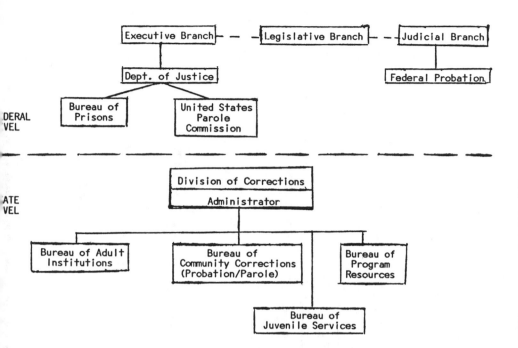

Figure 16-5
Organization of a Private Agency
Focussing on Correctional Clients
(Wisconsin Correctional Service, Milwaukee, Wisconsin) *

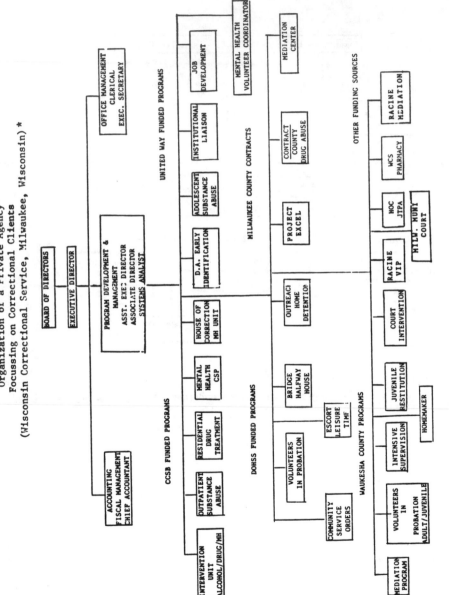

* Source: Organization chart of the Wisconsin Correctional Service, Milwaukee, Wisconsin: Wisconsin Correctional Service, 1986. Reprinted with the permission of the Wisconsin Correctional Service.

524

- Financial assistance through other agencies via purchase of service
- Maintaining contact with families
- Foster care
- Group homes
- Generalized family and marital counseling
- Financial counseling and management.

OCCUPATIONS and PROFESSIONS

The corrections network, is predominantly staffed by custo-dial personnel for security purposes, however employs a wide range of human service occupations and professions. Figure 16-6 shows a selected range of human service occupations and profes-sions employed in the corrections network.

In general, 33.418 percent of the selected human service occupations and professions are employed in treatment or rehabilitative forms of employment and 66.582 percent in custo-dial or security forms of employment. One should note that 13.793 percent of the employees are in social work (probation and parole and institutional services). Other professions which are involved in probation and parole and institutional services include, criminal justice, sociology, psychology amongst others.

In general when one discusses probation and parole services and institutional social services, these tasks are performed by a variety of occupations and professions. Since about 1940 a background in a social science, psychology, sociology, or in an allied area like social welfare, social work, and criminal justice are part of the educational requirements for employment in the social service functions of the corrections network.

Similar to the process of specialization which has been occuring in other human service professions, there are now programs designed more specifically for an individual interested in corrections. These educational programs may be called criminal justice (since 1970), correctional administration (which could be in sociology or political science), human resource management (which could be in business or political science), social work and corrections, criminal justice and social work, etc. Since no one social science profession dominates the corrections network, a variety of disciplines and interdisciplinary programs are used for training personnel who provide social services.

Figure 16-6
Number and Percent of Selected Human Service Occupations
and Professions Employed In the Justice, Public Order and
Safety Industrial Classification (Emphasis Corrections
Network) in 1980*

Selected Occupation and Profession	Number	Percent
Corrections Officer	84,730 [1]	66.582
Social Work	17,553	13.793
Teachers	8,169	6.419
Counselor Education/Vocational Rehabilitation	2,440	1.917
Librarians	729	.572
Psychologist	1,370	1.076
Clergy/Religious Worker	984	.773
Recreation Worker	337	.264
Physician	589	.462
Dentist	252	.198
Nurse	1,901	1.493
Therapist	878	.689
Physicians Asst.	5,110	4.025
Clinical Lab Technician	408	.321
Licensed Practical Nurse	649	.509
Child Care	938	.737
Painter Sculptor	114	.089
Health Records	104	.081
TOTAL	127,255	100.000

*Source: Adapted from United States Department of Commerce, Bureau of the Census, 1980 Census of Population: Vol. 2 Subject Reports Part 7C: Occupation by Industry, Washington, D.C.: U.S. Government Printing Office, 1984, pp. 295-664.

The industrial classification of justice, public order and safety represents the protective services, judical and corrections networks. The subject report is not detailed enough to clearly identify the corrections network. Some occupations are clearly corrections such as corrections officer, or clearly judicial, such as judges, or clearly protective service, such as police and detectives. The above listing of occupations represents an attempt to identify those which were working in the corrections network. This list is obviously representative and not exhaustive.

[1] It should be obvious, but most corrections officers are employed in the justice, public order and safety industrial classification.

526

DOMINANT OCCUPATIONS and PROFESSIONS

The major occupational groupings of the selected human service occupations and professions employed in the corrections network is the custodial staff, corrections officer and child care work which comprise 66.582 percent of the employed personnel (see Figure 16-6). There is a movement today to upgrade both of these occupations through in-service training, staff development and post secondary educational programs.

CORRECTIONS OFFICER--The National Manpower Survey of 1974-1975 indicated an estimated 73 percent of the corrections officers had a high school education or less, and of the 27 percent which had a post secondary education, they generally held an associate of arts or a bachelor's degree. No state had a requirement beyond high school graduation for employment and 20 states had less than high school graduation as a requirement. The recommended requirement by the American Correctional Association is a high school diploma. Figure 16-7 shows the employment of corrections officer by industrial classification. Of the corrections officers 97.8 percent are employed in the industrial classification of justice, public order and safety.

In 1984, there were an estimated 99,078 corrections officers guards of which 91,011 or 91.9 percent were male, and 8,067 or 8.1 percent were female. The ratio of corrections officers to inmate population varies from state to state with Alaska having a ratio of 1:2 and South Carolina and Texas with a ratio of 8:3.

Since the corrections officer has more contact with the inmates of institutions than any other person, there have been requests that corrections officer training be upgraded to include topics, such as counseling techniques, human relations, minority perspectives, alcohol and drugs, correctional law, as well as the usual topics of department policies, control and prevention of escapes, supervision of inmates, security, weapons, etc. As a consequence of attempts to upgrade the position of the corrections officer, some states now have a specialized associate of arts degree program for corrections officers, such as the Morraine Park Technical Institute located in Fond du Lac, Wisconsin. In addition to technical training, 32 states have developed their own specialized in service training program in the form of academies, training units, etc.

Although the corrections officer is beginning to assume some functions of a human relations role, their function is still focused on security. The primary functions of a corrections officer include the following:

Figure 16-7
Number and Percent of Corrections Officers Employed in the
Industrial Classification of Public Administration in 1980*

Industrial Classification	Number	Percent
General Government	1,393	1.608
Justice, Public Order, Safety	84,730	97.826
National Security (Military)	490	.566
Total[1]	86,613	100.000

*Source: Adapted from Department of Commerce, Bureau of the Census, 1980 Census of Population: Subject Reports Vol. 2: Occupation by Industry, Washington, D.C.: U.S. Government Printing Office, 1984, pp. 295-664.

[1] No corrections officers are employed outside the public administration industrial classification.

- Observe and control movement of inmates
- Intervene in conflicts amongst inmates
- Monitor feeding of inmates and prevent disruptions
- Search cells of inmates and critical areas of the institution for contraband material
- Assign tasks to inmates and monitor performance
- Advise inmates on personal, work or adjustment problems (in some jurisdictions the corrections officer becomes an active participant in group counseling programs)
- Respond to any emergency as required.

CHILD CARE WORKER—In juvenile institutions the corrections officer (is called a child care worker in some states) has taken on a more flexible role, than in adult institutions. Consequently, there has been more emphasis on human relations than in adult institutions. Generally, educational levels of juvenile child care workers are higher than those of corrections officers with about 48 percent having a high school education or less, and 52 percent having some post secondary education of which a higher proportion have a bachelor's degree. Generally, a high school education is required for employment and in 40 states beyond high school was recommended.

The juvenile child care worker is somewhat different than the corrections officer in orientation since many juveniles do not go to state institutions, but private or public residential treatment facilities. Consequently child care workers and their educational advancement has received more attention than the adult corrections officer. When one looks at state institutions, training programs for juvenile child care workers have been more human relations oriented than those for adult corrections officers. The type of in service training given to juvenile child care workers is similar to that of a corrections officer. More emphasis in staff development is placed on counseling techniques, uniqueness of the juvenile law, family relations, sex education and child and adolescent psychology. Although the general format of training is similar, differences occur because of the younger population and their specific needs. Specific educational programs are developing at both the associate of arts degree level for child care workers, and more recently at the university level, such as the program at the University of Wisconsin-Milwaukee. The functions of a child care worker include the following:

- Intervene in conflicts between residents to maintain order
- Respond to emergency situations
- Observe and control movement of residents
- Search resident's and critical areas for contraband material
- Monitor feeding of residents to avoid disruption
- Advise residents concerning personal or other problems (in some jurisdictions the child care worker becomes an active participant in group programs and counseling)
- Assign tasks to residents and monitors performance
- Individual and group counseling.[6]

SOCIAL WORK

Estimates on the number of social workers in the corrections network are unreliable since in many cases, the function of a group is given but not the professional discipline, i.e., probation and parole. It is known from the Manpower Survey of the Criminal Justice System in 1974-1975, that social workers are employed in all parts of the corrections network, however, it is not a dominant profession. Figure 16-6 shows an estimated 17,553 social workers employed in the corrections network in 1980. Social workers are employed in all areas of the corrections network identified in Figure 16-3.

Social work as one of the helping professions has been involved to a greater or less extent in the corrections network since the establishment of state systems in the early 1870's. The role of social work in the corrections network has been variable, depending upon the specific part of the corrections network and the historical time period. In general, examples of jurisdictions which have extensively used social workers in the corrections network include the Federal System, California, Michigan, Minnesota, New Jersey and Wisconsin. What the social worker does in corrections varies from individual work to community organization, and whether one is employed in probation and parole services or institutional services. A minority of social workers are involved in strictly treatment programs.

INDIVIDUAL LEVEL

A social worker may be employed as a probation and parole agent, service worker in an institution or providing individual services in a private agency. Generally, at this level, one becomes involved in casework which would range from providing a concrete service to providing counseling. In some situations a person may become involved in depth therapy for individuals and work with families and their problems. Some of the tasks expected of social workers in corrections include pre-sentence investigation reports, social histories, court and agency reports.

GROUP LEVEL

Numerous individuals in addition to casework, employ group work skills in attempting to enable individuals to cope with problems of a psychological nature or with the social and economic environment. Groups can be either didactic, in which the function is to provide information, or therapy, in which the function is to resolve underlying psychological problems. Groups can be devised for general purposes, such as coping skills, or for specific problem areas, such as drugs, alcohol or sexual functioning.

COMMUNITY LEVEL

With the trend toward community treatment programs, community organizing skills are becoming more important. An individual must be able to relate to a specific community and mobilize community support for the establishment of community centers. In addition to helping develop community centers, there is a wide range of tasks involving the coordination of services and relating to various community interest groups.[7]

PROBATION and PAROLE SERVICES

Whether probation and parole is organized as a companion service or as a separate service, the general tasks for the agent are similar. In general the typical tasks of a probation or parole agent include the following:

- Pre-sentence investigation-(a social history of the offender to aid the judge in sentencing and provide basic information for the institition)
- Pre-parole plans-(a short report to verify the plans one has upon release from an institution)
- Special reports-(checks on employment, acquaintences, etc.)
- Supervision of the offender
- Providing counseling to the offender and their family
- Cooperate with other law enforcement agencies on investigations.[8]

INSTITUTIONAL SERVICES

Depending upon the institution, the specific tasks of the social worker will vary. In general, the institutional social service employee becomes involved in some or all of the following activities:

- Reception reports and assessment while the inmate is in observation or reception status. This means to obtain information on the inmate and their background from the inmates perspective. At the end of the reception period the worker is to develop an overall behavioral and adjustment report.

- Classification and preparole reports which means to make an assessment of an individual and to prepare a recommendation for the classification committee on the type of institution and program the individual should be assigned to.

- Cooperate with the parole agent and the individual in developing a parole plan.

- Maintain contact with the family.

- Provide individual and group counseling.

- Help resolve practical day to day problems to better enable the individual to cope within the institution.

531

PERSONAL SOCIAL SERVICES

The corrections network, like other networks, has a personal social service component (see chapter 22, Personal Social Service). Some examples of the personal social services in the corrections network are as follows:

PROTECTIVE SERVICES

Special programs for the older offender, counseling for offenders committing child or spouse abuse. Some examples include One America Rehabilitation Division, One America Inc., Washington, D.C. and Mother's in Prison Project, Minneapolis, Minnesota.

UTILITARIAN SERVICES

Legal aid, legal libraries. Some examples include Were Here Inc., Milwaukee, Wisconsin and Probationers and Parolees Organization, San Francisco, California.

DEVELOPMENTAL and SOCIALIZATION SERVICES

Family counseling. Some examples include Self Development Group, Boston Massachusetts; Project Reentry, Syracuse, New York and All for One Community Counseling Center, San Jose, California.

REHABILITATIVE and THERAPEUTIC SERVICES

Specialized alcohol and drug programs and sex offender programs. Some examples include Wisconsin Correctional Service, Milwaukee, Wisconsin and John Howard Association, Honolulu, Hawaii.

SPECIAL POPULATIONS

The corrections network has as its clientele representatives from all segments of society and subsequently representatives from all special populations. (See Chapter 25, Special Populations and Chapter 24 Rehabilitation). Some examples of programs for special populations in the corrections network include the following:

ASIAN

Linkage with the Asian community to provide support for the offender and their family. Some examples include the John Howard Society of Honolulu, Hawaii and Prisoner's Component, Seattle, Washington.

BLACK

Cultural awareness programs and organized groups. Some examples include the Commando Project, Milwaukee, Wisconsin; Brooklyn Core (Congress of Racial Equality), Brooklyn, New York and Illinois Prisoner's Association, Chicago, Illinois.

EUROPEAN ETHNIC

Cultural awareness programs and support groups. Some examples include the International Institutes in St. Paul, Minnesota and Milwaukee, Wisconsin; Catholic Charities of Buffalo, New York and Lutheran Social Services, Milwaukee, Wisconsin.

NATIVE AMERICAN

Support and sensitivity groups; linkage with the tribe and community. Some examples include Indians of All Tribes, Monroe Washington; Indian Offender Rehabilitation Program, Topeka, Kansas and Project Phoenix, Milwaukee, Wisconsin.

SAME SEX PREFERENCE

Support and sensitivity groups. Some examples include Join Hands, San Francisco, California and Prisoner Parole and Probation Program, Gay Community Services Center, Los Angeles, California.

SPANISH SPEAKING

Bilingual education, support and sensitivity groups. Some examples include Active Mexicanos, Seattle, Washington and Spanish Center, Milwaukee, Wisconsin.

WOMEN

Special educational programs and family follow-up while the individual is incarcerated. Some examples include the St. Benedict Center for Criminal Justice, Milwaukee, Wisconsin; the Women's Prison Association, New York, New York and Women Helping Offenders, Inc., Minneapolis, Minnesota.

ISSUES

The corrections network in the United States is undergoing rapid development and change in the 1970's and 1980's. These changes will undoubtedly alter and affect the functions of human service personnel in the system. These changes can be grouped into the broad categories of legality, education, purpose of correc- tions and future directions.

LEGALITY ISSUES

Prior to 1950 limited attention was devoted to the correc- tions network by the legal profession. Few people questioned the authority of probation and parole agencies, parole boards and institutional policies, nor paid attention to the legal rights of the individual involved in the corrections network. Since the beginning of the 1960's, lawyers and courts have challenged the authority of the probation and parole agencies resulting in modification of the decision making process in most states. There have been challenges to the authority of parole boards and in some states certain parole board decisions must be reviewed by a court prior to implementation. Institutional procedures, such as mail censorship, banned material, visiting rights, etc., have been challenged and modified.

A significant social, political and legal debate today surrounds the issue of determinate and indeterminate sentenc- ing. A determinate sentence is a fixed period of time or a flat sentence. The concept behind the fixed sentence is to match the punishment to the crime (the "just deserts model"). An indeter- minate sentence is a variable sentence with a minimum and a maximum period of time. A parole authority can release the individual, based upon their procedures between those two periods of time. The concept behind an indeterminate sentence is matching the punishment with the offender (the rehabilitation model).

If society uses a system of a determinate sentence, there is a minimum need of a parole authority to make decisions, since a release date has been determined at the time of one's sentence. If a society uses a system of an indeterminate sentence, then some parole authority or other authority has to make decisions. Currently, society is moving toward some variation of the deter- minate sentence and away from the indeterminate sentence. The impact on parole authority, parole board policies and procedures is unclear at this time. In 1986, some of the states which adopted some form of a determinate sentence are reconsidering those legislative decisions.

EDUCATION

There is no specific discipline which has predominance in the corrections network. On one hand, the majority of personnel are employed in custody and security, on the other, there is a growing reliance on individuals trained at the university level. Generally custody and security personnel are individuals

534

with high school degrees or less and human service personnel are college graduates from diverse areas which include criminal justice, correctional administration, social work, psychology, sociology, education, urban affairs, etc. Some individuals argue that a specialty should be created in corrections, others in criminal justice, and others prefer an eclectic approach. Social work education will need to modify its curriculum to develop content areas in correctional law, knowledge of the network, and emphasize other roles of social work beyond treatment.

One of the consequences of this lack of clarity on education, is the growing importance of staff development and in service training programs developed by corrections agencies.

PURPOSE of CORRECTIONS

The dual function of corrections as a network has been incarceration and rehabilitation and which one is dominate changes over time. Up until 1945 the function of incarceration was dominant, from 1945 to 1970 there had been an emphasis on rehabilitation, and from 1975-1987 a movement toward the "just deserts" model of punishment or incarceration has been dominant.

These changes in the focus of corrections are directly related to broader social, political and philosophical aspects of our society and viewpoints about criminality. In general, the function of incarceration closely parallels models of criminality which stress individual responsibility and the concept that punishment should fit the crime (Classical School of Criminality). The function of rehabilitation closely parallels models of criminality which stress the causative factors of criminality (social, psychological, educational, economic, etc.) and the concept that punishment should fit the offender (Positivistic School of Criminology). Currently, the "just deserts" model is in vogue which focuses more on equity in sentencing (same sentence for similar crimes) which is a variation on the theme of punishment should fit the crime.[9]

Some individuals argue that this duality in function is creating internal discontinuity, therefore corrections is unable to effectively meet either objective. As the corrections network changes, it is speculated there will be a split between incarceration functions and rehabilitative functions. Individuals employed would predominantly have one or the other function. The practical impact is that most rehabilitation would be implemented outside of the institutional environment. Part of this trend to decrease the conflict between incarceration and rehabilitation is reflected in the movement toward determinate

535

and shorter sentences except in cases of assaultive behavior and specifically sexual assault.

FUTURE DIRECTIONS

The trend is toward smaller community corrections centers, smaller institutions and improvement in educational and work programs. Private corporations between 1975 and 1987 have been established to build prisons as an alternative to public expenditures and sponsorship.

Rehabilitation programs will be expanded, however a heavy emphasis will be placed on locating these programs in other facilities than the correctional institutions, as well as purchasing these services from other agencies.

SUMMARY

Corrections is a complex but large network, with expenditures of at least 8.9 billion dollars in 1984, employing at least 342,470 individuals and having approximately 2.5 million individuals under the jurisdiction of the network. A brief history of the major components of the corrections network, i.e., jails and house of correction, prison, probation and parole and private agencies was provided to show the divergence within the network as well as the complexity of the network.

An overview of selected human service occupations and professions indicated that 33.4 percent of the selected human service occupations and professions employed in the corrections network were involved in treatment and rehabilitative functions and 66.582 percent in custody and incarceration functions. The dominate occupations were those of a corrections officer and the child care worker (juvenile corrections officer). No one profession dominates the corrections network. The primary professions used today include (amongst others), criminal justice, sociology, psychology, psychiatry, management and administration, and social work. The role of social work was discussed in the provision of social services. Some of the current issues in the field, such as education, philosophical direction and legal rights were highlighted.

FOOTNOTES

* This chapter was reviewed for comments by William Feyerherm, Associate Professor, Criminal Justice, School of Social Welfare, University of Wisconsin-Milwaukee, Milwaukee, Wisconsin.

1. These estimates of the extent of private social service agency participation in corrections is taken from the "Directory of Corrections Service Agencies." Correctional Service Federation of the United States, and Helga Croner and Kurt Guggenheim National Directory of Private Social Agencies, 1986 Queens Village, New York: Croner Publishing Co., 1986 (updated annually).

2. Other places of detention as a means of holding individuals were used long before 800 A.D. Many times these places of detention were in watch towers, palaces, the basement of a building, shackles, etc. Referring to the jail since 800 means a specific building or place of detention designed specifically for that purpose. Accounts of dungeons, church related places of detention during the inquisition of the 1200's, etc., are well documented. Jails were used well into the 19th century for holding prisoner's as well as the housing of the poor (debtor), mentally ill, etc. The focus here, is on the jail as we perceive it today.

3. For a history of work release and study release programs the reader is referred to James Hall, Criminal Justice Administration: The American Plan. Dubuque, Iowa: Kendall Hunt Publishing Co., 1976.

4. For a brief discussion of the poorhouse, workhouse and the Bridewell (house of correction) movement see Gerald Handel. Social Welfare in Western Society. New York, New York: Random House, 1982 pp. 97-101.

5. The organizational context of the corrections network is extremely varied and complex. The corrections network consists of juvenile detention, juvenile probation, juvenile institutions, juvenile aftercare (parole), misdemeanent probation, adult local probation, probation (state and federal), local institutions and jails, adult state and federal institutions and adult state and federal parole.

   In addition to public and private facilities and agencies for providing services to the individual involved in the corrections network a folk system still exists consisting of peer and colleague pressure, family relations and at times the family feud. For example in December, 1979 in Milwaukee, Wisconsin, there was a situation involving a Serbian family feud and the family resorted to appropriate action as they perceived the situation (a killing) to resolve the problem.

6. The tasks performed by both adult corrections officers and juvenile child care workers is adapted from the National Institute of Law Enforcement and Criminal Justice, National

Manpower Survey of the Criminal Justice System: Volume 3 Corrections, Washington, D.C.: U.S. Government Printing Office, 1978, pp. 99, 112. Some examples of professional organizations in the corrections network include the following: American Association of Correctional Officers, 1474 Willow Avenue, Des Plaines, Illinois 60016; National Association for Child Care and Management, 1800 M Street, NW, Suite 1030 M, Washington, DC 20030; American Correctional Association, 4321 Hartwick Road, Suite 6208, College Park, Maryland 20740; Academy of Criminal Justice Sciences, 1313 Farnam on the Mall, University of Nebraska at Omaha, Omaha, Nebraska 68181; Correctional Service Federation USA, c/o John Howard Association, 67 East Madison Street, Suite 1216, Chicago, Illinois; American Association of Correctional Training Personnel, 1800 Hagen Street, Elmburst, New York 11370 and National Association of Juvenile Correctional Agencies, 36 Locksley Lane, Springfield, Illinois 62704.

7. For further information on social work in the corrections network the reader is referred to the National Association of Social Workers, 7981 Eastern Avenue, Silver Spring, Maryland 20910, or contact the local office of the National Association of Social Workers.

8. Standards for corrections have been proposed by many groups, such as the American Correctional Association Manual of Correctional Standards, 1966, and The Academy of Criminal Justice, Criminal Justice Accreditation Council, 1979.

    The preferred standard for probation and parole, for example is completion of a master's degree in social work or comparable study in criminology, sociology, criminal justice, etc., and the minimum standard is a bachelor's degree in a behavioral science or social work. See National Manpower Survey, op cit p.69.

9. For a discussion of the conflict between the "just deserts" model and the rehabilitation model, the reader should review the book by Francis Cullen and Karen Gilbert Reaffirming Rehabilitation Cincinnati, Ohio: Anderson Publishing Co., 1982.

SUGGESTED READINGS

Harry Barnes. The Story of Punishment. Montclair, New Jersey: Patterson Smith, Inc. 1972. For an individual interested in the historical approach to the various methods society has used to treat the criminal this book is an excellent source.

Francis Cullen and Karen Gilbert. <u>Reaffirming Rehabilitation</u>. Cincinnati, Ohio: Anderson Publishing Co., 1982. This book is a critical analysis of the "just deserts" and "rehabilitation" models of criminal justice and strongly suggests that both models have a function in the corrections network.

David Duffey and Robert Fitch. <u>An Introduction to Corrections: A Policy and Systems Approach</u>. Pacific Palisades, CA: Goodyear Publishing Co., 1976. For a critical analysis of the corrections network, this book is an excellent resource.

Hayes Hatcher. <u>Correctional Casework and Counseling</u>. Engelwood Cliffs, NJ: Prentice Hall Inc., 1978. This book provides a general overview of the treatment process in corrections. Although dated the book is useful.

Leonard Hippchen (Ed.). <u>Correctional Classification and Treatment</u>. Cincinnati, OH: The W. H. Anderson Co., 1975. A fundamental process in the corrections system today is classification of the offender. This edited series of articles, links the process of classification to varied types of treatment programs.

Otto Kirchheimer and Geary Rusche. <u>Punishment and Social Structure</u>. New York, New York: Columbia University Press, 1939. For the individual interested in a classic book which uses historiography to analyze the manner in which society punishes the law violater, this book is a must.

Albert Roberts (Ed.). <u>Social Work in Juvenile and Criminal Justice Settings</u>. Springfield, IL: Charles C. Thomas Co., 1983. This collection of readings is the first book to be published in close to 10 years which focuses on the role of social work in the criminal justice system. This book is an excellent resource for an individual who desires to obtain a broad overview of social work in corrections and other parts of the criminal justice system.

David Rudoysky, Alan Bronstein and Edward Koren. <u>The Rights of Prisoners</u>. New York, New York: Bantam Books, 1983. A significant issue in corrections today (and in criminal justice) are the legal rights of individuals in the corrections network. This book is an excellent introduction into some of the legal issues and provides a solid list of resources and references.

REFERENCES

Abadinsky, Howard. <u>Social Services in Criminal Justice</u>. Englewood Cliffs, New Jersey: Prentice Hall, Inc., 1979.

Allen, Harry and Clifford Simonsen. Corrections in America: An Introduction. Beverly Hills, California: Glencoe Press, 1975.

Barnes, Harry. The Story of Punishment. Montclair, New Jersey: Patterson Smith Inc., 1972.

Carney, Louis. Corrections and the Community. Englewood Cliffs, New Jersey: Prentice Hall Inc., 1977.

Carter, Robert. Probation, Parole and Community Corrections. New York, New York: John Wiley Inc., 1976.

Croner, Helga and Kurt Guggenheim. National Directory of Private Social Agencies. 1986 Queens Village, New York: Croner Publishing Co., 1986 (updated annually).

Cull, John and Richard Hardy. Fundamentals of Criminal Behavior and Correctional Systems. Springfield, Illinois: Charles C Thomas Publisher, 1973.

Cullen, Francis and Karen Gilbert, Reaffirming Rehabilitation, Cincinnati, Ohio: Anderson Publishing Co., 1982.

Duffey, David and Robert Fitch. An Introduction to Corrections: A Policy and Systems Approach. Pacific Palisades, California: Goodyear Publishing Co., 1976.

Galaway, Burt, Joe Hudson, and David Holister. Community Corrections: A Reader. Springfield, Illinois: Charles C. Thomas Publishers, 1976.

Handel, Gerald. Social Welfare in Western Society. New York, New York: Random House, 1982.

Hardy, Richard and John Cull. Introduction to Correctional Rehabilitation. Springfield, Illinois: Charles C Thomas Publisher, 1973.

Hatcher, Hayes. Correctional Casework and Counseling. Englewood Cliffs, New Jersey: Prentice Hall Inc., 1978.

Hippchen, Leonard (Ed.). Correctional Classification and Treatment. Cincinnati, Ohio: The W H Anderson Co., 1975.

Karlen, Delmar. Anglo-American Criminal Justice. New York, New York: Oxford University Press, 1967.

Kirchheimer, Otto and Geary Rusche. Punishment and Social Structure. New York, New York: Columbia University Press, 1939.

Law Enforcement Assistance Administration, Two Hundred Years of American Justice. Washington, D.C.: U.S. Government Printing Office, 1976.

Mangrum, Claude. The Professional Practitioner in Probation. Springfield, Illinois: Charles C Thomas Publisher, 1975.

Minahan, Anne (Ed.). Encyclopedia of Social Work, 18th Issue. Washington, D.C.: National Association of Social Workers, 1986.

National Institute of Law Enforcement and Criminal Justice, The National Manpower Survey of the Criminal Justice System: Volume 3: Corrections. Washington, D.C.: U.S. Government Printing Office, 1978.

Newman, Charles. Sourcebook on Probation, Parole and Pardons, 3rd ed. Springfield, Illinois: Charles C. Thomas Publisher, 1968.

Norton, Thomas. The Constitution of the United States. New York, New York: Committee for Constitutional Government. 1956.

Office of the Federal Register, United States Government Manual 1985-86, Washington, D.C.: U.S. Government Printing Office, 1985.

Peoples, Edward. Readings in Correctional Casework and Counseling. Pacific Palisades, California: Goodyear Publishing Co., 1975.

President's Commission on Law Enforcement and Administration of Justice, Task Force Report: Corrections. Washington, D.C.: U.S. Government Printing Office, 1967.

Roberts, Albert (Ed.) Social Work in Juvenile and Criminal Justice Settings. Springfield, Illinois: Charles C. Thomas Co., 1983.

Rudovsky, David, Alvin Bronstein and Edward Koren. The Rights of Prisoners. New York, New York: Bantam Books, 1983.

Scheurell, Robert. "Social Work Ethics in Probation and Parole."
    pp. 241-251 in Albert Roberts (Ed.). Social Work in
    Juvenile and Criminal Justice Settings. Springfield, IL:
    Charles C. Thomas Co., 1983.

Studt, Elliot. Education for Social Workers in the Correctional
    Field, Vol. 5: A Project Report of the Curriculum Study.
    New York, New York: Council on Social Work Education, 1959.

Travisono, Diana (Ed.). American Correctional Association
    Directory - 1986. College Park, Maryland: American
    Correctional Association, 1986.

Travisono, Diana (Ed.). National Jail and Adult Detention
    Directory - 1981 2nd Edition. College Park, Maryland:
    American Correctional Association, 1980.

United States Department of Justice, Bureau of Justice
    Statistics, Sourcebook of Criminal Justice Statistics
    --1984. Washington, D.C.: U.S. Government Printing Office,
    1985.

United States Department of Commerce, Bureau of the Census,
    1980 Census of Population, Vol. 2: Subject Reports Part 7C:
    Occupation by Industry, Washington, D.C.: U.S. Government
    Printing Office, 1984.

United States Department of Commerce, Bureau of the Census,
    Statistical Abstract of the United States: 1986 (106th
    Edition), Washington, D.C.: U.S. Government Printing
    Office, 1985.

United States Department of Commerce, Bureau of the Census.
    Public Employment in 1984, Washingotn, D.C.: U.S.
    Government Printing Office, 1985.

United States Department of Justice, National Institute of
    Justice, Private Sector Involvement in Prison Based
    Businesses, Washington, D.C.: U.S. Government Printing
    Office, 1985.

United States, Department of Justice, National Institute of
    Justice, The Privatization of Corrections, Washington,
    D.C.: U.S. Government Printing Office, 1985.

Wisconsin Legislative Reference Bureau, Wisconsin Blue Book
    1985-86, Madison, Wisconsin: Department of Administration,
    1985.

CHAPTER 17

EMPLOYMENT and MANPOWER NETWORK*

"The nation is becoming increasingly concerned over the utilization of its human
resources. In recent years public discussion has centered on levels of unemployment;
rates of unemployment; labor market problems
of young workers and school dropouts; and
retraining problems of older workers,
minority groups and the female labor
force." (Haber and Krueger:1964:1).

INTRODUCTION

The employment and manpower network in the United States
since 1850 has seen a steady decline for the need of workers in
the agriculture industrial classification with a corresponding
rise for the need of workers in the goods and services production industrial classifications. This means, holding a job for
"someone else" has become the central means of employment, or as
some authors indicate, we have a "job economy". A job economy
requires a vehicle or mechanism for; individuals to secure
employment, employers to secure employees, and maximizing the
utilization of a labor pool. These two societal concerns of
employment and maximizing a labor pool are addressed through the
employment and manpower network.

In 1985, there were an estimated 108,072,000 individuals
employed in the United States of which 57,181,000 or 53 percent
were male and 50,891,000 or 47 percent were female. Of the
female employees, 12,925,000 or 25.4 percent were single,
29,755,000 or 58.5 percent were married, and 8,211,000 or 16.1
percent were widowed or divorced. In the same year unemployment
was estimated at 8,413,000 or 7.3 percent of the civilian labor
pool. Of the unemployed, 4,649,000 or 55.3 percent were male,
3,764,000 or 44.7 percent were female, 6,451,000 or 76.7 percent
were white, 1,718,000 or 20.4 percent were Black and 244,000 or
2.9 percent were other populations. The highest rates of
unemployment were for teenagers (age 16-19) 18.9 percent, Black
teenagers, 42.7 percent, Native Americans, 13.2 percent (1980)
and the age group 25-44 years old, 43.4 percent. In 1986, the
overall unemployment rate was estimated at 6.9 percent of the
civilian work force. In addition, it was estimated that
63,313,000 individuals or 35 percent of potential individuals
for the work force were not seeking employment.

In the United States the traditional mechanisms for securing employment have been; individual initiative, informal contacts, advertisements, private employment agencies, and more recently (1933) the combined federal and state Employment Service (Job Service). In addition to employment agencies (both public and private), there are numerous manpower training facilities including the vocational technical education system, public manpower training centers and private manpower training centers, such as the Opportunity Industrialization Center. This chapter describes the employment and manpower network, with an emphasis on the role of the various occupations and professions, such as employment counselor, employment interviewer, and the potential role of social work.

SIZE

The employment and manpower network consists of public employment agencies (federal and state employment services), private employment agencies, and training facilities including the vocational and technical education programs (See Chapter 8 Education Network for a discussion of vocational and technical education).

The federal and state employment services, in 1984, had an estimated 2,700 local offices throughout the United States, employing 123,320 individuals, with expenditures of an estimated 6.5 billion dollars and served an estimated 15 million individuals.[1]

Private employment agencies were estimated at 16,136 in 1982, employing an estimated 608,779 individuals, with expenditures of an estimated 5.6 billion dollars, and serving 8 million plus individuals.[2]

The manpower training network consists of private facilities, utilization of vocational and technical education programs, higher education programs, and specialized subsidized programs by the federal government, such as Job Opportunities in Business (JOBS) (replaced by Private Sector Initiative Program, PSIP, in 1973), Concentrated Employment Training Act (CETA) (replaced by the Job Training and Partnership Act, JTPA, in 1982), amongst others. In 1982-1984, there were an estimated 4,875 manpower training agencies, employing an estimated 209,507 individuals with expenditures of 6.2 billion dollars and serving an estimated 3.3 million individuals.[3] Figure 17-1 shows the estimated size of the employment and manpower network.[4]

Selected Characteristic	Type of System			
	Private Employment Agency	Public Employment Agency	Manpower Training Agency [1]	Total
Number of Facilities	16,136	2,700	4,875	23,711
Expenditure (Dollars)	5,631,924,000	6,558,000,000	6,240,062,000	18,429,986,000
Number of Employees	608,779	123,320[2]	209,507	941,606
Population Served (Million)	8.0+	15.0	3.3	26.3

*Source: United States Department of Commerce, Bureau of the Census, Public Employment in 1984, Washington, D.C.: U.S. Government Printing Office, 1985, p.3; Martinez Thomas. The Human Marketplace: An Examination of Private Employment Agencies, New Brunswick, New Jersey: Transaction Books, 1976; United States, Department of Commerce, Bureau of the Census, Statistical Abstract of the United States: 1986 (106th Edition, Washington, D.C.: U.S. Government Printing Office, 1985, p. 357,359, 325; and United States Department of Commerce, Bureau of the Census, 1982 Census of Service Industries, Washington, D.C.: U.S. Government Printing Office, 1984, p. 4.

[1] Includes some overlap with rehabilitation agencies.

[2] Includes employees in social insurance programs which overlap with unemployment insurance and compensation.

HISTORICAL DEVELOPMENT

Although employment of individuals has always been a concern in society, the development of formalized systems of employment services, and manpower training programs is essentially a product of the 20th Century. For this historical review, employment services and manpower training programs are discussed separately.

EMPLOYMENT SERVICES

There are a variety of ways for individuals to seek and obtain employment, such as applying directly to employers, contacting friends, and relatives, answering ads, public employment services, private employment services, contacting teachers, school placement services, etc.[5] The focus in this historical review is on the private and public employment agencies. Figure 17-2 shows a historical time line of the development of the employment and manpower network.

GENERAL DEVELOPMENT - Historically some means of securing employment were usually available for the unemployed. In ancient civilizations like Sumeria (2,000 B.C.) the unemployed workers would congregate around the temple, and the priest would assign any available work to the individuals, and send the individual to the employer. The temple priest would receive a percentage fee for this service. The parable in the Holy Bible on the laborers in the vineyard, is a description of this type of system. In Greece (500 B.C.), the Colonas (public square) was a specific place in a city for the unemployed to congregate, and employers would select individuals for hiring, and negotiate wages.

Medieval Europe (450 to 1500 A.D.), had a variety of mechanisms to secure employment. In cities, the unemployed would congregate for living purposes in specific houses on the back streets, which had cheap rent, and use the public square, or the main church as a meeting area to negotiate employment with prospective employers. The guilds (craft unions) were another source of employment through the apprentice system.[6] In rural areas where feudalism (serfdom and vassalage) was dominate, the Bishopric or lord, would contract for a fee, with an "employment locater" (one who finds employment) to utilize their unemployed laborers for employment in other geographical areas. In some cases an individual, such as a "land speculator", would contract with a local lord or bishop for a specified number of laborers (for a fee or a percentage of the new land or both) to help populate an unpopulated area. The local lord or bishop would then encourage unemployed people to move to specific locations for land development and employment.

Figure 17-2

HISTORICAL TIME LINE of the EMPLOYMENT and MANPOWER NETWORK

2000 BC	Unemployed congregate by the temple; apprenticeship
500 BC	Colonas (Public Square) in Greece; apprenticeship
100	Village square as a gathering place; apprenticeship
1200	Guild, craft union or church as a gathering place
1600	Indentured servitude; apprenticeship
1700	Immigrant Agent; apprenticeship
1819	Employment agency for domestic servants (private)
1834	New York City employment exchange
1907	United States Employment Service, Bureau of Immigration and Naturalization
1909	National Employment Service and Private Agencies
1914	United States Employment Service, Department of Labor
1917	The Smith Act (vocational training)
1933	Wagner Peyser Act - Federal and State Employment Service
1935	Social Security Act (Unemployment Insurance)
1938	National Apprenticeship Act
1960	Opportunity Industrialization Center
1962	Manpower Development Training Act (MDTA)
1964	Economic Opportunity Act (EOA) - War on Poverty
1967	Concentrated Employment Program (CEP)
1968	Opportunities in the Business Sector (JOBS)
	Work Incentive Program (WIN)
1973	Comprehensive Employment Training Act (CETA)
1974	Dismantling the War on Poverty
1977	Youth Employment and Demonstration Project Act (YEDPA)
	Economic Stimulus Appropriation Act (both acts amended CETA)
1978	Full Employment and Balanced Growth Act
1981	Reduction of Title II and III programs of CETA
1982	CETA replaced by Job training and partnership Act (JTPA)

547

Through these mechanisms many areas which were sparsely populated, such as Silesia in Poland (1300 A.D.) were then populated with a different population group.

A variation of this pattern of a land speculator was the padrone system, used by the Dutch in the United States in the 1600s. An individual was granted a large patent of land, and individuals who went with this person to settle the land were assigned a portion of this patent to live on and work. For example Ryche's patent in New York state (New York city area). By 1600 a system of indentured servitude was also used to secure employment for the unemployed in the New World (the Americas). An "immigrant agent" was given a fee for each person assigned as an indentured servant to be imported to the new land, like the United States and later Australia.[7] The immigrant agent was called other names, such as soul seller, spirit seller, and newlander. The immigrant agent, was a predecessor of the private employment services. With the expansion of the use of newspapers by the public, some individuals and employers began to place ads for specific positions or jobs which were available, such as France (1733).

PRIVATE EMPLOYMENT AGENCIES - In the United States private employment services had an early development in 1819 with the Employers Servants Protestant Agency in New York, which was established to better regulate the hiring of domestic servants. This agency was a commercial establishment, operated on a fee basis. Some immigrant groups, such as the Irish in 1816, established employment services as part of their Immigrant Aid Society. In order to supply laborers for the newly developing clothing industry, a system of private enterprise was developed by 1846 to secure employees for that industry. A "slaver" would ride a circuit through the New England states, recruiting female laborers at $1 a head for specific employers. With the rapid increase of immigration toward the middle of the 19th Century, and the crowded urban centers, private employment agencies developed rapidly, such as New York city, where private firms were actively advertising in newpapers as early as 1851. Immigrant societies were established to encourage foreign immigration, such as the American Immigrant Society, established in 1863. All of these agencies were on a commercial fee basis to attract and recruit laborers.

Early employment agencies focussed on blue-collar and domestic employment, with an emphasis on white-collar employment, developing after 1917. The private employment agency prior to any form of state or municipal regulations, could have consisted of: one person operating out of their home, one person recruiting in saloons, pool halls or union halls, or a large multi personnel agency. The employment agency was at

548

one time called the "intelligence office". With the rapid
expansion of private employment agencies, there developed a need
for coordination of effort, regulation and licensing by
governmental agencies. In 1909 a National Employment Exchange
was established in New York which became the forerunner of the
professional association for private employment agencies.[8] By
1914, twenty four states had statutes directly regulating
private employment agencies, and nineteen states had statutes
indirectly regulating private agencies. Currently all states
have some form of regulation for private employment agencies.[9]

PUBLIC EMPLOYMENT AGENCIES - Pubic employment services
initially began as a city and state enterprise, such as New York
city (1834), San Francisco (1868), Minnesota (1885), New York
(1888) and Ohio (1890). By 1907 there were seventeen states
(including Wisconsin) with employment services and eleven municipalities. The current system of federal and state employment
services (now called Job Service) is an outgrowth of the United
States employment service which was established in 1907, under
the Division of Information, Bureau of Immigration and Naturalization. The function of this agency was to enable immigrants
to secure employment. In 1913, the agency was transferred to
the Department of Labor and in 1914 was called the Employment
Service, becoming independent from the Immigration Bureau.
During World War I, there was an expansion of the employment
services, in order to mobilize the nation's resources for the
war effort. A National Labor Exchange was organized for: farm
labor, young adults, the Mexican Expedition (1916), Veteran's,
women and seamen. As the United States mobilized for war in
1917, the employment exchange was further expanded to include
aging and shipyard employment. During this time period, the
local Post Office was used as the agency to implement the
employment services. In 1918, the Employment Service was
reorganized to use state offices instead of the Post Office, and
included special services for blacks and women.

The current system of federal and state employment services
was established in 1933 under the Wagner Peyser act, which
provided 50 percent of the funding by the federal government for
participating states. In 1935 the Social Security Act expanded
the functions of the employment services to include unemployment
insurance (Titles III, VII, IX and XII - See Chapter 19 Income
Maintenance network). Since the 1935 Social Security Act, there
has been a tension in the employment services between the
employment service function, and the unemployment insurance
function. There has been further expansion of the function of
the employment services, into manpower training with, the
implementation of the Manpower Development Training Act of 1962,
and the Economic Opportunity Act of 1964 (War on Poverty), with
programs, such as Job Corp, Neighborhood Youth Corp, Work

Incentive, Youth Opportunity Center, Human Resource Development, etc. Further changes in the employment services were made in 1967 with the Concentrated Employment Program, and in 1973 with the Comprehensive Employment Training Act (CETA). The Comprehensive Employment Training Act attempted to combine efforts toward employment and manpower by providing jobs which train the person at the same time. The period of the 1980's is experiencing a decline in public funding for the employment and manpower network as indicated in the 1986 federal budget with reductions of monies for CETA programs (which was replaced by the Job Training and Partnership Act - JTPA) and these budget cuts resulted in some employee counselors in the combined federal and state employment system to become unemployed and seek other employment.

MANPOWER TRAINING and DEVELOPMENT

GENERAL DEVELOPMENT - The concept of human resource development or a coordinated effort at manpower training is rather recent, developing as late as 1960 in the United States. Although governmental policies are rather recent there have been some historical precedents in the training of individuals for employment.

Manpower training for much of historical time, was on the job training, with a person either learning a specific job, or becoming an apprentice to a craftsman in order to learn a trade. For example, the Medieval Guild trained an apprentice, or an indentured servant would learn a specific craft. Even in professions, such as medicine, law, etc., a person would learn, by working with someone else until late into the 19th Century. The predecessor of manpower training in the United States is the vocational education system which was established in 1917 under the Smith Hughes Act. This act provided a system of federal funding for vocational technical and adult education programs, and was very quickly followed by the Vocational Rehabilitation Act of 1920, which contained provisions for the training of disabled individuals.[10] The current system of manpower development and training is a combination of private and public resources.

PRIVATE MANPOWER TRAINING and DEVELOPMENT - The private component of manpower training and development consists of specialized programs, such as the Opportunity Industrialization Center, industrial programs, union programs, training schools, and special government subsidized programs which includes Job Opportunities in Business Sector (Jobs) established in 1968 (replaced by the Private Sector Initiative Program in 1973).[11] Other examples of private involvement in manpower development include business schools, diesel truck drivers schools, heavy equipment schools, electronic and computer schools and institutes.

One example of the private sector involvement in manpower development is the Opportunity Industrialization Center (OIC), established in Philadelphia, Pennsylvania in 1960 under the leadership of Leon Sullivan. The OIC movement began as an attempt to train and secure employment for unemployed blacks in Philadelphia. As of 1983, there were over 110 OIC centers in the United States providing a full range of services, such as vocational guidance, testing, social services, training, adult education and personal counseling. The OIC movement is a community based, self-help approach which currently provides services to a range of population groups and has expanded beyond the black community.[12]

PUBLIC MANPOWER and TRAINING DEVELOPMENT – The predecessor of manpower development and training programs, was the Vocational Educational Act of 1917, and the Rehabilitation Act of 1920. Efforts at manpower development and training are a combination of job creation and job training programs. Early legislation in manpower development and training emerged during the period of the depression of 1929-1943 and its various programs, such as Civilian Conservation Corp (1933-1942), Federal Emergency Relief Administration (1933-35) and Works Progress Administration (1935-1942). From 1945 to 1960 little effort was expended on manpower development and training since the United States had a booming economy with a small percentage of unemployment. The only major legislation consisted of the Full Employment Act of 1945, and the National Defense Act of 1958. During the 1960s, which was a period of social consciousness, a recognition that poverty and unemployment existed in large numbers, and concern for opportunity and equality for minority groups, resulted in a large number of manpower development and training type programs, such as The Area Redevelopment Act of 1961 with its training provisions, the Manpower Development Training Act of 1962, the Economic Opportunity Act of 1964 (War on Poverty) with its broad programs (Job Corp, Neighborhood Youth Corp, Work Experience, Public Works, Work Study, Youth Opportunity Center, Work Incentive, Indian Employment, Migrant Employment Programs, etc.),[13] and the Concentrated Employment Act of 1967 which was the first effort to coordinate manpower development and training programs which were distributed between a dozen or so federal departments and agencies.

The 1970s was a decade of reorganization and decentralization of federal programs. Programs under the auspices of the Office of Economic Opportunity were transferred to various other federal departments, and local governments were given more authority over specialty programs. Manpower development and training programs were expanded to include New Careers (1969), Public Employment (1971) and the Public Service Employment Act of 1973. The Comprehensive Employment Training Act of 1973 (CETA) coordinated many of the federal efforts in manpower development and training and replaced the Manpower Development and Training Act of 1962 and the Economic Opportunity Act of 1964.[14] In 1982 the Jobs and Training Partnership Act (JTPA) replaced the Comprehensive Employment Training Act. After two decades of expansion of manpower development and training programs, the 1986 federal budget has reduced expenditures for manpower development and training, and has dismantled some manpower development and training programs at the federal level.

STRUCTURE

Since many of the services in the employment and manpower network are sponsored totally or partially by the government, the organizational context closely follows the governmental structure. In addition to the governmental context, the structure of the employment and manpower network includes services provided, occupations and professions and dominant occupations and professions.

ORGANIZATIONAL CONTEXT

Figure 17-3 shows the federal government organization of the employment and manpower network. Figure 17-4 shows a typical state government organizational structure.

In addition to the federal and state governmental organization, both employment and manpower development and training agencies have their specific structure for implementation of programs at the local level which will vary from location to location. Figure 17-5 shows the organization of a private manpower development and training program.

SERVICES PROVIDED

The variety of services provided in the employment and manpower network is rather extensive, subsequently a representative listing of services is as follows:

- Vocational dexterity tests
- Vocational aptitude tests
- Training programs
- Psychological tests
- Vocational guidance services
- General counseling

Figure 17-3

Idealized Organization of the Employment and Manpower
Network at the Federal Level*

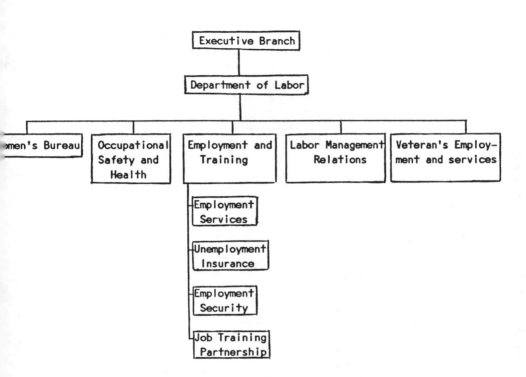

Source: Adapted from Office of Federal Register, United States Government Manual
1985/86, Washington, D.C.: U.S. Government Printing Office, 1985, p. 846.

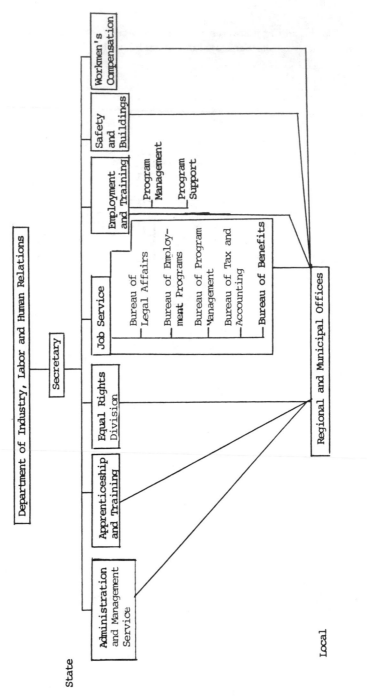

Figure 17-4

IDEALIZED ORGANIZATION OF THE EMPLOYMENT AND MANPOWER
NETWORK AT THE STATE AND LOCAL LEVEL*

Department of Industry, Labor and Human Relations

Secretary

Administration and Management Service

Apprenticeship and Training

Equal Rights Division

Job Service

Employment and Training

Safety and Buildings

Workmen's Compensation

Bureau of Legal Affairs

Bureau of Employment Programs

Bureau of Program Management

Bureau of Tax and Accounting

Bureau of Benefits

Program Management

Program Support

Regional and Municipal Offices

State

Local

*Source: Adapted from Wisconsin Legislative Reference Bureau, Wisconsin Blue Book 1985-1986, Madison, Wisconsin: Department of Administration, 1985, p. 531.

Figure 17-5

ORGANIZATION OF A PRIVATE MANPOWER TRAINING AGENCY*

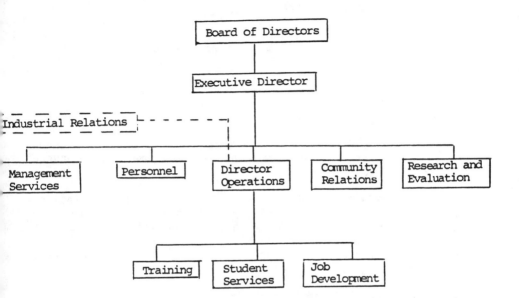

- Placement and referral counseling
- Placement follow-up
- Adult basic education
- Community referral
- Outreach
- Veterans counseling
- Psychiatric referral
- Career information and development
- Referral to unemployment insurance and compensation offices
- Job development with business
- Special services for minorities and women.

OCCUPATIONS and PROFESSIONS

Figure 17-6 shows a selected number of human service occupations and professions employed in the employment and manpower network.

Of the selected human service occupations and professions employed in the industrial classification of job training and vocational rehabilitation (employment network), 7,169 were employed as counselors in 1980 (24.8 percent) and 21,743, or 75.2 percent were other human service occupations and professions, including 6,551 social workers.

DOMINANT OCCUPATIONS and PROFESSIONS

In the employment services component of the employment and manpower network, a dominant profession is that of employment counselor and a dominant occupation is that of employment interviewer. In the manpower development and training component of the employment and manpower network the dominant profession is vocational education followed by vocational guidance. Figure 17-7 shows the employment of counselors by industrial classification in 1980.

EMPLOYMENT COUNSELOR - Only 6.4 percent of the public employment service employees are employment counselors with advanced degrees. The ideal educational qualification for an employment counselor (also called guidance counselor or vocational counselor) is a minimum of 30 graduate credits in counseling or a masters degree in counseling. Employment counseling is one subspecialty of the general counseling profession. The counseling profession began with the vocational guidance movement in 1909 with Frank Parsons, who developed the Vocational Bureau in a settlement house in Boston, Massachusetts. The first counselor training program was established at Harvard University in 1917 by Meyer Bloomfield. The National Vocational Guidance Association was established in 1913. The general field

556

Figure 17-6

Number and Percent of Selected Human Service Occupations and
Professions Employed in the Industrial Classification of
Job Training and Vocational Rehabilitation of the
Social Service Industrial Classification in 1980*

Selected Occupation and Profession	Number	Percent
Counselor (Education, Vocational Rehabilitation)	7,169 ----------	24.795
Social Work	6,551 ----------	22.658
Welfare Aide	521 ----------	1.812
Therapist (such as occupational, corrective, speech correction, recreation, art, dance etc.)	2,066 ----------	7.145
Teacher	4,963 ----------	17.165
Physician	88 ----------	.304
Nurse	604 ----------	2.089
Dietician	42 ----------	.145
Psychologist	514 ----------	1.777
Librarian	57 ----------	.197
Recreation	219 ----------	.757
Clergy/Religious Worker	245 ----------	.847
Lawyer	51 ----------	.176
Painter/Sculpter	78 ----------	.269
Licensed Practical Nurse	292 ----------	1.009
Guards/Watchmen	380 ----------	1.314
Nursing Aide	1,376 ----------	4.759
Child Care	1,390 ----------	4.807
Personnel Training/ Relations	2,306 ----------	7.975
TOTAL	28,912	100.000

*Source: Adapted from United States Department of Commerce, Bureau of the Census, 1980 Census of Population. Vol. 2 Subject Reports, Part 7C: Occupation by Industry. Washington, D.C.: U.S. Government Printing Office, 1984, pp. 295-664.

This listing of occupations and professions is representative not exhaustive. Since the designation of counselor includes education (guidance) vocational and rehabilitation, one needs to estimate of the 7,169 counselors in the Job training/rehabilitation industrial classification how many are vocational counselors. Most education counselors work in education, and most rehabilitation counselors work in health related areas. The bulk of the counselors if not all listed under job training and rehabilitation would be vocational or guidance counselors.

Figure 17-7

Number and Percent of Counselors (Education,
Vocational, Rehabilitation) Employed by
Industrial Classification in 1980*

Industrial Classification	Number	Percent
Agriculture	76	.039
Mining	9	.005
Construction	104	.053
Manufacturing	932	.482
Transportation, Communication, Public Utilities	295	.153
Wholesale Trade	117	.060
Retail Trade	295	.153
Finance/Real Estate	811	.429
Business/Repair	1,779	.920
Entertainment/Recreation	285	.147
Personal Services	336	.173
Professional and Related (Except Health Care and Social Service, Education)	2,652	1.371
Health Care	7,818	4.046
Social Service (Other)	5,042	2.608
Job Training/Voc. Rehab.	7,169	3.710
Education	147,131	76.146
Public Administration	18,368	9.505
TOTAL	193,219	100.000

*Source: Adapted from United States Department of Commerce, Bureau of the Census, 1980 Census of Population Vol. 2 Subject Reports, Part 7C: Occupation by Industry, Washington, D.C.: U.S. Government Printing Office, 1984, pp. 295-664.

The occupational classification of counselor includes education, vocational and rehabilitation. One can assume that those employed in health care, social service and public administration are primarily rehabilitation counselors. Those counselors employed in education are primarily education or guidance. The majority of those in job training and rehabilitation are vocational counselors.

of counseling expanded and there were further developments of subspecialties, such as student counseling in 1937 and development of masters degree programs in 1936. The National Vocational Guidance Association in 1952 changed its name to the American Personnel and Guidance Association and in 1984 to the American Association for Counseling and Development. The American Association for Counseling and Development has the following subdivisions: American College Personnel Association; Association for Counselor Education and Supervision; National Vocational Guidance Association; American School Counselor Association; American Rehabilitation Counseling Association; Association for Measurement and Evaluation in Counseling and Development; National Employment Counseling Association; Association for Non White Concerns in Personnel and Guidance; Association for Religious and Value Issues in Counseling; Association for Specialists in Group Work; Public Offender Counselor Association and American Mental Health Counselors Association.[15]

The employment counselor generally engages in the following activities:

- Vocational aptitude testing
- Career development counseling
- General counseling
- Job placement referral
- Vocational dexterity testing.

EMPLOYMENT INTERVIEWER - The employment interviewer usually has a bachelors degree in a social science. The employment interviewer has the following functions:

- Assesses the vocational and employment interest of an
-   individual,
- Matches the individual's interest with an employment
-   opportunity and
- Refers an individual to a prospective employer for an
  interview.

The individual who was referred for an employment interview, then follows-up on the job referral and hopefully secures employment. Other individuals in the employment services include paraprofessionals (a high school diploma), who may be called an outreach worker, and essentially are used for outreach purposes with minority groups, such as Native Americans, Spanish speaking groups, Blacks, etc.

In the manpower development and training component of the employment and manpower network component, the dominant profession is that of a vocational guidance counselor.[16] The role of the vocational guidance counselor is very similar to that of an employment counselor.

SOCIAL WORK

In 1980, there were an estimated 6,551 social workers employed in the job training and rehabilitation industrial classification of the service industries. Of these, 10 percent or 655 were employed directly in the employment and manpower network. A social worker would be employed in the employment and manpower network for a combination of their skills in working with individuals, and their skills in community organization.

INDIVIDUAL WORK

In the employment services component of the network, the social worker would be supportive to the employment counselor in coping with difficult situations which would involve more than counseling on a career development basis. There are numerous situations, where an individual would need other forms of individual casework as well as referral to other community resources. In the manpower development and training component of the employment and manpower network, the social worker can be utilized in a supportive role to the vocational counselor.

COMMUNITY ORGANIZATION

The social worker can become involved with private business in the development of job placement. Working with the business community involves community organization skills and there have been some circumstances where social workers have become involved in community organization activities, in order to maximize the potentialities of job placement.[17]

PERSONAL SOCIAL SERVICES

The employment and manpower network with its emphasis on the unemployed has as its clients individuals with a variety of poor work records and in some cases numerous personal problems. Subsequently, there is a close linkage between the personal social service network and the employment and manpower network (see Chapter 22, Personal Social Service). Some examples of the personal social services and the employment and manpower network include the following:

PROTECTIVE SERVICES

Spouse and child abuse counseling, special counselors in Job Services who are sensitive to these problems, and the local Opportunity Industrialization Center.

UTILITARIAN SERVICES

Day care is provided by some agencies to provide release time for mothers to take a training program and seek employment, such as the local Opportunity Industrialization Center.

DEVELOPMENTAL and SOCIALIZATION SERVICES

Family counseling is available in some of the employment agencies and most of the manpower development and training programs with comprehensive services, such as the local Opportunity Industrialization Center.

REHABILITATIVE and THERAPEUTIC SERVICES

Alcohol and drug counseling is available in some employment agencies and in most comprehensive manpower development and training agencies, such as the local Opportunity Industrialization Center.

SPECIAL POPULATIONS

The special populations in our society are mainly those who suffer the most from unemployment, lack of training and limited accessability to the employment and manpower network (see Chapter 25, Special Populations, and Chapter 24, Rehabilitation). Some examples of organizations and programs for special populations in the employment and manpower network include the following:

ASIAN

Affirmative action programs and employment and manpower agencies, such as the Asian Manpower Services Inc, Oakland California and Asian Counseling and Referral Services, Seattle, Washington.

BLACK

Affirmative action programs and employment and manpower agencies, such as the Opportunity Industrialization Centers in Philadelphia, Pennsylvania and Milwaukee, Wisconsin; Afro youth Community Incorporated, Chicago, Illinois and Alabama Council on Human Relations, Auburn, Alabama.

561

EUROPEAN ETHNIC

Affirmative action programs and organizations, such as the German Society of the City of New York, New York and American Fund for Czechoslovak Refugees, New York, New York.

NATIVE AMERICAN

Affirmative action programs and employment and manpower agencies such as the American Indian Opportunity Industrialization Center, Minneapolis, Minnesota; American Indian Employment Services, Oakland, California and the American Indian Center, Dallas, Texas.

SAME SEX PREFERENCE

Affirmative action programs and general resource agencies, such as the Homosexual Information Center, Hollywood, California and Lesbian Resource Center, Minneapolis, Minnesota.

SPANISH SPEAKING

Affirmative action programs and employment and manpower agencies, such as the Mexican Manpower Development Association, San Jose, California and El Centro de Services Sociales, Lorain, Ohio.

WOMEN

Affirmative action programs and organizations such as the Advocates for Women, San Francisco, California; Better Jobs for Women, Denver Colorado and Options for Women, Philadelphia, Pennsylvania.

ISSUES

Issues in the employment and manpower network include the conflict over the appropriate function of the employment service, affirmative action and employment access, and content in social work on employment and manpower.

ORGANIZATIONAL CONFLICT

Since the development of the federal and state employment system in 1933, there has been an organizational conflict between whether the emphasis should be on job referral, unemployment insurance or currently the provision of manpower development and training services or personal counseling. This organizational conflict still exists within the employment services today. There were attempts in the 1960s to expand the

562

employment services to include manpower development and training as well as personal counseling.

For employment counselors there has to be a recognition that referral of an individual to a prospective employer is only one aspect of a person's employment problem situation. There is a vast difference between whether an individual is employable, or whether that individual can become gainfully employed. For the economically disadvantaged individual pending employment does not solve a person's problems. There are other potential problems, such as employment continuation, further training, financial resources, family and personal readjustment etc. The private employment services in many situations, have now become specialty employment agencies, such as business, education, etc. There should be consistent regulations regarding the private employment services, since there have been numerous abuses of their clientele in the past where individuals were charged an exorbitant fee in order to find employment. There are also instances where private employment agencies have mismatched individuals, resulting in further hardship for the individual who is seeking employment.

AFFIRMATIVE ACTION and ACCESS

Some of the major issues in the employment and manpower network relate to affirmative action programs, and accessability and opportunity programs for minority groups and the economically disadvantaged. There are numerous examples of discrimination in employment, based upon sex, race, age, disability, and social status (ex-offender). As the United States economy shifts into a "service economy", and a more technological modernized productive system, there will be employment dislocation. This employment dislocation will be a consequence of many newer jobs requiring technical training or education, subsequently, the unemployment rate is expected to remain high.

Programs, such as Help Through Industry Retraining (HIRE), Private Sector Initiative Program (PSIP) and On the Job Training (OJT), should be expanded. With changes in the work force, such as a higher percentage of women, especially married women, programs like day care, child care, flex hours, etc. should be explored and expanded. As unemployment continues, and employment opportunities will be linked with positions needing training or education, efforts in affirmative action programs must be continued. There are attempts in 1986 to limit the impact of affirmative action programs with numerous challenges to quota systems of hiring.

SOCIAL WORK EDUCATION

In social work education there should be an emphasis on social policies relating to the employment and manpower network as these impact on social work practice. There should be a recognition of the historical development and role of both public and private employment and manpower agencies, and potential roles of social work in the employment and manpower network should be stressed.

SUMMARY

The United States has been termed a "job economy," since for most individuals employment for someone else is a key aspect of one's life. In 1986 the unemployment rate was 6.9 percent of the civilian labor force with various population groups having a much higher unemployment rate, such as blacks 14 percent and Native Americans 13.2 percent. The development of both employment services and manpower development and training programs are a product of the 20th Century. There are both private and public employment services in the United States, with the former, having been established in approximately 1819 and the later in 1933. Manpower development and training as a governmental policy had its development in the 1960s with the Manpower Development Training Act of 1962.

The public (federal and state) employment service system in 1984, now called Job Service, had over 2,700 local offices employing an estimated 123,320 individuals, with expenditures estimated at 6.5 billion dollars and serving an estimated 15.0 million individuals. The private employment service of the employment and manpower network in 1982 was estimated at over 16,136 agencies, employing an estimated 608,779 individuals, with expenditures estimated at 5.6 billion dollars and serving 8 million individuals per year. The manpower development and training component of the employment and manpower network consists of both private and public facilities including the vocational technical adult education programs. Estimates for this component of the employment and manpower network are at least 4,875 agencies, employing an estimated 209,507 individuals with expenditures of 6.2 billion dollars and serving an estimated 3.3 million individuals.

In the employment services, the dominant occupation or professions are those of an employment counselor and employment interviewer. In manpower training and development the dominant occupations and profession is the vocational guidance or employment counselor. The roles of both these professions are compared and contrasted with that of social work.

In the area of employment some of the major issues include the conflict of goals for the public employment services which results in organizational confusion. For example, the public employment services has as one goal the job placement of individuals, a second goal, counseling of individuals, a third goal manpower development and training and a fourth goal the provision of unemployment insurance benefits. These goals are at times incompatible with each other.

Historically, there have been abuses within the private employment agencies, such as excessive fee charging, misrepresentation of services, etc. However, many of these abuses have been minimized by state regulation and legislation. In manpower development and training, a major issue is continuation of many of the programs since they rely on federal funding. Since manpower development and training programs are attempting to train the hard core unemployed, there has not been sufficient emphasis placed upon understanding specific training needs for minority group members.

For social work education, there needs to be a greater emphasis and understanding on the role that employment and manpower development and training programs play in the United States in a "job economy". This means a change and modification of course content to include social policy issues as they relate to employment services and manpower development and training programs.

FOOTNOTES

*This chapter was reviewed for comments by Philip Lerman, Director, Employment and Training Institute, University of Wisconsin-Milwaukee and Ernest Spaights, Sullivan Professor, School of Social Welfare, Professor Educational Psychology, and Social Work, University of Wisconsin-Milwaukee, Milwaukee, Wisconsin.

1. Estimates on the size of the United States Employment Service component of the employment and manpower network, are adapted from: United States Department of Commerce, Bureau of the Census, Public Employment in 1984, Washington, D.C.: U.S. Government Printing Office, 1985 p. 3 and United States Department of Commerce, Bureau of the Census, Statistical Abstract of the United States: 1986 (106th Ed.), Washington, D.C.: U.S. Government Printing Office, 1985 p. 325, 357-359.

2. Estimates on the number of private employment agencies involved in the employment and manpower network are adapted from the United States Department of Commerce, Bureau of the Census, 1982 Census of Service Industries, Washington, D.C.: U.S. Government Printing Office, 1984 p. 4.

3. Estimates on the size of the manpower network are adapted from 1982 Census of Service Industries, Op Cit p. 4 and Statistical Abstracts 1986 Op Cit p. 325, 357, 359.

4. For a more detailed description of related programs see Chapter 8, Education Network, Chapter 19, Income Maintenance Network, and Chapter 24, Rehabilitation Network.

5. An interesting survey of how people seek employment was conducted by the Department of Labor in 1972, United States Department of Labor, Bureau of Labor Statistics, Job Seeking Methods Used by American Workers, Washington, D.C.: U.S. Government Printing Office, 1975.. This survey covered approximately 10 million workers and asked which means they had used for seeking and securing employment. The general results of the survey showed the methods an individual used in seeking job information included: application direct to employer 66 percent, answering of ads 57 percent, asked friends 50 percent, used public employment agency 33 percent and 21 percent used a private employment agency. The methods an individual used in securing employment included: application direct to the employer 35 percent, answering ads 13 percent, asking friends 12 percent, using private employment agency 6 percent, and using public employment agency 5 percent. This survey indicates that the folk system or informal mechanisms (friends, relatives, contacts etc.) were more significant in seeking employment than the formal channels, like the public employment service (Job Service).

6. The United States, Department of Labor, Bureau of Statistics, Handbook of Labor Statistics: 1984, Washington D.C.: U.S. Government Printing Office, 1985 p. 88 had similar statistics on how the unemployed use various methods in seeking employment. In 1983 of the 8,800,000 jobseekers, 2,147,200 or 24.4 percent used the public employment agency, 457,600 or 5.2 percent a private employment agency, 6,978,400 or 79.3 percent went to the employer directly, 2,974,400 or 33.8 percent placed or answered ads, 1,469,600 or 16.7 percent used friends or relatives and 431,200 or 4.9 percent used other methods. Individuals tended to use more than one method to seek employment and the average number of methods an individual used was 1.6.

For a more detailed description of the guild system see Chapter 5 Economic Network and Chapter 21 Mutual Support Network.

7. Some authorities estimated that 50% of the immigrants to the United States in the 1600s were indentured servants.

8. An example of a national organization for private employment agencies is the National Employment Association, 2000 Case Street N.W., Washington D.C. 20006. Some examples of private employment agencies include the following; Butter-fields Employment Service, Associate Career Counseling, Dunhill Inc., and Snelling and Snelling. In addition to the agencies which are securing full-time employment for people, there are a number of agencies for temporary help, such as Manpower Temporary Employment Service, Instant Help, and Flexiforce. Most of these agencies can be found in any large city.

9. In addition to private employment agencies other services in the private sector include unions, mutual aid societies and fraternal organizations, which provide employment informa-tion for their members.

10. For a detailed description of vocational education the reader is referred to Chapter 8 Education Network, and Chapter 24 Rehabilitation Network.

11. Examples of industrial programs include: General Motors, Ford, IBM, etc. In a survey of business in 1982, 700,000 corporations had training and retraining programs serving approximately 2.5 million workers. An example of union programs providing training and retraining programs include the International Brotherhood of Electrical Workers, and United Auto Workers. Some companies have joint programs sponsored by the corporation and the union, such as the Armour Company and International Telegraph.

12. Although the Opportunity Industrialization Centers began with private funding, their current budget consists of a combination of private and federal funding.

13. The War on Poverty, or the Economic Opportunity Act of 1964, focused heavily on employment training, and employment accessibility as a key to alleviate and prevent poverty. The Economic Opportunity Act of 1964 developed the following programs:

1. Title I - Youth programs, such as Job Corp, work training (Neighborhood Youth Corp) and work study for college students.

2. Title II - Established the Community Action Program (CAP), which was an umbrella agency for anti-poverty programs in a community. The intent was to involve the poor (maximum feasible participation) in developing remedies for problems they were facing. Examples of programs initiated include day care, homemaking, and services to the elderly (See Chapter 22 Personal Social Service).

3. Title III - Established programs for alleviating rural poverty. Programs were established for migrant workers and other minorities, such as Head Start, Upward Bound (See Chapter 8 Education Network), migrant workers (See Chapter 25 Special Populations) and loans for farm investment.

4. Title IV - Loans for small business.

5. Title V - Work experience program for unemployed fathers on Aid to Families with Dependent Children, and other training programs for other Public Assistance recipients (See Chapter 19, Income Maintenance Network).

6. Title VI - Unemployment Compensation Income (See Chapter 19 Income Maintenance Network)

7. Title VII - Administration and Coordination - Established Volunteers in Service to America (VISTA) (See Chapter 21 Mutual Support Network).

Initially an Office of Economic Opportunity, coordinated these programs. By 1969, programs established under the Office of Economic Opportunity were transferred to various agencies, such as Department of Labor, Department of Education, Action, Department of Health and Human Services, etc. The Office of Economic Opportunity was abolished, and replaced with the Community Service Administration in 1974 with substantially reduced funding.

14. The Comprehensive Employment and Training Act of 1973, reorganized administratively manpower programs and developed some new programs. The Comprehensive Employment and Training Act (CETA) consisted of the following:

1.	Title I - Nationwide program of comprehensive local services, including training, employment, counseling and testing.

2.	Title II - Programs for transitional public service employment.

3.	Title III - National sponsored training, employment and job placement programs for special groups. Some examples of programs include Skill Training Improvement Program (SKIP), Indian and Native American Employment and Training Program (INAETP), youth programs, migrant worker programs, Help Through Industry Retraining and Employment Program (HIRE).

4.	Title IV - Reestablished the Job Corp Program.

5.	Title V - Established a national Commission for Manpower Policy.

6.	Title VI - Established countercyclical Public Service Employment Programs, programs for disabled, veterans, ex-offenders.

7.	Title VII - Established private sector opportunity for the economically disadvantaged. Examples of programs include the Private Sector Initiative Program (PSIP) which replaced the 1968 Opportunities in the Business Sector Program (JOBS).

8.	Title VIII - established a Young Adult Conservation Corps (YACC).

Amendments of the Act in 1977, consolidated programs from Titles I and II into Title II. For details on programs implemented through CETA, the reader is referred to special reports of the Department of Labor. The 1981 federal budget, had reduced part of the training programs under CETA, specifically, programs under Titles II and III. In 1982 the Job Training and Partnership Act (JTPA) replaced CETA as a program.

15. Examples of major professional organizations in employment counseling include the following: National Vocational Guidance Association, (NVGA 5999 Stevenson Ave., Alexandria, Virginia 22304; The National Employment Counselors Association (NECA) at the same address and the American Association for Counseling and Development, 5999 Stevenson Ave., Alexandria, Virginia 22304. Accreditation of counselor

programs is the responsibility of the association for Counselor Education and Supervision (ACES), a division of the American Association for Counseling and Development.

An example of major professional organizations in manpower development include the Association of Training and Employment Professionals, P.O. Box 221, 100 Bidwell Road, South Windsor, Connecticut 06074 and National Employment and Training Association, P.O. Box 1773, Upland, California 91786.

An association which represents the private employment agency is the National Association of Personnel Consultants 1432 Duke Street, Alexandria, Virginia 22314.

16. Since the history of vocational education and that of teaching was discussed in Chapter 8 Education Network, no discussion of vocational education is included in this chapter.

17. For further information on social work in the employment and manpower network the reader is referred to the National Association of Social Workers, 7981 Eastern Avenue, Silver Spring, Maryland 20910 or the local chapter of the National Association of Social Workers.

SUGGESTED READINGS

Bernard Anderson. The Opportunities Industrialization Center: A Decade of Community Based Manpower Programs. Philadelphia, PA: University of Pennsylvania, 1976. For a history of a private manpower development system, this book focusses on the community based type which started in Philadelphia, Pennsylvania.

Joseph Becker. In Aid of the Employed. Baltimore, MD: John Hopkins Press, 1975. For the individual interested in the history of services and programs for the unemployed this is a highly recommended reading.

Walter Friedlander and Robert Apte. Introduction to Social Welfare, 5th Ed. Englewood Cliffs, NJ: Prentice Hall Inc., 1980. This comprehensive textbook has one chapter devoted to employment and manpower and the potential role of social work in that network.

Thomas Martinez. The Human Marketplace: An Examination of
Private Employment Agencies. New Brunswick, NJ: Transaction Books, 1976. For a history and overview of private
employment agencies, this book is an excellent resource.

John McGowan. Counselor Development in American Society.
Washington, DC: U.S. Government Printing Office, 1975.
This publication presents a general history of the
development of counseling as a profession and is an
excellent resource book.

Stanley Ruttenberg and Jocelyn Gutchess. The Federal State
Employment Service: A Critique. Baltimore, MD: John
Hopkins Press, 1970. Although dated, this book is a sound
analysis of the state and federal employment service and
highlights many of the conflicts and issues of this joint
state and federal program. This book, in addition, provides
the reader with numerous other resource materials.

John Williamson. Strategies Against Poverty in America. New
York, NY: John Wiley and Sons, 1975. This book provides a
general overview of programs to alleviate poverty which
includes comprehensive chapters on employment and manpower
programs.

REFERENCES

Adams, Leonard. The Public Employment Service in Transition,
1933-1968. Ithaca, New York: Cornell University Press,
1969.

Anderson, Bernard. The Opportunities Industrialization
Centers: A Decade of Community Based Manpower Services,
Philadelphia, Penn: University of Pennsylvania, 1976.

Becker, Joseph. In Aid of the Unemployed. Baltimore,
Maryland: John Hopkins Press, 1965.

Cassell, Frank. The Public Employment Service: Organization in
Change. Washington D.C.: Center for Manpower Policy
Studies, 1968.

Claque, Ewan and Leo Kramer. Manpower Policies and Programs: A
Review of 1963-75. Kalamazoo, Michigan: W.E. Upjohn
Institute for Employment Research, 1976.

Council of State Governments. Book of the States: 1984-85 Vol. 27. Lexington, KY: Council of State Governments, 1984.

Department of Labor. Employment and Training Report of the President. Washington, D.C.: U.S. Government Printing Office, 1979.

Ferman, Louis, Joyce Kornbluh and Alan Haber. Poverty in America. Ann Arbor, Michigan: University of Michigan Press, 1965.

Friedlander, Walter and Robert Apte. Introduction to Social Welfare, 5th Edition. Englewood Cliffs, NJ: Prentice Hall, Inc., 1980.

Gordon, Robert. Toward a Manpower Policy. New York, New York: John Wiley and Sons, 1967.

Haber, William and Daniel Krueger. The Role of the United States Employment Services in a Changing Society. Kalamazoo, MI: W.E. Upjohn Institute for Employment Research, 1964.

Harper, Maxwell and Arthur Pell. Starting and Managing an Employment Agency. Washington D.C.: U.S. Government Printing Office, 1971.

Hoos, Ida. Retraining the Work Force. Berkeley, CA: University of California Press, 1967.

Mangum, Garth. Employability, Employment and Income. Salt Lake City, UT: Olympus Publishing, 1976.

Martinez, Thomas. The Human Marketplace: An Examination of Private Employment Agencies. New Brunswick, NJ: Transaction Books, 1976.

McGowan, John. Counselor Development in American Society. Washington, D.C.: U.S. Government Printing Office, 1975.

Minahan, Anne (Ed.). Encyclopedia of Social Work. 18th Issue. Washington, D.C.: National Association of Social Workers, 1986.

Office of the Federal Register. United States Government Manual, 1985/86. Washington D.C.: U.S. Government Printing Office, 1985.

Ruttenberg, Stanley and Jocelyn Gutchess. The Federal State Employment Service: A Critique. Baltimore, Maryland: John Hopkins Press, 1970.

Somers, Herald. Retraining the Unemployed. Madison, Wisconsin: University of Wisconsin Press, 1968.

State Department of Education. Guidelines for Employment Counseling and Placement. Richmond, Virginia: State Department of Education, 1976.

United States Department of Commerce, Bureau of the Census, Public Employment in 1984, Washington D.C.: U.S. Government Printing Office, 1985.

United States Department of Commerce, Bureau of the Census, 1982 Census of Service Industries, Washington, D.C.: U.S. Government Printing Office, 1984.

United States Department of Commerce, Bureau of the Census. Statistical Abstract of the United States: 1986 (106th Edition). Washington, D.C.: U.S. Government Printing Office, 1985.

United States Department of Labor, Bureau of Labor Statistics, Occupational Outlook Handbook 1986/87, Washington D.C.: U.S. Government Printing Office, 1986.

United States Department of Labor, Bureau of Labor Statistics, Handbook of Labor Statistics: 1984, Washington D.C.: U.S. Government Printing Office, 1985.

United States Department of Labor, Bureau of Labor Statistics, Job Seeking Methods Used by American Workers, Washington, D.C.: U.S. Government Printing Office, 1975.

Wilcox, Claire. Toward Social Welfare. Homewood, IL: Richard D. Irwin Company, 1968.

Williamson, John. Strategies Against Poverty in America. New York, New York: John Wiley & Sons, 1975.

Wisconsin Legislative Reference Bureau. Wisconsin Blue Book 1985/86, Madison, WI: Department of Administration, 1985.

CHAPTER 18

HOUSING NETWORK*

We believe that there is a need for substantially more
public housing, but we believe that the emphasis of
the program should be changed from the traditional
publicly-built, slum based, high-rise project to
smaller units on scattered sites. Where traditional
high rise projects are constructed, facilities for
social services should be included in the design, and
a broad range of such services provided for tenants."
(Wicker:1968:478)

INTRODUCTION

The housing network in the United States consists primarily
of establishments operating in the private sector of the economy
with only about 2.3 percent of all housing units operated and
built by a governmental unit. Adequate housing which meets
housing and sanitary codes has been the objective of various
levels of government since 1935.

In spite of advances made in the enforcement of housing
codes and regulations, there are still sizeable pockets of
substandard housing particularly in central cities and in rural
areas. In 1983, it was estimated that 26 percent of occupied
housing units were built since 1970, 35.1 percent between
1950-1970, 9 percent between 1940 and 1950 and the remaining
29.9 percent before 1940. Strides have been made in providing
adequate housing when one compares 1940 to 1983. For example,
in 1940, 44.6 percent of all housing units had inadequate or no
plumbing facilities, and in 1983, this figure was reduced to
2.4 percent, or in 1940 20 percent of dwelling units had more
than 1 person per room as an average in comparison to 5 percent
in 1983.

Adequacy of housing varies from population group to population group. If you look at plumbing (having water and indoor
bathroom), in 1980, 1.7 percent of dwellings occupied by whites
lacked such facilities, in comparison to 10.8 percent of Native
Americans and 5.5 percent of Blacks. Conveniences most of us
take for granted in 1980 are lacking in a surprising number of
dwellings: 16.4 percent lacked running water, 26 percent of
dwellings lacked a sewer system, 17.2 percent do not have central heating, .8 percent do not have a kitchen, and 7.1 percent
do not have a telephone. A major concern in the housing network
is the average age of some of the dwellings, 29.9 percent were
built prior to 1940, and the potential cost to maintain these

dwellings in compliance with more strict housing codes and regulations is high.

Although not discussed in this chapter, a significant and growing problem is the number of "homeless individuals and families" who live off of or on the streets, in emergency shelters, cars, tents, etc. Estimates of this population group vary from 1 million to 2 million individuals. For example, a family in Racine, Wisconsin, lived in a car and tent for six months since the father was unemployed and the family did not want to accept public assistance payments (Milwaukee Journal, 5/16/85).

The focus of this chapter is on low-rent public housing which has developed since 1935. The use of social services in public low rent housing projects is discussed, along with the use of human service occupations and professions including urban planning, architecture, housing managers and social work.

SIZE

The housing network in the United States consists of public low-rent housing (housing projects), private and commercial housing, such as single family dwellings, duplexes, apartment buildings, condominiums, cooperatives, etc. In 1984 the housing network in the United States consisted of an estimated 93.5 million housing units, which employed an estimated 4.3 million individuals (97 percent in construction and related trades), had expenditures estimated at 146.3 billion dollars, and served the entire population of 236 million people. Figure 18-1 shows the estimated size of the housing network. Of the 93.5 million housing units in 1983, 98 percent were year-round units and 2 percent seasonal units. Of the 91,675,000 year-round units, 59.7 percent were owner occupied, 32.7 percent were rental occupied and 7.6 percent were vacant (for sale or rent).[1]

Our concern is low-rent public housing. In 1984 there were an estimated 2.1 million low-rent public housing units (2.3 percent of the total housing units), which employed an estimated 111,393 individuals, had expenditures estimated at 9.0 billion dollars and served an estimated 3.6 million individuals, or 1.4 percent of the population. In 1982 there were an estimated 10,000 housing projects in the United States under the jurisdiction of 2,700 local public housing authorities.

Public housing units focus on the lower income and elderly populations. In 1982, 5.2 million individuals in public housing projects represented 139,667 families of which, 73 percent were receiving public welfare, 33 percent were elderly, 43 percent were white, 42 percent were black, 10 percent Spanish, 2.5 percent Native American and 2.5 percent Asian. The majority of

ESTIMATED SIZE OF THE HOUSING NETWORK in 1983-84*

Selected Characteristic	Type of Housing		Total
	Public[1]	Private/Commercial	
Number of Housing Units	2,180,000	91,339,000	93,519,000
Number of Employees	111,393	275,000 [2]	4,386,393
Expenditures (Dollars)	9,090,000,000	137,240,000,000	146,300,000,000
Population Served (Number)	3,668,000	232,332,000	236,000,000

*Adapted from: United States Department of Commerce, Bureau of the Census, Statistical Abstract of the United States: 1986 (106th Edition), Washington, D.C.: U.S. Government Printing Office 1985, pp. 325, 354, 355, 719, 729, 732-735,; United States Department of Housing and Urban Development, Problems Affecting Low Rent Families, Washington, D.C.: U.S. Government Printing Office, 1979 and United States Department of Commerce, Bureau of the Census, Public Employment in 1984, Washington, D.C.: U.S. Government Printing Office, 1985, p. 3.

1. There are an estimated 10,000 public housing projects, under the jurisdiction of 2,700 Public Housing Authorities.
2. Construction and other specialized builders.

the public housing projects are family oriented, 70 percent, and 30 percent focus specifically on the elderly.[2]

HISTORICAL DEVELOPMENT

Housing as a social problem is closely linked to the development of cities, specifically urban centers. In general, as societies responded to housing as a problem, three different aspects of housing became a concern: city and urban planning, housing codes, and public low-rent housing. Figure 18-2 shows a historical time line of planning, housing codes, and public low-rent housing.

CITY and URBAN PLANNING

City and urban planning, up until the early 1900s, was closely linked to the profession of architecture. Architecture as an occupation and profession has been in existence since the time of Imahotep, in Egypt (2700 B.C.). There was a close affiliation of architecture with the arts (sculpture, painting) during the Renassance of the 1400-1600's and with engineering until the 1720's. Although planning as a distinct profession did not emerge until the 20th century, there was historically a profession of a planner/architect/engineer.

CLASSICAL SOCIETY - PRE 450 - Early civilizations planned their cities along water ways and transportation routes, usually on a grid system or a geometric design with temples, a public plaza, and other public buildings as the central part of the city. Examples of these early planner/architects include Hippodramus of Miletus in Greece (500 B.C.), Ictanus in Greece (47 B.C.) who designed the Parthenon and Philon in Greece (330 B.C.). The Romans continued the planning tradition of the Greeks adding public auditoriums, large boulevards and scattered public plazas under planner/architects, such as Vitruvius (25 B.C.), Severius (60 A.D.) and Appollodarus (100 A.D.). The planner/architect/engineer was a respected individual and ranked high in the socioeconomic order. The classical civilizations, at least in the public arena, did have some notions of hygiene, sanitation, and housing codes.

MEDIEVAL EUROPE - 450-1500 A.D. - With the decline of the Roman empire and the development of the feudal system with small independent city states, the status of the planner/architect declined to that of a craftsman. The grid system was used to build the cities with a wall built around the city for protection. The church, public mall, and other public buildings were the central part of the city. Little concern was shown for housing and sanitation codes. The city, like classical times (Greece and Rome), consisted of merchants, tradesmen, religious

578

Figure 18-2

HISTORICAL TIME LINE of the HOUSING NETWORK

	City and Urban Planning	Housing Standards and Codes	Public Low-Rent Housing
2,700 BC	Egypt - architect/planners		
500 BC	(Architect/Planners) Greece - **Hippodramus**	500 BC-Sanitation and Health Codes for	
47 BC	Greece Ictanus (Architect/Planners)	Cities in Greece	
25 - 100 AD	Rome - Vitruvius Severius Appolodarus	100 AD-Sanitation and Housing Codes for Rome	
450 - 1500 AD	Medieval Europe (Architect/Planners/ Engineers) City State-Central Plazas		
1500 - 1600	Renaissance Europe (Artist/Architect/ Planners) Brunelleschi, Rafael, Filippe Alberti, Michelangelo		
1771	Engineering/Planners		
1798	Architect/Planners		
1857	American Institute of Architecture	1867-New York City Code San Francisco Code 1879-New York Code	
1901	First City Planning Board Hartford, Conn.	1894-National Municipal League	1918-War Laborer Housing
1903	City Plan-Cleveland Ohio	1919-Most Large Cities	1919-Milwauke, Wis.
1909	Landscape Architecure Course (Frederick Olmsted, Jr.)	Have Codes	
1917	American City Planning Institute		
1929	School of City Planning		1932-Emergency Relief Act.
1935	Greenbelt Towns		1934-Housing Act
1954	Housing Act 1954		1937-Public Housing 1949-Project Housing 1956-National Assoc. of Housing and Redevelopment Officials 1954-Urban Renewal 1963-Tenants Union 1966-Model Cities Act 1968-Neighborhood Development Program 1978-Housing Voucher Program 1986-Budget Reduction

and political leaders, with the majority of the common people living outside the city. The period of the Renaissance (1400-1600), was one of building large plazas, public buildings, cathedrals, etc., with many of the planners having an architecture or art background. Some examples of these individuals were Filippi Brunelleschi (1377-1446), Rafael (1483-1520), Michelangelo (1475-1564) and Leon Alberti (1404-1472). Planning was seen as part of the world of the architect and the architect was partly concerned about the development of an aesthetic product, i.e. the arts.

EARLY INDUSTRIAL - From 1600-1800 there was a slow differentiation of the planner and architect as a profession from both the professions of art and engineering. Separate organizations were established for engineering in 1771, i.e., civil engineering and mechanical engineering (1793). An architecture club was established in Paris, France in 1791, with a school for architecture established in 1798 known as the Ecole Nationale et Special des Beau Arts. Architect/planners were primarily concerned with plazas, public buildings, and malls, and not with private housing and its development, nor the social needs of the population of a city.

1800 ON - The 19th century, and its changing economic base from agriculture to industry, resulted in the rise of a new type of city. Workers needed to live close to the place of employment which was usually located in the center of the city adjacent to rivers, or transportation routes which resulted in population density and overcrowding. The development of railroad car tenements (five to six stories high with no sanitation, limited health or space provisions) and a lack of recreation or open space began to cause a series of health problems. The merchants and more wealthy individuals tended to move away from the city to the suburbs. In response to a neglect of the problems of urban centers, planners and landscape architects began to incorporate parks, open spaces, into planning proposals, as well as, greenbelt areas (parkways surrounding and interspersed in a city), the concept of new towns (planned cities), garden cities (designed space usage), and single family and duplex family structures into city plans.

By 1900, planner/architects, such as Frederick Olmsted, Jr. and Daniel Burnham were quickly developing the foundation for a planning profession. Burnham developed comprehensive city plans for Cleveland, Ohio in 1903 and Chicago, Illinois (1909).

The first local board for city planning was established in Hartford, Connecticut in 1901 followed swiftly with the establishment of planning boards in other cities, such as Milwaukee, Wisconsin (1909). Planners, as a profession, organized the

American City Planning Institute in 1917 which became the American Institute of Planning in 1939. During the Depression of the 1930s planners became involved in the development of greenbelt towns, such as Greendale, Wisconsin, under the Resettlement Administration Act of 1935 and in the development of pubic housing in 1937. The major impetus for expansion of the planning profession was the Housing Act of 1954 which provided federal matching funds for the development of local planning commissions, and for a comprehensive community plan prior to that community receiving federal funds.

Slowly, planners shifted concepts from public buildings to city plans, to comprehensive city plans (public and private construction), to metropolitan and regional planning. Metropolitan and regional planning is comprehensive focusing on housing, transportation, education, leisure and recreation, social services, health facilities, utilities, sanitation, and social needs. In the broadest sense, planners currently ideally incorporate all aspects of a region's development including the environment.

HOUSING CODES

Development of housing codes and regulation of private housing paralleled the growth of the planning and architecture professions. Until the late 1800s, when problems of crowded cities, such as tenement houses, lack of health facilities, leisure and recreation activities, etc., became apparent, little attention was paid to regulation of housing or the zoning of cities. In the United States, the predominant attitude was that the construction and ownership of housing was a private activity and the state had no right to intervene.

Health and sanitation problems were becoming quite severe in large cities like New York by 1850 and citizen groups were calling for housing reforms. Initial legislation for regulation of housing occurred at the local level, such as the 1867 ordinance in New York which placed limitations on further development of railroad flats, and in San Francisco, California where slaughter houses and other industries were prohibited in certain parts of the city. New York, in 1879, developed minimal standards for the building of tenement housing, i.e. space, sanitation, and light regulations, followed by Boston, Massachusetts, in 1898, which regulated the height of buildings. The National Municipal League was formed in 1894 and this organization early advocated for housing regulations pertaining to health, building codes, and zoning ordinances. By 1900, most large cities began to develop housing codes and zoning ordinances.

A significant period for the establishment of housing codes and zoning was 1901-1909. In 1901, New York established codes for sanitation, air space, light, etc., and in 1909 the United States Supreme Court in <u>Welch vs. Swasey</u> upheld the right of state and local governments to enforce housing codes and zoning restrictions. All areas, urban and rural now have regulations on housing codes and construction and zoning practices for the construction of buildings.

PUBLIC LOW-RENT HOUSING

Historically, housing and its development was the prerogative of private developers and private construction firms. Planning and architecture, until recently, focused on public buildings, transportation systems, and large private developments. Little attention was paid to the housing of common citizens until the urban centers became crowded in the mid-1800s with problems of health, congestion, etc.

In the United States, public housing for low income populations did not develop until the depression of the 1930s. There were early precedents in public housing, such as the federal government provided housing for laborers in war plants (1918), Milwaukee, Wisconsin (1919) developed a joint program between the municipality and a private corporation to build housing, the Emergency Relief and Recovery Act (1932) which provided loans for low-income housing, Housing Act (1937) which provided for low-income housing through the Public Works Administration, and the development of greenbelt cities (spacious lots and numerous parkways) through the Resettlement Administration Act (1934).

Public housing, as we know it, is a consequence of the Housing Act of 1937 which established the United States Housing Authority and provided grants to local governments to establish a public housing authority and housing projects. The emphasis in this early time period was on public housing for the poor and these were built on scattered sites in neighborhoods (using vacant land which was available).

The Housing Act of 1949 changed the focus of low-rent public housing, from scattered site low-income project housing, to slum clearance and urban redevelopment. Slum clearance meant the rebuilding of a small neighborhood and the relocation of many families. The broadened intent of the act was to shift planning from specific projects to revitalization of a neighborhood. The Housing Act of 1954 further expanded the planning concept to include urban renewal with an emphasis on housing projects in conjunction with rehabilitation of an entire section of a city. This Housing Act required citizen participation (in the planning stages) in the housing project and reaffirmed relocation aid as a service.

In the 1960s, there was a shift from large scale high-rise projects to the use of scattered sites, leased housing, and projects for the elderly. Other programs were added, such as Operation Turn-Key (housing built with government money and turned over to private developers for operation), rent supplement (rental allowance for the poor) etc. The Model Cities Act of 1966 provided 80 percent federal funding for redevelopment of entire sections of the city, however, the planning process was to include education, training, employment, rehabilitation, social services, etc. The Model Cities Demonstration Act was to provide a broad range of services for individuals in order to break the cycle of poverty. Since the 1966 Model Cities Act, there have been further extensions of aid to the urban centers, such as the concept of urban homesteading, for a small fee the person buys a house in an impoverished area and agrees to rehabilitate and live in the house.

In addition to federal-local funding for housing projects and other housing related programs, the 1960s was a period of social activism. In 1963, a tenants union was formed in Harlem, New York, which rapidly spread throughout the United States, and by 1969 there were over 700 local Tenants Unions established. A national organization was developed in 1969, called the National Tenants Organization. Tenants unions are concerned with more than public housing, i.e. the range of landlord and tenant problems, however their activities overlap with the concerns of tenants in public housing through their resident councils. The 1980's have seen a reduction of funding for public low rent housing and a reduction of funding in other federally sponsored housing programs.

STRUCTURE

Since the focus of this chapter is on public low-income housing and related programs, the structure presented will focus on this component of the housing network and not on private construction and development. The structure of the housing network has an organizational context, services provided, occupations and professions, and dominant occupations and professions.

ORGANIZATIONAL CONTEXT

Housing programs are implemented through a myriad of federal, state and local agencies. Figure 18-3 shows an abbreviated organization of the Department of Housing and Urban Development and its programs for public and low-income housing.

583

A typical state and local governmental structure for low-income public housing is shown in Figures 18-4 and 18-5.

There are a variety of patterns at the local level for the organization of public housing authorities ranging from an independent standing agency, a part of another related agency or department, to an integrated system which includes urban renewal, city planning, public housing, and other related areas. The model of a local housing authority shown in Figure 18-5 is that of an integrated system.[3]

SERVICES PROVIDED

The housing network has a variety of programs and services directly related to the housing projects for low-income individuals, as well as, encouraging individuals to rehabilitate and own their own housing. Examples of some of the services offered through the housing network are as follows:

- Low-income housing projects
- Urban renewal programs
- Relocation services
- Rent assistance
- Turn-Key programs
- Urban homesteading
- Recreation programs
- Social services (counseling, public welfare, etc.)
- Education and self-help classes
- Day care
- Resident councils
- Special programs for the elderly and disabled
- Physical health services
- Reading and library services
- Hot lunches
- Volunteer help
- Psychological and psychiatric counseling
- Pharmaceutical services
- Legal services

OCCUPATIONS and PROFESSIONS

In the housing network, no specific profession is dominant, however the major ones are urban planners, architects, and housing managers. Depending upon the organization of the specific public housing authority, there is utilization of lawyers, physicians, nurses, guards and security watchmen, social workers, psychologists, housing code enforcement, and public health specialists. Figure 18-6 shows a selected range of human

584

Figure 18-3

Idealized Organization of the Housing Network
at the Federal Level*

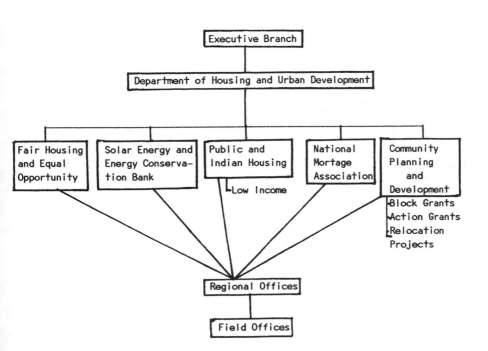

*Source: Adapted from Office of Federal Register, <u>United States Government Manual</u>
<u>1985-86</u>, Washington, D.C.: U.S. Government Printing Office, 1985, p. 843.

585

Figure 18–4

ORGANIZATION OF THE HOUSING NETWORK AT THE STATE LEVEL*

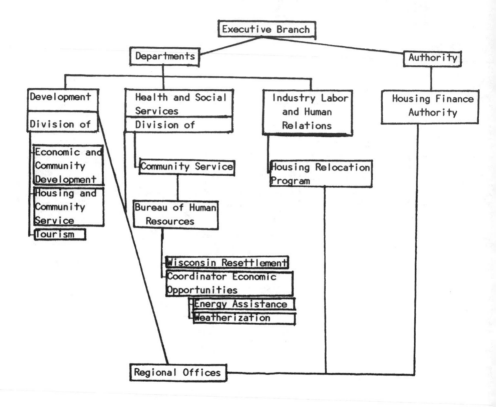

*Source: Adapted from Wisconsin Legislative Reference Bureau, <u>Wisconsin Blue Book</u>, <u>1985–86</u>, Madison, Wisconsin: Department of Administration, 1985, p. 437, 510, 531.

ORGANIZATION OF A TYPICAL PUBLIC HOUSING AUTHORITY PROJECT*

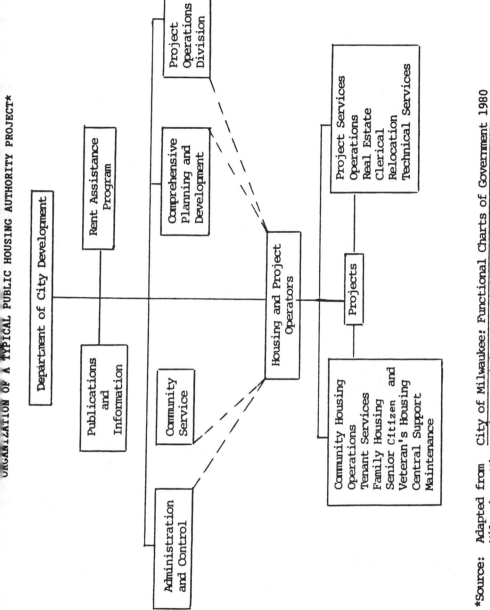

*Source: Adapted from City of Milwaukee: Functional Charts of Government 1980 Milwaukee, Wisconsin: Municipal Reference Library, 1980.

service occupations and professions involved in the public housing network.

DOMINANT OCCUPATIONS and PROFESSIONS

Two professions which are peripheral to human services (see discussion in Chapter 2), such as planning and architecture, are discussed because of their central role in the development of public housing and in planning functions, which at times overlap with the planning function of a social worker. An occupation which is currently seeking professional status is that of the housing manager, which is the occupation most directly related to the implementation of public housing programs. Figure 18-7 shows the employment of planners and architects by industrial classification in 1980.

Approximately 78.9 percent of urban planners are employed in the public administration industrial classification, i.e., governmental planning agencies, and only 1.2 percent in the industrial classification of architectural and engineering firms and the remaining 19.9 percent in other industrial classifications. Architects on the other hand had only 4.8 percent employed in the industrial classification of public administration, 63.2 percent employed in the industrial classifications of architectural and engineering firms and the remaining 32 percent in other industrial classifications.

PLANNING - The planning profession is rather recent in its development and has its roots in landscape architecture. In the United States, Harvard University, under the leadership of Frederick Olmsted, developed the first course in planning in 1909 in the School of Landscape Architecture, the first degree program in planning in 1923, and the first School of City Planning in 1929. There was initially, a slow development of academic programs, i.e., nine by 1949, with a rapid expansion after the 1954 Housing Act. That particular Act provided matching federal funding for the development of local planning commissions to implement the planning process which was mandated in the Housing Act. By 1969, there were over 60 programs in planning.

The profession of planning began to organize early with the establishment of the American City Planning Institute in 1917 (renamed American Institute of Planning in 1939), and the American Society of Planning Officials in 1934. Both of these organizations merged into one organization in 1978.[4] Current educational standards for city and urban planners are a bachelors degree in a related field to qualify for training engineering and public administration. The professional in positions, such as architecture, landscape architecture, civil

Figure 18-6

NUMBER AND PERCENT OF SELECTED HUMAN
SERVICE OCCUPATIONS AND PROFESSIONS EMPLOYED IN THE
INDUSTRIAL CLASSIFICATION OF ADMINISTRATION OF
ENVIRONMENTAL AND HOUSING PROGRAMS IN 1980*

Occupation and Profession	Number	Percent
Housing Manager and Aide	20,000	63.613
Health - other	129	.411
Administrator	4,125	13.121
Protective Service	1,600	5.089
Physician	7	.023
Nurse	20	.064
Social Work and Welfare Aide	210	.667
Dietician	20	.063
Counselor	50	.159
Teacher	500	1.591
Urban Planner	2,055	6.536
Architect	1,017	3.234
Recreation Work	320	1.017
Clergy	10	.033
Lawyer	300	.954
Psychologist	15	.048
Librarian	80	.254
Author/Painter/Dancer	110	.349
Child Care	164	.522
Therapist	15	.048
Personnel/Labor Relations	603	1.918
TOTAL	31,440	100.000

*Source: Adapted from United States Department of Commerce, Bureau of the Census, 1980 Census of Population. Vol. 2 Subject Reports, Part 7C: Occupation by Industry, Washington, D.C.: U.S. Government Printing Office, 1984, pp. 295-664 and United States Department of Commerce, Bureau of the Census, Public Employment in 1984, Washington, D.C.: U.S. Government Printing Office, 1985, p. 3.

The estimate for human service personnel in the housing network is derived from using figures from Public Employment 1984 and estimating the number of individuals who would be employed in the industrial classification of administration of environmental and housing programs. The estimates used to derive a figure was 20 percent of employees in housing, 35 percent in environment protection and 45 percent in leisure and recreation.

589

Figure 18-7

NUMBER AND PERCENT OF URBAN PLANNERS AND ARCHITECTS EMPLOYED BY
INDUSTRIAL CLASSIFICATION IN 1980*

Industrial Classification	Urban Planner Number	Percent	Architects Number	Percent
Agriculture/Fishery/Forestry	13	.100	17,010	16.188
Mining	6	.046	89	.085
Construction	98	.753	4,545	4.325
Manufacturing	113	.868	1,716	1.632
Transportation/Communication/ Public Utilities	145	1.113	1,126	1.072
Wholesale/Retail Trade	35	.269	1,865	1.775
Finances/Real Estate	324	2.488	2,877	2.738
Business/Repair	531	4.077	853	.811
Entertainment/Recreation	13	.100	164	.156
Personal Services	1	.008	162	.154
Professional and Related	1,307	10.036	3,124	2.973
Architectural/Engineering	159	1.220	66,463	63.251
Public Administration	10,278	78.922	5,085	4.840
TOTAL	13,023	100.000	105,079	100.000

*Source: Adapted from United States Department of Commerce, Bureau of the Census, 1980 Census of Population. Vol. 2 Subject Reports, Part 7C: Occupation by Industry, Washington, D.C.: Government Printing Office, 1984, pp. 294-664.

planning usually has a masters degree in planning. Certification procedures for planning are changing. For example, New Jersey in 1962 began to require state certification for planners.

The urban planner has responsibility for comprehensive planning of a city, metropolitan and regional geographical area which includes the following services:

- Utilities
- Transportation
- Health

590

- Social services
- Zoning
- Subdivisions
- Recreation
- Leisure
- Cultural activities
- Industrial growth
- Housing
- Education.

The planner should be able to develop a general global model for the development of an entire city, metropolitan area, or geographical region. Some planners are more sensitive to social needs than others, and some planners have used citizen participation and social workers to assess the needs of a community. Part of the task of the planner is to develop models for the coordination of various services within a community.

ARCHITECTURE--Architecture as a professional group, has been in existence since at least 2700 B.C., however educational standards and a university education is a more recent development. In the United States, the American Institute of Architecture as a professional association, was established in 1857, with the first school of architecture developed at the Massachusetts Institute of Technology in 1868.[5] Licensing of architects was first used in Illinois (1897) and in 1902 the American Institute of Architects established the standard of graduation from an approved school and/or passage of the National Architectural Accrediting Board Exam.

Currently, an individual interested in architecture can enter the profession through one of three routes: general liberal arts college for three years then two years of architecture school, graduation from a school of architecture and practice/experience. In all three situations, it is necessary for the individual to pass the examination of the National Architectural Accrediting Board. It is significant that architecture is primarily practiced in private offices (68 percent), which means that an individual from high school could learn the trade through a period of employment and/or experience in a private firm.

The role of the architect has some similarity to that of the planner except more emphasis is placed on the design and landscaping aspect of specific buildings and geographical areas. The architect usually performs the following functions:

- Design of building
- Design of malls, parks

- Landscaping design
- Plans for a city, metropolitan area
- Design of transportation routes
- Overall plan in addressing social service needs in design plans
- Public relations in a community in support of overall planning.

In some schools of architecture there is an emphasis on incorporating social needs into design plans.[6]

HOUSING MANAGER - The public housing authorities have developed a specialized career line in housing management to implement on a daily basis housing programs. The first courses taught in housing management were in 1945, and the first degree program in housing management was at Temple University in Pennsylvania. Like other occupations, there were early attempts to organize into professional groups, such as the National Association of Housing and Redevelopment Officials established in 1933.[7] There are an estimated 10,000 housing managers in the United States. The preferred degree in higher positions is a bachelors degree in housing management, plus experience. Currently there are certificate programs for housing managers, bachelor's programs and master's programs, such as the master's in urban affairs from Old Dominion University, Norfolk, Virginia. A description of career lines in housing management is outlined in "Professional Career Systems in Housing Management," (1979). This document indicates general career lines ranging from those having no education to those with a university degree and describes the following positions: housing management aide, management trainee, assistant housing manager, housing manager, assistant director of housing management and director of housing management.

These career lines in housing management attempt to provide nonprofessional and professional positions. Instead of describing the tasks at each level, an example of the role of the nonprofessional, i.e. the housing management aide, and the professional housing manager and assistant director positions, are used for illustrative purposes.

The functions of a housing management aide includes the following:

- Visit project residents to explore their social interests and suggest the use of community facilities when necessary
- Assist in coordination of all the programs in the project
- Assist residents in utilizing community health and welfare services

- Schedules the use of community activity facilities
- Monitors the need for physical repair and maintenance of facilities
- Maintains files of records and reports
- Works with the resident council
- Recommends to the housing manager specific ways to solve problems as needed.

The functions of a housing manager include the following:

- Plan, assign and review the work of the housing management aides
- Train employees in duties and responsibilities
- Conducts staff meetings
- Interviews prospective residents
- Shows units to prospective residents
- Completes necessary forms for the project
- Prepares necessary reports
- Inspects the project on a periodic basis
- Deals with problems within the unit.

The functions of the assistant director of housing includes the following:

- inspects the various projects
- arranges for the transfer of personnel to various projects
- reviews the work of subordinates
- handles problems which cannot be resolved by other individuals
- prepares various reports
- develops recommendations for improving operating procedures
- participates in the development of new plans and procedures designed to improve project management.[8]

SOCIAL WORK

The number of social workers and aides employed in the housing network is estimated at approximately 210 in 1980 (see Figure 18-6). Social workers early became involved in housing as a social problem both as reformers in the early 1900s and as direct service workers providing social services under a project's community services division. Examples of some early individuals in social work involved in housing include Octavia Hill and Jane Adams. The social worker can be employed in a public housing project or depending upon their specific skills could become more involved in the area of social planning.

PUBLIC HOUSING

The tasks of a social worker in a public housing project are described by David Preston (Social Work, 1964). He describes the role of the social worker in both direct and indirect services. Direct services include social assessments, short-term casework, long-term casework, relocation problems, group work skills with recreation activities, and community organization skills in working with the resident councils and tenant unions. Indirect skills would include staff development, consultation, planning and advocating for changes in various policies.

SOCIAL PLANNING

Frank So in "The Practice of Local Government Planning," (1979), discusses what is called social planning. Social planning involves both policy development, the coordination of human services systems, establishment of management by objective programs (MBO), planning through the process of planning programming and budget systems (PPBS), as well as using the sensitivity of social workers to alert physical planners to the social needs of a population. So indicates that for social planning, individuals should have a high degree of sensitivity to the needs of others and subsequently concludes that social planning is one aspect of social work education. Social workers who are interested in the planning aspect of a community should develop a closer linkage with schools of architecture and schools of planning.

PERSONAL SOCIAL SERVICES

The housing network, like other societal networks has personal social service programs (see Chapter 22 Personal Social Service). Some examples of organizations or programs which provide personal social services in the housing network include the following:

PROTECTIVE SERVICES

A department of social services liaison person who goes to the housing project, such as Chicago, Illinois and Milwaukee, Wisconsin.

UTILITARIAN SERVICES

A homemaker who goes to the housing project through the sponsorship of the local social service department, such as Milwaukee, Wisconsin.

DEVELOPMENTAL and SOCIALIZATION SERVICES

A social worker who goes to the housing project to council an unwed mother or the elderly, such as St. Louis, Missouri and San Francisco, California.

REHABILITATIVE and THERAPEUTIC SERVICES

An alcohol and drug counselor who goes to the housing project, such as San Francisco, California and New York, New York.

SPECIAL POPULATIONS

The focus of low-rent public housing is on the poor, minorities and elderly, consequently a large percentage of their clientele consists of what is referred to as special populations (see Chapter 25 Special Populations and Chapter 24 Rehabilitation). Some examples of organizations which focus on special populations and the housing network include the following:

ASIAN

Support group organized by a resident council in a housing project and organizations, such as the Asian Neighborhood Design, San Francisco, California; Indochinese Assistance Center, Sacramento, California and Chinese Community Housing Corporation, San Francisco, California.

BLACK

Support group organized by a resident council in a housing project and organizations, such as the Delta Housing Development Corporation, Indianola, Mississippi; Neighborhood Institute, Chicago, Illinois and Neighborhood Housing Services, Pittsburg, Pennsylvania.

EUROPEAN ETHNIC

Support group organized around a specific population, such as the Americans for Czechoslovak Refugees, New York, New York; Jewish Association for the Aged, New York, New York and Mennonite Disaster Service, Akron, Pennsylvania.

NATIVE AMERICAN

Support group organized by a resident council in a housing project and organizations, such as the Miccosukee Tribe of Indians of Florida, Miami, Florida; American Indian Center, Fort

Worth, Texas and Kalakilegoning Indian Community Council, Watersmeet, Michigan.

SAME SEX PREFERENCE

Support group organized by a resident council and organizations, such as the Homosexual Community Counseling Center, New York, New York and Lesbian Resource Center, Minneapolis, Minnesota.

SPANISH SPEAKING

Support group organized by a resident council in a housing project and organizations, such as the Chicano Affairs Center, Eugene, Oregon; Hispanos En Minnesota, St. Paul, Minnesota and Eastern Farmworkers Association, Bellport, New York.

WOMEN

Support group organized by a resident council and organizations, such as the Women's Law Fund, Cleveland, Ohio and National Organization for Women, Chicago, Illinois.

ISSUES

The United States should review the focus of planning which historically has been on the physical or structural aspects of planning. It is obvious that the environmental impact of various projects are going to be of more concern, especially since the passage of recent legislation on environment, such as 1974 and 1979, and greater attention needs to be paid to systems of rapid transportation as envisioned in the 1972 Transportation Act. Specifically, there are some issues which must be faced by the planning, architecture, housing management and social work professions.

PLANNING

For the planning profession, some of the issues are: planning for the immediate future versus the long range future, incremental planning versus comprehensive planning, public versus private decision-making, local planning versus interdependence of various regions and legal problems as they relate to the planning perspective. The planning profession should pay more attention to the social psychological needs of the community and clientele which they are serving.

ARCHITECTURE

Architecture as it continues in the combined role of architect and planner, has some of the same problems and issues that
the professional planner faces. That is, the social psychological aspect of the models and designs they are developing, legal
concerns, localism versus regional interdependence, incremental
versus comprehensive planning, immediate goals, long-range
goals, etc.

HOUSING MANAGER

Housing management as a career, is striving for professional
status. The requirements for a housing management position
include content and skill in property and real estate management
which is not oriented toward the resolution of interpersonal
problems amongst the residents. Consequently, in their strive
for professional status, housing managers should be aware of the
differences between their tasks and duties as they relate to
other helping professions, such as social work in the area of
interpersonal counseling. Problems of housing projects have
been well articulated in a document by the Department of Housing
and Urban Development entitled "Problems Affecting Low-Rent
Public Housing Projects," (1979). These problems range from
selection and screening of residents for the project, discipline
and behavior problems, security problems, inadequate facilities
and lack of funding.

SOCIAL WORK

Social work has had a limited role in the area of housing,
however the potential need for direct services and indirect
services is rather obvious. Social work education should
incorporate more curriculum content in the area of housing to
encourage individuals to take an interest in the area and to
understand the roles of the planner, architect and housing
manager. An under-utilized area for social work education is
the combination of social work/planner. Social workers should
establish liaison with the profession of planning and the
profession of architecture to see where there are overlapping
and potential roles for them in social planning. Many social
workers view social planning from the clinical perspective of
organizing groups and changing policies, but have not adequately
perceived a different level of planning in conjunction with
planners and architects.

SUMMARY

Housing as a social problem is a product of the Industrial
Revolution with the changing function of the city becoming the

597

living place for workers near their place of employment, and resultant problems of overcrowding, health and sanitation problems. The housing network in the United States actually consists of primarily private and commercial housing, and a small percentage of low-rent public housing. Within the housing network, there are an estimated 2.1 million low-rent public housing units accounting for approximately 2.3 percent of the total housing units in the United States. Public housing is implemented through 10,000 housing projects under the jurisdiction of 2,700 public housing authorities.

In reviewing the development of the housing network, it is apparent there are three related aspects of housing; city and urban planning, housing standards and codes and public low-rent housing. The planning profession is a relatively new profession developing out of landscape architecture in the early 1900s. Architecture, as a profession, has been in existence since at least, 2700 B.C. and there are numerous examples of a combination planner/architect/engineer. Architecture as a profession became autonomous from engineering in the early 1700s and then planning emerged from architecture in approximately 1900-1909. Housing codes and their development paralleled the growth of city planning in that prior to 1900 there were few cities that established any codes for housing. The first housing regulation was in New York in 1867 which placed limitations on the development of railroad flats. In 1879 New York had developed standards for construction, i.e. space, sanitation, light, etc. By 1900, most large cities had developed housing codes and zoning ordinances.

Public housing is essentially a product of the depression of the 1930s through the Housing Acts of 1934 and 1937. There were early precedents for public housing, such as the federal government providing housing for laborers in war plants (1918), and Milwaukee, Wisconsin (1919) which developed a joint housing program between the municipality and private corporations. There were further expansions of housing programs with the concept of urban renewal and public housing through acts passed in 1949, 1954, the Model Cities Demonstration Act of 1966, Neighborhood Development Act of 1968, and the Housing Voucher Program in 1978.

A range of professions are involved in the housing network and those selected for further analysis were those of planning, architecture, and housing management. Each of these professions was discussed in terms of their development, current educational standards and general roles and tasks they perform. The role of social work was then described both in terms of working for a public housing authority, providing direct and indirect services and the potential role of social work in the planning process.

Issues in the area of housing were briefly discussed in each of the areas of planning, architecture, housing management, and social work. Some of the issues faced by the planner are very similar to those faced by the architect, such as the concept of incremental versus comprehensive planning, short-term planning versus long-range planning, local responsibility versus regional interdependence, etc.

FOOTNOTES

*This chapter was discussed with Fred Cox, Dean, School of Social Welfare, University of Wisconsin-Milwaukee.

[1]Overall statistics for the housing network were taken from United States Department of Commerce, Bureau of the Census, Statistical Abstract of the United States: 1986 (106th Edition), Washington, D.C.: U.S. Government Printing Office, 1985, pp. 325, 354, 355, 719, 729, 732-735; Department of Commerce, Bureau of the Census, 1980 Census of Housing: United States Summary, Washington, D.C.: U.S. Government Printing Office, 1983, p. 1-8; Department of Commerce, Bureau of the Cenus, 1980 Census of Housing Summary of Detailed Housing Characteristics, Washington, D.C.: U.S. Government Printing Office, 1983, p. 1-8, 10, 11, 12 and United States Department of Commerce, Bureau of the Census, Public Employment in 1984, Washington, D.C.: U.S. Government Printing Office, 1985, p. 3.

[2]Estimates on the size of the public housing system were taken from the Department of Housing and Urban Development, Crime in Public Housing, Washington, D.C.: U.S. Government Printing Office, 1978 and various summary reports of the Department of Housing and Urban Development. An additional publication which will be helpful to the reader in understanding public housing is the publication by the Department of Housing and Urban Development, Problems Affecting Low-Rent Public Housing, Washington, D.C.: U.S. Government Printing Office, 1979.

[3]In addition to the formal organization for housing, an informal or folk system exists for rehabilitating individual houses. For example, numerous individuals in the Amish community will respond and replace a barn or a house in 1 to 2 days. That is, one can use family members, relatives, neighbors, friends and even the community to handle housing needs.

[4]Examples of professional associations for city and urban planners are the American Institute of Planners, 1776 Massachusetts Avenue, N.W., Washington, D.C. 20036 and the American Society of Planning Officials, 1313 East 60th Street, Chicago, Illinois 60637.

[5]Examples of professional associations for architecture are the American Institute of Architecture, 1735 New York Avenue, N.W., Washington, D.C. 20006 and the American Society of Landscape Architecture, 1750 Old Meadow Road, McLean, Virginia 12201.

[6]The School of Architecture at the University of Wisconsin-Milwaukee has courses on social problems, human service needs, and social planning. This is one of the schools of architecture which has attempted to create a balance between social and physical planning.

[7]Examples of professional organizations in housing and community development include: the National Association of Housing and Redevelopment Officials, 1320 18th St. N.W., Washington, D.C. 20036; National Association for Community Development, 1424 16th Street, N.W., Washington, D.C. 20036; National Tenants Organization, 425 13th Street, N.W., Washington, D.C. 20004; National Center for Housing Management, 1228 M Street N.W., Washington, D.C. 20005; National Federation of Housing Counselors, 2700 Ontario Road N.W., Washington, D.C. 20007; Public Housing Authority Director's Association, Hall of the States, 444 N. Capital Street N.W., Suite 403, Washington, D.C. 20001 and Low Income Housing Information Service, 323 Eighth Street, Washington, D.C. 20002.

[8]Other occupational and professional groups, such as housing code enforcers, public health specialists, and Department of Housing and Urban Development employees, were not discussed in this chapter as a matter of expediency.

[9]For information on social work and the housing network the reader is referred to the National Association of Social Workers, 7981 Eastern Avenue, Silver Spring, Maryland 20910 or the local chapter of the National Association of Social Workers.

SUGGESTED READINGS

Glen Beyer. Housing and Society New York, New York: Macmillan Press, 1965. For a history of housing this book although dated is a good resource. The book provides an overview of housing styles as well as social policies affecting housing.

600

Walter Friedlander and Robert Apte. Introduction to Social Welfare. 5th Ed. Englewood Cliffs, New Jersey: Prentice Hall Inc. 1980. This standard textbook in social welfare has one chapter devoted to housing and the role of social work in the housing network.

Spiro Kostaff. The Architect: Chapters in the History of the Profession. New York, New York: Oxford University Press, 1977. For the individual interested in the history of professions, this is an excellent resource for the history of architecture.

David Preston. "Human Dimensions in Public Housing". Social Work Vol. 19, No. 1 (January 1964), pp 29-37. This brief article although dated provides a brief description of the role of social work in the housing network.

United States Department of Housing and Urban Development, Professional Career Patterns in Housing Management, Washington, D.C.: U.S. Government Printing Office, 1979. This government publication describes the variety of careers in housing and is a useful publication for an individual not acquainted with these areas of employment.

United States Department of Housing and Urban Development, The Manager and Social Services, Washington, D.C.: U.S. Government Printing Office, 1979. This useful publication describes the types of social services which are needed in low income public housing projects. For individuals who are not aware of social services and housing, this is a sound resource book.

Robert Walker. "The History of Modern City Planning". Urban Planning 1949, pp. 3-46. This article provides a concise history of the development of planning as a profession. The article is non-technical and contains many useful references.

REFERENCES

Abrams, Charles. Man's Struggle for Shelter in an Urbanizing World, Cambridge, Massachusetts: MIT Press, 1964..

Adams, Thomas. Outline of Town and City Planning. New York, NY: Russell Sage Foundation, 1935.

Beyer, Glen. Housing and Society. New York, New York: Macmillan Press, 1965.

Congressional Quarterly. <u>Housing A Nation</u>. Washington, D.C.: U.S. Government Printing Office, 1965.

Department of City Development. City of Milwaukee. <u>Community Housing in Milwaukee, 5th Edition</u>. Milwaukee, WI: Department of City Development for the Housing Authority of the City of Milwaukee, 1977.

Ewald, William. <u>Environment for Man: The Next Fifty Years</u>. Bloomington, IN: Indiana University Press, 1967.

Fish, Gertrude. <u>The Story of Housing</u>. New York, NY: Macmillan Publishing Company, 1979.

Fisher, Robert. <u>Twenty Years of Public Housing</u>. New York, NY: Harper and Brothers, 1959.

Friedlander, Walter and Robert Apte. <u>Introduction to Social Welfare, 5th Edition</u>. Englewood Cliffs, NJ: Prentice-Hall, Inc., 1980.

Kostoff, Spiro. <u>The Architect: Chapters in the History of the Profession</u>. New York, NY: Oxford University Press, 1977.

Lubove, Roy. <u>The Urban Community: Housing and Planning in the Progressive Era</u>. Englewood Cliffs, NJ: Prentice-Hall, Inc., 1967.

Minahan, Anne. <u>Encyclopedia of Social Work, 18th Issue</u>. Washington, D.C.: National Association of Social Workers, 1986.

National Association of Housing and Redevelopment. <u>Urban Careers Guide</u>. Washington, D.C.: National Association of Housing and Redevelopment, 1973.

Office of the Federal Register. <u>Government Organization Manual, 1985-86</u>. Washington, D.C.: U.S. Government Printing Office, 1985.

Preston, David. "Human Dimensions in Public Housing," <u>Social Work</u>, Vol. 19, No. 1 (January, 1964), pp 29-37.

Smailes, Arthur. <u>The Geography of Towns</u>. London, England: Hutchison's University Library, 1957.

So, Frank, Israel Stodlman, Frank Beal, Daniel Arnald. <u>The Practice of Local Government Planning</u>. Washington, D.C.: International City Management Association, 1979.

United States Department of Commerce, Bureau of the Census,
   Public   Employment   in   1984,   Washington,   D.C.:   U.S.
   Government Printing Office, 1985.

United States Department of Commerce, Bureau of the Census,
   1980 Census of Housing: United States Summary, Washington,
   D.C.: U.S. Government Printing Office, 1983.

United States Department of Commerce, Bureau of the Census, 1980
   Census of Housing: Summary of Detailed Housing Characteristics, Washington, D.C.: U.S. Government Printing Office,
   1983.

United States Department of Commerce, Bureau of the Census, 1980
   Census of Population: Vol. 2 Subject Reports Part 7C:
   Occupation by Industry. Washington, D.C.: U.S. Government
   Printing Office, 1984.

United States Department of Commerce, Bureau of the Census,
   Statistical Abstract of the United States: 1986 (106th
   Edition).   Washington,   D.C.:   U.S.   Government   Printing
   Office, 1985.

United States Civil Service Commission, Occupations of Federal
   White-Collar   Workers,   1979,   Washington,   D.C.:   U.S.
   Government Printing Office, 1981.

United States Department of Housing and Urban Development, The
   Manager   and   Social   Services,   Washington,   D.C.:   U.S.
   Government Printing Office, 1979.

United States Department of Housing and Urban Development,
   Professional   Career   Patterns   in   Housing   Management.
   Washington, D.C.: U.S. Government Printing Office, 1979.

United States Department of Housing and Urban Development,
   Crime in Public Housing Washington, D.C.: U.S. Government
   Printing Office, 1978.

United States Department of Housing and Urban Development,
   Problems   Affecting   Low-Rent   Public   Housing   Projects,
   Washington, D.C.: U.S. Government Printing Office, 1979.

Wald, Patricia. Law and Poverty: 1965. Washington, D.C.: U.S.
   Government Printing Office, 1965.

Walker, Robert. "The History of Modern City Planning," Urban
   Planning 1949, pp. 3-46.

603

Wicker, Tom. Report of the National Advisory Committee on Civil
    Disorders. New York, NY: Bantam Books, 1968.

Wilcox, Claire. Towards Social Welfare. Homewood, IL: Richard
    D. Irwin Inc., 1969.

Williamson, John. Strategies Against Poverty in America. New
    York, NY: John Wiley and Sons, Inc., 1975.

Wisconsin Legislative Reference Bureau, Wisconsin Blue Book,
    1985-86. Madison, WI: Department of Administration, 1985.

CHAPTER 19

INCOME MAINTENANCE NETWORK*

"In no country at no time have income and wealth been distributed equally. Everywhere and always there have been some people who were relatively rich, others who were relatively poor. The extent of inequality has varied from place to place and from time to time." (Wilcox:1969:1)

INTRODUCTION

Economic or financial security (income maintenance network) is a problem existing in every society at anytime. The manner and extent to which societies develop resources to ameliorate or alleviate the problem of economic security varies from self help and mutual aid groups, such as the Amish religious denomination to highly complex and bureaucratic public and/or private programs, such as the social security program and retirement and pension programs. In some societies, like the United States, the income maintenance network consists of a vast array of programs, for example, employee benefit and pension plans, union welfare funds, public assistance programs, social security and other financial programs.[1]

This chapter describes the nature and extent of the income maintenance network, primarily from the perspective of government funding. The variety of human service occupations and professions employed in the network are indicated with a discussion of the occupations and professions of welfare worker, social security claims examiner, social security administrator, veteran's insurance examiner/counselor and the role of social work.

SIZE

Contrary to public opinion, the income maintenance network in the United States is not only for individuals below the poverty level. In 1984, there were 33,700,000 individuals below the poverty level which was 14.4 percent of the population yet an estimated 65,563,000 individuals or 27.6 percent of the population received cash benefits from social insurance or public assistance programs excluding medical care and other non cash benefits, such as food stamps, school lunches, nutrition programs and emergency food service. Definitions of poverty status are relative to one's self concept, income level, standard of living, expectations etc. The poverty level as established by the United States, Department of Health and Human Services was estimated at $10,000 annual income for a family of four (including parents) in 1984, and in 1986 at $11,000 annual income for a family of four (including parents).

The percentage of the population estimated to be below the poverty level actually decreased since 1959. In 1959, it was estimated that 22.4 percent (27.5 million) of the population was below the poverty level, and in 1984, 14.4 percent (33.7 million) of the population was below the poverty level. This decrease in the percentage of the population below the poverty level between 1959 and 1984 seems significant. However, one must keep in mind that in 1979 11.7 percent (26.1 million) of the population was below the poverty level. In effect, between 1979 and 1984 the percentage of the population below the poverty level actually increased by 23.0 percent. When one looks at the number of families below the poverty level, a similar trend emerges. In 1959, 18.5 percent (8,320,000) of the families in the United States were below the poverty level. In 1979, 9.1 percent (5,320,000) of the families, and in 1984, 11.6 percent (7,277,000) of the families were below the poverty level. In effect between 1979 and 1984 there was a 27 percent increase in the number of families below the poverty level.

Poverty does not effect all segments of the population equally. Of the 33,700,000 individuals below the poverty level in 1984, 23 million or 68.0 percent were white, 9.5 million or 28.0 percent were black and 1.2 million or 4 percent were other minority groups. For specific population groups the percentages below the poverty level were as follows: 11.5 percent of the whites, 33.8 percent of the Blacks, 28.4 percent of the Spanish speaking, 13.1 percent of the Asians, and 27.5 percent of the Native Americans.

Of concern when one reviews the figures for specific groups below the poverty level, one finds a high proportion of female headed households and children. The concept "feminization of poverty" refers to the fact many of the households below the poverty level are headed by women. In 1984, of the 86,789,000 households in the United States, 60,025,000 or 69.2 percent were headed by a male and 26,764,000 or 30.8 percent were headed by a female. Of the 60.025,000 male headed households 7,443,100 or 12.4 percent were below the poverty level and of the 26,764,000 female headed households 19,892,500 or 40.7 percent were below the poverty level. Of the 60,025,000 male headed households 2,013,000 or 3.3 percent had children living with them and the male was married with the wife absent, widowed, divorced or

606

single. Of the 26,764,000 female headed households 9,469,000 or 35.4 percent had children living with them and the female was married with the husband absent, widowed, divorced or single. Of the estimated 62,281,000 children (under age 18), 13,400,000 or 21.5 percent were below the poverty level.

A common assumption made by many individuals is that those individuals who are below poverty are not working and that those families receiving cash benefits from the Aid to Families with Dependent Children program are predominantly adults. In 1984 of the 7,258,000 families below the poverty level the householder had been employed in 3,574,000 or 49.2 percent of the families, and in 3,684,000 or 50.8 percent of the families the householder was not employed. In fact, of the 3,574,000 employed house-holders, 1,577,000 or 44.1 percent worked full time and 1,997,000 or 55.9 percent worked part time. This means there are a large number of what is called the "working poor". In 1984, there were 3,674,000 families receiving cash benefits from the Aid to Families with Dependent Children program which in-cluded 10,763,000 individuals of which 3,707,000 or 34.4 percent were adults and 7,056,000 or 65.6 percent were children. An interesting but little known fact about the Aid to Families with Dependent Children program is that in approximately 1.3 percent of the cases the mother is absent. In 1982 the reasons for families receiving cash benefits from the Aid to Families with Dependent Children program were as follows: the father is deceased, 9 percent, incapacitated 3.5 percent, unemployed 6.0 percent; parents are divorced 20.5 percent, separated 19.0 percent; never married 46.5 percent; other 2.2 percent and mother absent in 1.3 percent of the cases. Another assumption by many individuals is that once on AFDC always on AFDC. In 1982, it was estimated that 31.8 percent of the recipients received benefits for less than one year, 29.5 percent between 1-3 years, 14.5 percent between 4-5 years, 16.2 percent between 6-10 years and 8.0 percent for over 10 years. The majority of recipients on AFDC, 61.3 percent received benefits for less than 3 years.

When one looks at the number of households in the United States below and above the poverty level in 1984, 18,312,400 or 21.2 percent were below the poverty level and 68,477,000 or 78.8 percent were above the poverty level. The number of households which received some form of government income maintenance bene-fits (cash and noncash) in 1984 was estimated at 32,329,000 or 37.3 percent of all households of which 18,312,000 or 56.6 per-cent were below the poverty level and 14,017,000 or 43.4 percent were above the poverty level. This means at least 43 percent of public income maintenance benefits go to the working and middle classes and is referred to as "middle class welfare." In effect, public income maintenance programs have prevented at least an additional 2-3 million households from falling below the poverty level. As budgetary cuts and restrictions occur in the social insurance programs in the 1980's a number of families which are above the poverty level will fall below the poverty level.

The major public income maintenance programs include the following: Social Security (OASDHI), Public Employee Retirement, Railroad Retirement, Veteran's Pension and Compensation, Unemployment Insurance, Temporary Disability, Workmen's Compensation (including Black Lung Disease), Public Assistance and Supplemental Security Income).[2] Figure 19-1 shows an estimated size of the income maintenance network for the public programs of Public Assistance, Social Security, Veteran's and Unemployment Insurance in 1982.

The four representative income maintenance programs in Figure 19-1 are implemented through a variety of federal, state, county, city and township governmental units. A conservative estimate of the number of agencies participating is 8,020 of which about 7,000 are in the local communities and 1,020 are regional state and federal offices. A small number of agencies (about 250) are operated by the township or city, with most local offices run by the state or county.

The estimated expenditures for the four representative income maintenance programs in Figure 19-1 for 1984 were 322.1 billion dollars excluding medical care and noncash benefits. In 1984, 67.2 million individuals received cash benefits from these four programs, which is 28.3 percent of the population of the United States. Of the 67.2 million individuals receiving cash benefits, it was estimated that 33.7 million individuals or 50.1 percent were below the poverty level and 35.5 million individuals or 49.9 percent were above the poverty level. The number of employees to implement the four representative income maintenance programs in 1984 was estimated at 547,831 of which 407,000 or 74.3 percent were employed at the local level of government (city, township, county) in the public assistance programs and the remaining 140,831 or 25.7 percent were employed by the state and federal government.

HISTORICAL DEVELOPMENT

With the variety of programs providing income maintenance benefits, only the major ones which represent different philosophies and historical development will be discussed, such as Public Assistance, Social Security, Veteran's Programs and Unemployment Insurance.

Figure 19-1

Estimated Size of the Income
Maintenance Network in 1984-85*

	INCOME MAINTENANCE NETWORK[1]			
Selected Attribute	Public Assistance	Social Security and Supplemental Security Income	Veteran's Assistance	Unemployment Insurance
Number of Agencies	3,500	1,320	500	2,700
Expenditures	56.6	236.4	3.8	25.3
Number of Employees	407,000	32,774[2]	3,057[2]	105,000[3]
Population Served (Million)	11.9	41.8	2.3	11.2

*Sources: Adapted from: United States Department of Commerce, Bureau of the Census Statistical Abstract of the United States: 1986 (106th Ed.), Washington, DC: U.S. Government Printing Office, 1985 p 354,325,355,357; United States Civil Service Commission, Occupations of Federal White Collar Workers, 1979, Washington, DC: U.S. Government Printing Office, 1981; United States Department of Commerce, Bureau of the Census, Public Employment in 1984, Washington, DC: U.S. Government Printing Office, 1985 p 3 and Amy Weinstein Public Welfare Directory: 1986/87 Washington D.C.: American Public Welfare Association, 1986.

[1]These figures do not include medical costs and other noncash benefits.
[2]Figure is of social insurance examiners (social security and veteran's examiners) employed at the federal level.
[3]Figure is of social insurance examiners (unemployment examiners) including Job Services.

PUBLIC ASSISTANCE PROGRAMS

Public aid for the poor and unfortunate, has always been a part of any society. The mechanism for granting this aid and the philosophy behind granting aid has varied. Many societies utilize a mutual aid concept where, because of kinship or community bonds, the fortunate help the unfortunate in time of need. The current public assistance programs in the United States consists of General Assistance and Aid to Families with Dependent Children. The history of public assistance has the following themes: church control to secular control, private organization to public organization and local control to state and federal control.

CLASSICAL CIVILIZATIONS, PRE 450 AD--The Greeks by 400 BC used philanthropy (individual benefactor gives money to a city, state, religious or fraternal organization) for the purpose of aiding the poor. The poor were seen as worthy or unworthy of recieving aid. The worthy poor could receive monies or food from the emergency fund of the city, state, religious or fraternal organizations. The unworthy poor (the lowest classes and the uneducated) were expected to make it as best as they could which included begging. Greek philanthropy was motivated by a concept of honor and not a concern for the weak and helpless. Roman society 100 BC followed similar practices in aiding the poor as Greece.

MEDIEVAL EUROPE, 450-1500 A.D.--Western Europe relied on church institutions to provide assistance to the needy as well as other unfortunate individuals, i.e., mentally ill, aged, sick, etc. The giving of charity to others was seen as a Christian obligation. Poverty was viewed as a matter of unfortunate circumstances, therefore, being poor was not a social stigma. Medieval society recognized that people were poor for a variety of reasons, such as holy poverty (voluntary choice), unfortunate circumstances and societal parasites (thiefs, vagabonds and scoundrels). The system of individual charity, as well as, monastery relief and housing, parish relief and housing, and hospital (hospice) relief and housing were all utilized. Most of these programs for helping the poor were in-kind services and not cash benefits.

MERCANTILISM 1600-1700--In late Medieval Europe and in the period of the Renaissance and Reformation which corresponded with Mercantilist economics a series of social, religious, and technological changes occurred, shifting the burden of poor relief from the church to public institutions, such as the county, parish or state. In this period of time there was the emergence of the nation state, religious reformation (Protestant

Reformation), and a change in technology from agriculture to small business (mercantilism). With these massive changes in society, concurrent changes occurred in the treatment of the poor and in controlling individuals displaced by the changing economic system.[3] The famous Elizabethan Poor Laws of 1601 were passed stressing the following themes: secular control (public control of the programs to aid the poor) and local control of programs (parish or county which established an overseer of the poor for each parish or county). With these societal changes there concurrently occurred a change of philosphy towards the poor. A distinction was made between the worthy poor (sick, disabled, aged, etc.) and the unworthy poor (able bodied). In England the worthy poor received aid through the local relief agencies, and the unworthy poor were sent to the almshouse (poorhouse 1596, London, England), the workhouse established 1595, or the house of correction initially called the Bridewell established in 1555 in London, England.

LAISSEZ FAIRE ECONOMICS, 1800-1935--In England, there was a short lived movement to transfer responsibility for the working poor to employers by establishing minimum wages or a minimum level of living standards through the Speenhamland Plan of 1795. The basic concept behind the Speenhamland plan was a "right to a living wage" through a wage supplementation allowance to be paid out of general tax revenues. The wage for a laborer was to be adjusted with the price of bread (a crude cost of living index). If the employer's wage was less than the price of bread, a wage supplement was to be paid to the laborer. The wage supplement system was to prevent the working laborer from falling into poverty. By 1834, with an increasing number of poor, increasing tax burden and a more conservative economic and political climate the wage supplementation system was abolished and replaced with a philosophy of deterrence and the concept that "nobody owes the laborer a living wage." The conservative concept of the 1834 Poor Law was to deter people from seeking public assistance and the philosophy of a laborer is entitled only to the income they can earn even though the income was not sufficient to make a living. After 1834 relief for the poor was left to public officials for parish or county relief and the almshouse.

The United States initially followed the pattern developed in England of having the local community taking responsibility for financial assistance through a series of programs which included the following: outdoor relief (institutions, such as the poorhouse, almshouse), indoor relief (in one's own home), apprenticeship, warming out (individual forced out of a community), contract out (some one cares for the person for a small fee) and private philanthrophy. The intent was to provide public assistance as a last resort, therefore policies of deterrence were established. Deterrence policies were a means to discourage individuals from utilizing the public assistance programs for aid. Because of the stigma attached to being poor there were a number of laws which officially sanctioned the legal status of a pauper (a second class citizen).

In both England and the United States, there was an increased emphasis placed upon private philanthropy in providing financial assistance. The Charity Organization Movement of the 1870's used "scientific methods" to differentiate between the worthy and unworthy poor (see chapter 3, Social Work as a Helping Profession for a fuller discussion of "scientific methods"). The worthy poor were accepted initially by private agencies for individual counseling and guidance, and the unworthy poor were sent to the public institutions, (almshouse, workhouse, house of correction). Later, by 1910, private agencies were providing financial assistance as well. The period of private philanthropy lasted until the depression of 1929-1941, and the New Deal when public welfare became predominant.

In addition to the general relief programs established by both public and private agencies, there was a slow growth in the development of state plans for aging, disabled and widowed women prior to 1935. For example, 34 states had old age pension laws in addition to general assistance or relief prior to 1935, 27 states had pensions or grants for blind individuals prior to 1935 and 17 states had a mother's pension for widows by 1935. Only one state prior to 1935 had provisions for the disabled and this was Wisconsin.[4]

WELFARE CAPITALIST ECONOMIC'S 1935 on--The 1930's and the Great Depression resulted in a total reorganization of public assistance programs in the United States. The Social Security Act of 1935 developed a multiple system for helping the poor in the United States, which was in addition to township and county public assistance (relief programs).

The Social Security Act of 1935 established the following federal and state programs in public assistance known as the categorical aids: Old Age Assistance (OAA-Title 1), Aid to the Blind (BA-Title 10) and Aid to Dependent Children (ADC-Title 4). Finances for the programs were shared by the federal, state, and local governments (from general tax revenues), with implementation of the programs at the local level. The county welfare department (now called social service or human service department) was normally the implementing agency. The local governmental unit (county, city or township) was still responsible for the granting of relief or general assistance (GA) from their own funds. By 1960, in most jurisdictions, the county implemented the general assistance programs instead of the city or township. In addition to the public assistance programs, the county welfare departments were responsible for social services to children (Title V of the Social Security Act).

A number of changes have occurred in public assistance programs since 1935. Some of the major changes are as follows:

1. 1950 – Aid to Disabled (DA – Title XIIII of the Social Security Act).

2. 1952 – Law enforcement to be notified of a deserted or abandoned child.

3. 1961 – Medical Assistance to the Aged program Work experience program established for welfare recipients.

4. 1962 – A) Aid to Dependent Children programs, changed to Aid to Families with Dependent Children (AFDC). This change reflected the growing number of unwed mothers on the program, and a shift to a family orientation.

   B) Social Services were provided for public assistance beneficiaries with the federal government contributing 75 percent of the cost. The concept of purchase of service care or third party vendor payments began to emerge at this time. Purchase of service care refers to a public agency contracting out to another agency to provide a specific social service, such as psychotherapy.

   C) Unemployed fathers eligible for AFDC (UF-AFDC) depending upon the state adopting the program.

5. 1964 – Economic Opportunity Act – War on poverty, specifically, those sections relating to work experience and AFDC[5]

6. 1965 – Medicaid – title XIX – medical program for public assistance recipients (replaces medical assistance for the aged).

7.　1967 –　Work incentive program for public assistance recipients.

Purchase of services expanded for public assistance recipients.

8.　1972 –　A)　Categorical programs of OAA, BA, DA, transferred to the Social Security Administration as Supplemental Security Income (SSI).

B)　States could establish an Optional Supplemental Security Income program, to provide assistance for recipients of SSI (about 25 states currently provide this option (1986).

C)　Distinction made between providing financial assistance and social services.

9.　1974 –　Social Service Plans – Title XX. Each state is to develop a comprehensive plan for the provision of social services with five major goals: reduce dependency; achieve self sufficiency; prevent or remedy abuse, neglect and exploitation of children and adults; prevent, or reduce inappropriate institutional care and securing institutional care when necessary. Each state plan must be approved by the federal government.

Services under Title XX are at no cost to public welfare recipients and for nonpublic welfare recipients, based upon income (a sliding fee scale can be charged based upon income level). Services can be provided by a public agency, or by a private agency through purchase of care and subcontracting of programs. Title XX also provided grants to educational institutions for training and educational purposes.

10.　1981 –　A)　Block Grants – Funding for Title XX is made directly to the state, although at a reduced level and states would no longer need prior approval of the federal government for disbursing of the funds.

                    B)   A tightening of eligibility and funding
                         for AFDC.

11. 1986   A retrenchment on cost of living increases
                    for AFDC recipients and further reduction of
                    medical coverage.

SOCIAL SECURITY PROGRAMS

     Social Security as an insurance program in the United States
has had a recent development beginning with the Social Security
Act of 1935.[6]

     The Social Security Act of 1935, specifically set up an
insurance fund to cover employees as they reached retirement
age. The Social Security program is a federally sponsored and
operated program through a combined system of employer and
employee contributions (payroll tax and individual tax).   In
contrast to public assistance and its reliance on county government and employees, the Social Security System relies upon federal employees with regional, district and field offices.   In
contrast to public assistance programs, which are seen as programs for emergency and temporary aid based upon need and as a
privilege, Social Security programs are seen as a matter of
rights (eligibility) and provides retirement and other benefits
for the poor, as well as, the non-poor. Figure 19-2 compares
the Aid to Families with Dependent Children program (public
assistance) with Social Security (social insurance).

     The original program under the Social Security Act of 1935
consisted of a Retirement Fund - Title II. Like the public
assistance programs the Social Security program has undergone
numerous changes since 1935. Some examples of the major changes
include the following:

     1)   1939 - Survivors insurance, including children under 18.
     2)   1950 - Self employed covered by Social Security.
     3)   1954 - A freezing of wage records, for a person who is
                  disabled.
     4)   1956 - A) Disability program for workers and dependents
                  B) Women could retire at 62.
                  C) Veteran's covered by Social Security.
     5)   1965 - Medicare - Title XVIII (Health insurance)
     6)   1966 - Special program for individuals over age 72.
     7)   1972 - Supplemental Security Income program,
                  transferred from local government, to the Social
                  Security Administration (is actually a public
                  assistance program but under the Social Security
                  Administration).

Figure 19-2

Comparison of the Aid to Families With Dependent
Children and Social Security Programs

Characteristics	Program	
	Aid to Families Dependent Children	Social Security
Philosophy	A privilege	A right
Relation to earnings	Non work related	Work related
Proof of need	Means test	Eligibility
System of funding	Budget grants	Flat grants
Source of funding	General taxation	Special Funds
Individual Participation	Noncontributory	Contributory
Repayment Provision	System of recovery	Non recovery
Jurisdiction	County program	Federal program

8) 1981 – Budgetary cutback on minimun income benefits
under Medicare, and proposals to increase the
retirement age to 68.
9) 1985 – Limit set on cost of living increase.
10) 1986 – Further reductions for medical coverage and in
financial benefits

There were many other changes in the Social Security program, such as the percentage of salary from compulsory contributions made to support the system, benefits for children
attending school to age 25, increases in monetary benefit,
changes in who was covered and early retirement. Benefits under
the Social Security program have been expanding rapidly, with a
concurrent increase in expenditures. The first reduction in
social security benefits occurred in 1981, as an attempt to

maintain the system in the light of increased costs. The period of the 1980's has seen a number of reductions in Social Security benefits as part of a broader program to reduce government expenditures at the federal level.

VETERANS PROGRAMS

The concept of providing benefits to veterans of military service in a society is not new. In Europe, benefits to individuals for military service date back to the Hundred Years War in 1400. In the United States, some benefits were available for disabled veterans and widows as early as 1636, such as Plymouth County, Massachusetts. In the United States the most usual early form of veteran's benefit was a granting of bounty land (1753 French and Indian War, Revolutionary War and War of 1812). The veteran was granted title to land on the frontier for serving in the military (usually 160 acres). A monetary pension for the veterans of the Revolutionary War (1776-1783) was provided, however, this was based upon financial need of the veteran or having the rank of an officer. A pension was provided for individuals serving in the War of 1812, Indian wars, Mexican War, Civil War, Spanish-American War, World War I, World War II, Korean conflict, and the Vietnam conflict. [7]

The Bureau of Pensions, for Military Veterans, initially was under the War Department, transferred to the Treasury Department in 1914, with the formation of the Veteran's Bureau as an independent agency in 1921. The current Veteran's Administration was established in 1931. Veterans pensions are viewed by most individuals, as not part of the income maintenance network, since these benefits are granted as a matter of rights, and not privilege. Yet these programs are as much a part of the income maintenance network as are Social Security, Public Assistance and Unemployment Insurance. In many instances, an individual can apply to the county social service department for veterans benefits through cooperative arrangements between the Veterans Administration and the county social service offices. Some states have specialized veteran's programs, such as Wisconsin which are supplemental to any federal benefits.

UNEMPLOYMENT INSURANCE PROGRAMS

There were some early precedents for unemployment insurance, such as the trade union movement in England (1824), and the United States (1831). The first country to adopt an Unemployment Insurance system was England (1911).

In the United States, little attention was paid to unemployment benefits outside of a few voluntary companies until the

Great Depression of 1929 and thereafter. Wisconsin was the first state to develop a state-wide compulsory unemployment benefit program (1932).

The current system of unemployment insurance was part of the Social Security Act of 1935 (Title III, VIII, IX and XII). The Unemployment Insurance program is a joint federal and state endeavor, implemented through state employees and financed by a payroll tax on the employer with matching federal funding. It is a program for decreasing the financial strain on the unemployed and to prevent families from becoming public assistance clients. Like the Aid to Families with Dependent Children and Social Security programs, the Unemployment Insurance program has experienced numerous changes since its inception in 1935 on the amount of benefits payable, under what circumstances and for how long. [8]

Except for the public assistance programs for income maintenance, most individuals perceive the other parts of the income maintenance network as a matter of right and not as a matter of privilege. Yet, all of these programs make a significant contribution towards preventing individuals and families from falling below the poverty level. Figure 19-3 shows a historical time line in the development of Public Assistance, Social Security, Veteran's and Unemployment Insurance programs.

STRUCTURE

With the maze of agencies, jurisdictions and purposes of various segments of the income maintenance network, it is no wonder a person may become confused as to who is responsible for which program, which personnel are involved, and what functions they perform. The structure of the income maintenance network can be viewed from its organizational context, services provided, occupations and professions and dominant occupations and professions.

ORGANIZATIONAL CONTEXT

Each of the major components of the income maintenance network has a separate structure for program implementation. Public assistance, although implemented through county and local departments, has a close relationship to state and federal agencies. Social Security and Supplemental Security Income programs are implemented through the Social Security Administration at regional and field offices. Veteran's programs are implemented through the Veteran's Administration, which is an independent federal agency, along with a specific states' Veteran's Affairs Departments and their representatives at the various county departments of social service. Unemployment insurance program's

Figure 19-3

Historical Time Line of the Income
Maintenance Network

Time Period	PROGRAM			
	Public Assistance (GA or AFDC)	Social Security	Veterans Programs	Unemployment Insurance
Ancient Civilization 2000 BC– 450 AD	Philanthropy (Religious Organizations, individual)	Non-Existent	Non-Existent	Non-Existent
Medieval Europe 450–1500 AD	Church relief and Parish programs	Non-Existent	Early programs in France 1400	Non Existent
Mercantilism 1500–1800	General Assistance Contract Out Elizabethan Poor Law 1601 Alms House 1595	Non-Existent	1636–Massachusetts Land Grant 1778 Land Grants Pensions for indigent	Non Existent
Laissez Faire Economics 1800–1935	Speenhamland plan – Parish (County) relief State (County) programs	Development of Social Insurance Programs in Europe	1812 Land Grants 1864 Hospitals 1918 Rehabilitation and training	Development of programs in Europe
Welfare Capitalist Economics 1935–1980	1935 Aid to Dependent Children Categorical Aids 1965–Medicaid 1972 Supplemental Security Income 1974 Title XX	1935 Social Security United States 1954 Disability 1965 Medicare	1944 GI Bill 1953 Korean Conflict Bill 1965 Vietnam Conflict Bill	1935 Unemployment Insurance– (Federal and State) cooperative program
Service Economics 1980 on	1982 Block grants Cutback Medicaid	1981 Cutback Medicare and other programs under Social Security	Discussion of eliminating or cutting back on specific benefits	Period of eligibility for funding increases or decreases depending upon the economy (recession or boom period)

are implemented through state offices under federal and state guidelines. Figures 19-4 through 19-7 show the governmental organization for these programs.

In addition to the public agencies, there are about 2,900 private agencies which provide some form of emergency financial assistance. Many individuals make use of lending institutions, (banks) as well as a folk system of mutual aid, such as bartering to alleviate a tight economic situation. This means individuals use family members, friends and colleagues for emergency financial assistance.

SERVICES PROVIDED

Except for the county social service departments, most of the financial service programs provided by the income maintenance network have as their primary function the determination of eligibility for specific programs and insuring that the eligible individual receives the authorized payment.

PUBLIC ASSISTANCE PROGRAMS--In the county social service department the major programs for income maintenance are:

- General Assistance or relief
- Aid to Families with Dependent Children (includes unwed
- mothers, unwed fathers, and in some states unemployed fathers)
- Food stamps
- Medicaid
- Work assistance (in cooperation with the employment services)
- Veteran's aid (cooperative arrangement between the Veteran's Administration, State Department of Veteran's Affairs, and county social service departments).

In addition, the county social service department is responsible for a wide-range of allied personal social services, such as:

- Protective services for children (abuse, neglect, runaways)
- Family counseling
- Adoption
- Foster-care
- Other substitute care (institutions such as nursing homes, residential treatment care centers)
- Home-making
- Self-support (cooperative with employment services)
- Financial management and counseling
- Legal advice.

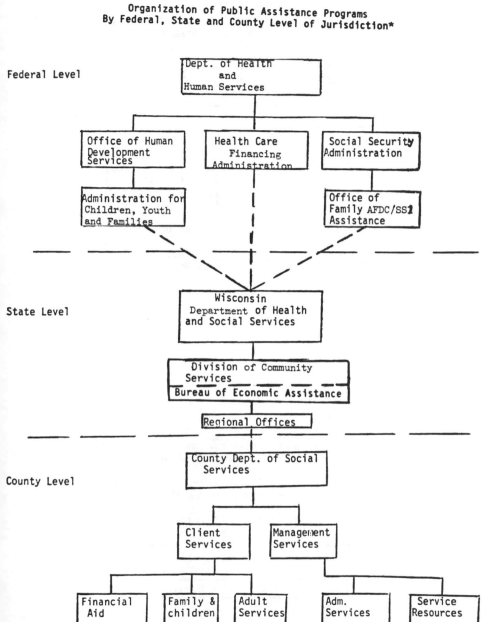

Figure 19-4

Organization of Public Assistance Programs
By Federal, State and County Level of Jurisdiction*

Federal Level

Dept. of Health
and
Human Services

Office of Human
Development
Services

Health Care
Financing
Administration

Social Security
Administration

Administration for
Children, Youth
and Families

Office of
Family AFDC/SSI
Assistance

State Level

Wisconsin
Department of Health
and Social Services

Division of Community
Services
Bureau of Economic Assistance

Regional Offices

County Level

County Dept. of Social
Services

Client
Services

Management
Services

Financial
Aid

Family &
children

Adult
Services

Adm.
Services

Service
Resources

*Sources: Adapted from Office of Federal Register, United States Government
Manual 1985-86, Washington, D.C.: U.S. Government Printing Office, 1985,
p. 842; Wisconsin Legislative Reference Bureau, Wisconsin Blue Book 1985-86,
Madison, Wisconsin: Department of Administration, 1985 p. 512; and the
Milwaukee County Social Services Department.

621

Figure 19-5

Organization of Social Security and Supplemental
Security Income Programs*

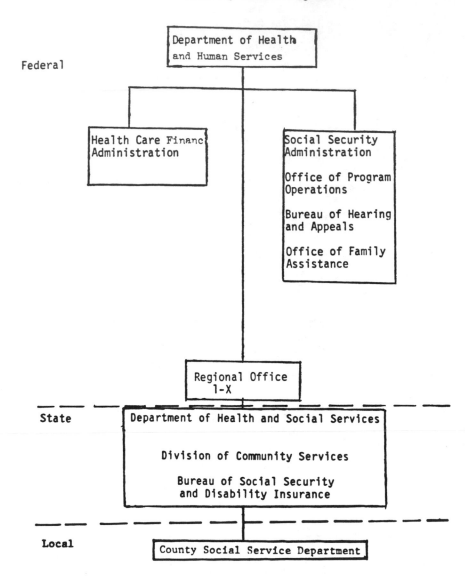

*Source: Office of Federal Register, United States Government Manual 1985-8
Washington, D.C. U.S. Government Printing Office, 1985 p. 842; Wisconsin
Legislative Reference Bureau, Wisconsin Blue Book 1985-86, Madison, Wisconsin
Department of Administration, 1985 p. 512, 518.

622

Figure 19-6

Organization of Veteran's Income Maintenance Programs
By Level of Jurisdiction*

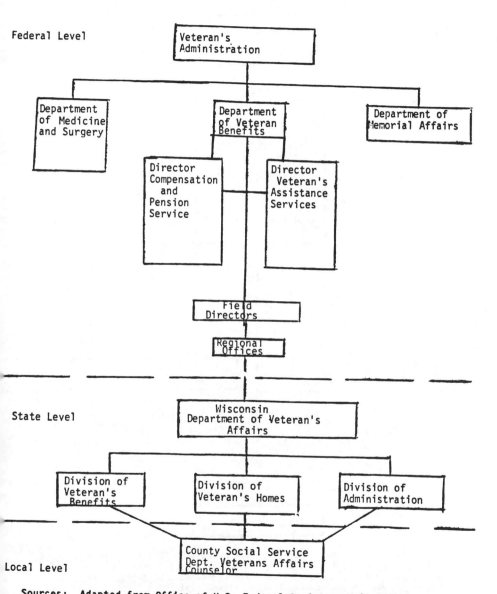

Sources: Adapted from Office of U.S. Federal Register, United States Government Manual 1985-86, Washington, D.C.: U.S. Government Printing Office, 1985, p. 874 and Wisconsin Legislative Reference Bureau, Wisconsin Blue Book, 1985-1986, Madison, Wisconsin: Dept. of Administration, 1985, p. 549.

Figure 19-7

Organization of Unemployment Insurance Programs
By Level of Jurisdiction*

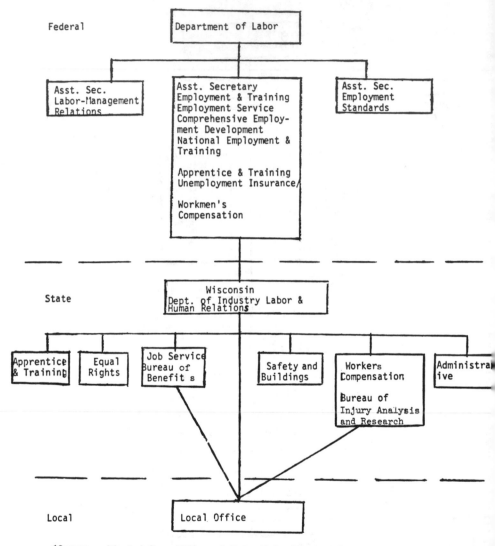

*Source: Adapted from Office of Federal Register, <u>United States Government</u>
<u>Manual 1985-86</u>, Washington, D.C.: U. S. Government Printing Office, 1985,
p. 846 and Wisconsin Legislative Reference Bureau, <u>Wisconsin Blue Book</u>
<u>1985-1986</u>, Madison, Wisconsin: Dept. of Administration, 1985, p. 531.

SOCIAL SECURITY PROGRAMS--The Social Security Administration has responsibility for the following programs:

- Retirement benefits
- Survivors benefits
- Disability benefits
- Medicare (hospital and medical)
- Supplemental security income programs (blind aid, disabled aid, old-age aid)
- Referral services to vocational rehabilitation service programs and county social service departments.

VETERAN'S PROGRAMS--The Veteran's Administration and Department of Veteran's Affairs in cooperation with county social services, has responsibility for the following programs:

- Veteran's emergency assistance
- Veteran's pensions
- Veteran's counseling.

UNEMPLOYMENT INSURANCE PROGRAMS--The unemployment insurance agency (employment services area offices) has responsibility for the following programs:

- Unemployment insurance benefits
- Referral to employment services. [9]

OCCUPATIONS and PROFESSIONS

Since each component of the income maintenance network has a specific function, one would expect the types of occupations and professions involved in implementing these programs to vary from program to program. Figure 19-8 shows selected human service occupations and professions employed in the income maintenance network in 1980. All of these occupations and professions listed in Figure 19-8 are employed in the industrial classification of public administration and subcategory administration of human resources. [10]

DOMINANT OCCUPATIONS and PROFESSIONS

Each of the major programs in the income maintenance network has a dominant occupation or profession. In the public assistance programs (whether General Assistance or Aid to Families with Dependent Children), the dominant occupation or profession is that of the financial aide assistant, welfare worker, and social worker; in Social Security, the dominant occupation or profession is that of the social insurance claims examiner and social insurance administrator; in Veterans programs the dominant occupation or profession is the veteran's insurance

Figure 19-8

Number and Percent of Selected Human Service Occupations and
Professions Employed In the Industrial Classification of
Administration of Human Resources (Income Maintenance Network) In 1980*

Occupation and Profession	Number	Percent
Administrator	39,001	12.213
Personnel Relations	36,117	11.211
Architect	3,132	.981
Physician	2,985	.935
Other Health	3,393	1.063
Registered	12,536	3.926
Dietician	1,364	.427
Therapist	2,497	.782
Teacher[1]	4,214	1.319
Counselor	8,802	2.747
Librarian	754	.236
Psychologist	3,126	.978
Urban Planner	506	.158
Social Work	85,064	26.953
Recreation Work	469	.147
Clergy/Religious Work	250	.077
Lawyer	4,077	1.277
Judge	1,753	.548
Author, Musician, Painter, Actor	794	.249
Health Records	151	.047
Licensed Practical Nurse	1,259	.394
Police, guards, detectives	938	.294
Health Aide	1,686	.528
Nurse Aide	8,826	2.764
Welfare Aide	5,571	1.745
Child Care	4,219	1.321
Social Insurance Examinor and		
Administrator	32,774	10.164
Veteran's Examiner	3,057	.957
Unemployment Examiner[2]	50,000	15.659
TOTAL	319,315	100.000

* Source: Adapted from United States Department of Commerce, Bureau of the Census, 1980
Census of Population Vol. 2 Subject Reports Part 7C: Occupation by Industry, Washington,
DC: U.S. Government Printing Office, 1984, pp. 225-664.

This Industrial classification Includes the following programs and agencies: public
assistance, social security, veteran's administration, unemployment/employment, public
instruction, Bureau of Indian Affairs and vocational rehabilitation. These figures are
somewhat Inflated because of the last four categories which account for about 10 percent
of the selected human service occupation and professions.

[1] The author assumes most of the teachers would be employed In the public Instruction
category of administration of human resources and not in income maintenance programs.

[2] This figure Is an estimate only assuming approximately 40-45 percent of the 112,000
employees In employment/unemployment programs would be In unemployment and the remainder
In employment functions.

examiner/counselor and in Unemployment Insurance the dominant occupation and profession is the unemployment insurance examiner. All of these individuals are employed in the public sector and in the industrial classification of administration of human resources (income maintenance).

PUBLIC ASSISTANCE PROGRAMS--Figure 19-8 shows 85,064 social workers (includes welfare worker) and 5,571 welfare aides employed in the industrial classification of administration of human resources (income maintenance network) in 1980. The classification social worker refers to an occupational title and not whether the person has a professional degree in social work. The financial aide or case aide falls under the classification of NEC (not elsewhere classified).

Prior to 1972, the task of determining eligibility and providing personal social services for the public assistance programs was performed by case workers or welfare workers, who normally held a bachelor's degree, preferrably, in the social sciences, including social welfare or social work. [11] With the division of responsibilities between financial assistance eligibility and providing personal social services, in 1972, these two tasks became separate and are now performed by two different occupational groups.

The function or tasks of the <u>financial assistance aide</u> or case aide include the following:

- Provide information on the program
- Obtain information from the applicant
- Process the applications for assistance
- Determine eligibility for assistance
- Determine the amount of assistance, and
  follow up on the case.

Educational requirements for a financial assistant aide varies from less than a high school education to an associate of arts degree from a junior college.

<u>Welfare Workers</u> have the function of implementing the personal social service programs which includes the following tasks:

- Home visits
- Investigation of abuse/neglect cases
- Develop social histories
- Provide individual and group counseling (depending upon academic degree)
- Provide therapeutic services (depending upon academic degree)

- Represent the agency in court hearings
- Public relations
- Referral of individuals to other agencies.

Educational standards for welfare workers vary from less than a bachelor's degree, to a bachelor's degree in social science or social welfare and social work, to a master's degree in social work or an allied profession. These educational standards will vary from state to state and county to county. In most jurisdictions, the proportion of professional social workers, (bachelor's or master's degree in social work) is relatively low in proportion to non-social workers. There is tremendous confusion in the eyes of the public of the role of social work in public assistance programs. Since many county departments of social services call their employees case workers, welfare workers, or social workers, the assumption is that all personnel are trained in the profession of social work. [12]

SOCIAL SECURITY PROGRAMS--The primary employee in social security programs is the social insurance claims examiner or the social insurance administrator. Figure 19-8 shows 32,774 social insurance examiners and administrators employed in the industrial classification of administration of human resources (income maintenance network) in 1980. In general, a bachelor's degree is required, preferably in one of the social sciences. The general functions of the claims examiner include the following:

- Provide information on programs to the general public
- Answer specific questions on specific cases
- Take applications for initial benefits
- Follow-up on cases already determined to be eligible
- Referral of individuals to other social service programs. [13]

VETERAN'S PROGRAMS--The primary employee in the veterans program is a veteran's insurance examiner/counselor. Figure 19-8 shows 3,057 veteran's examiners/counselors employed in the industrial classification of administration of human resources (income maintenance network) in 1980. The general functions of the claims examiner include the following:

- Gathering of information
- Determining a veteran's eligibility status
- Determination of benefits
- Referral of the individual to other social service agencies.

As indicated earlier, the Veteran's Administation and State Departments of Veterans Affairs work in cooperation with the county department of social services in processing applications for veteran's assistance. In this situation, the employee may be a financial assistance worker in an agency or a specialized veteran's counselor. Veteran's counselors usually have a bachelor's degree in one of the social sciences and is usually a veteran. [14]

UNEMPLOYMENT INSURANCE PROGRAMS--The primary employees of this program is the unemployment insurance examiner. Figure 19-8 shows an estimated 50,000 unemployment examiners employed in the industrial classification of administration of human resources (income maintenance network) in 1980. This position usually requires a bachelor's degree in one of the social sciences or advanced training in vocational guidance. The primary functions of the unemployment insurance examiner include the following:

- Gathering information on the applicant's circumstances
- Determine eligibility for programs
- Follow-up on eligibility
- Referral to the employment section and/or other social service agency for services. [15]

The primary role or function of the dominant occupations or professions in the income maintenance network is generally restricted to the processing of applicants, determining eligibility, follow-up service, and occassionally public relations except in public assistance programs which provides a variety of personal social services.

SOCIAL WORK

Of the estimated 85,000 social workers employed in the income maintenance network, the vast majority are employed in public assistance programs (see Figure 19-8). Of the 85,000 individuals who were identified as social workers approximately 35 percent have a professional degree in social work, (bachelor's or masters) and the remaining 65 percent have degrees in other disciplines. The task the social worker performs in the agency may be the same as the welfare worker or caseworker or may be different depending upon the agency. The author, in discussing the role of the social worker in the income maintenance network is somewhat idealistic since many social workers do not perform these tasks.

PUBLIC ASSISTANCE PROGRAMS

The primary task of the social worker would be ancillary or supportive to the functions of determining financial need and amount of assistance granted. The role of the social worker in public assistance programs will vary depending whether upon one is looking at the individual/group level, community level, and supervisory and administrative level of tasks.

INDIVIDUAL and GROUP WORK--the social worker should be involved in the following:

- A concentrated team approach (use of multiple helping professions in providing treatment programs)
- Individual counseling
- Development of group counseling techniques for juveniles and/or adults
- Family or marital counseling.

In addition to these specific tasks in the treatment area, the social worker would perform some of the same tasks as a welfare worker. The social worker should have a more knowledgeable basis upon which to make decisions, should have a better grasp of interviewing techniques and a better grasp of interventive techniques, than the welfare worker. That is, the social worker should be more adept at interpersonal relationships than the welfare worker because of training and/or experience.

COMMUNITY--depending upon the particular agency, the social worker should be involved in the following tasks:

- Coordinating agency activities with the community
- Locating housing
- Providing transportation
- Facilities for meetings
- Developing employment opportunity for welfare clients.

Since a chronic need is for the establishment of residential treatment care centers, half-way houses, foster homes, etc., the worker may be involved in community organization tactics in order to establish specific houses for a particular clientele.

SUPERVISORY and ADMINISTRATIVE--the social worker should be involved in the following tasks:

- In-service training
- Maintenance of the operations of a specific unit
- Providing supportive advice and counseling for employees
- Seeking modification of agency policy and/or directions when they become counter-productive in providing services to the population concerned.

The social work role should be a broader role than that of the welfare worker and caseworker.

SOCIAL SECURITY PROGRAMS

Although working with the public on social security claims takes knowledge of the income maintenance network, and some basic skills of communication, such as interviewing, social work skills of an individual or group intervention nature are not essential. Consequently, a social worker will assume a different role than that of the social insurance claims examiner. A social worker could be utilized in the following tasks:

- Consultant on service systems
- Consultant on individual problematic situations
- Potentially become involved in staff development and in-service training.

VETERANS and UNEMPLOYMENT INSURANCE PROGRAMS

In both of these programs the primary concern is the determination of eligibility, consequently, there is no need for a sophisticated level of social work skills and intervention. Similar to Social Security programming, there is a need for basic communication and interviewing skills. The social worker could be utilized in the following tasks:

- Consultation in problematic situations
- Referral services
- Development of in-service training programs for employees. [16]

PERSONAL SOCIAL SERVICES

The income maintenance network with its focus on financial programs has implemented a wide variety of personal social service programs (see Chapter 22 Personal Social Service). Some examples of personal social service programs in the income maintenance network include the following:

PROTECTIVE SERVICES

Child abuse investigations, child welfare services offered by the local department of social services (social welfare), such as Cook County, Chicago, Illinois and San Francisco County, San Francisco, California.

UTILITARIAN SERVICES

Homemaking, day care services offered by the local department of social services (social welfare), such as Los Angeles County, Los Angeles, California and St. Louis County, St. Louis, Missouri.

DEVELOPMENTAL and SOCIALIZATION SERVICES

Family and marital counseling, programs for unwed mothers offered by the local department of social services (social welfare), such as Milwaukee County, Milwaukee, Wisconsin and Philadelphia, Pennsylvania.

REHABILITATIVE and THERAPEUTIC SERVICES

Alocohol and drug counseling offered by the local department of social services (social welfare), such as New York, New York; Philadelphia, Pennsylvania and San Diego, California.

SPECIAL POPULATIONS

The income maintenance network has a high percentage of special populations as recipients of these services, since a higher percentage of special populations are poor in comparison to the total population (see Chapter 25, Special Populations and Chapter 24 Rehabilitation). Some examples of programs for special populations in the income maintenance network include the following:

ASIAN

Refugee programs for the Indochinese, Vietnamese, Cambodians and Loatians, such as Los Angeles County Welfare Dept., Los Angeles, California and Milwaukee County Social Service Department, Milwaukee, Wisconsin.

BLACK

Refugee programs for Haitians, such as Department of Health and Rehabilitation District Offices in Miami and Pensacola, Florida.

EUROPEAN ETHNIC

Bilingual workers and agencies, such as Irish Charities of America, New York, New York

NATIVE AMERICAN

Indian social services and Indian General Assistance programs through the Bureau of Indian Affairs, Department of Interior, United States Government.

SAME SEX PREFERENCE

Awareness and sensitivity programs, such as the Homosexual Resource Center, Hollywood, California

SPANISH SPEAKING

Bilingual workers and programs, such as migrant assistance, Cuban refugee programs Milwaukee County Social Service Department, Milwaukee, Wisconsin and Department of Health and Rehabilitation, Miami, Florida.

WOMEN

Awareness and sensitivity programs and agencies, such as Women in Transition, Philadelphia, Pennsylvania

ISSUES

Income maintenance is a network designed to both alleviate the problem of poverty (public assistance), as well as prevent poverty (social insurance). The income maintenance network has within it a number of significant issues which includes the following: gaps in service, conflicting philosophies and limited programs.

GAPS in SERVICE

The major programs for income maintenance have been designed for a specific population, such as destitute poor, (public assistance) the aged, (Social Security) veterans, and the unemployed. There is no one overall program of income maintenance which generally focuses on all populations of the United States which are poor or on the verge of poverty. Consequently, the United States has gaps in provisions of services, such as family allowances, maternity benefits, students, able bodied and the related problems of medical insurance and programs for the working poor. Programs, such as food stamps, retraining, personal social services under Title XX are designed for both the poor (destitute) and the working poor.

CONFLICTING PHILOSOPHIES

There is a conflict between the ideologies of providing income maintenance as a right (institutional social welfare), and insurance programs, such as Social Security, Veterans, and Unemployment, or as a privilege (residual social welfare) and emergency programs, such as Aid to Families with Dependent Children, Supplemental Security Income and General Assistance. If the programs are expected to be only of the insurance type (prevent poverty), then social services are provided by other individuals and agencies. If agencies are of the emergency type (alleviate poverty), than social services can be provided by the same agency. It is the recognition of this conflict in ideology between the roles of providing financial aid or providing personal social services, which resulted in the division of these two functions in 1972 in public assistance agencies, and the development of Title XX of the Social Security Act (Social Service Funding). Additional conflicts of ideology surround the concept of the work ethic (1967 Work Incentive Programs) and a cutback of financial resources for public assistance programs. The 1986 federal budget is an example of these conflicts since a number of income maintenance programs had reduced expenditures. The concept of the federal government paying for personal social services under Titles XVIII, XIX and XX of the Social Security Act is being challenged in 1986.

A role conflict is also seen in the Unemployment Insurance program between the role of the insurance claims examiner and the employment counselor. Some individuals have been arguing for a division between these two tasks, which is similar to the division, which was made in the public assistance programs in 1972. Similar role conflicts can be seen in the Social Security Administration and Veteran's programs.

LIMITED PROGRAMS

A major concern is the amount of benefits available to individuals, especially with past inflation and the cost of living increasing. Many of the individuals receiving income maintenance benefits are on fixed incomes, and the benefits are of a fixed income nature. Consequently, these families are unable to keep up with the rising cost of living.

Many individuals have multiple needs including financial, medical, housing, etc. Since the income maintenance programs are organizationally under separate jurisdiction and separate agencies, this means an individual can be referred from agency to agency in an attempt to seek services. Some individuals receive multiple benefits, such as Social Security and Veterans and others may obtain assistance from one form of program. It is partly this concern, about multiple and autonomous agencies and programs, which is leading to a movement toward program integration and coordination, and in some cases, a multiple service center at the county level. The trend toward having county social service departments develop personal social service programs for many areas of need is part of this movement toward integration and coordination of human services.

SUMMARY

The United States and the income maintenance network has a variety of programs to serve different population groups. Only the major programs are discussed in this chapter which are the following: public assistance programs (Aid to Families with Dependent Children and General Assistance), Social Security, Veteran's and Unemployment Insurance programs. Sixty-seven million individuals received benefits from these programs in 1984 which represents 32.3 million households or 37.3 percent of the households in the United States. Of these 32.3 million households 56.6 percent were below the poverty line and 43.4 percent above the poverty level. The estimated expenditures for the four representative programs in 1984 was 332.1 billion dollars with approximately 8,020 agencies and 547,831 employees.

The income maintenance network is large and complex, since governmental jurisdiction ranges from federal, state, county, municipal to township. In addition, numerous financial assistance programs are offered through private agencies and the United Nations. Each of the major programs in the income maintenance network has a distinct historical development. Public assistance programs, (a residual emergency type of aid), dates back to late Medieval Europe. Social security programs and Unemployment programs (a institutional preventative type of aid), are of rather recent origin in the United States, since 1935. Veterans programs of some form have been in existence since at least 1400, however, the United States developed its special programs after the Revolutionary War of 1776-1783.

The complexity of the organizational structure of the income maintenance network was discussed, showing the variability of the structure, (federal/state, local) with a brief indication of specific programs and services provided. The variety of human service occupations and professions was discussed and in particular the dominant profession and occupation in each of the major programs. For example, in public assistance, the dominant occupation is that of the financial assistance aide and the welfare worker or caseworker, in social security, it is the social insurance claims examiner/counselor and administrator, in veteran's programs it is the veterans insurance examiner/counselor and in unemployment it is the unemployment insurance examiner. The functions of these occupations and professions were contrasted with an idealized role of social work in the income maintenance network.

The income maintenance network, like other human service networks has built in problems. Some problems of the income maintenance network discussed include: gaps in programs and services, conflicting philosophies, (insurance versus aid, institutional versus residual programming or alleviating poverty versus preventing poverty) and limitations of programs. It was earlier indicated that the United States has numerous other programs involving income maintenance, however, these programs are relatively small in size. Ancillary social services are usually provided to the beneficiaries of income maintenance programs either by the same agency or through different agencies.

FOOTNOTES

*This chapter was reviewed for comments by Robert Magill, Associate Professor, School of Social Welfare, University of Wisconsin-Milwaukee, Milwaukee, Wisconsin.

[1] The income maintenance network has linkages with all of the other networks in society. Specifically, other important related networks include the following: Economic Network, Chapter 5; Military Network, Chapter 6; Religious Network, Chapter 15; Employment and Manpower Network, Chapter 17, and Housing Network, Chapter 18.

[2] Estimates of the poverty level and individuals and families below the poverty level are adapted from the United States Department of Commerce, Bureau of the Census, Statistical Abstract of the United States: 1986 (106th Edition), Washington, D.C.: U.S. Government Printing Office, 1985, pp. 456-461; and "Milwaukee Journal," June 16, 1985.

Definitions of income maintenance programs is that used by the United States Department of Commerce Bureau of the Census. Statistical Abstract of the United States: 1986, (106th Edition), pp. 358-359. It is recognized there are a large variety of other programs involving income maintenance payments, about 171 at the federal level, and 633 at the state and local levels. The reader is referred to William Laurence and Stephen Leeds An Inventory of Federal Income Transfer Programs, White Plains, New York: Institute for Socioeconomic Studies, 1980 and An Inventory of State and Local Income Transfer Programs fiscal year 1977, White Plains, New York: Institute for Socioeconomic Studies, 1978.) For simplicity and comparative purposes, only the major programs are used as examples. The estimates on income maintenance program costs do not include the associated cost of related employees, the varied social service programs and medical and child welfare services. If one adds figures for more than the four representative programs in Figure 19-1, the expenditures would be about 400 billion dollars and covers about 35 percent of the population of the United States.

3 For a more in depth discussion of these changes in the economic network, the reader is referred to Chapter 5 Economic Network. The Elizabethan Poor Laws of 1601 were a codification of numerous laws passed between 1400-1600.

4 An excellent review of public assistance programs and social security is contained in Helen Clarke, Social Legislation. New York, NY: Appleton-Century Crofts, Inc., 1957, chapters 17-25. These estimates on the state programs available prior to 1935 are from Helen Clarke, op cit. pp. 544, 581, 584, 588.

5 The War on Poverty (Economic Opportunity Act of 1964) consisted of a variety of programs, primarily directed at employment and educational programs to enable individuals to achieve self sufficiency.

6 The United States, in general, has lagged far behind other European countries in establishing insurance for employed workers. For example, England established such programs in 1908, Australia, 1908, France, 1923 and Germany, 1870.

7 Veterans of military service are eligible for more than pension benefits from the Department of Defense and Veteran's Administration. Approximately 17 states have special programs for veterans, including Vietnam Veterans. Some examples, include Pennsylvania, New York, Louisiana, Wisconsin and Connecticut. Programs at the state level may or may not include the following: hospital, psychiatric and social service facilities, personal social services, real estate programs and educational benefits. The specific benefit under discussion in this chapter is the veteran's assistance benefit, (income maintenance). Other aspects of programs for military personnel and veterans are discussed in chapter 6, Military Network.

8 The Employment Services are responsible for more than Unemployment Insurance. The Employment Service is responsible for finding employment, manpower development and training, vocational guidance, etc. These other functions of the Employment

Service are discussed in chapter 17, Employment and Manpower Network. The War on Poverty in 1964 had as one of its main goals, employability of people through programs, such as the Job Corp, Neighborhood Youth Corp, etc. A related program to Unemployment Insurance is Workmen's Compensation, which provides benefits in case of accident. Workmen's Compensation programs are all administered by the states. The earliest workmen's compansation program, was developed in Wisconsin in 1911, and by 1948 all states had worker compensation laws.

[9] Services discussed are those related to the income maintenance portion of programs. It is recognized that agencies like the Veteran's Administration and Employment Service, provide other forms of social service and have other forms of programs. However, these other programs and services are described in other chapters (see footnote 10).

[10] Occupations discussed for Social Security, Veterans programs and Unemployment Insurance are limited to the income maintenance function of each particular agency. Other occupations and professions are involved in other functions of each agency. These functions are described in other chapters focusing on the Military Network, Chapter 6 and Employment and Manpower Network, Chapter 17.

[11] Harold Wilensky and Charles LeBeaux, in Industrial Society and Social Welfare, New York, New York: Free Press, 1965, for example, estimated that 4 percent of employees in public assistance programs had a master's degree in social work.

[12] An example of a professional organization for public assistance programs is the American Public Welfare Association, 1125 15th NW, Suite 300, Washington, D.C., 20005.

[13] An example of a professional organization for social security programs is the National Conference of State Social Security Administrators, Public Employee Retirement system, P.O. Box 1953, Sacramento, California. For more details on Social Security, the reader is referred to the nearest regional office of the Social Security Administration or the Social Security Administration in Washington, D.C.

[14] An example of a professional organization for veterans programs is the National Association of State Director's/Veterans Affairs, 941 N. Capital St., NW, Room 1211F, Washington, D.C. 20421. For further information on programs for veterans, the reader is referred to the nearest regional office of the Veteran's Administration or the Veteran's Administration in Washington, D.C. or the State Department of Veteran's Affairs.

[15] An example of a professional organization for unemployment programs is the Interstate Conference of Employment Security Agencies, 444 N. Capital St., NW, Suite 126, Washington,
D.C. 20001. For further details on unemployment programs, the
reader is referred to the local office of the state Employment
Service.

[16] For further information on the profession of social
work, the reader is referred to the National Association of
Social Workers, 7981 Eastern Avenue, Silver Spring, Maryland
10910 or the local chapter of the National Association of Social
Workers.

SUGGESTED READINGS

Helen Clarke. Social Legislation, 2nd Ed. New York: NY:
    Appleton Century Crofts Inc., 1957. Although dated, this is
    a classic book which describes the history of programs and
    services for the poor. For the individual interested in
    history and a book with numerous resources and references,
    this book is highly recommended.

Blanche Coll. Perspectives in Public Welfare: A History.
    Washington, D.C.: U.S. Government Printing Office, 1969.
    For a non-technical overview of the development of public
    welfare in the United States, this government publication is
    an excellent resource.

Walter Friedlander and Robert Apte. Introduction to Social
    Welfare, 5th ed. Englewood Cliffs, NJ: Prentice Hall,
    Inc., 1980. This basic text in social welfare has one
    chapter on poverty and public welfare and the role of social
    work in poverty and public welfare programs.

Gerald Handel. Social Welfare in Western Society. New York,
    NY: Random House, 1982. This book interweaves the follow-
    ing systems of providing social welfare programs to the
    unfortunate from a historical perspective; charity and
    philanthropy, social assistance, mutual aid, social insur-
    ance and social services.

Arthur Hands. Charities and Social Aid in Greece and Rome.
    Ithaca, NY: Cornell University Press, 1968. For the
    individual who is interested in classical societies and the
    use of mutual aid societies and charity/philanthropy to
    provide for the unfortunate, this is a highly recommended
    book.

Samuel Mencher. <u>Poor Law to Poverty Program</u>. Pittsburg, PA: University of Pittsburg Press, 1967. The uniqueness of this book is the interweaving of economic, social and political thought in developing a history of social welfare programs for the unfortunate. This book is highly recommended because of its historical and sociological approach.

Charles Schottland. <u>The Social Security Program in the United States</u>. New York, NY: Appleton Press, 1963. This book is an indepth history of the development of the Social Security program and explains in detail the political process in passing the Social Security Act of 1935.

Walter Trattner. <u>From Poor Law to Welfare State</u>, 2nd Ed. Chicago, IL: Free Press, Inc. 1979. Although this book discusses the development of social work as a profession, the focus is on poverty and society's response to the problem. The book is highly recommended for its blending of the problem of poverty and the development of social services and a specific profession.

REFERENCES

Clarke, Helen. <u>Social Legislation 2nd Edition</u>. New York, NY: Appleton-Century Crofts, Inc., 1957.

Coll, Blanche. <u>Perspectives in Public Welfare: A History</u>. Washington, D.C.: U.S. Government Printing Office, 1969.

Dye, Thomas. <u>Understanding Public Policy, 5th Edition</u>. Englewood Cliffs, NJ: Prentice-Hall, Inc., 1984.

Ferguson, Elizabeth. <u>Social Work: An Introduction, 3rd Edition</u>. Philadelphia, PA: J.B. Lippincott and Co., 1975.

Friedlander, Walter and Robert Apte. <u>Introduction to Social Welfare, 5th Edition</u>. Englewood Cliffs, NJ: Prentice-Hall, Inc., 1980.

Haber, William, Wilbur Cohen and Merrill Murray. <u>Unemployment Insurance in the American Economy</u>. Homewood, Illinois: Irwin Press, 1966.

Handel, Gerald. <u>Social Welfare in Western Society</u>. New York, New York: Random House, 1982

Hands, Arthur. <u>Charities and Social Aid in Greece and Rome</u>. Ithaca, New York: Cornell University Press, 1968.

Lawrence, William and Stephen Leeds. An Inventory of State and Local Income Transfer Programs: Fiscal Year 1977. White Plains, NY: Institute for Socioeconomic Studies, 1978.

Lawrence, William and Stephen Leeds. An Inventory of Federal Income Transfer Programs: Fiscal Year 1977. White Plains, NY: Institute for Socioeconomic Studies, 1980.

Macarov, David. The Design of Social Welfare. New York, NY: Holt, Rinehart and Winston, Inc., 1978.

Mencher, Samuel. Poor Law to Poverty Program. Pittsburgh, PA: University of Pittsburgh Press, 1967.

Milwaukee Journal. "America's Children are Becoming Better Acquainted with Poverty," June 16, 1985.

Minahan, Anne (Ed.) Encyclopedia of Social Work 18th Issue Washington, DC: National Association of Social Workers, 1986.

Ruttenberg, Stanley. Federal, State Employment Service: A Critique. Baltimore, MD: John Hopkins Press, 1970.

Office of the Federal Register, United States Government Manual, 1985-86, Washington, DC: U.S. Government Printing Office, 1985.

Schottland, Charles. The Social Security Program in the United States. New York, New York: Appleton Press, 1963.

Trattner, Walter. From Poor Law to Welfare State, 2nd Edition. Chicago, IL: Free Press, Inc., 1979.

United States Civil Service Commission, Occupation of Federal White Collar Workers; 1979. Washington, DC: U.S. Government Printing Office, 1981.

United States Department of Commerce, Bureau of the Census, Public Employment in 1984, Washington, DC: U.S. Government Printing Office, 1985.

United States Department of Commerce, Bureau of the Census, Statistical Abstract of the United States: 1986 (106th Ed.), Washington, DC: U.S. Government Printing Office, 1985.

United States Department of Commerce, Bureau of the Census. 1980 Census of Population: Vol. 2 Subject Reports Part 7C: Occupation by Industry, Washington, DC: U.S. Government Printing Office, 1984.

Vonhoff, Heinz. People Who Care: An Illustrated History of Human Compassion. Philadelphia, Pennsylvania: Fortress Press, 1971.

Weber, Gustavus and Lawrence Schmeckebier. The Veteran's Administration. Washington, DC: Brookings Institute, 1934.

Weinstein, Amy. Public Welfare Directory 1986/87, Washington, D.C.: American Public Welfare Association, 1986.

Wilcox, Clair. Toward Social Welfare. Homewood, IL: Richard D. Irwin, Inc., 1969.

Wilensky, Harold and Charles LeBeaux. Industrial Society and Social Welfare. New York, New York: Free Press, 1965.

Williamson, John. Strategies Against Poverty in America. New York, NY: John Wiley and Sons, Inc., 1975.

Wisconsin Legislative Reference Bureau, Wisconsin Blue Book 1985/86, Madison, Wisconsin: Department of Administration, 1985.

CHAPTER 20

MENTAL HEALTH NETWORK*

"In utilizing its own rationality, the mind also
realizes the presence in itself of elements which are
not rational. These irrational elements may appear to
dominant only the minds of madmen, yet, devoted as the
20th Century is to the reign of reason, it has often
failed to recognize the irrational elements which shape
conceptions and definitions of rational behavior."
(Neaman:1975:5)

INTRODUCTION

The mental health network has undergone massive changes
since 1945 with an emphasis on short term, out-patient care and
use of pharmacological techniques for intervention. On the
other hand, many experts are still debating the existing nomen-
clature, definitions, dimensions and parameters of mental illness. It is ironic that the 20th Century does not know what
mental illness is, yet, the Medieval theologians (1200 A.D.),
made distinctions between the mentally ill, the mad, and the
possessed. In spite of advances in the mental health network,
we still carry many of the negative values and attitudes toward
the mentally ill, and their problems as have past generations.

The mental health network has a variety of occupations and
professions implementing the delivery of social services.
Unlike some of the other networks of society discussed, there is
no one profession dominating the mental health network. It is
customary to list four professions as constituting the core of
the treatment team in mental health which are: psychiatry,
psychology, psychiatric nursing and psychiatric social work.
Each of these occupations and professions are discussed.

SIZE

The mental health network in the United States has been
undergoing profound changes since 1950, and one of these changes
is the increase in outpatient care in contrast to inpatient
care. This change is reflected in Figure 20-1, which shows the
estimated size of the mental health network by it's inpatient
and outpatient components.

In 1982-84 there were an estimated 4,302 mental health
facilities in the United States serving an estimated 6.5 million

643

Figure 20-1

ESTIMATED SIZE OF THE MENTAL HEALTH NETWORK
IN 1982-1984 *

Selected Characteristic	Type of Facility		
	In Patient	Out Patient	Total
Number of Facilities	2,487	1,815	4,302
Number of Patient Care Episodes	1,720,000	4,823,000	6,543,000
Number of Employees	264,000	117,300	381,300
Expenditures (Billion)	8,169,000,000	3,998,000,000	12,167,000,000

*Sources: Adapted from United States Department of Commerce, Bureau of the Census, Statistical Abstract of the United States 1986 (106th Edition, Washington, DC: U.S. Government Printing Office, 1985 p. 49, 106, 107, 113, 116, 117.

¹Estimates on the incidence of mental illness in the United States is 15 percent of the population or about 35.5 million people. Estimates of the number of individuals who see psychiatrists, psychologists and social workers in private practice is estimated at 1.3 million. United States Department of Health Education and Welfare, Health United States, Washington, D.C.: U.S. Government Printing Office, 1979 p. 302.

644

patient episodes, employing approximately 381,320 individuals and having expenditures estimated at 12 billion dollars.[1]

Outpatient care serves more individuals, has more facilities, and costs less than inpatient care and has fewer employees.[2] Although the mental health network directly serves an estimated 6.5 million patient episodes annually, the actual incidence of mental illness in the United States is estimated at 15 percent of the American population (237 million in 1986) or approximately 35.5 million individuals. Of these 35.5 million people it is estimated that 5 million are seeking help on a private basis, 17 million are not receiving any formal service, 6.5 million appear in the statistics of the mental health network, and the remaining 7 million individuals are either seeking help sporadically, or utilizing an informal or folk system.

HISTORICAL DEVELOPMENT

In Western culture the mentally ill were shunned, tortured, incarcerated, and in many cases executed in prior centuries. Programs for the more humane treatment of the mentally ill are a product of the last 100 years. Historically perceptions on the cause of mental illness changed from, notions of the supernatural and external possession by demons or spirits, to psychological and socio-biological factors. Along with the changing concepts of the causation of mental illness came modifications and innovations in the methods of treating the mentally ill. Figure 20-2 shows a historical time line of the mental health network.

In some prehistoric societies the cause of mental illness was perceived as a bodily invasion of the individual by an external spirit or supernatural force. A medicine man performed various rituals to exorcise or force the supernatural spirit to leave. In performing these rituals the medicine man would use herbs or drugs, body massages, and other measures to relax the patient. There are numerous archeological reports of the use of surgery i.e. trephaning, or skull surgery, to release the demon spirit.

CLASSICAL CIVILIZATIONS PRE 450 A.D.

Early civilizations like, Egypt (4000 B.C.), Sumeria (2000 B.C.), used priest/physicians to treat the mentally ill. As indicated in the chapter on Physical Health (Chapter 23), there were 3 classes of priest/physicians: the holy healer, medicine healer, and surgeon. The holy healer was the one who treated those with a mental illness. Mental illness was seen as supernatural in origin, caused by external forces, consequently exorcism of the supernatural force was necessary. The person

645

Figure 20-2

HISTORICAL TIME LINE OF THE MENTAL HEALTH NETWORK

Time Period	Aspects of Mental Health Network			
	Cause	Personnel	Treatment	Significant Figures
Prehistoric pre 4000 BC	Supernatural	Medicine man	Ritual, Prayer, Exorcism	
Early Civilization 4000 BC - 300 BC	Supernatural	Priest/Physician (Holy Healer)	Ritual, Prayer Exorcism	
Greek/Roman 300 BC - 450 AD	Natural/super-natural	Physician	Ritual, Prayer, Sleep Therapy, general Hygiene, Logical Persuasion	Hippocrates Soranus Ariteaus
Medieval 450-1500	Supernatural	Priest/Physician	Prayer, Exorcism	Johannes Weyer Paracelsus
Renaissance and Reformation 1500-1700	Early development of Natural causes/ environmental causes	Physician	Special Hospitals Blood Letting or Purging	Thomas Sydenham George Cheyne Felix Platter
Enlightenment 1700-1800	Natural Causes	Physician	Hospitalzation	Phillipe Pinel William Tuke Jean Esquiral
19th Century 1800-1900	Organic	Physician/Psychiatrist	Hospitalization Some Medication	Franz Gall Anton Messmer Emil Kraepelin
20th Century 1900 on	Organic/ Psychological Sociological	Physician - Psychiatrist, Psychologist, Psychiatric Nurse, Psychiatric Social Work...	Hospitalization Out patient care Psychotherapy Medication	Sigmund Freud Wilhelm Wundt John Dewey William James

was treated either at home or in the healing temple. The Egyptians also used relaxation methods, music therapy, sleep therapy and recreation activity as a means to treat the mentally ill. The Hebrews used dreams and dream interpretation as a means to treat the mentally ill.

Greek civilization (400 B.C.) attempted to look for natural causes and used the humoral theory or imbalance of humors as the cause of mental illness.[3] A classification or typolgy of mental illness was developed consisting of: phrenetia, mania and melancholia. Treatment was by a physician either at home or in the Aesculapian Temple named after the Greek god of medicine Aesculapius. Some techniques used for treating the mentally ill included drugs, music therapy, sleep therapy, general hygiene, bloodletting, purging and leeching. Hippocrates (460-377 B.C.) is the most famous of the Greek physicians. Roman civilization continued the same medical practices of the Greeks through individuals, such as Ariteaus of Cappadocia (150), Galen (130-201) and Soranus of Ephesus (100). The Romans under Soranus added the concept of logical persuasion or talking a person out of illness, and advocated humanitarian treatment. Treatment was usually at home, however, some separate part of the public infirmaries used by the lower classes and slave population were set aside for the housing of the mentally ill. The general population did not accept natural causes as an explanation for mental illness and therefore looked at the supernatural for an explanation.

MEDIEVAL EUROPE - 450-1500

The decline of the Roman Empire resulted in a regression or a backwards movement in the humane treatment of the mentally ill and a return to supernatural explanations. The cause of mental illness was viewed either as punishment for past sins or transgression of an individual, and/or their ancestors, or possession by an evil spirit. The priest had responsibility for exorcising the evil spirit. Distinctions were made between degrees of mental illness. An individual who was harmless and non-heretical by church doctrine in their behavior, was left to roam the streets and have the community take care of them. Some of the more severe cases were placed in monastery hospices or asylums, such as St. Galls (720), or a special colony like Gheel Belgium (580). Upon release from either the hospice or colony, the person was to wear a red badge indicating they were released from a monastery "hospice" and the community was expected to provide care for them. This was an early form of a parole plan for the mentally ill, since the person was released back to the local community for care. However, this plan quickly degenerated, as criminals began to steal the badges from the mentally ill person and dispose of the person in order to obtain free community aid. An additional factor for the decline of the "parole plan" was the fear the general population had of the person who was mentally ill, since they viewed that person as being or having been possessed by the devil. Consequently many of the people who were mentally ill in the community were stoned to death. Of importance in the treatment of mental illness was the Middle East, in places, such as Baghdad, Iraq (750), Cairo, Egypt (873) and Damascus, Syria (800) where special hospitals were established for treatment of the mentally ill. These hospitals (hospices) were located in natural environments of great beauty, with the hospitals surrounded by exquisite gardens with charming fountains.

By 600 these early measures for treating mental illness were changing. An added factor which increased the fear of the general population toward the mentally ill was the decision made at the Council of Tolous (500) which sanctioned the notion of devil possession as a cause of mental illness, instead of a generalized possession by an evil spirit. The substitution of devil (satanical) possession for general evil spirit possession paved the way for devil cults, and the confusion of mental illness, with witchcraft and heresy. A classical portrayal of devil possession appears in the book by Heinrich Kraemer and Jakob Sprenger <u>Witches Hammer</u> written in 1486. Since mental illness was perceived to be caused by devil possession the mentally ill were beaten, tortured, executed, thrown into dungeons, or early jails where no medical or sanitary care was provided. The United States counterpart of this harsh treatment of the mentally ill was the Salem Witch trials of 1670.

In spite of these harsh measures, there were early voices which proposed humanitarian treatment for the mentally ill and dared suggest that perhaps there were other causes for mental illness than diabolical possession. Cornelius Agrippa (1486-1535) was a physician at Metz, France, in one of the jail/prisons for the insane. He was appalled at the inhumane treatment and advocated better sanitary conditions, such as padded cells, non use of chains, adequate food and heat. He further postulated that mental illness was not caused by possession by the devil, but by other natural causes. For his activities he was branded a heretic and had to flee from France before the inquisitors could imprison him for heresy. Other early reformers in the treatment of the mentally ill included: Paracelsus (1491-1541) developed a classification system for mental illness and Johannis Weyer (1515-1588) further advanced the concept of natural causation, humane treatment and has been called the founder of psychiatry.

RENAISSANCE and REFORMATION - 1500-1700

Special hospitals (institutions) were developed during this time period as an alternative to execution and death for devil possession. Felix Platter (1536-1614), Thomas Sydenham (1624-1689), George Cheyne (1631-1743), and Thomas Willis (1621-1690), were all physicians who began to look at abnormal behavior as an illness. Willis has been called the father of neurology, a special branch of medicine, which ultimately led to psychiatry as a medical speciality by 1850. These physicians postulated that mental illness was the consequence of social and psychological conditions and continued to advocate for special institutions. Two parallel systems were developed for the treatment of the mentally ill: public network i.e., insane asylums, and pauper prisons for the poor and private institutions and home care for the wealthy.

ENLIGHTENMENT 1700-1800

Psychiatry emerged as an independent field of medical practice, with subsequent changes in the treatment of the mentally ill, yet at the same time, there was a rapid increase in the use of insane asylums for the mentally ill. It was a period when the housing of the mentally ill were warehoused under extremely unsanitary conditions. Common practices for treating the mentally ill included: inadequate heating, food, clothing, and beating the mentally ill into submission, chaining the individual indefinitely in various uncomfortable positions, and exhibiting the mentally ill to the general public for a fee. Because of these abuses many physicians became concerned about the welfare of the mentally ill and began to advocate naturalistic theories of causation and reforms in the treatment of the mentally ill.

New theories on the causation of mental illness were developed, such as George Stahl (1650-1734) and his theory of animism. Stahl postulated that disease is a consequence of the fight between the anima (soul), which directs the physical and chemical reactions of the body, and the external environment. The anima serves to ward off and to fight the negative influences of a psychological and physical nature. Stahl viewed mental illness in a twofold classification: sympathetic or organic (physical) in nature, and pathetic or non organic (psychological) in nature. Frans (Frederick Anton) Mesmer (1734-1815) developed a theory of animal magnetism which was called mesmerism. Each individual has a psychological force called magnetism. Mental illness is a consequence of a disruption or imbalance of this force. These early theories of animism, mesmerism, and attempted classification of illness led to attempts to develop psychological, and organic theories of causation.

Concurrent with the search for natural causes of mental illness, was the development of a variety of treatment techniques and humanitarian reforms of the insane asylums. Pierre Cabanis (1757-1808) advanced a theoretical base for psychotherapy. A variety of physical treatments were developed, such as the Darwins Chair (a shaking chair), electric shock (the use of electric eels), straight jackets and the use of some drugs. Phillipe Pinel (1745-1826), Jean Esquiral (1772-1840) and William Tuke (1732-1822) revolutionized the treatment of individuals housed in insane asylums. In 1793 Pinel shocked the medical profession and the citizens of Paris by releasing the mentally ill from their chains at the Bicetre Insane Asylum. Pinel advocated that the asylum should become a primary treatment facility and there should be a full program of work, physical activity, physical and psychological treatment, as well as, humane living circumstances. In addition, Pinel observed cases and used the clinical model of observation to differentiate between different disease patterns. Jean Esquirol, a student of Pinel's continued in Pinel's work. William Tuke in England, established a special hospital for the insane in 1793. In the United States Benjamin Rush (1745-1813) developed a hospital for the insane and advocated humane treatment and identified alcoholism as one of the possible causes of insanity. Benjamin Rush has been considered the founder of American psychiatry. The 18th Century laid the foundation for the development of psychiatry as a specialty in medicine, psychology as a social science, and the utilization of treatment methods in mental institutions instead of warehousing the mentally ill.

NINETEENTH CENTURY - 1800-1900

During the 19th Century there was the development of a psychiatric classification, Freudian theory, and its offshots, and psychology as a discipline. Dorthea Dix (1802- 1887) championed reforms for treatment of the mentally ill, including the development of public mental institutions. Jean Charcot (1825-1893) studied hypnosis as a therapeutic technique and through his prize pupil Sigmund Freud (1856-1939) and his works there was the development of depth psychology, psychoanalysis and eventually the understanding of psychodynamics. William Griesinger (1817-1868) has been labeled the first genuine psychiatrist because of his extensive research and orientation toward the problem of mental illness. One of Griesingers followers Emil Kraepelin (1855-1926), made extensive studies of mental illness and devised the classification system of mental illness still in use today. Kraepelin because of his background in neurology leaned toward the organic branch of psychiatry.

Psychology as a discipline, distinct from philosophy had early developments with the work of Anton (Frederick Anton) Mesmer (1734-1815) the founder of mesmerism, Franz Gall (1758-1828) founder of phrenology, Wilhelm Wundt (1832-1921) and Francis Galton (1822-1911). Psychology as an applied science was developing with the work of Hugo Munsterberg (1863-1916). Lichtner Witmer (1867-1956) developed the first psychology clinic, and the giants of American psychology John Dewey (1859-1952) and William James (1842-1910) developed academic programs. By 1900 psychology and psychiatry were both established as independent fields of study and practice. Psychology had its origins in social philosophy and experimentation, whereas psychiatry had its origins in medicine. The mental institution remained as the primary vehicle for the treatment of the mentally ill while progress was made in understanding the behavior of the mentally ill. The common person still perceived mental illness as negative, with many individuals still viewing mental illness as caused by possession of the devil or the consequence of sin.

TWENTIETH CENTURY - 1900-ON

In the early 20th Century psychiatric social work developed in child guidance clinics (1909) and was a subspeciality of social work by 1926. Psychiatric nursing as a subspecialty began as early as 1841, with courses offered in the field by 1882 and a mental health division in the nursing association by 1911. Psychiatric nursing was not formally approved as a speciality by the American Nurses Association until 1937.

Up until 1950, the predominate means of treatment in the mental health network was the state hospital for the lower socioeconomic groups, and private hospitals or private care for the more affluent socioeconomic groups. Since 1950, there has been a gradual revolution in the mental health network with an increasing deemphasis on long-term institutional care, the growing importance of outpatient treatment facilities and the establishment of inpatient and outpatient facilities in local (general) hospitals. An impetus for this change in the mental health network was the 1946 Mental Health Act, which mandated the development of community mental health centers, and provided funding for the training of various professions in mental health. Other significant legislation affecting the mental health network includes the 1956 study commission, the establishment of the National Institute of Mental Health in 1946 and the 1963 Mental Health Act, establishing community mental health facilities. As a consequence of these legislative acts, there has been a rapid development of community mental health centers, day hospitals, neighborhood health stations, and the use of indigenous paraprofessionals. Although a difference still exists between psychiatric care available for members of the higher socioeconomic groups, and lower socioeconomic groups, accessibility to services has been made available to all citizens, and the quality of service is not necessarily dependent upon income. Since the 1960's numerous health plans now include treatment of mental illness under insurance coverage. The 1980's is a period where there has been a budgetary reduction of federal monies available for the treatment of mental illness consequently both the quality of service and accessability of service to the lower socioeconomic populations has been reduced.

STRUCTURE

Like the other societal networks which utilize human service professions, the structure of the mental health network can be described from its organizational context, services provided, occupations and professions and dominant occupations and professions.

ORGANIZATIONAL CONTEXT

The mental health network consists of public and private, agencies with varying degrees of governmental organization. An idealized model of the mental health network is shown in figure 20-3.

Numerous governmental units are part of the mental health network. Examples of the federal and state government structure are shown in Figure 20-4.

Most psychiatric hospitals and outpatient clinics have either a physician or a professional administrator as the director. The social service department may or may not be an independent unit based upon the uniqueness of the structure of the facility. Figures 20-5 and 20-6 show a typical organizational chart of a private and a public psychiatric hospital with the location of the social service department i.e., social work within the medical sector, and as an autonomous unit. In addition to the formal mental health network, individuals may use an informal or folk system to try to solve problems, such as relatives, friends, co-workers, religious cult groups and so on.

Figure 20-3

IDEALIZED MODEL OF THE MENTAL HEALTH NETWORK

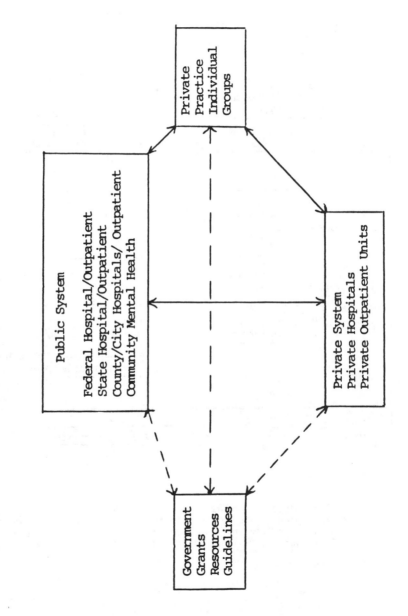

653

Figure 20-4

ORGANIZATION OF GOVERNMENTAL SERVICES
IN THE MENTAL HEALTH NETWORK BY LEVEL OF ADMINISTRATION

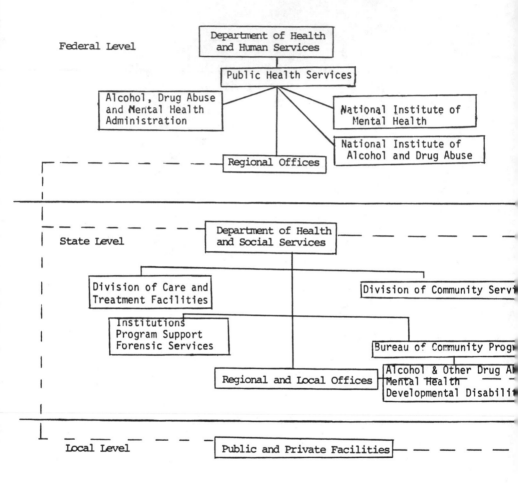

*Sources: Adapted from Office of the Federal Register, <u>United States
Government Manual 1985-86</u>, Washington, D.C.: U.S. Government Printing
Office, 1985, p. 842 and Wisconsin Legislative Reference Bureau, <u>Wisconsin
Blue Book 1985-86</u>, Madison, Wisconsin: Department of Administration 1985 p.
512, 517, 518.

Figure 20-5

MODEL OF THE ORGANIZATION OF A
TYPICAL PRIVATE PSYCHIATRIC HOSPITAL*

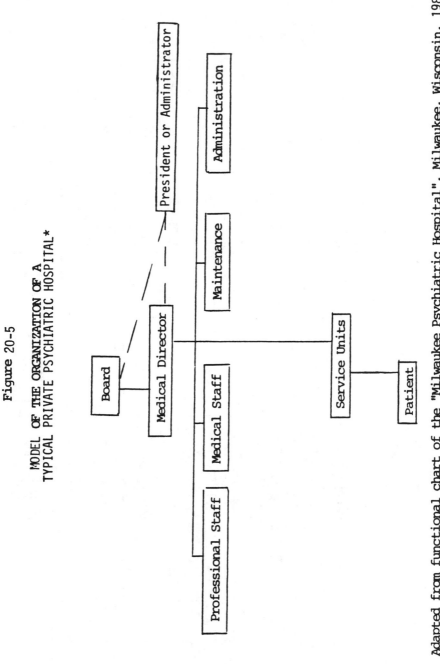

*Source: Adapted from functional chart of the "Milwaukee Psychiatric Hospital", Milwaukee, Wisconsin, 1982.

Figure 20-6

ORGANIZATION OF THE CLEMENT J. ZABLOCKI MEDICAL CENTER
VETERANS ADMINISTRATION, MILWAUKEE, WISCONSIN

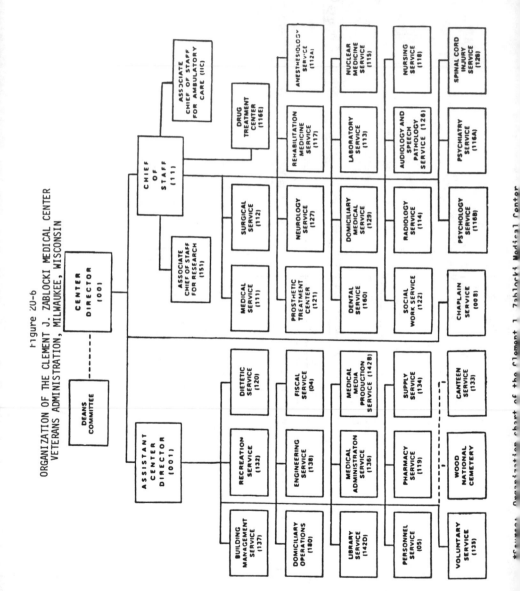

*Source: Organization chart of the Clement J. Zablocki Medical Center

SERVICES PROVIDED

The mental health network provides the following services:

- Long-term patient care
- Acute patient care
- Partial hospitalixation (or day hospital)
- Outpatient care
- Medication, physical, and psychiatric treatments
- Individual and group counseling
- Individual and group therapy
- Family and couples counseling and therapy
- Recreation therapy and activities
- Aesthetic therapies, (i.e., art, music, dance)
- Rehabilitation and vocational counseling
- Mental health assessment and diagnosis
- Pre-discharge planning and referral
- Library resources
- Work activity
- Religious counseling activity
- Examinations, medical and psychiatric
- Psychological testing and evaluation
- Educational programs
- Social activities
- Home and relative visitations
- Medical prescriptions and surgery
- Support groups
- Dental care.

OCCUPATIONS and PROFESSIONS

In 1980-1981, the mental health network employed an estimated 387,337 individuals who could be classified as human service occupations and professions. Of these selected human service occupations and professions, 122,514 or 31.6 percent were mental health aides which is a paraprofessional group. Figure 20-7 shows a selected variety of human service occupations and professions employed in the mental health network. It has been customary to consider psychiatry, psychology, psychiatric social work and psychiatric nursing as the core professions in mental health. These four professions account for 196,155 individuals or 50.6 percent of the selected human service occupations and professions employed in the mental health network and the remaining 191,182 or 49.4 percent consisted of a variety of other occupations and professions. Mental health careers generally consist of the following: physician (psychiatry), psychology, psychoanalyst, psychiatric social work, psychiatric nursing, nurse clinician, occupational therapist, recreational therapist, art therapist, music

657

FIGURE 20-7

NUMBER AND PERCENT OF SELECTED HUMAN SERVICE

OCCUPATIONS AND PROFESSIONS EMPLOYED IN THE MENTAL

HEALTH NETWORK IN 1980-1981*

Occupation and Profession	Number	Percent
Psychiatry	31,490	8.2
Psychiatric Nursing[1]	51,564	13.3
Licensed Practical Nurse	16,587	4.2
Social Work	96,600	24.9
Psychology[1]	16,501	4.2
Vocational Rehabilitation/ Teacher, Occupational Therapy	39,363	10.1
Physical Health Profession (Dentist, Dental Technician Pharmacist, Dietician)	9,684	2.5
Mental Health Staff (less than a BA/BS degree, mental health aides)	122,514	31.6
Physicians	3,034	.1
TOTAL	387,337	100.0

* Sources: Adapted from United States Department of Commerce, Bureau of the Census 1980 Census of Population Vol. 2. Subject Reports Part 7C: Occupation by Industry, Washington, DC: U.S. Government Printing Office, 1984, pp 295-664; American Nurses Association, Facts About Nursing, 1984-85, Kansas City, Missouri: American Nurses Association, 1985, pp 56, 77, 281; and United States Department of Health and Human Services, Public Health Service, Mental Health United States: 1983, Washington, DC: U.S. Government Printing Office, 1983.

[1] Depending upon the source used there is some discrepancy between figure 20-7 and 20-8 on the number of professions employed in mental health. The census material did not sufficiently detail the area of mental health, subsequently some estimates were made. The American Nurses Association Facts about Nursing 1984-85 Kansas City, Missouri: American Nurses Association 1985 showed a figure of 33,142 psychiatrists in 1982 and 28,635 registered nurses.

therapist, dance therapist, biblio therapist, poetry therapist, psychiatric aide, (technician), clergy, counselor, community worker, human service generalist and volunteer.[4]

DOMINANT OCCUPATIONS and PROFESSIONS

As indicated earlier, the core professions in mental health are: psychiatry, psychology, psychiatric nursing, and psychiatric social work. Figure 20-8 shows the employment of a psychiatrist, psychologist and psychiatric nurse by industrial classification in 1980.[5]

PSYCHIATRY - In 1980, there were an estimated 31,490 psychiatrists employed in the mental health area mental health network (see Figures 20-7). Figure 20-8 shows employment of psychiatrists by industrial classification. The discrepancy in numbers between figure 20-7 and 20-8 is a consequence of using a different method of calculation and in incorporating materials from the American Psychiatric Association. In 1980, there were an estimated 29,722 psychiatrists employed in the mental health area (mental health and public administration) which represents 95 percent of the psychiatrists in the United States. The remaining 1,579 or 5.0 percent of psychiatrists are employed in other industrial classifications. Of the 29,772 psychiatrists employed in the mental health and public administration industrial classifications, 20,156 or 67.7 percent were employed in private practice, 7,612 or 25.6 percent in psychiatric hospitals and 2,004 or 6.7 percent in administration.

Psychiatry, as described earlier, became a separate branch of medicine in the mid-1800s. The first professional organization in psychiatry in the United States was organized in 1844 called the Association of Medical Superintendents of American Institutions for the Insane. This organization changed its name to the American Medico-Psychological Association in 1890, and in 1921 was renamed American Psychiatric Association. Currently, an individual must have an M.D. degree, successfully complete a residence in psychiatry, and be certified by the American Board of psychiatry, which was established in 1936. Psychiatry as a field, has focused on psychological manifestations of illness and has tended to use some form of the psychodynamic approach (unconscious drive, defense mechanisms, adaptation to anxiety, etc.) as part of its approach in understanding mental illness. A psychiatrist engages in the following tasks:

- Diagnosis and evaluation of mental illness
- Individual and group therapy (usually from a psychodynamic approach)
- Prescribes medication

FIGURE 20-8

Number and Percent of Psychiatrists, Psychologists

and Psychiatric Nurses Employed by Industrial

Classification in 1980*[1]

Industrial Classification	Psychiatrist[4] Number	Percent	Psychologist Number	Percent	Psychiatric Nurse[4] Number	Percent
Agriculture/Forestry Fishery			—	—		
Mining			19	.020		
Construction			26	.028		
Manufacturing			588	.648	279	.6
Transportation/						
Communication Utilities			235	.259		
Wholesale/Retail Trade			128	.141		
Financial/Real Estate			236	.259		
Business/Repair[2]	141	.4	1,054	1.161	375	.7
Entertainment/Recreation			44	.048		
Personal Services			156	.172	395	.8
Professional/Related						
(Except Health)[3]	1,439	4.6	34,798	38.313	3,887	8.1
Health-Physical			15,716	17.303	2,291	4.7
Health-Mental	27,718	88.6	30,187	33.237	35,823	73.9
Public Administration	2,004	6.4	7,639	8.411	5,456	11.2
TOTAL	31,301	100.0	90,826	100.00	48,506	100.0

*Source: Adapted from United States Department of Commerce, Bureau of the Census, 1980 Census of Population Vol. 2 Subject Reports, Part 7C: Occupation by Industry, Washington, D.C.: U.S. Government Printing Office, 1984, pp. 295-664; Communication received from the American Psychiatric Association and American Nurses Association (1985); United States Department of Health and Human Services, Public Health Service. Mental Health United States, 1983, Washington, DC: U.S. Government Printing Office, 1983.

[1] Social work as an occupation is discussed in Chapter 3.

[2] Of the 1,054 psychologists in the industrial classification of business and repair, 311 were employed in research, 531 in consulting and 212 in computers.

[3] Includes 1,062 psychiatrists engaged in research activity.

[4] The 1980 census data did not specifically indicate the professions of psychiatry and psychiatric nursing by industrial classification. Letters to the American Psychiatric Association and American Nurses's Association in 1985 provided some useful information. The information received from these professional associations was not compatible with format used for this figure and estimates were made for these groups. The American Nurses Association Facts About Nursing 1984-85 Kansas City, Missouri American Nurses Association, 1985 p. 281 indicated 29,674 practicing psychiatrists in 1982 and an additional 3,468 psychiatrists specializing in child psychiatry for a total of 33,142 and 28,635 registered nurses in mental health.

- Psychiatric histories
- Consultation
- Educational programs.[6]

PSYCHOLOGY - In 1980, there were an estimated 16,501 psychologists employed in the mental health network (see figure 20-7). Figure 20-8 shows employment of psychologists by industrial classification. The discrepancy in numbers between figures 20-7 and 20-8 is a consequence of using a different method of calculation and incorporating materials from the American Psychological Association. In 1980, there were an estimated 90,826 psychologists in the United States, of which 37,826, or 41.6 percent, were employed in the mental health or public administration industrial classifications, and the remaining 53,000 or 58.4 percent were employed in other industrial classifications. Of the 37,826 psychologists in the mental health and public administration industrial classification 30,187 or 79.8 percent were employed in clinical settings and the remaining 7,639 or 20.2 percent were employed in administration.

Psychology as a discipline and a profession developed from social philosophy in the mid-1800s and the application of experimental methodology to the study of human behavior. The psychologist focuses on normal development, learned behavior, or bodily response to stimulus (stimulus/response), behavior modification, field psychology, testing and measurement, etc. in understanding behavior.

The American Psychological Association was formed in 1892 and has recognized a specialty in clinical psychology and psychometrics. Examples of other specialties in psychology include: school psychology, community, consulting, educational psychology, developmental psychology, social psychology, physiological psychology, experimental psychology, industrial psychology, etc. The first course in the United States in psychology was taught by William James at Harvard University in 1875. The first doctoral program in psychology in the United States was established at Harvard, and the first Ph.D. recipient was Stanley Hall in 1881. Generally, the practicing psychologist has at minimum a masters degree (psychometrics), and in most cases a Ph.D. (clinical psychology). A number of states currently require licensing of a psychologist if one is to practice independently as a clinical psychologist or as a psychometrician. The psychologist generally engages in the following activities:

- Testing and measurement
- Behavioral assessment
- Individual and group therapy (from a psychological perspective)

- Behavior modification
- Consultation
- Couples and family therapy
- Educational programs.[7]

PSYCHIATRIC NURSING - In 1980, (Figure 20-7) there were an estimated 1,272,900 registered nurses in the United States of which 51,564 or 4.1 percent were employed in mental health, and the remaining 1,221,336 or 95.9 percent in other areas (see figure 20-8). Estimates on the employment of psychiatric nurses by industrial classification in 1980 (from the American Nurses Association) are shown in figure 20-8. These estimates are slightly lower than the ones indicated in the United States census of 1980, but the general trend is similar. Of the 48,056 psychiatric nurses (3.8 percent of all registered nurses), 35,823 or 73.9 percent are employed in mental health, 5,456 or 11.2 percent in public administration, 2,291 or 4.7 percent in physical health and the remaining 4,936 or 10.2 percent in other industrial classifications.

Of the 41,279 psychiatric nurses employed in the mental health and public administration industrial classification, it was estimated that 35,823 or 86.7 percent were employed in clinical settings and 5,456 or 13.3 percent in administration. Figures from the Fact Book of Nursing 1984-85 shows an estimated 1,404,200 registered nurses in 1983 of which 28,635 or 2.0 percent were employed in mental health. Of these 28,635 registered nurses, 7,904 or 27.6 percent had a master's degree, 20,731 or 72.4 percent had less than a master's degree and in 1985 6,322 or 22 percent were certified by the American Nurses Association.[8]

Psychiatric nursing as a subspeciality of nursing developed in 1882 when a course was taught at McLean Hospital in Waverly, Massachusetts. In 1911, the American Nurses Association recognized a specialty practice area in mental hygiene and developed curriculum guidelines by 1917. Psychiatric nursing was formally sanctioned as a specialty in 1937. Since requirements for nursing are shifting from diploma schools, i.e., hospital training schools, to bachelors education at the university level, the requirements for a psychiatric nurse are in flux. The desired requirement is that of a masters degree in nursing, however, a bachelors degree is currently acceptable for employment in many places.

In addition to many of the standard nursing functions, the psychiatric nurse will engage in some of the following activities:

- Individual and group therapy
- Enhance practical problem solving on hospital wards for patients
- Create a positive atmosphere in the hospital setting conducive to better medical and psychiatric care
- Monitoring reaction of patients to prescribed drugs and medication
- Create a positive environment for social, recreation and rehabilitation programs
- Supervision of mental health aides and other nursing personnel.[9]

SOCIAL WORK

In 1980 (see figure 20-7), there were an estimated 345,000 social workers in the United States of which 96,600 or 28.0 percent were employed in the mental health network, and the remaining 248,400 or 72.0 percent were employed in other industrial classifications. Social work, in mental health began in child guidance clinics (1909), the Boston Psychopathic Hospital (1905) with the work of Mary Jarres and expanded to psychiatric hospitals. The American Association of Psychiatric Social Workers was established in 1926, and merged with six other social work organizations to form the National Association of Social Workers in 1955.

Standards for psychiatric social work are a masters degree from an accredited school of social work (including appropriate internship), and in some cases a bachelors degree in social work and a period of post-bachelors degree experience. The focus of social work is an eclectic discipline in comparison to the other mental health professions discussed. Social work utilizes knowledge from psychiatry, psychology, sociology and other social sciences. General functions of a psychiatric social worker include the following:

- Individual/group therapy (from the social work perspective)
- Family and marital therapy
- Pre-discharge planning and post-release followup
- Home visitations
- Community referral and followup
- Social histories
- Evaluation of functioning.

The social worker generally employs casework and group work skills in the treatment process, acts as a liaison with other community agencies, and may engage in community organization, staff development, consultation and research services.

INDIVIDUAL CASEWORK

This task involves a one to one relationship, where the worker is discussing with the person their problems and perceptions of reality. Techniques used could be confrontation, clarification, non directed intervention etc. In addition to psychological discussion, casework could also mean a concrete service, such as a home visit, helping a person find a job or assisting an individual or group on an education or recreation trip.

GROUP WORK

This task generally involves 3-12 persons discussing and exploring mutual problems. The structure of the group could vary from an in depth discussion of feelings and perceptions, to group cooperative efforts in solving a specific problem, such as ways to look for a job, how to obtain information in order to take a bus, etc.

COMMUNITY ORGANIZATION

These activities vary from environmental manipulation, to attempting to influence policy at the local or state level concerning the treatment of the mentally ill, to organizing a group of discharged patients to enable themselves to advocate for policies in their own behalf.

STAFF DEVELOPMENT

These activities include holding seminars on psychopathology, understanding the affect of cultural difference on behavior, or an analysis of a specific treatment technique. A common vehicle for staff development is the case analysis where one or two cases are presented to elaborate on specific treatment techniques or to point out how the clients behavior can be best understood in terms of their cultural backgrounds.

CONSULTATION and RESEARCH

This activity usually involves program evaluation, an analysis of an organizations structure, analysis of staff development programs, research on specific techniques of treatment and their success rate, and causes of mental illness.

As indicated earlier, all four core professions overlap in the provision of therapeutic activities, however the focus or direction of these activities will vary depending upon training and orientation. Each of the four professions has a uniqueness which distinguishes it from the other three. Figure 20-9 shows a comparison of the four core professions in mental health, on selected characteristics.

PERSONAL SOCIAL SERVICES

The mental health network since it focuses on emotional problems has a close linkage with the personal social services (see Chapter 22 Personal Social Service). Some examples of personal social service programs in the mental health network include the following:

PROTECTIVE SERVICES

Spouse abuse programs sponsored through a mental health counseling center, such as Nevermore, Milwaukee, Wisconsin and the Domestic Violence Unit, Mount Sinai Hospital, Milwaukee, Wisconsin.

UTILITARIAN SERVICES

Day care programs sponsored by a psychiatric hospital and information referral services, such as Day Care Center, Family Hospital, Milwaukee, Wisconsin and the Hayden M. Donahue Mental Health Institute, Norman, Oklahoma.

DEVELOPMENTAL and SOCIALIZATION SERVICES

Family and marital counseling programs through community mental health centers, such as the Behavioral Health Agency of Central Arizona, Casa Grande, Arizona and the Albany County Mental health Clinic, Albany, New York.

REHABILITATIVE and THERAPEUTIC SERVICES

Alcohol, drugs, suicide programs sponsored by the community mental health center or a specialized agency, such as the Albany County Mental Health Clinic, Albany, New York and Catalyst (sex therapy) Milwaukee, Wisconsin

SPECIAL POPULATIONS

Particular groups may have more difficulty in handling the stress of every day life and in coping with society since their culture or perspectives on life may differ from the broader society. Consequently, the mental health network should be more sensitive to the needs of special populations (see Chapter 25, Special Populations and Chapter 24 Rehabilitation). Some examples of organizations and programs focusing on special populations in the mental health network include the following:

Figure 20-9

COMPARISON OF THE FOUR CORE PROFESSIONS
IN THE MENTAL HEALTH NETWORK

Characteristic	Core Profession			
	Psychiatry	Psychology	Social Work (Psychiatric)	Nursing (Psychiatric)
Parent Academic Discipline	Natural Science	Social Science	Social Science	Natural Science
Specific Academic Discipline	Neurology/Psychiatry (inter psychic process)	Behaviorism/Learning Theory	Eclectic bio/ psycho/social	Neurology/Psychiatry (Inter Psychic Process)
Training/Education	Bachelor's Degree/ Medical Degree/ + internship/residency	Bachelor's Degree, Master's Degree, PHD	Bachelor's Degree Master's Degree	Bachelor's Degree Master's Degree
Historical Period of Specialization	1850-1900	1890	1905	1895
Focus	Medical/Therapy	Testing/Therapy	Psycho/Social Therapy	Medical/Therapy/ Home Environment

ASIAN

Asian Human Services of Chicago, Illinois, Chicago, Illinois; Asian Community mental Health Services, Oakland, California and the Waialua Mental Health Clinic, Waialua, Hawaii.

BLACK

Black Counseling and Guidance Center, Milwaukee, Wisconsin; Black Counseling Services, Ithaca, New York; Crispus Attucks Center, New York, New York; Change Incorporated, Berkeley, California and the Seattle Atlantic City Street Center, Seattle, Washington.

EUROPEAN ETHNIC

Ethnic Minority Mental Health Center, Seattle, Washington; Greek American Counseling Center, Meerick, New York; Jewish Family and Childrens Service Society, Milwaukee, Wisconsin; Counseling Center Bangor, Maine (French) and the South Oaks Hospital, The Long Island Home, Amityville, New York (German, Italian, Hebrew).

NATIVE AMERICAN

Milwaukee Indian Health Boards of Milwaukee, Wisconsin and St. Paul, Minnesota; American Indian Center, Omaha, Nebraska and the Hayden H. Donahue Mental Health Institute, Norman, Oklahoma.

SAME SEX PREFERENCE

Homosexual Information Center, Hollywood, California; Gay Union, Milwaukee, Wisconsin; Parents of Lesbians and Gays, New York, New York and the Gay Community Services Center, Los Angeles, California.

SPANISH SPEAKING

Andromeda Hispano Mental Health Center, Washington, D.C.; El Centro de Services Sociales, Lorain, Ohio and the Association Puertorriquenos en Marcho Incorporated, Philadelphia, Pennsylvania.

WOMEN

Counseling Women, New York, New York; Women's Survival Center, Pontiac, Michigan; Women, San Francisco, California;

The Women's Touch, Indianapolis, Indiana and The Wives Self Help Foundation. Chiltenhan, Pennsylvania.

ISSUES

The mental health network has undergone profound changes in the past twenty years with the introduction of drugs, deinstitutionalization of mental patients and the use of general hospitals with psychiatric wards. Issues in the mental health network relate to the above changes and can be classified as systemic issues and professional issues.

SYSTEMIC ISSUES

Since 1950, there has been a general shift away from placing the mentally ill in a state mental institution to the use of general hospitals, as the latter are more readily accessible to the patient population and their relatives. There has been an extensive utilization of paraprofessionals in mental health since 1960, and it is expected that this trend will continue. In addition to the use of paraprofessionals, there has been a rapid development of a variety of other disciplines which have been incorporated into the treatment team, such as art therapy, dance therapy, music therapy, recreation therapy, human service generalist etc. Each of these professions are developing their own specialized training programs and will have further impact on future changes within the mental health network. In addition to the modifications already indicated, of note, is the increasing use of nursing homes for the elderly mentally ill, the development of community mental health centers, and a variety of pre-payment insurance plans for mental health services and purchase of service contracts through Titles XIX and XX of the Social Security Act (see Chapter 19, Income Maintenance).

Since the attempted assasination of President Reagan there has been a growing concern about using mental illness as a defense for a criminal act. Some states have changed their laws to require a determination of guilt or innocence first, and then determination of mental capacity. The development of pre-paid mental health service plans by unions, companies, etc., is leading to a rapid increase in the development of third party contracts and private practice. Private practice for psychiatric nursing and for social work is relatively new, but is an expanding area of clinical activity.

PROFESSIONAL ISSUES

In psychiatry, one of the current trends is to make use of drugs on a more extensive basis, and in viewing the whole person in terms of treatment (the holistic approach). There is a shift away from the strict psychoanalytical approach as developed in the early 1900s. In psychology, there has been a growing emphasis on the use of behavior modification and reality therapy. A number of legal and ethical issues have received a high degree of publicity in the last ten years. Some of these ethical issues include the use of inmates of psychiatric hospitals for drug experimentation and the fact a number of therapists have sex relations with their clients under the guise of sex therapy. For a psychiatric nurse, there are changing standards for practice and licensing and there needs to be a clearer definition of the role of the psychiatric nurse in comparison to both the psychiatrist and the social worker. A growing concern in nursing, as in social work, is the role of private practice. There are a number of ethical issues regarding private practice which have to be dealt with, such as fee standards, licensing and accountability.

In social work it is necessary to take a closer look at staff development and consultation roles. In social work there should be a greater appreciation of cultural variables as they affect behavior and the perceived causes of mental illness. Different cultures, such as Native Americans, have a different perception of mental illness than the majority culture, and these different perceptions will have an impact upon the treatment of mental illness. That is, not all ethnic and racial groups will exhibit the same symptoms as others, and therefore, when one is dealing with individuals one has to be aware of different cultural backgrounds and different perceptions of what causes mental illness.

SUMMARY

The mental health network in the United States is large and diverse, having an estimated 4,302 facilities, serving directly approximately 6.5 million patient episodes, employing 381,300 individuals and having expenditures of approximately 12.0 billion dollars. These estimates are for direct service, yet the incidence of mental illness in the United States is estimated at 15 percent of the population, or about 35.5 million people.

A historical analysis of the development of the mental health network showed that perceptions of the causation of mental illness have evolved from supernatural sources, and possession by evil spirits to a hypothesized organic or psychological etiology. Along with the changing concept of the cause of mental illness was a change in individuals responsible for treating the mentally ill from the medicine man to a priest/physician, to a lay physician, and more recently, psychiatrists, psychologists, psychiatric nurses and psychiatric social workers.

Although the four occupations listed above are considered to be the core professions in providing mental health services, there are a variety of new mental health careers developing, such as art therapy, music therapy, dance therapy, recreation therapy, human service generalist etc., and each of these groups are developing their own knowledge base and specialized training. With the formation of specialized professional groups in the treatment of the mentally ill, there has been a concurrent shift from the utilization of mental institutions or long-term inpatient care facilities as the primary vehicle for treatment, to the increased utilization of outpatient units and the general hospital for treatment purposes.

A number of issues and trends were discussed in relationship to the mental health network, such as the shift from inpatient to outpatient, the development of new careers, including the use of paraprofessionals, legal defense of mental incapacitation, ethical concerns related to practice and the development of third party contracts and pre-payment programs for mental health services.

FOOTNOTES

*This chapter was reviewed for comments by Milton Silva, Professor of Psychiatry, Medical College of Wisconsin, and Director of Psychiatric Services, Columbia Hospital, Milwaukee, Wisconsin.

[1]These estimates on the size of the mental health network have some duplication with the physical health network. Since many general hospitals now provide psychiatric services, it is difficult to completely separate mental health from physical health statistics. The size of the mental health network was estimated from the United States Department of Commerce, Bureau of the Census, Statistical Abstract of the United States: 1986 (106th Ed.), Washington, D.C.: U.S. Government Printing Office, 1985 pp. 49, 106, 107, 113, 116, 117..

[2]Institutional care or inpatient care takes more employees than outpatient care, since an institution must provide ancillary services, such as food, clothing, laundry service etc. The ratio of patient episode to employees in inpatient care is 15:1, whereas for outpatient care, the ratio of patient episode to employee is 24:1.

[3]Humoral theory was postulated by Hippocrates (460 B.C.) viewing the cause of illness, physical or mental, as a consequence of the imbalance of a humoral element in the body. The four

humors in the body are equivalent to the four elements in nature which are: blood (air), yellow bile (fire), black bile (earth), and phlegm (water).

[4]The professions of art, dance and music therapy are discussed in Chapter 4 Aesthetic Network, recreation therapy in Chapter 14 Leisure and Recreation Network, occupational therapy in Chapter 23 Physical Health Network, rehabilitation counseling in Chapter 24 Rehabilitation Network, general nursing, physicians and other health professions, in Chapter 23 Physical Health Network and human service generalist in Chapter 22 Personal Social Service Network.

[5]The inconsistency in the numbers and percent used for the various professions in figures 20-7 and 20-8 is the result of slightly different data bases used for each figure.

[6]A listing of physicians by industrial classification is contained in Chapter 23 Physical Health Network. An example of a professional association is the American Psychiatric Association, 1400 K St. NW, Washington D.C. 20005. The American Board of Psychiatry and Neurology is located at One American Plaza, Suite 808, Evanston, Illinois 60201.

[7]Examples of professional associations include: the American Psychological Association 1200 17th St. NW, Washington D.C. 20036; American Board of Professional Psychology, 2025 Eye St. NW, Suite 405, Washington, D.C. 20006 and the Psychometric Society, Darvie Hall, University of North Carolina, Chapel Hill, North Carolina 27514.

[8]The Publication Facts About Nursing 1984-85 by the American Nurses Association (1985), provides an overview of where nurses are employed in the United States including psychiatric nurses.

[9]A listing of nurses, and where they are employed by industrial classification, is contained in Chapter 23 Physical Health Network. The American Nurses Association listed in the footnotes of Chapter 23 Physical Health Network has a division on psychiatric and mental health nursing. In addition to the registered nurse there are approximately 13,483 licensed practical nurses employed in the mental health network and 65,299 ancillary nursing personnel (aides, orderlies, attendants).

[10]A listing of social workers, and where they are employed by industrial classification, is contained in Chapter 3 Social Work as a Helping Profession. The estimate by the National Association of Social Workers of the number of social workers employed in mental health in 1982 is 28 percent of all social workers or

96,600. For information on social work in the mental health network, contact The National Association of Social Workers, 7981 Eastern Avenue, Silver Spring, Maryland 20910 or the local chapter of the National Association of Social Workers.

SUGGESTED READINGS

Franz Alexander and Sheldon Selesnick. The History of Psychiatry. New York, New York: Harper and Row, 1966. Although this book is dated it does provide an indepth history of psychiatry which should be of interest to an individual with a historical focus.

Albert Deutsch. The Mentally Ill in America. Garden City, New York: Doubleday, Doran and Co., 1937. This is a classic book about the treatment of the mentally ill in the United States. For the individual who wishes to focus on the United States, this book is highly recommended.

James Dugger. The New Professional: Introduction for the Human Services/Mental Health Worker Monterey, California: Brooks/Cole Publishing Co. 1975. An emerging occupation and profession is that of the human services generalist. This book describes this newer occupation and its development.

Marion Kalkman and Ann Davies. New Dimensions in Mental Health: Psychiatric Nursing, 5th Ed. New York, New York: McGraw Hill Book Co., 1980. This is a basic text about psychiatric nursing which describes its development, current standards and knowledge base needed for the field.

Abraham Roback. History of Psychology and Psychiatry. New York, New York: Greenwood Press Publishing Co., 1969. Although dated, this book provides an overview of two of the core professions in mental health.

Peter Vallitutte and Florence Christoplos. Interdisciplinary Approaches to Human Services. Baltimore, Maryland: University Park Press, 1977. This edited book of articles contains brief descriptions of the four core professions in mental health: psychiatry, psychology, psychiatric nursing and psychiatric social work.

REFERENCES

Alexander, Franz and Sheldon Selesnick. The History of Psychiatry. New York, NY: Harper and Row, 1966.

American Nurses Association. Standards for Psychiatric and Mental Health Nursing Practice. Kansas City, Missouri. American Nurses Association, 1973.

American Nurses Association. Facts About Nursing 1984-85, Kansas City, Missouri: American Nurses Association, 1985.

American Psychological Association. Ethical Standards of Psychology. Washington, D.C.: American Psychological Association, 1967.

Atkinson, Erwin. A Short History of Psychiatry 2nd Edition. New York, NY: Haffner Publishing Co., 1968.

Bromberg, Walter. The Mind of Man; the Story of Man's Conquest of Mental Illness. New York, New York: Harper and Brothers, 1937.

Caplan, Gerald. Concepts in Mental Health and Consultation in Public Health Social Work. Washington, D.C.: U.S. Government Printing Office, 1959.

Clark, Kenneth. American Psychologists: A Survey of a Growing Profession. Washington, D.C.: American Psychological Association, 1957.

Connaughton, James. "Psychiatry," pp. 307-336, in Vallittute, Peter and Florence Christoplos, Interdisciplinary Approaches to Human Services, Baltimore, MD: University Park Press, 1977.

Detlefsen, Ellen. The National Directory of Mental Health. New York, NY: John Wiley and Sons, 1980.

Deutsch, Albert. The Mentally Ill in America. Garden City, NY: Doubleday, Doran and Co., 1937.

Dugger, James. The New Professional: Introduction for the Human Services/Mental Health Worker. Monterey, CA: Brooks/Cole Publishing Co., 1975.

Ehrenwald, Jan. From Medicine Man to Freud: An Anthology. New York, NY: Dell Publishing Co., 1956.

Friedlander, Walter. <u>Introduction to Social Welfare, 5th</u>
    <u>Edition</u>. Englewood Cliffs, NJ: Prentice-Hall, Inc., 1980.

Hershey, William, Jr. "Social Work" pp. 373-396, in Vallittute,
    Peter and Florence Christoplos, <u>Interdisciplinary Approaches</u>
    <u>to Human Services</u>, Baltimore, MD: University Park Press,
    1977.

Howells, John G. and Livia Osborn. <u>A Reference Companion to the</u>
    <u>History of Abnormal Psychology</u>. Westport, Connecticut:
    Greenwood, Press, 1984.

Kalkman, Marion and Ann Davis. <u>New Dimensions in Mental</u>
    <u>Health: Psychiatric Nursing, 5th Edition</u>. New York, NY:
    McGraw Hill Book, Co., 1980.

Kasschau, Richard et al. <u>Careers in Psychology</u>. Washington,
    D.C.: American Psychological Association, 1975.

Minahan, Anne (Ed.). <u>Encyclopedia of Social Work, 18th Issue</u>.
    Washington, D.C.: National Association of Social Workers,
    1986.

Neaman, Judith. <u>Suggestions of the Devil: The Origins of</u>
    <u>Madness</u>. Garden City, NY: Anchor Books, 1975.

Office of the Federal Register, <u>United States Government Manual</u>
    <u>1985/86</u>, Washington, D.C.: U.S. Government Printing Office,
    1985.

Roback, Abraham. <u>History of Psychology and Psychiatry</u>. New
    York, NY: Greenwood Press Publishing Co., 1969.

Rose, Arnold. <u>Mental Health and Mental Disorder</u>. New York,
    NY: W.W. Norton Company, 1955.

Schneck, Jerome. <u>History of Psychiatry</u>. Springfield, IL:
    Charles C. Thomas Co., 1960.

Soddy, Ken and Robert Ahrenfeldt. <u>Mental Health and</u>
    <u>Contemporary Thought</u>. Philadelphia, PA: J.B. Lippincott
    Co., 1967.

Thackeray, Milton, Rex Skidmore and O. William Farley.
    <u>Introduction to Mental Health, Field and Practice</u>.
    Englewood Cliffs, NJ: Prentice Hall Inc., 1979.

United States Department of Commerce, Bureau of the Census
1980 Census of the Population Vol. 2 Subject Reports, Part
7C: Occupation by Industry, Washington, D.C.: U.S.
Government Printing Office, 1984.

United States Department of Commerce, Bureau of the Census,
Statistical Abstract of the United States: 1986 (106th
Ed), Washington, D.C.: U.S. Government Printing Office,
1985.

United States, Department of Health, Education and Welfare,
Health: United States: 1978. Washington, D.C.: U.S.
Government Printing Office, 1978.

United States, Department of Health, Education and Welfare,
Staffing of Mental Health Facilities: United States: 1974,
Washington, D.C.: U.S. Government Printing Office, 1976.

United States Department of Health and Human Services, Public
Health Service, Mental Health United States: 1983,
Washington, DC: U.S. Government Printing Office, 1983.

United States, Department of Health and Human Services, Public
Health Service, Mental Health Directory: 1985, Washington,
D.C.: U.S. Government Printing Office, 1985.

Wellner, Alfred. "Psychology" pp. 336-356 in Vallittute, Peter
and Florence Christoplos, Interdisciplinary Approaches to
Human Services, Baltimore, MD: University Park Press, 1977.

Wisconsin Legislative Reference Bureau, Wisconsin Blue Book
1985/86. Madison, Wisconsin: Department of Administration,
1985.

CHAPTER 21

MUTUAL SUPPORT NETWORK*

"Perhaps because of the complexity of modern living,
the growth in welfare programs, seemingly intractable
social problems, and the changed structure of society,
some discussions of social welfare assume that mutual
aid [support] no longer takes place or decry the
decrease they assume. Some such thinking seems based
on a nostalgic view of an idealized past. Whether
there is less mutual aid today than there was at some
given point in history is subject to empirical
investigation, but that there still exists considerable
mutual aid [support] in families, groups and neighborhoods among other places seems irrefutable."
(Macarov:1978:66)

INTRODUCTION

Implicit in the above quotation from Macarov, is the assumption that mutual aid and support groups are a significant part
of American society, and have been generally neglected as a
major topic of discussion by professional human service
workers. The assumptions that mutual aid no longer exists and
that the use of mutual aid groups is still decreasing, were
semi-accurate observations until rather recently (1975). Since
1975, the professional human service worker has become more
concerned with the concept of and implementation of mutual aid
and support groups (Gartner and Riessman, 1977; Caplan and
Killilea, 1976; Katz and Bender, 1976; and Collins and Pancoast,
1976).

Macarov (1978) generally describes a mutual support network
as the essence of human relationships, forming the basis for
individual social existence, and is one of the primary motiva-
tions of social welfare programs. He classifies the mutual
support network as:

- The family
- Guilds, unions and mutual aid societies
- Small groups i.e. self help, support, encounter
- Social and personal growth, human relations community and
  neighborhood groups
- Cooperatives, collectivities and communes.

677

The focus of this chapter is on the classification of small groups (although often large in size and number), such as self-help, support, encounter groups, etc. These small groups often rely on the participants of a problem or the consumers themselves as a primary driving force behind the group's formation and development. Since the group's purpose is largely directed at problem solving, personal enhancement, or emotional and psychological support, many of these groups are sustained through volunteers who provide services. Volunteers often give of their time, effort and expertise to motivate, provide direction and sustain many small group efforts. The role of volunteers in the mutual support network is dissucssed and an idealized role for social work is described.

SIZE

The mutual support network is composed of both highly and loosely structured organizations, ranging in size from thousands of individuals to a small group of five or less individuals. Accurate figures on the number of these groups is almost impossible and even a simple task of classifying these groups is difficult. Some authors have suggested a classification of twenty separate types of groups (Caplan and Killilea, 1976) and other authors have grouped them into four major categories (Katz and Bender, 1976). A common sense type of classification for mutual suppport groups would be as follows:

- Groups organized around a <u>specific problem</u>, such as alcoholics anonymous
- Groups organized for self-fullfillment, <u>personal growth</u> and self actualization purposes, such as encounter and sensitivity groups
- Groups organized for <u>support</u>, such as peer groups, natural networks i.e. relatives, friends, etc.

Some estimates on the size of the mutual support network, regardless of the method of classification are as follows: 500,000 groups in the United States having a membership of over 125 million individuals, utilizing an estimated 94.5 million volunteers, and adding an estimated $80 billion of work productivity to the economy and serving about 125 million individuals.[1] Figure 21-1 shows the estimated size of the mutual support network in 1983.

HISTORICAL DEVELOPMENT

Mutual aid and support networks have been with humankind since the formation of early societies, however, formalization of these networks outside of kinship groupings came much later in the development of society. Figure 21-2 shows a historical time line and the utilization of mutual support groups.

GENERAL DEVELOPMENT

Peter Kropotkin (1921) wrote a classic book on the utilization of mutual aid groups in Western society. The clan and tribal organization was the primary form of mutual aid utilized in both classical Greece and Rome. In addition there was an informal network of self-help groups based upon ones status in life, i.e. slave, poor, artisan, etc. and a more formal network linked to one's participation in a specific religious group.

PRE 450 A.D. - Concurrent with the decline of the classical empires (for example Rome in 400-450 A.D.), a village community network of mutual aid developed to fill the void of organized political structure for the purposes of defense, health, transportation, etc. Each village, city, and feudal lord (and his fiefdom) became self-supporting and relied upon its inhabitants for defense and welfare purposes. Examples of the early village community network included the Celts (100 A.D.) and Saxon and Normans (300 A.D.). The village community means the entire village helped out someone who was in an unfortunate circumstance and needed aid. An early example of mutual aid for a specific purpose was the Welsh Cyvar, which was a network of various individuals working jointly to complete a task. Individuals would band together for a specific task, such as building a house, defense, welfare etc. In the older traditions of the Welsh Cyvar agricultural land was seen as community or village property and a joint team effort was used to plant and harvest the crops.

Early Christians, (50 A.D.) formed themselves into religious communities and communes which relied heavily on mutual aid and support. Although each community was independent from the other, in times of crisis or trouble, each Christian community would look to another community for aid and support. As the village and community grew larger there was the beginning of cities and independent villages.

MEDIEVAL EUROPE - 450-1500 - In addition to the village and community concept, individuals began to organize around one's status in life, such as craft union, serf, freeman, burger, or around a specific activity, such as hunters, fishermen, etc. By 800 A.D. the masses of people organized around the concept of God's Peace known as Treuga Dei in order to preserve peace and harmony. The Treuga Dei was a series of days in which the community banned together to maintain peace. By 970 there was the development of the early guilds established in Lyon, France with the Cambrai, which was a craft union for the cloth or linen

FIGURE 21-1

Estimated size of the Mutual Support
Network 1983*

Number of Organizations	500,000 plus
Expenditures	80 billion
Number of Volunteers	94.5 million
Population Served	125 million

*Source: Adapted from Gene Glover and Michele Mickelson. Volunteerism: A Workbook on How to Build or Improve a Volunteer Program. Madison, Wisconsin: University of Wisconsin Extension, 1981; Giving USA, 1982, p. 7 and United States Department of Commerce, Bureau of the Census, Statistical Abstract of the United States: 1986 (106th Edition), Washington D.C.: U.S. Government Printing Office, 1985 p. 383-385.

workers. The guild network of Medieval Europe provided mutual support for protection, education, welfare, etc. Those individuals not belonging to guilds relied on community volunteer aid, church organizations, or their families for support.

RENNAISSANCE and REFORMATION – 1500-1700 – In the late 1500's concurrent with the development of the nation state, shifting technology, and religious reformation, the role of the Medieval guild began to decline. In the place of the Medieval guild the focus of mutual aid groups during this period of time shifted toward religious groups. Some examples of religious groups include the Anta-Baptist community (1521),the Jewish community (1550) and the Hutterite community (1533). The peasants banned together in this period of time partly as an attempt to defend themselves in the religious wars which were part of the Reformation.

ENLIGHTENMENT – 1700-1800 – By 1700, a further shift in technology toward a fledging factory system resulted in the development of Friendly Societies in England. The purpose of these societies was to enhance a group's economic and social position. The most rapid development of Friendly Societies in England occurred from 1700 to 1800. Examples of these societies in England include the Norman Society (1703), Goldsmith Friendly

680

FIGURE 21-2

HISTORICAL TIME LINE OF THE MUTUAL SUPPORT NETWORK

Pre Historic Groups for defense and welfare

3000 - 50 BC Greece   ----Groups based upon status:
              Rome   slave
                               artisan
                               stranger

50BC - 200 AD Europe - Religious self help groups and village, community groups

200 - 450 AD Europe - Village/City groups for defense and welfare

450 - 1500   Europe - Guild system (worker's form mutual aid groups)

1500-1700   Europe - Religious self help groups - Hutterite 1533

1700-1800   England - Friendly societies - Goldsmith society 1712,
                        Glassmakers society 1755

              Cooperative Societies

1800-1900   United States - Utopian Communities - 1820's
                              Immigrant society - 1813
                              Religious society - 1843
                              Trade Unions - 1870
                              Charitable society - 1873

1900 on   United States - Problem focus group - alcoholics anonymous - 1935
                              Personal Growth Groups - T groups - 1935
                              Sensitivity Groups - 1946
                              Peer support groups - Miami University 1969
                              Volunteerism - National Committee on
                                             Volunteers - 1933
                                             Peace Corp - 1961
                                             Vista - 1964
                                             ACTION - 1981

Society (1712), Ancient Society of Gardeners (1716) and the
Brotherhood of Master Glassmakers (1755).

By 1800, over 191 Friendly Societies existed in England.
There was concern about the political activity of these organizations as they began to oppose the policies of the government,

681

subsequently these organizations were declared illegal in 1799 by the Combinations Act.[2] The Combinations Act was passed as an attempt to prevent workers from participating in strikes against the employer. The prevailing attitude of the employer was that the individual employee contracted with the employer for employment and that labor organizations were incompatible with this philosophy. The movement to establish mutual aid groups, although banned in England, flourished with the development of labor unions, and cooperative societies (inside England as well as other countries), such as Rochdale and other Utopian communities. These forms of mutual aid societies still exist today and were the forerunners of mutual aid and support groups found today.

UNITED STATES – Since its beginning, the United States relied heavily on mutual aid groups and voluntary participation of its citizens for protection, welfare, work activity and general morale. DeTocqueville, in his visit to the young American republic in 1831, commented as follows:

"I met with several kinds of associations in America of which I confess I have no previous notion: and I have often admired the extreme skill with which the inhabitants of the United States succeed in proposing a common object to the exertion of a great many, and in inducing them voluntarily to pursue it. I have since traveled over England, whence the Americans have taken some of their laws and many of their customs; and it seems to me that the principle of association was by no means so constantly or adroitly used in that country. The English often perform great things singly, where the Americans form associations for the smallest undertakings."[3]

In colonial days, there was heavy reliance on voluntary groups and community involvement. Like European countries in the early 1800's, there was further development of mutual aid groups based on: religion or ethnicity, such as B'nai B'rith (1843) Irish Immigrant Society (1813); utopian communities, such as Fanny Wright Community and the Owen Community (1820); and the Oneida Community (1848); cooperative societies, such as Farmer's Cooperative (1820) ; trade unions, such as the Soverign's of Industry (1870), the women's trade unions (1905) and the combination of volunteer and religious organizations, such as St. Vincent DePaul (1845), Association for the Advancement of the Poor (1843), Jewish Aid Society (1853) and the Charity Organization Society (1873). Until the Depression of 1929-1942 the United States relied on the use of the religious network, volunteers and mutual aid societies for many of its social services and for alleviating social problems.[4] Since 1935,

the public system of human and welfare services has been
dominate, however the decades of the 1970's and the 1980's has
seen a resurgence in mutual support groups and volunteer
activity.

SPECIFIC DEVELOPMENT

PROBLEM FOCUS GROUPS - A typical example of a problem
focussed group is that of Alcoholics Anonymous Association which
was organized in 1935. This group was organized through the
efforts of Dr. Bob and Bill W., who were part of a larger movement known as the Oxford Movement of the 1930's.[5] Alcoholics
Anonymous uses professionals for consultation and advice but the
main task of solving or working with the problem, is accomplished through non-professional volunteers and self-participa-
tion. Alcoholics Anonymous, in 1973, had over 14,000 local
chapters and over 400,000 members.

Other groups with a specific problem focus have developed,
such as Abused Women's Aid in Crisis, Narcotics Anonymous,
Checks Anonymous, Divorce Anonymous, Riddle-to-Riddle, Parents
Anonymous, Weight Watchers, Recovery Incorporated, Synanon, Take
Off Pounds Sensibly, Smoke Watchers, Prison Families Anonymous,
Multiple Sclerosis, Grey Panthers, Emphysema Anonymous, etc.[6]

PERSONAL GROWTH GROUPS - Since 1945 there has been a rapid
expansion of groups focussing on personal growth and sensitivity
of individuals involved. These groups can be called T groups,
Gestalt Groups, encounter groups, sensitivity groups, marathon
groups, etc. The commonality of these groups is personal growth
using the group experience and social psychological techniques.
Most, if not all, of these groups are an outgrowth of psychotherapeutic techniques which have developed since 1900 and the
application of social psychology to small groups since 1945.

The development of psychotherapeutic techniques is generally
attributed to the following individuals: Joseph Pratt (1905),
Sigmund Freud (1914), Jacob Morino (1935), Abraham Law (1933)
and Gerald Slawson (1935). The theories and techniques these
individuals developed in the fields of psychology, psychoanalysis, psychiatry, psychodrama, social psychology and psychology of groups formed the nucleus of theoretical thought and
background for the development of sensitivity and encounter
groups.

The social movement for the development of sensitivity
groups grew out of the experiences of Kenneth Benne, Leland
Bradford, Ronald Lippitt and Kurt Lewin in 1946 at the New
Britain Teachers College in Connecticut. These social psychologists were having staff sessions on group leadership. At one

683

session the participants of the program indicated the perspectives of the staff were different than the perspectives of the participants in the program. In discussing these differences, the idea of sensitivity sessions emerged. Since this beginning, sensitivity groups have rapidly expanded, some formal, some informal, into a wide variety of agency and private practice settings, informal settings and formal research settings. Some examples of formalized group practice include the following: Gestalt Therapy Institute of San Diego, California, Senoi Counseling and Growth Center, Eugene, Oregon, Training Consultants International in Minneapolis, Minnesota, the Employee Assistance Program at the Illinois Gulf Central Railroad, Chicago, Illinois and at universities, such as Brigham Young in Utah.[7]

SUPPORT GROUPS - In contrast to the problem and sensitivity focussed groups, the support group was developed to enable a person to cope with a specific situation. The focus of a support group is one's specific status and how to obtain the optimum benefits from the status or situation one is in, or to advocate for changes in policies which affect one's status if they have a negative impact. This type of group developed out of the social consciousness and individual advocacy perspectives of the 1960's. Examples of such types of groups include the following: student support groups (1969), Volunteer Services, (1965), welfare rights groups, gay rights groups, women's support groups, etc.

VOLUNTEERS - The role of volunteers in the development of human services was significant in the United States. An early example of the volunteer approach was that of Benjamin Franklin who organized at the grass roots level utilizing volunteers who were indispensable in the development of the Library Company (1731), the Philadelphia Academy (1749) and the Pennsylvania Hospital (1751). An example of a mass appeal for volunteer help was the Boston blockade in 1775 during the early phases of the Revolutionary War. Volunteers were indispensable in the development of various social service programs, such as the Charity Organization Society (1882), Boys Clubs (1906), Boy Scouts (1910), Girl Scouts (1912), etc.

A national organization was developed in 1933 on volunteerism called the National Committee on Volunteers in Social Work. The function of this committee was to recognize the significance of the volunteer as an integral part of social services and to develop guidelines for in-service training of the volunteer. This specific group was expanded in 1941 in order to concentrate and coordinate volunteer efforts for World War II. Professional recognition of volunteers was indicated by the fact that the

Council on Social Work Education had sponsored workshops addressed to the training needs of volunteers in 1945 and 1959, and currently voluminous material is produced on the utilization and training of volunteers in social service agencies.

Some formalization of volunteer activities began to occur in 1961 with the development of the Peace Corp and VISTA (Volunteers in Service to America), in 1964 which is now part of ACTION at the federal level. There are other volunteer programs of a formal nature, such as universities which grant credit for volunteer programs where students are encouraged to volunteer efforts to various organizations, such as the aged, women's groups, etc.

STRUCTURE

The mutual support network, unlike other networks is both loosely defined and has an organized structure. One can view the structure of the mutual support network from its organizational context, services provided, occupations and professions and dominant occupations and professions.

ORGANIZATIONAL CONTEXT

The mutual support network is a constellation of a variety of groups at the local level which engages volunteers in programs and may or may not have a dependence on a centralized government hierarchy. Although most volunteers are at the local level, there has been some development in the 1960's of federal and state programs attempting to organize volunteers. Figure 21-3 shows an idealized structure of the mutual support network and the organized governmental efforts at volunteer activities.[8]

SERVICES PROVIDED

Since the mutual support network consists of groups focussing on specific problems, personal growth and support groups, the type of services provided by the type of group will vary. In addition to the types of group, the quality of services will vary depending upon the intensity and type of training volunteers receive from an agency, the type of previous experiences they have had and the degree of training the professional has had in working with volunteers. The following is an exemplary listing of services provided in the mutual support network:

- Concrete services, such as automobile trip, shopping, looking for an apartment, moving, painting, etc.
- Individual counseling
- Group counseling

- Community activities, such as fund raising, block visitation, speeches, public relations
- Personal growth lessons
- Home visitation
- Emotional support
- Hotline/helpline services
- Referral services for social agencies
- Employment information
- Helping the disabled
- Student and peer advising.

OCCUPATIONS and PROFESSIONS

The mutual support network engages self-participants and volunteers as the primary source of personnel. Professionals in human services perform back-up, administrative and consultation functions. Consequently, there is no dominant profession, nor an adequate listing of professions employed in the mutual support network. One can only assume that representatives from all of the human service professions at some point become involved in volunteer activity. Subsequently, the range of human service professions participating in the mutual support network would approximate the entire range of human service professions.

DOMINANT OCCUPATIONS and PROFESSIONS

In a survey taken by the Department of Labor in 1965, it was estimated that 16 percent of the people over age 14, or 22 million people, volunteered their time to various groups and agencies. This same survey estimated that by 1980, volunteers would contribute about $80 billion dollars of work productivity to the economy.[9]

In 1982, it was estimated that 94.5 million individuals volunteered their time to various activities. The type of activity in which individuals volunteered their time and the percentage of volunteerism include the following: religious organization 37 percent, health organization 23 percent, education organization 23 percent, recreation organization 13 percent, political organization 11 percent, citizenship organization 11 percent, community action organization 11 percent, social welfare organization 10 percent, informal volunteering 44 percent, work related volunteering 11 percent and fund raising activity 11 percent (percentages equal more than 100 since individuals volunteer for more than one organization).

There has been an upsurge in volunteerism since 1963. Volunteers are performing tasks which are not otherwise performed by professionals. These tasks can be supplemental and

IDEALIZED GOVERNMENT ORGANIZATION OF THE MUTUAL SUPPORT NETWORK*

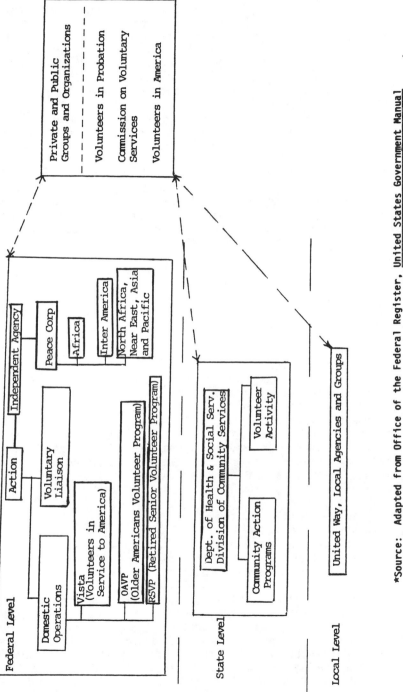

*Source: Adapted from Office of the Federal Register, United States Government Manual
1985-86, Washington, DC: U.S. Government Printing Office, 1985, p. 850, 854 and Wisconsin
Legislative Reference Bureau, Wisconsin Blue Book 1985-1986, Madison, Wisconsin:
Department of Administration, 1985, p. 512, 518.

supportive to agency programs, an integral part of agency programs and innovative to an agency's program. The motivation for a person to volunteer their services are varied but include the following:

- A sense of duty
- Idealized notion to help people
- To enjoy an activity
- Personal satisfaction from working with people
- Someone asked them to be a volunteer (felt an obligation to respond to a specific request).

Most social service agencies and mutual support groups have some system of in-service training and staff development which can be rather formalized and structured, or more informal with a person learning by doing. Examples of volunteer training programs which are more formalized and structured include the Women's Crisis Center and Volunteers in Probation of Milwaukee, Wisconsin.[10]

The Women's Crisis Center has the following format for training volunteers. A volunteer receives 18 weeks of in-service training for a total of 64 hours which includes the following major items:

- Telephone skill
- Understanding the community
- Knowledge of social service agencies
- Verbal response patterns
- Telephone assessment
- Women's issues.

The Volunteers in Probation has the following format for training volunteers. A volunteer receives 6 weeks of in-service training for a total of 24 hours which includes the following items:

- Criminal justice system
- General human behavior
- Developing a relationship
- Listening and lay counseling skills
- Knowledge of community resources.

The role of the volunteer is different than the professional, and it is not necessarily a matter of personal competence which separates the volunteer and the professional. Gartner and Reismann (1977) have succinctly described the differences between the volunteer and the professional as follows: the volunteer ideally is more concrete, subjective, experiential, and intuitive as compared to the professional who ideally is more socially distant, has a broader perspective, is more effective, and has more systematic knowledge in understanding behavior.

Volunteerism and more extensive use of the mutual support networks has been highly encouraged by the political and economic environment of the 1980's. There is a growing recognition that some social problems must be dealt with through a mutual support network and not a formalized system of help. One consequence of the growing significance of volunteerism is the concept of a "professional volunteer". A professional volunteer means one of three things or a combination of the following:

1. A person is a full time volunteer and receives some payment or reimbursement for their efforts (usually minimal and not full time payment).

2. A person has received extensive in-service training on volunteerism (management, program, fund raising, staff development, screening and recruitment).

3. A person has received some formal education in volunteerism which could include a bachelor's degree. An example of a professional educational program in volunteerism is that of Temple University in Pennsylvania established in 1976.

The volunteer depending upon the agency for which they are working would perform some of the following functions:

- Concrete services, such as transportantion, food, finding a house, finding employment, etc.
- Emotional support or listening to a person and their problems
- Community activities, such as fund raising, speeches and public relations
- Referral to other agencies
- Home visitation for specific problems
- Operation of hotlines and helpline services

Although volunteerism has not previously been seen as an occupation, as the service economy continues to expand, the role of the volunteer will expand. As the role of the volunteer expands, volunteerism will be given more societal recognition as a full time occupation. Volunteerism will be given further social recognition as society develops educational programs for "professional volunteers". This process is no different than the one previously described (see Chapter 2) as an occupation moves toward professionalism.[11]

No adequate figures exist on the number of social workers involved in the mutual support network either as volunteers or as paid professionals. Since the mutual support network usually has professionals like social workers acting in support of volunteers, the role of the social worker is ideally substantially different than that of the usual direct service role they assume in many other situations.

The social worker, as a supportive back-up and change type of professional, ideally should assume the following types of activities in the mutual support network:

PROGRAM EVALUATION

The social worker, based upon research experience and knowledge of social programs should be able to help a mutual support group look at its own program and determine whether it is effective and efficient, or both.

STAFF DEVELOPMENT

Since the social worker has a background in human behavior and human relations, they should be able to provide content and training sessions for the volunteers.

CONSULTATION

The social worker should be able to provide advice on development of programs, procurement of funding, organization of a program, etc.

ADMINISTRATION

In some situations, the mutual support group will hire a professional to administer the program, but not become involved in day-to-day services.

BACK-UP SERVICE

In some mutual support groups, the paid professional who is an administrator of a program, should be expected to provide back-up services in case other volunteers and personnel are not available.

START-UP ROLE

As part of the backup role of a social worker, an individual may be asked to develop a program or start a program. Once a program has been initiated, the social worker could become the administrator and perform the roles of a supportive or back up professional and when necessary a change agent.

PUBLIC RELATIONS

To secure funding, make speeches, and present a positive image of the program to a broader audience like the community.

Depending upon the type of mutual support group, such as a sensitivity or encounter group, a social worker may take a more direct and active role in group discussions, assessing individual and group growth, monitoring programs, and experientially using different techniques in order to create a positive atmosphere suitable for open discussion.

Ideally, the social worker in the mutual support network, should take a secondary role to the volunteers and self-participants, who are the primary implementors of the mutual support network.[12]

PERSONAL SOCIAL SERVICES

Like other networks, the mutual support network has a linkage with the personal social service network (see chapter 22 Personal Social Service). Some examples of services available and organizations focussing on the personal social services in the mutual support network include the following:

PROTECTIVE SERVICES

Spouse and child abuse counseling, such as Women, San Francisco, California and Sojourner Truth House, Milwaukee, Wisconsin.

UTILITARIAN SERVICES

Homemaking and legal aid, such as Legal Aid of Wisconsin, Milwaukee, Wisconsin.

DEVELOPMENTAL and SOCIALIZATION SERVICES

Family and marital counseling, such as Divorce Anonymous, Chicago, Illinois and women Pro Se, Inc., Milwaukee, Wisconsin.

REHABILITATIVE and THERAPEUTIC SERVICES

Alcoholics Anonymous and its local Chapters and Narcotics Anonymous and its local Chapters.

SPECIAL POPULATIONS

The mutual support network because of its focus on self help has numerous programs and services for the often times neglected groups of our society which are called special populations (see Chapter 25, Special Populations and Chapter 24 Rehabilitation). Some examples of organizations and programs for special populations and the mutual support network include the following:

ASIAN

Chinese American Union, San Francisco, California; Vietnamese American Refugee Center, San Francisco, California and the Asian American Voluntary Action Center, Los Angeles, California.

BLACK

Adams Morgan Association, Washington, D.C. and Black and White Men Together, San Francisco, California.

EUROPEAN ETHNIC

Association Canado Americaino (French Canadian), Manchester, New Hampshire; Daughters of Penelope, Washington, D.C. (Greek) and the American Society for Croation Migration, Cleveland, Ohio.

NATIVE AMERICAN

Abenaki Self Help Association, Swanton, Vermont; Alaska Native Brotherhood, Juneau, Alaska; American Indian Volunteers, Los Angeles, California, Americans for Indian Opportunity, Albuquerque, New Mexico and Arrow Incorporated, Washington, D.C.

SAME SEX PREFERENCE

Gay Union, Milwaukee, Wisconsin; Daughters of Bilitis, San Francisco, California and Friends for Lesbian and Gay Concerns, Sunneytown, Pennsylvania.

SPANISH SPEAKING

National Council of Puerto Rican Volunteers, Mount Vernon, New York; Coalition Accion Latina, Chicago, Illinois and Xanthos, Alameda, California.

WOMEN

Women's Awareness Centers, such as National Organization for Women, Chicago, Illinois; Older Women's League, Washington, D.C. and Women in Transition, Philadelphia, Pennsylvania.

ISSUES

General issues related to the mutual support network can be classified into those which pertain to the support groups themselves and those which pertain to social work education.

MUTUAL SUPPORT GROUPS

For the mutual support groups, there are some issues related to the concept of professionalism and how group participants relate to other human service professionals. In general, there is some degree of an anti-professional orientation and a mistrust of a professional, and vice versa there is some degree of an anti-volunteer and mistrust of the volunteer by the professional. At times there is an over-emphasis on the "self" as a volunteer and what they can obtain from the volunteer experience (the helper/therapy principle). Instead of viewing the people they work with as "equals", the volunteer may begin to relate to them as if they themselves were the only experts. The major concern here is not the professional orientation of volunteers in the support groups, but the fact that because of the mistrust of the professional they may not be seeking the appropriate advice and consultation which may or may not be needed. The situation may be reversed for the professional in human services who does not seek the advice or feedback of the volunteer.

There is a concern about the lack of training for the volunteer, and some authors have proposed some form of certification process for a qualified volunteer. A potential problem with sensitivity groups, such as encounter groups and marathon sessions is what is called "repressed behavior", or getting involved over one's head. It has been speculated that at least 10 percent of individuals who become involved in these groups are unable to cope with their emotions or the subjects discussed, therefore instead of being helped, actually become worse. In some mutual support groups there has been a lack of an organized structure which in itself may not be a problem. The concern about the lack of structure in some organizations is when this results in non-accountability, or lack of services, etc. Therefore some authors argue for a more clearly articulated organizational structure.

SOCIAL WORK

Some of the issues in social work education involve the benign neglect in many schools of social work in the teaching of group content both as social group work, and the role of the group in modern society. There should be a greater emphasis on the use of groups in society and some content on the mutual support network and the role of volunteers within this network.

Specifically, content is needed on how to train and supervise volunteers. Since 1975, there has been an emphasis in some schools of social work on the natural helping process (natural helping groups, such as friends, and family).

SUMMARY

In contrast to popular notions, the role of the mutual support network in American society has been expanding rapidly since approximately 1945. It is estimated in 1983 there were over 500,000 such groups in the United States, having a membership of at least 125 million, utilizing an estimated 94.5 million volunteers, and providing an estimated $80 billion of donated services to the human service networks.

Mutual support groups have been a part of American society since its inception. When one looks at such groups from a historical perspective one can see different focal points for the organization of such groups. For example, in Medieval Europe the focal point of such groups was the guild and trade union, in the 1600's religion, in 1700 and 1800 the work place and unions, and in the 20th century social problems and personal growth.

Mutual aid and support groups can be classified according to the primary focus of the group: problem focus, such as Alcoholics Anonymous, personal growth, such as T groups and sensitivity groups, and support focus, such as student support groups, welfare mothers, etc. In all of these groups the volunteer and/or self-participant is the predominant individual involved, with the human service professional ideally participating in an indirect role in the provision of these services.

The mutual support network is a constellation of a diverse number of organizations, agencies and groups, consequently there may or may not be a well defined organization or structure to the mutual support network. Since 1960 there has been some attempts to establish on a formal basis volunteer activity at various levels of government, such as the Peace Corp (1961), Volunteers in Service to America (1964) and currently ACTION (1986). The role of the volunteer and self-participant in the mutual support network was described as well as the ideal role of social work.

Some issues regarding the mutual support network were discussed, such as certification and professional education for volunteers, the "helper/therapy principle," the anti-professional orientation of some volunteers, the anti-volunteer orientation of some professionals, and the lack of a well defined structure in some organizations. For social work, some

of the issues related to the mutual support network include the
development of course content on group and group activity, the
role of the volunteer in the mutual support network and the
training and supervision of volunteers.

FOOTNOTES

* This chapter was reviewed for comments by William Winter,
Criminal Justice Institute, University of Wisconsin Exten-
sion, Milwaukee, Wisconsin, and vice president of the
Wisconsin Association for Volunteers in Adult and Juvenile
Justice.

1. These estimates on the size of the mutual support network
are adapted from Gene Glover and Michele Mickelson. Volun-
teerism: A Workbook on How to Build or Improve a Volunteer
Program, Madison, Wisconsin. University of Wisconsin
Extension, 1981; Giving USA, 1982, p. 7 and United States,
Department of Commerce, Bureau of the Census, Statistical
Abstract of the United States: 1986 (106th Edition).
Washington, D.C.: U.S. Government Printing Office, 1985, p.
383-385.

2. The attempt in England to ban worker and other forms of
mutual aid groups was short-lived since the development of
the union movement resulted in legislation in 1825 to
recognize these societies. Other parts of Europe were
slower to recognize worker's rights to organize, such as
France (1825), Germany (1886) and Russia (1917). Although
Russia was slow in recognizing unions and other forms of
mutual aid groups, other groups were allowed to flourish,
such as the Reliance of Mothers (1872) which was a self-
support group for women who were in poverty and had children, and the Medical Academy for Women (1887), which was a
support group for women who wanted to become physicians.

3. Alexis deTocqueville, Democracy in America, edited by
Richard Heffner, New York, NY: Metro Books, 1956. This is
a classic book on a Frenchman's perspective of American
society in 1831 and is an excellent source for viewing the
politics of America at that time.

4. The reader is referred to chapter 15 Religious Network for a
detailed description of the development of religious and
private organizations in human services.

5. The Oxford Movement stressed the relationship of man to God,
and the reliance on this individual relationship to handle

social and life situations. That is, each person is responsible for their behavior, therefore correcting the problem
involves correcting oneself.

6. A complete listing of problem focus groups is impractical.
This listing provides some examples of various groups. For
a fuller listing of organizations the reader is referred to
Allan Gartner and Frank Riessman Self-Help in the Human
Services, San Francisco, California: Jossey-Bass Publica-
tions, 1977.

7. A complete listing of sensitivity encounter groups is impossible. This listing provides some examples of various
groups. For a fuller listing of such organizations and
groups the reader is referred to Jane Howard Please Touch:
A Guided Tour of the Human Potential Movement, New York,
NY: McGraw Hill Book Company, 1970.

8. The emphasis in this chapter has been on the more formalized
mutual support network. In addition there is a vast array
of more informal mutual support services one receives
through the folk or informal system consisting of parents,
relatives, friends, colleagues, acquaintances, etc.

9. This survey of volunteers indicate that the majority of
volunteers were participating in educational agencies, 30
percent, followed by social service agencies, 24 percent and
the remaining 46 percent in a vast array of diverse groups.
The typical volunteer was age 24 to 44, unemployed, a female
with a working husband. For further details, see United
States Department of Labor, Americans Volunteer, Washington,
D.C.: U.S. Government Printing Office, 1969.

In 1983 The Statistical Abstract of the United States: 1986
(106th Edition) indicate that the largest percentage of
volunteerism is with religious organizations or informal
organizations, such as mutual support groups.

10. Material on the in-service training programs is adapted from
the following sources: Training Manual for the Women's
Crisis Center and Volunteers in Probation, Milwaukee, WI.

11. National organizations where a person can obtain general
information on volunteer activities is the Commission on
Voluntary Services Action, 475 Riverside Drive, New York, NY
10027; National Self-Help Clearinghouse, 184 5th Avenue, New
York, NY 10026; Clearinghouse of the National Center for
Voluntary Action, 1735 Eye Street, NW, Washington, D.C.
20006 and Volunteers of America, 3813 N. Causeway Blvd.,
Metairie, Louisiana 70002.

12. For information on social work as a profession contact the National Association of Social Workers, 7981 Eastern Avenue, Silver Spring, Maryland 20910 or the local chapter of the National Association of Social Workers.

SUGGESTED READINGS

Alice Collins and Diane Pancoast. Natural Helping Networks: A Strategy for Prevention. Washington, DC: National Association of Social Workers, 1976. This book is one of the earlier books in social work to focus on social networks as a means of changing individual and group behavior.

John Cull and Richard Hardy. Volunteerism: An Emerging Profession. Springfield, Illinois: Charles C. Thomas Co., 1974. This book describes the development of volunteerism, its movement toward professionalism and some of the issues facing the field. This book is very useful as a resource book.

Alan Gartner and Frank Reissman. Self Help in the Human Services. San Francisco, California: Jossey Bass Publications, 1977. For the individual interested in self help groups and their application to alleviating problems, this is a highly recommended book.

Alan Gartner and Frank Riessman. The Self Help Revolution. New York, New York: Human Sciences Press, 1984. The decade of the 1980's is one where there has been a growing significance of self help groups. This book analyzes this movement.

P.H. Gosdin. Self Help: Voluntary Associations in the 19th Century. London, England: B.T. Botsford, Ltd. 1973. For a person interested in history, this book is an in depth analysis of the variety of self help groups developing in the 18th century and analyzes the reasons for their development.

Hurvitz, Nathan. "The Origins of the Peer Self-Help Psychotherapy Movement" Journal of Applied Behavioral Science. Vol. 12 No. 3 (July/August/September), 1976, pp 283-294. This brief article succinctly describes the development of the peer self help group. For the individual interested in the social climate of a movement this is an excellent resource.

Alfred Katz and Eugene Bender. "Self Help Groups in Western Society: History and Prospects". Journal of Applied Behavioral Science Vol. 12 No. 3 (July/August/September), 1976, pp 265-283. This lengthy article provides a concise history of self help groups and is an excellent resource and reference.

Peter Kropotkin. Mutual Aid: A Factor of Evolution. New York, New York: Alfred Knopf Co., 1921. This is a classic book on mutual aid. It is rather detailed in its use of examples but is highly recommended for its historical-sociological approach.

United States Department of Labor, Manpower Administration, Americans Volunteer, Washington, DC: U.S. Government Printing Office, 1969. Although dated, this publication provides some useful information on who volunteers, why, where and what they do.

George Weber and Lucy Cohen. Beliefs and Self Help. New York, New York: Human Sciences Press, 1982. This book adopts a cross cultural approach in analyzing self help groups. For an individual who is interested in this type of approach, this book is highly recommended.

REFERENCES

Abrahams, S. Ruby. "Mutual Help for the Widow," Social Work, Vol. 17, No. 5 (January 1972), pp. 55-63.

Back, Kurt and Rebecca Taylor. "Self-Help Groups: Tool or Symbol, "Journal of Applied Behavioral Science, Vol. 12 No. 3 (July/August/September 1976), pp. 295-309.

Back, Kurt. Beyond Words: The Story of Sensitivity Training and the Encounter Movement. New York, NY: Russell Sage Foundation, 1972.

Borman, L.D. Explorations in Self-Help Mutual Aid. Evanston, IL: Northwestern University Press, 1975.

Caplan, Gerald and M. Killilea (ed). Support Systems in Mutual Help: Multi-disciplinary Explanations. New York, NY: Green and Stratton Co., 1976.

Caplan, Gerald. Support Systems. New York, NY: Behavioral Publications, 1974.

Cohn, Nathan. The Citizen Volunteer. New York, NY: Harper and Brothers,1960.

Collins, Alice and Diane Pancoast. Natural Helping Networks: A Strategy for Prevention. Washington, D.C.: National Association of Social Workers, 1976.

Croner, Helga and Kurt Guggenheim. National Directory of Private Social Agencies 1986. Queens Village, New York: Croner Publishing Co., 1986 (updated annually).

Cull, John and Richard Hardy. Volunteerism: An Emerging Profession, Springfield, Illinois: Charles Thomas Co. 1974.

David, Anne. A Guide to Volunteer Services New York, New York: Cornerstone Library, 1970.

DeTocqueville, Alexis. Democracy in America. New York, NY: Mentor Books, 1956.

Friedlander, Walter and Robert Apte. Introduction to Social Welfare, 5th Edition. Englewood Cliffs, NJ: Prentice-Hall, Inc., 1980.

Gartner, Alan and Frank Riessman. Self-Help in the Human Services. San Francisco, CA: Jossey-Bass Publications, 1977.

Gartner, Alan and Frank Riessman. The Service Economy and the Consumer Vanguard. New York, NY: Harper Row, Inc., 1974.

Gartner, Alan and Frank Riessman. The Self Help Revolution. New York, New York: Human Sciences Press, 1984.

Glover, Gene and Michele Mickelson. Volunteerism: A Workbook on How to Build or Improve a Volunteer Program. Madison, Wisconsin: University of Wisconsin Extension, 1981.

Gosdin, P.H. Self-Help: Voluntary Associations in the 19th Century. London, England: B.T. Botsford, Ltd., 1973.

Hardy, Richard and John Cull. Applied Volunteerism in Community Development. Springfield, IL: Charles C. Thomas Co., 1973.

Howard, Jane. Please Touch: A Guided Tour of the Human Potential Movement. New York, NY: McGraw Hill Book Co., 1970.

699

Hurvitz, Nathan. "The Origins of the Peer Self-Help Psychotherapy Movement," Journal of Applied Behavioral Science,
Vol. 12 No. 3 (July/August/September 1976), pp. 283-294.

Jones, John and John Herrick. Citizens in Service: Volunteers
in Social Welfare During the Depression of 1929-1941.
Lansing, MI: Michigan State University Press, 1976.

Katz, Alfred and Eugene Bender. The Strength In Us: Self-Help
Groups in the Modern World. New York, NY: Franklin Watts
Co., 1976.

Katz, Alfred and Eugene Bender. "Self-Help Groups in Western
Society: History and Prospects," Journal of Applied
Behavioral Science, Vol. 12 No. 3 (July/August/September
1976), pp. 265-283.

Katz, Alfred. "Application of Self-Help Concepts in Current
Social Welfare," Social Work, Vol. 10, No. 3, (July 1965),
pp. 68-74.

Katz, Alfred. "Self-Help Organizations and Volunteer
Participation in Social Welfare," Social Work, Vol. 15, No.
1 (January 1970), pp. 51-60.

Konopka, Gisela. Social Group Work: A Helping Process, 2nd
Edition. Englewood Cliffs, NJ: Prentice-Hall, Inc., 1972.

Kropotkin, Peter. Mutual Aid: A Factor of Evolution. New
York, NY: Alfred Knopf Co., 1921.

Levy, Leon. "Self-Help Groups: Types and Psychological
Process," Journal of Applied Behavioral Science, Vol. 12 No.
3 (July/August/September 1976), pp. 310-322.

Macarov, David. The Design of Social Welfare. New York, NY:
Holt, Rinehart and Winston, Inc., 1978.

Manser, Gordon and Rosemary Cass. Volunteerism at the
Crossroads. New York, New York: Family Service Association,
1976.

Minahan, Anne (ed.). Encyclopedia of Social Work, 18th Issue.
Washington, D.C.: National Association of Social Workers,
1986.

Office of the Federal Register. United States Government
Manual, 1985/86. Washington, D.C.: U.S. Government
Printing Office, 1985.

Rosenbaum, Max and Alvin Snadowsky. The Intensive Group
    Experience. New York, NY: The Free Press, 1976.

Routh, Thomas. The Volunteer and Community Agencies.
    Springfield, Illinois: Charles C. Thomas Co., 1972.

Stenzel, Anne and Helen Feeney. Volunteer Training and
    Development: A Manual. New York, NY: Seabury Press, 1976.

United States Department of Commerce, Bureau of the Census,
    Statistical Abstract of the United States: 1986 (106th
    Edition), Washington, D.C.: U.S. Government Printing
    Office, 1985.

United States Department of Labor, Manpower Administration,
    Americans Volunteer, Washington, D.C.: U.S. Government
    Printing Office, 1969.

Vattano, Anthony. "Power to the People: Self-Help Groups,"
    Social Work, Vol. 17, No. 4 (July 1972), pp. 7-15.

Weber, George and Lucy Cohen. Beliefs and Self Help. New York,
    New York: Human Sciences Press, 1982.

Whittaker, James and James Garbarino. Social Support Network.
    Hawthorne, New York: Aldine Publishing Co., 1983.

Wisconsin Criminal Justice Institute. "Volunteers in Probation
    Report." (Mimeographed sheet, 1980).

Wisconsin Legislative Reference Bureau. Wisconsin Blue Book
    1985/86, Madison,Wisconsin: Department of Administration,
    1985.

Women's Crisis Line of Milwaukee Wisconsin. (Mimeographed
    Sheet, 1980.)

Chapter 22

PERSONAL SOCIAL SERVICE NETWORK*

"Historically, five major social welfare or human service
systems have been identified: education, income maintenance, health, housing, and employment/labor power. Recent
comparative international studies have led to the identification of a sixth system--personal social services--with a
long tradition which now appears to be coalescing into a
coherent system to meet the normal and anticipated social
needs which arise in modern industrial nations." (Dolgoff
and Feldstein: 1984:206)

INTRODUCTION

The personal social service network (also referred to as
general social services) consists of a variety of social
services implemented by other societal networks, and more
recently is beginning to assume its own autonomous identity as a
network. Each of the networks previously described, such as
income maintenance, education, physical health, mental health,
etc., have some personal social services connected with them.

The personal social service network can be defined as "those
communal responses (programs, activities) to meet individual and
group needs which are not met, or are not the primary focus of
other societal networks.[1] The personal social service network
consists of individualized and group forms of services (programs
and activities) and relies on interpersonal contact or relationships for implementation of programs. A useful classification
of the personal social service network is one discussed by
Compton (1980) and modified here.[2] A classification or
typology of the personal social service network is as follows:

PROTECTIVE SERVICES

These are programs and activities for specific population
groups which are vulnerable in society and need special attention. Examples of programs and activities under protective
services include the following: services for children, such as
child welfare, adoption, foster care, substitute care, alternate
living, dependency, neglect; abuse and exploitation, such as
incest, child pornography, pedophilia (molesting of children);
services for victims of family violence, such as spouse abuse,
child abuse and parent abuse; services for the mature adult

(aged), such as nursing homes, consumer fraud, incompetency legislation, guardianship, etc.

UTILITARIAN SERVICES

These are programs and activities which are practical or useful in providing needed information, coordinating various programs, advocating for individuals and groups, and providing other concrete services. Examples of programs and activities under utilitarian services include the following: services for those individuals and groups needing information, such as <u>information</u> and <u>referral</u>; services for organizations and agencies to <u>coordinate</u> services and to prepare appropriate legislation, such as politics and community organization; services for individuals and groups needing an <u>advocate</u>, such as legal advice regarding both civil and criminal cases; and services to individuals and groups needing <u>concrete aid</u>, such as day care, homemaking, meals on wheels, food, clothing, shelter (emergency housing) and institutional care.

DEVELOPMENTAL and SOCIALIZATION SERVICES

These are programs and activities which focus on different aspects of the life cycle. Examples of programs and activities under developmental and socialization services include the following: services for <u>families and couples</u>, such as family and marriage counseling; services for <u>unwed mothers</u>, such as family planning, personal counseling, etc.; and services for <u>youth</u>, such as camps, YMCAs or YWCAs.

REHABILITATIVE and THERAPEUTIC SERVICES

These are programs and activities which focus on changing or managing a specific or a series of behaviors. That is, the focus is to change one's psychosocial functioning or to resolve one's psychosocial conflicts. Examples of programs and activities under rehabilitative and therapeutic services include the following: services for individuals exhibiting a <u>substance addiction</u>, such as alcohol, drugs, smoking, etc.; services for individuals exhibiting <u>self-destructive</u> behavior, such as suicide; services for individuals in which there are problems of <u>sexual functioning</u> which can be of a general nature (psychological/emotional) or of a specific nature (physiological); <u>sexual assault</u> or abusive behavior; <u>aberrant behavior</u> (sexual deviation), such as necrophilia, voyeurism, pedophilia, bestiality; and <u>problematic behavior</u>, such as prostitution, pornography, child sexual exploitation, fornication, adultery and sexual harassment.

Since the personal social service network interlocks with every other societal network, only those not previously described in detail elsewhere are the focus of this chapter. Of significance in the personal social service network is the profession of social work which has traditionally provided these services. This chapter provides an overview of the personal social service network and discusses social work which is one of the dominant professions in this network.

SIZE

The full range of the personal social service network is quite extensive. Consequently, only selected examples of the personal social services in each major category will be discussed, such as protective, utilitarian, developmental and socialization, and rehabilitative and therapeutic services.

PROTECTIVE SERVICES

The major services which are discussed in this category include: children and child welfare, such as adoption, foster home services and child neglect; victims of family violence, such as spouse abuse, child abuse, and parent abuse against the mature adult (aged).

CHILDREN (CHILD WELFARE) - There are an estimated 11,000 agencies in the United States which provide services listed under child welfare. Of these 11,000 agencies, approximately 3,500 are county welfare departments, 2,000 are homes for dependent children, and the remainder are private agencies. It is estimated that approximately 27,000 social workers and 100,000 child care workers focus on child welfare work. A conservative estimate of the expenditures for these services is approximately 800 million dollars and an annual population of at least five million individuals receiving services. In 1980, there were an estimated 38,000 children in homes for dependent and neglected children. In 1983, there were 1,001,400 reported cases of child neglect and abuse. In 1984, there were an estimated 2,388,000 orphans in the United States.

VICTIMS of FAMILY VIOLENCE - There are at least 6,000 agencies which provide services to victims of family abuse. Of these 6,000 agencies, approximately 3,500 are county welfare departments, at least eighty are transitional homes for battered women and men, and the remainder are private agencies. Some agencies in the judicial network (see Chapter 13) provide services for this population and are not included here. The number of individuals working in this area and the cost of services is distributed amongst other networks and programs such as family and marital counseling, legal services, etc. It is estimated that approximately 1.9 million children are severely battered each year, approximately 1.8 million wives, and 100,000 husbands. According to Murry Strauss (1980), about one in three marriages have physical conflicts which is of a chronic nature and has occurred in maybe once in an additional one out of three marriages. The above figures do not include violence in connection with sexual assault and abuse (see section on sexual assault). In 1983, there were a reported 1,001,400 cases of child abuse and neglect and in 1984, 33,000 arrests for crimes against the family and children.

MATURE ADULTS (AGED) - There are at least 11,000 agencies focussing on the aged population. Of these 11,000 agencies about 3,500 are county welfare departments, about 4,500 are senior centers, and the remainder are private agencies. These estimates do not include nursing homes, Social Security programs, and Veterans programs. Expenditures for operating senior centers alone was estimated at 270 million dollars per year. Employees for programs for the mature adult are distributed throughout many of the other networks. The potential population of service is about 28 million individuals or about 11.8 percent of the population, which was over age 65 in 1984. This figure is in sharp contrast to 1900, when there were an estimated three million people over the age of 65, or four percent of the population.[3] Some older adults are also victims of family violence, consequently, there is some overlap between agencies focussing on family violence and those focussing on the mature adult. In 1980, there were 2,492,000 individuals residing in homes for the aged.

UTILITARIAN SERVICES

The major services to be discussed in this category are for individuals and groups needing concrete aid, such as day care and homemaking programs.

DAY CARE - There are an estimated 18,000 day care programs in the United States, employing an estimated 1.2 million individuals. Expenditures for day care programs was estimated at 1.2 billion dollars and served an estimated one million children.

In 1982 there were an estimated 5,086,000 women who had young children and were employed. These women used a variety of methods to provide for day care services. Of the 5,086,000 women, 1,556,316 or 30.6 percent used their own home (father, relative, non-relative), 2,044, 572 or 40.2 percent used another home, 752,728 or 14,8 percent used group care facilities, 462,826 tried to care for the children themselves, and 10,172 or .02 percent used other methods.

706

HOMEMAKING -There are an estimated 6,500 agencies providing homemaking services. Of these 6,500 agencies, approximately 3,000 are private agencies and the remainder are county welfare departments. At least 18,000 individuals are employed in homemaking. Expenditures for this service are distributed amongst other networks. The number of families served annually is at least 25,000.[4]

DEVELOPMENTAL and SOCIALIZATION SERVICES

The major services to be discussed in this category include families and couples, unwed mothers, and youth.

FAMILIES and COUPLES - In 1984 there were an estimated 53.5 million married couples, 2.4 million marriages, and 1.1 million divorces. In other words, almost one out of every two marriages, or 46.7 percent end in divorce. In 1984, of 169.5 million individuals over 18, 36.9 million, or 21,8 percent, were single, 107.1 million or 63.2 percent were married, 13.2 million or 7.8 percent were widowed and 12.3 million or 7.2 percent were divorced. It is estimated there are at least 9,000 agencies focussing on family and marital problems. Of these 9,000 agencies, approximately 5,500 are private agencies, and the remainder are county welfare departments. The number of employees and the cost of family services is distributed throughout other networks. These figures do not include private marriage counselors, psychologists, or mutual support groups, etc.

Estimates on the number of families seeking counseling are difficult to ascertain, however, it has been estimated that 68 percent of marriages have some degree of conflict, 20 percent of adults find their sex life to be unsatisfactory, and 50 percent of marriages have sexual and personal problems. Using these estimates of marital problems and a numerical base of 53 million married couples, then approximately 26.5 million couples may need some form of social service intervention in order to maintain their marriage and family.

UNWED MOTHERS - In 1982, there were 715,000 live births to unmarried women between the ages of 18-49. In 1984, there were an estimated 2.3 million unmarried (never married) women between the ages of 18-49 with children. In 1985, it was estimated that 18 percent of live births were to unmarried women between the ages of 18-44. In 1980 the comparable figure was 14 percent. Of the unmarried women having children between the ages of 18-44, 11.7 percent were white, 54.9 percent black, and the remaining 33.4 percent other ethnic groups. Of the unmarried women having children between the ages of 18-24, 20.2 percent were white, 74.5 percent black, and the remaining 5.3 percent other ethnic groups. The age group with the highest percentage of unwed motherhood is 15-18 followed by 18-24. The national rate of unmarried teenage women having children is 50 live births per 1,000 teenagers. There are at least an estimated 6,400 agencies focussing on services to the unwed mother. Of these 6,400 agencies, approximately 105 are special institutions, 3,500 are county welfare departments, and the remainder are private agencies. These figures do not include mutual support groups, employment programs, educational programs, etc.

Institutions for unwed mothers in 1980 employed an estimated 20,000 individuals and had expenditures of approximately 6 billion dollars and served 2,000 women. Employees and expenditures for providing services to unwed mothers are distributed amongst other programs and social networks. The potential population base which could use these services is estimated at over ten million individuals.

YOUTH PROGRAMS--In 1984, there were an estimated 44.8 million individuals between the ages of five and seventeen in the United States, or 18.9 percent of the population. This population group is served by a variety of private and public agencies. There are at least 10,000 separate agencies which focus on the youth population and the numbers served by these agencies runs into the millions. Expenditures and employees for these services are distributed throughout other social networks.

REHABILITATIVE and THERAPEUTIC SERVICES

The major services to be discussed in this category include the following: individuals exhibiting substance abuse problems, such as alcohol, drugs; individuals exhibiting self-destructive behavior, such as suicide; and individuals and groups exhibiting problems around sexual functioning. Problems related to sexual functioning include: general functioning, (psychological and emotional) and specific functioning (physiological), assaultive behavior, aberrant behavior, and problematic behavior, such as pornography, prostitution and sexual harassment.[5]

SUBSTANCE ABUSE PROBLEMS - In 1984 there were an estimated eight million alcoholics in the United States, and about seventeen million problem drinkers over age 18. In 1982, approximately 80 percent of the population of the United States has used alcoholic beverages, and about 50 percent are chronic users. In 1984, there were 886,000 arrests for drunkenness and 1,347,000 arrests for drunken driving. There are an estimated 40,000 agencies focussing on alcohol abuse and alcoholism. Of these 40,000 agencies, 4,000 are specialized agencies, 800 are

specialized hospitals, and the remaining are specialized programs in conjunction with other public and private agencies. Of
those agencies focussing strictly on alcohol abuse and alcoholism, there are about 47,000 employees. Expenditures for alcohol
programs was approximately 800 million dollars in 1980, and
served close to two million people. Estimates of the cost to
employers for lost productivity due to excessive alcohol use was
estimated at 66 billion dollars in 1986.

The use of drugs is a closely related problem to alcoholism
and other substance abuse. In 1980 there were an estimated
500,000 drug addicts. About 20 percent of the United States
population has used drugs, and about 10 percent are current
users of drugs. In 1984, there were 562,000 arrests for drug
violations. There are an estimated 3,700 agencies focussing on
drug abuse alone. Of these 3,500 agencies, 85 are specialized
institutions and the remainder are specialized outpatient
programs in conjunction with other programs. Many, if not most
of these specialized programs, use some form of federal money.
These agencies employ approximately 34,000 individuals, and in
1982 expenditures were approximately 600 million dollars. In
1982 these agencies served approximately 200,000 individuals.
Estimates of the cost to employers for lost productivity due to
drug use was estimated at 33 billion dollars in 1986.

SUICIDE--In 1984 there were an estimated 28,242 reported
suicides in the United States. The suicide rate is estimated at
12.2 per 100,000 population, and the ratio between male and
female is 4:1. According to Dublin (1967), the reported rate of
completed suicides is three out of four; however, the attempted
suicide rate is ten times higher than that figure. Consequently, at least 280,000 individuals probably attempted suicide
in that year. There are an estimated 760 agencies focussing on
suicide. Of these 760 agencies, 360 are suicide prevention
centers, and 400 are community mental health centers. The
number of employees is estimated at about 35,000 and the expenditures are estimated at 4 billion dollars. The number of
people who attempt suicide or obtain services for this behavior
are difficult to ascertain, since they may seek help under other
general problems (mental and physical health). If only those
who have attempted suicide sought some form of social services,
then the estimated population for service would be at least
280,000 individuals.

SEXUAL FUNCTIONING--Behavior discussed under this category
includes: general functioning, assaultive or abusive behavior,
aberrant behavior, (sexual deviation), and problematic
behavior. General sexual functioning can be defined as individuals having difficulty coping with sexual activity, either as

a marital partner, with members of the opposite sex, or as a non-marital partner. It has been estimated that 20 percent of the adult population has an unsatisfactory sex life, and about 50 percent of all marriages have sexual problems. Problems related to sexual functioning can be classified into two types: general problems (psychological and emotional), such as anxiety, low self-esteem, lack of communication, lack of respect, etc.; specific problems (physiological), such as the inability of the male to obtain an erection, premature ejaculation, retarded ejaculation (incompetence), and dypareunia (painful erection). In the female, some of these problems include primary (no orgasm) and secondary orgasm (occasional orgasm) dysfunctioning, dyspareunia (painful vaginal penetration), and vaginismus (prevention of coital interpenetration).[6]

Estimates on the size of the network for general and specific sexual functions are difficult to ascertain since individuals will be seen as part of family counseling services and the physical health or mental health network.

Assaultive and abusive sexual behavior refers to rape, incest, child exploitation and molestation (pedophilia). There were an estimated 76,000 reported rapes in the United States in 1982 and in 1984, 28,000 arrests for this behavior. It is further estimated that only one out of four rapes are reported, which means, there are approximately 300,000 rapes occurring annually. It has been further estimated that one out of five rape victims are under age twelve Geiser (1979). Since 1970, there has been a rapid increase in the number of sexual assault treatment centers. Prior to 1970, there may have been five or six in the United States, whereas in 1980 there were at least 200 specialized sexual assault treatment centers.

Incest, although a problem since the beginning of humankind, has only recently been seen as a significant social problem. Since 1962, with the studies on child abuse, incest has been highlighted as one form of abuse. Geiser (1979) estimated that about 250,000 cases of incest occur per year, but other studies indicate that about one in ten cases are reported. The most common form of incest is brother and sister, followed by father and daughter. A less common form of incest is mother and son. Social services for this problem are usually provided as part of sexual assault and treatment centers, as part of general family counseling, or in some cases, focussing on an individual as engaging in aberrant behavior and classified as a sexual offender and receiving services through the corrections or mental health network.

Child molestation and exploitation includes a variety of behaviors, such as pedophilia (child intercourse), paederasty

710

(sexual foreplay with a child), pornography, sex rings for foreplay, prostitution, etc. Geiser (1979) has estimated that one
in three children, male or female, has been a victim of sexual
abuse or assault in one form or another before they reach age
eighteen. Psychological consequences of abuse seem to be more
damaging for female children, with the exception of mother and
son incest. Some authors have speculated that most male
children may have been exposed once or twice to some form of
abuse and exploitation in comparison to the multiple exposure of
female children to some form of abuse and exploitation. It has
been extimated that as many as 1.2 million children under age 18
have been exposed to, or are engaged in pornography and prostitution. For every female under twelve raped, it has been
estimated that the rate of abuse for males as victims is about
one-half that of the rate for young females. Since the Mann Act
focussed on females as victims, there has been a neglect of
looking at the problem of young males who unwillingly become
involved in sexual practices. The Mann Act has recently been
revised in 1978 to include young males.

Aberrant behavior refers to behaviors, such as exhibitionism
(showing one's self), voyeurism (peeping Tom), sado-masochistic
behavior (flagellation), coprolalia (obscene phone calls),
necrophilia (use of a corpse for a sexual act), bestiality (use
of animals for a sexual act), etc. In 1984 there were approximately 76,000 arrests for varied sexual offenses, excluding rape
and prostitution. It has been estimated that 10 percent of the
adult population engages in these forms of behavior. Reported
cases of aberrant behavior are one in twenty. The number of
specialized facilities for aberrant behavior or for sex
offenders is relatively small in the United States, consisting
of less than one hundred specialized facilities. Most of the
individuals involved in aberrant behavior are handled through
the mental health network, although a small number are handled
through the corrections network.

Problematic behavior refers to a variety of behaviors, such
as pornography, prostitution, sexual harassment, etc. Pornography in the United States is big business, grossing over
3 billion dollars per year. It is estimated that 90 percent of
the males and 80 percent of the females have been exposed to
pornographic literature. The number of chronic users of pornographic materials is considerably smaller, about 15 percent of
the population.[7] This estimate on the chronic use of pornography varies for males, about 10 percent and females about
5 percent.

Prostitution in the United States, like pornography, is big
business. A rather conservative estimate of the number of
prostitutes in the United States is between one to three

million, and between 300,000 and 500,000 children are involved in prostitution. Although there were 88,000 arrests in 1984 for prositution, it is estimated that one in twenty was arrested. It should be of interest to note that for every 1,000 prostitutes arrested, only two tricks or Johns are arrested.

Sexual harassment among employed women is a major problem in the United States. Sexual harassment includes behaviors, such as ogling, or leering at one's body, constant brushing against one's body, squeezing or pinching a woman's body, forced intimacy, outright propositions, losing one's job or promotion for refusing to accept harassment and forced sexual relations. Surveys on sexual harassment show a range of between 49 to 80 percent of female workers have been victims of some form of sexual harassment.[8] On a general basis, a reasonable figure for the frequency of sexual harassment seems to be approximately 60 percent of working women. Redbook Magazine in 1976 had a special article on sexual harassment and projected a figure of 60 percent. The economic and social cost of sexual harassment is difficult to assess, although the number of people involved can be counted in the millions. Figure 22-1 shows the estimated size of the personal social service network.[9]

HISTORICAL DEVELOPMENT

Since the personal social service network consists of a variety of services each of the major categories will be briefly described and selected services within each category will be highlighted.

PROTECTIVE SERVICES

Selected services under the category of protective services include the following: services for children, services for victims of family violence, and services to the mature adult or the aged population.

CHILDREN (CHILD WELFARE)--The early history of child welfare services is closely linked to the treatment of the poor in society. Dependent and neglected children in Medieval Europe (450-1500) were placed in monasteries or hospitals (hospice) for care, or were apprenticed (indentured) to individuals for a specific period of time in order to learn a trade. Most of the institutions for child welfare services were built and managed under religious organizations and institutions.

In 1601 under the Elizabethean Poor Laws, the care of dependent and neglected children became the responsibility of relatives, or the parish (county). The parish developed a

Figure 22-1

ESTIMATED SIZE OF THE PERSONAL
SOCIAL SERVICE NETWORK in 1980-85*

Component of Network	Number of Agencies[1]
Protective Services	27,525+
Utilitarian	22,039+
Developmental and Socialization	15,270+
Rehabilitative and Therapeutic	43,370+
Total Agencies	108,204

*   Sources: Adapted   from   the   following   resources;   Amy
    Weinstein, Public Welfare Directory 1986-87 Washington,
    D.C.:   American   Public   Welfare   Association,   1986;   Helga
    Croner, National Directory of Private Social Agencies 1986,
    Queens Village, New York: Croner Press, 1986;   United States
    Department   of   Commerce,   Bureau   of   the   Census, Statistical
    Abstract   of   the   United   States: 1986   (106th   Edition),
    Washington,   D.C.:   U.S.   Government   Printing   Office,   1985;
    pp.   24,   35-37;   40,   45-49;   62-66;   78-79,   118-119,   172-173,
    355,   382-384;   Department   of   Health,   Education   and   Welfare,
    Day Care Centers in the United States, Washington, D.C.:
    U.S. Government Printing Office, 1979; United States Depart-
    ment   of   Health   Education   and   Welfare,   Public   Health   Service,
    National   Directory   of   Drug   Abuse   and   Alcohol   Treatment
    Programs,   Washington,   D.C.:   U.S.   Government   Printing
    Office,   1982   and   1982 Census of Service Industries
    Washington,   D.C.:   U.S.   Government   Printing   Office,   1984,
    pp. 5-7.

1   The 1982 Census of Service Industries shows as estimated
    61,938   agencies,   an   estimated   667,000   employees   and
    expenditures of 16.3 billion dollars for establishments in
    the following categories: individual and family services,
    child care and other social service.

system   of   almshouses   which   housed   the   young,   aged,   sick,
vagrants,   criminals,   etc.   In   the   United   States,   during   the
colonial   period   (1609-1783),   the   most   common   public   means   of

caring for dependent and neglected children were: the almshouse (New York, 1700; Pennsylvania, 1767); indentured servitude or apprenticeship (Plymouth Colony, Massachusetts, 1635 and New York, 1703); and in some cases, outdoor relief or financial relief in ones own home.

A private system of services for dependent and neglected children slowly developed, such as the Ursuline Convent in New Orleans (1779), the Society for the Relief of Poor Widows and Small Children in New York (1797), private child welfare agencies in New York (1807), the Children's Aid Society under Charles Brace in New York (1853) and the Society for the Prevention for Cruelty to Animals and Children in New York (1875). From this dual system of public and private agencies there developed institutions, such as county homes (Ohio, 1866), state homes (Wisconsin, 1866, Massachusetts, 1883), foster care and boarding out placements (Massachusetts, 1863 and 1868), and adoption services (Massachusetts, 1851 and Wisconsin, 1853). During the latter part of the nineteenth century 1875-1900 there was a rapid development of child welfare services culminating in the juvenile court movement in 1899, and the child welfare and the child labor law movements from 1900-1925. The juvenile court movement established a separate system of courts for youthful offenders as distinct from adult courts. Prior to 1899, the youthful offender (age 7 and up) was treated as an adult (see Chapter 16, Corrections Network).

The child welfare movement focussed on adequate care of children including housing, medical care, food, clothes, education, etc. The child labor movement focussed on protective legislation for youthful workers, including medical care, salary, hours, protective conditions of the work situation, etc. There were numerous national conferences focusing on child welfare concerns, such as the White House Conference of 1909, 1919 and every decade thereafter. As a consequence of public pressure, the Children's Bureau was established at the national level in 1912 which currently is under the Department of Health and Human Services. The Children's Bureau provides funds for child welfare services, such as foster care, and provides literature and guide lines for social service programs. Concurrent with the development of federal agencies, there was a development of international organizations focussing on child welfare, such as the International Union for the Promotion of Child Welfare, established in 1920, and professional organizations in the United States of a private nature, such as the Child Welfare League in 1919. Currently all states have child welfare agencies and legislation related to foster care, adoption and child labor laws.

714

A service program which is related to child welfare is that of Widow's Pensions now called Aid to Families with Dependent Children under the income maintenance network (see Chapter 19 – Income Maintenance Network). The first state to authorize a mother's or widow's pension was Illinois in 1911. By 1935, all but two states had some form of mother's aid. The passage of the Social Security Act in 1935 and its provisions for Aid to Families with Dependent Children superseded all existing state programs. A recent development in the area of adoption (permanent transfer of custody and guardianship to one other than one's natural parents) and foster care (temporary transfer of custody to one other than one's natural parents) is the possibility of allowing single individuals and parents to adopt children and become foster and adoptive parents.[10]

VICTIMS of FAMILY VIOLENCE – Family discord, violence and conflict is not a new phenomenon in the United States since it has been around for centuries. What is changing is societies attitudes toward this behavior and its toleration, or lack of toleration of the behavior and recognition of family violence as a significant social problem. Family violence includes behaviors, such as spouse abuse, child abuse, sexual exploitation of a child (incest and sexual molestation) and parent abuse. Abuse directed at women as a marital partner (spouse abuse) or in a relationship has been acceptable or at least condoned behavior historically in many societies. Women in many societies have been subordinated legally and socially to the male. In Egyptian and Roman society women had certain legal and social rights. On the other hand Teutonic (Germanic tribes of Europe) and in India (after 200 BC), China (600 BC), and Medieval Europe (450-1500) women were viewed as inferior and under the domination and protection of the husband. Famous Medieval European philosophers and churchmen, such as St. Augustine (354-430), and Thomas Aquinas (1225-1274), advocated the philosophy of male dominance. English Common Law followed the traditions of Medieval Europe and these attitudes of male domination carried over into the United States. Male legal and social domination of women included items, such as the personal property of a woman, income of a woman and personal behavior of a woman. The male was expected to provide corrective discipline to the woman for personal behavior when necessary. The male was perceived as having the right to use forceful measures to assure appropriate behavior of their spouse. An example of this attitude was expressed in Freedoms Ferment by Alice Tyler.

"Wife beating with a reasonable instrument was legal in almost every state as late as 1850. In Massachusetts, Judge Buller defined a legal instrument as a stick no thicker than my thumb, and in New York, the courts upheld a worthy

Methodist exhorter for beating his wife with a horse whip every few weeks in order to keep her in proper subjection and prevent her scolding."[11]

Public attitudes condoned or ignored spouse abuse until the social consciousness and the feminist movement of the 1960's. An early publication which signaled a concern about spouse abuse was that of Richard Gelles in 1972 entitled, The Violent Family. In 1972 a hotline was established in St. Paul, Minnesota for battered women and later, in 1974, a safe house or residence was established called the Women's Advocate House. In 1978 there were an estimated 75 transitional and temporary homes for battered women and their children and two for battered men. These homes provide a broad range of social, legal and financial services for women such as the Sojourner Truth House in Milwaukee, Wisconsin.[12]

Child abuse and exploitation has been acceptable in many societies historically. Children held a similar status to women in many societies in that they were under the total subordination or control of the father. Children did not have separate social or legal rights. In Greece (621 BC) a father had the right to sell the child and discipline the child to correct their behavior. In the case of a malformed or sick child, the father could leave a child exposed to the environment to die. Roman society around 50 BC followed similar customs as Grecian society. A greater emphasis was placed upon the family in Roman society as an important entity in society, consequently by 200, Roman society had restricted the father's right of punishment to that of chastisement but still condoned the potential selling of children. Under Christianity, the domination of the father continued as illustrated in the works of St. Augustine (354-430) and Thomas Aquinas (1225-1274). In Medieval Europe (450-1500), abandonment of children and infanticide (the killing of a baby) were as common as selling single children for sexual purposes. English Common Law continued the tradition of father dominance which was then transferred over into the legal traditions of the United States. Although the father had full legal and social authority over his children in the United States, there was a concept that excessive cruelty and the killing and selling of a child was not warranted. There was little societal support for regulating the authority of a father in any meaningful fashion until after 1900.

In 1866, the Society for the Prevention of Cruelty to Animals was organized in New York. As a consequence of the Mary Ellen case of 1874 when no social service agency would come to her aid, the Society for the Prevention of Cruelty to Animals accepted the case and argued the case in court and expanded its focus to cover children. As a consequence of this court case a separate organization known as the Society for the Prevention of Cruelty to Children was established.[13] By 1900 many social service agencies were concerned about child abuse and sexual exploitation, such as incest, child prostitution, etc. The public was not ready to recognize this behavior as a major social problem at that time. By 1960, national attention was focussing on child abuse and legislation was endorsed in many states mandating professionals in the human services, such as physicians, nurses, social workers, and psychologists to report a suspected case of child abuse. By 1963 as general societal attitudes were shifting to accept child abuse as a problem, there was the concurrent development of legislation to define and protect the legal rights of children.[14]

Parent abuse as problematic behavior has become recognized as a social problem in the late 1970's and early 1980's. As the population became older in terms of expected life span (1900 an expected life span of 49 years and in 1986, 75 years) and suffers from more long-term chronic illnesses, the numbers of reported cases of parent abuse are increasing. Reported cases of parent abuse are usually related to the frustrations of taking care of a forgetful, senile parent, or because of physical disability, the parent is unable to perform routine tasks of living. Numerous stories are in the newspapers quite regularly highlighting physical abuse toward the elderly parent.

MATURE ADULT (AGED)--The elderly in society and their treatment has been closely related to those programs established for the poor, such as income maintenance programs, and voluntary efforts to provide social and recreational outlets. The family and relatives historically were the prime mechanisms for handling the problems of the poor and destitute aged.

If the aged person was poor, those programs which were available were those connected with the poor laws. In Medieval Europe (450-1500) the system for handling the aged poor consisted of: parish or county relief, monastery relief, hospitals, and individual charity. With the Elizabethan Poor Laws of 1601, the workhouse was established which later became the almshouse and later the old folks home, along with the use of parish or county relief. In the United States urban areas primarily used the workhouse or almshouse and the rural areas primarily used outdoor relief. By 1923, some states had developed old age pensions, such as Montana (1923), and by 1934, 34 states had some form of old age pension law. The New Deal of 1935 resulted in the development of the current Social Security system, and the Old Age Assistance program (became part of the Supplemental Security Income program in 1974, see Chapter 19 - Income

717

Maintenance Network). Additions were made to these laws to cover institutionalization, such as nursing homes in 1950, and later hospital and medical care. The utilization of nursing homes has been rapidly expanding since 1965 (see Chapter 23, Physical Health Network). Prior to 1950, the poor and the aged were housed in public institutions and private and public old age homes.

Prior to 1945, little attention was paid to the aged as a group except for the poor since they constituted a small percentage of the population. As the United States population grows older, more attention has been focussed on this particular population group. In 1945, the Gerontological Society was formed. A conference was held in Aspen, Colorado by the Council on Social Work Education focussing on the elderly, and in 1961 the first White House Conference on Aging was held. During the decade of the 1960's there was a rapid development of social services to the aged which includes senior centers. The National Council on Aging was formed in 1950 which had a strong role in developing one of the first senior centers (the Hodson Center in New York - 1961). Family Social Service and Jewish Social Service Agencies developed specialized programs for the aged in 1961, and the Older American Act of 1965 and its amendments of 1973 provided for the development of social services for the aged. The Older Americans Act specifically provided funding for the establishment of senior community centers. The aged in addition to securing services from the federal, state, and local governments began to organize on their own behalf. The National Council on Senior Citizens was organized in 1961 and a political activist group called the Grey Panthers was organized in 1971. The aged as a group have moved from the position of a lack of political power and social visibility in 1940 to a significant social political force by 1986.[15]

UTILITARIAN SERVICES

Selected services discussed in this section include day care and homemaking.

DAY CARE SERVICES--Day care services in the United States developed from a children's nursery which was established in Children's Hospital in New York City (1854) where a room was set aside to take care of the mother's children while she was visiting patients. The first permanent day care center was established in 1863 and by 1900 there were 175 such centers. A professional organization was developed in 1898 called the National Federation of Day Nurseries which in 1960 changed its name to the National Committee for Day Care of Children, and currently is called the Child Development Association

Consortium. Day care as a service is distinct from nurseries and nursery schools although there are common origins in their development. There has been a slow but steady movement to professionalize day care and child care work in the United States.[16] It is estimated that thirty percent of the married women use day care facilities in the United States. The Public Welfare amendment of 1962 provided funding for the establishment of day care centers to allow welfare mothers to take their children to day care centers while they were involved in the Work Incentive Training program. As more and more women in the United States work on a full or part time basis, it is anticipated that the need for day care centers will increase.

HOMEMAKING SERVICES--Families may need homemaking services as a consequence of mental and physical health emergencies, chronic absence of a spouse, or there is only one spouse in the family which is usually not home. Homemaking service may be a practical service in preventing a family from becoming a welfare recipient, helping to keep a family together or for those individuals who are on welfare providing needed assistance in order to cope with problems of daily living. One of the first homemaking services was established in 1903 through the Family Service Bureau Association for the Improvement of the Conditions of the Poor in New York City. This service was essentially a visiting housewife service using volunteers. By 1923 organized programs for homemaking services were established through the Jewish Family Welfare Society in Philadelphia, Pennsylvania. An impetuous for the development of homemaking services was the establishment of homemaking programs in 1935 under the Work Progress Administration. In 1939 a voluntary group was organized known as the Committee on Supervised Housekeeping Services. This group became the National Committee on Homemaking Services in 1946 and changed its name to the National Council on Homemaking Services (1970) and currently is known as the National Homecare Council. The major local organization for implementing homemaking services usually is the social service department (the welfare department) at the county level. Most social service departments have a specialized unit for homemaking and provides funds and staff for this particular purpose. Generally, homemaking services are performed by volunteers or paraprofessionals who are paid to essentially take care of the house and are given minimal training.[17]

DEVELOPMENTAL and SOCIALIZATION SERVICES

Selected Services discussed in this section include services for families and couples, unwed mothers and youth.

FAMILY and COUPLES SERVICES - The family however defined has been a basic social unit since the beginning of humankind, however, the form or structure of the family has changed over the years and undoubtedly will continue to change. Currently the family in the United States is generally perceived to be a nuclear, conjugal, patriarical or companionate type of family, which means parents and children who are related by blood, with the male as the head of the household and shared decision making between the spouses and in some cases with the children.[18]

The nuclear family from a historical perspective has been in existence since about 1700 with other types of family structure preceding it. The focal point of any family unit has been the mother-child relationship. In some societies, the mother and her kinship lines are predominant in establishing kinship lines, property rights and authority in the family (matriarichy). In other societies, the father and his kinship lines are predominant in establishing kinship lines, property rights and authority in the family (patriarchy). An anthropological example of a matriarchy is the Fante tribe of the Gold Coast in Africa. In this tribe the mother took care of the children, was the authority figure in the family, had property and housing rights, and resided with the mother and her kinship group. The father was viewed as a peripheral part of the family and the children barely knew their father. An anthropological example of a patriarchy is the Buna Tribe of the Ivory Coast of Africa. In this case authority in the family resided with the husband, and property, housing and kinship rights followed his line of descent.[19]

By 4000 B.C. the family unit consisted of parents, children and relatives, that is, an extended family with family loyalties and allegiances equal to or more important than the government. In Egyptian society (1400 B.C.), the family was matriarchial, whereas in Grecian society (400 B.C.), Roman society (100 B.C.), Chinese society (500 B.C.), and Hebrew society (1200 B.C.), the family was patriarchial, with an emphasis on the extended family. Family problems were handled by family members or by consultation from the clergy or in drastic cases a divorce or a separation was recognized. Most marriages were monogamous, however, some provisions were made for polygamous marriages.[20] Marriages were generally civil in nature, although some groups had both civil and religious marriages, such as the Hebrews.

Medieval Europe (450-1500) continued the practice of monogamous marriages, and the conjugal relationship (husband, wife and children) was primary. Although the conjugal relationship was recognized, allegiances were still to ones kin and ones other family members (extended family). Marriage was recognized as a religious sacrament (in contrast to a civil or religious ceremony) in the fourth book of Peter Lombard's "Sentences"

(1164), which later was reaffirmed by the Council of Florence (1439) and the Council of Trent (1543-1563). Divorce was frowned upon and not recognized in most cases although some cases of annulment and separation were recognized. Family and marital problems were generally taken to the clergy for resolution. During the Renaissance and Reformation (1500-1700), the nuclear conjugal family became dominant in Western society. The decline of the extended family in parts of Western Europe and later in the United States was related to the rise of the nation-state, and the changing economic system, which resulted in a different social organization, which emphasized an individualistic thought process and philosophy. As the nuclear conjugal family unit became the primary focus of family life, more attention and concern was expressed about the nature of the conjugal relationship, which means the marital relationship. Later, the companionate context of the marital relationship was stressed. Changes were made in divorce laws, allowing for divorce and separation, and there was recognition of civil, religious and common law marriages. Family and marital problems were generally handled by family members, clergy, friends and on an occasional basis the physician.

The movement toward the development of family and marital counseling services as a specialty was evident through the establishment of professional organizations and academic training by the late 1800's. The Family Service Association was organized in 1874 (changed its name to the Family Service Association of America in 1911), and the establishment of the American Hygiene Association in 1914 are examples of professional organizations which focussed on the family and its problems.

Some courses on marriage and family counseling were offered at various colleges and universities by 1893 and an Institute of Family Relations was established in 1930. Ernest Groves is considered to be the prime catalyst for the development of academic courses in marriage and the family and the family relations movement in the United States, when he established the field of family relations (1937). Family and marital counseling as a subspeciality and a practice area, is related to the development of the sexual counseling movement. The Berlin Institute on the Study of Sex, under Magnus Hershfled (1919), concentrated on the study of sexual behavior and developed clinics which dealt with marital problems. These marital clinics spread rapidly throughout Europe and the United States, with a marriage counseling center established in New York under Abraham and Hanna Stone (1929). Concurrent with the academic aspect of marriage and family relations, and agencies focussing on marriage counseling, professional organizations and practice standards emerged. In

1942 the American Association of Marriage Counselors was established. The American Association of Marriage Counselors initiated professional practice standards (1948), a code of ethics (1962), and a process of professional certification (1967). This organization changed its name to the American Association of Marriage and Family Counselors in 1970, and as of 1978 is known as the American Association for Marriage and Family Therapy. Currently some states require licensing and certification in order to practice as a marital counselor. Certification standards as a marriage counselor or therapist by the American Association for Marriage and Family Therapy include the following: a Ph.D. in psychology, sociology or education, or an M.D. degree, or an M.S. degree in social work, or a degree in divinity; three years experience; and completion of a training program which is approved by the American Association for Marriage and Family Therapy. Although, standards have been established for marital counseling and therapy, numerous individuals and agencies engage in counseling, and may not be a member of the American Association for Marriage and Family Therapy.[21]

UNWED MOTHERS--Historically the treatment of unwed mothers was closely related to child welfare services and treatment of the poor. Current concepts on single unwed parentage refer to either the mother or the father. Children who are conceived outside of the marital relationship is not a new problem, since this behavior has been in existence since the earliest days of humankind. Societal responses to the unwed mother have varied from acceptance of illegitimate children to punishment of the women, and condemnation and/or killing of the child. Among some North American Indian tribes the illegitimate child was taken care of by relatives with no social stigma attached to the mother or child, such as the Algonquin tribe, in contrast to the Aztec tribe in Mexico which practiced infanticide (killing the child). In Greece, around 400 B.C., children of unmarried couples were sold into slavery, or killed. In Rome, around 100 B.C., the practice of infanticide was common. In Hebrew society, the child was either killed or taken care of by the community. Amongst Teutonic tribes in Germany, the child was cared for by the mother, and if the mother was unable to take care of the child, relatives would take care of the child. In earlier Moslem societies, the mother, or the child, or both were killed.

In Medieval Europe (450-1500), chastity was viewed as a highly esteemed virtue, consequently the unwed mother was viewed as one who committed a grievious sin. The mother and child had no legal rights, and in some cases, the mother was killed, in numerous cases the child was killed, anonymously placed for care with a church or monastery, or placed with a close relative.[22] Many of the illegitimate children were handled as poor orphans and dependent children. At the Council of Nicaea (352), the church began to sponsor homes for the sick and poor, called the xenodocheion, with these homes also used for abandoned infants. Archbishop Datheus of Milan (787) established a foundling home (home for infants) for abandoned children. Pope Innocent the III (1300), established a system known as a turn box, where unwed mothers could place a child anonymously in a box outside of a church, and have the church authorities take care of the child. A special home for foundlings (infants) was established at St. Katherines in England (1414) and the St. Vincent De Paul Society established special infant homes (1633). The problem of infanticide (killing the child) in Medieval Europe was so severe, that in 1623, the practice of infanticide was punishable by death.

An unwed mother in later time periods was severly chastised for her behavior, as indicated by an English law of 1609, which stipulated that the mother was to be committed to the house of corrections for one year, or, in 1744 the mother was to be publicly whipped and then sent to the house of corrections for 6 months. In the United States similar attitudes prevailed, as indicated by a system of potentially branding the mother in Hawthorn's The Scarlet Letter.[23]

By 1800, the illegitimate child was placed in an orphanage, poorhouse (almshouse), or if fortunate may have been placed with relatives or legally adopted by others. Public attitudes remained negative toward both the mother and the child. It was not until 1891 in England in a court case Barnaby vs. McHugh that an unwed mother obtained legal rights for her child. In the United States this did not occur until a court case in the state of Arizona (1915).

A series of maternity homes, poorhouses, and orphanages were the main system for providing services for the unwed mother until the incorporation of programs and services for unwed mothers under the Social Security Act of 1935, which made them eligible for the Aid to Families with Dependent Children program (see Chapter 19 - Income Maintenance). Support payments are normally expected from the father for the children of the unwed mother when paternity has been established. There were earlier precedents for the payment of nonsupport by the father, such as Wisconsin (1865). Attitudes towards unwed mothers have slowly changed from stigma and punishment to one of grudging acceptance. The population group having the highest number of unwed motherhood is the age group of 15 to 19 which has led some authors to refer to the problem as an "epidemic of illegitimacy" in the United States.[24]

YOUTH SERVICES - Many of the agencies involved in the provision of services for youth are products of the later part of the nineteenth century and are generally operated by religious or nonsecretarian agencies. These services overlap with the religious network (see Chapter 15) education network (see Chapter 8) and the leisure and recreation network (see Chapter 14).

Organized services for youth were a response to the crowded urban conditions of the mid and late 1800's with the development of leisure and recreation agencies, park and municipal recreation leagues, socialization agencies, and non-secretarian agencies, such as the YMCA, YWCA, Boy Scouts, Girl Scouts, etc. Most communities today have a variety of public and private facilities which cater to youth including cultural and aesthetic activities, such as bands, and special musical series. The information and referral network (see Chapter 10) through the library system has developed special programs which appeal to the youth. These programs and activities use a variety of funding sources, such as federal, state and local. Programs and activities include day care, nursery, short term and extended term camping and other leisure and recreation activities. The focus of these agencies has shifted throughout the years from a moral philosophical approach and perspective to one of cultural understanding and awareness, which includes family relationships.[25]

REHABILITATIVE and THERAPEUTIC SERVICES

Selected services for discussion in this category include individuals exhibiting substance abuse problems (alcohol, drugs, etc.), individuals exhibiting self destructive behavior (suicide) and individuals and groups exhibiting problems around sexual functioning.

SUBSTANCE ABUSE - Substance abuse consists of alcohol, drugs, stimulants, barbituates, coffee, smoking, etc. The two selected areas for further discussion are alcohol and drug abuse.

Alcohol abuse or the use of alcohol in some fashion has a long history since at least 6400 BC. Archeologists have uncovered evidence of the use of hackberry wine and beer from Catal Huyuk, Anatolia (region in Turkey) dating from approximately 6400 BC. All of the pre-Christian era societies such as Egyptian, Grecian, Roman, Chinese, Indian, etc. have references in their literature to the use of alcohol. For example, in Egypt (2500 BC) there was an awareness of an alcohol problem since soldiers were forbidden from drinking. In Rome it was reported that a general in the First Punic War (264 - 241 BC), lost a major battle because his troops were drunk. Julius

Caeser in the Gallic Wars of 47 BC many times waited until the Gauls were drunk before attacking them and was almost always assured of a military victory.

Societal attempts to control the drinking of alcoholic beverages is also of long duration as indicated by the Code of Hammurabi in Babylonia (2400 BC), which attempted to restrict the sale of alcoholic beverages. Noah, in the Hebrew tradition, (1700 BC) condemned the use of alcohol, and China (1766 BC) condemned the use of alcohol. Many societies have accepted drinking but condemned drunkenness. Alcohol use was widespread in Medieval Europe (450 to 1500), during the Renaissance and Reformation (1500-1700), in Puritan, England (1600) and in the colonial period of the United States (1600-1783). Public drunkeness became a crime in England (1552). England had a reputation for excessive drinking during the period of Cromwell and Puritanism (1649-1660) and was called the "land of the drunkards."

Although drunkeness was widespread, alcoholism as a major problem developed after distilled liquors, such as whiskey, gin, etc. became inexpensive enough for the common person to purchase them around 1650. Prior to 1650, the common person usually drank beer or ale and it was primarily the wealthy who could afford distilled products, such as brandy and whiskey. England had passed legislation to control gin use (1729 and 1736). The increase on taxes for gin in 1736 led to the "gin riots" by the laborers, since their own salaries were rather low and they felt the high taxes on alcohol were unjustified.

In the United States the use of alcohol was accepted and like England, drunkenness was punished. Drunkenness was viewed as a sin therefore the person had to be reformed, redeemed or punished for their sinful ways. Attempts were made to regulate the use of alcohol through "Blue Laws", licensing, taxation and in some cases outright prohibition. The Blue Laws refer to restrictions on the use of alcoholic beverages on the sabbath, as well as, at other social and recreational events. By 1700 distilled spirits like rum and whiskey were increasing in use and problems of public drunkenness were becoming more visible. The church and political leaders were becoming more concerned about the problem. The state of Georgia under Governor John Oglethorp attempted prohibition from 1733 to 1742. This prohibition movement failed almost immediately as widespread smuggling occurred and individuals began making their own alcohol. John Wesley (Methodist clergyman, 1773) advocated for total abstinence as a solution to the problem and by 1780 other clergymen, such as Anthony Benezet, Bishop Asbury, James Finley, and Ebenezer Sparhawk managed to establish an early temperance

movement. The United States like England had violence surrounding an increase in taxes for whiskey with the "whiskey rebellion" in New England (1794). The Temperance Movement in the
United States can be divided into three phases: 1811-1865,
1870-1900, 1910-1933.

The first phase of the Temperance Movement (1811-1865),
initially relied on total abstinence and moral persuasion as a
means to treat the problem. In its later phases, the movement
shifted its focus to advocate for state and local legislation
regulating the use of alcohol. Lymon and Catherine Beecher, and
Justin Edwards were leaders in this early movement and helped
establish the American Society for the Promotion of Temperance
(1826). By 1833 there were over 4000 local temperance societies
in the organization and in 1836 the name was changed to the
American Temperance Society. Women and their participation were
extremely important in the temperance movement. Some examples
of significant women in the temperance movement include:
Susan B. Anthony, Elizabeth Stanton, Lucy Stone, Abbey Foster,
and Antionette Brown. All of these individuals were significant
in the development of a Women's State Temperance Society in New
York (1852).

A related organization in the early temperance movement was
the Washingtonian Movement established by John Hawkins and John
Gaugh (1840). The Washingtonian Movement stressed individual
reform of the drunkard by taking the pledge and signing an
agreement not to drink, and using group techniques of confession
and a narration of one's own life experiences to stay sober.
(The Alcoholics Anonymous organization which was developed in
1935 uses similar techniques). In addition to the individual
appeal, the Washingtonian societies developed private sani-
tariums for the treatment of alcoholism (1841). During this
time period, some private hospitals began to admit alcoholics
for medical treatment. By 1845 the Washingtonian Movement as a
separate entity became part of the broader temperance movement.

Individual states in response to the temperance movement
passed various laws regulating the use of alcohol, such as
Massachusetts (1838) and Maine (1846). Other states banned the
sale of alcohol in particular time periods, days, etc. By 1855,
15 states had passed such laws. These early prohibition laws
were unpopular with the new immigrants from Europe, veterans of
the Civil War and other groups. Consequently most of those
states which passed prohibition laws repealed these laws by
1865. This first phase of the temperance movement, which
focussed on individual redemption and moral persuasion, faltered
and collapsed as reformers became more concerned with the
slavery issue and the Civil War.

The second phase of the temperance movement (1870-1900) stressed the development of political activism and legislation restricting the use of alcohol, and the utilization of private agencies to work with the alcohol abuser. A National Temperance Prohibition Party was established (1869), and the Women's Christian Temperance Union (1874). The focus of this phase of the temperance movement was on education, political campaigns in support of candidates who would endorse temperance legislation, militant activism and general public relations. Attempts were made to have the public schools educate students about the negative impact of alcohol, such as New York (1882). An active force in this movement was the Anti-Saloon League (1893), under the leadership of Carrie Nation. This organization gained national recognition when Carrie Nation walked into saloons with a hatchet and broke beer barrels in the bar. A large number of states passed prohibition and regulatory laws between 1875 and 1900. By 1906, 30 states allowed local options for banning the sale of alcoholic beverages. Again these laws were unpopular and many of these state laws were repealed or modified. The treatment of the alcohol abuser was viewed as a private individual concern. Consequently most of the agencies providing services were of a private nature, such as sanitarians, individual physician consultation, commitment to private mental institutions and the use of private agencies, such as the Salvation Army. In the United States, the Salvation Army (established in 1898), developed a series of social services, such as Rescue Missions, Men's Social Service Centers, and used moral persuasion to reform the alcohol abuser.

The third phase of the temperance movement (1910 to 1933) used the same tactics as the second phase to enhance the temperance cause except to focus on national legislation instead of local legislation. From 1907 to 1917, twenty five states had laws restricting the sale and use of alcohol and this movement culminated in the Volstead Act of 1919, the Eighteenth Amendment to the United States Constitution (Prohibition). National prohibition began in 1920 and by 1923 illegal trade (smuggling) and the illegal distillation of alcohol increased. The use of bootleg liquor rapidly increased after 1923, with over 15,000 physicians and 57,000 pharmacists applying for licenses to prescribe alcohol for medicinal purposes. With the coming of the depression, the anti-prohibition forces began to organize and increased political pressure was placed on congress until prohibition was repealed in 1933.

The prohibition movement failed to eradicate alcohol abuse and other means were emerging for the study and treatment of alcohol abuse. Since 1933, there has been a slow development of an attitudinal change toward alcohol abuse from the perspective

727

of viewing the cause as an individual moral character weakness and individual sin to perceiving alcohol abuse as an illness. The Yale Center for Alcoholic Studies (established in 1932) helped organize the National Council for Alcoholism in 1942. Alcoholics Anonymous, a mutual support group was established in 1935 (see Chapter 21 - Mutual Support Network).

Recognition of alcohol abuse as a major social problem was reflected in legislation, such as the Alcoholic and Narcotic Act (1962) which provided federal funding for community treatment programs which allows alcoholics to be eligible for rehabilitation programs. The National Institute on Alcohol Abuse was established in 1974 under the Department of Health, Education and Welfare (now Health and Human Services). In the court decision of Powell vs. Texas (1966) the perspective taken was that individuals with an alcohol problem need treatment and not incarceration. The treatment of alcohol abuse is currently viewed primarily as part of the mental health network and certification programs for alcohol counselors are rapidly developing.[26]

The 1980's is a decade where alcohol use and abuse is seen as a major social problem and a period of conflict over underlying ideology and social policy directions. There is debate over the term alcoholism, the criteria for alcoholism and the best approach to its treatment. There is less tolerance for drunkeness and groups are encouraging strong punishment for drivers who are legally intoxicated, such as incarceration instead of treatment or educational and awareness programs. Other groups are encouraging a legal drinking age of 21, which most states currently have, instead of 19, which has led to heated emotional political debates in some states. Regardless of what directions social policy makers politically endorse in the 1980's, it is clear there is less tolerance and acceptability of public drunkeness in 1986, than in 1960, especially when one is driving an automobile.

Educational programs appear to be having some impact, since more individuals are aware that alcohol is a depressent, which leads to an initial euphoria and then impairs reflexes both physically, and intellectually with various degrees of emotional instability. In effect, individuals are more aware of the fact that alcohol is a mind altering substance and understand the effects of long term use, such as physiological withdrawal, lack of adequate nutrition, irritability and rapid mood swings. Although the problem of alcohol abuse is seen as severe, the reduction of federal money available for programs between 1980-1986 has resulted in a reduction of service available.

Drug Abuse is not a product of the twentieth century since use of various substances dates back to at least 2000 BC. Coffee was viewed as a problem by 1500 in some Moslem countries, such as Turkey, which banned its use because coffee was viewed as an aphrodisiac, a stimulant and therefore sinful to use. Tobacco was viewed as a problem by 1600 in some countries and its use was banned or restricted. For example, China (1638) had a death penalty for the use of tobacco, and in the United States, fourteen states had laws prohibiting the use of tobacco between 1900 and 1925. On the other hand, some societies used tobacco as part of their religious ceremonies, such as some of the American Indian tribes. England, in the 1600's viewed tobacco as part of the medical means for the treatment of certain diseases.

A concept used today is that of polyabuse (more than one psychoactive substance) since many people use more than one psychoactive substance, such as alcohol, smoking, and coffee, or cannabis, stimulants, coffee, alcohol, etc.

The major concern in this section on substance abuse is the use of drugs, such as opiates, cocaine, cannabis or marijuana, hallucinogens, sedatives, stimulants and inhalants.

The opiates are a psycho-active substance derived from the poppy plant and includes opium and its more refined products, such as morphine, heroin and codeine. As a narcotic, the opiates are a depressant and initially result in a state of euphoria, then a period of drowsiness and impaired functioning. The opiates are used medically to relieve pain. After long term use an individual has mood swings, becomes irritable, suffers physiological withdrawal and has impaired memory and intellectual functioning.

Opiates and their use date back to Sumeria (4000 BC), Egypt (3500 BC), Greece (2000 BC) and Rome (100). At that time, its use was primarily for medical and religious purposes. Although opiates were used in Medevial Europe, its use was primarily for medicinal purposes since the cost of drugs was extremely high. In 1700, opiates were proclaimed to be a cure for diseases including the common toothache, cancer and venereal diseases. With the development of laboratory refined and more concentrated opiate derivites, such as morphine (1805), codeine (1832) and heroin (1898). With the development of the hypodermic needle (1853), the cost of opiate substances was decreasing and there was an easy means to use these drugs. Severe problems with the use of opiates began to develop after the Civil War with many of the soldiers returning from the war having become addicted to the use of morphine as a consequence of coping with the pain of battle wounds and surgery (Solder's Sickness).

729

By 1900, the medical profession had become aware of the dangers of opiate addiction. Public attitudes toward the use of opiates began to change and this attitudinal change was reinforced by the negative image of opium dens used by the Chinese on the West Coast. The opium den was viewed as a place where individuals became high on drugs and engaged in many evil and illegal activities. Treatment for individuals addicted to one of the opiates consisted of private individual contact with physicians or placement in a private sanitarium. By 1912, all states had some laws prohibiting the use and selling of opiates and the federal government with the Harrison Act (1914) banned the sale, production and distribution of opiate products except for medicinal purposes. Heroin was added to the list of drugs covered under the Harrison Act in 1934.

Shortly after the Harrison Act was passed a number of local medical clinics were developed to treat or to maintain the opiate addict. By 1919, there were 44 such medical clinics. These medical clinics, such as Knoxville, Tennessee, were closed by 1925. These medical clinics were closed because it was thought that medical care was not solving the problem but only maintaining the opiate addict. The United States government authorized two narcotic farms in 1929 which later became the Federal Hospitals in Lexington, Kentucky and Fort Worth, Texas. The only other form of treatment for the opiate addict was commitment to a mental hospital which was authorized by 34 states for conviction under the criminal statutes. The opiate addict was now viewed as a criminal and the primary implementator of the Harrison Act was the Bureau of Narcotics and Dangerous Drugs which was established in 1930.

Little was done to treat the problem outside of the law enforcement perspective (the person viewed as a criminal, therefore incarceration as a means of control) until opiate use became wide spread in the late 1950's. A support group known as Synanon was developed by Charles Diedrich (1959), which was a modified version of a therapeutic community (each individual was part of the group, the group makes all the decisions). Synanon has departed from its original goals and has taken on the characteristic of a commune or a religious cult. The criminal and legalistic approaches which were dominate from 1939-1960 were having minimal success in reducing the problem of opiate use.

In 1962, a White House Conference was held on narcotic and drug abuse which made recommendations for the development of a treatment approach. In 1964 narcotic addicts were included under rehabilitation programs and in 1966 the Narcotic Addict Rehabilitation Act was passed which provided federal funding for community based treatment programs. These acts were further modified in 1970 and 1972 along with the development of the National Institute on Drug Abuse which was organized in 1970. The current methods of treating the opiate addict are: hospitalization, drug free treatment (a clinic which reduces drug use through reduced dosages of the drug), therapeutic communities (a group environment), methodone maintenance programs (substitute drugs), antagonistic drug treatment (incompatible drug program) and multi modality approaches or one which combines different forms of treatment. A program for the treatment of drug users is known as TASC (Treatment Alternatives to Street Crimes) which is part of the newer orientation to drug addiction along with the Drug Enforcement Administration under the Department of Justice. Unfortunately many of these treatment programs rely on the infusion of federal money and with budgetary cutbacks between 1980 and 1986 a number of these treatment centers will be forced to close. The impact of the newly declared "War on Drugs" in 1986 is unclear since its focus appears to be more legalistic and law enforcement oriented rather than rehabilitative oriented.

Cocaine is derived from the erythrorylon coca plant and is a stimulant. The drug is a mood elevator. After the initial feeling of euphoria has subsided, the person becomes restless, irritable and there can be damage to the nose membranes if one is snorting or sniffing the drug.

The use of cocaine is documented at least as far back as 1230 in the Inca Empire in Peru for religious and medicinal purposes. The rapid use of cocaine developed after 1859 when an economically means of producing the drug was developed. Cocaine was praised as a wonder drug for medicinal purposes by such well known figures as Sigmund Freud (1884). Its use spread rapidly and it was used as an ingredient in Coca Cola from 1885 to 1903. By 1900 a high degree of concern was expressed over cocaine use and its sale and distribution was prohibited under the Harrison Act of 1914. Attitudes towards the cocaine addict and treatment methods for the addict are very similar to that of the opiate addict. The cocaine problem is receiving wide public exposure, partly as a response to two young prominent athletes dying as a consequence of its use in 1986.

The use of cocaine between 1980-86, had dramatically increased in the United States and is now seen as the main drug of choice, replacing marijuana. Both experts in the field of narcotics and the public press refer to this increase in the use of cocaine as the "blizzard." It has been estimated that in 1974, 5.4 million individuals had used cocaine and by 1982 this estimate increased to over 21.6 million individuals. One reason for the increase in cocaine use is the development of cheaper varieties of the drug such as "crack" (a smokable form of the drug) and a paste. A "war on drugs" was declared, late in 1986, however the impact of this program is unclear since its orientation is primarily legalistic and law enforcement, instead of rehabilitation.

Cannabis or marijuana is derived from the cannabis setiva plant and results in a feeling of relaxation and euphoria. After this feeling of euphoria subsides some individuals experience panic reactions and have an inability to function intellectually.

The use of marijuana is documented as far back as 2700 BC in China where it was used for religious and medicinal purposes. Marijuana use was known to exist amongst the Scythians (430 BC), limited use amongst the Greeks in (300 BC), and in Medevial Europe (450-1500 AD) for medicinal purposes. The use of marijuana (also known as Ganja) for non-medicinal purposes developed in India and Asia Minor about 1800. In the United States, the drug was used in the Southwest amongst the Mexican laborers and others between 1900 and 1910. In 1906, the Pure Food and Drug Administration classified marijuana as a dangerous drug and in 1915 the United States prohibited its importation except for medical purposes.

The period of most rapid increase of its use in the United States corresponded with the Prohibition years of 1920-1933, when it became a substitute for alcohol, although 29 states had laws prohibiting its use except for medicinal purposes. By 1933, there was a general social concern over its use and in 1937 the Marijuana Tax Act was passed. Debate continues today over the effects of marijuana use. Those groups supporting the use of the drug indicate it is safer and has a less harmful effect than smoking or the use of alcohol. Those groups opposing use of the drug indicate there are long range effects physically, mentally, behaviorally, and in sexual functioning. Societal attitudes vacillate between treating the person as a criminal, a person needing therapy, or a matter of individual conscience with each person making the decision to use or not use the drug.

The decade of the 1960s was one in which the use of marijuana drastically increased amongst all population groups. The use of marijuana seemed to decrease in the 1970's, and in the 1980's, cocaine has replaced marijuana as the drug of first choice.

The hallucinogens include a variety of drugs which distort ones perception and provides an altered state of consciousness and includes: LSD (lysergic acid diethylamide) which is produced chemically or from the ergot fungus; peyote (from the mescal cactus); mescaline (from the mescal cactus and maguey plant) and PCP (phencycledine) which is produced chemically. These drugs result in visual distortion, auditory distortion, rapid heartbeat etc. A person can experience flashbacks of the "trip" or their experience months after they have taken the drug. Individuals who have paranoid tendencies could easily withdraw or become aggressive while having a trip. It is common to experience anxiety or depression with these drugs.

Sedatives, stimulants and inhalants include a variety of drugs used to relax a person or to obtain a quick high. Sedatives are a depressant and decreases ones physiological, intellectual and emotional functioning. These drugs are produced chemically. The more common sedatives are seconal, nembutal, secobarbital, valium, phemothiazme, librium and quaolude. These drugs produce a feeling of relaxation, relief of tension and anxiety and some euphoria, along with drowsiness. Stimulants include caffeine (from the thea sinensis plant, coffee from the coffea arabuca plant), cocoa (from the theobroma cacao plant), nicotine (from the nicotiana tobacum plant), and a variety of amphetamines which are chemically produced, such as dexedrine, preludin, riliten, etc. The stimulant of our immediate concern are the amphetamines. Use of these drugs results in an increased alertness and reduces fatigue. Long term use results in restlessness, irritability and in some cases a toxic psychosis. Other mood elevators include the tranqualizers and antidepressants, such as thorazine, haldal, elavel, tofranil, etc. As mood elevators these tranqualizers calm a person down but as the effects of the drug subside, a person becomes restless and irritable. The inhalants or anesthetic gases and chemicals are a depressant and includes toxic substances, such as gasoline, nitricoxide, chloroform, glue, paint, aerosal can propellents, etc. Extensive use of these chemicals can result in liver, kidney and brain damage. The individual obtains a high or a feeling of euphoria from use of these chemicals.

Hallucinogens/Sedatives/Stimulants/Inhalents and their use have became widespread after 1945. There were some drugs, such as peyote and mescaline, which were used earlier in some societies for religious ceremonies. For example, some of the American Indian and Mexican Indians tribes. A period of rapid increase in the use of these drugs was the late 1950's and 1960's for an assortment of problems including obesity, general dieting, mild depression, anti-depression, high blood pressure, manic styles of behavior, deliberate highs, escape etc. At first the use of these drugs was seen as positive since the results were positive. In the late 1960's it was recognized that individuals could become addicted to their use and concern developed over the abuse of these psycho-active substances. The general attitude today is to use these psycho-active drugs in moderation, but no consistent approach has been taken on how to address or handle this specific problem.

Similar to alcohol abuse, the problem of drug abuse is leading to educational awareness programs, strictor law enforcement measures (the newly declared War on Drugs) and a specialization in human services as a drug counselor with a certification or credentialing procedure for individuals interested in or engaged in drug counseling.[27]

SUICIDE - The thought of a person taking their own life in our society is considered to be an act of hopelessness and alien to the predominate Judaic-Christian tradition. Yet, suicide is a significant problem in the United States. Individuals become upset when a person they know commits suicide and are horrified and perplexed when a case of mass suicide occurs, such as the Jonestown incident in Guyana in 1978. In Jonestown 900 individuals committed suicide either voluntarily or forced, to avoid repercussions of the slaying of Congressman William Ryan. Historically suicide has been condemned by most societies. Some societies have made allowances for acts of patriotism (United States), maintain honor (Japan), avoiding pain (classical Roman society) and a process of bereavement (India). Early societies frowned on suicide because through this act there was a loss of a warrior or a mother and it showed contempt for society. This condemnation of suicide was carried over into taboos, rituals and later into religious beliefs. All of the pre-Christian era societies generally condemned suicide, such as China, India and Japan but made allowances for acts of suicide involving bereavement or for saving face. In Hebrew society suicide was generally condemned and rare, but allowances were made for various acts for religious purposes. Some historical examples of Jewish individuals or groups which committed some form of suicide include Sampson who destroyed himself in a Philistine temple (about 1125 BC), Saul who killed himself by torture (about 1004 BC) and the mass suicide of the Jewish zealots at Masada under the leadership of Eleazar Benjair (73). In both Grecian and Roman society suicide was severely condemned amongst the slave population. The masses would tolerate the behavior, but it was acceptable in the higher classes in order to preserve honor, avoid pain, express bereavement, or for patriotic reasons.

Medieval Europe (450-1500) initially accepted suicide for religious purposes, such as martyrdom, but began to condemn this behavior after 400. There were allowable reasons for suicide in

Christian Medieval Europe, such as a woman to protect her chastity in avoiding a rape or a religious ascetic who goes on a fast until they die. Since humans are a creature of God, suicide was considered a grievious sin if one destroyed a creature of God. Consequently, if one took their own life, it was a grievious sin against both humankind and God. These attitudes condemning suicide slowly developed through a series of church announcements which both condemned suicide and developed policies pertaining to property rights, legal rights, etc. Some examples of these policies include: the Council of Arles (452) which condemned suicide and the estate of the deceased was forfeited to the church; Council of Braga (563) where religious rights for the body of the suicide victim were denied; Antisidor Council (590) which proclaimed a series of penalties against the body of the suicide victim; and the Synod of Nimes which denied a Christian burial for the suicide victim, and the individual's body could not be interred in a Christian cemetery. As a consequence of these harsh attitudes towards suicide in church policy, customs developed, such as taking the body out of the home through a window or hole in the wall, mutilating the body, and burying the body in the middle of a crossroad so the ghost of the deceased would not be able to find its way back to haunt the family. In spite of the condemnation of suicide, individuals still committed suicide and even mass suicide occurred, such as a Jewish group in York, England (1190) and the Albigenses a reformanist religious group in France (1218).

During the Renaissance and Reformation (1500 to 1700) there was a softening or easing of the attitudes of condemnation and sinfulness towards suicide amongst the nobility and mercantile classes but not amongst the masses or the clergy. Shakespeare in his works has numerous examples of suicide in plays such as "Macbeth" where Lady Macbeth committed suicide. From 1700 to 1900 suicide was condemned and viewed as a sin by most individuals. Some attitudinal changes were slowly taking place towards suicide by scholars and physicians who were looking for natural causes of the behavior, such as Merian (1783), Madome DeStael (1814), Esquiral (1838) and Emile Durkheim (1897). These scholars and physicians began to investigate suicide as a social and psychological phenomenon, as well as, looking for medical reasons for suicide. Merian and Esquiral investigated psychological motivation, Durkheim investigated social and economic causes, and DeStael was investigating medical causes. Emile Durkheim, in his classic work "Suicide" (1897), developed a classification system consisting of: anomic suicide - caused by a feeling of hopelessness; altruistic suicide - caused by looking for a higher principle; egoistic suicide - caused by an individual failing to live up to individual expectations; and

735

fatalistic suicide - caused by a feeling of fate or fatalism. No major attempts were made at preventing suicide or models developed for the treatment of the person who unsuccessfully attempted suicide until approximately 1950. Most European countries and the United States viewed suicide as a sin, condemned it, and some states had laws prosecuting the individual who attmpted suicide as an attempted murder, as recently as the 1980's. There was a situation in 1984 where an individual in the state of Iowa had attempted suicide and there was serious consideration given to charging the individual with attempted murder.

An early attempt at suicide prevention was developed in 1906 through the National Save a Life League in New York City. The beginnings of a treatment movement for suicide began with Louis Dublin (1933), who is called the father of suicidology, and his extensive articles and monographs attempting to create public awareness of the problem. The first suicide prevention center was established in 1958 in Los Angeles, California by Norman Farberow and Edwin Schneiderman. Some mutual support groups began to form, such as Friends in Miami, Florida (1959), Lifeline in Miami, Florida (1967) and the Samaritans in England (1953) under the leadership of Reverend Chad Varah. A person who was contemplating suicide could call one of these mutual support groups for emergency counseling and emotional support. After 1963 there was a rapid development of suicide prevention centers as a consequence of the Mental Health Center Act of 1963, which provided federal funding for local communities to develop emergency psychiatric services. National attention was focusing on suicide as a major social problem with the establishment of a Center for the Study of Suicide Prevention in 1968. A specialized program of study was established for post masters degree work in suicidology at Johns Hopkins University and a professional association was established in 1968 called the American Association of Suicidology. These developments show the recency of recognizing suicide as a major social problem with the beginning specialization of treatment facilities and professional personnel. The Center for the Study of Suicide Prevention was merged in 1972 with the National Institute of Mental Health. In 1986 there were over 175 suicide prevention centers in the United States and an additional 591 community mental health centers which provide emergency psychiatric service. These services focussing on suicide prevention have been curtailed as a consequence of federal monies available between 1980-1986.[28]

SEXUAL FUNCTIONING - Selected behaviors described under this category include the following: general sexual functioning which refers to individuals having difficulty in coping with sexual activity either as marital partners, with members of the opposite sex, or as non-marital partners; <u>sexual assaultative and abusive behavior</u>, which refers to rape, incest, child molestation and exploitation: <u>aberrant behavior</u>, which refers to exhibitionism, voyeurism, sadomasochistic behavior, coprolalia, necrophilia, beastiality, etc.; and <u>problematic behavior</u> which refers to pornography, prostitution and sexual harassment.

<u>General sexual functioning</u> overlaps with the area of family and couple counseling (see earlier section this chapter). Behaviors included under general sexual functioning can be classified as general (psychological and emotional problems), such as anxiety, low self esteem, or specific (physiological), such as dypareunia. Societal attitudes toward sexuality have ranged from openness in classical Grecian and Roman society to extreme repression of the behavior between 1800 and 1900 in the United States and England. Little concern was paid to treating problems of sexual functioning outside of moral admonition and exhortation until the latter part of the eighteenth century. Some early individuals writing on general sexual functions include the following: Soranus of Rome (100) and his writings on sexual theory, Galen of Rome (400) and his writings on contraceptives, Erasmus of Germany (1466-1536) and his classic work "Collequia Familiaria," and Rosseau of France (1712-1718) and his classic work "Emille."

The scientific study of sexual functioning was ignored by the scientific community until the work of Kaan in Russia (1843), Morel in France (1857), Krafft-Ebing in Germany (1886) and William Acton in England. Some of these early studies and treatment techniques focussing on medical intervention for sexual functioning were somewhat crude and in fact dangerous. For example, in order to avoid masturbation or to cure one from engaging in masturbation electric shock treatments to the sexual organs was prescribed, or to avoid an erection in the male from looking at a female, a metal spiked harness was worn around the penis. This harsh treatment, which is extremely repressive and dangerous, slowly gave way to a therapeutic school of thought of a psychological nature.

The works of Sigmund Freud (1856-1939) on psychosexual development, Margaret Mead (1901), and Bronislaw Malinowski on crosscultural studies, Havelock Ellis, (1859-1939) on sexuality, and Magnus Hirchfield (1865-1935) on sexual counseling, led to a more positive approach to a discussion of sexual issues and to a study of sexuality. Hirshfield is credited with developing the first institute for Sex Science in 1919 in Berlin, Germany. A sexual counseling center was opened in New York City in 1929. More recent developments in the study of sexual functioning and counseling include the work of Alfred Kinsey (1894-1956), at the Institute for Sex Research established in Bloomington, Indiana in 1947, and his prize pupil, Paul Gebhard, and the works of William Masters and Virginia Johnson at the Masters and Johnson Institute in St. Louis, Missouri in 1964. More recently, a professional organization attempting to establish standards for sex therapy was formed in 1974, known as the American Association of Sex Educators, Counselors and Therapists.[29]

Sexual assaultive and abusive behavior has become a serious concern in the United States. Some sexual behaviors involve violence or threats of violence, coercion or abuse toward others, such as rape, incest, molestation and exploitation of children. Rape and other sexual assaults as a social problem has recently been recognized as one of serious magnitude, as evidenced by the establishment of the National Center for the Prevention and Control of Rape in 1975. Prior to the 1960s little attention was given to rape as a social problem. Yet this behavior is one of the oldest crimes in history. Societal attitudes towards this behavior has varied from a total lack of concern to viewing it as a serious crime.

In many preliterate societies rape of women from a different tribe was accepted as part of the spoils of war. Rape of an individual in one's own tribe was often punishable by death. In Greece (500 B.C.), the laws established a death penalty for the rapist, and abduction of women for sexual purposes was illegal. Enforcement of these laws was extremely lax, and many times individuals refused to press charges. In Babylonia (1000 B.C.), a rapist was either executed or required to marry the victim if both parties were eligible and agreeable. In Rome (100), rape was punishable by death. Enforcement of rape laws depended upon one's status in society, i.e., whether the woman was rich or poor, a member of a religious order, or the rapist was rich or poor. Hebrew culture (300 B.C.) prescribed various penalties for rape, including execution or marrying the victim, depending upon the circumstances of the victim, such as the age of the victim, whether married or unmarried, whether betrothed or engaged or not. Medieval Europe (450-1500) prescribed the death penalty or other alternatives, depending upon the circumstances of the victim, such as age of the victim, member of a religious order, married, etc. Enforcement of these laws was lax because of the inferior social and legal status of women. An English law of 1309 made rape a felony crime with a death penalty or a fine, depending upon the circumstances.

Early legislation in the United States focussing on rape, such as the Colony of Massachusetts (1642) were similar to those of England. The rapist could be executed if the victim was married or betrothed or under age ten. Some other sentence was stipulated if the victim was unmarried, such as public whipping, placing one in the stocks, marriage, etc. Over time, the death penalty was replaced by fines, jail terms, etc. A system of specialized services for the rape victim developed out of the social consciousness of the 1960s. The passage in 1975 of the Sexual Assault and Rape Prevention Act provided monies for the establishment of sexual assault centers through the Law Enforcement Assistance Administration and other federal agencies. Funding for sexual assault treatment centers has been reduced at the federal level between 1980-1986.

Incest has as its most common form brother and sister, but the most common form reported to authorities is father and daughter. Prior to 1960, incest as a social problem was a taboo subject and most individuals assumed it was a behavior which rarely occurred. In a survey of women published by Hunt (1974), 7 percent of the sample had sexual intercourse with a relative and in a survey of undergraduate students by Finkelhor (1980), 15 percent of the female respondents and 10 percent of the male respondents had a sexual experience with a brother or sister. If incest is viewed more broadly than sexual intercourse, and includes foreplay, the incestuous experience is rather common.

Almost all societies have a strong moral taboo against incest behavior and in many circumstances was punishable by death. An exception to the incest taboo was the Egyptian nobility in the pre-Christian era, where it was an acceptable behavior. The recognition that incest was a relatively common form of behavior emerged concurrently with the recognition of child abuse and spouse beating or family violence as social problems in the 1960's which is related to the social consciousness of the United States of that decade. Many mutual support groups have been established to help individuals cope with the psychological consequences of incestuous behavior.

Molestation and exploitation of children includes the use of children for sexual purposes, such as sexual intercourse, foreplay, pornography and prostitution. In the late 1970s and 1980s these forms of behavior were beginning to receive widespread attention as part of the broader concern regarding child abuse and neglect. The Child Abuse and Prevention Treatment Act of 1974 is a major national effort to address this problem. The 1974 Act created a National Center for Child Abuse and Neglect which provides funds for the provision of social services for agencies working with the abused child. Child abuse programs include services for the sexually abused child, as well, as the physically and emotionally abused child. Children historically have been viewed as under the total control of the father and consequently were not provided with legal rights. Since 1960, concern has been expressed over the growing problem of exploitation of young children for pornographic purposes. The Commission on Obscenity and Pornography in 1970 as part of its report included testimony on the use of children for pornographic purposes. In 1978 Congress passed the Act Against Child Exploitation which begins to address this problem.[30]

Aberrant behavior includes behaviors, such as exhibitionism (showing one's sex organs), voyeurism (peeping Tom), sado-masochistic behavior (flagellation), coprolalia (obscene phone calls), necrophilia (use of a corpse for a sexual act), bestiality (sexual intercourse with animals) amongst others. These behaviors are generally considered to be unacceptable in a community, and individuals engaging in such behaviors are generally termed deviant, mentally ill, or in some communities the sexually perverse or sexually deviant individual.

Depending upon the society, such behavior was termed unnatural, immoral, a crime, or partly acceptable. In pre-Christian societies like Greece and Rome, there was a more tolerant attitude toward certain forms of these behaviors, but they had laws restricting this behavior. That is, if the behavior was engaged in with children, the penalty was death, and if the behavior was engaged through a forceful, non-consented act, the penalty was death. Hebrew society (100 B.C.), viewed these behaviors as unnatural and punishable by death. Medieval Europe (450-1500), held the same views as Hebrew society, and all these behaviors were condemned. A person was branded as a sinner, a heretic, or a person in league with the Devil, and could be executed. Both English and American attitudes still condemn this behavior. Individuals were treated as sinners, a criminal, or a person who was mentally ill. Scientific studies of sexual offenders and their behavior were initiated by Krafft-Ebing, in his classic work, "Psychopathia Sexualis" (1886). Currently, the focal point for treatment involving aberrant behavior rests with the physical and mental health networks, although there is some overlap with the corrections network.[31]

Problematic behavior refers to a variety of sexually related behaviors which are condemned, condoned, or accepted by various societies at different times and includes prostitution, pornography and sexual harassment.[32] These behaviors need not involve rehabilitative intervention techniques unless the behavior is causing family, marital or personal problems. These forms of behavior have been in existence since the earliest times, however, societal viewpoints have varied.

Prostitution has been practiced since humankind has been in existence. Attitudes toward prostitution varied depending upon the society and the time. For example, in classical Greece there were three types of prostitutes: the hetairae (a companion for the upper classes), the auletrides (dancers who performed sexual favors) and the dicteriades (streetwalkers and brothel employees). Prostitution in early Greecian society was seen as an alternative to adultery.

In Roman society the attitudes varied depending upon the time span. Early Roman society (100 BC), severely regulated and restricted prostitution. Later Roman society (100), was rather open sexually. The early Christian society tolerated prostitution, but by 1100 severly condemned prostitution.

In the United States prostitution was tolerated until the 1920's. Most large cities had "red light districts" and recognized brothels, such as New York, New York; San Francisco, California; Chicago, Illinois; New Orleans, Louisiana and Milwaukee, Wisconsin. Brothel's existed in most large cities until the close of World War II or about 1945. As brothels declined, prostitution became less organized except for the system of call girls and escort services. Many prostitutes are street and bar workers, and dancers who perform sexual favors on the side. The 1980's has seen a high degree of concern over prostitution and some communities are arresting the John or trick, as well as, the prostitute. Some groups argue for legalization of prostitution and other groups for its elimination.

Pornography is not a new issue. Prior to the 17th century (1600) there was no or minimal concern about sexually stimulating literature. With the rise of Puritanism in England in the 1600's there was a high degree of concern about the use of pornographic material, but this movement was short lived. Legislation against pornography developed in England in 1824 and earlier in the United States with the Puritan influence in Massachusetts in 1711.

It has been estimated that 90 percent of the male population and 80 percent of the female population has been exposed to or occasionally used pornographic materials. Chronic users of pornography has been estimated at 10 percent of the male population and 5 percent of the female population. A growing concern in the United States is the increasing use of children under age 12 for pornographic purposes. There are legal issues related to pornography, such as does pornography come under the first and fourteenth amendment of the constitution, what is socially unredeeming material, what are the prevailing standards of the community, etc.

The Commission on Obscenity and Pornography established in 1968 had as its objective the gathering of factual material on this problem and presented their final report in 1970. The major recommendation of this commission was that the availability of material of a sexually explicit nature has no consequences of a grave national concern and suggested liberalization of the current laws. Shortly thereafter the Supreme Court in the Kaplan versus California decision (1973) by a narrow margin rejected the Commission's recommendations and suggested a more restrictive approach.

A second National Commission on Pornography was established in 1985, with their final report published in 1986. News accounts of this Commission indicate that the membership is more conservative than the 1968 Commission, however, the members were still divided on some issues. The Commission divided pornographic materials into erotica, soft pornography and hard core pornography. The definitions of each are somewhat nebulous. Erotica generally means sexual titillating materials, such as Playboy. Soft pornography generally means nudity and simulated sexual acts, such as Hustler and other more explicit magazines. Hard core pornography generally refers to materials explicitly showing the sexual act in a variety of positions. Hard core pornography also explicitly shows violence and degradation of women, such as self flagellation, beatings etc. The major finding of the 1985 Commission is that hard core pornography stimulates violent behavior. This conclusion by the Commission on Pornography is not shared by many social scientists. As a consequence of the Commissions report and finding in 1986 there has been numerous demands and proposals for a more restrictive legalistic and law enforcement approach to remedy this problem.

A further indication of the changing values in American society about this problem, is the fact that between 1980-86 a number of groups have been organized in Wisconsin, Minnesota, New York and other states seeking stronger anti-pornography legislation.

Sexual harassment like other forms of sexual behavior is not a new problem, but the toleration and condonation of the behavior is changing. Sexual harassment can occur at work, in education settings, in psychotherapy and on the street. Since the mid and late 1900's when more women were employed outside the home, women were exposed to sexual harassment on the job and in numerous instances their initial employment and promotional opportunity depended upon the granting of sexual favors. Sexual harassment is not only directed at women, but occasionally at men. A Redbook survey in 1976, found that 90 percent of the female respondents (sample of 9000) indicated they had been exposed to some form of sexual harassment, however only a small percentage of these cases resulted in sexual contact. In 1977, the United States Supreme Court in Alexander vs. Yale, construed sexual harassment to be a violation of the 1964 Civil Rights Act and all companies, corporations and educational institutions must have a policy on sexual harassment. These behaviors are included here as potential areas of involvement for the human service worker depending upon the specific situation and circumstances.[33] A historical time line of the personal social service network is shown in Figure 22-2.

STRUCTURE

The structure of the personal social service network can be viewed from its organizational context, services provided, occupations and professions and dominant occupations and professions.

ORGANIZATIONAL CONTEXT

The personal social service network overlaps with all other societal networks. An idealized model providing examples of the overlapping between the personal social service network and other societal networks is shown in Figure 22-3.

Figures 22-4 and 22-5 show an idealized model of federal and state agencies involved in the personal social service network. Figure 22-6 shows a private corrections agency within the personal social service network which has become heavily involved in alcohol, drugs and other mental health problems. Many individuals when having problems reject help from the formal network for their problem. Instead, they attempt to solve the problems themselves, or use an informal or folk system, such as family, relatives, friends, acquaintances, colleagues and even strangers.

SERVICES PROVIDED

Detailed descriptions of the types of social services provided within the personal social service network were outlined on pages 703-705. The personal social service network also overlaps with all other social networks and those social services are described in other chapters.

OCCUPATIONS and PROFESSIONS

In the personal social service network, a large variety of human service occupations and professions are employed. An

743

FIGURE 22-2

HISTORICAL TIME LINE OF THE PROTECTIVE
AND UTILITARIAN PERSONAL SOCIAL SERVICES

PROTECTIVE SERVICES   UTILITARIAN SERVICES

1601 —— English Poor Law –
          Aged, Child Welfare

1700 —— Almshouse

1729 —— Ursuline Convent

1797 —— Relief of Widows – New York

1850 —— Wife Beating legal in most
          states. Children under control
          of father.

1853 —— Children's Aid Society

                                       1854 —— Nursery School – New York

                                       1863 —— First permanent Day Care

1866 —— County Homes, Foster Care,
          Boarding Out, Adoption

1875 —— Society for the Prevention of
          Cruelty to Animals and Children.

                                       1898 —— National Federation of Day Nurseries

1899 —— Juvenile Court

                                       1903 —— Visiting Housewives

1919 —— Child Welfare League

1923 —— Old Age Pension – States   1923 —— Homemaking Service

1935 —— Social Security Act,   1935 —— Works Progress Administration
          Aging, Dependent Children
                                       1939 —— Committee on Supervised Housekeeping

1950 —— National Council on Aging
                                       1960 —— National Committee for Day Care

1961 —— Conference on Aging
                                       1962 —— Day Care included in Public Welfare

1963 —— Societal Attention Focuses
          on Child Abuse   1964 —— National Council on Homemaker
                                                Service

1965 —— Older American Act

1971 —— Gray Panthers

1972 —— Women's Hotline

1974 —— Wife Beating Centers

FIGURE 22-2 (continued)

HISTORICAL TIME LINE OF THE DEVELOPMENTAL AND SOCIALIZATION
AND REHABILITATIVE AND THERAPEUTIC PERSONAL SOCIAL SERVICES

**DEVELOPMENTAL AND
SOCIALIZATION SERVICES**

1300	-Turn Box System
1414	-St. Kathryn's
1609	-Unwed mother sent to House of Corrections
1633	-Foundling Hospital St. Vincent De Paul
1854	-YMCA's YWCA's
1874	-Family Service Association
1888	-Charity Organization Society
1912	-Boy Scouts, Girl Scouts
1915	-Unwed mother obtains legal rights to child
1919	-Institute on the study of sex in Berlin
1929	-Marriage Counseling Agency in New York
1930	-American Institute of Family Relations
1935	-Social Security Act (Unwed mothers)
1942	-American Association of Marriage Counselors

REHABILITATIVE AND THERAPEUTIC SERVICES

1733	
1742	-Georgia; Prohibition
1773	-Early Temperance Movement
1794	Wesley, Benezet
1805	-Morphine developed
1811	-Temperance Movement
1865	Moral Persuasion Edwards, Beecher, Washingtonians
1875	-Temperance Movement
1900	State and local option Carrie Nation
1866	- Krafft-Ebing
1905	-Sigmund Freud
1906	-National Save a Life League
1910	-Temperance Movement
1920	Federal Regulation of alcohol 18th Amendment
1914	-Harrison Act
1919	-Institute on the study of sex in Berlin
1920-1933	Prohibition
1935	-Alcoholics Anonymous
1937	-Marijuana Tax Act
1945	-Use of amphetamines
1958	-Suicide Prevention Center
1963	-Mental Health Center Act Center for Suicidology
1964	-Narcotic Addicts Rehabilitation Act, Masters and Johnson
1966	-Alcoholism - disease concept
1970	-National Institute on Alcohol Abuse and Alcoholism Comprehensive Drug Act Prevention Act. President's Commission on Pornography
1974	-Child Abuse Prevention and Treatment Act, National Institute on Drug Abuse
1975	-National Center for the Prevention and Control of Rape
1986	-President's Commission on Pornography

FIGURE 22-3

IDEALIZED RELATIONSHIP OF SELECTED PERSONAL SOCIAL
SERVICE TO SOCIETAL NETWORKS

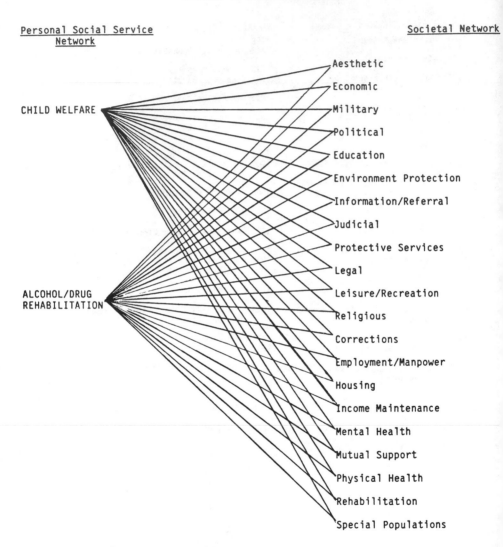

746

FIGURE 22-4

IDEALIZED ORGANIZATION OF THE FEDERAL GOVERNMENT
IN THE PERSONAL SOCIAL SERVICE NETWORK*

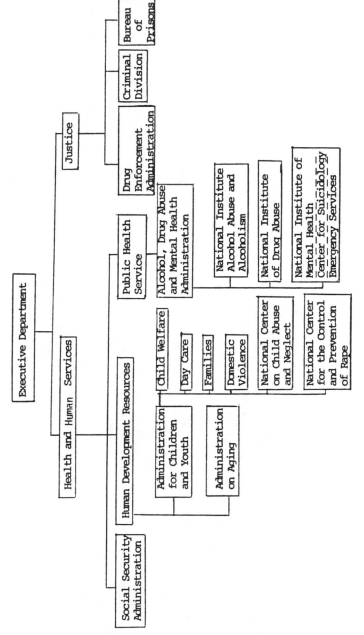

*Source: Adapted from Office of Federal Register, United States Government Manual 1985-86, Washington, D.C.: U.S. Government Printing Office, 1985, pp. 842, 845.

747

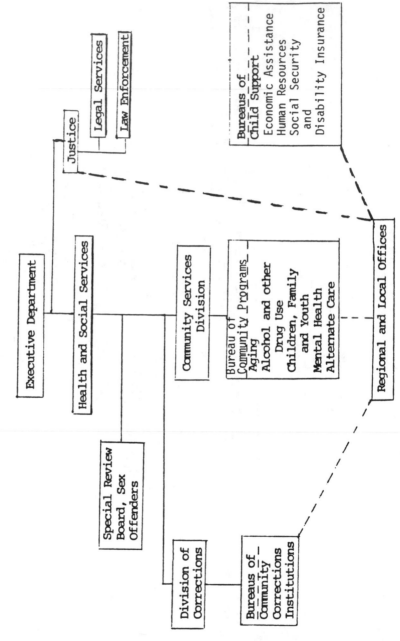

FIGURE 22-5

IDEALIZED ORGANIZATION OF A TYPICAL STATE GOVERNMENT IN THE
PERSONAL SOCIAL SERVICE NETWORK*

Executive Department

Justice

Legal Services

Law Enforcement

Health and Social Services

Community Services Division

Bureau of Community Programs
Aging
Alcohol and other Drug Use
Children, Family and Youth
Mental Health
Alternate Care

Special Review Board, Sex Offenders

Division of Corrections

Bureaus of Community Corrections
Institutions

Bureaus of Child Support
Economic Assistance
Human Resources
Social Security and Disability Insurance

Regional and Local offices

*Source: Adapted from Wisconsin Legislative Reference Bureau, The State of Wisconsin Blue Book, 1985-1986,

748

ORGANIZATION OF A PRIVATE AGENCY FOCUSING ON ALCOHOL AND DRUGS (WISCONSIN CORRECTIONAL SERVICE, MILWAUKEE, WISCONSIN)*

BOARD OF DIRECTORS

EXECUTIVE DIRECTOR

PROGRAM DEVELOPMENT & MANAGEMENT
ASST. EXEC. DIRECTOR
ASSOCIATE DIRECTOR
SYSTEMS ANALYST

OFFICE MANAGEMENT
CLERICAL
EXEC. SECRETARY

ACCOUNTING
FISCAL MANAGEMENT
CHIEF ACCOUNTANT

CCSB FUNDED PROGRAMS

INTERVENTION UNIT ALCOHOL/DRUG/MH

OUTPATIENT SUBSTANCE ABUSE

RESIDENTIAL DRUG TREATMENT

MENTAL HEALTH CSP

HOUSE OF CORRECTION MH UNIT

UNITED WAY FUNDED PROGRAMS

D.A. EARLY IDENTIFICATION

ADOLESCENT SUBSTANCE ABUSE

INSTITUTIONAL LIAISON

JOB DEVELOPMENT

MENTAL HEALTH VOLUNTEER COORDINATOR

DOHSS FUNDED PROGRAMS

COMMUNITY SERVICE ORDERS

VOLUNTEERS IN PROBATION

ESCORT LEISURE TIME

BRIDGE HALFWAY HOUSE

OUTREACH HOME DETENTION

MILWAUKEE COUNTY CONTRACTS

PROJECT EXCEL

CONTRACT COUNTY DRUG ABUSE

MEDIATION CENTER

WAUKESHA COUNTY PROGRAMS

MEDIATION PROGRAM

VOLUNTEERS IN PROBATION ADULT/JUVENILE

INTENSIVE SUPERVISION

HOMEMAKER

JUVENILE RESTITUTION

COURT INTERVENTION

OTHER FUNDING SOURCES

RACINE VIP

MILW. MUNI COURT

HOC JTPA

WCS PHARMACY

RACINE MEDIATION

*Source: Organization chart of the Wisconsin Correctional Service, Milwaukee, Wisconsin: Wisconsin Correctional Service, 1986. Reprinted with permission of the Wisconsin Correctional Service.

749

estimate of the variety of occupations and professions employed in the personal social service network was derived from using the industrial classifications of child care, day care, residential care (non-nursing), and non-specified social services according to the 1980 census. Figure 22-7 shows a range of selected human service occupations and professions employed in the personal social service network.

DOMINANT OCCUPATIONS and PROFESSIONS

In England, the personal social services are usually associated with the profession of social work. Salinsburg, in The Personal Social Services, writes:

"Social work is the rationale for the existence of the personal social services. Personal social services could exist without the social workers. But what has emerged in recent years is a growing compatibility between the objectives of the personal social services and the values and techniques of social work."[34]

It is clear that not all of the individuals involved in the personal social service network are social workers. On the other hand, not all of the individuals who are professional social workers involved in the personal social service network are identified as social workers. For example, a person in probation or parole services (and specialties, such as alcohol, drugs, sex offenders, etc.) could be trained as a professional social worker, but instead of identifying themselves as a social worker, they would identify themselves as a corrections agent or they could be classified as a social worker and have their degree in some other area.

In any event, what appears to have occurred in England is equally true in the United States. Figure 22-7 shows that at a minimum, 35.2 percent of the selected human service occupations and professions employed in the personal social service network were classified as social work. If one excludes teachers from these figures, since their function is primarily educational and part of the education network and excludes child care work, which could be part of the mental health or corrections networks, the percentage of those classified as social work in the personal social service network increases to 69.3 percent. Regardless of which way one counts the figures, social work is one of the dominant professions in the personal social service network. Since social work is described in the following section, two emerging professions in the personal social service network are described further.

Figure 22-7

NUMBER AND PERCENT OF SELECTED HUMAN SERVICE OCCUPATIONS AND PROFESSIONS
EMPLOYED IN THE INDUSTRIAL CLASSIFICATIONS OF CHILD/DAY,
RESIDENTIAL CARE AND SOCIAL SERVICE NOT SPECIFIED IN 1980[*]

cupation and Profession	Number	Percent
cial Work and Aide	212,730	35.288
ild Care	152,942	25.536
acher and Aide	142,111	23.573
rsonnel and Public Relations	8,147	1.351
nagers	23,675	3.927
chitect	120	.029
ysician	981	.163
her Health	2,833	.469
rse	13,756	2.282
etician	2,265	.375
erapist	4,233	.702
unselor	5,042	.837
brarian	800	.132
ychologist	3,853	.638
ban Planner	379	.062
creation Work	2,718	.450
ergy/Religious Work	3,276	.543
wyer and Asst.	2,014	.334
thor/Musisian, Etc.	883	.146
censed Practical Nurse	2,191	.363
ards	3,323	.551
rse Aide	10,229	1.696
alth Aide	3,337	.553
TOTAL	602,837	100.000

Source: Adapted from United States Department of Commerce, Bureau of the
Census, 1980 Census of Population Vol. 2 Subject Reports Part 7C:
Occupation by Industry, Washington, D.C.: U.S. Government Printing Office
1984, pp. 295-664.

These industrial classifications are those primarily involved in the
personal social services. The classification child care/day care somewhat
inflates the role of teachers in the network. Most of the teachers are
involved in day care and not child care. Taking this into consideration,
the two occupations and professions which are dominate in the network are
social work and child care. Excluding teachers, social work, accounts for
46.2 percent of the selected human service employees in the network and
child care workers, 33.4 percent of the selected human service employees,
and these two groups account for 79.65 percent of selected human service
employees.

751

Two occupations which are seeking professional status in some parts of the personal social service network are the child care worker and human service generalist.

CHILD CARE WORK--An emerging profession closely related to child welfare activities and the personal social service network is that of the child care worker. A child care worker is usually employed in an institution for dependent, neglected, and emotionally disturbed children which may involve some pre-delinquent children. A professional organization has been established called the National Association for Child Care Management.

A small number of states are beginning to certify child care workers. An example is the Wisconsin Association of Child Care Workers, Inc. The criteria established in Wisconsin for certification as a child care worker include one of the following: a master's or bachelor's degree with a specialization in child care from an accredited university or college program which includes two semesters of field instruction at child care agencies; or a bachelor's degree with a specialization in child care from an accredited university or college program and one year's experience in child care; a bachelor's degree and one year's experience and completion of a child care inservice training program. Provisions are also made for recipients of an associate of arts degree and a high school diploma to obtain certification.

The child care worker would perform some of the following tasks or activities:

- Monitor daily behavior of a resident of an institution
- Lead social and recreational activities
- Provide emotional support for the resident of an institution
- Mediate problems between the residents of an institution
- Engage in emergency counseling when necessary
- Public relations
- Operate on a team basis with social workers, psychologists, psychiatrists, etc.

HUMAN SERVICE GENERALIST--The human service generalist is sometimes referred to as the human service worker. The basic concept behind this newer occupation is the idea that the older professions, such as social work and psychology, in the personal social service network, have become too specialized. The function of the human service generalist is to be able to initially respond to a variety of personal and social problems, and make a referral to one of the other professions in the personal social services, when needed.

Any emerging occupation and profession goes through a series of stages in its development which relate to professional organizations and educational standards. Two professional organizations related to the human service generalist are the National Organization of Human Service Educators and the National Organization of Human Services.

Educational standards and certification standards for the human service generalist are in flux, consisting of 2-year academic programs (Associate of Arts degree), four year programs (Bachelors degree) and graduate programs (master's degree). An example of a 2-year academic program is the Human Services Associate of Arts degree program at the Milwaukee Area Technical College, Milwaukee, Wisconsin. An example of a four year academic program is the College for Human Services, New York, New York. An example of a graduate program is the National College of Education, Evanston, Illinois. There is some degree of role diffusion and confusion between the emerging profession of human service generalist and the older professions of psychology and social work.

Some of the roles of a human service generalist include the following:

- Preliminary interviews and client screening
- Make home visits
- Preparation of reports
- Leading discussion groups
- Referral to another agency
- Providing transportation
- Enabling one to find employment.[35]

SOCIAL WORK

Social workers who are employed in the personal social service network can be described from the general roles they perform, the methods used to implement a service and a field of practice.

GENERAL ROLES

Some of the general roles of social work in the personal social service network include the following:

- Administrator - implement and plan a series of service programs for an agency or a group.

- Broker - have a knowledge of community resources and link a person with a problem to an appropriate service.

753

- Advocate - help a person obtain services.

- Information processor - assess problems and obtain information from or for ones client.

- Behavior change - through social work methods, and techniques enable a person to change specific behaviors.

METHOD

From a traditional perspective, social work methods can be classified as individual casework, group work, community organization, administration and supervision.

Social workers who are employed in the personal social service network usually utilize one or more of the following methods.

INDIVIDUAL CASEWORK--This method uses interviewing techniques, listening and communication skills in helping a person cope with practical or emotional problems. The levels of casework range from a concrete level (providing transportation) to an indepth psychotherapeutic level (therapy).

GROUP WORK--This method uses a group process and communication skills in helping a group or members of a group cope with practical or emotional problems. The levels of group work can vary from a didactic level (information) to a psychotherapeutic level (therapy).

COMMUNITY ORGANIZATION--This method uses knowledge of a community and politics to help a group in a community or a group with a specific interest to solve a problem, advocate or change social policies or lobby at a political level for clarification or changes in legislation. The level of community organization can vary from a small group within an organization to state and federal legislation.

ADMINISTRATION and SUPERVISION--Many social workers become a director of a social service program or are responsible for supervising or monitoring the work of other employees in the same agency.

FIELD of PRACTICE

One can view social work from the perspective of fields of practice or programs in which they are employed within the personal social service network. Examples of the personal social service network and its overlapping with other social networks were provided in each of the earlier chapters. Some examples of social work programs and organizations in the personal social service network include the following:

PROTECTIVE SERVICES--Social Service Department (welfare dept.) in the local community; Nevermore, Milwaukee, Wisconsin and Project Involve, Milwaukee, Wisconsin.

UTILITARIAN SERVICES--Day Care Services in the local community and local social service or welfare department.

DEVELOPMENTAL and SOCIALIZATION SERVICES--Neighborhood Center, Milwaukee, Wisconsin and other local organizations, Lutheran and Catholic Social Services in the local community.

REHABILITATIVE and THERAPEUTIC SERVICES--DePaul Rehabilitation Center, Milwaukee, Wisconsin (alcohol/drugs); local Council on Alcohol and Drugs; American Association of Suicidology, Denver, Colorado; Sexual Assault Treatment Center, Milwaukee, Wisconsin; Adults Molested as Children United, San, Jose, California; Treatment Program for Sex Offenders, Buena Vista, California; Catalyst Counseling Center, Milwaukee, Wisconsin; Working Women's Institute, New York, New York; Overcome, Minneapolis, Minnesota and Mistresses Anonymous, Islip, New York.[36]

PERSONAL SOCIAL SERVICES

Although the footnotes to this chapter have numerous examples of organizations which have specialized services in the personal social service network, it may be helpful to the reader to have an example of an organization which focusses on a specific personal social service. For example some organizations in the personal social network include the following:

PROTECTIVE SERVICES

CHILD WELFARE--Child Welfare League of America, New York, New York.

FAMILY VIOLENCE--Nevermore, Milwaukee, Wisconsin.

MATURE ADULT (AGED)--Project Involve, Milwaukee, Wisconsin.

UTILITARIAN SERVICES

DAY CARE--Day Care Services for children and their local offices.

755

HOMEMAKING--Catholic Social Services and their local office, and the local department of social services (welfare department).

DEVELOPMENTAL and SOCIALIZATION SERVICES

FAMILY and COUPLE COUNSELING--Lutheran Social Services and their local office.

SERVICES to UNWED MOTHERS--Local Social Service or welfare department.

SERVICES to YOUTH--Young Men's Christian Association and their local office, Boys Club of America and their local office.

REHABILITATIVE and THERAPEUTIC SERVICES

ALCOHOL--Council on Alcoholism and the various local organizations and Alcoholic Anonymous and their local organizations.

DRUGS--Council on Drug Abuse and the various local organizations and Narcotics Anonymous and their local organizations.

SUICIDE--National Save a Life League and their local organizations and Parents of Suicides, Palisades Park, New Jersey.

SEXUAL ASSAULTIVE and ABUSIVE BEHAVIOR--Open Door Mental Health Center, Aspen, Colorado and Santa Monica Valley Rape Center, Santa Monica, California.

SEXUAL PROBLEMS--

Sexual functioning - Catalyst Counseling Center, Milwaukee, Wisconsin (sex therapy).

Aberrant behavior - Treatment Programs for Sex offenders, Buena Park, California.

Problematic Behavior - Working Women's Institute, New York, New York (Sexual Harassment); Project Overcome, Minneapolis, Minnesota (Prostitution) and Mistresses Anonymous, Islip, New York (Adultery).

SPECIAL POPULATIONS

The personal social service network with its emphasis on individual and group problems has a vast array of services for special populations. (See Chapter 25 Special Populations and Chapter 24 Rehabilitation.) Some examples of programs for special populations in the personal social service network include the following:

ASIAN

Asian American Counseling Center, Chicago, Illinois and Asian American Homemakers, National City, California.

BLACK

Crispus Attucks Center, York, Pennsylvania and Alabama Caucus on Black Aged, Montgomery, Alabama.

EUROPEAN ETHNIC

Greek American Counseling Center, Meerick, New York and Jewish Association for the Aged, New York, New York.

NATIVE AMERICANS

American Indian Council on Alcoholism, Milwaukee, Wisconsin and Native American Urban Transition Program, Denver, Colorado.

SAME SEX PREFERENCE

Lesbian Resource Center, Minneapolis, Minnesota and New York City Parents of Lesbians and Gay Men, New York, New York.

SPANISH SPEAKING

Mexican American Council on Alcoholism, San Jose, California.

WOMEN

Women in Transition, Philadelphia, Pennsylvania and Women, San Francisco, California.

ISSUES

A major issue in the personal social service network is the recent development or recognition of these services as a specialized network. However, this network does not stand by itself but is implemented through a variety of other networks. Some of the major issues in the personal social network include the following: reduction of financial support, integration and coordination of services, access to services and emerging occupations and professions.

REDUCTION of FINANCIAL SUPPORT

Federal legislation of the 1960s and 1970s was focussed on employment, poverty, family problems, health care services, alcohol and drugs, psychotherapy, etc., which are all examples of the development of a personal social service network.

There are five assumptions underlying the personal social service network as it developed in the 1960's, all of which are being challenged in the 1980's. These assumptions are: government has an obligation to underwrite programs financially; government has an obligation to assist the unfortunate; public service funds should on a priority basis be utilized for programs to help the lower income population; funding for the personal social services is not a substitute for other existing social service programs; and use of these services should be on a voluntary basis (except for cases of crisis emergency intervention). Much of the federal funding for these programs has been under serious debate in Congress in 1984 through 1986 and there has been a reduction in the amount of federal monies available for the personal social services since 1981. There is an early trend to have more responsibility for the personal social services to be placed in the private sector, with the assumptions of a priority for lower income levels, and voluntary use of services seriously being questioned.

INTEGRATION and COORDINATION of SERVICES

As the personal social service network emerged in the United States, a central issue was the organizational structure of the public agencies to integrate and coordinate various services. That is, should there be separate agencies for public welfare, mental health, corrections, education, etc. The federal government and many state and county governments developed an umbrella agency variously known as a Department of Human Services, Department of Health and Human Services which combined a multitude of previously independent or some independent agencies and programs.

In addition to governmental reorganization to enhance the integration and coordination of services, the governmental agencies at the state and county level developed closer linkages with private agencies in order to enhance the coordination of services. Although many government agencies have been reorganized and closer liaison with private agencies exist, there are still numerous problems relating to the integration and coordination of services, such as duplication of services, and individuals not able to obtain services since they do not meet eligibility requirements for specific services.

ACCESS to SERVICES

With reduced funding, some individuals are unable to obtain services. A large segment of the United States population does not speak English or has serious difficulties with English (about 10 percent) and this creates problems in obtaining services. Transportation is a barrier to obtaining services in some areas, primarily rural, but it can be a major problem in large metropolitan cities for the poorer populations.

Another access issue is when an individual is already receiving some form of service like a resident of mental institution, but cannot be discharged because there is no place to live which is the responsibility of a different part of the personal social service network. Another barrier to services is the lack or inadequacy of the services available, such as day care, homemaking and shelters for the homeless.

EMERGING OCCUPATIONS and PROFESSIONS

Two occupations which have become recognized since 1960 are those of a child care worker and a human service generalist. Both of these occupations were initially considered paraprofessional, but in the past ten years have devloped four year and graduate level educational programs. The functions of these emerging occupations and the roles they perform in the personal social service network are at times confused with older professions, such as psychology and social work. For both occupations, professional and educational standards are in flux.

SUMMARY

This chapter on the personal social service network departed from the general format followed for describing the other networks. Most of the material in this chapter focussed on a historical perspective and the variety of the personal social services. The actual services provided within the personal social service network are discussed in each of the other specific nerworks, such as education, mental health and so forth.

What is apparent from the historic overview is that those social problems which comprise the personal social service network, such as child welfare, family violence, mature adult (aged), and problems of alcohol and drug abuse, suicide, and so forth, are not recent problems, but have been with humankind since the beginning of time. Other problem areas within the personal services are of a more recent origin, such as day care, homemaking services, and the use of specific forms of substance abuse, such as amphetamines. A central thrust of the historical

overview, was to show that the development of programs and
services for most of the personal social services were initially
sponsored by private and religious organizations, and did not
enter the public realm until the 20th Century. In addition, the
concept of treatment programs and rehabilitation is a product of
the 20th Century.

The personal social service network emerged in the 1960,s
with five assumptions relating to the role of government:
government has an obligation to financially underwrite programs;
government has an obligation to assist the unfortunate; priority
should be on lower income groups; public programs are not a
substitute for private programs and use of these services should
be voluntary. Each of these assumptions underlying the personal
social service network are being challenged in the 1980's.
There has been a reduction in financial support and in the
number of services available. Other issues in the personal
social service network include the integration and coordination
of services, access to services and emerging occupations and
professions.

FOOTNOTES

*This chapter was reviewed for comments by Charles Zastrow,
Professor, Department of Social Welfare, University of
Wisconsin-Whitewater, Whitewater, Wisconsin, and Robert
Holzhauer, Professor Emeritus, School of Social Welfare,
University of Wisconsin-Milwaukee, Milwaukee, Wisconsin.

1. The reader is referred to Chapter 2 Human Services and
   Helping Professions for a more detailed discussion of
   concepts, such as social services, human services, social
   welfare, personal social service and social work. A brief
   review at this point may be helpful.

   Social service means a series of (programs, activities) for
   individuals and groups who have a specific need and are
   implemented through human service or social welfare organizations. Human service means a communal (programs, activities) response to generalized individual and group needs.
   Specific societal networks have been established in order to
   meet these needs, such as education, religion, etc.

   Social welfare means a communal response (programs,
   activities) to specific individual and group needs or a
   specific social problem. In this case, a specific societal
   network has been established to meet this specific need,

such as income maintenance, housing, physical health, mental health, corrections, etc. Personal social service means a communal response (programs, activities) to meet individual and group needs which are not met nor are the primary focus of other networks. That is, the personal social services are a variety of programs and activities to ameliorate individual and group concerns for which a major social network has not been established.

Social work means a specific profession which has major responsibilities for implementing a variety of programs and activities within the personal social service network.

2. This classification of the personal social services, into protective, utilitarian, developmental and socialization, and rehabilitative and therapeutic services, does not imply a mutually exclusive grouping. That is, a program in child welfare, although under protective services, could also be part of the utilitarian, developmental and socialization, or the rehabilitative and therapeutic services classification. There is an overlapping between these classifications with the typology being one of conceptual convenience. (The reader is referred to Chapter 3, Social Work As a Helping Profession, for a discussion of social work and the personal social services). One can readily see the interdependence of the personal social service network with other networks described in this book. However, it is useful to indicate the major forms of the personal social services. A general schema of the personal social services is that used by Beulah Compton, Introduction to Social Welfare and Social Work: Structure, Function and Processes, Homewood, IL Dorsey Press, 1980. For further information, the reader is referred to Alfred Kahn, Social Policy and Services, New York, NY: Random House, Inc., 1973, and Eric Salinsburg, The Personal Social Services, London, England, Pittman Publishing Company, 1977. Instead of a detailed description of all the personal social services, the reader is referred to specific chapters for details on the historical development of various networks, such as education, information and referral, environment protection, mental health, etc.

3. Nursing home care is a growing response to the medical needs of an aging population. Nursing homes are described in Chapter 23, Physical Health Network. For Social Security and Veterans programs, see Chapter 19, Income Maintenance.

4. As indicated in the text, other parts of the utilitarian services are discussed in specific chapters, such as Chapter 10, Information and Referral; Chapter 7, Political Network; Chapter 11, Judicial Network; Chapter 13, Legal Network;

Chapter 21, Mutual Support Network; Chapter 19, Income Maintenance Network; Chapter 16, Corrections Network; Chapter 20, Mental Health Network; Chapter 23, Physical Health Network and Chapter 24, Rehabilitation Network.

5. The area of physical and mental health, and disability and rehabilitation overlap with the classification of rehabilitative and therapeutic services. The reader is referred to Chapter 23, Physical Health Network, Chapter 20, Mental Health Network and Chapter 24, Rehabilitation Network, for further details.

6. Behaviors, such as homosexuality (same sex preference), bisexualism, and transvestitism are viewed as different lifestyles. These behaviors are discussed in Chapter 25, Special Populations.

7. The reader is referred to the United States Commission on Obscenity and Pornography, Report of the Commission on Obscenity and Pornography 1970, Washington, D.C.: U.S. Government Printing Office, 1974 and Benjamin Sadock, Harold Kaplan and Alfred Freedman. The Sexual Experience, Baltimore, Maryland: The Williams and Wilkens Company, 1976.

8. The reader is referred to Benjamin Sadock, Harold Kaplan and Alfred Freedman. The Sexual Experience, Baltimore, Maryland: The Williams and Wilkens Co., 1976 and Janet Hyde, Half the Human Experience: The Psychology of Women Lexington, Kentucky: DC Heath and Company, 1985.

9. Due to the diversity of programs and activities in the personal social service network, no one single source of information contains an estimate on the size of this network. Consequently, estimates on the size of the personal social service network are derived from a multiplicity of resources which include the following: United States Department of Commerce, Bureau of the Census, Statistical Abstract of the United States: 1986 (106th Edition), Washington, D.C.: U.S. Government Printing Office, 1985; 1982 Census of Service Industries, Washington, D.C.: U.S. Government Printing Office, 1984; Department of Health, Education and Welfare, Day Care Centers in the United States, Washington D.C.: U.S. Government Printing Office, 1979; Alfred Kadushin, Child Welfare Services, 3rd edition, New York, NY: Macmillan Company, 1980; Ann Shyne and Anita Schroeder, National Study of Social Services to Children and their Families: An Overview, Washington, D.C.: U.S. Government Printing Office, 1978; National Institute on Alcohol Abuse and Alcoholism, Fourth Special

Report to the United States Congress on Alcohol and Health, Washington, D.C.: U.S. Government Printing Office, 1981; Department of Health, Education and Welfare, Child Abuse and Neglect Programs, Washington, D.C.: U.S. Government Printing Office, 1978; Department of Health, Education and Welfare, National Directory of Drug Abuse and Alcoholism Treatment and Prevention Programs, Washington, D.C.: U.S. Government Printing Office, 1983; Department of Health, Education and Welfare, Inpatient Health Facilities, Washington, DC: U.S. Government Printing Office, 1980; United States Department of Justice, Uniform Crime Reports, 1979, Washington, DC: U.S. Government Printing Office, 1980; Robert Geiser, Hidden Victims: The Sexually Abused Child, Boston, MA: Beacon Press, 1979; Jane Chapman, and Margaret Gates, (Editors), The Victimization of Women, Beverly Hills, California: Sage Publications, 1978; Department of Health, Education and Welfare, Health Resources-- United States: 1978, Washington, DC: U.S. Government Printing Office, 1979; Amy Weinstein. Public Welfare Directory 1986-87, Washington, DC: American Public Welfare Association, 1986; Helga E.Croner and Kurt Guggenheim National Directory of Private Social Agencies 1986, Queens Village, New York: Croner Publishing Co., 1986; Edward L. Purcell, The Book of the States 1984/85: Lexington, Kentucky: The Council of State Governments, 1984; Murray Strauss and Gerald Hotating, The Social Causes of Husband and Wife Violence, Minneapolis, MN: University of Minnesota Press, 1980 and Murray Strauss, Richard Gelles, and Suzane Steinmetz, Behind Closed Doors, New York, NY: Anchor Books, 1980.

10. Until the 1940s the majority of child welfare services were provided by private, volunteer, religious and non-sectarian agencies. Readers are referred to Chapter 15, Religious Network, for further details. The Aid to Families with Dependent Children program is discussed in Chapter 19, Income Maintenance Network.

Examples of organizations which focus on child welfare include the following: Child Welfare League of America, 67 Irvine Place, New York, NY, 10003; Children's Rights, Inc., 3443 Seventeenth Street, N.W., Washington, DC, 20010; North American Center on Adoption, 67 Irvine Place, New York, NY, 10003 and the International Union for the Promotion of Child Welfare, International Center, Rue de Varembue 1, CH 1211, Geneva 20, Switzerland. The Child Welfare League has established guidelines for agencies for the implementation of adoption, foster care, and protective service programs. Agencies can be certified as meeting the standards of the Child Welfare League.

11. Alice Tyler, <u>Freedom's Ferment</u>, New York, NY: Harper & Row Publishers, 1944, p. 26.

12. An estimate on the number of transitional homes for spouse abuse is adapted from Terry Davidson's <u>Conjugal Crime</u>, New York, NY: Hawthorne Books, Inc., 1978. Examples of organizations which focus on family violence include the following: Abused Women's Aid in Crisis, P.O. Box 1699, New York, NY, 10001 and Women Against Violence Against Women, 543 N. Fairfax Avenue, Los Angeles, California 90030.

13. The Mary Ellen case of 1874 involved a foster child who was severely beaten and neglected by her foster parents in New York City. Church workers attempted to obtain some means of intervention through social service agencies. Failing to receive any form of intervention or help from the social service agencies, the church workers turned to the Society for the Prevention of Cruelty to Animals for help. This agency agreed to help the church workers, thereby expanding its interest to include cruelty to children. In this case, the foster parents were given jail terms for cruelty. The following year, 1875, the Society for the Prevention of Cruelty to Children was formed.

14. Examples of organizations which focus on child abuse include the following: National Committee for the Prevention of Child Abuse, 332 S. Michigan Avenue, Suite 250, Chicago, IL, 60604; National Center on Child Abuse and Neglect, Children's Bureau, Department of Health and Human Services, Washington, DC, 20006 and the National Center for the Prevention and Treatment of Child Abuse and Neglect, 7929-30, University of Colorado Medical Center, 1205 Oneida Street, Denver, CO, 80220.

15. Examples of organizations which focus on aging include the following: National Council on Aging, 1828 Sixth Street, N.W., Washington, DC, 20036 and National Association of Aging Americans, 12 Electric Street, West Alexandria, OH, 45381.

16. Day care refers to physical, emotional and social care of a child when the mother is working or otherwise not able to care for the child. Nursery school refers to a pre-kindergarten educational and social program.

17. Examples of organizations which focus on day care include the following: Day Care and Child Development Council of America, 520 Southern Building, 805 15the Street, NW, Washington, DC, 20005 and the Child Development Association

Consortium, 1427 Rhode Island Avenue, NW, Washington, DC, 20009. This last organization has developed guidelines and standards for day care centers and has a process for certifying or providing credentials for day care centers. This process of credentialing is in addition to any state or local government requirements. The Child Welfare League of America (see Child Welfare) has also established guidelines for day care.

Examples of organizations which focus on homemaking include: National Homecaring Council, 67 Irvine Place, New York, NY 10003 (this organization has developed guidelines and standards for homemaking and has an agency accreditation for certification procedure); National Council for Home-making and Health Aid, 235 Park Ave., S., New York, New York 10003 and the National Council for Homemaker Services, 235 Park Ave., S., New York, New York 10003.

18. Many individuals perceive the family as consisting of the marital couple, man and wife, and their children. Marriage is a distinct institution which for many years was a civil institution and was formalized as a religious sacrament with the publication of Peter Lombard's "Sentences" in 1164. In the United States there are families with one parent, common-law families, communal families, mixed homosexual and straight families, homosexual families, and parental surrogate or substitute families. Terminology used in this section is as follows: nuclear family--means husband, wife and children; conjugal family--means the marital relation-ship or husband and wife; matriarchal family--means a family dominated by the female; patriarchal family means a family dominated by the male; companiate family means a shared responsibility between the family members.

19. For further details on "mother right" the reader is referred to E.S. Hartland, "Mother Rights," pp. 182-202, in V.F. Calverton, editor, The Making of Man: An Outline of Anthropology New York, New York: Random House Inc. 1931.

20. As the family unit changed over historical time, marital practices have also changed. The monogamous (one spouse pattern) is predominant in Western culture, however, this is not always the case. For example the Chukahi of Siberia practice a group marriage, with the husband upon marrying an eligible woman also married the other eligible women of the same family. The Tungus of Northern Asia and the Tilinkit of the Northwest United States practiced wife exchange between brothers when a husband was gone for an extended period of time. The Mormons of the United States practiced

polygny (more than one wife) until 1890 when Utah became a state. Although the Mormons generally do not practice polygny today, there are still numerous individuals in that cultural group who engage in this marital practice. Some groups practice a communal marriage and others engage in sexual hospitality.

21. Examples of organizations which focus on family and marital counseling include the following: American Association for Marriage and Family Therapy, 924 W. 9th Street, Upland, CA 91786; National Council on Family Relations, 1219 University Avenue, S.E., Minneapolis, MN 55414 and Family Service of America, Corporate Headquarters, 11700 W. Lake Park Drive, Milwaukee, Wisconsin 53224. The American Association for Marriage and Family Therapy has a certification procedure for marriage counselors and therapists.

22. Although the child nor the mother had legal rights, there are notable exceptions to this rule amongst the upper classes. For example, William the Conqueror (1066) was an illegitimate child, as well as, Erasmus (1486), Leonardo da Vinci (1512) and Alexander Hamilton (1755-1804) in the United States. An excellent source for the history of social legislation as it affects the unwed mothers the reader is referred to Helen Clarke, Social Legislation, 2nd edition, New York, NY: Appleton Century Crofts, Inc., 1957.

23. Nathaniel Hawthorne, in the Scarlet Letter, described the situation in Puritan New England where the unwed mother was branded with an "A" on her forehead to indicate she was an adulteress with a bastard child and to warn other people in the community about this loose and immoral woman.

24. An example of an organization which has a focus on services to unwed mothers is the Child Welfare League of America, 67 Irvine Place, New York, NY 10003.

25. Examples of organizations which focus on youth activities include the following: Young Men's Christian Association, 219 Broadway, New York, NY 10007; Boys Clubs of America, 771 First Avenue, New York, NY 10017 and Young Women's Christian Association, 1600 Lexington Avenue, New York, NY 10022.

26. Examples of organizations which focus on alcohol abuse include the following: National Institute on Alcohol Abuse and Alcoholism, Public Health Service, Department of Health and Human Services, 5600 Fishers Lane, Rockville, MD 20857; The American Council on Alcohol Problems, 119 Constitution Avenue N.E., Washington, DC 20002; National Council on Alcoholism, 733 Third Avenue, New York, NY 10017; General

Service Board of Alcoholics Anonymous, 468 Park Avenue, New York, NY 10016 and various state associations for alcohol and drug counselors.

The National Institute on Alcohol Abuse and Alcoholism since 1972 has developed guidelines and training materials for alcohol counselors. The National Institute has encouraged states to develop a system for certification or credentials of alcohol counselors. By 1980, thirty four states had a program for certifying alcohol and drug counselors. Since each state has different standards for certification, there will be some variation from the following general guide-lines: one year of experience as an alcohol counselor and completion of the state certification examinations in six areas of competency. The areas of competency included within the examination are as follows: knowledge of commun-ity resources, knowledge of alcohol use and its effects, knowledge and skill in case evaluation assessment, knowledge and skill in case planning, knowledge on resources for information and referral and knowledge and skill in counsel-ing and treatment approaches. The reader is referred to the National Institute on Alcohol Abuse and Alcoholism for further details.

27. Examples of organizations which focus on drugs and other substance abuse include the following: National Institute of Drug Abuse, Public Health Service, Department of Health and Human Services, 5600 Fishers Lane, Rockville, MD 20857; National Council on Drug Abuse, 571 W. Jackson Street, Chicago, IL 60606; National Association of Drug Abuse Problems, 355 Lexington Avenue, New York, NY 10017 and Narcotics Anonymous, Box 622, Sun Valley, CA 91352.

The National Institute of Drug Abuse has established a series of guidelines and training materials for drug counselors. States have been encouraged to develop certification procedures for drug counselors which are similar to those established for alcohol counselors (see Footnote 26). For further information the reader is referred to the National Institute on Drug Abuse.

28. Examples of organizations which focus on suicide include the following: American Association of Suicidology, 2459 S. Ash St., Denver, Colorado 80222; National Save A Life League, 4520 Fourth Ave., Suite MH 3 New York, NY 11220 and Parents of Suicides, 15 E. Brinkerhoff Ave., 2nd Floor, Palisades Park, New Jersey, 07650. The American Association of Suicidology has been attempting to develop professional standards for practice and subsequently a procedure to certify suicide counselors.

Since 1972 there has been a reduction of funding available for a specialization in suicidology through the use of federal monies.

29. Examples of organizations which focus on general sexual functions include the following: American Association of Sex Educators, Counselors and Therapists, 5010 Wisconsin Avenue N.W., Washington, DC 20016; Sex Information and Education Council of the United States (SIECUS), 85 Fifth Avenue, Suite 407, New York, NY 10011; Academy of Psychologists in Marital Sex and Family Therapy, C. W. Post Center, Long Island University, Greenvale, NY 11548; Institute for Sex Research, Inc., Morrison Hall, Room 416, Indiana University, Bloomington, IN 14701 and the Masters and Johnson Institute, 4910 Forest Park Blvd., St. Louis, Missouri 63108. The American Association of Sex Educators, Counselors and Therapists has developed minimal standards for certification as a sex therapist which include the following: a master's degree plus one thousand hours of case clinical experience (this is a grandfather clause to allow current practitioners to become members of the organization), or an M.A. in a clinical field and an internship with a certified sex therapist, plus one thousand hours of paid clinical experience, passing an examination of a written nature, a personal interview with the Board, and a completion of a two-day workshop sponsored by the American Association, or an M.A. degree, either in nonclinical field plus the other requirements as stipulated above.

In addition to professional certification, a specialized school has been developed granting master's and Ph.Ds in human sexuality which is the Institute for Advanced Study of Human Sexuality, 1523 Franklin Street, San Francisco, CA 94109, which was established in 1976.

30. Examples of organizations which focus on sexual assault and abusive behavior include the following: Rape Crisis Center, P.O. Box 21005, Washington, DC 20009; Abused Women's Aid in Crisis, P.O. Box 1699, New York, NY 10001; the National Center for the Prevention and Control of Rape, National Institute of Mental Health, 5600 Fishers Lane, Rockville, Maryland, 20857; the National Coalition Against Sexual Assault, c/o Austin Rape Crisis Center, P.O. Box 7156, Austin, Texas 78712; Incest Survivors Resource Network, Friends Meeting House, 15 Rutherland Drive, New York, New York 10003 and Adults Molested as Children United, P.O. Box 952 San Jose, California 95108.

31. Some forms of sexual behavior are viewed as deviant and/or aberrant and individuals are either viewed as mentally ill or having an emotional problem, such as exhibitionism, voyeurism, pedophilia, transvestitism, sado-masochistic behavior, etc. Discussions of these forms of behavior are beyond the scope of this book, and the services for these individuals usually involve a combination of the mental health or corrections network. Examples of organizations which focus on forms of aberrant sexual behavior include the following: Institute for Sex Research, Inc., Morrison Hall, Room 4161, Indiana University, Bloomington, IN 14701; the Masters and Johnson Institute, 4910 Forest Park Blvd., St. Louis, Missouri 63108; Sexaholics, P.O. Box 300, Simi Valley, California 93062 and CoDependents of Sexual Addicts, P.O.Box 14537, Minneapolis, Minnesota 55408.

32. Other forms of sexual behavior, such as adultery or fornication, etc., may be problematic and are not the focus of this chapter. There are some states that have changed the statutes and no longer consider fornication between two eligible, mutually consenting adults as a crime. As these statutes are changing, states are still maintaining the statutes relating to adultery.

33. Examples of organizations which focus on problematic sexual behavior include the following: Women Against Pornography, 358 W. 47th St., New York, NY 10036; Morality in Media, 475 Riverside Drive, New York, NY 10027; National Task Force on Prostitution, P.O.Box 2635, San Francisco, California 94126; Johns and Call Girls United Against Repression, P.O.Box 1011, Brooklyn, New York 11202; Project Overcome, 1900 Hennepin Ave., Minneapolis, Minnesota 55403, (Prostitution); Mistresses Anonymous, P.O.Box 151, Islip, New York, 11751 (Adultery) and Working Women's Institute, 593 Park Avenue, New York, New York 10021 (Sexual Harassment).

34. Eric Salinsburg, The Personal Social Services, London, England: Pittman Publishing Company, 1977, p. 24.

35. An example of a professional organization for child care workers is the National Association for Child Care Management, 800 M St. NW Suite 1030N, Washington, DC 20036: For further information on certification as a child care worker, the reader is referred to the national association listed above.

The major professional organizations in human services are the National Organization of Human Service Educators, c/o MHT Program, 214 Morton Hall, Ohio University, Athens, Ohio

45701 and the National Organization of Human Services, PO Box 999, Loretto Station, Denver, Colorado 80236. This organization is also responsible for certification of the graduates of human service programs.

36. For information on social work as a profession, the reader is referred to the National Association of Social Workers, 7981 Eastern Avenue, Silver Spring, Maryland 10910 or the local chapter of the National Association of Social Workers.

SUGGESTED READINGS

Richard Blum and Associates. Society and Drugs. San Francisco, CA: Jossey Bass Press, 1967. For a general review of the history of drug use and abuse and society's response to it, this is a highly recommended reading.

Vern Bullogh. Sexual Variation in Society and History. Chicago, IL: University of Chicago Press, 1976. For a nonsophisticated overview of the attitudes toward sexual behavior in society, this book is a sound reference.

Vern Bullogh. Sex, Society and History. New York, NY: Science History Publications, 1976. This is a companion volume to the one on sexual variation. Reading both volumes should give a reader a rather comprehensive overview of the shifting societal attitudes towards sexuality and sexual behavior.

Helen Clarke. Social Legislation. 2nd ed. New York, NY: Appleton Century Crofts Inc., 1957. Although this book is dated, the historical content on child welfare and the family is concise and well documented.

Terry Davidson. Conjugal Crime: Understanding and Changing a Wife Beating Pattern. New York, NY: Hawthorne Books, 1978. For a beginning understanding of the problem of spouse abuse this book is highly recommended.

Robert Geiser. Hidden Victims: The Sexually Abused Child. Boston, MA: Beacon Press, 1979. This book provides an overview of the varieties of sexual abuse with children and documents the incidence, causes and consequences of the behavior.

Paul Halmos. The Personal Service Society. New York, NY: Schocken Books, 1970. Although this book foscusses more on the role of a counselor, its discussion of the personal services provides insight into the changing nature of the social service delivery system.

Alfred Kadushin. Child Welfare Services 3rd Ed. New York, NY: Macmillan Co., 1980. This standard text in child welfare provides an overview and history of these services. The text is well documented and is an excellent reference and resource book.

Alfred Kahn and Sheila Kamerman. Social Services in the United States. Philadelphia, Pennsylvania: University of Pennsylvania Press, 1976. This book describes social services in the United States and uses the concept of the personal social services as the organizing theme.

Lewis Loery. Social Work with the Aging. New York, NY: Harper and Row, Inc., 1979. The aging population is a significant population group in the United States. This text provides a comprehensive overview of the problems of the aged, programs and services available, and developing issues.

Raymond McCarthy. Drinking and Intoxication. Glencoe, IL: Free Press, 1959. Although dated, this book provides a useful historical perspective on the problem of alcohol use and abuse.

Charles Rosenberg. The Family in History. Philadelphia, PA: University of Pennsylvania Press, 1975. For a general overview of the family in history, this book provides a comprehensive perspective and is well documented.

Erik Salinsburg. The Personal Social Services. London, England: Pittman Publishing Co., 1977. This book is an analysis of the development of the personal social services as a societal institution in England, and describes its major features and changes in the service delivery system. For an understanding of the concept of the personal social services, this book is highly recommended.

Gail Sheehy. Hustling: Prostitution in a Wide Open Society. New York, NY: Delacote Press, 1973. This is a rather interesting book since it provides an overview of prostitution in the United States including child and teenage prostitution. For an individual who is not well versed in this problem area, this book should provide some valuable insights.

United States Department of Health, Education and Welfare. National Institute on Drug Abuse, Perspectives on the History of Psycho-Active Substance Use. Washington, DC: U.S. Government Printing Office, 1978. This publication provides a well documented historical overview of the history and current problems of drug use and abuse. For the individual who has no knowledge of this problem area, this publication is highly recommended.

United States. Federal Commission on Obscenity and Pornography, Report of the Commission on Obscenity and Pornography 1970, Washington, DC: U.S. Government Printing Office, 1974. This publication develops a concise history and provides well documented material on the current use of pornography in the United States including child pornography. The publication outlines in detail the social and legal problems associated with pornography. This is a form of behavior which today is provoking highly emotional responses and this publication provides valuable insights into the problem. In addition the reader should consult the report of the 1985 Commission on Pornography.

Louis Weksteen. Handbook of Suicidology. New York, NY: Brunner/Mazell Publishers, 1979. This book provides a comprehensive overview of the problem and has excellent resource and reference material.

REFERENCES

Ard, Ben Jr. and Constance Ard, Hand Book of Marriage Counseling, Palo Alto, California: Science and Behavior Books, 1967.

Belliview, Fred and Lyn Richter, Understanding Human Sexual Inadequacy, Boston, Massachusetts: Little Brown and Co., 1967.

Blum, Richard and Associates, Society and Drugs, San Francisco, California: Jossey Bass Press, 1967.

Briffault, Robert, "Group Marriage and Sexual Communism", pps 202-233 in V.F. Calverton (Editor) The Making of Man: An Outline of Anthropology, New York, NY: Random House Inc., 1931.

Bullogh, Vern, Sexual Variation in Society and History, Chicago, Illinois: University of Chicago Press, 1976.

Bullogh, Vern, Sex, Society and History, New York, NY, Science History Publications, 1976.

Chamblis, Rollin, Social Thought From Hammurabi to Comte, New York, NY: Henry Holt and Co., 1954.

Champman, Jane and Margaret Gates (Editors), The Victimization of Women, Beverly Hills, California: Sage Publication, 1978.

Child Protection Report. National Directory of Children and Youth Services 1981-82. Washington, D.C.: Children's Protection Report, Directory Service Co., 1981.

Clarke, Helen, Social Legislation, 2nd Ed. New York, NY: Appleton Century Croft Inc., 1957.

Compton, Beulah, Introduction to Social Welfare and Social Work, Homewood, Illinois: Dorsey Press, 1980.

Croner, Helga and Kurt Guggenheim, National Directory of Private Social Agencies 1986, Queens Village, New York: Croner Publishing Co., 1986.

Croner, Helga and Kurt Guggenhein. Narcotics and Drug Abuse: A-Z. Queen's Village, New York: Croner Publishing Co., 1985.

Davidson, Terry, Conjugal Crime: Understanding and Changing a Wife Beating Pattern, New York: NY, Hawthorne Books Inc., 1978.

Dolgoff, Ralph and Donald Feldstein, Understanding Social Welfare, 2nd Ed. New York, NY: Longman Inc., 1984.

Dublin, Lewis "Suicide: An Overview of A Health and Social Problem" Bulletin of Suicidology, December 1967 pps. 25-30.

Dzieck, Billie and Linda Weiner. The Lecherous Professor: Sexual Harassment, Boston, Massachusetts: Beacon Press, 1983.

Farberow, Norman, "Cultural History of Suicide", pps. 30-34, in Jan Waldenstrom et al Suicide and Attempted Suicide, Stockholm, Sweden: Nordiska Bokhandelns Farlao, Co., 1972.

Finkelhor, D., "Sex Among Siblings", Archives of Sexual Behavior, Vol. 9, (1980) pp. 171-194.

Frederickson, Hazel, and R.A. Mulligan, A Child and His Welfare, San Francisco, California: W. H. Freeman & Co., 1972.

Friedlander, Walter and Robert Apte, Introduction to Social
    Welfare, 5th Edition, Englewood Cliffs, New Jersey: Prentice
    Hall Inc., 1980.

Geiser, Robert, Hidden Victims: The Sexually Abused Child,
    Boston, Massachusetts: Beacon Press, 1979.

Gelles, Richard, The Violent Home, Beverly Hills, California:
    Sage Publications, 1972.

Gill, David, Child Abuse and Violence, New York, NY: EMS Press,
    1979.

Greenstome, James and Sharon Leviton. Hotline Crisis
    Intervention Directory. New York, New York: Facts on File
    Inc., 1981.

Haeberly, Erwin, The Sex Atlas, New York, NY: Seabury Press,
    1978.

Halmos, Paul, The Personal Service Society, New York, NY:
    Schocken Books, 1970.

Hartland, E.S., "Mother Rights," pps. 182-202 in V.F. Calverton
    (Ed.), The Making of Man: An Outline of Anthropology, New
    York, NY: Random House, Inc., 1931.

Hawton, Keith, Sex Therapy, Oxford New York: Oxford University
    Press, 1985.

Hunt, M., Sexual Behavior in the 1970's. Chicago, Illinois:
    Playboy Press, 1974.

Hyde, Janet, Half the Human Experience: The Psychology of Women,
    Lexington, Massachusetts: D.C. Heath and Co., 1985.

Inelis, Ruth, Sins of the Fathers: A Study of the Physical, and
    Emotional Abuse of Children, New York, NY: Saint Martins
    Press, 1978.

Kadushin, Alfred, Child Welfare Services - Third Edition, New
    York, NY: Macmillan Co., 1980.

Kahn, Alfred, Social Policy and Social Services, New York, NY:
    Random House Inc., 1973.

Kahn, Alfred and Sheila Kamerman, Social Services in the United
    States,   Philadelphia,   Pennsylvania: University   of
    Pennsylvania Press, 1976.

Krafft-Ebing R. Von <u>Psychopathia Sexualis</u>, Philadelphia, Pennsylvania: F. A. Davis Co., 1893.

Krohne, Eric, <u>Sex Therapy Handbook</u>, Jamaica, New York: Spectrum Publishing Co., 1981.

Loery, Lewis, <u>Social Work With The Aging</u>, New York, NY: Harper and Row, Inc., 1979.

McCarthy, Raymond, <u>Drinking and Intoxication</u>, Glencoe, Illinois: Free Press, 1959.

McGee, Richard, <u>Crisis Intervention in the Community</u>, Baltimore, Maryland: University Park Press, 1974.

Morris, Robert, <u>Social Policy of the American Welfare State: An Introduction to Policy Analysis</u>, New York: NY: Harper and Row Publishers, 1979.

Minahan, Anne (Ed.). <u>Encyclopedia of Social Work - 18th Edition</u>, Washington, DC: National Association of Social Workers, 1986.

Motto, Jerome, Richard Brooks, Charlotte Ross, and Nancy Allen, <u>Standards for Suicide Prevention in Crisis Centers</u>, New York, NY: Human Sciences Press, 1974.

Norback, Judith and Patricia Weitz, <u>Sourcebook of Sex Therapy, Counseling and Family Planning</u>, New York, New York: Van Nostrand Reinhold Co., 1983.

Office of the Federal Register, <u>United States Government Manual 1985-86</u>. Washington, DC: U.S. Government Printing Office, 1985.

Offir, Carole, <u>Human Sexuality</u>, New York, New York: Harcourt, Brace, Jovanovich Co., 1982.

Palmare, Erdman, <u>Handbook on the Aged in the United States</u>, Westport, Connecticut: Greenwood Press, 1984.

Peterson, Deena, <u>A Practical Guide to the Women's Movement</u>, Brooklyn, New York: Women's Action Alliance, 1975.

Purcell, Edward, <u>The Book of the States 1984/85</u>, Lexington, Kentucky: The Council of State Governments, 1984.

Rosenberg, Charles, <u>The Family in History</u>, Philadelphia, Pennsylvania: University of Pennsylvania Press, 1975.

Roy, Maria, Battered Women, New York, NY: Van Nostrand Rineholt Co., 1967.

Russo, Francis and George Willis. Human Services in America. Englewood Cliffs, New Jersey: Prentice Hall Inc., 1986.

Sadock, Benjamin, Gerald Kaplan and Alfred Freedman, The Sexual Experience, Baltimore, Maryland: Williams and Wilkins Co., 1976.

Salinsburg, Erik, The Personal Social Services, London, England: Pittman Publishing Co., 1977.

Schmolling, Paul Jr., Merrill Youkeles and William R. Burger. Human Services in Contemporary America. Monterey, California: Brooks Cole Publishing Co., 1985.

Sheehy, Gail, Hustling: Prostitution in a Wide Open Society, New York, NY: Delacote Press, 1973.

Shyne, Ann and Anita Schroeder, National Study of Social Services to Children and Their Families: Overview, Washington, DC: U.S. Government Printing Office, 1978.

Skidmore, Rex and Milt Thackery, Introduction to Social Work - Second Edition Englewood Cliffs New Jersey: Prentice Hall Inc., 1976.

Stahman, Robert and William Hiebert, Klemmer's Counseling in Marital and Sexual Problems - Second Edition, Baltimore, Maryland: Wilkins Co., 1977.

Strauss, Murray and Gerald Hotating, The Social Causes of Husband and Wife Violence, Minneapolis, Minnesota: University of Minnesota Press, 1980.

Strauss, Murray, Richard Gelles, and Suzane Steinmetz, Behind Closed Doors, New York, NY: Anchor Books, 1980.

Tyler, Alice, Freedoms Ferment: Phases of American Social History From the Colonial Period to the Outbreak of the Civil War, New York, NY: Harper and Row Publishers, 1944.

United States Department of Commerce, Bureau of the Census, Statistical Abstract of the United States: 1986 (106th Edition). Washington, DC: U.S. Government Printing Office, 1985.

United States Department of Commerce, Bureau of the Census, 1980 Census of Population, Vol. 2 Subject Reports Part 7C: Occupation by Industry, Washington, DC: U.S. Government Printing Office, 1984.

United States, Department of Commerce, Bureau of the Census, 1982 Census of Service Industries, Washington, D.C.: U.S. Government Printing Office, 1984.

United States Department of Health Education and Welfare, Office of Human Development, Child Abuse and Neglect Programs, Washington, DC: U.S. Government Printing Office, 1978.

United States Department of Health Education and Welfare, Public Health Service, National Directory of Drug Abuse and Alcoholism Treatment and Prevention Programs, Washington, DC: U.S. Government Printing Office, 1982.

United States Department of Health Education and Welfare, National Institute on Drug Abuse, Perspectives on the History of Psycho-Active Substance Use, Washington, DC: U.S. Government Printing Office, 1978.

United States Department of Health Education and Welfare, In-patient Health Facilities, Washington, DC: U.S. Government Printing Office, 1980.

United States, Department of Health and Human Services, Public Health Service, National Directory of Alcoholism Treatment Programs, Washington, D.C.: U.S. Government Printing Office, 1981.

United States Department of Health Education and Welfare, Health Statistics Division, Health Resources United States: 1978, Washington, DC: U.S. Government Printing Office, 1978.

United States Department of Health Education and Welfare, Day Care Centers in the United States. Washington, DC: U.S. Government Printing Office, 1979.

United States Department of Justice, Uniform Crime Reports 1983, Washington, DC: U.S. Government Printing Office, 1984.

United States Federal Commission on Obscenity and Pornography, Report of the Commission on Obscenity and Pornography: 1970, Washington, DC: U.S. Government Printing Office, 1974.

United States National Institute on Alcohol Abuse and
   Alcoholism, <u>Fourth Special Report to United States Congress</u>
   <u>on Alcohol and Health</u>, Washington, DC: U.S. Government
   Printing Office, 1981.

United States Strategy Council on Drug Abuse, <u>Federal Strategy</u>
   <u>for Drug Use and Drug Traffic Prevention 1975</u>, Washington,
   DC: U.S. Government Printing Office, 1975.

United States National Commission on Marijuana and Drug Use,
   <u>Drug Use in America: Problem in Perspective</u>, Washington, DC:
   U.S. Government Printing Office, 1973.

Walters, David, <u>Physical and Sexual Abuse of Children</u>,
   Bloomington, Indiana: Indiana University Press, 1976.

Weinstein, Amy, <u>Public Welfare Directory 1986/87</u>, Washington,
   DC: American Public Welfare Association, 1986.

Weksteen, Louis, <u>Handbook of Suicidology</u>, New York, NY:
   Brunner/Mazel Publishers, 1979.

Wisconsin Legislative Reference Bureau, <u>Wisconsin Blue Book</u>
   <u>1985-86</u>,   Madison,   WI: Wisconsin   Department   of
   Administration, 1985.

Women's Action Alliance. <u>Women Helping Women</u>, New York, New
   York: Neal Schuman Publishing Inc., 1981.

Chapter 23

PHYSICAL HEALTH NETWORK*

"The individual physician in private practice has been the dominant figure in medical care since the colonial era and the genesis of American individualism. The public role has been far more limited than in many other countries, and has been focused on the sick poor, and on specific disease areas, such as tuberculosis and mental health. Medical care was considered by many physicians to be a 'privilege' and there developed two levels of care in the United States -- superior for those who could afford it, and inferior for those who could not. The later faced a major hurdle and gained access to care." (Bowers:1977:155)

INTRODUCTION

The physical health network in the United States is under-going rapid changes, such as dominance of the hospital setting, reemergence of home health care, prepaid insurance plans, public health programs, specialization and expansion of the health professions, health maintenance programs (HMO's), increasing demand and cost of medical care with the emergence of health system agencies (HSA's) to contain cost increases, reevaluation of ethical codes in the professions, an increasingly sophisticated technology and an emphasis on holistic and preventive medicine.

The physical health network of today is vastly different than the physical health network of the 1900s. The number of occupations and professions involved in the physical health network are diverse and varied ranging from a physician, to an operating room attendant. This chapter briefly describes the physical health network, with an emphasis on the professions of medicine, nursing and social work.

SIZE

Estimates on the size of the physical health network vary depending upon the source of statistics used, however, one of the most comprehensive reports is the survey of health resources compiled by the Department of Health, Education and Welfare entitled Health The United States: 1978.[1] The estimated size of the physical health network is shown in Figure 23-1. In 1982-84 there were an estimated 374,410 medical facilities (including private offices), which employed an estimated 6.1

Figure 23-1

ESTIMATED SIZE OF THE PHYSICAL HEALTH
NETWORK IN 1982-84*

Selected Characteristic	Major Type of Facility			Total
	Nursing Home	Hospital	Other	
Number of Facilities	25,849	6,324	342,237	374,410
Number of Employees	918,000	3,443,000	1,818,970	6,179,970
Expenditures (Billion)	32.0	157.9	181.7	371.6
Use of the Health Network (Duplicate Count)[1]	1,493,000, Residents)	861,000 (Residents)	1,553,000,000 (Patient Visits)[3]	3,907,000,000

*SOURCES: Adapted from United States Department of Commerce, Bureau of the Census Statistical Abstract of the United States: 1986 (106th Ed.) Washington, D. Government Printing Office, 1985 pp. 96, 97, 104, 105, 106, 107, 110, 111, 112; Uni States Department of Commerce, Bureau of the Census, 1980 Census of Population: Vol Subject Reports Part 7C: Occupation by Industry, Washington, D.C.: U.S. Governm Printing Office, 1984, pp. 295-664 and United States Department of Commerce, Bureau the Census, 1982 Census of Service Industries, Washington, D.C.: U.S. Governm Printing Office, 1984, p. 5-7.

1. Duplicate count means one individual can be counted more than once since they move to different nursing homes or may leave a specific home and return to the s home later.

2. Includes office of physician, dentist, osteopath, chiropractor, optometrist, etc.

3. It is estimated that on an average, an individual sees a physician 5 times a y and 50 percent of the population a dentist once a year.

million individuals, with expenditures of 371.6 billion dollars. The number of individuals in nursing or other skilled nursing facilities and hospitals was estimated at 2,354,000 and there were an estimated 1,553,000,000 patient visits to the office of a physician and dentist.

The above estimates of the physical health network, divide the network into nursing homes, hospitals, and other care, i.e., physician's office, outpatient care, etc. It is estimated that an individual visits a physician five terms per year, and about half of the population sees a dentist once a year. Nursing homes are listed separately, since they are the majority of inpatient or resident population facilities. Nursing homes were a small percentage of the physical health facilities available pre-1950, however with the growing aging population and various federal legislation for funding, it is anticipated that the nursing home and its function will continue to grow.

HISTORICAL DEVELOPMENT

The physical health network as we know it, is essentially a product of the last 100 years. The network has a number of separate but interrelated parts: the professions of medicine and nursing, hospitals, public health programs, and a variety of allied health professions.[2] Each of these components of the physical health network has its own distinctive historical development. Figure 23-2 summarizes a historical time line for each of these different components of the physical health network.

MEDICINE

The profession of medicine, which is currently dominated by the physician, has had a long history with periods of growth and prestige, and periods of stagnation and suspicion.

PRE-CLASSICAL and CLASSICAL CIVILIATION-PRE-450 A.D. - In prehistoric times the medicine man was the counterpart to the modern medical practitioner. The general concept of the causation of disease was bodily invasion from external supernatural sources. The Egyptians (4,000 B.C.) had a priest/physician who was trained and worked in the healing temple called the Aesculapian Temple. The physician at this time was also a pharmacist and a dentist. The Egyptians had a hierarchy of medical practitioners based upon prestige: the holy healer, the herb and medicine physician, and the surgeon. In Egypt, physicians became specialists in specific diseases.

A predecessor of modern medical care was Hippocrates (460 B.C.), of Greece, who used a clinical approach to medicine,

Figure 23-2

HISTORICAL TIME LINE OF THE PHYSICAL HEALTH NETWORK

Time Period	Aspect of the Physical Health Network				
	Medicine	Nursing	Place of Treatment (Hospital)	Public Health	Allied Health Professions
Pre Historic Pre 3,000 BC	Medicine Man	Nurturing woman (Independent from Medicine Man)	Home Care Sacred Place		Midwife
Egyptian 3,000 BC	Priest/physician (Including pharmacy, Dentistry)	Physician Aide (subservient to Physician)	Healing Temple Home Care	Hygiene Code	Midwife
Greek/Roman 500 BC-450 AD	Hippocrates 460 BC (Father of clinical medicine)	Trained Nurses	Home Care	Public Baths Sanitation Programs	Midwife
Early Medieval 450-700 AD	Priest/Physician	Deaconesses 58 AD Matrons 250 AD	Home Care/ Early Hospital 350 AD	Prior Programs Deteriorate	Barber/Surgeon Midwife
Middle Medieval 700-1200 AD	Priest/Physician	Monastic and Religious Orders	Home Care Hospital for Poor	Prior Programs Deteriorate	Barber/Surgeon Midwife
Late Medieval 1200-1500 AD	Priest/Physician Dentistry and Pharmacy become a distinct occupation	Military and Secular Orders	Home Care Hospital for Poor	Prior public Health Program Deteriorate	Barber/Surgeon Midwife, Pharmacy, Dentistry
Renaissance 1500 - 1700	Lay Physician/Some Educational Standards beginning	Religious orders Sisters of Charity	Home Care Hospital for poor	Health Program Decline	Dentistry, Pharmacy Midwife, Barber, Surgeon
1700-1800 AD	Physician/Surgeon	In the U.S. Women and mothers as nurse	Home Care Office Care	Health Program Decline	Dentistry, Pharmacy Midwife
1800-1900	Physician/Surgeon Obstetrics and Gynecology, Psychiatry	Florence Nightengale and modern nursing (Subservient to Physician)	Home Care Office Care	Develop health programs in cities	Dentistry, Pharmacy
1900 -	" " " " Numerous Subspecialties	Specialization in Nursing	Office Care, Hospital, Nursing Homes, Outpatient	Public Health Programs	Medical Social Work/ numerous other Professions

as well as, looking for natural causes of disease. He viewed diseases as a consequence of an imbalance of the humors, and developed a humoral theory of disease. The four humors were blood (air), yellow bile (fire), black bile (earth), and phlegm (water). The professional oath of the physician is called the Hippocratic Oath. The Romans (100) generally accepted the medical practices of Greece. Physicians were generally private practitioners and entrepreneurs who learned their trade through an apprentice type of system. There were some physicians who were hired by the municipality to handle sanitary conditions and a fledgling beginning of medical schools. In the classical societies of Greece and Rome the physician was in addition a pharmacist and dentist, but most surgery was done by what is known as a barber surgeon, which was still viewed as an occupation with low prestige.

MEDIEVAL PERIOD - 450-1500 - In the early Medieval European era (450-700), there was a movement to combine the roles of a priest/physician, such as St. Damien (500). In the middle Medieval European era (700-1200), the tradition of a priest/physician continued with the emergence of medical schools in some of the monasteries, such as St. Gall in France (720) and Salerno in Italy (1100), which was probably an offshoot of the Abbey of Monte Cassino. During the late Medieval European era (1200-1500), a university education became available for physicians, a differentiation occurred between the profession of a priest and a physician, a licensing procedure was established, and the growing importance of surgeons as an occupational group. In addition to changes in the position of a physician, other occupational groups were achieving autonomy from medicine. For example, pharmacy (apothecary) became a distinct occupation in about 1240, dentistry was becoming a separate occupation and associating itself with the barber surgeon. The physician treated wounds and diseases, but did not perform surgery, except in rare cases, and the priest still continued to handle mental illness.

RENAISSANCE and REFORMATION - 1500-1700 - This was a period of rapid change and advancement for the profession of medicine. The humoral theory of the Greeks was rejected and progress was made in the understanding of anatomy (Vesalius, 1513-1564) and blood circulation (Harvey, 1578-1657). Beginning efforts were made to include surgeons as part of medicine (Pare, 1510-1590), even though barber surgeons, as a group, were not a recognized guild until at least 1540. Even though advances were made in the biological sciences, most physicians were still trained through an apprentice system and not through a university education.

783

ENLIGHTENMENT - 1700-1800 - This time period laid the foundation for modern medicine. Surgery became a recognized specialization of medicine partly as a consequence of the work of John Hunter (1728-1793), inoculation procedures were developed, and in the United States the first medical school was established by John Morgan in 1765 in Philadelphia, Pennsylvania.

NINETEENTH CENTURY - Further advances in understanding disease occurred between 1800 and 1900 with the development of bacterial medicine through the works of Louis Pasteur (1822-1895) and Robert Koch (1843-1910). New medical technologies were developed, such as the use of x-rays (William Roentgen 1845-1922), use of radium (Marie and Pierre Curie 1898), use of chemotherapy (Paul Erlich 1854-1915), the use of antiseptics in hospitals (Lynz Semmelweiss 1818-1865, and Joseph Lister, 1827-1912), and the use of anesthetics in surgery (Crawford Lang 1815-1879 and William Morton 1819-1868).

Medical education was still in a state of flux, and it is estimated that as late as 1840, only one-third of the physicians had completed a program in a medical school. Most physicians were trained through a preceptor/apprentice type of system. The American Medical Association was formed in 1847 and one of their first tasks was to address the issue of medical education. An Association of University Medical Colleges was established in 1890. One of the major issues addressed through this association was medical education, since many medical schools were not keeping abreast of newer developments. Notable historical figures in medical education include Sir William Osler (1849-1919) and William Halsted (1859-1902) of John Hopkins University, Baltimore, Maryland.

TWENTIETH CENTURY - The American Medical Association asked for a national survey of medical education, which was completed in 1910 by Abraham Flexner. As a consequence of this survey, most proprietary schools (small, private, non-university related schools) were closed, the practice of a preceptor/apprentice system was abolished, and university medical schools (either private endowment or state supported) were established. Admission requirements for entrance to medical school expanded to high school graduation by 1914, one year of college by 1916, two years of college by 1918 and currently four years of college.

Advances in medical technology continued, such as miracle drugs, (Gerhard Domagh 1936), penicillin (Sir Alexander Fleming 1939), polio vaccine (Jonas Salk 1953), and more recently the development of sophisticated surgical techniques, drugs, diagnostic techniques, etc. The medical profession in the United States, like many of the other human service professions began to receive financial assistance from the federal government for educational facilities and student aid through legislation, such as the Public Health Service Act Amendments of 1966.

NURSING

The concept of a nurturing person for the sick, i.e., a nurse, is as old as the use of the priest/physician. Like medicine, the profession of nursing has had periods of acceptance and high status in society, and periods of suspicion and low status in society.

PRE-CLASSICAL and CLASSICAL CIVILIZATIONS - PRE-450 A.D. - In prehistoric times there were women who nurtured ill individuals and provided care before and after the medicine man saw the patient. In many cases, the nurturing women were totally responsible for the care of the ill individual who never saw a medicine man. In essence, the nurturing women were independent from the medicine man and were held in high esteem.

In Egypt (4,000 B.C.), this independent status was lost and the helping women who worked in the temples of healing were subservient to the priest/physician.[3] In Greece and Rome, the helping women were generally untrained, however, Hippocrates of Greece (460 B.C.), and Gallan of Rome (130), stressed the need for trained individuals.

During the early Christian era from about 50 to 450, emerged the tradition of the charity and giving aspect of Christianity. A group motivated by religious principles called the Order of the Deaconess was established in Rome, and were referred to as "Bearers of the Lamp," since they provided visiting nursing services. Notable historical figures in the Order of the Deaconesses include Phoebe (60) and St. Olympias (400). In addition, groups of Roman matrons provided nursing services, such as St. Helena (250-330), St. Paula (347-404) and St. Fabiola (390). Caring for the ill was considered to be a noble occupation and was the embodiment of the highest ideals of Christian charity. These early nurses were independent from the physician.

MEDIEVAL PERIOD - 450-1500 - During the Medieval European era, there was a shift from an independent religious order to monastic orders, and some training through the monastery. Examples of notable historical figures of this time period include St. Bridget (452-523), and St. Scholastica (500). During the Medieval period, there was a close relationship between the occupation and profession of a nun/nurse, like many physicians were priest/physicians. In the later Medieval European era there emerged military religious orders, and

785

Mendicant orders which were male dominated. Examples of these military religious orders include the Knights Hospitallers, (1050), Order of Trinitarians, (1197), and the Francisan Order (St. Francis of Assisi, 1182-1226) which provided nursing services. In addition, non-monastic and nun/nursing orders continued to expand, such as the Sisters of Common Life, and Order of Antonines (1095). There was extensive use of midwives who were a separate occupational grouping.

RENAISSANCE and REFORMATION - 1500-1700 - The close relationship between religion and nursing and their independence from physicians continued until the 1800s. The Sisters of Charity (1638), St. Francis de Sales (1657), and St. Francis de Paul (1576-1669), established new orders for treating the ill, and working with the poor. St. Vincent de Paul was an early advocate of visiting nursing, social services and training for individuals.[4]

ENLIGHTENMENT - 1700-1800 - In the United States, there was a lack of skilled nurses, consequently, the older religious orders or "wise women" and mothers provided care for the ill. The list of religious orders, which provided nursing services in the United States is lengthy. Some examples of these religious orders include the Ursuline Sisters (1740's), Sisters of St. Augustine, Sisters of Charity, Sisters of St. Mary, Sisters of St. John's House, Sisters of the Holy Communion and the Alexian Brothers. A notable historical figure is that of Elizabeth Bayley Seton (Mother Seton) 1774-1821) who established the Sisters of Charity in the United States.

NINETEENTH CENTURY - Modern nursing developed in a period of social reform which includes notable figures, such as Dorthea Dix (1850's), Clara Barton (1860's), Harriet Tubman (1820-1910), Louise Schuyler (1873) and Florence Nightingale (1820-1919). Florence Nightingale through her experiences in the Crimean War, of 1854, revolutionized modern nursing education and established training schools for nurses. The first modern nursing schools in the United States were established in 1873 at Belleview Hospital in New York, and in Hartford, Connecticut in 1877. Major issues that developed early in the education of nurses were: should they be educated as a combined nurse/social service professional, as a nurse professional, and whether educational programs should be located in hospital schools, independent schools or at the university level.

TWENTIETH CENTURY - Hospital and diploma schools dominated nursing education until the late 1960's, although some university programs developed, such as Minnesota (1909), and a practical nurse program in Boston, Massachusetts. As nursing emerged as a professional field, professional organizations quickly developed. The Nurses Associated Alumnae began in 1896, which became the American Nurses Association in 1911. The American Society of Superintendents of Training Schools for Nursing developed in 1893, and became the National league of Nursing in 1912, and more recently the National League for Nursing in 1952.

The trend away from hospital schools (diploma schools) is clearly seen when one compares figures for 1960 and 1983. In 1960, there were 1,137 programs for nursing education, of which 908 or 79.9 percent were diploma schools, 172 or 15.1 percent were university programs, and 57 or 5.0 percent were associate of art degree programs. In 1983, there were 1,490 programs for the education of nurses, of which 281 or 18.8 percent were diploma schools, 433 or 29.1 percent were university programs, and 776 or 52.1 percent were associate of art degree programs. An impetus for the expansion of nursing education was the Public Health Amendments Act of 1956, which provided financial grants for graduate education in nursing, and the Nurses Training Act of 1964, which provided financial grants for university education programs, and for students at the baccalaureate level.[5]

Practical Nursing as a field developed in the 1880's with programs at Ballard Hospital in New York City and Household Nursing in Boston, Massachusetts. In 1941, a National Association for Practical Nursing Education was formed which became the National Association for Practical Nursing Education and Services in 1959. Currently, the licensed practical nurse (LPN) or licensed vocational nurse (LVN), obtain either a 2 year associate of art degree, or a 1 year certificate. These programs constitute 50 percent of the nursing programs in the United States in 1983.

HOSPITALS

The hospital consisting of physicians, nurses, and a staff of allied health professions, is a product of the last 100 years. Prior to 1900, most health care was delivered at home or in the physician's office. The public hospital was for the low status socioeconomic groups and the private hospital was for the higher socioeconomic status groups.

CLASSICAL CIVILIZATION PRE-450 A.D. - The earliest form of a hospital was a temple of healing in Sumeria (4000 B.C.) and in Egyptian society (3000 B.C.). The Greeks (400 B.C.) had Aesculapian temples named after the Greek god of medicine, Aesculapius, and the Romans (100) had public infirmaries for the slaves and lower class citizens. The hospital was initially a hospice or hostel for the ill, aging, vagrants, etc. It was a place where the unfortunate could go for aid.

787

MEDIEVAL PERIOD - 450-1500 - In early Medieval Europe (450-700) there were hospices for the aged established by St. Helena (250-330), for the convalescent established by St. Fabiola (390) and the mentally ill established by St. Dymphania (580). Generally the hospices, or hospital, were not differentiated according to problems, such as aging, mentally ill, etc., but housed a variety of social, physical, mental, and psychological problems. The hospital essentially was a public endeavor to aid the poor. There were monastic hospitals established focussing on the poor, such as St. Basil (330-379), Hospital Dieu in Lyons France (542) and Santo Spirito Hospital in Italy (717). The hospital was primarily for the poor until the 1900's, since the primary setting for medical treatment was in the home.

UNITED STATES DEVELOPMENT - Some of the early hospitals in the United States included Blockley Hospital in Philadelphia (1731), Charity Hospital in New Orleans (1737) and the Pennsylvania Hospital of Philadelphia (1751). Hospital care in general was poor, inadequate and unsanitary, with these conditions remaining until the 20th Century.

Since 1900 there has been a complete reversal in the role of hospitals from a place to house the poor who were ill, training grounds for physicians and nurses, a place of last resort, to currently a medical health center for all citizens with an emphasis on curing and restoration. The hospital with its diagnostic facilities, surgical procedures, social and psychological services and allied health services, is now the mainstay of the physical health network. The changes in hospital functioning and structure since 1900 has indeed been remarkable. In 1900 some individuals refused to go to a hospital for care, since the mortality rate was well over 50 percent, and now most individuals "willingly" go to a hospital to participate in their own health care. This change in the role of the hospital is a consequence of technological changes, medical discoveries, educational programs and public/private funding.

Significant advances in hospital care were related to the work of Lynz Semmelweiss (1818-1865) and Joseph Lister (1827-1912) in the development of an antiseptic environment. A financial impetus for the use of hospitals, was the development of prepaid insurance programs, such as Blue Cross in 1929. As hospital organization and care changed with the newer technologies, a need emerged for standard setting for both hospital administrators and programs. An American College of Hospital Administrators was formed in 1933, and this organization began to accredit graduate education programs in 1934. The American Hospital Association was formed in 1898, and later hospital facilities were accredited by a Joint Commission on Accreditation of Hospitals.[6]

A second major impetus in the use of hospitals for health care was the Hill Burton Act of 1946, which provided funding for the construction of hospital facilities. This act, attempted to remedy the lack of health care in rural areas, consequently, one now finds numerous small hospitals throughout the United States, which are unable to keep abreast of newer and expensive technological advances.

Currently, there is a movement to consolidate and integrate hospital care, and the emergence of specialty hospitals and nursing homes. Specialty hospitals include family practice, cancer, heart and the hospice for the dying. The idea of a specialty hospital versus a general hospital is not new. In 1898 Rose Hawthorne Lathrop (1851-1926) opened St. Roses Home in New York City for cancer patients. The current hospice movement for terminal illness began in the 1960's with the scholarly work of Kubler-Ross on death and dying, and the practice orientation of Dr. Cecil Saunders in London, England. Dr. Saunders in 1965 opened St. Christopher's Hospice and initiated the current hospice movement which is growing rapidly in the United States. Nursing homes for the aged, developed rapidly since 1950 with the Medical Assistance to the Aged Program, and more recently with benefits under Title XIII and XIX of the amended Social Security Act in 1965.[7]

PUBLIC HEALTH PROGRAMS

Public health programs focus on prevention of disease instead of a curative or restorative function. Public health as a movement developed out of a public concern in three problem areas; housing and sanitation, community diseases and personal cleanliness.

CLASSICAL CIVILIZATIONS - PRE-450 A.D. - The Egyptians (4000 B.C.), Babylonians and the Code of Hammurabi (2000 B.C.), and the Hebrews in the Pentateuch (1000 B.C.), all had sanitary and hygienic codes. The Hebrews had established lay officials who became health inspectors. The Greeks and Romans had established public baths, sanitary and water systems, as well as, appointing lay health officials.

MEDIEVAL PERIOD to 1800 - After the decline of the Roman Empire in 450, systems for public health had rapidly declined and personal hygiene was at a low level. In fact, public health and preventive medicine did not again become a major con- cern until the redevelopment of urban centers in the early 1800's. Central authority was lacking after the decline of the Roman

789

Empire, consequently local communities and individuals were left to their own devices. Classical Greek and Roman med- ical knowledge, as well as, their sanitation procedures were abandoned. By 1300 Western Europe was beset with contagious diseases, such as typhoid, malaria, chlorea, small pox, and the great bubonic plague (black death) of 1346. It is estimated that these diseases decimated between 1/3 to 1/2 of the total population at that period of time.

In spite of the general lack of concern for sanitary mea- sures, there were some notable historical examples of indivi- duals who spoke out against the unsanitary conditions of the time. Balavignus in Germany (1310-1348) and Simmon De Covina in Italy (1340-1390) were early figures in attempting to reestab- lish some form of sanitary measures. Balavignus during the bubonic plague of 1345 encouraged the Jewish population in Strassburg, Germany to reduce the incidence of disease by burn- ing refuse, garbage, diseased clothing, and adhering to personal sanitation codes. When the fatality rate for the plague was reduced to 5 percent from the surrounding nonghetto (nonJewish) population fatality rate of 50 percent, he was accused of poisoning the Christians, and was executed. Simmon De Covina in 1377, noticed that the incidence of disease coming from the ships passing through Venice was higher than other parts of Italy. He quarantined for 30 days and than 40 days ships coming through Venice, and a decline in the incidence of certain diseases was noticed. These two figures by their actions clearly indicated the nature of communicable diseases and showed the importance of sanitation in controlling contagious diseases. Most large cities did have a health official at this time, however, most were lay individuals with limited, if any, medical knowledge.

UNITED STATES DEVELOPMENT - Like other Western European countries, the United States ignored public health concerns until the early 1800s. There was a concept of miasma, that is people became ill from unhealthy things in the air and the social environment, and a slow movement emerged regarding public health. It was not until after the Civil War when there was a high degree of social unrest over the crowded and unsanitary conditions in the cities that programs were established. Public health programs began at the local level of government and even- tually the state and federal governments developed public health programs.

One of the earlier cities to form a public health program was New York in 1866. With the crowded slums and tenements in New York there was a high degree of concern over the rapid increase in the death rate from communicable diseases, such as tuberculosis, small pox, etc. As a consequence, in 1866, after a period of agitation by citizens, a Metropolitan Health Board was established. An outbreak of chlorea developed in New York in 1866 and the Health Board took action to disinfect areas, establish sanitary areas, and recommended sanitary procedures for garbage and refuse. As a consequence, of these procedures the chlorea outbreak of 1866 was not as severe as anticipated. In 1869, the New York Metropolitan Health Board developed a system for analyzing water supplies, and in 1874-75 they established an inoculation system for smallpox. Concurrent with the Metropolitan Health Board, a system of visiting nurses was established in 1877 under Lillian Dock. The public health movement spread rapidly throughout other areas of the United States, such as Massachusetts (1869), Wisconsin (1876) and Milwaukee, Wisconsin (1876). In addition, programs of health care were established in public school systems in 1896 and 1902 in New York City. There was an expansion of the visiting nurse concept to other places like Philadelphia (1886), Chicago (1889) and Providence Rhode Island under Mary Gardiner. A professional public health association was formed and established in 1872.

Although local governments were the first to establish public health programs in the United States, the federal government had an early involvement, although limited, in the public health movement. In 1798 the Marine Hospital was established which provided services for the merchant seaman. In 1902 this service was renamed Public Health and Marine Hospital Service, and in 1912 it was renamed the Public Health Service. This unit of the federal government had expanded its activities which began with merchant seaman to include mental illness, alcohol and drugs, contagious diseases, health manpower, venereal diseases, food quality, etc.

The public health component of the physical health network, like other parts of the human services, developed its own professional identity through professional organizations and educational programs. The American Public Health Association was formed in 1872, and the first university programs were at Michigan (1910) and Massachusetts (1912). The first school of public health was in Pennsylvania. In 1941, an Association of Schools of Public Health was formed, which began accrediting educational programs in 1946.[8] The federal government provided financial support for educational programs in public health and for students through legislation, such as the Health Manpower Training Act in 1948, and the comprehensive Health Planning and Public Health Service Amendments of 1966.

Today, public health departments and community sanitation programs are established in all major areas in the United States with centralized laboratories tracking down communicable diseases, such as the legionnaires disease (1976) and acquired immune deficiency syndrome (AIDS) (1986) which is affecting a small percentage of the population but could spread rapidly. Services available in most public health departments include outpatient clinics, visiting nurses, social workers, outreach medical testing, educational programs, as well as inspection of facilities for eating and preparation of foods, etc.

ALLIED HEALTH PROFESSIONS

This component of the physical health network has developed mainly since 1900, although a few occupations and professions were established earlier. Allied health professions prior to 1900 included dentistry, pharmacy, nursing midwives and lay midwives. Dentistry was originally practiced by the medical profession but became an autonomous occupation from medicine around 1300-1400. Guy deChauliac, a surgeon, argued that operations on the teeth, was the proper jurisdiction of the barber/ surgeons and dentators. Pierre Fauchard 1690-1761 is considered to be the father of modern day dentistry. Early training for dentistry occurred primarily through the preceptor/apprentice method with the first dental school established in 1840 in Baltimore, Maryland and a Dental Professional Association in 1839.

Pharmacy (apothecary), like dentistry, had a common origin with medicine and became an autonomous occupation about 1240. Midwives and "wisewomen" have been practicing since prehistoric times. Midwives were a respected occupational group and remained independent from physicians. It was not until the early 1900's when the medical profession established a specialty in obstetrics and gynecology that the physician became the predominant figure in the delivery of babies and as a result the use of midwives declined. The nursing profession has had a specialty in midwivery for years, which is in addition to the development of lay midwives. Currently, there is a movement to use nursing midwives in the home as an alternate means of care, instead of hospitalization.

Medical social work was formally established in 1905 in Boston, Massachusetts, New York City and Baltimore, Maryland through the work of Mary and Elizabeth Cannon and Mary Wadleigh. There were earlier precedents of services similar to medical social work through organizations, such as the St. Vincent DePaul Society, The Lady Almoners of England in the 1860s, and individuals like Clara Barton (1863), Lillian Wald and Mary Brewster of the Henry Street Settlement House (1893), and Richard Cabot and Charles Emerson (1902).

Most of the allied health professions began latter in the 20th Century, such as dental hygiene (1913), dietetics (1917), hospital administration (1933), medical records administration, (1910), medical technician (1930), occupational therapy (1914), physical therapy (1916), physician's or medical assistant (1940's), paramedic (1960's), respiratory therapy (1950), etc.[9]

STRUCTURE

The structure of the physical health network is more diverse and complex than some of the other human service networks. The same format can be used to describe the structure of the physical health network as other networks: organizational context, services provided, occupations and professions and the dominant occupations and professions.

ORGANIZATIONAL CONTEXT

Since the physical health network consists of a combination of public and private components, an idealized model of this network is shown in Figure 23-3. The hospital currently is a primary component of this network with the use of prepaid insurance and public insurance programs covering many of the costs. A specialized emerging field of service delivery since 1970 is that of home health care and holistic medicine.

Figures 23-4 and 23-5 show respectively the idealized government organization, and the organization of a typical hospital, showing the location of medical social work. In addition to the formal components of the physical health network, many individuals use the informal or folk network for physical problems. Examples of the folk network include use of herbs, vitamins, voodoo cults, psychic surgery, home remedies, etc.

SERVICES PROVIDED

A total listing of services provided by the physical health network would be rather lengthy. Examples of services provided within the physical health network include the following:

- Long term nursing care
- Short term nursing care
- Diagnostic testing, formulating diagnosis
- Prescribing restorative drugs
- Surgery
- Changing life styles to adapt to physical conditions
- Emergency first aid and outpatient units
- Death and dying counseling
- Individual and group counseling
- Social histories
- Physical restoration services, such as physical and occupational therapy etc.

Figure 23-3

IDEALIZED MODEL OF THE PHYSICAL HEALTH NETWORK

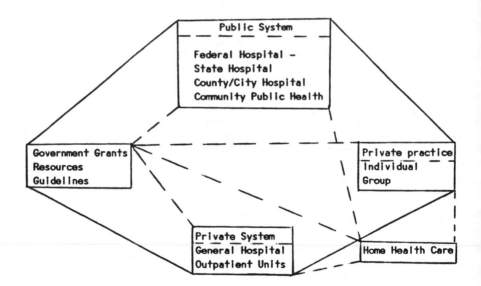

Figure 23-4

GOVERNMENT ORGANIZATION OF THE
PHYSICAL HEALTH NETWORK*

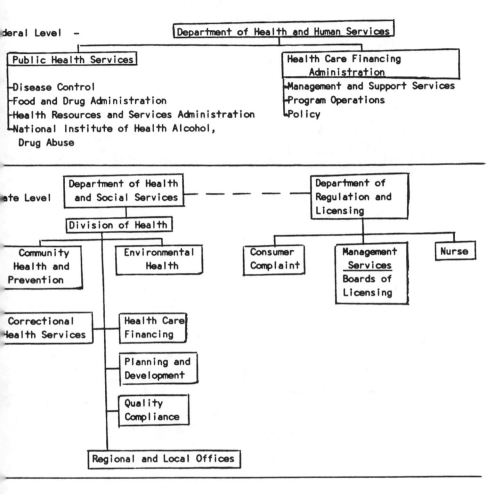

Federal Level —

Department of Health and Human Services

Public Health Services

⌐Disease Control
⌐Food and Drug Administration
⌐Health Resources and Services Administration
└National Institute of Health Alcohol,
  Drug Abuse

Health Care Financing
  Administration
⌐Management and Support Services
⌐Program Operations
└Policy

State Level

Department of Health
and Social Services

Division of Health

Department of
Regulation and
Licensing

Community
Health and
Prevention

Environmental
Health

Consumer
Complaint

Management
  Services
Boards of
Licensing

Nurse

Correctional
Health Services

Health Care
Financing

Planning and
Development

Quality
Compliance

Regional and Local Offices

Local Level   Public Health Units and Private Facilities

Source: Adapted from Office of the Federal Register. United States Government Manual
   1985/86, Washington, D.C.: U.S. Government Printing Office, 1985, p. 842 and
   Wisconsin Legislative Reference Bureau: Wisconsin Blue Book 1985/86, Madison,
   Wisconsin: Department of Administration, 1985 pp. 445, 512, 519.

Figure 23-5

Organization Chart of a Private Hospital
(Columbia Hospital, Milwaukee, Wisconsin)*

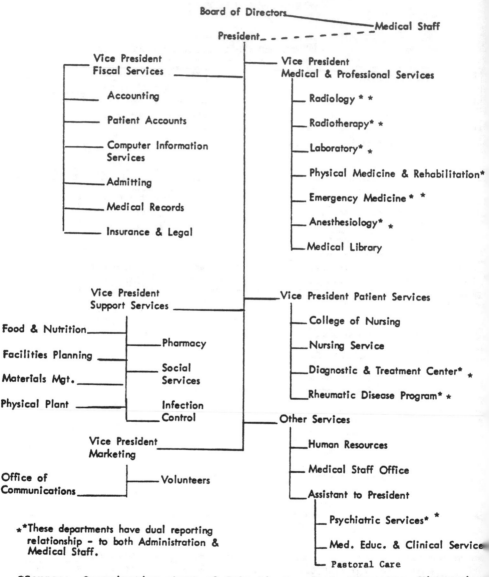

*Source: Organization chart of <u>Columbia Hospital</u>, Milwaukee, Wisconsin:
Columbia Hospital, Inc., 1985. Reprinted with the permission of Columbia
Hospital Corporation, Columbia Hospital, Inc. and Columbia Health, Inc.

- Tracing communicable diseases
- Home care (visiting nurses and social workers)
- Dental treatment and surgery
- Health education
- Industrial/office/occupational health care
- School health services
- Prepaid insurance plans/health maintenance organizations (HMO)
- Convalescent centers
- Speech correction
- Eye treatment and corrective lenses
- Sanitary health services etc.

OCCUPATIONS and PROFESSIONS

In the physical health network, there are over 100 medical specialities and a range of other human service professions which are involved in the network. Figure 23-6 shows a selected number of human service professions employed in various positions within the physical health network in 1980. The major professions are those of a physician (medicine) and nurse (nursing) which comprise about 34.04 percent of the selected human service employees. Other professions employed in the physical health network include social work, psychology, lawyer, clergy, therapist, etc. The largest occupations numerically are nurses aide (1,179,397), and health aide (242,961), however these are viewed as nonprofessional or paraprofessional positions.[10]

DOMINANT OCCUPATIONS and PROFESSIONS

The major professions in the physical health network are medicine (physician) and nursing (nurse).

MEDICINE - Figure 23-7 shows employment of physicians in 1980 by industrial classification. In 1980 there were an estimated 399,524 physicians in the United States. The vast majority of physicians are employed in the physical health network which includes public administration, 379,784 or 95.058 percent, 14,086 or 3.525 percent in other professional and related areas, and the remaining 5,654 or 1.417 percent in a variety of other industrial classifications. Figure 23-8 shows employment of physicians in the professional and related industrial classification in 1980. The majority of physicians are employed in an individual or group office, 169,276 or 62.049 percent, 88,065 or 32.281 percent are employed in hospitals, 7,251 or 2.659 percent are employed in other health related areas and the remaining 8,217 or 3.011 percent in a variety of other industrial classification.[11]

797

Figure 23-6

NUMBER AND PERCENT OF SELECTED HUMAN SERVICE
OCCUPATIONS AND PROFESSIONS EMPLOYED IN THE PHYSICAL
HEALTH NETWORK[1] IN 1980*

Selected Occupation and Profession	Number	Percent
Physician[1]	373,782	8.722
Optometrist	21,345	.497
Dentist	121,206	2.825
Podiatrist	7,282	.169
Nurse[1]	1,086,355	25.318
Pharmacist	36,483	.851
Dietician	51,127	1.191
Therapist	139,312	3.246
Physicians Assistant	17,659	.412
Social Work	68,655	1.600
Teacher	21,468	.501
Counselor	7,827	.182
Personnel Relations	25,640	.597
Administrator, Health, Education	104,947	2.445
Architect	381	.008
Psychologist	45,982	1.071
Urban Planner	98	.002
Recreation Work	12,234	.285
Clergy and Religious Work	7,638	.178
Lawyer	2,470	.057
Author	119	.003
Musician/Actor	299	.006
Painter	1,132	.026
Chemical Lab Technician	224,626	5.235
Dental Hygiene	43,802	1.020
Health Record	13,544	.315
Licensed Practical Nurse[1]	374,053	8.717
Guards	33,351	.777
Health Aide	242,961	5.662
Nurses Aide	1,179,397	27.487
Welfare Aide	6,832	.159
Child Care	18,715	.436
TOTAL	4,290,722	100.000

*Source: Adapted from United States Department of Commerce, Bureau of the Census, 1980 Census of Population Vol. 2 Subject Reports Part 7C: Occupation by Industry Washington, D.C.: U.S. Government Printing Office, 1984, pp. 295-664

[1] Excludes estimated figures for these occupations and professions which are employed in the mental health network.

798

Figure 23-7

NUMBER AND PERCENT OF PHYSICIANS AND NURSES
EMPLOYED BY INDUSTRIAL CLASSIFICATION IN 1980*

dustrial Classification	Physicians		Nurses	
	Number	Percent	Number	Percent
riculture/Forestry/Fishing	131	.033	461	.037
ning	57	.014	201	.016
nstruction	43	.011	326	.026
nufacturing	2,038	.511	15,582	1.277
ansportation/Communication tilities	450	.112	1,744	.143
olesale/Retail Trade	625	.157	2,147	.177
nances/Real Estate	1,146	.287	4,486	.369
siness and Repair	685	.172	20,735	1.708
rsonal Services	187	.047	6,067	.497
tertainment/Recreation	292	.073	546	.044
ofessional and Related (Except Health)	14,086	3.525	60,279	4.946
alth[1]	373,782	93.556	1,086,355	89.150
blic Administration	6,002	1.502	19,628	1.610
TAL	399,524	100.000	1,218,557	100.000

Source: Adapted from United States Department of Commerce, Bureau of the
Census,   1980 Census of Population Vol. 2.   Subject Reports Part 7C:
Occupation by Industry, Washington, DC: U.S. Government Printing Office,
1984 pp. 295–664.

The figures on health exclude estimates on those professions employed in
the mental health network.   The American Nurses Association Facts About
Nursing 1984–85, Kansas City Missouri: American Nurses Association, 1985,
p. 281, 20 estimates the number of physicians in 1982 as 449,389 (includes
residents) and the number of nurses in 1983 as 1,404,200.

Figure 23-8

NUMBER AND PERCENT OF PHYSICIANS AND NURSES EMPLOYED
IN THE PROFESSIONAL AND RELATED INDUSTRIAL CLASSIFICATION IN 1980*

Professional and Related Industrial Classification	PROFESSION			
	Physicians		Nurses	
	Number	Percent	Number	Percer
Physician Office	169,276	62.049	60,279	7.402
Hospital	88,065	32.281	566,934	69.6ᴜ.
Convalescent Home	586	.215	60,191	7.39
Other Health	6,665	2.444	58,379	7.168
Legal	126	.047	246	.03
Elementary and Secondary Education	786	.288	25,389	3.11
College and University Education	6,089	2.231	6,975	.85
Other Education Service	130	.047	669	.08
Religious Organization	374	.137	717	.08
Welfare Services	394	.144	33,101	4.06
Residential Welfare	53	.019	920	.11
Nonprofit membership Organization	265	.098	656	.08
Total	272,809[2]	100.000	814,456[2]	100.00

*Source: Adapted from United States, Department of Commerce, Bureau of the Census, !
Census of Population: Vol. 2 Subject Reports Part 7C: Occupation by Indust
Washington, D.C.: U.S. Government Printing Office, 1984.

[1] The American Nurses Association Facts About Nursing 1984-85 Kansas City, Missou
American Nurses Association, 1995 p. 56, 62, 281 estimates the number of physicians
office based practice in 1982 as 299, 191 or 66.6 percent and 109,472 or 24.4 percent
hospital based practice and the remaining 40,726 or 9 percent in other professio
practice. In 1983 there were an estimated 1,404,206 nurses of which 909,404 or 6
percent were employed in hospitals, 82,139 or 5.8 percent were employed in nursing
and the remaining 412,657 or 29.5 percent in other professional areas.

[2] The discrepancy in the totals between figures 23-7 and 23-8 is the exclusion of
specified professional and related from figure 23-8.

Medical education and practice has been revolutionized since 1910. Prior to that time, medical schools had minimal entrance requirements. Some physicians were educated in a university setting, a medical school, trained under an apprentice system, were intelligent lay readers, and others used folk medicines and a variety of pseudomedical remedies. Since 1910, partly as a consequence of the Flexner report (mentioned earlier), public pressure, and improvements in medical technology, both the educational system for training physicians and the form of medical practice changed. The major schools of medical practice can be classified as: homeopathic (emphasis on drugs), osteopathic (emphasis on musculoskeletal system), allopathic (alter disease process by acting against the causative agent, i.e., bacteria) and holistic (entire person approach). Most medical education today is of the allopathic school of medicine.

Currently the standards for a physician are: graduation from a medical school approved by the Council on Medical Education of the American Medical Association, license to practice in a specific state, participation in an approved training program in a specialty and certification by a specialty board.[12] Figure 23-9 shows the major specialties in medicine with the date a board was created to certify a physician in that specialty.

The physician in general performs the following major tasks in the role of a curative agent:

- Diagnostic workup
- Diagnosis of disease
- Medical histories
- Physical examinations
- Medical consultation
- Prescribe medication
- Perform surgery
- Emergency first aid
- Medical followup and referral.

Two recent developments in the medical health network are the role of a paramedic (1970's) and the physician's or medical assistant (1966). The paramedic is an emergency assistant who travels to the home or the scene of an accident to perform emergency first aid and provide initial diagnostic clues for the physicians. The intent is to enhance a critical diagnosis and treatment program for an individual who needs emergency care. The physician's or medical assistant has usually undergone an intensive short term training period of approximately one year. Some educational programs have developed a physician's or medical assistant curriculum leading to an associate of arts degree.

Figure 23-9

EXAMPLES OF SPECIALIZATIONS IN MEDICINE AND NURSING

Medicine	Nursing
General Practice	Aerospace
Opthalmology (1916)	Public Health (Community)
Otolaryngology (1924)	School Health
Obstectrics and Gynecology (1927)	Family (maternal and child care)
Dermatology (1923)	Psychiatric/Mental Health
Orthopedic Surgery (1934)	Occupational Health
Urology (1934)	Gerontology
Psychiatry (1934)	Medical/Surgical
Radiology (1934)	Nurse Anesthetist
(includes diagnostic and theraputic radiology)	Nurse/midwife
Colon and Rectal Surgery (1935)	Operating Room Nurse
Internal Medicine (1936)	Clinical Nurse Specialist
(includes gastroenteralogy, pulmonary, allergy,	Independent Nurse Practitioner
cardiovascular)	Administration
Forensic Pathology (1936)	Home Health Care
General Surgery (1937)	
Plastic Surgery (1939)	
Neurological Surgery (1940	
Neurology (1940)	
Anesthesiology (1941)	
Physical Medicine and Rehabilitation (1947)	
Thoracic Surgery (1948)	
Public Health (1948)	
Aerospace Medicine (1955)	
Occupational Medicine (1955)	
General Preventive medicine (1960	
Family Practice (1969)	
Nuclear Medicine (1971)	
Allergy and Immunology (1973)	
(Formerly pediatric allergy)	

*Source: Adapted from Henry Wechsler. Handbook of Medical Specialities New York, York: Human Sciences Press, 1976 and Josephine Dolar. Nursing in Socie Philadelphia, Penn: W.B. Saunders, Co., 1978 and American Nurses Association. Fa About Nursing 1984-85 Kansas City, Missouri: American Nurses Association, 1985.

NURSING--Figure 23-6 shows an estimated 1,086,355 nurses in the United States employed in the physical health network. Figure 23-7 shows 1,218,557 nurses employed in the United States by industrial classification. The vast majority of nurses are employed in the physical health network which includes public administration, 1,105,983 or 90.760 percent and the remaining 112,574 or 9.240 percent in other industrial classifications. Figure 23-8 shows registered nurses employed in the industrial classification of professional and related. In contrast to physicians, the vast majority of nurses are employed in hospitals, 566,934 or 69.609 percent, a small number in an individual or group office, 60,279 or 7.402 percent, an additional 118,570 or 14.559 percent in other health related areas, and the remaining 68,673 or 8.430 percent in a variety of other professional and related areas.[13]

There has been some system of registration for nurses required since 1903. Currently, the profession of nursing is divided into Registered Nurse and Licensed Practical Nurse, or Licensed Vocational Nurse. The registered nurse has completed a nursing program, either four year university, or a three year diploma school and has passed the State Board Examination. The state boards of nursing have used a uniform examination since 1950, consequently when a nurse passes a board examination of one state, they can become registered in a second state. The Licensed Practical Nurse or licensed vocational nurse has either completed a one year certificate program, or a two year associate of art degree program, and then takes specific state examinations. The current trend is to phase out the one year certificate programs and the three year diploma schools. Accreditation procedures for both registered nursing programs and licensed practical nursing programs have been achieved since 1949.[14]

In 1965 the American Nurses Association recommended the following minimal educational criteria for nursing; professional nurse - graduation from an accredited four year bachelor degree program in nursing, technical nurse - graduation from an accredited associate of arts degree program in practical nursing. The individual would then take the state exams to become a registered or licensed nurse. In addition, there are both master's and doctorate programs in nursing. As a consequence of the movement toward university based education and a bachelors degree as the entry professional degree, the number of diploma and hospital schools are decreasing. (See section on nursing history p. 787).

The role of a nurse is a restorative role as compared to the curative role of the physician. Nurses can be expected to perform the following functions:

- Nursing histories, and nursing diagnosis
- Patient and family nursing care and comfort measures
- Easing the psychological stress of physical or emotional illness
- General counseling and education regarding health status of client and family
- Evaluation of nursing care and monitoring the progress of a patient
- Implementing prescribed medical treatment
- Assisting the physician.

Specialization of the nursing profession has developed rapidly which is similar to the process occuring in medicine and the allied health professions. Figure 23-9 shows the major areas of specialization in nursing.

SOCIAL WORK

Figure 23-6 shows an estimated 68,655 social workers employed in the physical health network in 1980 in the approximately 3,418 medical hospitals which have social service departments.[15] Medical social work was formally established as a practice area in 1905 in New York and Boston. An individual generally needs a masters degree in social work from an accredited school of social work, however, there are provisions for nursing homes which allows an individual with a bachelors degree in social work from an accredited program to practice as a medical social worker. The general tasks of a medical social worker include:

- After care planning
- Home visitation
- Development of social histories
- Easing psychological stress of illness
- Easing psychological stress of hospital care
- Individual and family counseling.

The medical social worker, although employed primarily in hospitals, nursing homes and convalescent centers, engages in tasks at the individual, group, and community level.

INDIVIDUAL CASEWORK

This task would involve discussion with a patient on the nature of the hospital and what services are available. The medical social worker may discuss the patient's specific illness to alleviate their anxiety, and help them accept their medical condition and cope with it. For example, the task of helping an individual accept a terminal illness or hospice care is extremely difficult. Social workers assist people in the positive use

804

of whatever limited time is available to them. In many circumstances the social worker enables the individual patient to receive services through Title XIII and XIX of the Social Security Act and formalizes post discharge planning.

GROUP WORK

Social workers help to develop support groups of individuals with a common problem, such as burn victims, emphysema patients, etc. The purpose is to enable the person to see they are not the only ones with a problem, and to use the group for support.

COMMUNITY ORGANIZATION

This could involve many activities from lobbying for specific legislation, to having a community support a specific service program, such as a paramedic squad.

PERSONAL SOCIAL SERVICES

The physical health network in addition to physical elements of disease and trauma has recognized the significance of socio-emotional problems and the role of family members in the recovery of a patient. Consequently a variety of personal social services are offered within the physical health network (see Chapter 22 Personal Social Service). Some examples of personal social service programs in the physical health network include the following:

PROTECTIVE SERVICES

Spouse, child abuse and sexual assault programs, such as Domestic Assault and Sexual Assault treatment Center, Milwaukee, Wisconsin.

UTILITARIAN SERVICES

Day care and homemaking services, such as the Day Care Center at Family Hospital and Nursing Home, Milwaukee, Wisconsin.

DEVELOPMENTAL and SOCIALIZATION SERVICES

Counseling unwed mothers, such as Planned Parenthood, New York, New York and the various local chapters.

REHABILITATIVE and THERAPEUTIC SERVICES

Alcohol and drug counseling etc., such as DePaul Rehabilitation Hospital, Milwaukee, Wisconsin; Treatment Program for

Sex Offenders, Buena Park, California and Open Door Mental Health Center, Aspen Colorado.

SPECIAL POPULATIONS

The physical health network has contact with all segments of society and subsequently all different cultural and special populations (see Chapter 25 Special Populations and Chapter 24 Rehabilitation). Some examples of organizations and programs for special populations in the physical health network include the following:

ASIAN

Asian Health Services, Oakland, California; Pacific Asian Community Clinic, Los Angeles, California and Chinatown health Services, New York, New York.

BLACK

Watts Health Foundation, Los Angeles, California; Martin Luther King Health Center, Bronx, New York and Black Belt Community Health Center, Epes, Alabama.

EUROPEAN ETHNIC

Grenfell Association of America, New York, New York (French Canadian); Mennonite Health Assembly, Elkhart, Indiana (German) and Federation of Jewish Philanthropies, New York, New York.

NATIVE AMERICAN

Milwaukee Indian Health Board, Milwaukee, Wisconsin; American Indian Health Services, Chicago, Illinois; Auburn Indian Health Programs, Auburn, California and numerous facilities on reservations.

SAME SEX PREFERENCE

Special programs on medical problems, such as Homosexual Counseling Center, New York, New York and Lesbian Resource Center, Minneapolis, Minnesota.

SPANISH SPEAKING

Wisconsin Migrant Health Project, Wild Rose, Wisconsin; Borriquen Health Care Center, Miami, Florida; Barrio Comprehensive Child Health Care Center, San Antonio, Texas and Alianzo Centro Medico, Healdsburg, California.

WOMEN

Women's Health Institute (Good Samaritan Medical Center), and Bread and Roses, Milwaukee, Wisconsin; The Clinic for Women, Los Angeles, California and Cedar Rapids Clinic for Women, Cedar Rapids, Iowa.

ISSUES

There are some general issues in the physical health network which are reaching crisis proportions, such as cost, accessibility and other issues which relate to the professions.

COST ISSUES

Specifically, the cost of medical care has been increasing rapidly. For example, in 1955 the average cost of a room in a hospital per day was 23 dollars, and in 1986 over 200 dollars per day. This means that the average citizen is becoming more unable to afford medical care unless they have some form of prepaid health insurance program (3rd party payment), such as private insurance companies, employee benefits, etc. Long term care for the older population, or for a terminal illness is increasing, in comparison to short term care which increases the cost factor.

Two types of organizations which have developed since 1960 to help contain the cost of medical care are the Health Maintenance Organization (HMO's) and Health Systems Agency (HSA's). The Health Maintenance Organization attempts to reduce costs by having an individual utilize a specific medical service facility for all health needs. Upon joining an HMO an individual is not able to utilize any other medical service without the prior authorization of an HMO physician. A problem emerging with the HMO's is the failure to adequately address emergencies as perceived by the patients. That is, an individual may not be able to obtain prior authorization from an HMO physician for service, yet the physical condition may be life threatening. The Health System Agency (HSA) is a planning and coordinating body to reduce costs by avoiding duplication of services and coordinating services. A problem emerging with the HSA planning concept is that only one hospital in an area may have a specific service and the individual may have no means of transportation to get there, or when they are able to find transportation may not have insurance to cover the cost, or have adequate finances, which creates other problems.

Another cost containment measure is to place a limit or cap on how much insurance companies will pay for a specific service. At times this leads to inadequate service since certain tests or medical procedures will not be done since they are not covered by insurance. Lastly, the issue of rationing medical care has been suggested by some individuals. What it means, is one must assess whether the high cost of medical services should be utilized for individuals who are at high risk for recovery. This issue of rationing medical services or potentially excluding some populations from quality medical care is also a legal and ethical issue.

ACCESSIBILITY

A serious problem of medical care is developing amongst the poorer population group in the United States. Some individuals because of cost factors do not carry insurance, others lose insurance benefits because of unemployment, and others have restrictive or exclusionary insurance policies which excludes coverage on the illness they have.

Many of these individuals do not seek medical care or when they do are refused service from private hospitals or are given emergency service and transferred to a public hospital. A series of articles in the Milwaukee Journal (May 11-13, 1986) highlighted the problems the poor (who are ineligible for welfare programs) are having in obtaining health services.

PROFESSIONAL ISSUES

MEDICINE - For the profession of medicine a number of issues emerging are: the role of paramedics, exploration of new and unorthodox techniques, the concept of holistic and preventive medicine, bodily part transplants, ultra sonic scanning and diagnostic procedures and use of lasers and radiation for surgery and treatment. Of concern to the medical profession is the rapid development of specializations, each with their own professional organization. It is because of the rapid development of specializations that the American Medical Association has now recognized a specialty as a family physician or general practice. Since 1970, many ethical and legal issues have been raised. For example, in a case of terminal illness is euthanasia (mercy killing) acceptable, when does a person have a right to have life support systems halted, is clinical brain death 100 percent accurate. Other ethical questions include the practice of ghost operations (a different physician performs the surgery) and faulty prescriptions (antagnostic medication). A major issue facing the medical practitioner is the spector of a malpractice suit. The number of malpractice suits has been increasing, resulting in high financial cost for insurance, defensive medicine (performing more tests than needed which increases costs) and in some cases the practitioner leaving practice for other positions.

NURSING - In nursing, the debate regarding appropriate educational programs, such as diploma, university schools, or associate of arts degrees is a significant issue. Concurrent with the movement for university education, there is a concern about the issue of professional autonomy. The hospital nurse has been subservient to the physician, yet has a specific professional knowledge and expertise. There is some concern about specialization versus generalization in nursing, and the rapid development of independent nursing, or private practice and home health care. Similar to social work and other human service professions, private practice raises some ethical issues in terms of fees, selection of clients and accountability of the service. There is a further concern in nursing with the rapid development of the paraprofessional occupations, such as the one-year licensed practical nurse and this concern involves both the differentiation of tasks and educational qualifications

SOCIAL WORK - There is a need for social work to incorporate in their curriculum a cultural understanding of minority groups and their view of the physical health network and their perception of the causes of illness. That is, many individuals still use a folk system, herbs and may be suspicious of the formal physical health network, such as Native Americans. In addition, there is a growing awareness that the needs of women are somewhat different than the general population, therefore, the perception of women has become an extremely important element in the delivery of services in the physical health network. Social work has to have an adequate understanding of the physical health network, of medical terminology, of the causes of disease, and current trends in physical health.

SUMMARY

The physical health network in the United States actually consists of a variety of components, such as the professions of medicine and nursing, hospitals and nursing homes, public health, and allied health professions. In 1982-84 there were approximately 374,410 medical facilities, employing an estimated 6.1 million individuals, with expenditures of an estimated 371.6 billion dollars, an estimated 1.5 billion patient visits to physicians, hospitals, etc., and 2,354,000 resident patients.

There was a brief analysis of the historical development of each of the major components of the physical health network: the professions of medicine and nursing, hospitals, public health, and allied health professions. The physical health network as we know it, is a product of the last 100 years. There has been a slow development from the idea of supernatural and external causes of disease, and the use of medicine men and a priest/physician, to the concept of a lay physician, natural causes, and currently a high degree of specialization within the physical health network and related occupations and professions.

Examples of the variety of occupations and professions involved in the physical health network were discussed, with an emphasis on the fact there are over 100 specialized occupations and professions. The roles of the physician, nurse and social worker were discussed.

Some major issues were discussed, such as the increase in the cost of medical care, increases in long-term care, preventive medicine, and the role and development of paramedical services. In each of the major professions, medicine, nursing and social work, a number of issues were discussed which included the following: in medicine, the concept of holistic medicine and specialization, cost factors, accessability to health service by the poor, and ethical issues including malpractie; in nursing, the struggle for uniformity in educational standards and problems associated with home health care; and in social work, an understanding of the perspectives of minority groups of the causes of illness and their concept of the physical health network.

FOOTNOTES

*This chapter was reviewed for comments by Karen Robison, Associate Professor of Nursing, School of Nursing University of Wisconsin-Milwaukee, Milwaukee, Wisconsin.

[1]The estimates used to show the size of the physical health network, attempted to exclude figures from the mental health network. It is difficult to clearly differentiate between mental health and physical health since there is an overlapping of resources between the two networks. (Mental health is covered in Chapter 20 Mental Health Network). As a consequence of the overlapping between these two networks, the figures on physical health would contain some figures which also relate to the mental health network. The physical health network also includes, prepaid insurance programs, hospices for death and dying, and title XVIII and XIX of the Social Security Act. (See Chapter 19 Income Maintenance Network for the Social Security Act).

[2]The physical health network consists of at least 100 separate occupations and professions. It is impractical to explore all facets of physical health, consequently the focus of this chapter is on medicine, nursing, and social work.

[3]Of interest in reviewing the history of nursing, is the variation between cultures on the status of the nurse, or "wise woman," and whether it was a male or a female dominated occupation. The Hebrews held the "caring individual" in high esteem and they were primarily women and independent from the physician. In Celtic Ireland, the "wise woman," or a combination of mid-wife/nurse, was held in high esteem and was independent from the physician.

In Medieval Europe (400-1500) there was a mixture of male and female nurses and a small number of female physicians. Some early medical schools trained both men and women, and special military male nursing orders were established, such as the Knights Hospitallers (1050) and the Order of Trinitarins (1197). Male dominance of the medical profession has occurred since 1600, with a subservient role of nursing, until 1960. The female domination in the profession of nursing has occurred since 1700.

[4]In the preformal education era of nursing (pre-1850) there was a close relationship between religion/nursing and social services. Many of the same individuals that are important in the history of nursing are important in the history of social work, such as St. Dymphania (580), St. Vincent de Paul (1576), Sister Seton (1800), Dorthea Dix (1850), Louise Schuyler (1890), Clara Barton (1870) and Harriet Tubman (1820-1913). In particular with the historical figures of St. Vincent de Paul, and Clara Barton, there were the rudiments of early medical social work.

[5]These figures are taken from the American Journal of Nursing Vol. 18 No. 6 (June 1981), p. 112 and American Nurses Association Facts About Nursing 1984-85, Kansas City Missouri: American Nurses Association, 1985 p. 138. In 1965, the American Nursing Association had recommended the bachelors degree as the entry professional degree for registered nurses and the associate degree as the entry degree for licensed practical nurses.

[6]An example of a professional organization for hospital personnel is the American Hospital Association, 840 N. Lake Shore Drive, Chicago, Illinois 60611 organized in 1898. In addition, the organization responsible for accrediting hospitals is the Joint Commission on Accreditation of Hospitals, 875 Michigan Ave., Chicago, Illinois 60611 organized in 1951, and the organization for accrediting educational programs in hospital administration is the Accrediting Commission on Education for Health Services Administration, One Du Pont Circle, Suite 420, Washington, D.C., 20036, organized in 1961.

[7]Some professional associations for hospices and nursing homes include the following: National Hospice Organization 1901 N. Fort Myer Drive, Suite 402, Arlington, Virginia 22209; American College of Health Care Administrators, P.O. Box 5890. 4650 East-West Hwy. Bethseda, Maryland 20814 and American Health Care Association, 1200 15th Street NW, Washington, DC 20005.

[8] An example of a professional organization for personnel in public health is the American Public Health Association, 1015 15th St. NW, Wshington, D.C. 20005, organized in 1872. Educational programs in public health, have been accredited by the American Public Health Association since 1974.

[9]Other specialties were discussed in other chapters such as art, dance, and music therapy in Chapter 4, Asethetic Network; recreation therapy in Chapter 14 Leisure and Recreation Network; homemakers Chapter 22 Personal Social Service Network; rehabilitation counseling in Chapter 24 Rehabilitation Network, and psychiatric social work in Chapter 20 Mental Health Network.

In this historical overview, the segment of the physical health network known as prepaid insurance plans, group practice, and third party practice and payment, were not discussed. The main reason for exclusion of these parts of the network is one of expediency. It is impractical to delineate in detail all parts of a network that is as diverse as physical health.

[10]Occupations not included in Figure 23-6 are: dietetic aid, dietetic assistant, dietetic technician, nutritionist, health planner, long-term care administrator, nursing home administrator, community health educator, medical communicator, medical illustrator, medical photographer, public health education, school health educator, chemistry technologist, cysto technologist, hematology technologist, histologic technician, medical technologist, microbiological technologist, nuclear medical technologist, pathologist, cardiopulmonary technician, circulation technologist, dialysis technician, inhalation therapist, rehabilitation specialist (corrective, orthotist, prothetist), rehabilitation counselor, ophthalmic assistant, and technician. For a brief description of many of the physical health occupations and professions, and information on related professional associations, the reader is referred to Ann Allen, Introduction to Health Professions, 2nd Edition, St. Louis, Missouri, C.V. Mosby Co., 1976.

Some professional organizations in the allied health professions include the following: American Dental Association, 211 E. Chicago Avenue; Chicago, Illinois 60611; American Association of Medical Assistants. One E. Wacker Drive, Chicago, Illinois 60601; American Physical Therapy Association, 1156 15th St., NW,

Washington, D.C. 20005; Department of Allied Health Education, American Medical Association, 535 N. Dearborn St., Chicago, Illinois 60610; American Chiropractic Association, 2200 Grand Avenue, Des Moines, Iowa, 50312 and American Occupational Therapy Association, 6000 Executive Blvd, Suite 200, Rockville, Maryland 20852.

[11]This distribution of employment of physicians in 1980 is derived from American Nurses Association, Facts About Nursing 1984-85, Kansas City, Missouri: American Nurses Association,, 1985 p. 281 and adaptation of material from the United States Department of Commerce, Bureau of the Census. 1980 Census of Population Vol. 2 Subject Reports Part 7C: Occupation by Industry, Washington, D.C.: U.S. Government Printing Office, 1984 pp. 295-664.

These two resources have somewhat different totals on the number of physicians in the United States, however combining the two resources provides a reasonable distribution of where physicians are employed.

[12]In addition to the requirement for graduation from a medical school, a person must have a bachelor's degree prior to admission to medical school. For a more detailed description of medical specialities, the reader is referred to Henry Wechsler, Handbook of Medical Specialties, New York, New York: Human Sciences Press, 1976. This book contains the names and addresses of all the specialty certification boards. The main professional association for allopathic medicine is the American Medical Association, 135 N. Dearborn Street, Chicago, Illinois, 60610. Medical schools are accredited by the Council on Medical Education of the American Medical Association. This council receives feedback and input from the Liaison Committee on Medical Education (AMA) and the Association of Medical Colleges, One Dupont Circle NW, Washington, D.C. 20026. For the person who is interested in osteopathic medicine, the major organization is the American Osteopathic Association, 212 E. Ohio St., Chicago, Illinois 60611. The major professional organization for holistic medicine is the National Council on Holistic Therapeutics and Medicine, P.O. Box 15859, Philadelphia, Pennsylvania, 19103. The major professional organization for homeopathic medicine is the National Center for Homeopathy, 7297 H Lee Highway, Falls Church, Virginia 22042.

[13]Other aspects of nursing, such as licensed practical nurse, vocational practical nurse, are not discussed. The licensed practical nurse (LPN) is a significant proportion of employees in the physical health network. Approximately 525,980 LPN'S were employed in the physical health network in 1983. Many of these individuals are employed in the emerging field of home

health care (19,959 or 3.8 percent).   In addition there were an estimated 385,830 orderlies, aides, attendants, etc. employed in the physical health network in 1983.

[14]The major professional associations in nursing are the American Nurses Association, 2420 Pershing Rd., Kansas City, Missouri 64108 and the National League for Nursing, Ten Columbus Circle, New York, New York, 10019.   Nursing education programs whether baccalaureate and higher degree, diploma school, practical nurse or associate degree are accredited by the National League for Nursing.

[15]Figures are derived from the Department of Health, Education and Welfare, Health United States: 1978, Washington, D.C.: U.S. Government Printing Office, 1978.   Major professional associations in social work include the Council on Social Work Education, 1744 R St. NW, Suite 400, Washington, D.C. 20009 and the National Association of Social Workers, 7981 Eastern Ave., Silver Spring Maryland, 20910   or the local chapter of the National Association of Social Workers.   For a more detailed analysis of medical social work, the reader is referred to Jeanette Regensburg, Toward Education for Health Professions, New York, New York: Harper and Row Publishers, 1978.

Estimates on the number of medical social workers vary depending upon the source.   The 1980 census of population as indicated in Figure 23-6 shows an estimated 68,655 medical social workers and a survey by the National Association of Social Workers in 1982 has an estimate of 51,750.

SUGGESTED READINGS

Ann Allen.   Introduction to Health Professions. 2nd Ed.   St. Louis, Missouri: C. V. Mosby Co., 1976. This book provides a nontechnical overview of the variety of occupations and professions in the physical health network.

Donald Atkinson.   Magic, Myth and Medicine. Greenwich, Connecticut: Fawcett Publications, 1958.   For a short history of medicine and significant historical figures, this book is extremely useful. Although dated, the book provides a sound overview.

Josephine Dolan.   Nursing and Society: A Historical Perspective.   14th Ed.   Philadelphia, Pennsylvania: WB Saunders Co., 1978. This standard text in nursing is a comprehensive overview of the history of nursing, current organization and issues.

John Duffy. The Healers: The History of American Medicine.
Chicago, Illinois: University of Chicago Press, 1979. An
interesting book as it blends historical and sociological
approaches in analyzing the profession of medicine. For the
individual who desires to obtain a perspective on the profession of medicine and how it has changed this is a highly
recommended book.

Jeanette Regensburg. Toward Education for Health Professions.
New York, New York: Harper and Row Publishers, 1978. This
book explores the roles of human service professions, such
as the human service generalist and social work. For a
review of some of the allied health professions this book
serves as a nontechnical introduction.

George Rosen. History of Public Health. New York, New York:
MD Publications, 1958. This book provides some startling
insights into the poor sanitation and living conditions of
the majority of the population in Western Europe and the
United States until well into the 19th century. For the
individual who is not aware of the significance of the
public health movement this book is highly recommended.

Peter Vallitutte and Florence Christoplos. Interdisciplinary
Approaches to Human Services. Baltimore, Maryland: University Park Press, 1977. This collection of articles on the
human services has articles on the following physical health
and related professions: orthotics and prosthetics, dentistry; physical medicine and rehabilitation, nursing, speech,
hearing and language pathology, pediatrics, occupational
therapy, physical therapy, social work and medicine.

Henry Wechsler. Handbook of Medical Specialties. New York, New
York. Behavioral Publications Inc., 1976. For the individual who is seeking information on the various specialties in
medicine, this book is an excellent resource for information
and references.

REFERENCES

Allen, Ann. Introduction to Health Professions, 2nd Edition.
St. Louis, MO: C.V. Mosby Co., 1976.

American Hospital Association. Guide to the Health Care Field:
1985 Edition. Chicago, IL: American Hospital Association,
1985.

American Nurses' Association. Nursing: A Social Policy State-
    ment. Kansas City, Missouri: American Nurses Association,
    1980.

American Nurses Association. Standards for Psychiatric and
    Mental Health Nursing Practice, Kansas City, Missouri:
    American Nurses Association, 1973.

American Nurses Association. Facts About Nursing 1984-85.
    Kansas City, Missouri: American Nurses Association, 1985.

Atkinson, Donald. Magic, Myth and Medicine. Greenwich, CT:
    Fawcett Publications, 1958.

Bowers, John. An Introduction to American Medicine. Washing-
    ton, D.C.: U.S. Government Printing Office, 1975.

Clay, Rotha Mary. The Medieval Hospitals of England. New York,
    New York: Barnes and Noble Inc., 1966.

Conway, William, "The MRA and the Social Worker: Common Career
    Preparations" Medical Record News April 1978, pp. 26-31.

Dankmeyer, Charles, Jr. "Orthotics and Prosthetics," pp.
    237-252 in Vallitutte, Peter and Florence Christoplos,
    Interdisciplinary Approaches to Human Services. Baltimore,
    MD: University Park Press, 1977.

Dolan, Josephine. Nursing and Society: A Historical
    Perspective, 14th Edition. Philadelphia, PA: W.B. Saunders
    Co., 1978.

Duffy, John. The Healers: The History of American Medicine.
    Chicago, IL: University of Chicago Press, 1979.

Fox, Lawrence. "Dentistry," pp. 61-80, in Vallitutte, Peter and
    Florence Christoplos, Interdisciplinary Approaches to Human
    Services. Baltimore, MD: University Park Press, 1977.

Friedlander, Walter and Robert Apte. Introduction to Social
    Welfare, 5th Edition. Englewood Cliffs, NJ: Prentice-Hall
    Inc., 1980.

Goldstein, Louis. "Physical Medicine and Rehabilitation," pp.
    267-278, in Vallitutte, Peter and Florence Christoplos,
    Interdisciplinary Approaches to Human Services. Baltimore,
    MD: University Park Press, 1977.

Gordon-Davis, Karen and Judith Strasser. "Nursing," pp.
155-172, in Vallitutte, Peter and Florence Christoplos,
Interdisciplinary Approaches to Human Services. Baltimore,
MD: University Park Press, 1977.

Griffin, Gerald and Joan Griffin. History and Trends of
Professional Nursing, 7th Edition. St. Louis, MO: C.V.
Mosby Co., 1973.

Hoffnung, Audrey. "Speech, Hearing and Language Pathology," pp.
387-414 in Vallitutte, Peter and Florence Christoplos.
Interdisciplinary Approaches to Human Services. Baltimore,
Maryland: University Park Press, 1977.

Johnson, Robert. "Pediatrics," pp. 252-266, in Vallitutte,
Peter and Florence Christoplos, Interdisciplinary Approaches
to Human Services. Baltimore, MD: University Park Press,
1977.

Lansing, Stella and Pat Carlson. "Occupational Therapy," pp.
211-236, in Vallitutte, Peter and Florence Christoplos,
Interdisciplinary Approaches to Human Services. Baltimore,
MD: University Park Press, 1977.

Latimer, Ruth. "Physical Therapy," pp. 279-306, in Vallitutte,
Peter and Florence Christoplos, Interdisciplinary Approaches
to Human Services. Baltimore, MD: University Park Press,
1977.

Milwaukee Journal May 11-13, 1986

Minahan, Anne (Ed.). Encyclopedia of Social Work, 18th Edition.
Washington, D.C.: National Association of Social Workers,
1986.

"News" American Journal of Nursing. Vol. 18 No. 6 (June 1981).

Osler, William. The Evolution of Modern Medicine. New Haven,
CT: Yale University Press, 1921.

Office of the Federal Register, United States Government
Manual, 1985-86, Washington, D.C.: U.S. Government Printing
Office, 1985.

Regensburg, Jeanette. Toward Education for Health Professions.
New York, NY: Harper and Row Publisher, 1978.

Rosen, George. History of Public Health. New York, New York:
MD Publications, 1958.

Smillie, Wilson. <u>Public Health: Its Promise for the Future</u>. New York, New York: Macmillan Co., 1955.

Suchman, Edward. <u>Sociology and the Field of Public Health</u>. New York, New York: Russell Sage Foundation, 1963.

United States Department of Commerce Bureau of the Census, <u>Statistical Abstract of the United States: 1986 (106th Edition)</u>, Washington, D.C.: U.S. Government Printing Office, 1985.

United States Department of Commerce, Bureau of the Census, <u>1980 Census of Population Vol. 2. Subject Reports. Part 7C: Occupation by Industry</u>, Washington, D.C.: U.S. Government Printing Office, 1984.

United States Department of Commerce, Bureau of the Census, <u>1982 Census of Service Industries</u>, Washington, D.C.: U.S. Government Printing Office, 1984.

United States, Department of Health, Education and Welfare, <u>Health The United States: 1978</u>, Washington, D.C.: U.S. Government Printing Office, 1978.

United States Department of Health and Human Services, <u>Employees in Nursing Homes in the United States: 1977 National Nursing Home Survey</u>, Washington, DC: U.S. Government Printing Office, 1981.

Wechsler, Henry. <u>Handbook of Medical Specialties</u>. New York, NY: Behavioral Publications, Inc., 1976.

Wisconsin Legislative Reference Bureau, <u>Wisconsin Blue Book 1985-1986</u>, Madison, Wisconsin: Department of Administration, 1985.

Wilcox, Claire. <u>Towards Social Welfare</u>. Homewood, IL: Richard D. Irwin Co., 1969.

CHAPTER 24

REHABILITATION NETWORK*

"There is, however, a trend in rehabilitation toward
greater emphasis on independent living services for the
disabled. Consequently, the term "vocational rehabilitation" is gradually being replaced by "rehabilitation"
in legislation, agency names, and literature."
(Bitter:1979:IX).

INTRODUCTION

The disabled, historically in society at different times
have been: chastised, made the brunt of jokes, neglected, and
at other times have been denied services of a financial, psychological, and medical nature. For years, the treatment of the
disabled was related to the treatment of the poor, consequently,
the close linkage between income maintenance programs and the
treatment of the poor, and of the disabled continued into the
20th Century.

Development of a specialized rehabilitation network and subsequently a profession of rehabilitation counseling, was a
product of the mid 20th Century. Rehabilitation counseling's
initial focus was on the blind, deaf, and physically disabled,
and later expanded to include persons with mental and social
disability, including mental retardation. Since the late
1970's, the focus of the rehabilitation network has been less on
social disability, and more on physical and mental disability.
The initial focus of programs for the disabled was on vocational
rehabilitation. Social and psychological counseling was later
recognized as an important component of rehabilitation, and most
recently, the focus has been expanded to include independent
living. Although employment continues to be a crucial goal of
most programs serving the disabled, with the initiation of
independent living programs, services have been expanded to
include self-help activities directed toward assisting the disabled to live in the least restrictive environment possible.
This chapter describes the development of rehabilitation counseling as a profession, indicates the variety of human service
professions in the rehabilitation network and the role of social
work.

SIZE

For many years the rehabilitation network was almost synono-
mous with state vocational rehabilitation agencies, and specific

819

private agencies for helping the disabled. Since 1945 there has been a rapid increase in the development of rehabilitation centers and hospitals. Figure 24-1 provides some estimates on the size of the rehabilitation network.

In the United States in 1982-84 there were an estimated 25,055+ agencies working with different populations of disability. Of these agencies 95+ are part of the federal/state rehabilitation system and 24,960+ were private or public rehabilitation centers, hospitals, workshops, etc. Expenditures for these facilities were estimated at 12.4 billion dollars and employed an estimated 441,437 individuals. The rehabilitation network directly served an estimated 2.9 million individuals. There is some degree of overlap between the rehabilitation network, and the physical health network (see Chapter 23), the mental health network, (see Chapter 20), and the employment and manpower network (see Chapter 17) through the use of medical and convalescent homes, mental health facilities and job training facilities.

Estimates on the number of disabled individuals in the United States vary depending upon the source used. The National Arts and Handicapped Information service, estimated there were approximately 57.7 million people in the United States with some form of disability. The variety of disabilities include the following: 12.5 million individuals who are temporarily disabled due to injury, burns, etc.; 11.7 million individuals who are physically disabled, such as those who use wheel chairs, suffering from cerebral palsy, muscular dystrophy, etc; 11.0 million individuals with a hearing impairment; 8.2 million individuals with a visual impairment; 6.8 million individuals with a mental disability, such as mentally disturbed, ill and retarded; 2.4 million individuals who are deaf; 2.1 million individuals who are institutionalized for mental retardation and illness; 1.7 million individuals at home with a degenerative illness and 1.3 million individuals who are blind. In addition to the rehabilitation network described above, these disabled individuals also receive services from other networks, such as income maintenance, education, employment and manpower, etc.[1] This estimate on the number of disabled is consistent with the Statistical Abstract of the United States: 1986 (106th Edition) which has a figure of about 59 million.

HISTORICAL DEVELOPMENT

Services to the disabled i.e blind, deaf, etc. historically have been linked with the treatment of the poor, and these individuals were labeled as the unfortunate poor, or the worthy poor, and received some social services. In contrast, the able

Figure 24-1

ESTIMATED SIZE OF THE REHABILITATION NETWORK IN
1982 and 1984*

Rehabilitation Agency

Selected Characteristics	Federal/State Rehabilitation (1984)	Other Facility (1982) [1]	Total
Number of Agencies	95+	24,960+	25,055+
Expenditures (Dollars)	1,360,000,000	11,041,163,000	12,401,163,000
Number of Employees	34,000+	407,437	441,437
Population Served (Number)	936,000	1,978,297+*	2,914,297

* Sources: Adapted from United States Department of Commerce, Bureau of the Census, Statistical Abstract of the United States: 1986 (106th Ed.), Washington, D.C.: U.S. Government Printing Office, 1985 p. 48, 116, 117, 355, 378, 384; United States Department of Commerce, Bureau of the Census, 1982 Census of Service Industries, Washington, D.C.: U.S. Government Printing Office, 1984 p. 6, 7; United States Department of Commerce Bureau of the Census, 1980 Census of Population. Vol. 2 Subject Reports Part 7D: Persons in Institutions and Other Group Quarters, Washington, D.C.: U.S. Government Printing Office, 1984.

[1] Other facilities include sheltered workshops, private institutions, rehabilitation centers and homes for the disabled, mentally retarded etc.

bodied individuals were labeled as the unworthy poor, and social services were grudgingly provided. In spite of the close association of services for the disabled with the poor, some specialized programs for the disabled were developed within the religious network, and income maintenance networks (see Chapter 15, Religious Network and Chapter 19, Income Maintenance Network).

GENERAL DEVELOPMENT

DEAF--Some examples of early programs for the deaf include: St. John of Beverly England who taught deaf mutes (685); Juan Paulo Bonet of Spain developed teaching methods for deaf individuals (1584); John Bulwer developed a text book for the teaching of the deaf (1648); Johann Amman (1669-1724), became an early expert in the teaching of the deaf and the establishment of the first public school for treatment of the deaf was in Paris, France (1760). In the United States the father of treatment programs for the deaf was Thomas Gallaudet (1787-1851). Gallaudet founded the Hartford School for the Deaf in 1815, and used sign language as a primary technique for learning. Two of his sons, followed in his footsteps: Thomas Gallaudet opened a church for the deaf in New York City, and Edward Gallaudet was instrumental in the development and opening of Gallaudet College in Washington, D.C. (1864). Gallaudet College is a coeducational liberal arts college for the deaf, and has special programs for the training of teachers for the deaf.

BLIND--Some early examples of programs for the blind include: St. Basil (800), when he established a special hospice for individuals who were blind; the reign of Louis X of France, 1260 was instrumental in establishing a hospice in Paris for veterans who were blind returning from the crusades, and during the reign of Louis XVI of France in 1784 a special institution was established in Paris for the training of the blind. The father of training programs for the blind in the United States was Louis Braille (1809-1852). Braille developed the system of raised dot printing (braille) to teach the blind to read and write.

DISABLED--Some early programs for the physically disabled include the following: during the reign of Phillip IV in France, (1300), monasteries were used as a place to house disabled veterans returning from the crusades; during the reign of Elizabeth in England (1592) a disability pension was provided for veterans; during the reign of William IV in England (1833), some educational programs for the disabled were developed and in Bavaria, John Nepinak (1832) developed a specialized school for disabled individuals, which was the beginning of the movement for orthopedic oriented schools.

MENTAL RETARDATION--Some early programs which focused on the mentally retarded include: the St. Vincent DePaul Society (1576), and their institutions for the mentally ill; Jean Itard (1775-1838), and his work with the mentally ill in Paris, France and Edouard Seguin (1812-1880) who developed a set of teaching techniques for the retarded.[2]

UNITED STATES DEVELOPMENT

In the United States, early programs for the disabled were implemented through four separate but related systems: public assistance programs, veterans programs, religious and voluntary organization programs, and vocational technical education programs, including the state and federal vocational rehabilitation program.

PUBLIC ASSISTANCE PROGRAMS--Generally, disabled individuals were treated similarly to the poor and, when family members could no longer care for them, they were sent to almshouses, such as Boston, Massachusetts (1632), or if ill to a charitable hospital. Some individuals were provided financial assistance through the prevailing income maintenance program. These income maintenance programs prior to 1935 consisted of the state or local general assistance program and since 1935, Blind, Old Age and Disabled Assistance programs (since 1974 incorporated into the Supplemental Security Income program - see Chapter 19 Income Maintenance).

VETERANS PROGRAMS--The United States government provided a pension for veterans with a service connected disability beginning with the Revolutionary War in 1776. A specialized home for retired and homeless veterans, specifically naval personnel, was established in 1811, and a home for soldiers was established in 1853. After the Civil War (1861-64) there was an expansion of programs for veterans which included a home for veterans who were disabled at Togus, Maine (1866). The first World War with its mass armies and numerous veterans who were disabled provided an impetus for the development of vocational education and rehabilitation services for returning soldiers. In 1916, the National Defense Act recognized the necessity of providing rehabilitation services for veterans in the United States. The Smith Hughes Act of 1917 provided vocational education for veterans, and in 1918 a specialized rehabilitation program was established for veterans. The Veterans Bureau was organized in 1921, and later became the Veterans Administration (1933). The Veterans Administration is responsible for a wide range of programs including: vocational retraining, rehabilitation, medical care, GI bill and other services. Initial development of vocational rehabilitation programs was linked closely to services provided for veterans who were disabled (see Chapter 6 Military Network).

RELIGIOUS and VOLUNTARY ORGANIZATION PROGRAMS--Special institutions for the physically disabled were developed in New York (1863), and orthopedic hospitals were developed in New York, New York (1864), Philadelphia, Pennsylvania (1884), and Boston, Massachusetts (1893). Schools for the deaf were organized in Baltimore, MD (1812), and Hartford, Connecticut (1817). Schools for the mentally retarded were established in Massachusetts (1848) and Pennsylvania (1853). The use of religious and voluntary organizations for the disabled population developed rapidly after (1865) with programs, such as the Salvation Army (1879), the American Red Cross (1881), which established a hospital for the physically disabled under Clara Barton (1917), the National Tuberculosis Association under Dr. Lawrence Flick (1904), Goodwill Industries under Dr. Edgar Helms (1902), the Easter Seal Society under Edgar Allen (1907), the Curative Workshop of Milwaukee, Wisconsin (1919) and the Institute for the Crippled and Disabled in New York (1917) (see Chapter 15 Religious Network).

VOCATIONAL TECHNICAL EDUCATION and STATE and FEDERAL REHABILITATION PROGRAMS--A specialty area known as rehabilitation counseling, was an outgrowth of the three service programs mentioned above, and the development of state and federal programs in vocational education and rehabilitation. Early state programs in rehabilitation include: Minnesota (1917), and both Massachusetts and Wisconsin (1918). The initial federal legislation establishing both vocational education and state and federal rehabilitation programs, was between 1916 and 1920 and focussed on veterans who were disabled, and their vocational retraining.

In 1920, the Vocational Rehabilitation Act was passed which provided for a state and federal system of vocational rehabilitation. Within 18 months 34 states had enacted legislation to provide vocational rehabilitation services for citizens who were disabled. The focus of these early programs, was closely tied to vocational education training. The administration of these programs was initially with the Department of Labor, Federal Board of Vocational Education. By 1933 vocational education and vocational rehabilitation became separate administrative entities, however, the programs were still closely linked together. There was close cooperation between vocational education and vocational rehabilitation in the development and implementation of a program for an individual. Vocational rehabilitation ultimately came under the jurisdiction of the United States Department of Health, Education and Welfare in 1953 and in 1980 the United States Department of Education.

The state and federal program, as the central program for the rehabilitation of individuals who are disabled, has undergone a slow expansion of its functions since 1920. The Social Security Act of 1935 for the first time provided rehabilitation programs with a permanent base of federal support. In 1943 vocational rehabilitation amendments included persons who were mentally ill and mentally retarded as a disability, and eligible for rehabilitation programs. A critical piece of legislation for rehabilitation programs were the amendments of the Rehabilitation Act of 1954, which provided federal support for the training of human service professions in rehabilitation, and allied fields, such as social work. This legislation also programmatically separated rehabilitation, and vocational education as different service networks. As a consequence of this act, there was a rapid increase in educational programs in rehabilitation counseling from 10 programs in 1954, to the current 90+ programs in 1986. There was a corresponding increase in federal monies available to allied programs, such as social work, psychology, psychiatry, nursing and occupational therapy.

The 1965 Rehabilitation Act further expanded the definition of disability to include social disability, alcohol and drug use, and provided funds to promote the development of sheltered workshops. The rehabilitation network expanded from a primary focus on vocational retraining and placement to, a primary focus on counseling, and development of independent living arrangements for the disabled. With these changes in primary focus and the expanding population for services, the term vocational rehabilitation was slowly replaced with the term rehabilitation counseling. Along with the expansion of the state and federal system of rehabilitation, there has been a corresponding increase in rehabilitation centers and facilities of a private nature, which provide comprehensive medical, psychological, psychiatric, social and rehabilitation services. Many of these facilities are organized as independent private corporations and make use of matching federal and state monies for implementing their programs. This expansion of public rehabilitation programs and services is clearly reflected in the 1973 Rehabilitation Act and subsequent amendments. This legislation was focussed on ensuring that the severly disabled would receive priority attention for services, authorized independent living rehabilitation services, and established the National Institute of Handicapped Research. The decade of the 1980's has seen a retrenchment in financing of these programs. Figure 24-2 summarizes some of the major historical events in the development of services for the disabled.

Figure 24-2

HISTORICAL TIME LINE OF THE
REHABILITATION NETWORK

685 AD	St. John's Home for the deaf
800	St. Basil - Hospice for the blind
1300	Monasteries used for disabled veterans.
1576	St. Vincent De Paul Society - Home for the disabled.
1632	Disabled placed in poor house or hospital
1776	Disability Pension for Revolutionary War Veterans
1811	Home for Naval Personnel
1853	Soldiers Home established
1902	Goodwill Industries
1916	National Defense Act for Veterans
1917	Smith Hughes Act - vocational education for veterans
1919	Curative Workshop
1920	Vocational Rehabilitation Act
1927	National Rehabilitation Association
1933	Vocational rehabilitation administratively separated from vocational education
1943	Rehabilitation includes mental illness
1954	Training Act. Program and service seperation rehabilitation from vocational education.
1965	Rehabilitation includes alcohol and drugs
1968	Rehabilitation Counseling recognized as a distinct profession
1975	Accreditation of professional programs

STRUCTURE

The rehabilitation network and its structure can be described from: its organizational context, services provided, occupations and professions and dominant occupations and professions.

ORGANIZATIONAL CONTEXT

The formal rehabilitation network consists primarily of state and federal agencies and private agencies. In addition some individuals utilize an informal folk system, such as friends, relatives, and mutual support groups for psychological and at times financial support. The primary federal agency in rehabilitation is the Department of Education, Special Education, Rehabilitation Services, which oversees the specific state agencies and their programs. The organization of the rehabilitation network at the federal level, and in a typical state organization is shown in Figure 24-3.

Private facilities, such as Curative Rehabilitation Center, Goodwill Industries, Jewish Vocational service, etc., have a different organizational structure than the state and federal system. Although private agencies range from small workshops serving a few clients, to large rehabilitation centers providing comprehensive services, certain commonalities exist between them. In general, private facilities are accredited by the Commission on Accreditation of Rehabilitation Facilities (CARF) and cooperate through the various state associations of rehabilitation facilities.[3] Figure 24-4 shows the typical structure of a private rehabilitation agency.

SERVICES PROVIDED

Depending upon whether the rehabilitation program is part of the state and federal network, or a private facility the services provided will differ. In general, services provided in the rehabilitation network would include the following:

- Diagnostic study
- Vocational evaluation
- Vocational planning
- Vocational placement
- Casework service
- Counseling service
- Referral to other professions
- Assistance with the development of independent living arrangements
- Post employment follow-up

Figure 24-3

GOVERNMENT ORGANIZATION IN THE REHABILITATION NETWORK*

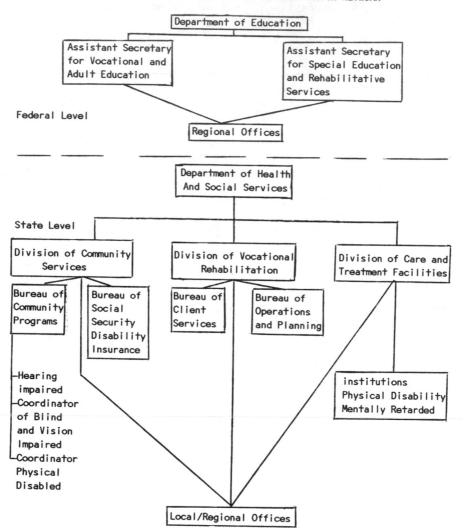

Sources: Adapted from: Office of the Federal Register, United States Govern-
ment Manual 1985-86, Washington D.C.: U.S. Government Printing
Office, 1985, p. 840 and Wisconsin Legislative Reference Bureau,
Wisconsin Blue Book 1985-1986 Madison, Wisconsin: Department of
Administration, 1985, p. 512, 517, 518, 521.

Figure 24-4

ORGANIZATION OF A PRIVATE MEDICAL
REHABILITATION AGENCY*

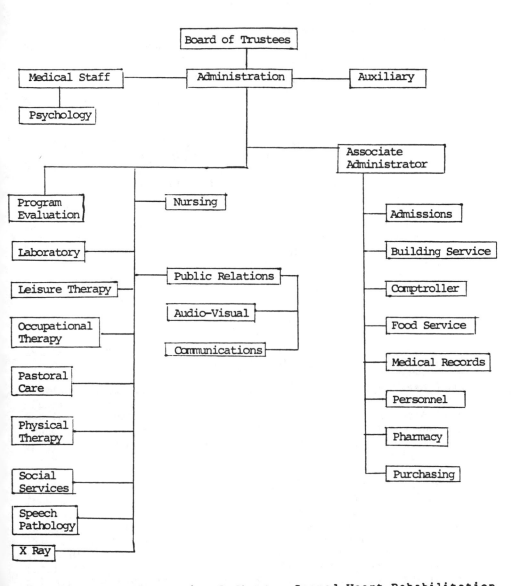

urce: Adapted from Functional Chart - Sacred Heart Rehabilitation
Hospital. Milwaukee, Wisconsin, 1982. Reprinted with the
permission of Sacred Heart Rehabilitation Hospital, Inc.

- Integrative planning (Supplemental Security Income, Social Security, Comprehensive Employment Training Act, Work Incentive Program, special education, etc.).

OCCUPATIONS and PROFESSIONS

Rehabilitation agencies such as the state and federal network and private facilities employ a wide range of human service professions. Figure 24-5 shows a selected number of human service professions employed in the rehabilitation network.

The following occupations and professions are involved in the rehabilitation network:

audiologist, corrective therapist, dance therapist, dentist, diet therapist, employment counselor, employment interviewer, guards and watchmen, law enforcement and security specialists, home economist, industrial therapist, librarian, manual arts therapist, medical records, music therapist, nurse, occupational therapist, ophthalmologist, optometrist, oralogical therapist, orthopedic, orthotist, pathologist, physical therapist, physician and physician specialties (psychiatrist, neurologist), prosthetist, psychologist, radiologist, recreation therapist, rehabilitation counselor, social worker, and vocational education teacher.

DOMINANT OCCUPATIONS and PROFESSIONS

Since the detailed classification of the 1980 Census of Population Occupation by Industry report only lists counselors as an occupational group (education, vocational, rehabilitation) under one classification it is difficult to accurately provide a figure on rehabilitation counselors. If one looks at the industrial areas where rehabilitation counselors are usually employed one can reasonably estimate the number of rehabilitation counselors. Figure 24-6 shows an estimate of counselors employed by industrial classification in 1980.

Assuming that rehabilitation counselors are usually employed in health care and social services one can estimate there are at least 20,029 rehabilitation counselors. A detailed breakdown of this estimated number shows the following distribution: 1,054 or 5.26 percent employed in residential care, 7,818 or 39.03 percent employed in health care, 3,988 or 19.92 percent in other social services, and 7,169 or 35.79 percent in vocational rehabilitation. This estimated figure of 20,029 rehabilitation counselors is consistent with an estimated number of 18,000 in 1976.[4]

830

Figure 24-5

Number and Percent of Selected Human Service Occupations and
Professions Employed in the Industrial Classification of
Job Training and vocational Rehabilitation of the Social Service
Industrial Classification in 1980*

Selected Occupation and Profession	Number	Percent
Counselor (Education, Vocational, Rehabilitation)	7,169	24.795
Social Work	6,551	22.658
Welfare Aide	521	1.812
Therapist (Occupational, Corrective, Speech Correction, Recreation, Art, Dance, etc.	2,066	7.145
Teacher	4,963	17.165
Physician[1]	88	.304
Nurse	604	2.089
Dietician	42	.145
Psychologist	514	1.777
Librarian	57	.197
Recreation Worker	219	.757
Clergy, Religious Worker	245	.847
Lawyer	51	.176
Painter/Sculpter	78	.269
Licensed Practical Nurse	292	1.009
Guards/Watchmen	380	1.314
Nursing Aide	1,376	4.759
Child Care	1,390	4.807
Personnel Training/Relations	2,306	7.975
Total	28,912	100.000

*Source: Adapted from United States Department of Commerce, Bureau of the
Census, 1980 Census of Population. Vol. 2 Special Reports Part 7C: Occupation
by Industry, Washington, D.C.: U.S. Government Printing Office, 1984 pp.
295-664. This listing is representative not exhaustive. In addition there
were 1,054 counselors in residential care, 7,818 in health care and 3,988 in
other social services. It is presumed that counselors in these other areas
are primarily rehabilitation counselors and that most counselors in job
training and voca- tional rehabilitation are rehabilitation counselors.

[1]The American Nurses Association, Facts About Nursing 1984-85. Kansas City,
Missouri: American Nurses Association, 1985, p. 281 shows a figure of 2,685
physicians specializing in physical medicine and rehabilitation in 1982.

Figure 24-6

Number and Percent of Counselors (Education, Vocational, Rehabilitation) Employed by Industrial Classification in 1980*

Industrial Classification	Number	Percent
Agriculture	76	.039
Mining	9	.005
Construction	104	.053
Manufacturing	932	.482
Transportation, Communication, Public Utilities	295	.153
Wholesale Trade	117	.060
Retail Trade	295	.153
Finance/Real Estate	811	.429
Business/Repair	1,779	.920
Entertainment/Recreation	285	.147
Personal Service	336	.173
Professional and Related (Except Health Care, Social Service, Education)	2,652	1.371
Health Care[1]	7,818	4.046
Social Service[1]	12,211	6.318
Education[1]	147,131	76.146
Public Administration	18,368	9.505
Total	193,219	100.000

*Source: Adapted from United States Department of Commerce, Bureau of the Census, 1980 Census of Population Vol. 2 Special Reports Part 7C: Occupation by Industry. Washington, D.C.: U.S. Government printing Office, 1984 pp. 295-664.

[1] The occupational classification of counselor includes education, vocational and rehabilitation. One can assume that those employed in health care, social service and public administration are primarily rehabilitation counselors. Those counselors employed in education are primarily education and vocational counselors.

Although the first rehabilitation counselor on a full time paid basis was Regina Dolan in 1918, rehabilitation counseling as a distinct profession developed since 1945. Development of rehabilitation counseling as a profession involved two concurrent movements: professional organizations, and educational standards. Shortly after passage of the Rehabilitation Act of 1920, individuals working in the field, such as William Faulkes of Wisconsin, amongst others, organized the National Civilian Rehabilitation Conference in 1924. This organization changed its name to the National Rehabilitation Association (NRA) in 1927, and a subdivision of this organization is the National Rehabilitation Counseling Association (NRCA). This association was the dominant professional association until the establishment of the American Rehabilitation Counseling Association (ARCA), which was established in 1957, as a division of the American Personnel and Guidance Association (APGA), which was organized in 1952 and changed its name to the American Association for Counseling and Development in 1985. The American Rehabilitation Counseling Association developed a code of ethics for the profession in 1968.

The National Rehabilitation Association and the American Rehabilitation Counseling Association formed a joint committee in 1974 for professional certification, and developed certification procedures through an independent body known as the Commission on Rehabilitation Counselor Certification (CRCC).[6] For certification as a rehabilitation counselor an individual must: 1) graduate from an accredited masters degree program in rehabilitation counseling, or possess a masters degree from a non-accredited program in rehabilitation counseling, or possess a masters degree in a related field, such as social work, or possess a bachelors degree in rehabilitation counseling, or a bachelors degree plus experience. 2) All graduates from other than accredited master's degree programs, must accumulate varying periods of experience, under the supervision of a certified rehabiliation counselor before becoming eligible to apply for certification. 3) complete successfully the certification examination. In 1976 of the estimated 18,000 rehabilitation counselors, 5,000 or 27.8 percent were certified through the Commission on Rehabilitation Counselor Certification.

Certification procedures as a rehabilitation counselor paralleled the development of accreditation standards for masters degree programs in the field. Educational guidelines emerged as rehabilitation counselor programs increased at the university level. Courses in vocational rehabilitation were offered as early as 1929 at Harvard University, and major programs in the field were offered at New York University (1941), Ohio State University (1944) and Wayne State University (1946).

With the impetus for the development of rehabilitation counseling programs, as a consequence of federal funding and the Rehabilitation Act of 1954, concern arose over the uniformity of educational programs. Guidelines for rehabilitation counseling as a profession were established in 1968 by the American Rehabilitation Counseling Association. The National Council of Rehabilitation Education was formed in 1970 representing educators at both the undergraduate and graduate level. This group in conjunction with the professional counseling associations established an independent body called, the Council on Rehabilitation Education (CORE) in 1971, which had as its charge the development of accreditation standards. This body developed procedures and guidelines for accreditation of professional programs at the graduate level in 1974, and implemented them in 1975.[7] Both certification and accreditation processes focus on graduate level education, however, guidelines are developing for certification of individuals with a bachelor's degree.

The following is a sampling of the type of problems a rehabilitation counselor is confronted with: alcohol, drugs, arthritis, blindness, cardiovascular problems, deafness, developmental disability, cerebral palsy, epilepsy, mental retardation, neurological disorders, orthopedic disabilities, psychiatric disability, renal failure, speech impairment, spinal cord problems, etc. The rehabilitation counselor generally follows a sequential process in providing services to individuals. A typical sequential process in rehabilitation counseling is as follows:

- Preliminary diagnostic study
- Referral and diagnostic study
- Extensive evaluation
- Written individual rehabilitation program
- Counseling and guidance
- Physical and mental restoration
- Training program, job placement
- Post employment services.

The rehabilitation counselor, although having a knowledge of counseling techniques similar to those possessed by other human service professions, such as social work and psychology, differs from these professions in having a more indepth knowledge of: disabilities, assessment techniques for vocational interest and aptitudes, placement procedures for training and a vocational development orientation. There is some overlap in function with social workers in the counseling and guidance process, and differences between the two professions occurs in the depth of psychological involvement, focus of intervention, and philosophical orientation toward the client. Rehabilitation counselors are more attuned to the social, psychological, and physical implications of the disabled status, as well as, vocational training and placement procedures and options. In addition, services which assist the disabled in achieving their independent living goals, are becoming an increasingly large part of the skills of the rehabilitation counselor.

SOCIAL WORK

In 1980, according to the Occupation by Industry Subject Report there were 95,260 social workers employed in the industrial classifications of health, residential care and vocational rehabilitation. Of this number 68,655 are probably medical social workers (which overlaps with rehabilitation) and the remaining 26,605 can be considered part of the rehabilitation network. Of these 26,605 social workers in the rehabilitation network, 20,054 or 75.38 percent are employed in residential care, and 6,551 or 24.62 percent are employed in job training and rehabilitation agencies (see Figure 24-5).

In general, the social worker employed in the rehabilitation network performs tasks and duties which are similar to those of a medical social worker. That is, the functions of a social worker include:

- Emotional support for individuals as they go through the stresses of illness and subsequent treatment
- Follow-up services for each individual
- An independent living circumstance when warranted
- Enable individuals to cope with a specific illness
- Diagnostic workups
- The understanding of a person's social and psychological background in order to determine whether some part of a person's disability are of a psychosomatic nature.

Although most social workers would be involved on an individual casework level there are opportunities for individuals to become involved in a group process with different types of cases, and to become involved in community organization activities, and policies for disabled individuals.[8]

CASEWORK

The social worker would discuss medical problems with the patient and their family. In this discussion one of the critical areas of concern is for the patient and the family to accept the disabling condition and find ways to cope with the disability to one's optimum level of performance. In some cases these discussions would involve plans for independent living.

GROUP WORK

The social worker would use a group process to discuss feelings, attitudes and ways in which one can cope with a disabling condition. The group could be specific to one form of disability, such as orthopedic, blind etc., or may be a general group or a mixture of individuals with a disabling condition and their non-disabled spouse.

COMMUNITY ORGANIZATION

The social worker could advocate for specific program changes, for legislation at the local, state and federal level, or become involved in fund raising. The social worker could organize a mutual support group or even a political action group.

PERSONAL SOCIAL SERVICES

The personal social service network, has linkages with all other networks (see Chapter 22 Personal Social Service). Some examples of the personal social service programs in the rehabilitation network are as follows:

PROTECTIVE SERVICES

Guardianship and custody for the mentally incompetent, transportation for the aged, nursing homes, housing projects, sheltered workshops, foster homes, group homes, child abuse programs, and an ombudsman program for the aged. Examples of some organizations include the Curative Rehabilitation Center, Sacred Heart Rehabilitation Hospital and Ombudsman Program for the Aging and Disabled in Milwaukee, Wisconsin.

UTILITARIAN SERVICE

Advocacy for consumer rights, home care and homemaking services, and day care centers. Examples of some organizations are the Disabled American Veteran's local chapter and United Association for Retarded Citizens local chapter.

DEVELOPMENTAL and SOCIALIZATION SERVICES

Summer camps for disabled youth and adults, recreation and sports programs, special olympics, family sensitivity programs, marital and family counseling and programs for independent living. Examples of some organizations which provide these services are the Easter Seal Society of the local community, the Young Men's Christian Association and Young Women's Christian Association of the local community.

REHABILITATIVE and THERAPEUTIC SERVICES

Special programs for alcohol and drug abuse, and sensitivity to individuals with low self-esteem who are possibly suicidal. Examples of some organizations which provide these services include Lutheran Social Services, public school systems and the Salvation Army.

SPECIAL POPULATIONS

The rehabilitation network like other networks has some programs and services oriented to members of special populations (see Chapter 25 Special Populations). The following are some examples of programs, oriented toward special populations:

ASIAN

Asian community centers and health services, such as Asian Health Services, Oakland, California; Greater Chinatown Community, New York, New York; Korean Association of Southern California, Los Angeles, California and the Oriental Service Center, Los Angeles, California.

BLACK

Black self-concept centers, Inner City Councils, health centers, such as the Black Belt Community Health Center, Epes, Alabama; Martin Luther King Jr. Health Center, Bronx, New York; National Urban League local chapter; Pride Inc. local chapter and Watts Health Foundation Inc., Los Angeles, California.

EUROPEAN ETHNIC

International Institutes, such as Milwaukee, Wisconsin and St. Paul, Minnesota.

NATIVE AMERICAN

Indian Social Services, Bureau of Indian Affairs, Indian Health Centers, such as the Milwaukee Indian Health Board, Milwaukee, Wisconsin; Indian Health Board of Minneapolis, Minneapolis, Minnesota; Bureau of Indian Affairs, Washington, D.C.; Native American Indian Center, Oklahoma City, Oklahoma and the Detroit American Indian Center, Detroit, Michigan.

SAME SEX PREFERENCE

Awareness Centers, support groups and counseling centers, such as the Gay Community Counseling Center in San Francisco, California.

SPANISH SPEAKING

Spanish Centers, such as Milwaukee, Wisconsin, Centro Hispano Catolico, Miami Florida; La Clinica De La Raza, Oakland California; Spanish Center of Racine, Kenosha and Walworth Co., Wisconsin and Spanish Catholic Center, Washington, D.C.

WOMEN

Self-concept centers and programs, such as the Women's Center, Waukesha, Wisconsin; local Women's Crisis Lines and New Concept Self-Development Center of Milwaukee, Wisconsin.

ISSUES

Some of the major issues facing the rehabilitation network are societies attitude toward disability, legal and ethical concerns, reduction in program funding and professional education.

ATTITUDES

Society in general has neglected the needs of the disabled. In the 1960's and 1970's there was a growing awareness and recognition of the special needs of the disabled. Since 1980 there has been less national and local attention on the disabled population and pre-1950 attitudes seem to be more prevalent.

LEGAL and ETHICAL CONCERNS

In 1982 and in 1986 there were two United States Supreme Court decisions regarding the rights of the parents to allow disabled infants to die instead of using extraordinary medical services to maintain the life of the child. In both Baby Jane Doe cases, the parents were given the right to allow the infants to die.

In 1986, a female with a master's degree in social work who was extremely disabled asked for the legal right to allow herself to die by refusing extraordinary medical services. In both cases, legal and ethical concerns are raised regarding the maintenance of life in certain cases and raises some questions on our attitudes toward the disabled.

REDUCTION of PROGRAMS

Many of the programs for the disabled which developed in the 1960's and 1970's relied on federal and state funds. With the budgetary reductions at the federal and state levels there has been a corresponding reduction in services available.

PROFESSIONAL ISSUES

Rehabilitation counseling developed as a subspecialty of the general field of counseling, and has had some difficulty in differentiating itself, from its earlier roots in vocational education and vocational training. A number of competing professional organizations, such as the National Rehabilitation Association (NRA), the National Rehabilitation Counseling Association (NRCA), and the American Rehabilitation Counseling Association (ARCA) have made it difficult to develop a united front in developing a professional identification. Since part of the task of a rehabilitation counselor, is to provide individual counseling with a disabled individual, there is some overlap with a variety of other human service professions, such as psychiatry, psychology and social work.

In social work education there should be an awareness that the need for rehabilitation services for the disabled in our society will increase, as the population of the United States becomes older, as the focus of service changes to include learning disabilities, and as the disabled are mainstreamed into American society. At an early date social work was involved with the disabled, however many schools do not have specific content about disabilities, unless it is associated with medical social work content. Further efforts on behalf of the schools of social work to include more content on the disabled should be encouraged. Since a social worker is working in conjunction with a rehabilitation counselor, it would be helpful for each of these professions to have a basic understanding and knowledge of each other's orientation, and the tasks which they are expected to perform.

SUMMARY

Historically the treatment of the disabled was closely linked with the treatment of the poor. It was not until the early 20th Century that specialized programs were developed for the disabled. The rehabilitation network consists of public rehabilitation agencies, of which there are approximately 95 state agencies, and a variety of private agencies which are estimated at about 24,960+. Expenditures for 1982-1984 were estimated 12.4 billion dollars. The network employs approximately 441,437 individuals and serves approximately 2.9 million individuals.

Although there was an early precedent for services with the blind, physically disabled, deaf, mentally retarded etc., these programs were operated primarily through the religious network and other voluntary agencies. The development of public programs on a large scale, did not occur until 1920, with the Vocational Rehabilitation Act. This early state and federal system was closely related to that of vocational education and training, with vocational rehabilitation developing as a separate system in 1933. Numerous religious, voluntary, and private agencies have been involved in rehabilitation, such as the Curative Rehabilitation Center of Milwaukee, Wisconsin which was established in 1919, Easter Seal Society, Goodwill Industries, Jewish Vocational services, etc.

Rehabilitation counseling as a profession, had a slow development between 1920 and 1954. With the passage of the Rehabilitation Act in 1954, there was an impetus for the development of rehabilitation counseling programs with the use of federal money. Since 1954 there has been a move to separate rehabilitation counseling from the general area of vocational education and vocational retraining, with different educational requirements. Subsequently, programs for training in rehabilitation counseling now consist of a master's degree in rehabilitation counseling, with allowances for allied disciplines, such as social work. Along with educational standards, a certification procedure has been developed and several states have implemented or are in the process of developing licensing requirements.

The role of the rehabilitation counselor and the social worker was discussed. The social worker in the rehabilitation network, performs tasks which are similar to those of a medical social worker. Some of the issues which face rehabilitation counseling as a profession include: professional identification, since there are at least two major professional groups in rehabilitation counseling, and some ambiguity between the role of a rehabilitation counselor in comparison to other human service professions. Social work education needs to develop curriculum content with an emphasis on the disabled. As the United States population increases in age, as learning disabilities are more readily recognized and as the disabled are mainstreamed into American society, the role of the rehabilitation network will take on added significance in human services. The United States has a number of issues related to the disabled, such as attitude (negative or neutral), reduction of funding and more recently legal and ethical issues related to the right to die and who makes these decisions.

FOOTNOTES

*This chapter was reviewed for comments by, Ann B. Meyer (Ph.D., CRC), Professor and Director/Rehabilitation Counselor Education Program, and Bobbie J. Atkins (Ph.D., CRC), Assistant Professor and Assistant Coordinator, Rehabiliation Counselor Education Program, School of Education, University of Wisconsin-Milwaukee, Milwaukee, Wisconsin.

1. Estimates on the size of the rehabilitation network are adapted from the following sources: Nancy Weinberg "Rehabilitation" in Donald Brieland, Lela Costin and Charles Atherton. Contemporary Social Work 2nd Ed., New York, New York: McGraw Hill, Inc., 1980, pp.301-302; United States Department of Commerce, Bureau of the Census, Statistical Abstract of the United States: 1986 (106th Edition), Washington, D.C.: U.S. Government Printing Office, 1985 pp. 48, 116, 117, 355, 378, 384 and 1982 Census of Service Industries, Washington, D.C.: Government Printing Office, 1984, p. 6, 7.

    The reader is referred to Chapter 19 Income Maintenance Network for more details on services for the blind, deaf, disabled, etc., Chapter 17, Employment and Manpower Network, and Chapter 23 Physical Health Network which overlap with the rehabilitation network.

2. Jean T. Itard and Edouard Seguin were well known for their work with the mentally ill. Historically there has been a close linkage of the treatment of the mentally ill with that of the mentally retarded. As indicated earlier, treatment of the disabled was closely related with that of treatment of the poor. For details on the mental health network, the reader is referred to Chapter 20 Mental Health Network.

3. The Commission on Accreditation of Rehabilitation Facilities is located at 2500 North Pantano Road, Tucson Arizona, 85715. The Commission has accredited about 1,300 facilities by 1981, with programs consisting of: physical restoration, personal and social development, vocational development, sheltered employment, work activity and speech pathology and audiology.

4. Estimates on the number of rehabilitaton counselors in the United States is taken from the Department of Commerce, Bureau of the Census, <u>1980 Census of Population, Vol. 2 Subject Reports Part 7C: Occupation by Industry</u>, Washington, D.C.: U.S. Government Printing Office 1984, and the Department of Health, Education and Welfare, <u>Health United States: 1978</u>, Washington D.C.: U.S. Government Printing Office, 1978.

5. Some examples of professional associations in the rehabilitation network include the following: The National Rehabilitation Association and its subdivision, the National Rehabilitation Counseling Association, 522 Case Street, N.W., Washington D.C. 20005; The American Rehabilitation Counseling Association and its parent organization the American Association for Counseling and Development, 5999 Stevenson Avenue, Alexandria, Virginia, 22304; Goodwill Industries of America, 9200 Wisconsin Ave., Washington, D.C., 20014; National Easter Seal Society for Crippled Children and Adults, 2023 W. Ogden Ave., Chicago, Illinois, 60612; National Association of Jewish Vocational Services, 600 Pennsylvania Ave. S.E., Washington, D.C., 20003 and American Coalition of Citizens with Disabilities Inc., 1346 Connecticut Ave. N.W., Washington, D.C., 20036.

6. The Commission on Rehabilitation Counselor Certification is located at 162 N. State Street, Suite 602, Chicago, IL 60601

7. The accrediting organization for rehabilitation counseling is the Council on Rehabilitation Counseling, 3101 S. Deerborn St., Chicago, IL 60616. An excellent resource book on the field of rehabilitation is Robert Goldenson, <u>Disability and Rehabilitation Handbook</u>, New York, New York: McGraw Hill Inc., 1978.

8. For further information on the profession of social work contact the National Association of Social Workers, 7981 Eastern Avenue, Silver Spring, Maryland 20910 or the local office of the National Association of Social Workers.

SUGGESTED READINGS

James Bitter, <u>Introduction to Rehabilitation</u>, St. Louis, Missouri: C. V. Mosby Co., 1979. This standard textbook provides a comprehensive overview of rehabilitation as a field of practice.

Brian Bolton and Marceline Jacques. Rehabilitation Counseling: Theory and Practice. Baltimore, MD: University Park Press, 1978. For the individual who desires more information on the profession of rehabilitation counseling, this book would be an excellent source.

John Cull and Richard Hardy. Vocational Rehabilitation: Profession and Process. Springfield, IL: Charles C. Thomas Co., 1972. Although this book is dated it does provide a historical perspective on the field of rehabilitation, its various subspecialties and the functions of rehabilitation counseling.

Alfred W. McCauley and Lewis Carr. Role Differentials in Rehabilitation Counseling and Social Work Serving the Disabled. Washington, D.C.: National Rehabilitation Counseling Association, 1972. Although dated this book develops a comparison between the role of a rehabilitation counselor and a social worker. For comparing these two professions this book is highly recommended.

C. Esco Obermann. A History of Vocational Rehabilitation in America. Minneapolis, MN: T. S. Denison and Company, Inc., 1967. Although dated, this book provides an indepth analysis of the treatment of the disabled in the United States and the emergence of professional groups.

Peter Vallitutte and Florence Christoplos. Interdisciplinary Approaches to Human Services. Baltimore, MD: University Park Press, 1977. This edited work of articles contains an article on rehabilitation counseling and social work.

REFERENCES

Bitter, James. Introduction to Rehabilitation. St. Louis, MO: C.V. Mosby Company, 1979.

Brieland, Donald, Lela Costin and Charles Atherton. Contemporary Social Work 2nd Ed. New York, New York: McGraw Hill Inc., 1980.

Bolton, Brian and Marceline Jaques. Rehabilitation Counseling: Theory and Practice. Baltimore, MD: University Park Press, 1978.

Committee for the Handicapped. Directory of Organizations Interested in the Handicapped 1976. Chicago Illinois: Committee for the Handicapped, 1976.

Cull, John and Richard Hardy. Vocational Rehabilitation: Profession and Process. Springfield, IL: Charles C. Thomas Company, 1972.

Friedlander, Walter and Robert Apte. Introduction to Social Welfare, 5th Edition. Englewood Cliffs, NJ: Prentice Hall Inc., 1980.

Goldenson, Robert ed. Disability and Rehabilitation Handbook. New York, New York: McGraw Hill Inc., 1978.

Goldstein, Louis. "Physical Medicine and Rehabilitation," pp. 267-278 in Vallitutte, Peter and Florence Christoplos. Interdisciplinary Approaches to Human Services: Baltimore, Maryland: University Park Press, 1977.

Howells, John G. and M. Livia Osborn. A Reference Companion to the History of Abnormal Psychology (2 Vol.), Westport, Connecticut: Greenwood Press, 1984.

McCauley, W. Alfred and Lewis Carr. Role Differentials in Rehabilitation Counseling and Social Work Serving the Disabled. Washington D.C.: National Rehabilitation Counseling Association, 1972.

Minahan, Anne (Ed.). Encyclopedia of Social Work, 18th Edition. Washington, D.C.: National Association of Social Workers, 1986.

National Rehabilitation Association. Ethnic Difference Influencing the Delivery of Rehabiliation Services: American Indian; Black American; Mexican American; Puerto Rican. Washington, D.C.: National Rehabilitation Association, 1971.

Obermann, C. Esco. A History of Vocational Rehabilitation in America. Minneapolis, MN: T.S. Denison and Company Inc., 1967.

Office of the Federal Register, United States Government Manual, 1985-86. Washington, D.C.: U.S. Government Printing Office, 1985.

President's committee on Employment for the Handicapped, A Program Profile 1973, Washington, D.C.: U.S. Government Printing Office, 1973.

Schumacher, Brockman. "Rehabilitation Counseling" pp. 357-372 in Peter Vallitutte and Florence Christoplos. Interdisciplinary Approaches to Human Services. Baltimore, MD: University Park Press, 1977.

Sussman, Marvin (Ed.) Sociology and Rehabilitation. Washington, D.C.: American Sociological Association, 1966.

United States Department of Commerce, Bureau of the Census, Statistical Abstract of the United States: 1986 (106th Edition). Washington D.C.: U.S. Government Printing Office, 1985.

United States Department of Commerce, Bureau of the Census, 1980 Census of Population: Vol. 2 Subject Reports Part 7C: Occupation by Industry, Washington, D.C.: U.S. Government Printing Office, 1984.

United States Department of Commerce, Bureau of the Census, 1982 Census of Service Industries, Washington, D.C.: U.S. Government Printing Office, 1984.

United States Department of Commerce, Bureau of the Census, 1980 Census of Population. Vol. 2 Subject Reports Part 7D: Persons in Institutions and Other Group Quarters, Washington, D.C.: U.S. Government Printing Office, 1984.

United States, Department of Education, Office of Special Education and Rehabilitative Services, Directory of National Information Sources on Handicapping Conditions and Related Services, Washington, D.C.: U.S. Government Printing Office, 1982.

United States Department of Health, Education and Welfare. Health: The United States: 1978, Washington, D.C.: U.S. Government Printing Office, 1978.

University of Wisconsin-Milwaukee. "Rehabilitation Counselor Education Program: Student Handbook, 1980". Milwaukee, WI: Department of Rehabilitation Counseling, 1980.

Wilcox, Claire. Toward Social Welfare. Homewood, IL: Richard D. Irwin Company, 1969.

Wisconsin Legislature Reference Bureau, Wisconsin Bluebook, 1985-1986, Madison, WI: Department of Administration, 1985.

Wright, George. Total Rehabilitation. Boston, Massachusetts: Little Brown and Co., 1980.

Vandergoot, David and John Worrall. Placement in Rehabilitation. Baltimore, MD: University Park Press, 1979.

SECTION 5

SPECIAL POPULATIONS and MAJOR THEMES and ISSUES
in HUMAN SERVICES and SOCIAL WORK

The United States is one of the more culturally pluralistic societies in the world, consequently a social service delivery system needs to address the specific needs of special populations. Chapter 25, Special Populations, provides an historical overview of Asians, Blacks, European Ethnic, Native Americans, Same Sex Preference, Spanish Speaking and Women and the role of social work with these groups. Chapter 26 is a review of the major themes of this book and speculates on issues which will be with us for the next 10-20 years

CHAPTER 25

SPECIAL POPULATIONS*

"Through all of recorded history, men have
dreamed of a world in which there would be
both complete equality of opportunity for
all and perfect fraternity of all. Yet,
such a world is still a Utopia - a world
that exists only in the minds of those who
have closed their eyes to facts and refuse
to face reality." (Brown and Roucek:
1952:3)

INTRODUCTION

Diversity of population groups as a consequence of sex,
race, religion, ethnicity, and related differences in values,
attitudes and life styles is a fact of life in American
society. In the 1940's and early 1950's the assumption was that
varied groups in the United States were becoming assimilated
into one mass culture in American society. The decade of the
1960's has shown the American people that cultural identification and discrimination against various populations is not
dead. There has been a resurgence of various groups attempting
to maintain their own cultural identification and uniqueness and
to reduce discrimination, yet become a viable part of American
society. Although the focus of this chapter is on cultural
diversity and pluralism, the term "special" is used to connote
that each group has had a unique and distinct history and has
distinct or special needs, social, legal, educational, etc.

Since many of the services for special populations are
implemented through other parts of society's networks, the focus
of this chapter is on a historical perspective and the treatment
of various special populations in American society. Special
populations covered in this chapter include: Asians, Blacks,
European Ethnic, Native American, Same Sex Preference, Spanish
Speaking and Women[1]. Similar to other chapters, some estimates are made on the size of each of these population groups
and information is provided on some major organizations providing services for and with these populations. Programs and
services for special populations and the role of human services
personnel including that of social work with special populations
are incorporated into other chapters.

The major special population groups in the United States include: Asian, Black, European Ethnic, Native American, Same Sex Preference, Spanish Speaking and Women. Another population group which is considered to be a special population is the disabled. (See Chapter 24, Rehabilitation Network.) Figure 25-1 shows the estimated size of the special population groups in comparison to the total United States population.[2]

In 1982, the largest special population group was Women, estimated at 119,035,000 or 51.30 percent of the population. The next largest group was Blacks, 27,589,000 or 11.89 percent of the population, followed by European Ethnics, 25,455,000 or 10.70 percent of the population, Same Sex preference, 17,000,000 or 7.3 percent of the population, Spanish Speaking, 14,608,673 or 6.30 percent of the population, Asian, 3,466,421 or 1.50 percent of the population and Native Americans, 1,423,043 or .61 percent of the population. When one looks at these special population groups, there are some enormous differences in population growth rates between 1970-1980. For example, the Native American population increased by 72 percent, the Spanish Speaking population by 61 percent, the Black population by 17.9 percent, the Asian population by 70 percent, Same Sex Preference for 1970 and 1980, no change, Women by 11.7 percent and European Ethnics (foreign born) by 2 percent.

The implications of demographic changes in special populations has not been fully realized since popular perceptions on population concentrations have primarily focussed on specific areas, such as the far West, Southwest and Northeast, with Spanish Speaking, Native American and European Ethnic populations. What population growth rates and geographical location eventually means for the political process, education programs, necessity for a bilingual society (Spanish and English) and social service delivery programs in the United States is still uncertain. Of interest in special populations is their expansion or distribution throughout the United States. This means that social services for a special population group is not restricted to a specific geographical area. The net result is that communities which were never concerned before about special populations must now be concerned whether it is in the Southwest, West or Midwest, etc.

It is difficult to estimate the number of agencies relating to special populations. A National Directory published by Katherine Cole in 1982, lists over 7,186 organizations focussing on special populations (excluding Same Sex Preference, European Ethnic and Women). This directory contains a listing of 103 organizations for Alaska Native Americans, 1,539 for American

Figure 25-1

Estimated Size of the Special Populations In 1980-1983*

Asian	Total[1]	3,466,421	1.50
	Chinese	812,178	.35
	Japanese	716,331	.31
	Korean	357,393	.15
	Filipino	781,894	.34
	Indochinese	313,956	.14
	Other[5]	484,669	.21
Black	Total[2]	27,589,000	11.89
	Afro-American	27,042,000	11.65
	Other[6]	547,000	.24
European Ethnic	Total[2] (Foreign born and first generation)	25,455,000	10.70
Native American	Total[1]	1,423,043	.61
	Lower 48 states	1,380,881	.60
	Alaska	42,162	.01
Same Sex Preference	Total[3]	17,000,000	7.3
Spanish Speaking	Total[1]	14,608,673	6.30
	Chicano	8,740,439	3.77
	Puerto Rican	2,013,945	.87
	Cuban	803,226	.35
	Other[7]	3,051,063	1.31
Women	Total[2]	119,035,000	51.30
Population Base	Total[2]	232,057,000	100.00[4]

*Sources: Adapted from the following resources.

[1]United States Department of Commerce, Bureau of the Census, 1980 Census of Population. Supplementary Report: Asian and Pacific Islander Population by State 1980, Washington DC: U.S. Government Printing Office, 1983, p. 2; American Indian Areas and Alaska Native Villages 1980, 1984, pp. 2-4; Persons of Spanish Origin by State 1980, 1982, p. 2.

[2]United States Department of Commerce, Bureau of the Census, Statistical Abstract of the United States: 1986 (106th Edition), Washington, DC: U.S. Government Printing Office, 1985, pp. 24, 25, 87 and Statistical Abstract of the United States: 1982/83 (103rd Edition), 1982, p. 36.

[3]News and World Report, August 8, 1983.

[4]Percentages when added equal more than 100.00 percent since an individual may belong to two or three categories and therefore the figures are a double count of population. Numbers when added equal more than 232,057,000 since an individual may belong to two or three categories. In 1984, the number of Blacks was estimated at 28,486,000, Women at 121, 446,000, Spanish Speaking at 16,740,000 and the total population at 236,681,000.

[5]Other includes Asian Indian, Thai, Pakastani, Indonesian, and miscellaneous groupings.

[6]Other includes African, Jamaican, Haitian and miscellaneous groupings.

[7]Other Includes South Americans, Central Americans, Carribeans, Spanish and Portuguese.

Indians, 1,115 for Blacks, 1,561 for Spanish Speaking; 1,943 general minority and 925 for Asians. Other directories for Same Sex Preference, European Ethnic and Women contain at least 15,000 organizations.[3]

HISTORICAL PERSPECTIVE

Each of the special population groups has a distinct history and consequently the major groups will briefly be discussed to show general attitudes and social treatment toward special populations in the United States. This section discusses the Asian, Black, European Ethnic, Native American, Same Sex Preference, Spanish Speaking and Women as special populations.

ASIANS

This population group is diverse since it includes: Chinese, Japanese, Korean, Filipino, Indochinese and other Asian groups. Many of these groups are of rather recent origin in the United States, such as the Vietnamese (post 1974), and others have been in the United States since the early 1800's (Chinese). In 1980, it was estimated that 2,246,700 individuals of Asian descent were foreign born. Of this population group, 1,902,0000 individuals spoke their native Asian languages and over 31 percent have difficulty with English.

CHINESE--In 1980 this population group was estimated at 812,178 or .35 percent of the population. Although the major immigration of the Chinese to the United States developed after 1850 there were some Chinese in California as early as 1571 as ship builders, laborers in the far west by 1788, and in New York City by 1807.[4] The first major immigration of Chinese was in 1820, but their immigration was not encouraged by either China or the United States. By 1850 there was a demand for labor on the west coast in the gold rush days which coincided with the Taiping Rebellion in China (1850-1864). These two factors encouraged the immigration of Chinese especially from the Guangdong province. Cooley labor was in demand because of the need for a cheap labor force to construct the continental railroad in 1864.

Although labor was needed, the Chinese population was discriminated against almost immediately after their arrival. The range of discriminatory practices included the following: 1) not eligible to become a citizen since they were viewed as aliens (California 1855), 2) could not sue or speak against whites in court (California 1854), 3) could not marry whites in some states, 4) placed in separate schools (1860), 5) were required to pay extra taxes in San Francisco, California, 6) required to reside in special sections of a town through housing covenants (1879, California), 7) could not be employed in a government job (1879), 8) were not allowed to purchase real estate (California 1872) and 9) foreign born Chinese could not become naturalized citizens of the United States (Supreme Court decision 1898). These forms of discriminatory practices were a consequence of pressures due to poor economic conditions which affected the majority population and subsequently led to numerous acts of violence against the Chinese, such as mob action in California in 1871, 1875, 1877 etc. Such external pressures most assuredly maintained and reinforced the isolated Chinatown concept over the next several generations, including the use of internal mutual support groups to resolve problems.

The anti-Chinese attitude on the west coast was so extensive, that the United States passed the Exclusion Act of 1882 barring further immigration of Chinese. The Exclusion Act was amended in 1905 to cover the territories of Hawaii, and the Phillipines, and was reinforced by a second exclusion act in 1924 which also barred the wives of Chinese from immigrating. In spite of this hostile reaction, the Chinese were industrious, developed their own communities, and used mutual aid groups for support and the resolution of problems. Some examples of mutual aid and support groups developed for protection by the Chinese include: the Six Companies, Chinese-American Citizens Alliance 1895 and the Gam King Association 1929.

Children born in the United States could become citizens (1898), but the immigrant themselves had to wait until 1946 when the United States allowed naturalization. Although stripped of almost all civil rights, numerous Chinese went to France in 1918 in support of the war effort and fought in World War II in support of their adopted country. The attitude of the United States began to change toward the Chinese after the invasion of China by Japan in 1935, and the fact they were allies in World War II. Since 1943, restrictions on the Chinese have been repealed. Chinese communities grew with refugees from Communist China between 1949 and 1953 and with liberalization of the immigration laws in 1965. This population group is beginning to disperse throughout the United States and is extremely active in social and political affairs making major contributions to American society.[5]

JAPANESE--In 1980 this population group was estimated at 716,331 or .31 percent of the population. The first Japanese in the United States were reported to have been John Mung and Joseph Hamada. John Mung's real name was Manjiro Nahahama who was a survivor of a shipwreck in 1843 and was taken to New Bedford, Massachusetts. Joseph Hecor Hikozo Hamada (Hikozaemon) was a survivor of a shipwreck in 1850 and was taken to San

Francisco, California. After the Development of formal relations with Japan in 1854 some early immigrants moved to Hawaii in 1868. Because of mistreatment of the Japanese in Hawaii, Japan halted immigration to Hawaii until 1886. Some initial immigrants came to the United States in California in 1869, however, major immigration did not occur until after the United States annexed Hawaii in 1898.

The Japanese were initially welcome as a source of cheap labor, but very quickly found themselves in the same position as the Chinese. The immigrant was viewed as an alien and therefore not eligible for citizenship (the children known as Nisei were eligible). A ladies agreement in 1921 banned immigration of picture brides and in 1922 the Cable Act denied citizenship to Japanese Women who married a noncitizen. Therefore some of the Nisei Women who married male immigrants lost the civil rights they had obtained, even though they were born in the United States. The cable act was revised in 1931 allowing citizenship for the Nisei. Land acts were passed forbidding ownership of land by noncitizens in 1913 (California) and the Japanese were placed in segregated schools in 1906 in San Francisco. As a consequence of this discrimination, the Japanese government refused to grant passports for immigration after 1900 under the Gentleman's Agreement to curb immigration, and in 1924 the Exclusion Act denied further immigration. Violence erupted and was directed toward the Japanese population in 1906 and 1907, and this violence was sporadic until after World War II. World War II had a significant impact on the Japanese in America since they were viewed as potential enemies and evacuated from the west coast to internment camps (1941-1945). This internment camp program paid no attention to legal, property and family rights. In 1986, there are still civil law suits against the United States government for improper internment of the Japanese population with the government agreeing to a monetary payment to individuals who were interred. In spite of this history of discrimination against them, the Japanese fought in the Spanish-American War (1898), World War I, World War II, Korean and Vietnam conflicts in defense of their adopted country. Japanese immigrants are now eligible for citizenship, have become active in social and political affairs and are making a significant contribution to American society.[6]

KOREANS--In 1980 this population group was estimated at 357,393 or .15 percent of the population. Similar to other Asiatic groups the Koreans were early discriminated against, but differed from the Chinese and Japanese, in that the early immigrants were Christians. The fact of having Christianity as their religion tended to moderate discrimination against them. The church and the village council called the Dong Hoi, were the dominant social and political forces in the Korean community.

After formal diplomatic relations were established with Korea in 1884, a few political refugees immigrated after social and political reforms in Korea failed. Some examples of some of these political refugees include Joe-p'il also known as Phillip Jaisahn, So Kwang-Bom and P'Yon Lee. Immigration from Korea began in 1901 with Peter Ryce and a group of Koreans who eventually migrated to the Hawaiian Islands in 1903. Korea, because of political concerns banned further immigration in 1903, and the United States included Koreans under the Exclusion Act of 1924. Like other Asiatic groups the Koreans were treated as aliens, therefore ineligible for citizenship, were used as strikebreakers in employment, and were included under the Alien Land Laws of 1932 which restricted the purchase of property. Although a small group, the Koreans were targets of anti-Asian feelings and demonstrations in the early 1900's.

The Koreans quickly developed the church, and church school as a mainstay of their community and the village councils (Dong Hoi) to handle community and personal problems. Other mutual support groups developed, such as the Mutual Cooperation Association (1905) and the Sworn Brotherhood Societies known as the Dongji Hoi (1921). Korean immigrants generally maintained their allegiance to the homeland, and actively supported Korean independence from Japan. Although the Koreans had no legal status in the United States they actively fought in World War II for the United States, and in 1948 Syngman Rhee, who lived in the United States, became the first president of the independent Republic of Korea. During World War II the Koreans were exempt from alien status and refugees came to the United Sates after the Korean conflict of 1950-1953. More recently Koreans have been immigrating to the United States under the liberalized Immigration Laws of 1965.[7]

FILIPINOS--In 1980 this population group was estimated at 781,894 or .34 percent of the population. The Filipinos were technically United States citizens after the Treaty of Paris (1898), when the territory of the Phillipines was annexed to the United States as a result of the Spanish-American War. The Filipino was denied citizenship by legislation which shifted their status from nationals to aliens in 1902 and 1925, except for those who served in the United States Navy. This legal situation of noncitizenship remained until 1934 with the Tydings McDuffie Act, which granted the Phillipine Islands independence within a ten year period (by 1944), but this act also denied citizenship to Filipinos born in the United States. The second world war, 1941-1945, delayed implementation of the Tydings McDuffie Act until the Phillipines were granted independence in 1946.

Initial immigration to the United States was under the Pensionado Program of 1906, which was a program to encourage students to come to the United States. A peak period of immigration occurred between 1924-34. Like other Asian groups the Filipino was subject to restrictive legislation and discrimination, such as alien land laws which restricted rights to purchase land, some states prohibited mixed racial marriages, discrimination in employment, housing and schools. Violence erupted toward the Filipino in the late 1920's and the early 1930's. The Filipino response was the development of mutual aid associations, such as the Cabaeleros de Dimas (1921), the Luneta Benevolent Association (1933) and the Filipino Benevolent Association (1939). From 1935 to 1940 Filipinos were not eligible for general relief, public welfare, social security, government jobs, etc, in order to encourage repatriation of the immigrant to the Phillipine Islands.

World War II and its aftermath quickly changed the social and legal status of the Filipino, and all laws pertaining to land exclusion were repealed by 1943, citizenship was granted by 1945, and laws against mixed racial marriages were repealed in 1948. The Filipinos in the United States actively supported the war effort in World War II (1941-1945). There was limited immigration of Filipino refugees after 1945, with a large immigration of Filipinos occurring after liberalization of the immigration laws in 1965. This population group like other Asians is making its contribution to American society and is beginning to disperse throughout the United Sates.[8]

INDOCHINESE--In 1980 this population group was estimated at 313,956 or .14 percent of the population. The Indochinese population group consists of: Vietnamese, Cambodians, Laotians and Hmong. Almost all of the Indochinese have migrated to the United States since 1975.[9] Congress authorized the Indochinese Refugee Assistance Program in 1975 and its revision in 1977 and 1980, which provided funding for resettlement, and reimbursed county and state welfare units for medical assistance and social services.

Initially, these political refugees were accepted into American communities with a cautious, reticent acceptance, but as economic conditions worsened in many communities and subsequent competition for jobs, covert and overt patterns of prejudice and discrimination emerged. In some communities violence has been directed at the Indochinese, such as Seaburg, Texas.[10]

OTHER ASIANS--This population group was estimated at 484,669 or .21 percent of the population in 1980. This group consists of a variety of cultural groups including: Asian Indian (India),

Thailander's, Pakistanis, Indonesians and other groups. Each of these groups have a distinct culture and unique history. A high proportion of this population group are involved in major professions, such as university teaching, medicine, nursing, social work, etc.

BLACK

This population group consists of Afro-Americans (descendents of the slave population) and a variety of other groups, such as Jamaicans, Haitians, etc.

BLACK (AFRO-AMERICAN)--In 1982 this population group was estimated at 27,042,000 or 11.65 percent of the population. In 1980, there were an estimated 128,300 individuals born in Africa, residing in the United States. The initial Black population in America were either indentured servants or free persons. For example, one of the captains sailing with Christopher Columbus in 1492 was a free Black; Balboa in his voyages in 1513 had free Blacks on board; Cabeza-de Vasca in his explorations of 1527 and 1539 of the Southwest United States had free Blacks in his company, and a free Black named Estevancio served with Francisco Coronado in 1540 in exploring the South West United States and in 1608 the French explorers in Canada and northern United States had free Blacks in their company.

Initial transportation of Blacks as slaves began with the Spanish in 1510-1511 in Puerto Rico and Cuba. The mass importation of Blacks to the United States in 1619 in Virginia was initially one of where the individual was either a slave or an indentured servant. Three classes of Blacks were recognized: freeman (indentured servants who were granted their freedom), bonded Christian and bonded non-Christian. During the early years of Colonial United States (1609-1641), free Blacks had farms, some small businesses such as ship owners, and some were craftsmen, such as shipbuilders. The latter two categories of Blacks initially were in a position of indentured servitude, and could (theoretically) eventually earn or gain their freedom. Within twenty years the colonial attitude shifted toward perpetual bondage (slavery). The first category of Blacks to be placed in a position of slavery was the bonded non-Christian, then the bonded Christian. By 1641, various colonies began to legally accept slavery, such as Massachusetts (1641), Maryland (1663) and Virginia (1682). By 1723, the subjugation of the Black population was complete, with many colonies not recognizing marriages, family structure, banning the process of manumission (freedom), and negating any legal and social identity for the Black population. Interracial marriages were common during the early colonial period, especially between "indentured

857

servants," subsequently, many colonies enacted laws banning interracial marriages.

Bondage of the Black population was not readily accepted by the Blacks as evidenced by periodic uprisings for freedom. Some examples of these uprisings for freedom include, Cato (1740), Gabriel Prosser (1800), Denmark Vesey (1822) and Nat Turner (1831). With the formation of the United States in 1787, Blacks were not included by name in the Constitution. Article 1, Section 3, of the United States Constitution used the phrase "three-fifths of all other persons" in reference to Blacks, and Article 1, Section 9, forbade the importation of slaves after 1808. Although slavery was well entrenched in the United States this did not mean acceptance of slavery by the total American population. An anti-slavery movement was evident in the North prior to (1787) through Quaker leaders, such as Benjamin Say (1737), Ralph Sandiford (1729), John Woolman (1774), and Anthony Benezet (1772).

By 1787, slavery was abolished in the states of Massa-chusetts, Vermont, New Hampshire, Connecticut, Rhode Island and declared illegal in the Northwest Territory (Illinois, Wisconsin, Indiana, Michigan, Minnesota and Ohio). In the South, numerous anti-slavery people moved North, such as Sara and Angelina Grimke from South Carolina in the 1840's, Levi Coffin from North Carolina in the 1830's and James Birney from Alabama in the 1840's, along with a number of free Blacks like David Walker in 1829. These individuals joined forces with the anti-slavery movement in the North under the leadership of Benjamin Lundy (1828), William Lloyd Garrison (1831), Lydia Marie Child (1833) and Harriet Beecher Stowe (1851).

The anti-slavery movement before the Civil War attempted politically to ban slavery and developed two alternative methods to free slaves: The American Colonization Society and the underground railroad. The American Colonization Society, estab-lished in 1817, attempted to induce slave owners to emancipate slaves and return the slaves to Africa and establish a colony of free Blacks. This country became known as Liberia. This plan for emancipation was not successful for economic, social, and psychological reasons. The underground railroad, established about 1800, attempted to move slaves from the South to Canada, circumventing both Article 4, Section 2, of the Constitution and the Fugitive Slave law of 1793. Safe houses on a route to Canada were developed in various places in northern states, such as Philadelphia, Pennsylvania as early as 1810 through the efforts of Isaac Tate Hopper. The underground railroad movement spread to Ohio and Indiana by 1830 through the efforts of Levi Coffin. There were multiple routes with safe houses through states, such as New York, Ohio, Indiana, Pennsylvania and

Wisconsin. An example of a safe house is the Joseph Goodrich House, Milton, Wisconsin (1844). This house had hidden rooms and an underground tunnel (See National Geographic Magazine July 1984). Freed slaves who made the journey to Canada, such as Harriet Tubman and Josiah Henson in the 1830's, were key figures in developing links for the underground railroad and returning to the South to help other slaves gain their freedom.

The Civil War (1861-1865) had some humanitarian overtones to end slavery. The war was primarily a political and economic conflict between different economic systems. The North was becoming industrialized and the South remained agrarian. At the close of the Civil War, the Freedman's Bureau was established (1865-1872) as a means to assist dislocated and freed Blacks. Constitutional amendments of 1865-68, 1870, 1875, were passed to ensure social, legal and property rights for the freed slaves. As reconstruction of the South was implemented the social, economic and legal rights of Blacks became restricted and negated through Supreme Court decisions in 1883 and 1896, such as Plessey vs. Ferguson (separate but equal facilities doctrine was constitutional) and the development of Jim Crow laws (local discrimination). As Blacks were losing newly won social and legal rights, organizations began to form to push for further reforms, such as the National Association for the Advancement of Colored People (1908), the National Association of Colored Women (1896) and the National Urban League (1901). Black leaders emerged, such as WEB Dubois, Booker T. Washington, William Trottor, George Haynes and Phillip Randolph. Many, if not most of the social services for the Black population at this time period were implemented through schools, churches, fraternal, organizations and voluntary associations, Some examples of these mutual support societies include the Free African Society (1787), the Friendly Society (1795) and the New York African Society for Mutual Aid (1810). It is ironic that the Black population had to fight for its own rights since many Black individuals had fought in the Revolutionary War, the War of 1812, the Mexican War, the Civil War, and subsequently, World War I, World War II, Korean and Vietnam conflicts in defense of "their Country." In fact, the first person to die in the Revolutionary War was Crispus Attucks, a Black at Bunker Hill in 1776.

The years from 1900 to 1945 were slow in the development of civil rights although a number of legal decisions were made affecting voter and housing rights, such as Guinn vs. United States (1915), which declared grandfather clauses unconstitutional and Buchanan vs. Warley (1917), which declared exclusion of Blacks from specific sections of a city as unconstitutional. After World War II, the United States was in an awkward position from a humanitarian and political perspective as the leader of

859

the free world. After having been instrumental in defeating Nazi Germany and Japan and facing a cold war with the Soviet Union, (totalitarian countries) in the name of freedom and democracy, the United States still denied equal social, legal and political rights to its own minority groups. Slowly an awareness of this social inequity toward Blacks and the political inconsistency with the values of a democracy was developing. The armed forces were desegregated by presidential order in 1948, and new organizations were developing focussing on concerns of the Blacks, such as the Congress of Social Equality (1942) with the leadership of James Farmer. Existing organizations were developing a new impetus, such as the Black Muslims (1927) with the leadership of Garvey, and obtaining a national significance under new leadership with El Malik Al Shabazal (Malcalm X). Black politicians were becoming extremely visible, such as Adam Clayton Powell in Harlem New York.

The 1950's was a decade which laid the ground work for the civil rights activities of the 1960's. In 1954, the United States Supreme Court in Brown vs Board of Education, declared school segregation and the doctrine of "separate but equal" facilities unconstitutional. A series of social and political protests developed after this court decision. The Southern Christian Leadership Conference was established by Martin Luther King Jr. (1957). After the assassination of Martin Luther King, Jr. (1968), Ralph Abernathy became the leader of the Southern Christian Leadership Conference. A Student Nonviolent Coordinating Committee was established in 1960 (changed its name to Student National Coordinating Committee) through the leadership of James Foreman, and later Stokley Carmichael and H. Rap Brown. Militant groups like the Black Panthers were organized in 1966 by Bobby Seale and Huey Newton, and later Stokley Carmichael and Eldridge Cleaver in response to internal protest (Little Rock, Arkansas school desegregation 1957, Selma, Alabama marches, etc.). The United States Congress adopted a weak civil rights law in 1957 and 1960. Many whites began to join forces with the Blacks, such as the Mississippi Freedom Riders (Viola Luizzo) in 1964 and housing marches and protests, like Father Groppi, Milwaukee, Wisconsin (1964). The United States Congress adopted a more effective civil rights law in 1964. In the same year the War on Poverty (Economic Opportunity Act) was enacted which established social service programs to provide access for the disadvantaged, including Blacks to economic, social, legal and educational opportunities.

During the 1970's, there was a reduction in monies available from the federal government for programs and a dismanteling of major programs established under the War on Poverty. There was a political disenchantment with the War on Poverty Programs,

860

since the impact of these programs in reducing poverty and raising the socioeconomic status of segments of the Black population
were not as effective as anticipated. The 1980's continued the
trend of a reduction in monies available through federal programs and completed a dismantling of many programs established
between 1964-1970. Although strides have been made since 1954
to enhance the social, legal, and economic opportunities of the
Black population, the problems of poverty, inadequate housing,
discrimination, and restrictive economic and social opportunities still remain. This population group until 1900 was predominantly in the southern states, but since then has dispersed
throughout the United States. The contributions of the Black
population to the United States as a society and a culture have
been enormous. In addition to some of the political leaders
mentioned earlier, it should be noted that Benjamin Banniker
surveyed the grounds for the white house and perfected the time
clock. Blood plasma was developed by a Black physician, and Jan
Ernst Matzeliger invented a shoe making machine. Some early
settlers in Chicago were Black,and numerous scientific contributions are attributed to Booker T. Washington.[11]

OTHER BLACK POPULATIONS--This population group is rather
small consisting of 547,000 individuals in 1980 or .24 percent
of the population. In 1980, there were an estimated 485,100
individuals in this population group which were foreign born.
Unfortunately, the general population of the United States has
not recognized cultural differences between various Black
population groups. The people of the United States almost
exclusively equate the term black with descendants of African
American slaves. The more realistic perspective is to recognize
a diversity amongst the Black population since there are immigrants from Africa and the Caribbean region. In particular at
least three other groups of Blacks which have a distinct
cultural identity are those from Jamaica, Virgin Islands and
Haiti.

In the 1980's there has been a large number of Haitian
refugees. These individuals have been treated distinctly
different than the Cuban or Vietnamese refugees, since most of
these individuals are considered illegal aliens and are held in
internment camps waiting for deportation back to Haiti. Haiti
as a country was initially controlled by the Spanish. After the
depletion of the Arawak and Carib Indians, the Spanish imported
slaves from Africa. Haiti became independent from Spain in 1804.

EUROPEAN ETHNIC

The term European Ethnic refers to population groups which
migrated to the United States from Western and Eastern Europe,
including Jewish populations from those geographical areas. In

1982, the number of people who were either foreign or first generation born was estimated at 25,455,000 or 10.70 percent of the population. Most of these individuals came from Western European countries. In 1980 the number of foreign-born from Europe was estimated at 4,743,600. It was estimated that at least 6,331,000 individuals speak European languages and that about 14-17 percent have difficulty understanding English. In addition to those individuals who were foreign-born or first generation, a large percentage of the population identifies themself with a specific ethnic group. In the 1980 census 83 percent of the population identified themself with an ethnic group, 10 percent gave no response and 7 percent listed American. The largest groups identified for ethnicity were: English, German, Irish (these three groups accounted for 139 million individuals or 59.8 percent of the population), French, Italian, Scottish, Polish, Dutch, Swedish, Norwegian, Russian, Czechoslovakian, Hungarian, Welsh, Danish, and Portuguese. States with a high diversity of ethnic groups include California, New York, Pennsylvania, Illinois, Michigan, Wisconsin, Minnesota, Washington and Ohio. Some states ranked high in concentrations of specific groups. For example, Wisconsin ranked high in the numbers of Norwegians, Czechoslovakian and Danish. Minnesota ranked high in the number of Norwegians and Danish, and California and New York had high numbers of most groups.

The United States has been labeled a country of immigrants, and indeed, outside of the Native Americans (who were early immigrants), all of the groups have immigrated in various patterns or waves of migration. One can view the history of European migration to the United States from five historical periods.

(1)   Early Colonial Settlement pre-1700--The English in Jamestown (1607) and in Plymouth, Massachusetts (1620); Swedish (1638) along the Delaware River in New Jersey and Pennsylvania; the Dutch (1609) at Manhattan, New York (included Jews 1654); French settlements along the Lake Champlain and Quebec regions (1608); Swiss (1670) in South Carolina and Germans (1683) in Pennsylvania. In addition to these settlements there were other small groups of Irish and Danish represented in this early period of settlement.

(2)   Later Colonial Settlement 1700-1787--These immigrants were primarily from the British Isles, such as Scotland, Wales, England and Ireland, southwest Germany, along with a smaller variety of other nationality groups,

(3)   Early Industrial Settlement 1787-1880--The major population groups immigrated from northern and western Europe, i.e., Ireland, the German states and Scandanavia

862

(4)   Later   Industrial   Settlement   --   1880-1920--The   major
population groups immigrated from eastern Europe and southern
Europe, such as Russia, Austria, Hungary, Italy and the Balkans.

(5)   Recent and Post-World War II Settlement -- 1920 on. A
variety of political refugees from various countries as a
consequence of totalitarian governments of World War II and
refugees from current political events, such as Hungary,
Czechoslovakia, Poland etc.

WEST and EAST EUROPEAN ETHNIC--The majority of the European
inhabitants of the United States pre-1787 were of a Protestant
religious denomination and of Western European ancestry.   The
major wave of immigration between 1787 and 1880 was from Western
Europe and primarily Catholics from Ireland and Germany.[12]   In
response to these immigrants who were culturally different the
Nativistic movement developed in 1834 under the leadership of
Rev.   Lyman   Beecher   and   others.   The   Nativistic   movement
continued intermittently throughout the nineteenth century.   The
Nativistic movement and its anti-foreign feeling resulted in a
variety of prejudicial and discriminatory actions taken against
these groups, specifically Roman Catholic groups.   Although the
anti-foreign hysteria was not constant, it continued into the
1890's and discrimination against these groups continued well
into the 20th century.   For example, in 1834 the Ursuline
Convent in Boston, Massachusetts was burned.   Violence against
the Irish was chronic between 1843 and 1845 with further
outbreaks connected with the draft riots in New York City in
1863.   Employment discrimination was conspicuous.   For example,
recruiting signs were placed in factories indicating that Irish
need not apply for work.   The Germans also were initially
discriminated against by Nativistic groups especially that group
of Germans which immigrated after 1848, because of their radical
socialistic politics.   Northern and midwestern states, such as
Massachusetts, Pennsylvania, Illinois, Wisconsin, Ohio and large
cities like Boston, New York, Chicago, and Milwaukee, became
centers of immigrant groups by 1850.   For example, Milwaukee,
Wisconsin in the 1850's was called the German State of the
union.[13]

Conflict was not always directed at the immigrant group
themselves, such as German, Irish, Italian, etc., but was
directed at times between immigrant groups, like the Irish
versus the German and at times between a specific immigrant
group like Corkian Irish (County cork) and Mayoan Irish (County
Mayo).   Immigrant Women were often discriminated against both
because of their foreignness and because of the fact they were
Women.   Sexual harassment and inuendos were rather frequent.
The immigrants responded to this mistreatment and for their own
protection by developing mutual support groups.   The Catholic

church for many of these groups was used as a source of guidance and support. In numerous cases the immigrant group developed its own schools, newspapers, and in exceptional cases its own hospitals, etc.

Immigrant groups who came to the United States from 1880 to 1945 experienced a similar process of prejudice and discrimination, such as Italian, Polish and Greek. Prejudice against the immigrant group has carried over in many cases through the third generation, and in some communities there is still blatant prejudice against the Polish, Hungarian, Norwegian, Greek, Serbian, etc.[14]

JEWISH ETHNIC--The Jewish population came from a variety of European countries and settled as a separate religious community instead of a country ethnic community. Jewish settlements from Spain and Portugal were in the United States as early as 1654. Major immigration of the Jewish population occurred after a number of political upheavels and religious pogroms (persecution and harassment), such as Germany 1840 to 1870, Russia 1890 to 1924, Germany 1933 to 1945, and after World War II in Russia. The Jewish population tended to cluster in large cities, such as Chicago, New York, Milwaukee, and so on. Like other immigrant groups, the Jewish population has experienced prejudice and discrimination, and this persists up to the present time. If one looks at the material produced by the Klu Klux Klan, the Arayans and the Posse Comitatus one would see that groups which reflect discrimination and prejudice toward some European Ethnics are very active today.[15]

The European Ethnic immigrant initially had difficulty adjusting to the United States and was openly discriminated against. A general pattern of accommodation developed in that most immigrant groups established their own schools, newspapers, churches and mutual support groups. The use of these measures has generally decreased by the third generation, however, there is still pride in maintaining the cultural identification of these groups. All of these immigrant groups have made a significant contribution to American society.[16]

NATIVE AMERICANS

This population group consists of two related, but distinctly different cultures: those residing in the lower 48 states and those residing in Alaska.

NATIVE AMERICANS (lower 48 states)--In 1980 this population group was estimated at 1,380,881 or .60 percent of the population. It is interesting to note that on the 1980 census, 6.7 million individuals identified themselves as Native American.

864

This population group is highly diverse consisting of at least 12 distinct cultural and language groups: Na-Dene, Algonquian-Ritwan-Kutenai, Iroquois-Caddoan, Gulf, Siouan-Yuchi, Utaztecan-Tanoan, Mosan, Penutian, Yukian, Hokaltecan, Keres and Zuni. The diversity of the Native American population is further highlighted by the fact there are approximately 493 tribes recognized by the Bureau of Indian Affairs, at least another 100 tribes not recognized by the Bureau of Indian Affairs and there are at least 250 different languages.

Contrary to popular notions most Native Americans live outside of reservations and identified Native American areas. In 1980, 876,355 or 63.5 percent of Native Americans lived outside of identified Native American and reservation areas, 339,987 or 24.6 percent lived on 278 reservations, and the remaining 164,539 or 11.9 percent lived on tribal trust lands or historical areas, such as Oklahoma. Those states with a high concentration of Native Americans are California, Oklahoma, Arizona, New Mexico (46 percent of the Native Americans) with the remaining 54 percent distributed throughout all of the states. States east of the Mississippi river which have a heavy concentration of Native Americans include New York, North Carolina, Michigan and Wisconsin.

Contact of Europeans with the Native Americans in America was intermittent from 1492 until the settling of Jamestown in 1607. Even in this early period of European exploration, reactions of the two cultural groups included open hostility on the part of the Native Americans and the Europeans, open warfare by both groups and hospitality by both groups. Early contact with the Native American population include the Portuguese and Spanish. Gasper Cortereal (Portuguese) landed in Labrador in 1501. He found the Native Americans to be hospitable and curious, and in return he kidnapped 57 men and Women taking them back to Portugal to be sold as slaves. Ponce de Leon (Spanish) in 1513 explored the area of Florida and apparently had no hostile altercations with the Native American population. When Ponce de Leon returned to Florida in 1521 there was open hostility and fighting as a consequence of the exploration and activity of Lucas Vasquez de Ayllon. Lucas de Ayllon in 1520, raided the coasts of Georgia, and South Carolina, looking for slaves to transport to Haiti to work in the mines. In 1542, Hernando deSoto explored the Mississippi Valley and surrounding territory. According to accounts of the Creek tribe of Georgia and Alabama, and the Nilco tribe of Arkansas, this expedition was received in a friendly manner. DeSoto in his attempts to show the strength of Spain, destroyed many Creek villages and the stronghold of the Nilco tribe. Francisco Coronado (1540) explored Arizona and New Mexico and generally acted with moderation and tolerance toward the Native American tribes.

Permanent settlement of the United States began with Jamestown, Virginia (1607), and Plymouth, Massachusetts (1620) settled by the English and New York which was settled by the Dutch (1609). Initial contacts were generally friendly but cautious with chiefs, such as Powhaten in Virginia, Massasoit in Massachusetts and Wyandance in Long Island, New York. Tension quickly developed between the two cultural groups because of different land use patterns, religion, culture etc. One of the first major outbreaks of armed conflict occurred under Chief Opechancanaugh and his followers in 1622-1634 around Jamestown, Virginia. A second major outbreak of violence occurred in 1644, when Chief Opechancanaugh and his followers were defeated in battle. For the next 270 years, until almost 1900, there was intermittent fighting and conflict between the Native Americans and the European settlers.[17]

Prior to the revolution of 1776, British policy was to negotiate with each tribe (of which there were about 400 in the United States) as a separate independent sovereign nation, and the signing of a peace treaty granting land rights to the European settlers in return for hunting, fishing and other rights for the Native Americans on other parcels of land. In 1763 a proclamation line for the limitation of European settlement was established at the Alleghany Mountain range. East of the line, European settlement was allowed, west of the line was Native American country. This proclamation and boundary line for settlement was almost immediately nullified and broken by European migration. After the close of the Revolutionary War in 1783, the United States Government continued the policy of the predecessor British Government, and incorporated these practices into the Northwest Ordinance Act of 1787. Native Americans were excluded as citizens of the United States according to Article 1 Section 2 of the Constitution and Article I section 8 which refers to the right of congress to regulate commerce with foreign nations, the states and Indian tribes.

As Western expansion continued, treaties were signed with various tribes and a Bureau of Indian Affairs was established under the War Department in 1824, which was transferred to the Department of Interior in 1849. Until 1854 the focus of concern in Native American and United States relations, was those Native American tribes east of the Mississippi River. Three simultaneous policies were developed as part of the United States and Native American relationship: signing of treaties and provision for Native American land, development of reservations and Native American removal.

Treaties were signed with various tribes for ceding use of designated land to the United States government, and the Native Americans were provided use of designated land. Examples of

866

these treaties include: Delaware tribe (1778); Delaware, Potawatomie, (Illinois Michigan, Ohio) and other tribes (1809); Chippewa tribe, (Wisconsin) (1817); Cherokee (Georgia) tribe (1785) and the Winnebago (Wisconsin) tribe (1816). As pressure from European settlers continued, new treaties were signed designating limited areas of land as reservations, such as the Lenapi and Lenani in New Jersey (1758); the Choctaw in Alabama (1805); the Cherokee in Georgia (1817-18); Oneida (1823) in Wisconsin and Menominee in Wisconsin (1854).

The development of indian territory and reservations was part of the Native American removal policy of 1833-1854. This policy had as its objective the removal of all Native Americans east of the Mississippi to west of the Mississippi River. Native American tribes were forcibly moved, such as the Delaware (1849 from Ohio and previously Delaware), the Choctaw (1831-southeast), Creek (1836-Southeast) the Winnebago (1832-50-Wisconsin) and the Cherokees (1838-from Georgia), known as the "Trail of Tears."[18] Between 1823-38, a reservation was established as Native American territory in Oklahoma for the five "civilized" tribes of the South East (Cherokee, Creek, Choctaw, Chickasaws, and Seminole). Other tribes were moved to areas, such as Kansas, Missouri and Minnesota.

With most of the Native Americans east of the Mississippi under treaty, on reservations, or forcibly removed by 1854, attention began to focus on tribes west of the Mississippi, such as the Sioux, in the Plain states (1854-1890), the Apache in the Southwest (1861-1900) and the Nez Perce and the Modac in the West and Northwest (1872-1877).[19] By 1871 the period of government treaties was over and tribes were dealt with through the Bureau of Indian Affairs. One of the last major military engagements was the massacre at Wounded Knee in 1890 of Women and children.

Native Americans in 1862 were considered to be under the trust and protection of the United States government and had a legal status similar to that of wards of the government and under the supervision of the Bureau of Indian Affairs. The Native American populations became totally dependent for support on the government, and from 1871-1934 the policy of the Bureau of Indian Affairs and the government was to acculturate and assimilate Native Americans into American Society. These policies had the effect of almost destroying Native American culture. For example, the practice of Native American religions was banned from 1882-1938, tribal organization and courts were banned from 1899-1934, use of tribal languages was banned, children were placed in boarding schools in order to assimilate them into the overall American culture from 1885-1940; and large amounts of Native American land was sold to white settlers and land developers as a consequence of the Allotment or Dawes Act of 1887. The Dawes Act developed a system where land on a reservation was allotted in 160 acre parcels to male heads of households, and the excess land was declared surplus and resold to white settlers and developers. The result of this policy was a reduction in reservation land, and later many Native Americans lost their individual parcels of land for failure to pay taxes, which was then resold to settlers or land developers.[20] In addition to these attempts to assimilate the Native Americans', the Native Americans were discriminated against in other ways, such as classed as non citizens until 1924 (except those granted citizenship by treaty) the sale of liquor was banned, mixed marriages between Native Americans and whites were banned in some states, etc.

A significant year for Native Americans in the United States was 1934, with the passage of the Howard/Wheeler Act, or Indian Retribalization Act. The Howard Wheeler act allowed tribal organizations to reorganize, the use of Native American language, use of religious practices, etc. Since 1934 many programs have been established to provide: better housing, under the public housing authority, education programs through the Johnson-O'Mally Act and the Indian Education Act of 1972, medical care through the Public Health Service and welfare benefits through the Indian Relief programs of the Bureau of Indian Affairs and local welfare departments. The Economic Opportunity Act of 1964 and its subsequent revisions had an impact on many Native American communities. In spite of progress made in many areas there were further attempts to modify the relationship of Native Americans to the government through the Termination Act of 1954. The Termination Act authorized Congress with the "consent" of the tribe, to terminate federal responsibility for the tribe. An example of termination is the Menominee tribe in Wisconsin which was terminated in 1960 and the reservation land became a separate county. After a few years of experimentation with termination the Menominee tribe successfully reversed the termination process in 1972, and again achieved reservation status. The Native American population has fought hard to maintain their own identity, reservation and other lands, and their special status with the federal government.

A major issue for the Native American population is the status of the urban or non-reservation Native American. Until the late 1950's, when an individual left the reservation they were no longer entitled to certain services from the Bureau of Indian Affairs. Consequently many urban Native Americans were left without adequate support when they relocated to large cities. Some cities where the Native American population is large include: Minneapolis, Minnesota; Milwaukee, Wisconsin;

Chicago, Illinois; Los Angeles, California and New York City, New York. Since 1950, each of these cities has developed a number of specialized social service agencies which address the specific needs of the Native American community, and in general are staffed by Native Americans. In spite of difficulties between the Native American population and the majority society, many Native Americans fought alongside the Americans in the Revolutionary War and the War of 1812. Native Americans subsequently have fought in defense of their country in the Civil War, World War I, II and Korean and Vietnam conflicts. The status of the Native American in the United States is different than other minority groups since they have dual citizenship, (the tribe and the United States), consequently a separate bill of rights was passed for Native Americans in 1968 which applied to tribal government. Other recent legislation pertaining to Native Americans include the Child Welfare Act of 1977, education funding trough the Elementary and Secondary Act of 1968 and health facilities through the Amended Public Health Act of 1964.[21]

ALAKSA (Eskimo/Aleuts)--This population group consisting of Eskimos and Aleuts in 1980 was estimated at 42,162 or .01 percent of the population. The Eskimo was estimated at 27,957 or .007 percent of the population and the Aleuts were estimated at 14,205 or .003 percent of the population. Both of these groups are highly concentrated in the state of Alaska with 81 percent of the Eskimos and 57 percent of the Aleuts residing in that state. Two other states with a concentration of these two population groups are California and Washington. A high percentage of these two groups living in Alaska resided in identifiable Native American areas which are Alaskan Native villages. Of the Eskimos, 16,774 or 60 percent resided in Native American areas and of the Aleuts 4,688 or 33 percent resided in Native villages or the Annette Islands Reserve, a reservation.

SAME SEX PREFERENCE

In 1982 it was estimated that 7.3 percent of the American population or about 17 million people had leanings to or had a Same Sex Preference.

Societal attitudes toward homosexual behavior (male) and lesbian behavior (female), has varied from acceptance, to toleration, to attempts at persecution and/or execution of individuals. Today there is a polarization of attitudes and perceptions between many homosexual and heterosexual individuals. In pre-Christian era societies, like Greece and Rome this polarization did not exist. In Greece around 200 B.C., homosexual behavior was tolerated as long as an individual was engaging in such behavior with mutual consent and with eligible

parties (another mutual consenting person who was over age 10).
Roman society around 100 B.C. to 400 A.D., held similar view
points toward homosexual behavior as Greek society. Consequently no polarization occurred between the viewpoints that one
was either homosexual or heterosexual. These societies did
place limits on acceptable behavior, for example, molestation of
a child before age 6 was punishable by death.

Negative attitudes toward homosexual behavior developed
amongst the Hebrews and other groups around 100 B.C., who viewed
all sexual behavior as oriented toward procreation. Any other
form of sexual behavior was frowned upon and not condoned. The
potential punishment for homosexual behavior was death. The
early Christian community (33-400) followed the Hebrew codes and
condemned homosexual behavior. The writings of St. Augustine
(354-430) and St. Jerome (340-420), are early examples of these
negative attitudes toward homosexual behavior. Both of these
authors condemned this behavior as unnatural. The Christian
community went one step further in linking homosexual behavior
with religious heresy. The penalty for heresy (and homosexual
behavior) was execution by burning, or a lengthy period of
penitence, like 20-22 years. In Medieval Europe (1000-1500),
homosexual behavior was viewed as evidence of witchcraft and
satanism. By the time of Henry the VII in England (1553) homosexual behavior became a felony crime, punishable by execution,
and this was reinforced by the Puritan Act of 1650. In spite of
these harsh measures homosexual behavior and other forms of
condemned sexual behavior were rampant in England in 1650 during
the period of Cromwell. Attitudes toward homosexual behavior in
the United States were similar to those of England, that is
treating the person as a moral sinner, a degenerate and a
criminal. Homosexual behavior was viewed as unnatural and
immoral, consequently the individual was viewed as being
different.

Early scientific study of homosexual behavior reinforced the
religious perspective, since the behavior was viewed as
degenerate (Morel 1857), or as a form of sexual perversion (Kaan
1843, and Krafft-Ebing 1886, in Psychopathia Sexualis), or as a
mental illness (Kraepelin 1883). The term homosexuality was not
used until 1869 when it was introduced by Dr. Benkert in
Hungary, and lesbianism as a term was not used until late in the
19th Century. Since homosexual behavior was viewed as a mental
illness, the individual was generally treated in a mental
institution, or in a private office using techniques of psychotherapy and later behavior modification. If one could not
afford private medical or psychotherapeutic treatment, they were
handled by the law enforcement and corrections network and
treated as a criminal.

The works of Sigmund Freud (1856-1939) were extremely
significant in continuing the viewpoint of homosexual behavior
as a deviation and this view point is found in books as recent
as 1976 and later.[22] Homosexual behavior according to psychological theory was a deviation from or an arrestment (blockage)
of normal psychosexual development and behavior. The homosexual
has been discriminated against in employment, housing, military
and civil rights.[23] Recently the American Psychiatric Association (1973) has reversed its traditional viewpoint of viewing
homosexual behavior as a mental illness, and no longer classifies homosexual behavior as a form of mental illness. Regardless of the psychiatric classification of homosexual behavior,
it is evident that prejudice, discrimination, and lack of
empathy or understanding of the social and psychological difficulties of individuals engaging in homosexual behavior are still
with us today.[24] In 1986, the U.S. Supreme Court upheld a
Georgia law which considers homosexual behavior as a crime.
Twenty-four states have laws which define homosexual behavior as
a crime. Of these twenty-four states, five refer to homosexual
behavior between homosexuals and 19 refer to homosexual behavior
whether it occurs beween homosexuals or a homosexual and
heterosexual or heterosexual. The U.S. Supreme Court, in this
decision, further indicated that this decision had no effect on
other laws regarding discrimination toward homosexuals in
employment, housing, etc.

SPANISH SPEAKING

A rapidly growing special population in the United States is
the Spanish Speaking. In some parts of the United States, it is
essential to be bilingual. The major Spanish Speaking groups
are: Chicano, Puerto Rican and Cuban. In 1980, there were
2,807,000 individuals in the United States who were born in
Mexico and Cuba. It was estimated that 11,116,000 individuals
spoke Spanish and that about 25 percent have difficulty with
English.

CHICANO--In 1980, this population group was estimated at
8,740,439 or 3.77 percent of the population. Until the 1970's
two terms were used to describe the Spanish Americans in the
United States: Chicano (Mexican immigrant) and the Spanish
American, (descendants of the Old Spanish in America). The term
Chicano as used here applies to both groups and is generally
labeled Spanish-American. The Chicano in general is of
Spanish/Indian and Mexican ancestry.

Spanish exploration in the continental United States dates
back to Ponce de Leon (1513) in Florida, Hernando Cortez (1519)
in Yucaton Mexico, Hernando de Sota (1542) in the Mississippi
Valley, Francisco Coronado (1540) in the Southwest and Juan

Rodriguez Cabrillo (1542) in California. The Spanish controlled and settled the territory in the current Southwest states by 1590. An early mission was established in Sante Fe, New Mexico, (1598), and California was settled through the explorations of Sebastian Vizcaino (1602), with a mission established in lower California (Baja Penninsula) by 1697. Upper California was settled under Gasper de Portola and Father Junipero Serra who developed missions in San Diego (1762) and San Francisco (1776). This territory remained under Spanish domination until 1821 when Mexico gained its freedom from Spain. The Mexican War of 1846-48 transferred this territory to the United States (California, New Mexico, Nevada, Utah, Arizona and parts of Colorado and Wyoming).

The Treaty of Guadalupe Hidalgo in 1848 ending the Mexican War, guaranteed land, legal and civil rights to the Spanish/ Mexican population living in the territory. The Gold Rush of 1849 left the original Spanish Americans as a minority group in California, and further expansion of American settlement resulted in the old Spanish Americans in Texas, Colorado, New Mexico and Arizona becoming a minority group. By 1851 California laws had excluded Spanish Americans from holding public office, land laws deprived them of the land guaranteed in the treaty of 1848 and Spanish was not to be taught in schools. Similar laws were endorsed in other parts of the old Spanish territory even though the Spanish Americans technically and legally were United States citizens. Some states passed laws forbidding mixed marriages between whites and Spanish Americans.

The degradation of the Spanish American did not occur without violence. Juan Flores and Pancho Daniel (1856) led an attack against the Anglos in Los Angeles and Juan Cortinas (1859) led a revolt in Texas. Tension between the two groups ran so high that Los Angeles county in California was divided into an Anglo and Spanish American section. Groups were formed to resist land appropriation, such as the Gorras Blancas and Mano Negros (1889-91). Other mutual support groups emerged, such as the Junto Colonizadara De Sonora (1855) under Jesus Isles and the Alianzo Hispano American (1894). The process of depriving the old Spanish Americans of many civil, legal, social and land rights was accomplished by 1870.

Between 1870 and 1920 there was a mass migration of many Mexicans to the United States legally and illegally, encouraged by better employment opportunity and leaving the poverty of Mexico. In particular, as an aftermath of the Mexican Revolu- tion of 1910 there was a high level of migration to the United States. This new wave of migration from Mexico led to a rapid increase in the Spanish American population. These newer immi- grants were primarily laborers in the fields and not property

872

owners. They became extremely active in labor movements, such as the International World Workers Union (1915), Lu Confederation de Unions Obreros Mexicanos (1922), amongst others. There have been periodic attempts to control and limit immigration of this population group into the United States, such as 1917, 1924, 1926, etc. There have been many informal and formal agreements between Mexico and the United States to limit illegal entry.

Conflict between the Spanish American and the dominant non-Spanish society, continues up to the present. Labor strife was rampant in the 1930's with attempts at deportation of illegal aliens, which continues today. In 1984, the Border Patrol apprehended 1,135,000 Mexicans who were illegal aliens and located an additional 1,100,000. During the 1940's and 1950's there was the Pachuco Movement (1943) and labor strikes in 1947 and 1952. Since 1960 there emerged more organized and militant Spanish American groups. Examples of these groups include: Cesare Chavez who formed the National Farmworker's Union (1962) and Reies Lopez Tyerina who formed the La Alianza Federal de Mercedes organization (1963). Reies Tyerina invaded a court house (1967), and temporarily settled on a state park in 1969 based on land grants which were to be recognized by the 1848 Treaty of Hidalgo. David Sanchaz formed the Brown Berets (1967) which disbanded in 1973. There were attempts at a unified Spanish American political party through the La Raza Unida Party formed in 1970. Social, economic and legal reforms were called for in the treatment of the Chicano. Examples of these reforms include: migrant workers under Jesus Salas in Wisconsin (1970), equity in civil rights, and ending discrimination in housing, schools, employment and public places. In 1964, the Civil Rights Act addressed many of the civil rights issues as they affected Spanish Americans. More recent legislation is the amended immigration law of 1984 which provides for citizenship of illegal aliens entering before 1982. Like other special populations in the United States, the Chicano's have made a significant contribution to American society which included fighting in the Civil War, Spanish-American War, World War I, and II, Korean and Vietnam conflicts in defense of their adopted country. Specialized social service agencies have developed in response to the needs of the Chicano community, such as Spanish centers and United Migrant Opportunity Centers.[25]

PUERTO RICANS--In 1980 this population group was estimated at 2,013,945 or .87 percent of the population. This population group, like the Filipinos, became United States nationals after the Treaty of Paris in 1898 at the close of the Spanish-American War, yet, they were not granted citizenship until 1917.

Puerto Rico was settled by the Spanish in 1508 under Ponce de Leon. The Borenguen or Arawak Indian population was enslaved after periodic struggle by 1550. With the rapid depletion of the Native American population through disease and warfare, the Spanish repopulated the island with Black slaves from Africa and began to import slaves in 1510. The country remained under Spanish control until 1898. The current islanders are mainly descendants of the Spanish and Black population groups.

Some Puerto Ricans were in the United States by at least 1838 in Boston, Massachusetts, where the Spanish Benevolent Society was formed to aid immigrants from Spain, Cuba and Puerto Rico. In addition to functioning as a mutual aid society, this group also collected funds and actively engaged in political activities to overthrow the Spanish government in Cuba and Puerto Rico. In New York City, a small number of Puerto Ricans were in residence by 1830, and like the Boston community, were linked together with Cubans to fight Spanish control.

Prior to the annexation of Puerto Rico by the United States in 1898, there was little immigration to the United States. There was a small flow of immigrants from Puerto Rico up to about 1950, and a sharp increase in migration since then due to poor economic conditions on the island. From 1909 to the 1950's, an average of 2,000 Puerto Ricans immigrated per year. In the 1950's-1960's the average immigration rate grew to 41,000 per year. The trend of immigration to the United States slowed in 1970 and currently (1986) there are an equal number of people who migrate to the United States as who return to Puerto Rico. This trend in immigration is directly related to economic and population pressures in Puerto Rico. There is conflict in Puerto Rico over their commonwealth status since some groups actively seek statehood, such as the New Progressive Party, and others seek independent status, such as the Independent Party. Like other special populations there is a militant organization seeking independence from the United States known as the Partido Nacionalista (Nationalist Party) established in 1922 and its militant wing the FLN which attempted to assassinate President Truman in 1950.

The immigrant from Puerto Rico, lacking an adequate under-standing of English, and poor education, holding low paying jobs in the community, soon found themselves discriminated against in employment, housing and tended to live in a Puerto Rican community. The Catholic church became a major institution in providing the Puerto Rican with an identity and helped in the development of mutual support societies which included political activities. Various groups were formed, such as the Spanish Catholic Action Group (1953), the council of Puerto Rican and Spanish Organizations (1952) and the National Association for

Puerto Rican Civil Rights (1964). This population group, although small, has attempted to maintain their identity and is striving to make a contribution to American society. From the major population centers in New York city, this population group is beginning to disperse throughout the United States.[26]

CUBANS--In 1980 this population group was estimated at 803,226 or .35 percent of the population. Major Cuban immigration to the United States has occurred since 1959 with a large number leaving Cuba as refugees after Fidel Castro gained political control. More recently, there has been an influx of Cuban refugees in 1980. Cuba has a similar history to that of Puerto Rico, with the Spanish settling the island in 1511, and enslaving the Arawak Indians. The Indian population rapidly decreased as a consequence of disease, warfare and slavery, with the importation of slaves from Africa as early as 1517. The current Cuban population are descendants of the Spanish and Black population groups.

Spain controlled the island for centuries, however, there were periodic attempts at revolt and independence, such as Jose Francisco Lemus (1821), continuous political agitation in 1843, 1846 and the Ten Year War against Carlos de Cespedes (1868-1878). There were further political revolts by Jose Marti (1895), which was part of the causes for the Spanish-American War of 1898. After the Treaty of Paris in 1898, at the close of the Spanish-American War, Cuba was ruled by the United States under a military government and was granted independence in 1902.

There were Cubans in New York City by 1783, in Key West Florida by 1800, a revolutionary group in Key West, Florida by 1843 and in Boston, Massachusetts by 1830. These early immigrants were individuals fighting for the independence of Cuba, whereas the refugees of 1959 and 1980 left independent Cuba as refugees from a totalitarian political regime. Cuban refugees are facing similar problems as the Puerto Ricans in the United States. Special programs have been developed to provide social services through the Cuban Refugee Assistance Act of 1966 and 1980. Cubans in the United States have fought in both World Wars in defense of their adopted country and are striving to make a significant contribution to American Society.[27]

OTHER SPANISH--In 1980 the estimated number of other Spanish speaking in the United States was 3,051,063 or 1.31 percent of the population. Other Spanish populations include individuals from Argentina, Chili, Panama, Guatemala, Nicaragua, El Salvador, Spain, Portugal, etc. In 1980, it was estimated that 718,500 individuals were foreign born and about 25 percent have difficulty understanding English. Each of these groups have a distinct culture and heritage. There is a cultural difference whether one comes from Spain, Portugal, Central America, Caribbean America or South America.

WOMEN

In 1982 the estimated number of Women in the United States was 119,035,000 or 51.30 percent of the population. The status of Women socially, economically, and legally varies from society to society. Women historically have been subservient to the position of men. This subservience to the male may not always have been the case as illustrated in Greecian mythology and in other traditions of Amazon Women. The Amazons (according to mythology) were a tribe of Women warriors, where they were the dominant force and resided in the Caucus Mountains region by the Black Sea. This is the region where the Scythians lived later, about 2,000 B.C. Similar traditions of an Amazon tribe are found among the Indian tribes of South America in the Amazon valley.

In pre-christian era societies, the position of Women varied from one of near equality in Babylonia, to one of total sub-serviance to the husband in China. In Babylonian society (1700 B.C.), upper-class Women were subserviant to men but had rights to: buy, sell, and own property; make wills and share in estates; legally had mandated support from the husband and the right to learn how to read and write. On the other hand, the husband could bind his wife out to pay debts, and could drown her if she neglected the house or humiliated the husband. In Egyptian society (1400 B.C.), Women were dependent upon men, but were held in high esteem socially. In Chinese society, (1100 B.C.), Women were totally subserviant to the male and had few rights. A woman was expected to obey her husband, if he died, to obey the eldest son. Asian Indian society and religion, (1500 B.C.), such as Hinduism, shared similar viewpoints to the Chinese. In Hebrew society, (1400 B.C.), and in Greek society (400 B.C.), Women were subserviant to men and had few rights, but were treated with respect. The status of Women in early Roman society, (300 B.C.), was one of total subserviance to the male and had no rights, whereas in later Roman society the prerogatives of the husband were severely restricted.

With the decline of the Roman Empire in 450 the position of Women continued to decline with a blending of: Teutonic view-points, such as Women were totally subserviant with no rights, Judaic-Christian viewpoints, where the husband is head of the household and early Roman traditions of male dominance. The status of Women very quickly declined to one of a subordinate and inferior position. Thomas Aquinas (1225-1274), indicated it was natural for Women to be subordinated to men, since they were created as helpmates to men. Male attitudes by 1400 viewed

Women as morally and mentally inferior to the male. An example of this male chauvinistic viewpoint is contained in a book called The Witch's Hammer written in 1486 by Heinrich Kraemer and Jacob Sprenger. This book was a compendium on witchcraft, and concludes that Women were more prone to participate in the satanic cult, because of their moral inferiority. These attitudes carried over into the Renaissance and Reformation Periods of 1500-1700 as evidenced by the dominance of Women involved in the Salem Witchcraft Trials in Massachusetts (1649-1692). In effect, there was an abstract adoration of Women, but in a practical sense they were scorned, degraded and had few legal and social rights.

English Common Law initially was a reflection of these earlier attitudes and Women had no legal or property rights, and were under the total dominance of the male. The section on family violence (see Chapter 22 Personal social service) showed that the male had rights to chastise a woman for her behavior, which included physically beating the woman. There was some modification of common law practice in the United States, as colonial life was harsh and necessitated a mutual working together between the husband and wife, in order to economically and physically survive. Some of these modifications in the United States included the right to financial support, share the home and restrictions on violence.

In the United States in 1617, the ratio of men to Women was three to one and marriageable Women were transported to Virginia to be sold as wives. The status of Women in the colonies varied. The general rule of thumb was, Women had few rights as evidenced by the fact that many Women (about one-third of the total immigrants) came to the United States as indentured servants. Since the woman could not sue in court, it is difficult to ascertain what few rights they had. Consequently, many Women, instead of applying for divorce, simply ran away. There were some exceptional situations where Women became involved in legal and political affairs, owned property, had their own money, took care of business and could read and write. Two early advocates for Women's rights were: Ann Hutchinson (1635-1636) who was declared a heretic in Massachusetts and exiled to Rhode island, and Margaret Brent (1639) in Maryland who was a practicing attorney, a property owner and an advocate for the woman's right to vote.

Before the Revolutionary War, there was the beginning of an early feminist movement. In 1749, it was recognized that Women needed an education and a boarding school was established in Bethlehem, Pennsylvania. Other examples of this early feminist movement include: Judith Murray (1770), who wrote articles on the rights of Women, Phillis Wheately (1753-1784), who was a

877

freed slave and wrote poems about the plight of Women, and Abigail Adams, who chided her husband, John Adams (1779) for not advocating the rights of Women in the drafting of the United States Constitution in 1789. New Jersey in 1776 gave Women the right to vote, but this legislation was repealed in 1807. Although Women had few rights, they played an active role in the Revolutionary War through activities, such as boycotting English products, organizing the Daughters of Liberty under Mercy Otis Warren and Abigail Adams, providing nursing services, acting as couriers, etc. After the British retreat at Lexington and Concord in 1775, Women in Groton, Massachusetts changed clothes, grabbed rifles and actively engaged British troops and were successful in capturing a squad of British soldiers who were retreating. Some Women received pensions for their military service, such as Mary Hayes and Deborah Gannet. Mary Ludwig Hayes was known as "Molly Pitcher", who fought in the Battle of Monmouth in 1778, and Deborah Sampson Gannett was also known as Timothy Thayer, or Robert Shurklife, who in 1781 was on the payroll of the Continental Army.[28]

The early 1800's saw a further decline in the position of Women, as early industry employed men away from home and a split occurred between men's work (income production), and Women's work, (keeping house or domestic service which is not income production). Even when Women (or children) went to work outside of the home, their income was viewed as pin money and supplemental to the family income. This trend for different and segregated roles for men and Women was in sharp contrast to the mutual dependency called for in colonial days, or on the frontier, such as the western states like Montana. The sexes became segregated, men began to talk to men, Women to Women, and there were restrictions on the appropriate behavior of Women (and men) and dress codes.

The feminist movement of 1960-1975 was a continuation of earlier feminist movements. Earlier movements for rights of Women include the following: social issues 1820-1870, suffrage and protective legislation issues 1870-1920. Examples of significant Women in the social issue era of 1820-1870 period include the following: the Temperance Movement of 1836, (Margaret Fuller and Anne Royal); the anti-slavery movement, 1833-1860 (Lydia Maria Child, Sarah and Angeline Grimke, Lucretia Mott, Elizabeth Cady Stanton, Sojourner Truth); educational issues for Women, 1839-1860, (Catherine Beecher, Emma Willard, Mary Lyon, Susan B. Anthony); Professional education for Women 1835-1860, (Harriet K. Hunt, Elizabeth and Edith Blackwell in medicine, Antoinette Brown and Lucy Stone in theology, Dorthea Dix in mental health and Harriet Tubman in nursing). Although society was socially and legally restrictive for Women, the period of time from 1800-1850 resulted in the involvement of Women in a variety of social and political issues.[29]

Although the focus of the time period from 1820-1860 was on social issues, Women had not neglected the fact they had few social and legal rights themselves and suffrage and protective legislation became an issue. In 1848, the First Conference on Women's Rights was held in Seneca Falls, New York under the leadership of Elizabeth Stanton, Susan B. Anthony, Lucretia Mott, Earnestine Rose and Clarina Nickels. With the pressure for Women's rights increasing, New York became the first state to grant married Women the right to have property in 1848. New York state also provided for joint guardianship of children, Women could keep their wages and sue in court by 1860. Schools began to accept Women on equal terms, such as Oberlin Collge (1833) and Iowa State University (1858). Some western states granted suffrage, for example, Wyoming (1869), Utah (1870), and Colorado and Idaho (1890). Two organizations were developed in 1869 to further the cause of Women's suffrage: the National Women's Suffrage Association under Elizabeth Stanton, and the American Women's Suffrage Association under Susan B. Anthony which joined forces as the National American Women's Suffrage Association in 1890. With the formation of one organization, other Women became prominent in the Women's rights movements, such as Jane Addams (social work), Jeanette Rankin (politician), Anna Shaw (labor movement), etc. The culmination of this political activity led to the passage of the 19th Amendment in 1920 granting Women the right to vote.

Individuals in the suffrage movement became involved in other Women's issues, such as protective legislation for Women and child laborers (Jane Addams, Ellen Star, Florence Kelley in 1887), and in the labor movement and the Knights of Labor (Rose Schneiderman, Josephine Carey and Elizabeth Hosanovitz in 1881 to 1886). Further important figures in the labor movement were Elizabeth Gurley Flynn and Mary Harris Jones through the Industrial Workers of the World (1912). Sexual harassment in industry was an issue addressed by Rose Schneiderman. The delicate ideological and political issue of birth control and abortion was raised through Margaret Sanger, Ethel Burn and Martha Goldman (1913). This period of visible political activity for Women's rights began to decrease in the 1920's.

After two periods of activity (social issues 1820-1860 and suffrage and protective legislation 1870-1920), the feminist movement entered a third phase in the United States in the 1960's, with pressure for equality, socially, economically and legally. As more married Women began to work outside of the home, for example in 1890 the number of married Women that worked outside of the home was 5 percent, in 1940 15 percent, in

1980 44.5 percent, in 1984, 47.4 percent, and as more Women became part of the labor market, for example in 1950, 23.8 percent and in 1984, 43.8 percent, demands were made for child care, homemaking and day care services. A concurrent trend was for more Women (as well as men) to remain single. In 1960, 27.7 percent of the population was single, in 1984, 36.9 percent. A serious question of appropriate sex roles began to emerge partly as a consequence of new roles demanded for Women, as well as, a general concern about the legal and social rights of Women.

This third phase of the Women's movement was signaled by two books. Simone de Beuvior's book (1953) entitled The Second Sex, and a more active phase for the Women's movement with Betty Friedan's book on the Feminine Mystique (1963). This movement for equality, also known as Women's liberation, coincided with the social consciousness of the 1960's with legislation, such as the Civil Rights Act of 1964, Equal Opportunity Act of 1964, the proposed and defeated Equal Rights Amendment of 1972 and the Commission on the Status of Women (1961). The 1960's proved to be a decade of social and political activity with the establish- ment of the National Organization of Women (1966), the National Welfare Rights Movement (1967), Women's Liberation Conference under Shirley Chisolm (1968), concern over assault and abuse with rape consciousness organizations developing in 1971, wife beating organizations in 1972, abortion and birth control organizations and day care organizations in 1967 and the Equal Rights Amendment in 1972.

Other issues relating to the role of Women in society are emerging, such as Women in the military, sexual harassment, education, single Women, problems of working Women, and so on. The Women's movement today spans the political spectrum from a radical approach, such as Gloria Steinem to a more conservative approach, such as Ann Giordano and Gwendolyn Brooks. Regardless of the political aspects of the movement, there is no question that Women are striving for equal rights and just treatment, and seeking to be recognized for the enormous contributions they have made to American society.[30]

Although all special populations have faced prejudice and discrimination, the extent of discrimination varied depending upon whether a population had a different religion (Eastern religions and Judaism), racial identity (Black and Spanish Speaking or legal status (Women and Same Sex Preference). A historical time line of special populations in the United States is shown in figure 25-2.

STRUCTURE

The same model for analyzing the other networks of society is used for a discussion of special populations which is the

FIGURE 25-2

HISTORICAL TIME LINE OF SPECIAL POPULATIONS

	BLACK	EUROPEAN ETHNIC	NATIVE AMERICAN
–Some Chinese in California	1510–1511 –Slaves Transported to Puerto Rico & Cuba	pre 1700 –Early settlement from England, Scotland, Wales, Netherland France, Spain	1492 –Columbus
–Some Chinese in the Far West	1513 –Spanish and French explorers had free Blacks		1501 –Cortereal
–Some Chinese in New York	1619 –Slaves transported to Virginia	1700 –Colonial settlement mainly British Isles	1513 –Ponce De Leon
–Initial migration of Chinese	1723 –Slavery recognized and legal in all colonies	1800 1870 –Early Industrial Immigration –Ireland, Germany, 1834–nativistic movement – violence toward foreigners	1540 –Coronado
–John Mung – first Japanese			1542 –DeSota
–Major immigration of Chinese	1740–1831 –Various slave revolts 1740, 1800, 1822, 1831		1609 –Powhaten
–Asian discrimination laws, California	1787 –Slavery abolished in New England	1870 1900 –Middle Industrial Immigration, Russia Latvia, Finland Norway, Poland	1622 –Opechancanaugh
–Early Japanese immigration	1808 –importation of slaves stopped		1675 –King Phillips War
–Violence & mob action toward Chinese	1817–1861 –anti slavery movement	1900 1945 –Late Industrial Migration, Italy Greece, Turkey Jewish	1680 –Pueblo War
–Exclusion Act for Chinese	1865–1875 –Freedman's Bureau; 13th, 14th, 15th Amendment Civil Rights Acts	1945 –Post World War II Immigration – Displaced Persons & various other refugees	1689–1763 –French and Indian Wars (Pontiac Rebellion)
–Major Japanese immigration			1763 –Proclamation Line
–Korean immigration	1875 –Jim Crow Laws		1785 –Cherokee Treaty
–Segregation laws for Japanese	1901 –Urban league		1789 –Northwest Ordinance Act
–Violence toward Japanese	1908 –NAACP		1809 –Treaty–Delaware Potawatomi
	1942 –Congress of Racial Equality		1811 –Tecumsah
–Alien laws			1813 –Seminole War (Oceola)
	1954 –Brown vs. Board of Education		1817 –Treaty Chippewa
–Exclusion Act toward Japanese, Chinese, & Korean	1957 –Southern Christian Leadership Conference Civil Rights Act		1823 –Oneida Reservation
			1829 –Delaware Removal (Delaware)
–Filipino immigration Alien status violence toward Filipino	1960 –SNCC 1964 –Civil Rights Act Equal Opportunity Act		1832 –Black Hawk War (Wisconsin) Winnebago Removal (Wisconsin)

FIGURE 25-2 (Continued)

ASIAN	BLACK	EUROPEAN ETHNIC	NATIVE AMERICAN
1941 —Japanese Internship	1968 —Black Panthers	1960 —Refugees Communist	1838 —Cherokee R (South Car
943 —Restrictions toward Chinese & Filipino repealed	1970 —Focus on political participation	1970 Countries 1980 —Political Refugees 1986 —Political Refugees	1854 —Menominee Reservatio (Wisconsin
946 —Chinese become naturalized Japanese " " Korean " " Filipino " "	1980 —Focus on employment/ education 1986 —Uncertainty on how to handle the Haitian problem		Plain Stat (Red Cloud Sitting Bu Southwest
965 —Liberalized Immigra- tion laws			1854 —(Cochise Geronimo)
1973 —Vietnam Refugees Cambodian Refugees Laotian Refugees			1871 —Treaty Pe Ends 1882 —Indian Re Banned
980 —Decrease in funds for programs for Indochinese			1887 —Dawes Act 1889 —Tribal or tion Bann
			1890 —Northwest conflict Joseph) Wounded K
986 —Political refugees Government makes financial payment to individuals interred during World War II			1924 —Granted Citizensh
			1934 —Indian Re ization A
			1954 —Terminati
			1968 —Indian Ci Rights Ac
			1972 —Terminati Repealed
			1980 —Maintenan status qu Native Am backlash treaty rig
			1986 —Concern ov treaty rig and minera rights

FIGURE 25-2 (Continued)

SAME SEX PREFERENCE

200 B.C.   Greece - homosexuality accepted with limitations and
           mutual consenting partners

100 B.C.   Rome - homosexuality accepted with limitations and
           mutual consenting partners

           Hebrews - not accepted--considered an unnatural act
           and against the laws of God. Potential sanction
           was execution

50 A.D.   Christian - followed the Hebrew tradition

400 A.D.   Viewed homosexuality as religious heresy

1000 A.D. Medieval Europe - linked homosexuality with Satanism
           and Witchcraft

1550   England - homosexuality a crime and punishable by
           execution

1650   Puritan Act of 1650 reinforced the
           earlier acts on homosexuality

1700   United States - followed the English tradition

1886   Viewed as a sexual perversion and
           as a mental illness (Krafft-Ebing)

1900   Freudian psychology continues the tradition
           of viewing homosexuality as an illness

1960   Development of mutual support groups,
           open discussion of the problem

1973   American Psychiatric Association deletes
           homosexuality as a mental illness

1980   Concern over social, legal and political
           rights

1986   Medical problems of AIDS, discrimination
           in the military

FIGURE 25-2 (Continued)

SPANISH	WOMEN
1510 -Importation of 1511 slaves to Puerto Rico & Cuba	1617 -Marriageable women trans- ported to Virginia & sold for wives
1513 -Ponce DeLeon, Florida	
1519 -Cortes, Yucaton Mexico	1635 -Anne Hutchinson
1540 -Coronado, Southwest United States	1639 -Margaret Brent 1770 -Early voices for equal rights: Murray Wheately, Jane Adams
1542 -De Sota, Mississippi Valley Cabrillo - Calif.	
1590 -Southwest settled by Spanish	1776 -Fight in Rev.War
1769 -California settled by Spanish	1783 -Molly Pitcher (Mary Hayes Deborah Gannett)
1783 -Cubans in New York City	1820 -Social Issue movement
1821 -Mexico Independent from Spain	1860 Temperance - Catherine Beecher, Margaret Fuller
1838 -Puerto Ricans & Cubans in Boston & New York	Anti slavery - Lydia Child; Sojourner Truth
1846 -Mexican War; Treaty 1848 of Guadalupe Hidalgo	Suffrage Elizabeth Stanton, Susan Anthony; Conference of 1848
1851 -Spanish/American 1870 settlers losing Civil Rights & land -Resistance by Spanish Americans-Flores & Daniel 1856, Cortines, 1859	Education - Catherine Beecher, Mary Lyon Theology - Antoinette Brown, Lucy Stone Medicine - Harriet Tubman, Harriet Hunt
1870 -Mass Immigration 1920 from Mexico	Welfare - Dorthea Dix, Clara Barton
1898 -Puerto Rico & Cuba are part of the United States	1860 -Suffrage Movement 1920 & Protective Legislation, Jane Adams, Ellen Starr, Rose Schneiderman Elizabeth Flynn Susan B. Anthony 19th Amendment
1902 -Cuba becomes Independent	
1930 -Violence Toward Spanish Americans	
1947 -Labor movement 1950 -Immigration from Puerto Rico	1953 -Equal Rights Movement or Fem- inist Movement Simone de Beavoir Commission on Women Betty Friedan
1959 -Cuban Refugees 1962 -Cesar Chavez 1967 -Tyerina; Brown Berets 1970 -Jesus Salas 1980 -Cuban refugees	
1986 Central American Refugees-El Salvadore Nicaragua Reduction in federal monies for bilingual programs	1964 Civil Rights Act National Organ- ization for Women
	1972 Rape & sexual Assault Commission Spouse beating Shelters
	1980 Equal Rights Amendment defeated
	1986 Comparative Worth in Employment

organizational context, services provided, occupations and
professions and dominant occupations and professions.

ORGANIZATIONAL CONTEXT

A focal point for programs for special populations relates
to federal and state governments and their affirmative action
programs, which are a consequence of the Civil Rights legislation of 1964 and thereafter. Figure 25-3 shows an ideal relationship between the special populations in American society,
and the rest of the societal networks. Figure 25-4 shows the
general government organizations responsible for affirmative
action for special populations in the United States.

The various members of the special populations rely heavily
on an informal or folk system to solve problems and obtain
services. Of particular importance for many of the special
populations in the informal system are family members, friends,
specific oriented mutual support groups and the religious
network.

SERVICES PROVIDED

Services provided for special populations is covered in the
other chapters of this book. Consequently, the reader is
referred to various other chapters for further details. Some
general examples of services include the following:

- Cultural programs
- Bilingual programs
- Financial support
- Legal aid
- Housing
- Clothing and emergency food
- Employment aid
- Educational programs.

OCCUPATIONS and PROFESSIONS

Many of the individuals working with special populations are
volunteers, and employment is not concentrated in any specific
profession. Individuals are involved because of their own self
interest and identification with a particular group. Individuals who have a professional capacity, such as a social
worker, a lawyer, physician, psychologist and so on have a high
degree of influence in terms of program development and evaluation of specific services and organizations.

Figure 25-3

Idealized Relationship of Affirmative Action
Programs for Special Populations and Other Societal Networks

Example of Special Population

Societal Netwo

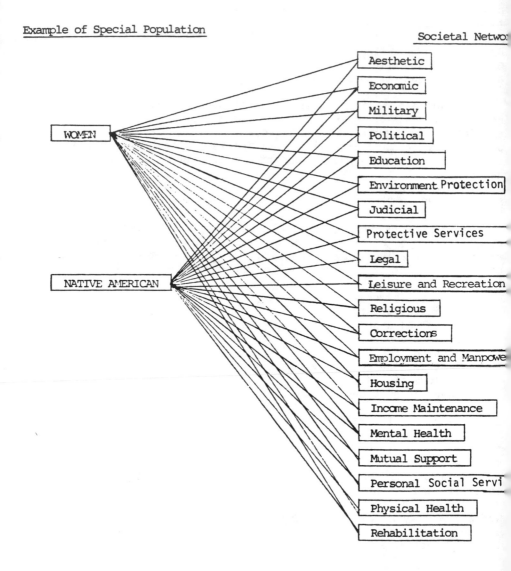

WOMEN	Aesthetic
	Economic
	Military
	Political
	Education
	Environment Protection
	Judicial
	Protective Services
	Legal
NATIVE AMERICAN	Leisure and Recreation
	Religious
	Corrections
	Employment and Manpowe
	Housing
	Income Maintenance
	Mental Health
	Mutual Support
	Personal Social Servi
	Physical Health
	Rehabilitation

Figure 25-4

Idealized Government Organization for Special Populations*

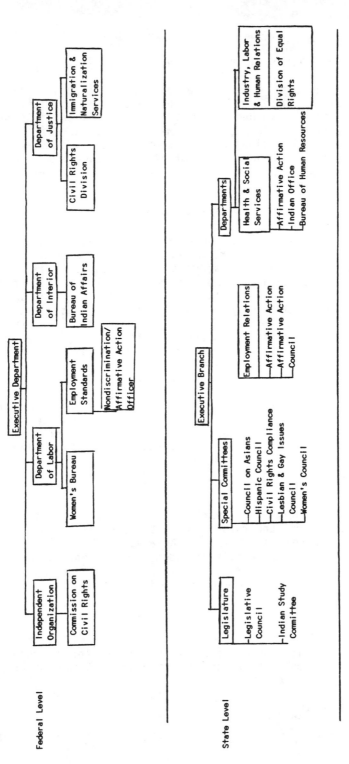

*Sources: Adapted from Office of the Federal Register, United States Government Manual 1985-86, Washington, DC: U.S. Government Printing Office, 1985, pp. 478, 844, 845, 846 and Wisconsin Legislative Reference Bureau, Wisconsin Blue Book 1985-86, Madison, Wisconsin: Department of Administration, 1985, pp. 331, 512, 531, 577.

887

DOMINANT OCCUPATIONS and PROFESSIONS

In working with special populations one practical criterion is a degree of identification with the special population and a commitment to the values and attitudes that a specific special population holds. Consequently, there is no specific dominant occupation or profession in the human services which is involved with special populations. All of the individuals who have some relationship with the human services are involved with special populations.

SOCIAL WORK

The role of social work with special populations is primarily that of a broker, advocate and an enabler to obtain particular objectives and services. The social worker may be involved with special populations as an individual citizen or as a professional. The specific role or task they would perform depends upon whether they are a member of a special population group themselves, advocating for certain positions on social policy, as an individual citizen, or whether they are advocating policies in terms of a generalized viewpoint based upon professional attitudes toward humanitarian concerns, such as equal justice, equity, etc. The specific role of a social worker with special populations will vary depending upon the societal network in which one is employed, for example, corrections, education, mental health, etc. The social worker would theoretically vary their methods or techniques of working with the special populations depending upon the specific population group one is working with.

CASEWORK

The social worker in working with special populations needs to have a cultural understanding of the specific group or groups they are working with, such as Asians, Native Americans, etc. For example, when working with some special populations either with individuals or families, one does not become verbally assertive, look people directly into the eyes, etc.

GROUP WORK

The social worker in establishing a specific group of a special population needs to be aware of whether the population group has a tradition of group discussion, group consensus or relies on individual discussion.

COMMUNITY ORGANIZATION

The needs of special populations will vary legally,

socially, economically, etc., therefore, the task of organizing a group and for what purpose will vary. For example, Native Americans are highly concerned about treaty rights, Asians are not.

ADMINISTRATION and SUPERVISION

When one directs an agency which has a focus on a specific special population, there are increased demands and expectations of providing service to that population and to implement these services in an individualistic and humanistic manner.

ORGANIZATIONS

Social workers themselves have professional organizations which address the needs of the special populations. Some examples of professional organizations and social work include the following:

ASIAN--Asian American Social Workers, Los Angeles, California and Asian American Social Workers of Western Washington, Seattle, Washington.

BLACK--Black Social Workers, Los Angeles California and Black Social Workers Association, Milwaukee, Wisconsin.

EUROPEAN ETHNIC--Ethnic Social Workers' Association, Chicago, Illinois.

NATIVE AMERICAN--Association of American Indian Social Workers, Portland, Oregon.

SAME SEX PREFERENCE--Gay and Lesbian Social Work Association, San Francisco, California.

SPANISH SPEAKING--Spanish Social Work Association, Phoenix, Arizona.

WOMEN--Women Social Workers' Association, Washington, D.C.

PERSONAL SOCIAL SERVICES

Many of the individuals identified as special populations utilize the personal social service network. (See Chapter 22 Personal Social Service.) Some examples of organizations and programs which provide personal social services which focus on special populations include the following:

PROTECTIVE SERVICES

Bay Area Black Child Advocacy Coalition, Oakland California and Urban Indian Child Resource Center, Oakland, California.

UTILITARIAN SERVICES

Asian American Homemakers, National City California; Asian American Legal Services, Los Angeles, California and United Migrant Opportunity Services, Grand Lodge Michigan and Milwaukee, Wisconsin.

DEVELOPMENTAL and SOCIALIZATION SERVICES

Black Caucus of Family Service Association of America, Wilmington, Delaware; Chinatown Youth Services, Boston, Massachusetts and National Indian Council on Aging, Albuquerque, New Mexico.

REHABILITATIVE and THERAPEUTIC SERVICES

American Indian Council on Alcoholism, Milwaukee, Wisconsin; Mexican American Council on Alcoholism, San Jose, California and Women for Sobriety, Quakertown, Pennsylvania.

SPECIAL POPULATIONS

Although the footnotes to this chapter have numerous examples of organizations which have specialized services for a specific special population group, it may be helpful to the reader to have an example of an organization which focusses on a specific special population group. A special population group not discussed in this chapter is the disabled (see Chapter 24, Rehabilitation Network). Examples of organizations for each special population group are as follows:

ASIAN

Asian American Community Center, Milwaukee, Wisconsin and Chinese American Citizen Alliance, San Francisco, California.

BLACK

Urban League, New York, New York and its local chapters and National Association for the Advancement of Colored People, New York, New York and its local chapters.

EUROPEAN ETHNIC

German Society of the City of New York, New York and Italian Charities of America, Elmhurst, New York.

NATIVE AMERICAN

Inter Tribal Council of California, Sacramento, California and United Indians of Milwaukee, Milwaukee, Wisconsin.

SAME SEX PREFERENCE

Homosexual Information Center, Hollywood, California and Lesbian Resource Center, Minneapolis, Minnesota.

SPANISH SPEAKING

Spanish Center, Milwaukee, Wisconsin and United Council of the Spanish Speaking Organizations, Martinez, California.

WOMEN

National Organization for Women, Chicago, Illinois and Women in Transition, Philadelphia, Pennsylvania.

ISSUES

Special populations in American society face a number of severe issues of which prejudice and discrimination are only symptoms. The major issues are socioeconomic, legal and cultural awareness.

SOCIOECONOMIC

Many of the individuals amongst the special populations are also at the same time, in the lower social economic class of society, have limited education, work skills etc. Therefore, questions of accessibility to social and legal services, education, employment and housing etc. are key issues. Although one may not be prejudicial in their relationship to other people, there is still the fact that many of these people in the special populations are in lower social economic positions and therefore in poverty or near poverty status. The major issue is whether the United States is able to afford and maintain a system where no individuals are below a particular level of socioeconomic security.

LEGAL

Equal rights under law, both civil rights and civil liber-ties, is a major issue since special populations historically have been denied access to the legal network. Even if these population groups had access to the legal network, they were still discriminated against in court, and legal decisions were based upon articulate but unequitable decisions.

CULTURAL AWARENESS

Cultural awareness and understanding is a critical issue since all of these special populations are not the same. It is imperative that human service professions and professionals be aware and respect cultural differences, historical traditions different perspectives on the family, physical and mental health, role of men and Women, etc.

SUMMARY

This chapter on special populations instead of attempting to define the specific services available for each of the special populations, focussed on a historical perspective to show the following:

1) That groups which were different than white, protestant, and Anglo Saxon (WASP), were victims of varied degrees of prejudice and discrimination.

2) The severity of discrimination varied in degrees between those populations which were European Ethnic versus those populations which were non European Ethnic.

3) Non European Ethnic populations were deprived of various legal, social and political rights in the United States.

4) All of the special population groups have fought for the United States in defense of their country, yet had to fight internally for their own civil, legal and social rights.

5) All of the special population groups have formed mutual aid and support societies, developed a political perspective, and through this political perspective attempted to obtain equal, social, legal and political rights in the United States.

6) Special population groups depending upon their size account for as little as .61 percent of the population and as high as 51.30 percent of the population. Depending upon the geographical location of a specific special population there are enormous political, educational, social service delivery and legal problems.

FOOTNOTES

*This chapter was reviewed for comments by Roger McNeely, Professor of Social Work, Elvira de Silva, Assistant Professor of Social Work, School of Social Welfare; Chan Kang-Ning (Adrian) Associate Professor, Educational Psychology, School of Education, and Victor Green, Professor, History, College of Letters and Science, University of Wisconsin-Milwaukee.

1. Individuals who are disabled, although having special needs, are not discussed in this chapter since Chapter 24, Rehabilitation Network, is devoted to disability.

   Within the context of this chapter, certain terms which are normally not capitalized are capitalized since the reference is to a specific, identifiable population group. The terms Asian, Black, European Ethnic, Native Americans, Same Sex Preference, Spanish Speaking and Women are capitalized.

2. These estimates on ethnicity do not include the current situation in Alaska for Korean immigration.

3. Estimates on the size of the special populations are derived from the following sources: United States Department of Commerce, Bureau of the Census, 1980 Census of Population Supplementary Report. Washington, D.C.: U.S. Government Printing Office; Asian and Pacific Islander Population by State, 1980, 1983, p. 2; American Indian Areas and Alaska Native Villages--1984 pp 2-4, Persons of Spanish Origin by State 1980, 1982 p. 2,; Statistical Abstract of the United States): 1986 (106th edition), 1985, pp. 24, 25, 32-36, 87 and 1982/83 (103rd edition) 1982, p. 36 and the News and World Week Report August 8, 1983.

4. Archeological evidence and some Native American traditions suggest that some Chinese were present in the western hemisphere before Columbus and more than likely before 100 A.D.

5. Some examples of organizations which focus on the Chinese include the following: Chinese American Citizen Alliance, 1044 Stockton St., San Francisco, CA 94108; Chinese American Civic Council, 2249 S. Wentworth St., Chicago, IL 60616; Chinese Development Council, 5 Division St., NY, NY 10002 and the National Association of Social Workers (Asian Social Workers) 7981 Eastern Ave., Silver Spring, Maryland 10910 or the local chapter of the National Association of Social Workers.

6. Some examples of organizations which focus on the Japanese include the following: Japanese American Citizens League, 22 Peace Plaza, San Francisco, CA 94115; Japanese Mutual Aid Society, 4410 N. Malden St., Chicago, IL 60600 and the National Association of Social Workers (Asian Social Workers) 7981 Eastern Ave., Silver Spring, Maryland 20910 or the local chapter of the National Association of Social Workers.

7. Some examples of organizations which focus on the Koreans include the following: Korean American Community Services, 3435 N. Sheffield St., Chicago, IL 60657; Korean National Association, 1368 W. Jefferson Blvd., Los Angeles, CA 90007 and the National Association of Social Workers (Asian Social Workers) 7981 Eastern Ave., Silver Spring, Maryland 10901 or the local chapter of the National Association of Social Workers.

8. Some examples of organizations which focus on the Filipinos include the following: Filipino American Political Association, 3156 Wilshire Blvd., Los Angeles, CA 90010; Club Filipino, 2734 Barry Ave., Los Angeles, CA 90064 and the National Association of Social Workers (Asian Social Workers) 7981 Eastern Ave., Silver Spring, Maryland 10910 or the local chapter of the National Association of Social Workers.

9. A general historical and cultural survey of the Indochinese population is contained in Chan, Kang-Ning (Adrian) in "Education for Chinese and Indochinese' Theory into Practice Vol. 20 No. 1 (Winter, 1981), pp. 35-44.

10. Some examples of organizations which focus on the Indochinese include the following: Vietnam Christian Service, 475 Riverside Dr., NY, NY 10027; International Committee of Conscience on Vietnam, P.O. Box 271, Nyack, NY 10960 and the National Association of Social Workers (Asian Social Workers) 7981 Eastern Ave., Silver Spring, Maryland 10901 or the local chapter of the National Association of Social Workers.

11. Some examples of organizations which focus on the Black population include the following: National Association for the Advancement of Colored People, 1790 Broadway St., NY, NY 11213; National Urban League, 55 E. 52nd St., NY, NY 10022; Southern Christian Leadership Conference, 330 Auburn Ave. N.E., Atlanta, GA 30303; Congress of Racial Equality, 200 W. 135th St., NY, NY 10030 and the National Association of Social Workers 7981 Eastern Ave., Silver Spring,

894

Maryland 20910 or the local chapter of the National
Association of Social Workers.

12. A listing of all immigrant groups and when they migrated to
the United States is beyond the scope of this text. The
reader is referred to Francis Brown and Joseph Roucek, One
America, New York, NY: Prentice Hall Inc., 1952, as a
source book on many of the immigrant groups in the United
States. The major groups of immigrants include the
following: British, Irish, Norwegian, Swedish, Danish,
Dutch, Belgian, French, German, Russian, Polish, Czech,
Slovak, Bohemian, Serbian, Croation, Bulgarian, Icelandic,
Latvian, Estonian, Lithuanian, Finish, Austrian, Hungarian,
Romanian, Canadian, Greek, Albanian, Italian, Turks,
Spanish, Portuguese, Swiss, Australian, New Zealanders,
Jewish, etc. In effect, the United States probably has a
representative from every country of the world. The
Asiatic, Black and Spanish Speaking immigrants were covered
in other parts of this chapter.

A group not discussed in this text are the various Arabic
groups, such as Egyptians, Libyans, Saudi Arabians,
Lebanese, etc. These groups have migrated, particularly
since 1945 and are a small proportion of the population.

13. The State of Wisconsin and the City of Milwaukee has been
called one of the most ethnic oriented states and cities of
the United States (Milwaukee Journal - special section, July
4, 1976). Milwaukee, Wisconsin in 1980 had population
groups from at least eight eastern European groups including
the following: Polish, Bohemian, Russian, Lithuanian,
Estonian, Croation, Slovakian and Latvian; five Scandanavian
groups including the following: Swedish, Finnish, Danish,
Norwegian and Icelandic; seven Native American tribes
including the following: Chippewa, Onieda, Potawatomie,
Winnebago, Stockbridge/Munsee, Brotherton and Menominee;
four British Isle groups: English, Scots, Irish and Welsh;
six west European groups including: German, Dutch, Belgian,
Swiss, Italian and French; four southern European groups:
Greek, Romanian, Armenian and Albanian; plus Asiatic groups;
Spanish Americans, Blacks and so on. The annual folk fair
held in Milwaukee represents this ethnic diversity, and in
1986 there were 45 ethnic groups participating in this
cultural activity. The cities of Chicago, Los Angeles, New
York, and Washington, D.C. are also known for their wide
diversity of European Ethnic groups.

14. Some examples of organizations which focus on European
ethnic immigrant groups include the following: The Ethnic
Foundation Inc., 562 Davis Bldg., Washington, DC 20006;

National Confederation of American Ethnic Groups, 1629 K. St. NW, Washington DC 20006; Ethnic Millions Political Action Committee, P.O. Box 48, Bayville, NY 11709; American Council for Nationalities Services, 20 W. 40th St., NY, NY 10018; International Institute of Milwaukee County Inc., 2810 W. Highland Blvd., Milwaukee, WI 53208 and the National Association of Social Workers (Ethnic Social Workers) 7981 Eastern Ave., Silver Spring, Maryland 10910 or the local chapter of the National Association of Social Workers.

15. Jewish organizations include B'Nai B'Rith and its local chapters and Jewish Family Services and the local agencies.

16. For a broad overview on ethnicity, the reader is referred to Francis Brown and Joseph Roucek, One America, New York, NY: Prentice Hall Inc., 1952 and various publications of the Oceana Press series on ethnicity, such as The Irish in America 1550-1972, The Japanese in America: 1843-1973, The Germans in America: 1607-1970 and other publications in this series.

17. The major Native American and European settler military engagements include the following: eastern state wars, Pequot War (1637) in Massachusetts and Connecticut; King Phillips War (1675-1678) in Massachusetts; French and Indian Wars of 1689-1763, which includes Pontiac's Rebellion in 1763; Lord Dunmore's War in Virginia (1774); Midwest State Wars, Chief Little Turtle in Indiana (1790-1794), Tecumsah (1811) in Ohio, Blackhawk (1832), in Wisconsin; Southern State Wars Creek (1813-1814 in Arkansas, Seminole Wars (1817-1818 and 1835-1842) under Osceola in Florida; Northern Plains State Wars, (1854-1890) with the following leaders, Little Crow (1862), Red Cloud, Sitting Bull and Crazy Horse (Sioux) (1876). These military engagements include Custer's Last Stand and the Massacre of Wounded Knee (1890); Southern Plains State Wars, the Sand Creek Massacre (1854); Black Kettle of the Cheyenne tribe, Satanta of the Kiowa tribe (1864-1874); Walkers War (1853) against the Utes, the Ute Blackhawk War (1865-1868) and Meekers War (1875) against the Utes; the northwest states, wars which include the Modac War under Captain Jack (1872-1873) and Chief Joseph of the Nez Perce (1877); and the Southwest State Wars, Apache (1861-1900) under Cochise, Victorio, Coloradus, Mangus and Geronimo and the Navaho wars (1843-1863).

18. In the process of removal some tribes refused to go to the Native American lands in Kansas and Missouri. Some tribes were removed, however, members of these tribes returned to their old tribal lands. Some of these bands were not

recognized as Native American tribes until the Howard-Wheeler Act of 1934, and at that time were provided with land. Examples of these tribes are the Winnebago of Wisconsin and the Mole Lake Potawatomie of Wisconsin. Native American lands in Kansas and Nebraska were open to white settlement in 1854, and in Oklahoma via the Homestead Act of 1862. Currently, there are about 490 recognized Native American tribes in the United States.

Some bands who resisted removal and fled the United states authorities are still fighting for recognition as a Native American tribe, such as the Kickapoo of Eagle Pass in Texas. This tribe fled to Mexico and resides along the border between Mexico and Texas and neither the United States nor Mexico claims responsibility for the tribe (Milwaukee Journal, 11-27-80).

A unique situation involves the Pueblo tribe of the Southwest. They were initially under the authority of Spain until 1822, then Mexico until 1848. The treaty of Hidalgo in 1848 grants them certain privileges based upon their prior treaties with Mexico. The net result is that the Pueblos have less constraints placed upon them by the United States government than other tribes.

19. The last 50 years of struggle between the Native American and White settlers is known for its great leaders, such as Sitting Bull, Red Cloud, Crazy Horse and Little Crow of the Sioux; and Cochise, Victorio and Geronimo of the Apache; and Chief Joseph of the Nez Perce.

20. Each tribe could vote to either allot the land to individuals or maintain the land in a tribal status dependig upon prior treaties. Most tribes voted for a combination of individual land and tribal allotment. The Menominees in Wisconsin partly based upon their treaty were able to maintain tribal land, consequently they were able to retain about 96 percent of the land granted to them in the treaty of 1854. In comparison the Chippewas in Wisconsin, lost about 50 percent of the land granted to them by their treaty of 1854.

21. Some examples of organizations which focus on Native Americans include the following: Indian Rights Association, 1505 Race St., Philadelphia, PA 19102; Coalition of Eastern Native Americans, 927 15th St., Washington, DC 20005; National Indian Education Association, Hubbard Bldg., 2675 University Ave., St. Paul, MN 55114; American Indian Movement, 555 Aurola Ave., St. Paul, MN 55101 and the National Association of Social Workers (Native American

social workers) 7981 Eastern Ave., Silver Spring, Maryland 20910 or the local chapter of the National Association of Social Workers.

22. An example is Benjamin Sadock et al. The Sexual Experience, Baltimore, MD: William and Wilkins Co., 1976. This book indicates that homosexual behavior is no longer classified as a mental illness but describes the behavior as a form of deviation and variation.

23. In the newspapers, about once a year, an article appears about an individual who has been coerced to leave positions in the military, education, religious or political organization because of their identification as a homosexual.

24. Some examples of organizations which focus on Same Sex Preference groups include the following: One Incorporated, 2256 Venice Blvd., Los Angeles CA   90006; National Gay Task Force, 80 Fifth Ave., New York, NY   10011; Lesbian Resource Center, 40 University YWCA, 4224 University Way NE, Seattle, WA   98105; United Sisters, P.O. Box 41, Garwood, NJ   07027 and the National Association of Social Workers (Gay Social Workers), 7981 Eastern Ave., Silver Spring, Maryland, 20910 or the local chapter of the National Association of Social Workers.

25. Some examples of organizations which focus on Chicanos' include the following: American-Spanish Committee, P.O. Box 119, Canal St. Station, NY, NY   10013; Spanish-American Association, 221 Swan St., Buffalo, NY   14204; National Latin American Federation, P.O. Box 342, Cheyenne, WY 82001; Division for the Spanish Speaking, 1312 Massachusetts Ave. NW, Washington, DC   20005; United Council of the Spanish Speaking Organizations Inc., 829 Main St., Martinez, CA   94553 and the National Association of Social Workers (Spanish American Social Workers) 7981 Eastern Ave., Silver Spring, Maryland   20910 or the local chapter of the National Association of Social Workers.

26. Some examples of organizations which focus on Puerto Ricans include the following: American Puerto Rican Action League, 75 E. 100 and 10th St., NY, NY   10029; National Association for Puerto Rican Civil Rights, 175 E. 116th St., NY, NY 10029; Puerto Rican Congress of Chicago, 2315 W. North Ave., Chicago, IL   60647 and the National Association of Social Workers (Spanish American Social Workers) 7981 Eastern Ave., Silver Spring, Maryland   20910 or the local chapter of the National Association of Social Workers.

27. Some examples of organizations which focus on Cubans include the following: Centrol Hispano Catolico, 130 NE 2nd St., Miami, FL 33132; Midwest Cuban Federation, 42 Buttermilk Park, Fort Mitchell, KY 41027; Cuban Municipalities in Exile, 1460 W. Flagler St., Miami, FL 33134 and the National Association of Social Workers (Spanish American Social Workers) 7981 Eastern Ave., Silver Spring, Maryland 10910 or the local chapter of the National Association of Social Workers.

Of interest in the history of Cuba is the direct role the United States played in supporting the revolutionary groups between 1843-1846, 1880, and more currently in 1961 with the tacit support of the Bay of Pigs invasion. At one point the United States attempted to purchase Cuba in 1844.

28. These two Women set a precedent which was not matched until 130 years later, when another Women was to receive a veterans pension on her own behalf for military service.

29. The chapters on the Education Network (8), Religious Network (15), Mental health Network (20) and Physical Health Network (23) contain further information on the role of Women in the development of social service programs.

30. Some examples of organizations which focus on Women include the following: National Organization for Women, 5 South Wabash St., Chicago, IL 60603; National Women's Studies Association, University of Maryland, College Park, MD 20742; Women's Educational and Industrial Union, 356 Boylston St., Boston, MA 02116; Women in Transition, 112 S. 16th St., Philadelphia, PA 19102 and the National Association of Social Workers (Women Social Workers), 7981 Eastern Ave. Silver Spring, Maryland 20910 or the local chapter of the National Association of Social Workers.

SUGGESTED READINGS

Rodolfo Acuna. Occupied America: The Chicano's Struggle Toward Liberation. San Francisco, California: Canfield Press, 1972. This book is an excellent indepth analysis of the history of the Chicano in the United States.

Edith Hoshino Altbach. Women in America. Lexington, Massachusetts: D.C. Heath Co., 1974. This book is a comprehensive overview of the treatment of Women in the United States. It is a well documented book and a good resource.

Derrick Bell, Jr. <u>Race, Racism and American Law</u>. Boston, Massachusetts: Little, Brown and Co., 1973. A technical but thought provoking book which clearly shows how the law for many years was interpreted and used to deny civil rights to minorities and more recently (1950 on) to enhance the civil rights of minorities.

Francis Brown and Joseph Roucek. <u>One America</u>. New York, New York: Prentice Hall, Inc., 1952. Although dated, this book is very useful as it contains a brief history of each of the major ethnic groups in the United States.

Frank Coppa and Thomas Curran. <u>The Immigrant Experience in America</u>. Boston, Massachusetts: Twayne Publishing Co., 1976. This book is a series of case studies describing the experiences of specific ethnic groups as they came to the United States. It is a book which has some useful insights and is a reminder of the difficulties various population groups experienced as they immigrated from their homeland.

Rupert Costo. <u>The American Indian Reader: History Vol. 4</u>. San Francisco, California: Indian History Press, 1974. This book provides a brief but comprehensive overview of Native American and white interaction in the United States.

Phillip Foner. <u>History of Black Americans</u>. Westport, Connecticut: Greenwood Press, 1975. This is a well documented comprehensive history of the treatment of the Black population in the United States. This book is highly recommended for those individuals seeking more information about this population group.

Erwin Haeberly. <u>The Sex Atlas</u>. New York, New York: Seabury Press, 1978. This book has one chapter on homosexual behavior which provides a broad overview of society's reactions and attitudes.

Carol Hymowitz and Michaele Weissman. <u>A History of Women in America</u>. New York, New York: Bantam Books, Inc., 1978. This is a nontechnical history of Women in the United States which provides a broad overview and highlights some interesting misperceptions about Women.

Alvin Josephy, Jr. <u>The Indian Heritage of America</u>. New York, New York: Bantam Books, 1973. This is a classic comprehensive overview of Native American history in North and South America. Some of the material is outdated, however it is a well documented book and highly recommended.

Stuart Levine and Nancy Lurie. The American Indian Today. Baltimore, Maryland: Penguin Books, Inc., 1968. This book is highly recommended since it focusses on the Native American today and their problems. Many individuals have numerous misperceptions about Native Americans since they are viewed from the past, pre-1930, and not from the perspective of a changing population.

Oceana Press. Series on ethnic studies 1971-1977. There are a series of publications from Oceana Press which focus on a brief history of specific population groups, such as Germans, Chicanos, Irish, Japanese, Filipinos, Koreans, Blacks, Chinese, etc. Each volume has a different author and provides a short historical overview. For the individual who is looking for a short, but intense overview of a variety of ethnic groups, this series is highly recommended.

Clarence Senior. The Puerto Ricans: Strangers - Then Neighbors. Chicago, Illinois: Quadrangle Books, 1965. This book provides insight into the problems and difficulties the Puerto Ricans have in adjusting to American society.

REFERENCES

Acuna, Rodolfo. Occupied America: The Chicano's Struggle Toward Liberation, San Francisco, CA: Canfield Press, 1972.

Altbach, Edith Hoshino. Women in America. Lexington, MA: D.C. Heath Company, 1974.

Bell, Jr. Derrick. Race, Racism and American Law. Boston, MA: Little, Brown & Co., 1973.

Bellview, Fred and Lyn Richter. Understanding Human Sexual Inadequacy. Boston, MA: Little, Brown & Co., 1970.

Blockson, Charles. "Escape from slavery: The Underground Railroad." National Geographic (July 1984), pp. 3-39.

Brotz, Howard (Ed.). Negro Social and Political Thought, 1850-1920. New, York, New York: Basic Books, Inc. 1966.

Brown, Francis and Joseph Roucek. One America, New York, New York: Prentice Hall Inc., 1952.

Bullough, Vern. Sexual Variation in Society and History. Chicago, Illinois: University of Chicago Press, 1976.

Bullough, Vern. Sex, Society and History. New York, NY: Science History Publications, 1976.

Chan Kang, Ning (Adrian). "Education for Chinese and Indochinese." Theory into Practice. Vol. 20 No. 1 (Winter 1981), pp. 35-44.

Cole, Katherine (Ed). Minority Organizations: A National Directory. Garret Park, Maryland: Garret Park Press, 1982.

Compton, Beulah. Introduction to Social Welfare and Social Work. Homewood, IL: Dorsey Press, 1980.

Coppa, Frank and Thomas Curran. The Immigrant Experience in America. Boston, MA: Twayne Publishing Co., 1976.

Costo, Rupert. The American Indian Reader: History Vol. 4. San Francisco, CA: Indian History Press, 1974.

Deloria, Vine Jr. Custer Died for Your Sins. New York, NY: Avon Books, 1969.

Foner, Phillip. History of Black Americans. Westport, CT: Greenwood Press, 1975.

Friedlander, Walter and Robert Apte. Introduction to Social Welfare, 5th Edition. Englewood Cliffs, NJ: Prentice Hall, Inc., 1980.

Furer, Howard. The Germans in America: 1607-1970. Dobbs Ferry, NY: Oceana Publications Inc., 1973.

Garcia, Richard. The Chicanos in America 1540-1974. Dobbs Ferry, NY: Oceana Publications, Inc., 1977.

Ginsberg, Eli and Alfred Eichner. The Troublesome Presence: American Democracy and the Negro. New York, NY: New American Library, 1964.

Griffin, William. The Irish in America: 1550-1972. Dobbs Ferry, NY: Oceana Publications, Inc., 1973.

Haeberly, Erwin. The Sex Atlas. New York, NY: Seabury Press, 1978.

Handlin, Oscar. Immigration as a Factor in American History. Englewood Cliffs, NJ: Prentice Hall Inc., 1959.

Herman, Masako. The Japanese in America: 1843-1973. Dobbs
     Ferry, NY: Oceana Publications Inc., 1974.

Hyde, Janet. Half the Human Experience: The Psychology of
     Women, 3rd Ed. Lexington, Massachusetts: D.C. Heath Co.,
     1985.

Hymowitz, Carol and Michaele Weissman. A History of Women in
     America. New York, NY: Bantam Books, Inc., 1978.

Josephy, Alvin. The Indian Heritage of America. New York, NY:
     Bantam Books, 1973.

Kim, Hyumg-Chan and Cynthia Mezia. The Filipinos in America:
     1898-1974. Dobbs Ferry, NY: Oceana Publications, Inc.,
     1976.

Kim Hyumg-Chan and Wayne Peterson. The Koreans in America:
     1882-1974. Dobbs Ferry, NY: Oceana Publications, Inc.,
     1974.

Krafft-Ebing, R. Von. Psychopathia Sexualis. Philadelphia,
     Pennsylvania: F.A. Davis Publishing Co., 1893.

Levine, Stuart and Nancy Lurie. The American Indian Today.
     Baltimore, MD: Penguin Books Inc., 1968.

Lurie, Nancy. Wisconsin Indians, Madison, Wisconsin: State
     Historical Society of Wisconsin, 1982.

Milwaukee Journal, July 4, 1976 (Special section: Two
     Centuries) and November 27, 1980 (Article Kickapoo Indians).

Minahan, Anne (Ed.) Encyclopedia of Social Work, 18th Issue.
     Washington, D.C.: National Association of Social Workers,
     1986.

News and World Report, August 8, 1983.

Norton, Thomas. The Constitution of the United States: Its
     Sources and Its Application. New York, NY: Committee for
     Constitutional Government, 1956.

Office of the Federal Register, United States Government Manual
     1985-86. Washington, D.C.: U.S. Government Printing
     Office, 1985.

Sadock, Benjamin, Harold Kaplan and Alfred Freedman. The Sexual
     Experience. Baltimore, Maryland: William and Wilkins Co.,
     1976.

Scott, Ann. The American Woman: Who Was She. Englewood Cliffs, NJ: Prentice Hall Inc., 1971.

Senior, Clarence. The Puerto Ricans: Strangers - Then Neighbors. Chicago, IL: Quadrangle Books, 1965.

Sloan, Irving. Blacks in America: 1492-1970. Dobbs Ferry, NY: Oceana Publications, Inc., 1971.

Tung, William. The Chinese in America: 1820-1973. Dobbs Ferry, NY: Oceana Publications, Inc., 1974.

Tyler, Alice. Freedoms Forment: Phases of American Social History from the Colonial Period to the Outbreak of the Civil War. New York, NY: Harper and Row Publishers, 1944.

United States Department of Commerce, Bureau of the Census, Statistical Abstract of the United States: 1982/83 (103rd Edition), Washington, D.C.: U.S. Government Printing Office, 1982 and Statistical Abstract of the United States: 1986 (106th Edition), Washington, D.C.: U.S. Government Printing Office, 1985.

United States Department of Commerce, Bureau of the Census, 1980 Census of Population, Supplementary Report: Asian and Pacific Islander Population by State 1980, Washington, D.C.: U.S. Government Printing Office, 1983.

United States Department of Commerce, Bureau of the Census, 1980 Census of Population, Supplementary Report: American Indian Areas and Alaska Native Villages 1980, Washington, D.C.: U.S. Government Printing Office, 1984.

United States Department of Commerce, Bureau of the Census, 1980 Census of Population. Supplementary Report: Persons of Spanish Origin by State 1980, Washington, D.C.: U.S. Government Printing Office, 1982.

United States Department of Commerce, Bureau of the Census, 1980 Census of Population, Supplementary Report: Ancestry of the Population by State 1980, Washington, D.C.: U.S. Government Printing Office, 1983.

United States Commission on Civil Rights, American Indian Civil Rights Handbook, Washington D.C.: U.S. Government Printing Office, 1972.

United States Commission on Civil Rights, <u>Puerto Ricans in the</u>
<u>Continental United States: An Uncertain Future</u>,
Washington, D.C.: U.S. Government Printing Office, 1976.

Wheeler, Thomas. <u>The Immigrant Experience: The Anguish of</u>
<u>Becoming an American</u>. New York, NY: Penguin Books Inc.,
1975.

Wisconsin Legislative Reference Bureau, <u>Wisconsin Blue Book</u>
<u>1985-86</u>, Madison, Wisconsin: Department of Administration,
1985.

Wright, Kathleen. <u>The Other Americans: Minorities in American</u>
<u>History</u>. Greenwich, CT: Lawrence Publishing Co., 1969.

CHAPTER 26

MAJOR THEMES and ISSUES

"It is rare that social services can exist in isolation. Often they represent an aspect of a combined effort to improve the effectiveness of education, for instance, or adequate health care and hospitals, nursing homes or similar institutions. The reality of social services is that it requires the most carefully executed adaption of that system with other social systems. It also requires on the part of social service manpower, an ability to work with other professionals, such as medical personnel, lawyers, physical planners, accountants, judges, wardens, and so on."
(Thursz and Vigilanti: 1975:27)

INTRODUCTION

The above quotation reflects a major theme of this book, the interdependence and interrelatedness of the human service networks and occupations and professions. One cannot adequately understand the role of social work as a profession without looking at the larger social networks (social institutions) of society of which it is a part. In describing the interdependence of the human service professions, a number of themes were discussed: development of a service economy, each social network (social institution) has a social service component, the interdependence and relatedness of the human service occupations and professions, the commonality and differences between the various human service occupations and professions and the role of social work.

As the United States economic system shifts more into a service oriented economy, some authors have called it a social-industrial economy (Kleinberg, 1973) and others a service information economy (Naisbitt, 1984). Some basic questions facing the human services as American society changes are as follows:

ORGANIZATIONAL

What is the focus of social service practice? What is the role of the state bureaucracy? Should services be centralized or decentralized?

PROFESSIONAL

What kind of personnel is appropriate for the human services? Should there be an interdisciplinary degree or interdisciplinary programs? What type of accountability should there be for the human services professional? What is the appropriate role of professional organizations? What type of education for the human services is most appropriate?

SOCIETAL QUESTIONS

Should the emphasis be on public, private or combined public and private programs? Should programs be universal or specific or a matter of equity?

This chapter briefly reviews the major themes of the book and some of: the major issues facing the human service professions as the reorganization of America's postindustrial economic network continues.

MAJOR THEMES

Throughout the book the major themes which were interwoven, include the concepts of a service economy, network of associations, relatedness of the human services, commonality and differences between the various human services, the role of human service professions and the role of social work.

SERVICE ECONOMY

The United States is undergoing a slow but steady transformation of its economic network from a goods producing system, also called the military industrial complex, to a service producing system, called a social industrial complex, service economy or service information economy. Service industries include transportation, utilities, communication, trade (wholesale and retail), finance, insurance, real estate, personal service, business and repair, professional and related, and public administration (including military). In 1900, 32 percent of the labor force was employed in service industries. By 1980, the percentage of the labor force employed in service industries increased to 69.8 percent, in 1982, 72.4 percent and in 1984, 72.6 percent. Human services are included under service industries and are part of the industrial classification of professional and related and public administration (including military). In 1900, 10 percent of the labor force was employed in the industrial classification of professional and related and public adminstration. By 1980, the percentage of the labor force employed in the industrial classification of professional and related and public administration increased to 35.6 percent and in 1984 to 36.2 percent. The number of people employed in human services has increased from approximately 2 percent of the labor force in 1900 to 20 percent of the labor force in 1980 and 24.7 percent in 1984.

As the service economy develops an overall concern will be an emphasis on the quality of life, such as health, environment, self actualization, etc. Since services are becoming an integral part of our economic network, it is no longer feasible to conceptualize human services as private versus governmental services. A private business will incorporate many social service functions, such as medical care, retirement plans, employee assistant programs, etc. Consequently authors like Kleinberg (1973) have indicated that the United States is moving from an economic network dominated by the military industrial complex to a social industrial complex, or the service aspect of society. The current retrenchment of the 1980's in social service programs is not a retreat from the service economy, but a reshuffling of who has responsibility for the provision of services, the type and level of services, who receives services, the role of government (which level) or nongovernment in providing services, and which occupations and professions will provide the services.

NETWORK of ASSOCIATIONS (SOCIAL INSTITUTIONS)

Since a coalition or a partnership will exist between private business and government one should find each major societal network having some social service function. The conceptual focus of the various chapters was an analysis of each major social network (social institution) and a description of the human services involved in that network. The major networks of association (social institutions) discussed include: aesthetic, economic, military, political, education, environment protection, information and referral, judicial, protective service, legal, leisure and recreation, religious, corrections, employment and manpower, housing, income maintenance, mental health, mutual support, personal social service, physical health, rehabilitation and special populations. Each of these networks has some human service function and a dominant occupation or profession, and social workers perform specific functions in each network.

RELATEDNESS of the HUMAN SERVICES

Within each of the societal networks, such as mental health, physical health, education, etc., there are a variety of human service occupations and professions employed. For example, in the education network there are teachers, guidance counselors, social workers, psychologists, psychiatrists, nurses, lawyers, clergy, etc. Each of these occupations and professions relate to each other within the education network, and the education network as a whole relates to other networks, such as physical health, mental health, housing, employment and manpower, corrections, etc. Consequently there is an interdependence of the human service occupations and professions within one social network, as well as, between social networks.

COMMONALITY and DIFFERENCES BETWEEN the VARIOUS HUMAN SERVICES

Regardless of the specific human service profession, a number of characteristics are common to all of them which includes the following: intangible product, specialization, working for large organizations, credentials, parallel systems (public, private and folk), service orientation, and labor extensive, meaning that when working with people it is extremely difficult to increase efficiency through technology.

The human service professions also share commonalities in the processes they use in working with people which include the following: problem solving process, communication skills both oral and written and development of a relationship with their clientele or target population.

A model showing the ideal differences between the various professions was described using the following criteria: knowledge base, value base, intervention methodology, historical precedent in terms of the establishment of a specialized professional grouping, and degree of sanction or degree of independence given to a profession by society. This model was then applied to the professions of medicine, law, theology and social work, but the model can be used for comparing any profession.

ROLE of the HUMAN SERVICE PROFESSIONS and SOCIAL WORK

In each of the networks the role of various professions and of social work was described. The role of a social worker would vary depending upon the specific social network and setting in which a person is employed. One aspect of social work (as well as other human service professions) which will be increasing is that of a private practitioner. One of the characteristics of a service economy is the system of subcontracting services out to private agencies, which means that more and more individuals will be coming involved in private practice. The increasing reliance on contracting out and private practice is a theme which involves all of the professions described in the various networks.

MAJOR ISSUES

In each of the specific social networks which employ human service occupations and professions, such as corrections, economic, military, etc., some issues were discussed which related to the specific social network under discussion. However, there are major societal issues which relate to the organization and implementation of the human services as a whole, which transcend each specific area. These major issues can be grouped into organizational, professional and societal issues.

ORGANIZATIONAL ISSUES

Organizational issues relate to items, such as the focus of practice, the role of bureaucracy, the concept of centralization versus decentralization of services and the role of government.

FOCUS of PRACTICE--From approximately 1870 to 1900 the focus of human service practice was predominantly in private agencies and organizations. Since 1900 there has been a shifting of the focus of practice into large public organizations, especially since 1935. A current trend is the development of private, solo and group practitioners in many of the human services. This trend toward private practice is directly related to the fact that some forms of social services are paid for or reimbursed through health insurance provisions, medical/employee contracts or third party payments of various services to private practitioners. As the focus of practice begins to shift from large scale organizations to private practice this calls for a different system of accountability, which is described later.

ROLE of BUREAUCRACY--Large scale organizations have been the structural unit in many areas of the human services since 1935. As long as society is providing human services to a mass population, some form of organization is essential and will continue. The issue regarding large scale organization is whether services can be provided from a humanistic perspective within a large scale organization. Along with the issue of humanism is the issue of professional autonomy and flexibility to make decisions in an organizational setting. In many areas of the human services, attempts are now developing to provide social services in smaller organizational units and even in one's home.

CENTRALIZATION VERSUS DECENTRALIZATION--The issue of centralization vs. decentralization of services is related to both of the other issues of practice focus and organizational structure. Should services be centralized into a large organization at a regional or a local level or should services be dispersed throughout the community in a variety of outreach offices? Current practice is predominantly the centralization model and it has been documented that centralization of services has resulted in large scale and at times ineffective organizations, with the added difficulty of the inability of the human service worker to be a part of the community and cope with the problems at that level. Decentralization of services has been one offshoot of Reaganomics and the concept of reduced federalism. Decentralization of services should enhance a more humanistic model and ideally an individualized approach, which should be used when one is working with people.

ROLE of GOVERNMENT--The degree and level of governmental involvement in the area of human services varies from social network to social network. Generally, in the delivery of human services there was minimal involvement of the federal government until 1935. Prior to 1935 the general concept was local or state government. From 1935-1970, there was an increasing reliance on the federal government with a centralization of decision making in Washington, D.C.

Beginning in 1970 there was a movement to decentralize decision making at the federal level to regional and local offices. Although decentralization was occurring, there was still an increased consolidation of activities and programs at the federal level. Beginning in 1980, the process of increased federal involvement was reversing. Decentralization as a concept was replaced by the concept "get the federal government out of certain programs" which means reversing the trend toward centralization at the federal level and return certain programs back to the states and local communities. The full impact of this trend has not been fully felt as yet, and this trend could reshape the delivery system for human services for the next 10-20 years.

Related to the role of government and attempts to place certain social service programs into the hands of state and local authorities is the Gramm-Rudman Act of 1985 which calls for a specified percentage decrease in spending at the federal level until a balanced budget is reached. The effect of this arbitrary method of balancing the federal budget will have a great impact on the local community and their budgets and programs. In some communities programs are already being cut (1986) with an attempt to have these programs transferred to voluntary and religious agencies, and in many instances unsuccessfully.

PROFESSIONAL ISSUES

Major issues refer to personnel, interdisciplinary focus, and accountability.

PERSONNEL--The personnel issue involves both the preparation and utilization of trained professionals as well as the use of paraprofessionals and volunteers. From about 1850-1900 the basic personnel in many human services was that of the volunteer, paraprofessional or minimally trained individual. Since 1900 there has been a rapid growth in the development of educational standards for professional personnel in the human services. In addition to the development of professional personnel in human services there was an increase in specialization. One of the concerns about professionalism is the social distance created between the professional and the client with whom they are working. There is a movement today to utilize paraprofessionals who have some degree of training, but less than a bachelor's degree, and to provide a viable and meaningful role for volunteers. The human services will need to develop a system which utilizes all three types of personnel (professional, paraprofessional and volunteer).

A related issue for personnel in the human services is the use of newer computerized technologies in the educational process and in practice. Some examples of the newer existing technology through computerization including the following: diagnosis of a mental health problem, diagnosis of a medical problem, simulation of treatment techniques, video disks for educational purposes and digital compact disk technology for the storage and retrieval of information for educational and teaching purposes, home educational programs, including courses for credit on television, etc. The impact of these newer technologies on the human services professions is just beginning to be felt and the full impact will not be known for 10-15 years.

INTERDISCIPLINARY FOCUS--As professionalism, specialization, and subspecialization emerges amongst the human services professions, training programs develop for particular areas, such as health, education, social work, rehabilitation counseling etc. For example, the profession of medicine has over 100 specialities, and social work has approximately 35 different specialities. Because of the increase in specialization the approach to a person's problem has become segmented, in that each professional group talks a different language, and has a specific perspective. Consequently one of the concerns is to develop a holistic perspective regarding the individual and social problems, which calls for an interdisciplinary focus. A major issue which has developed is the feasiblility of developing a generalist human service profession which can respond to all needs, or should specialization continue, but with an interdisciplinary approach to individual and social problems.

If one assumes, in a service economy, specialization, will continue, because of technology and knowledge growth it would

913

seem an overall human service profession for all human service areas is unfeasible. However it is practical to develop a human service generalist who would be able to recognize specific needs, refer cases to other professions for longer range or specialized intervention, act as a gatekeeper occupation and provide emergency and immediate service. For example, an individual may be able to recognize whether a problem is a medical, educational, psychological, income security problem, etc., provide immediate on the spot counseling and then refer to other appropriate professions for longer range intervention. It is anticipated with the developing concern for an interdisciplinary focus for the human services, the team approach will be utilized more than it has in the past. The concept of an interdisciplinary approach also has implications for educational institutions, in that each of the human service professions should have a concept of where other human service professions fit into the various social networks, and in general the type of knowledge required for each of the professions.

ACCOUNTABILITY—As the focus of practice partially shifts from large organizations to smaller organizational units and to private practice, a different form of accountability is required. There should be a renewed concern over ethical, financial, programatic and legal accountibility.

Ethical codes are a part of all human service professions. When one works for an organization, such as a bureaucracy, the general rule of thumb is that a person's behavior should be consistent with those expected by the organization. When one moves into private practice ethical issues, such as confidentiality, relationship to clients, relationship to colleagues and legal issues become important. Prior to 1970 few courts would review cases of "unprofessional behavior" since it was anticipated the professional organization would implement a code of ethics. Since 1970 a number of court cases have been filed or have been completed regarding ethical principles and values as they relate to the human service professions. The assumption is, the professional organizations have been unable or unwilling to implement a code of ethics, consequently a stronger measure is needed to enforce a code of ethics. For example, the Tarasoff vs. California case in 1974 concluded that in a case of a third party threat (intention to harm or murder) confidentiality can be legally breeched. Another example is where states require reporting suspected child abuse even though the information may have been provided within a confidential relationship. A growing problem (or at least awareness of the problem) is sexual relationships or contacts between a therapist and a client and the use of "involuntary subjects" for research, such as mental patients, prisoners, etc.

Financial accountability is a concern regardless of whether the focus of practice is goverment bureaucracy, private practice or industry. That is, programs will have to have a very accurate set of accounting procedures since the funding which they will be using will be based upon insurance provisions (third party contracts), governmental monies or proprietary monies (private funding).

Programatic accountability refers to a system of research and evaluation where one is measuring the impact of a specific program on the clientele to be served. This means practitioners will have to be more aware of research procedures, and aware of steps involved in the development and evaluation of programs. Since many practioners are trained in the area of intervention, one of the possible implications of an emphasis on programtic accountability is the utilization of trained researchers, and program evaluators in many of the areas of human service practice.

Legal accountability refers to the process of certification, regulation or licensing of a specific occupation or profession through a professional accrediting association and their certification boards or through state laws on licensing and certification and their boards. A related legal issue is that of liability in the case of malpractice or neglect. In some human service professions, such as medicine, the cost of malpractice insurance is extremely high, resulting in defensive medicine (more tests than needed) which increases the cost of medical service, and in some cases resulting in the physician leaving direct practice.

SOCIETAL ISSUES

The human services are part of the broader institutional context of our society. As a consequence some issues relate broadly to society as a whole, such as should human services be public, private, or a combined public/private endeavor, societal obligation for the personal social services, should services be universal or specific to populations, ethical/legal issues, the issue of equity or the distribution of services to people based upon social needs and not income and finally ecological crisis.

PUBLIC/PRIVATE/COMBINED SERVICES--If the United States economy is in fact moving to a social industrial, or service information type, the distinction between public enterprise and private enterprise for the delivery of services becomes a moot issue. Since about 1960 integration between public and private enterprise has been developing at a rapid pace. For example; if one looks at the Lockheed Aircraft Corporation and the Chrysler Automobile Corporation, one finds that goverment funds are being used to maintain a private enterprise, and conversely the AT&T Corporation developed a satellite which is used by the military. The trend for social services in the United States appears to be, to develop a social service system for the population regardless of whether the individual or social need is to be funded in the private sector or public sector of the economic network. Private industry will develop more social service programs for its employees, and consequently expand the range of human services, in which private industry is currently involved. The government (public sector) on the other hand will begin to provide some services which have typically been provided by private enterprise.

SOCIETAL OBLIGATION

The concept of the personal social services as an obligation of society (government) and the recognition of the personal social service network as an identifiable network is a product of the 1960s. There are five assumptions or principles underlying the personal social services: government has an obligation to provide service; govermment has an obligation to financially underwrite the personal social services; priority for services should be the lower income groups; government services are not a substitute for other services (voluntary and private) and services should be voluntary. All five of these underlying assumptions have either been challenged by society as a whole in the 1980s and the early 1990s will be a period of lively political debate on the role of government in the provision of the personal social services, especially the assumptions of government obligations in financing, priority on lower income groups and the voluntary nature of services.

UNIVERSAL or SPECIFIC--One of the major issues in the development of human services is, should services be provided to all individuals regardless of socioeconomic status (universal), or provided to a very specific population with a specific need (specific). For some services, such as income maintenance, medical care, education, the United States already has already developed the basic groundwork for the provision of universal services. However, in certain areas, such as general family and individual counseling, sexual counseling, family services, mental health counseling, etc., the services are generally dispensed throughout the human service network according to a person's ability to pay, consequently a specific service. Other specific services relate to a specific problem and population, such as housing and corrections. As the United States moves into a service economy, one of the assumptions should be, all individuals regardless of income would have access to a full range of social services.

ETHICAL/LEGAL ISSUES

In some of the human services, ethical/legal issues relate to decisions whether to maintain or not maintain life. Two United States Supreme Court decisions in 1982 and 1986 (Baby Jane Doe) granted the parents the right to not continue life support medical treatment on their disabled infants, thereby allowing the infant to die. In 1986, a female in her twenties, with a master's degree in social work was fighting for the right to die since she was totally incapacitated.

This issue of euthanasia raises significant ethical and legal questions, as well as, issues, such as abortion, denial of medical service, mandatory drug and alcohol testing (and treatment?), the proposals by a well known politician to have colleagues inform on each other, and electronic surveillance of individuals on probation and parole. In essence, the next 10 years will see numerous court cases involving the rights of individuals versus the good of society.

EQUITY--Refers to access of special populations, such as Asians, Blacks, Disabled, European Ethnic, Native Americans, Same Sex Preference, Spanish Speaking and Women to social service programs. Are these groups being discriminated against by society? If they are, and as a consequence, not receiving the form and quality of services they should obtain what measures and actions should be taken? Some related groups which are also discriminated against are welfare mothers, ex-convicts, etc. The issue is one of distributive equity in society, and that is, are social services available to individuals regardless of one's status as a special population, or social, economic and legal status. An important part of the concept of equity is the concept of access to a service, socially, legally and financially. The question is do all individuals have equal access to social services? The answer is no, since access may be limited because of finances, special population status, societal regulations, etc.

ECOLOGICAL CRISIS

The environment, how it is used or abused is an issue for all of us, even though it is not directly a human service issue. Most individuals and politicans are aware of the potential ecological crisis facing the world. Problems exist as a consequence of pollution, the breakdown of the ozone layer, acid rain, over population and the finite nature of many natural resources. Added to these problems is the growing danger of radioactive wastes and the threat of nuclear war. The major issue for society is, can we take a long range perspective on our social policies and their impact 25-50 years later (or

917

more), instead of viewing social policies in terms of the immediate (2-4 years) and near future (5-10 years). It seems in many areas of social policy, society and the politicians should be adopting a long range perspective.

Assuming the trend toward a service society continues, the number of human service occupations and professions will continue to proliferate with varying degrees of specialization. As this occurs, it is essential that individuals have a perspective of human services which incorporates the relatedness and interdependence of the various human service occupations and professions, as well as their differences. As the economic system continues to slowly change from an agrarian economy (pre-1900), to an industrial economy, (1900 to 1950), to a military industrial complex, (1950 to 1980), and to a social industrial or service/information complex (1980-2000), there will be continued periods of economic tightness and dislocation, with recessions and unemployment. In spite of these economic trends, the human services will continue to expand to meet the demands and needs of a service/information economic network. However, the focus of practice, such as specific employment opportunities will change to meet the needs of the changing economic network.

SUMMARY

The economic, political and other social networks (institutions) of the United States society are constantly changing. Those social networks which deliver human services to the population are no exception.

The system for delivering human services has undergone profound changes between 1935-1960, 1960-1980 and currently. There has been the emergence of a personal social service network, a proliferation of occupations and professions, a shifting in the financial responsibility of government and an increase in human services in social networks which did not normally deliver human services, such as economic, military, information and referral, etc.

The United States is a service economy, consequently one does find some form of human service in all of society's networks. There is a shifting of some human services from the public sector to the private sector, such as private corrections and employee assistance programs. The human service occupations and professions will slowly expand to meet the needs of a service economy, however, which professions engage in whch tasks, where the human service programs are implemented (public or private), and how programs are administered and funded, and which population groups will receive human services will become central issues.

SUGGESTED READINGS

Elliot Friedson, (Ed.). The Professions and Their Prospects, Beverly Hills, CA: Sage Publications, 1971. This book is a sociological analysis of professions and highlights some of the organizational and professional issues.

Benjamin Kleinberg. American Society in the Postindustrial Age. Columbus, OH: Charles E. Merrill Publishing Co., 1973. Although dated, this book analyzes American society and indicates the changes which will occur in our economic network. For the individual who is interested in broad generalizations of a society this is a highly recommended book.

John Naisbitt. Megatrends. New York: Warner Books, 1984. This book begins where Benjamin Kleinberg ends. The book acknowledges the role of high technology and computers in our society and refers to the American economy as a service/information economy. This is a thought provoking and stimulating commentary on the trends in our society.

REFERENCES

Friedson, Elliot (Ed.). The Professions and Their Prospects. Beverly Hills, CA: Sage Publications, 1971.

Gersuny, Carl and William Rosengren. The Service Society. Cambridge, MA: Schenkman Publishing Co., 1973.

Kleinberg, Benjamin. American Society in the Postindustrial Age. Columbus, OH: Charles E. Merrill Publishing Co., 1973.

Naisbitt, John. Megatrends. New York, New York: Warner Books, 1984.

Thursz, Daniel and Joseph Vigilanti (Ed.). Meeting Human Needs: Volume 1 An Overview of Nine Countries. Beverly Hills, CA: Sage Publications, 1975.

922

931

935

ABOUT the AUTHOR

Robert Scheurell, MS Social Work and MS Sociology is an Associate Professor, Social Work Program, School of Social Welfare, University of Wisconsin-Milwaukee, Milwaukee, Wisconsin. Prior to entering academics as a career, the author was employed in the field of public assistance and corrections. The author began his teaching career in sociology and has spent the last 19 years teaching in undergraduate and graduate social work programs. For 13 years, the author served in various administrative capacities such as undergraduate field internship (2 years), administrator of an undergraduate social work program (13 years), assistant dean (2 years) and the coordinator of a social work and Native American project (2 years).

The author has written a variety of articles on topical areas which include undergraduate curriculum, undergraduate field placement, social networks, social work in corrections, international social welfare, lower class incest, genealogy and social science and social work ethics. The author has contributed a chapter and other materials in Charles Zastrow Introduction to Social Welfare, 1978, 1982, 1986 and Albert Roberts Social Work in Juvenile and Criminal Justice Settings 1983, and currently is developing two volumes on international social welfare.